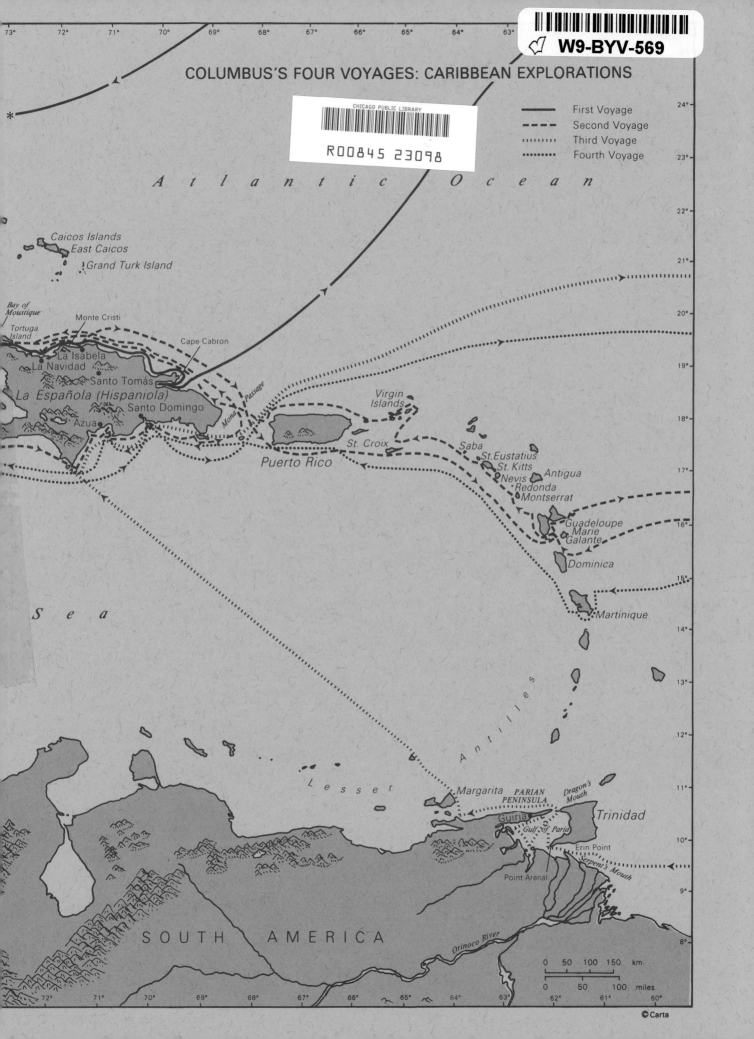

COLUMBUS'S FOUR VOYAGES: CARIBBEAN EXPLORATIONS

Legend:
— First Voyage
-- Second Voyage
···· Third Voyage
•••• Fourth Voyage

A t l a n t i c   O c e a n

Caicos Islands
East Caicos
Grand Turk Island

Bay of Moustique
Monte Cristi
Tortuga Island
Cape Cabron
La Isabela
La Navidad
Santo Tomás
La Española (Hispaniola)
Santo Domingo
Azua
Mona Passage

Virgin Islands
St. Croix
Puerto Rico
Saba
St. Eustatius
St. Kitts
Nevis
Redonda
Montserrat
Antigua
Guadeloupe
Marie Galante
Dominica

Martinique

S e a

L e s s e r   *A n t i l l e s*

Margarita
PARIAN PENINSULA
Dragon's Mouth
Guiria
Trinidad
Gulf of Paria
Erin Point
Point Arenal
Serpent's Mouth

SOUTH AMERICA

Orinoco River

0   50   100 150 km.
0   50   100 miles

© Carta

The
Christopher Columbus
Encyclopedia

The Christopher Columbus Encyclopedia

SILVIO A. BEDINI, Editor
Emeritus, The Smithsonian Institution

Editorial Board

DAVID BUISSERET
The Newberry Library

HELEN NADER
Indiana University

WILCOMB E. WASHBURN
The Smithsonian Institution

PAULINE MOFFIT WATTS
Sarah Lawrence College

Volume 1

SIMON & SCHUSTER
A Paramount Communications Company

New York   London   Toronto   Sydney   Tokyo   Singapore

Copyright © 1992 by

Simon & Schuster Inc.

Academic Reference Division
Simon and Schuster
15 Columbus Circle
New York, New York 10023

Printed in the United States of America

printing number
2 3 4 5 6 7 8 9 10

Library of Congress Cataloging-in-Publication Data

The Christopher Columbus Encyclopedia

Silvio A. Bedini, Editor in Chief

Includes bibliographies and index.
1. Columbus, Christopher—Encyclopedias.
2. America—Discovery and exploration—Encyclopedias.

E111.0774 1992   970.01'5'03—dc20   90-29253

ISBN 0-13-142662-1 (set)
ISBN 0-13-142670-2 (v. 1)

*Acknowledgments of sources, copyrights, and
permissions to use previously printed materials
are made throughout the work.*

Editorial and Production Staff

Publisher
Charles E. Smith

Editorial Director
Paul Bernabeo

Manuscript Editors
Mary Edwardsen   Stephen Wagley   Cecile Watters

Illustration Editor
David Sassian

Proofreader
Dorothy Bauhoff Kachouh

Executive Assistant
Glady Villegas Delgado

Assistant Project Editors
Debra H. Alpern   Robert M. Salkin

Compositor
The Clarinda Company
Clarinda, Iowa

Illustration Researcher
PAR / NYC Inc.
New York

Illustrator
A Good Thing Inc.
New York

Cartographer
Carta
Jerusalem

Indexer
AEIOU Inc.
Pleasantville, New York

Manufacturing Manager
Margaret Rizzi

Preface

By the end of the fifteenth century, the European states of Portugal and Spain were ready technologically and politically to explore and colonize thousands of miles from their own shores. Although Christopher Columbus was not the first European to arrive in the part of the world soon to be named after Amerigo Vespucci, another European explorer who followed Columbus westward, it was Columbus's first voyage across the Atlantic Ocean that initiated sustained European exploration, colonization, and conquest of what to Europeans was a new world.

The editors of this encyclopedia have planned a series of articles that provides a panoramic view of the age of European exploration from the late fifteenth century to the middle of the seventeenth century, including entries that examine the cultural and political motivations for European exploration as well as the maritime technologies that made this exploration possible. The core of the work includes articles treating Columbus's life and writings in detail. Related entries explore the Columbian legacy in literature, plastic and pictorial arts, and popular culture. The editors have also solicited articles that describe modern research techniques and the ongoing recovery of source materials for this period of history.

In addition to covering Columbus's life, the encyclopedia treats numerous other men and women who participated in the momentous events of his age. Included are the innovators of science and technology, the European leaders who sponsored overseas expansion, and the colonizers who left one world to gain another. Several other entries describe the indigenous ecologies and cultures of the New World encountered by Europeans in the century following Columbus's voyages. The exploitation of the natural resources of the Americas is addressed as is the impact of invasion, conquest, enslavement, and disease upon their human inhabitants.

The aim of this collection of articles, contributed by an international team of scholars, is to illuminate events that promoted the emergence of the modern West. In employing the word *discovery* to refer to Columbus's landfall in the Caribbean on October 12, 1492, our contributors do not deny the prior existence of the so-called discovered.

Nor do we, in referring to the lands previously unknown to Europeans as "the New World," suggest that this world and its peoples did not exist before. We do recognize, however, that what follows from that meeting of cultures, remembered today as the Columbian encounter, is indeed something new in history—a blending of peoples and cultures that constitutes the Americas as we know them today. The name *America* is itself of European origin, and use of the term *Indian* is a European misnomer. Where possible, the following articles are explicit about which Amerindians are under discussion, but ultimately it did not seem practical to abandon conventionally acceptable meanings of the terms *Indian* and *America*.

This encyclopedia does not attempt to trace the entire story of the colonization of the New World. Rather, it focuses on European and American subjects that figure prominently in the European expansionism of the sixteenth century and early seventeenth century. Every plan must set time limits, and ours is the year 1620. Hence, emphasis rests on the Caribbean region and European impact there, but articles are also included that discuss peoples, cultures, and events farther to the north and south, including England's search for the Northwest Passage and the histories of the Incas of Peru and the Tupinambás of Brazil. Pre-Columbian voyages are also covered, for example, in an overview of exploration before 1492, and, more particularly, in entries on Leif Ericsson, Vinland, and Portugal's exploration of Africa.

Thanks are due the more than one hundred scholars who have provided the accumulated learning collected herein. Each of them has played an important part and each is acknowledged within the work for the contribution of particular entries. Special thanks can be paid to Rebecca Catz for unfailing assistance concerning translation and bibliography related to Portuguese topics. Advice was frequently sought and generously given by the project's advisers: Professor Kathleen Deagan of the University of Florida, concerning archaeology; Admiral William Lemos (U.S. Navy, retired), concerning navigation; Vice President Paolo Emilio Taviani, Senate of the Republic of Italy, concerning the European background of the Columbian age; and Commander David W. Waters, honorary member of the Royal Institute of Navigation, Brighton, concerning scientific instruments. Dr. William C. Sturtevant of the Smithsonian Institution was central to the development of articles concerning native American peoples.

Acknowledgment of sources of illustrative material can be found in captions accompanying illustrations. Because so many of the objects illustrated are several hundred years old, special care has been taken to reproduce them faithfully, by electronic means. Translators are acknowledged at the end of each article that has been rendered into English from a foreign language.

The spelling and use of certain names and terms required editorial solutions specially tailored to this work. It was our policy to avoid overturning well-ingrained, common usage and to forgo provoking consternation among general readers by employing a full complement of unfamiliar diacritics in transliterated names. On the other hand, we were eager to balance this service to familiarity with our concern for scholarship. Thus, we have selected forms of personal and geographic names that approximate authentic forms. Cross-references appear throughout the work, including the index, to guide readers to the information they seek under variant forms of names. In addition, where it would not interfere with ease of reading, alternate forms of names are often included within parentheses immediately following the preferred forms.

The very name *Columbus* presented its own special editorial vexations. The encyclopedia discusses several members of the Columbus family who lived in different parts of the world and who spoke, wrote, and are referred to in original sources in various languages, among them, Italian, Portuguese, and Spanish. Members of the Columbus family whose lives centered in Italy are referred to by the Italian form of their name, *Colombo*; those whose lives centered in Spain or in Spanish America, by the Spanish name, *Colón*. To use the Italian *Cristoforo Colombo* or the Spanish *Cristóbal Colón* to refer to the main subject of our work would have been a serious breach of familiarity; therefore, we use the form common in English, *Christopher Columbus*.

Numerous other Europeans and Amerindians are known popularly by various forms of their names derived from different languages. We usually employ authentic forms; thus, the Spanish monarchs who sponsored Columbus's enterprise are known herein by the Spanish forms of their names: Isabel and Fernando; the Aztec emperor of Mexico is known herein as Motecuhzoma, a form of his name reflecting its Nahuatl origins. For these names as well as for numerous others—both personal and geographic—cross-references, parenthetical remarks, and the index will guide the reader to appropriate entries.

The Editors

Directory of Contributors

A

D. K. ABBASS
Newport, Rhode Island
Domesticated Animals; Metal

ANN U. ABRAMS
Atlanta, Georgia
Iconography, *article on* American
Painting

MAUREEN AHERN
Ohio State University
Cabeza de Vaca, Alvar Núñez;
Coronado, Francisco Vázquez de

LUÍS DE ALBUQUERQUE
*Comissão Nacional para as
Comemorações dos Descobrimentos
Portugueses, Lisbon, Portugal*
Dias, Bartolomeu; Indies, The; Lunar
Phenomena; Solar Phenomena;
Southern Cross; Tristão, Nuno;
Vizinho, José; Zacuto, Abraham

ANGEL ALCALÁ
*Brooklyn College of the City University
of New York*
Inquisition; Jews, *articles on* Jews in
Spain, Conversos, Expulsion from
Spain; Torquemada, Tomás de

RICARDO E. ALEGRÍA
*Centro de Estudios Avanzados de
Puerto Rico y El Caribe, San Juan*
Indian America, *article on* Taínos

GLENN J. AMES
University of Toledo
Henry the Navigator

JOSÉ JUAN ARROM
North Haven, Connecticut
Pané, Ramón

B

SELMA HUXLEY BARKHAM
Chichester, England
Exploration and Discovery, *article on*
Basque Exploration and Discovery

FREDERIC J. BAUMGARTNER
*Virginia Polytechnic Institute and State
University*
Charles VIII; France; Louis XI; Louis
XII

SILVIO A. BEDINI
Emeritus, The Smithsonian Institution
America, Naming of; Coat of Arms;
Compass, *article on* Declination of the
Compass; Humboldt, Alexander von;
Museums and Archives, *article on*
Collections of Columbus Memorabilia;
Signature; Timetelling; Waldseemüller,
Martin

STEPHEN P. BENSCH
Swarthmore College
Barcelona

JERRY H. BENTLEY
University of Hawaii
Fernández de Córdoba, Gonzalo

FRANCES E. BERDAN
*California State University, San
Bernadino*
Malinche

GORDON BLEULER
Dallas, Texas
Iconography, *article on* Philately

ARIE BOOMERT
Alkmaar, The Netherlands
Indian America, *article on* Arawaks and
Caribs

KATHLEEN BRAGDON
*Colonial Williamsburg Foundation,
Williamsburg, Virginia*
Indian America, *article on* Indians of
New England, Roanoke, Virginia, and
the St. Lawrence Valley

SYLVIA M. BROADBENT
University of California, Riverside
Indian America, *article on* Chibchas

GENE A. BRUCKER
University of California at Berkeley
Florence; Medici Family

DAVID BUISSERET
The Newberry Library, Chicago
Bahamas; Cartography; Colonization,
overview article; Cuba; Española, La;
Jamaica; Puerto Rico; West Indies

AMY TURNER BUSHNELL
University of California, Irvine
Women in the Americas

JOSEPH P. BYRNE
West Georgia College
Cadamosto; Carpini, Giovanni da Pian
del; Conti, Niccolò de'; Trade, *article
on* Mediterranean Trade; Vivaldi,
Ugolino, and Vadino Vivaldi

C

ILARIA LUZZANA CARACI
*Istituto de Scienze Geografiche,
Università de Genova*
Vespucci, Amerigo

IX

REBECCA CATZ
University of California, Berkeley
Almeida, Francisco de; Cabral, Pedro
Álvares; China; Cipangu; Columbus,
Christopher, *article on* Columbus in
Portugal; Gama, Vasco da; Madeira;
Pinto, Fernão Mendes; Portugal

S. L. CLINE
*California State University, San
Bernadino*
Cuauhtemoc

D

KATHLEEN DEAGAN
University of Florida
Archaeology, *article on* Land
Archaeology; Settlements, *articles on*
La Navidad, La Isabela

SUSAN M. DEEDS
Northern Arizona University
Indian America, *article on* Indians of
Northern Mexico, Baja, California, and
Southwestern North America

ANGEL DELGADO-GOMEZ
University of Notre Dame
Alvarado, Pedro de; Cortés,
Hernando; Díaz del Castillo, Bernal;
Fernández de Córdoba, Francisco

O. A. W. DILKE
Emeritus, University of Leeds
Marinus of Tyre; Pius II; Ptolemy;
Ruysch, Johan; Strabo; Toscanelli,
Paolo dal Pozzo

JAMES P. DOOLIN
Dallas, Texas
Iconography, *article on* Philately

SIMONE DREYFUS-GAMELON
*École des Hautes Études en Sciences
Sociales, Paris*
Indian America, *article on* Island Caribs

FRANCIS A. DUTRA
University of California, Santa Barbara
Cunha, Tristão da; Elcano, Juan
Sebastián de; Pacheco Pereira, Duarte

E

THERESA EARENFIGHT
Fordham University
Afonso V; Catherine of Aragón;
Charles V; Enrique IV; Isabel; Isidore
of Seville; João II; Juan; Juan II; Juana
de Castilla; Juana I; Manuel I;
Margaret of Austria; María; Maximilian
I; Santángel, Luis de

JUDITH LAIKIN ELKIN
University of Michigan
Jews, *article on* Jews in the New World

DAVID ELTIS
Queen's University, Kingston, Canada
Slavery

HELEN S. ETTLINGER
Central Michigan University
Art and Architecture

F

DONALD L. FIXICO
Western Michigan University
Quincentenary, *article on* American
Indian Perspectives

DONALD W. FORSYTH
Brigham Young University
Indian America, *article on* Tupinambás

G. S. P. FREEMAN-GRENVILLE
York, England
Africa

JOHN BLOCK FRIEDMAN
University of Illinois
Geography, Imaginary

PETER T. FURST
University of Pennsylvania
Flora, *articles on* Psychotropic Flora,
Tobacco

G

FRANCISCO GAGO JOVER
University of Wisconsin
Valladolid

MICHAEL V. GANNON
University of Florida
Exploration and Discovery, *article on*
European Exploration and Discovery
after 1492; Oviedo, Gonzalo Fernández
de

MARGERY ANN GANZ
Spelman College
Verrazano, Giovanni da

STEPHEN D. GLAZIER
Kearney State College
Religion, *article on* Amerindian
Traditions

JOAN B. GOLDSMITH
Northwestern University
England; Henry VII; Henry VIII

BARRY GOUGH
*Wilfrid Laurier University, Waterloo,
Canada*
Canada

EDWARD GRANT
Indiana University
Science, *article on* Science in the Late
Fifteenth Century

CLIVE GRIFFIN
Oxford University
Printing

BARBARA GROSECLOSE
The Ohio State University
Monuments and Memorials

JACQUELINE GUIRAL-HADJIIOSSIF
Université de Nancy II
Valencia

H

J. B. HARLEY
University of Wisconsin at Milwaukee
Cosa, Juan de la

EINAR HAUGEN
Harvard University
Icelandic Sagas

JOHN HÉBERT
Library of Congress
Celebrations

MARY W. HELMS
University of North Carolina at Greensboro
Indian America, *article on* Indians of the Spanish Main and Central America

DAVID HENIGE
University of Wisconsin-Madison
Writings, *article on* Journal

PAUL E. HOFFMAN
Louisiana State University
Ayllón, Lucas Vázquez de (1480–1520); Ayllón, Lucas Vázquez de (1514–1565); Colón, Diego (Columbus's son); Colonization, *article on* Spanish Colonization; Díaz de Solís, Juan; Encomienda; Jiménez de Quesada, Gonzalo; Martínez de Irala, Domingo; Mendoza, Antonio de; Montejo, Francisco de; Orellana, Francisco de; Toledo y Rojas, María de

CHARLES HUDSON
University of Georgia
Indian America, *article on* Indians of La Florida; Soto, Hernando de

I

HELGE INGSTAD
Oslo, Norway
Ericsson, Leif; Vinland

J

CORNELIUS J. JAENEN
University of Ottawa
Cartier, Jacques; Colonization, *article on* French Colonization

WILLIAM R. JONES
University of New Hampshire
Polo, Marco

K

ROBERT W. KARROW, JR.
The Newberry Library, Chicago
Gemma Frisius; Mercator, Gerardus; Ortelius, Abraham

CHRISTOPHER J. KAUFFMAN
Catholic University of America
Columbianism; Columbian Societies

WILLIAM F. KEEGAN
Florida Museum of Natural History, Gainesville
Pacification, Conquest, and Genocide

BENJAMIN KEEN
Santa Fe, New Mexico
Benzoni, Girolamo; Black Legend; Bry, Théodor de; Las Casas, Bartolomé de

HARRY KELSEY
Huntington Library, San Marino, California
Cabrillo, Juan Rodriguez; Narváez, Pánfilo de

MARGARET L. KING
Brooklyn College
Venetian Republic

FRED F. KRAVATH
United States Navy, Retired
Circumference; Distance, Measurement of

L

ASELA R. LAGUNA
Rutgers University
Literature, *article on* Columbus in Hispanic Literature

URSULA LAMB
Tucson, Arizona
Casa de la Contratación; Lawsuits; Ovando, Nicolás de; Santa Fe Capitulations

COLLEEN LEARY
Atmospheric Science Group, Texas Tech University
Azores; Canary Islands; Cape of Good Hope; Cape Verde Islands; Weather and Wind

WILLIAM LEMOS
United States Navy, Retired
Arana, Diego de; Arana, Pedro de; Arms, Armor, and Armament; Equipment, Clothing, and Rations; Méndez, Diego; Niña; Niño, Juan; Niño, Peralonso; Ojeda, Alonso de; Pinta; Pinzón, Francisco Martín; Pinzón, Martín Alonso; Pinzón, Vicente Yáñez; Quintero de Algruta, Juan; Santa María; Shipbuilding; Ships and Crews; Torres, Antonio de; Voyages of Columbus

RUDI PAUL LINDNER
University of Michigan
Ottoman Empire

PEGGY K. LISS
Washington, D.C.
Isabel and Fernando

PATRICK LOUGHNEY
Library of Congress
Iconography, *article on* Film

EUGENE LYON
Flagler College
Menéndez de Avilés, Pedro

M

FRANCIS MADDISON
Oxford University
Armillary Sphere; Astrolabe; Compass, *article on* Marine Compass; Cross-staff; Kamal; Lead and Line; Lodestone; Navigation, *article on* Instruments of Navigation; Quadrant; Timeglass

WILLIAM S. MALTBY
University of Missouri, St. Louis
Guzmán, Enrique de; Philip II;

JOHN A. MARINO
  University of California, San Diego
  Naples; Social and Economic
  Institutions

TERENCE MARTIN
  Indiana University
  Literature, *article on* Columbus in
  American Literature

DARIO G. MARTINI
  Edizione Culturali Internationali, Genoa
  Literature, *article on* Columbus in
  European Literature

LINDA MARTZ
  Bethesda, Maryland
  Jiménez de Cisneros, Francisco;
  Toledo

SCOTT MCPARTLAND
  *Marymount Manhattan College, New
    York*
  Science, *article on* Science and
  Technology in the Age of Discovery

MICHAEL C. MEYER
  University of Arizona
  Medicine and Health

NELSON H. MINNICH
  The Catholic University of America
  Alexander VI; Innocent VIII; Papacy;
  Rome

FRANK MOYA PONS
  University of Florida
  Bobadilla, Francisco de; Settlements,
  article on Santo Domingo; Trade,
  article on Caribbean Trade

JOHN V. MURRA
  *Institute of Andean Research, New
    York*
  Indian America, *article on* Incas and
  Their Neighbors

N

HELEN NADER
  Indiana University
  Bernáldez, Andrés; Book of Privileges;
  Burial Places of Columbus; Columbus,
  Christopher, *articles on* Adolescence
  and Youth, Early Maritime Experience,
  Columbus in Spain, The Final Years,
  Illness, and Death; Deza, Diego de;
  Fonseca, Antonio de; Fonseca, Juan
  Rodriguez de; Granada; Medina
  Sidonia, Duke of; Medinaceli, Duke
  of; Mendoza, Pedro González de;
  Palos de la Frontera; Rábida, La;
  Spain; Writings, *overview article,
  article on* Last Will and Testament

H. B. NICHOLSON
  University of California, Los Angeles
  Indian America, *article on* Aztecs and
  Their Neighbors; Motecuhzoma II

ANITA WAINGORT NOVINSKY
  Universidade de São Paulo
  Lisbon

O

JOSEPH F. O'CALLAGHAN
  Fordham University
  Alfonso X; Boabdil; Herrera y
  Tordesillas, Antonio de; Line of
  Demarcation; Madrid; Political
  Institutions; Reconquista; Treaty of
  Alcáçovas; Treaty of Tordesillas

SANDRA L. ORELLANA
  *California State University, Dominguez
    Hills*
  Indian America, *article on* Mayas

P

PAUL PADILLA
  University of California, Los Angeles
  Alfraganus

DEBORAH PEARSALL
  University of Missouri, Columbia
  Flora, *overview article*

EUGENIO PÉREZ MONTÁS
  *Museo de las Casas Reales, Santo
    Domingo*
  Settlements, *article on* Concepción de
  la Vega

MARY E. PERRY
  University of California, Los Angeles
  Seville

CARLA RAHN PHILLIPS
  University of Minnesota, Minneapolis
  Atlantic Rivalry; Iconography, *article on*
  Early European Portraits; Myth of
  Columbus

WILLIAM D. PHILLIPS
  University of Minnesota, Minneapolis
  Córdoba; Europe and the Wider World
  in 1492

ALFREDO PINHEIRO MARQUES
  Universidade de Coimbra
  Behaim, Martin; Cão, Diogo;
  Colonization, *article on* Portuguese
  Colonization of Brazil; Martellus,
  Henricus; Pizzigano Chart

CHARLES W. POLZER
  University of Arizona
  Museums and Archives, *article on*
  Overview of Documentary Sources

FOSTER PROVOST
  Duquesne University
  Bibliography

Q

DAVID B. QUINN
  *Emeritus, University of Liverpool
    Liverpool, England*
  Brendan; Cabot, John; Cabot,
  Sebastian; Colonization, *article on*
  English Colonization

R

ISABELLE RAYNAUD-NGUYEN
  Agrégrée de l'Université, Sèvres
  Mappamundi; Nautical Charts;
  Portolanos; Sailing Directions

ELIZABETH J. REITZ
University of Georgia
Fauna

PHILIP RICHARDSON
*The Woods Hole Oceanographic
Institution*
Tides and Currents

M. W. RICHEY
*Formerly Director, Royal Institute of
Navigation, Brighton*
Altura Sailing; Astronomy and
Astrology; Columbus the Navigator;
Dead Reckoning; Latitude; Longitude;
Navigation, *article on* Art, Practice, and
Theory; Piloting

JOHN M. RIDDLE
North Carolina State University
Spices

TEOFILO RUIZ
Brooklyn College
Chanca, Diego Alvarez; Fonseca,
Alfonso de; Talavera, Hernando de

RUSSELL RULAU
Iola, Wisconsin
Iconography, *article on* Numismatics

S

NICHOLAS SANCHEZ-ALBORNOZ
New York University
Quincentenary, *article on* Hispanic
Perspectives

JOHN F. SCHWALLER
Florida Atlantic University
Ávila, Pedro Arias de; Balboa, Vasco
Núñez de; Missionary Movement

JEANETTE SHERBONDY
Washington College
Atahualpa; Cuzco; Huascar; Huayna
Capac; Pizarro, Francisco; Pizarro,
Gonzalo; Pizarro, Hernando; Pizarro,
Juan

J. DONALD SILVA
University of New Hampshire
Funchal; Porto Santo

ROGER C. SMITH
*Bureau of Archaeological Research,
Tallahassee, Florida*
Archaeology, *article on* Underwater
Archaeology

WILLIAM C. STURTEVANT
The Smithsonian Institution
Cannibalism; Indian America, *article
on* First Visual Impressions in Europe

T

PAOLO EMILIO TAVIANI
Senate of the Republic of Italy
Arana, Beatriz Enríquez de; Bobadilla,
Beatriz de; Colombo, Domenico;
Colombo, Giovanni; Colombo,
Giovanni Antonio; Colón, Diego
(Columbus's brother); Colón,
Fernando; Columbus, Christopher,
article on Birth and Origins; Cuneo,
Michele da; Fieschi, Bartolomeo;
Fontanarossa, Susanna; Gallo,
Antonio; Genoa; Geraldini,
Alessandro; Perestrelo y Moniz, Felipa;
Pinelli, Francesco

DAVID W. TILTON
University of Wisconsin at Milwaukee
Cosa, Juan de la

AURELIO TIÓ
*Academia Puertorriqueña de la Historia,
San Juan*
Grijalba, Juan de; Ponce de León, Juan

DEBORAH TRUHAN
New York University
Quincentenary, *article on* Hispanic
Perspectives

U

DOUGLAS B. UBELAKER
The Smithsonian Institution
Disease and Demography; Syphilis

V

CONSUELO VARELA
*Escuela de Estudios
Hispano-Americanos, Seville*
Writings, *article on* Letters

DAVID VASSBERG
Pan American University
Agriculture

W

ERIKA WAGNER
*Instituto Venezolano de
Investigaciones Cientificas, Caracas*
Settlements, *article on* Nueva Cádiz

MARILYN ROBINSON WALDMAN
The Ohio State University
Muslims in Spain

HELEN WALLIS
The British Museum
Globes; Northwest Passage

WILCOMB E. WASHBURN
The Smithsonian Institution
Exploration and Discovery, *article on*
Exploration and Discovery before 1492;
Landfall Controversy; Vinland Map

PAULINE MOFFITT WATTS
Sarah Lawrence College
Ailly, Pierre d'; Antichrist; Bacon,
Roger; Grand Khan; Prester John;
Religion, *article on* European
Traditions; Spirituality of Columbus;
Terrestrial Paradise; Writings, *article on*
Book of Prophecies

DELNO C. WEST
Northern Arizona University
Library of Columbus; Writings, *article
on* Marginalia

GEORGE D. WINIUS
University of Leiden
Magellan, Ferdinand; Mineral
Resources

SYLVIA WYNTER
Stanford University
Anghiera, Pietro Martire d';
Quincentenary, *article on* Caribbean
Perspectives; Settlements, *article on*
Sevilla la Nueva

Z _____

CHRISTIAN ZACHER
The Ohio State University
Mandeville, John; Travel Literature

Alphabetical List of Entries

Abbreviations and Symbols Used in This Work

A.D. *anno Domini,* in the year of (our) Lord
A.H. *anno Hegirae,* in the year of the Hijrah
Ala. Alabama
A.M. *ante meridiem,* before noon
Ariz. Arizona
Ark. Arkansas
b. born
B.C. before Christ
B.C.E. before the common era
c. *circa,* about, approximately
Calif. California
C.E. of the common era
cf. *confer,* compare
chap. chapter (pl., chaps.)
cm centimeters
Colo. Colorado
Conn. Connecticut
d. died
D.C. District of Columbia
Del. Delaware
diss. dissertation
ed. editor (pl., **eds.**); edition; edited by
e.g. *exempli gratia,* for example

Eng. England
enl. enlarged
esp. especially
et al. *et alii,* and others
etc. *et cetera,* and so forth
exp. expanded
f. and following (pl., **ff.**)
fl. *floruit,* flourished
Fla. Florida
frag. fragment
ft. feet
Ga. Georgia
ibid. *ibidem,* in the same place (as the one immediately preceding)
i.e. *id est,* that is
Ill. Illinois
Ind. Indiana
Kans. Kansas
km kilometers
Ky. Kentucky
La. Louisiana
m meters
M.A. Master of Arts
Mass. Massachusetts
mi. miles
Mich. Michigan
Minn. Minnesota
Miss. Mississippi
Mo. Missouri

Mont. Montana
n. note
N.C. North Carolina
n.d. no date
N.Dak. North Dakota
Neb. Nebraska
Nev. Nevada
N.H. New Hampshire
N.J. New Jersey
N.Mex. New Mexico
no. number (pl., **nos.**)
n.p. no place
n.s. new series
N.Y. New York
Okla. Oklahoma
Oreg. Oregon
p. page (pl., **pp.**)
Pa. Pennsylvania
pl. plural, plate (pl., **pls.**)
P.M. *post meridiem,* after noon
Port. Portuguese
pt. part (pl., **pts.**)
r. reigned; ruled
rev. revised
R.I. Rhode Island
sc. *scilicet,* namely
S.C. South Carolina
S.Dak. South Dakota
sec. section (pl., **secs.**)

ser. series
sing. singular
sq. square
supp. supplement; supplementary
Tenn. Tennessee
Tex. Texas
trans. translator, translators; translated by; translation
U.S. United States
USNR. United States Naval Reserve
U.S.S.R. Union of Soviet Socialist Republics
v. verse (pl., **vv.**)
Va. Virginia
var. variant; variation
vol. volume (pl., **vols.**)
Vt. Vermont
Wash. Washington
Wis. Wisconsin
W.Va. West Virginia
Wyo. Wyoming
? uncertain; possibly; perhaps
° degrees

A Note on Monetary Systems

Various monetary systems were in use in the Columbian era. The maravedi was a unit of account only, used to record salaries and payments. The Spanish and Genoese maravedi were roughly equal in value and related to different forms of currency as follows:

375 maravedis to 1 gold ducat,
435 maravedis to 1 gold castellano (or peso d'oro),
870 maravedis to 1 gold excelente.

The
Christopher Columbus
Encyclopedia

A

AENEAS SILVIUS. See *Pius II.*

AFONSO V (1432–1481), king of Portugal (1438–1481). Known as Afonso the African, Afonso V used his military campaigns against the Turks in northwestern Africa to further the exploration of land and sea routes to the spices and gold of the Indies. By 1471 the Portuguese controlled territory in Africa from the Strait of Gibraltar to Tangier. The Portuguese navigators who charted the African coastline enabled Bartolomeu Dias to sail around the Cape of Good Hope.

Son of Duarte I and nephew of Prince Henry the Navigator, Afonso inherited his kingdom at the age of six, but his mother, Leonor, served as regent until Afonso reached his majority in 1446. He married Isabel of Coimbra who bore him two children, Juana and João, later King João II. After Isabel's death Afonso became the suitor and military supporter of Juana de Castilla (la Beltraneja), the alleged daughter and heiress of King Enrique of Castile. Afonso's commitment to Juana resulted in a succession crisis and prolonged war with Castile, which ended in 1479 with the Treaty of Alcáçovas. By the terms of this treaty Afonso renounced his claim to the Castilian throne, but more important for the future discoveries in the New World, Afonso also renounced Portuguese claims to the Canary Islands in return for Castilian recognition of Portuguese territorial rights in Africa. It was the Treaty of Alcáçovas that King João II invoked to support his claim to the lands discovered by Columbus in 1492. During the final years of his reign, Afonso delegated most of the work of overseas expansion to his son, João.

BIBLIOGRAPHY

Albuquerque, Luís. *Introdução a história dos descobrimentos.* Coimbra, 1962.

CHRONICLE OF KING AFONSO V. By Rui de Pina, fifteenth century. The chronicle recounts the life of the Portuguese monarch, the signer of the Treaty of Alcáçovas, an early attempt to address the conflicting claims arising from the voyages of discovery. The illumination in the left-hand column depicts the manuscript of the chronicle being presented to Afonso's nephew, Manuel I.

ARQUIVO NACIONAL DA TORRE DO TOMBO, LISBON

Boxer, C. R. *The Portuguese Seaborne Empire, 1415–1825.* New York, 1969.

Oliveira Marquês, A. H. de. *History of Portugal.* 2 vols. New York, 1972.

Peres, Damião. *História dos descobrimentos portuguêses.* Porto, 1943.

Perez Embid, Florentino. *Descubrimientos del Atlántico y la rivalidad castelano-portugesa hasta el tratado de Tordesillas.* Madrid, 1948.

Theresa Earenfight

AFRICA. Columbus's Atlantic voyages had African predecessors. Before 1312, Abu Bakari II, king of Mali, had sent two hundred canoes westward, with orders not to return until they reached the ocean's limits. Only one returned. He then sent two thousand more, but not a single one was seen again. Even though it failed, this initiative was unparalleled among neighboring African states in the Guinea region and on the southern Saharan border.

Trade in gold, salt, and slaves was the basis of an economy linked to the Mediterranean by four trunk routes. From the gold-bearing region and the Niger Bend, two routes converged at Sijilmasa to reach Morocco; two independent routes linked the southeastern Saharan states with Tunis and Tripoli. These and other North African ports linked with Europe. In all western Africa, constitutional monarchies had evolved, some into veritable empires, as economic complexity demanded more organized societies. The easternmost trade route joined the system to Cairo, which, under Mamluk rule since 1250, was the most advanced city of its time. No merchant city in Europe could compare with it in luxury or learning, wealth or splendor. It possessed great palaces, mosques and *madrassa*s (collegiate teaching mosques), hospitals, libraries, khans (hotels) for merchant caravansaries, and dervish monasteries. The whole Islamic world flocked to the university mosque of al-Azhar.

The Mamluk slave dynasty originated from a corps of

The African continent. Detail from Diego Ribeiro's *mappamundi*, 1529.

professional soldiers instituted by Saladin. They were recruited in their youth chiefly from southern Russia, and their primary loyalty was to the regiment that trained them. This ruling stratum was separate from the Egyptians, who, as agriculturalists, pursued a rural life wholly remote from Cairo and the great seaport of Alexandria. These were cosmopolitan cities, with commercial tentacles that stretched throughout the Mediterranean to western Africa, from Arabia and Syria as far as China, and down the eastern African coast to Kilwa and Mozambique. Chinese porcelain tableware was common among the well-to-do, and in the early fifteenth century a Chinese fleet had voyaged as far as Aden and eastern Africa. The commercial elite included Jews (whose records survive), Armenians, Greeks, and native Coptic Christians. As long as these minorities paid their taxes, they suffered little molestation.

To the south lay small Nubian kingdoms, which to now had been Christian but were giving way to Islam. They were in economic decline. Having burned their forests and made a desert, they could no longer smelt their gold and iron or grow crops. Yet farther south, Ethiopia was beleaguered in its mountains by a ring of small Somali states that controlled the trade routes in the plains. The only Christian state in Africa, Ethiopia had a highly sophisticated polity. It had long enjoyed links with Jerusalem and, through Rome, with Europe. Much of this society was to be destroyed by the Somali Ahmed Grañ's attacks from 1533 to 1535.

Along the eastern coast was a series of city-states, mostly trading centers, like Mogadishu and Pate. Kilwa, however, had a veritable seaborne empire which controlled the coast from the Rufiji to Sofala. Kilwa was a carrying trade entrepôt for the gold of Zimbabwe, which it exported to India. The Kilwa sultans had no internal territorial ambitions; more important were trade connections with Malacca and China.

We know nothing of the peoples who may have lived between the coast and the Great Lakes. Northwest of Lake Victoria a group of kingdoms emerged in Kitara in the twelfth century that had no known contact with the coast. This was the origin of present-day Uganda. In western Africa they had a counterpart south of the Rio Zaire, where highly sophisticated kingdoms emerged before the fifteenth century, albeit with no connection with the outer world. By contrast, in Zimbabwe an empire of Monomotapa had grown up round a local mining industry dependent on Arab and Swahili commercial contacts. All these states were Bantu, from stock that long before had emigrated from the Cameroon Mountains. Family groups were still expanding south of the Limpopo River, pushing the Khoi-San into the Kalahari Desert. These Bantu developed no tribal organizations before the nineteenth century.

Outsiders could have had no overall view of Africa in 1500; European knowledge of Africa was fragmentary. Only one European state had any access to information—Portugal, the poorest of all in wealth and manpower. Labor in Portugal was so short that by 1375 slaves were being imported from Morocco to till the fields. In 1415 Portugal seized Ceuta to serve as a trading base in Africa, and in the same year the half-English prince Henry the Navigator set up a school of navigation at Sagres on the mainland opposite Ceuta.

By the time of Henry's death in 1460, Portuguese trade along the western African coast had been established as far as Sierra Leone. By 1474 Fernão Gomes had advanced trade as far as Cape St. Catherine, south of the Bight of Benin; and by 1486 Diogo Cão had reached Walvis Bay. In 1488 Bartolomeu Dias sailed as far as the Cape of Storms (Cape of Good Hope); although forced to turn back by his seamen, he had nevertheless gained useful knowledge and experience. In the same year Pero da Covilhã was sent to gather intelligence in India and Africa. His story remains veiled in secrecy. From Cairo he traveled down India to Calicut and then back through Aden, along the eastern African coast as far as Sofala. After he returned to Cairo, his report was taken back to Lisbon by the rabbi of Beja while he continued on to Ethiopia. He had performed a journey that was unique for his time. In Ethiopia he was detained at the emperor's court until his death after 1526.

In 1497, therefore, Vasco da Gama set out on a well-reconnoitered route. He reached Natal by Christmas and then sailed up the coast, visiting Mombasa and Malindi. Crossing the Indian Ocean to Calicut he had as guide Ahmed ibn Majid al-Najdi, the foremost pilot of the age. Within a few years the Portuguese had taken Goa; their string of trading posts encircled Africa and reached Macao, off present-day Hong Kong. They now dominated the Indian Ocean commercially and had wrested the spice trade from the Arabs, Egypt, and Venice.

The Portuguese ascendancy had momentous consequences. It inflicted a deathblow on the Mamluk economy, which had depended on the eastern trade. The Mamluks even appealed to the pope to stop the Portuguese. But worse was to come for the Mamluks. In 1516 the Ottoman Turks seized Syria and in 1517 all Egypt. In 1518 Barbarossa (Khayr ad-Din) took the northern African coast as far as Morocco: the whole southern shore of the Mediterranean was now in Ottoman hands. Cairo was reduced to a provincial backwater, although it maintained its status as a center of Islamic learning. Shortly the northern African ports would shelter nests of pirates. Only Morocco, with gold from the south, was able to fend off the Ottomans with arms provided by Elizabeth I of England. In eastern Africa the Portuguese ruined the port towns by maintaining a strict trade monopoly. On the western coast, despite papal prohibitions, Portugal developed a series of slaving ports, chiefly on the coast of present-day Ghana. In the seventeenth century the Dutch, and then the English, followed them. At first the slaves, captured inland by coastal African rulers, were destined chiefly for Brazil and the Spanish colonies. Only in the seventeenth century did the slave trade have much importance north of the Gulf of Mexico, reaching its heyday in the eighteenth century.

The voyages of discovery brought Africa no benefits. The Turks and the Portuguese radically altered the pattern of economic life on the coasts. Cairo was ruined. On the east coast, there would be no stone building for two centuries; on the west, Portugal exploited the Angolan mines; farther north, what eventually numbered forty-two slaving forts drained the continent of manpower. Nevertheless, aside from the periphery that was affected by the Ottomans, Portugal, and, later, other European powers, African states continued to develop along their own lines. The Ottomans never interfered with the trans-Saharan trade. In western Africa, states and empires continued to develop. In the east, Ethiopia went through a long period of disunity and feebleness, threatened by the Somali. Among the Bantu in central Africa, states were developing into empires, to be checked only in the nineteenth century.

BIBLIOGRAPHY

Axelson, E. *South-East Africa, 1488–1530*. London, 1940.

Cambridge History of Africa. 8 vols. Edited by R. Oliver. Cambridge, 1975–.

Freeman-Grenville, G. S. P. *The New Atlas of African History*. New York, 1991.

Lane-Poole, Stanley. *A History of Egypt in the Middle Ages*. London, 1901.

The Oxford History of South Africa. Edited by Monica Wilson and Leonard Thompson. 2 vols. Oxford, 1969, 1971.

G. S. P. Freeman-Grenville

AGRICULTURE. Until the European voyages of discovery in the late 1400s and early 1500s, the Atlantic and Pacific oceans provided a barrier that effectively isolated the Americas from Europe, Asia, and Africa. Because of this isolation, the agricultural systems of the Old World and the New developed independently, along quite different lines.

Old World Agriculture

European agriculture in the fifteenth century was based on a complementary relationship between plant cultivation (mainly of wheat, barley, and rye) and animal husbandry (cattle, horses, poultry, pigs, goats, and sheep). The system was heavily indebted to the ancient Greeks and Romans. Mediterranean Europe continued for the most part the ancient Roman crop-and-fallow system, in which half the arable land was planted each year, while the other half was left idle, to store up moisture and to regain fertility. After harvest, the grain stubble was burned, and animal manure, a fertilizer, was spread among the ashes. In southern Europe, fruits and vegetables—grapes, olives, citrus, figs—were grown in addition to grain. Whereas most European agriculture relied upon natural rainfall, there was some irrigation in the Mediterranean area, mainly on intensively cultivated fruit and vegetable plots along rivers. In some places, intercropping (planting field crops between vines or fruit trees) was practiced, but crops were normally grown separately. Southern Europeans still used the Roman scratch-plow, which did not invert the soil, but merely made a shallow cut in the ground. Plows were almost invariably pulled by oxen.

In northern Europe, fields were worked primarily with horses pulling wheeled moldboard plows. Crops were more heavily fertilized with animal manure than in southern Europe, and through much of the north were planted according to a compulsory three-course rotational schedule (fall grain, spring grain, and fallow or legumes). Northern agriculture was in general more intensive than that of the south: fodder crops were often planted on what would otherwise have been fallow land, thus allowing for the expansion of animal husbandry, and increased attention was paid to selective livestock breeding and to the care of animals within a relatively confined space of pasture and barn. In Mediterranean Europe, by contrast, animals were usually herded over more extensive territory and received comparatively little care.

Agricultural tools throughout fifteenth century Europe remained much the same as in ancient times. Wood was still the basic material for the spade, hoe, pitchfork, rake, harrow, sickle, scythe, and plow. But many of these were tipped with iron for greater durability. An important medieval innovation was the heavy moldboard plow, which permitted the cultivation of tight, well-watered northern European soils that had been impenetrable to the Roman scratch-plow. At the same time, horseshoeing became widespread, and there were numerous improvements in harnessing. In northern Europe, the horse, a faster and more versatile draft animal, increasingly took the place of the ox, which was not displaced until the sixteenth century in southern Europe.

The landowning structure of fifteenth-century Europe was highly complex. The monarchs held ultimate claim to the ownership of all the lands in their kingdoms, but over the centuries they granted enormous territories to nobles, the church, military orders, municipalities, and private citizens. Furthermore, throughout Europe there were ancient communitarian traditions that gave rural villagers free access to certain lands. For example, it was normal to have the right of free use of common pastures. These might be owned by the municipality, by the Crown, or even, in some circumstances, by private parties.

There were infinite variations in the landholding structure. The lands of some agricultural villages were wholly owned by the local bishop, a noble, or a monastery. In such cases, the villagers tended to be tenants or sharecroppers. At the other extreme were villages where all arable land was owned by the villagers themselves. The norm was probably somewhere in between, with the average European peasant/farmer using some land of his own, some rented land, and some common land.

In Spain the livestock sector had become extraordinarily important as a consequence of the Reconquista, the eighth-century Christian reconquest of Muslim territory. During the Reconquista, which ended in 1492, the insecurity of the frontier made animal husbandry preferable in economic terms to crop cultivation. As Christian Spaniards expanded into Extremadura (western Spain), they invented cattle ranching, a means of exploiting the semi-arid expanses of the newly won territory with a limited labor force.

New World Agriculture

Agriculture in the Americas probably began somewhat later than in the Old World, and the crops were quite different. By the time of Columbus, agriculture was practiced nearly everywhere in the hemisphere except the frigid far north. There were thousands of different Indian communities, with greatly divergent cultures and economies, but, in general, pre-Columbian Indian peoples depended principally upon agriculture for their food. Hunting, fishing, and food gathering were of secondary importance.

Maize (Indian corn) was the most widely cultivated crop in pre-Columbian America. It was almost invariably grown in conjunction with beans, squashes, and other food plants, combinations that provided a diet with a good balance of proteins and carbohydrates. Maize growers were thus able to expand into geographic areas where it was difficult to obtain animal protein through hunting or fishing.

Maize was the predominant staple of the Indian communities of the eastern part of the present-day United States. Almost all other foods were mixed with corn gruel or baked in little corn cakes. The villages of the Algonquians and Iroquois were surrounded by cultivated fields, which were tended almost exclusively by women and children. Corn and squashes were planted alongside bean plants, which added nitrogen to the soil. But the beans never put into the soil as much nitrogen as corn and other

crops removed. Consequently, fields gradually declined in fertility and were abandoned for new fields cleared from adjacent forest. When the new fields became inconveniently far from the village, the community simply moved the village to a new site, usually only a few miles away. Thus most North American Indians practiced a semipermanent agriculture, remaining in one place only until diminished fertility forced a move.

The Indians of the arid Great Basin and Southwest learned to cultivate crops even under extremely unfavorable natural conditions. The Hopi, for example, developed drought-resistant varieties of maize and irrigated their fields with the silt-enriched floodwaters of desert rainstorms.

In tropical America, manioc, or cassava, became the major food crop. Manioc, a plant native to South America, produces a starchy root that can be made into gruel or bread. The domestication of manioc was of enormous importance to tropical communities, because the plant yields more food per acre than any other crop. Furthermore, manioc tolerates a wide range of soil types, altitudes, and levels of precipitation. Its cultivation is limited to tropical areas, however, as it does not tolerate cold.

One of the most important food plants developed in pre-Columbian America was the potato (now called inaccurately the "Irish" potato), first cultivated in the highlands of South America. The tubers of the potato plant also produced high yields under varied conditions. Though the potato did not grow well in the tropics, the sweet potato (another American root crop) thrived in both temperate and tropical zones. Other crops included the peanut, tomato, papaya, pineapple, avocado, chile pepper, cotton, and cocoa (or cacao). The Mayas and Aztecs valued cocoa highly as a beverage and even used cocoa beans as a medium of exchange.

It took a complex sociopolitical structure to construct, equitably administer, and maintain irrigation systems. The civilizations of Peru and Mexico produced such systems, and a less-complex irrigation was practiced in many other areas. Extensive terracing was used in various parts of the Americas, most notably in the Andean highlands, to permit the cultivation and irrigation of mountain slopes.

In swampy or marshy areas, pre-Columbian agriculturalists developed the technique of farming raised fields (also called ridged, riverbank, and drained fields). These were prepared by digging ditches for drainage and by using the displaced earth (perhaps mixed with upland soil) to raise the level of the area to be planted. The resulting raised fields were above the water level but moist enough to promote growth. This method was labor intensive but also highly productive if more than one crop was grown each year.

Communities in different parts of the Americas developed various techniques to maintain soil fertility. Manuring was done with fish heads (or even whole fish) and with human, bird, bat, and other animal droppings. And green manure (vegetable matter) and fertile silt were sometimes added to fields. Another method of forestalling soil depletion was mixed-cropping: throughout the Americas, maize was almost invariably planted together with nitrogen-producing beans, and the Incas rotated their staple potatoes with beans.

Perhaps the most primitive method of conserving soil fertility is to cultivate periodically, rather than steadily, with a long fallow period between plantings. Clearings for fields cultivated in this system were typically made in the forest. Hence the system is often called "forest fallow," although it was not always practiced in forests but also in areas with scrub brush, reeds, or other low-set vegetation. The large trees were felled, the branches and trunks burned, and crops were planted directly in the ashes. Forest fallow was widely practiced in the pre-Columbian Americas and also in parts of the Old World where climatic and soil conditions were not conducive to permanent agriculture. After several years of planting, fields with unacceptably declining yields were abandoned for periods as long as thirty years or more, depending upon rainfall and other local conditions. This allowed the forest or other spontaneous vegetation to regrow. Meanwhile, cultivation would be shifted to new fields cleared in other areas, until they in turn were abandoned. After the long fallow, the soil would have recovered much of its original fertility and could be cultivated anew, after clearing and burning again.

This long-fallow system of shifting agriculture (also called swidden, *milpa*, *conuco*, or slash-and-burn) offered several advantages: it was an efficient way to prepare large plots for cultivation with a minimum of human labor; the fire loosened the soil and killed weed seeds; and the ashes temporarily enriched the soil. The system continued to be practiced in late twentieth-century American tropical forests, and it was widely blamed for soil erosion and permanent deforestation.

Whereas the pre-Columbian Indians were eminently successful cultivators of plants, they had a poor record as domesticators of animals. Pre-1492 American agriculture had no draft animals, which meant that all cultivation had to be done with hand tools. This limited the scale and organizational level of agriculture. The only domesticated grazing animals were the llama and alpaca of the Andean mountains. These animals provided fiber, manure, and meat, but they were raised only in the central Andes. The dog was domesticated throughout the hemisphere and sometimes was eaten (apparently mainly on ceremonial occasions). Other animals raised for meat included the

turkey (despite its name, native to America) and the guinea pig. But domesticated animals provided only a tiny proportion of the diet of pre-Columbian Indians—far less than that of Europeans of the time.

The landholding system of the pre-Columbian Indians was overwhelmingly communitarian, although the Aztec and Inca ruling classes held private hereditary estates. Lands used by the common people were typically controlled by clan and kinship units that allotted arable land to each family. Land was communally owned, and individuals could merely use it. Under this communitarian system, land could neither be sold nor inherited; hence it could not be accumulated as wealth.

The basic agricultural tool throughout pre-Columbian America was the digging stick, or planting stick. In its crudest form, it was no more than a pointed stick. But some had stone tips, or were weighted, to help in breaking clods. Some Indian agriculturalists also used spades and hoes. There were no plows because there was a lack of draft animals to pull them.

Changes in Agriculture after 1492

Within half a century of the voyage of Columbus, Spain had conquered the Aztec, Maya, and Inca civilizations and established an enormous colonial empire spanning North, Central, and South America. The Spanish conquest did not completely destroy the pre-Columbian agrarian system. Instead, it introduced Old World plants, animals, tools, and methods that coexisted with the Indian system. Eventually, each system borrowed elements from the other, irrevocably changing the agriculture of both the Old and New World.

The Spanish—and the other Europeans who followed them—attempted to recreate in America the Old World agricultural system with which they were familiar. The Spanish introduced cattle, horses, donkeys, pigs, goats, sheep, and chickens to their colonies. These Old World animals adapted with astonishing speed to New World conditions. By the mid-1500s, European livestock were abundant, and meat was cheap. Many animals escaped domestication, forming feral herds that thrived on virgin grasslands and in the forests; their numbers quickly multiplied in the virtual absence of natural enemies. These untended herds, and the animals of Spanish ranchers, brought conflict between cultivated agriculture and animal husbandry for the first time in the history of the hemisphere. Spanish colonial authorities introduced the traditional Spanish concept of common pasture rights on woodlands, grasslands, and grain fields after harvest (where the stubble could be foraged). The result was that poorly supervised herds roamed the countryside, often straying into Indian crops and damaging them. The Indians began to erect fences—a new feature on the landscape—to protect their fields. This helped develop the concept of private land ownership among peoples whose previous experience had been almost wholly communitarian.

The Indians immediately recognized the superiority of European iron and steel axes, knives, hoes, and other tools, and it was not long before stone was virtually eliminated as a material for toolmaking. In the Spanish colonies, some Indian villages adopted Old World plows and oxen, while others clung to their pre-conquest planting sticks. By the 1700s, oxen and plows had become fairly common in Spanish-ruled Indian communities.

Cattle and horses, however, were not easily absorbed into pre-Columbian culture and long remained linked primarily to European immigrant agriculture. But if the Indians found it difficult to integrate cattle and horses into their agricultural system, they found that they could readily adjust to the use of smaller animals. Pigs and chickens were relatively inexpensive to acquire and maintain, and Indian families were able to fit them into the niche formerly occupied by pre-Hispanic dogs, turkeys, and guinea pigs. Other small animals, notably goats and sheep, blended easily with the Indian agricultural system, because they required little care and could live off the vegetation on hillside slopes not suited for cultivation.

The importation of ox, horse, and donkey revolutionized transport and travel and encouraged long-distance trade, thus providing new market opportunities for agriculture. Moreover, the tractional power of these animals encouraged an unprecedented expansion of cultivation. The ox (and the horse and mule favored by northern Europeans) could pull a plow through soils that had been too heavy, or too matted with roots, to be penetrated by the Indian planting stick. Livestock as a source of food also became important, as the result of the establishment of ranching on the vast plains of the New World. This began in the Spanish colonies in the sixteenth century and gradually spread into other areas. The result was a massive increase in the amount of animal protein available for human consumption. European colonists and their descendants were the primary beneficiaries, but eventually many Indian communities also turned to Old World animals as a substantial component of their social and economic life.

Desiring familiar foods, European immigrants in America brought with them the full complement of Old World crops. Nevertheless, out of necessity and experimentation, immigrants and their descendants gradually learned to eat maize, manioc, potatoes, and other native American foods. In addition to staple Old World crops, Europeans introduced sugarcane, originally from Asia. Europe seemed to have an insatiable appetite for sugar, even at high prices, and spectacular profits could be made from

its cultivation. But sugar production required a considerable capital investment, expensive machinery, and a large and continuously supervised work force. Sugarcane came to be grown primarily on large plantations worked by imported African slaves, after the native American population could no longer provide an adequate labor supply. European capitalists also imported African slaves to grow cotton (a native American crop) for the world market. Thus a zone of plantations was established, mainly along the coast, from the Chesapeake Bay to Rio de Janeiro, that depended on a work force of slaves imported from Africa. The institution of slavery, which had practically died out in Europe by 1492, was given new vigor in the New World colonies of the Spanish, Portuguese, French, English, and Dutch.

European colonists also introduced rice and bananas, which thrived in warm and humid American lowlands, often in soils not well suited for other crops. There were numerous other Old World crops that could be cultivated on lands not suitable for indigenous crops. Wheat, barley, and European broadbeans, for example, could be grown on mountain slopes at higher altitudes than maize.

Some Old World plants were readily accepted by the Indians. This was the case with many fruits, which were simply added to the Indian food list. Other crops could not easily be integrated into the Indian system. Old World grains, for example, were not normally grown by Indians. And it proved difficult for Indians to engage in large-scale livestock ranching or cash-crop production, because these activities had technological and social requirements that were alien to the indigenous cultures.

The Indian communities of the sixteenth to eighteenth centuries suffered catastrophic population losses to epidemics of Old World diseases to which native Americans had no inborn resistance. This enabled Europeans to encroach on supposedly inviolable Indian lands. The European colonial governments gradually legalized these land seizures, and this led to an increasingly Europeanized and privatized landowning structure.

The post-1492 exchange of plants, animals, tools, and methods of production between Old World and New brought vast alterations to the agricultural patterns of both hemispheres. Farmers now had a greatly increased number of food crops from which to choose. This made it easier to match crops to local soil and weather conditions. They discovered that the immigrant plants often would produce in soils that had been considered unsuitable for agriculture. The greater variety of crops brought not only a greater diversity of foods but also a more dependable food supply, because where one species was damaged by disease, pests, or unfavorable weather, another species often thrived. The increase in food production benefited all humankind, and made possible the massive increase in world population in the nineteenth and twentieth centuries.

The New World was changed far more than the Old. The pre-Columbian Indians had already modified the ecological balance of the Americas with their slash-and-burn agriculture, their irrigation and terracing, and various other practices. But the introduction of Old World agriculture drastically—and perhaps irrevocably—altered the ecology of vast areas of the Western Hemisphere. Cultivation with European plows and overgrazing by European animals brought an acceleration of deforestation and soil erosion. As a consequence of the Europeanization of American agriculture, countless species of native plants and animals were destroyed or reduced in numbers. Their place was taken by a far smaller number of specialized (often Old World) crops and herds and flocks of Old World animals.

Since 1492 the agriculture of the world has become not only more specialized and market-oriented but also more homogeneous. Such changes must be seen in the context of a general trend toward specialized production and the development of an ever more uniform global culture.

[See also *Domesticated Animals; Fauna; Flora; Metal.*]

BIBLIOGRAPHY

Chevalier, François. *Land and Society in Colonial Mexico: The Great Hacienda.* Translated by Alvin Eustis and edited by Lesley Byrd Simpson. Berkeley, 1970.

Crosby, Alfred W., Jr. *The Columbian Exchange: Biological and Cultural Consequences of 1492.* Westport, Conn., 1972.

Donkin, R. A. *Agricultural Terracing in the Aboriginal New World.* Tucson, Ariz., 1979.

Driver, Harold E. *Indians of North America.* Chicago, 1961.

Fussell, G. E. *The Classical Tradition in West European Farming.* Newton Abbot, United Kingdom, 1972.

García de Cortázar, José Angel. *La sociedad rural en la España medieval.* Madrid, 1988.

Hopkins, Joseph W. *Irrigation and the Cuicatec Ecosystem: A Study of Agriculture and Civilization in North Central Oaxaca.* Ann Arbor, Mich., 1984.

Pohl, Mary, ed. *Prehistoric Lowland Maya Environment and Subsistence Economy.* Papers of the Peabody Museum of Archaeology and Ethnology, Harvard University, vol. 77. Cambridge, Mass., 1985.

Sanoja, Mario. *Los hombres de la yuca y el maíz: Un ensayo sobre el origen y desarrollo de los sistemas agrarios en el Nuevo Mundo.* Caracas, 1981.

Slicher van Bath, B. H. *The Agrarian History of Western Europe, A.D. 500–1850.* Translated by Olive Ordish. London, 1963.

Sturtevant, William C., ed. *Handbook of North American Indians.* (20 volumes planned; vols. 4, 5, 6, 8, 9, 10, 11, and 15 published). Washington, D.C., 1978–.

Vassberg, David E. *Land and Society in Golden Age Castile.* Cambridge, 1984.

DAVID E. VASSBERG

AILLY, PIERRE D' (1350–1420), late medieval theologian and conciliarist. Born in Compiègne, d'Ailly was educated at the University of Paris, where he received his doctorate in theology in 1381. Subsequently a prominent administrative figure at Paris, he was named rector of the College of Navarre in 1384 and chancellor of the university in 1389. He was made bishop of Cambrai in 1397 and a cardinal in 1412 by Pope John XXIII. These ecclesiastical offices involved him in the complex conflicts among secular forces, adherents of conciliarism, and competing claimants to the papal throne that marked the Great Schism of the late fourteenth century. He played an active role in both the Council of Pisa (1409) and the Council of Constance (1413–1418).

D'Ailly wrote in both Latin and French. The commentaries, sermons, letters, and treatises that survive reflect the concerns of the academic and political worlds in which he moved. His commentaries on Lombard's *Sentences* and on Aristotle, and the opuscula (minor works) on cosmography and geography derive from his studies at Paris. Other letters and treatises such as *De materia concilii generalis* (1403) were occasioned by his participation in the Councils of Pisa and Constance and related negotiations. A third body of works were predominantly doctrinal or devotional in nature. These include commentaries on selected psalms and the *Song of Songs*, and meditations such as *Speculum considerationis, Compendium contemplationis,* and *De quatuor gradibus spiritualis.*

In the second decade of the fifteenth century, d'Ailly composed a cluster of interrelated works on cosmography, history, and astrology, which proved to be of particular significance in the genesis of Christopher Columbus's "Enterprise of the Indies" later in that same century. These include *Imago mundi* (1410) and *Tractatus de legibus et sectis contra supersticiosos astronomos, Tractatus de concordia astronomice veritatis cum theologia, Tractatus de concordia astronomice veritatis et narrationis hystorice,* and *Elucidarium astronomice concordie cum theologia et hystorica veritate,* all probably composed around 1414. Derived from d'Ailly's reading of a variety of late antique and medieval texts, they explore the interrelationships among Divine Providence, celestial configurations, and significant historical events.

Columbus read and annotated an incunabulum of these works. Published by John of Westphalia between 1480 and 1483, it survives in the Biblioteca Colombina in Seville. Columbus's marginalia indicate that *Imago mundi* was an important source for his plan to reach the Far East by sailing west across the Atlantic Ocean. The opuscula mentioned above supplied him with a larger prophetic and providential framework within which to establish the significance of the discoveries resulting from the "Enterprise of the Indies." These works of d'Ailly thus played an

PAGE FROM D'AILLY'S *IMAGO MUNDI*. Columbus's own copy, showing his notations on length of days at various latitudes.

LIBRARY OF CONGRESS, RARE BOOK DIVISION

important role in Columbus's conceptualizing of the voyage that led to the discovery of the Americas and in his understanding of its historical implications.

[See also *Writings,* article on *Marginalia.*]

BIBLIOGRAPHY

Buron, Edmond. *Imago mundi de Pierre d'Ailly.* 3 vols. Paris, 1930. (Includes Columbus's marginal annotations.)

Watts, Pauline Moffitt. "Prophecy and Discovery: On the Spiritual Origins of Christopher Columbus's 'Enterprise of the Indies.'" *American Historical Review* 90 (1985): 73–102.

PAULINE MOFFITT WATTS

ALCÁÇOVAS, TREATY OF. See *Treaty of Alcáçovas.*

ALEXANDER VI (c. 1431–1503), pope (1492–1503). Born Rodrigo de Borja y Borja at Játiva near Valencia in Aragón, the future pope was the son of local nobility. His father was Jofré de Borja y Doms and his mother was Isabel de Borja y Martí, the sister of Alonso, then bishop of Valencia.

As a youth Borja entered the clerical state and received benefices from his uncle Alonso, whom he followed to Italy, where he studied canon law at Bologna and received a doctorate in 1456. After Alonso was elected pope (as Calixtus III, r. 1455–1458), Borja was appointed administrator of the dioceses of Gerona (1457) and Valencia (1458), and a cardinal (1456) and vice-chancellor of the church (1457), a major post he continued to hold until his own election as pope. Even after the death of his uncle, Borja continued to accumulate lucrative church offices often in Spain.

Borja at first looked to the royal house of his native Aragón to further his own and his family's ambitions (he fathered illegitimately at least four sons and three daughters). In 1472–1473 he returned to the kingdom as papal legate. Although he failed in his primary task of securing Aragonese assistance for a crusade against the Turks, Borja succeeded in putting the heir to the throne, Fernando, forever in his debt.

Entrusted by Sixtus IV to grant or withhold at his discretion a papal dispensation from the impediment of consanguinity, Borja regularized Fernando's earlier (1469) marriage to his cousin Isabel of Castile and worked to secure the support of other Spanish prelates for this marriage, which led eventually to the political union of their kingdoms. As king, Fernando reciprocated the favor by asking Borja to crown his sister Juana as queen of Naples (1477) and to be godfather to his son. The king's kindnesses also extended to the cardinal's children: Cesare and Jofré were legitimized so they could receive Spanish benefices, Pedro Luis was granted the title of duke of Gandia (1485) and betrothed to the king's cousin María Enriquez, Juan succeeded to his brother's title and fiancée, and Lucrezia was initially betrothed successively to two Spanish noblemen. The cordial relations between the king and cardinal were briefly disrupted when Borja secured appointment to the metropolitan see of Seville (1484), which Fernando had wanted for his bastard son Alfonso. But amity was restored in 1486 when the prelate helped the Spanish ruler protect his cousins in Naples by patching up the differences between Ferrante I of Naples (r. 1458–1494) and Innocent VIII. When Fernando and Isabel completed the conquest of Granada in 1492, Borja provided lavish congratulatory celebrations in Rome.

During his thirty-six-year career as a cardinal, Borja earned a mixed reputation in Rome. His enemies saw him as greedy, ambitious, proud, unscrupulous, and lascivious. His friends pointed to his energy and knowledge of canon law, his skills as a diplomat, speaker, and administrator, and his orthodoxy and conventional piety. At the conclave of 1484, Borja was almost elected pope, but for the opposition of his archrival, Cardinal Giuliano della Rovere. With the help of Cardinal Ascanio Sforza, however, Borja triumphed in the conclave of 1492.

As Pope Alexander VI, he continued to further the careers and dynastic ambitions of the Borja family, but now its base shifted primarily to Italy. He often secured for his children there feudal titles and favorable matches. Thus, four of them were married into the nobility of Rome, the ducal family of Ferrara, and the royal house of Naples. His notorious son, Cesare, however, after a career as cardinal (1493–1498), was laicized and then appointed duke of Valence in France by Louis XII and married (1499) to Charlotte d'Albret, the sister of the king of Navarre. With his father's assistance, he nonetheless tried to carve out for himself a dukedom in the Romagna region of the Papal States.

In his foreign policy Alexander proved timorous and uncertain, and was often influenced by Cesare. He initially joined the League of San Marco, allying himself with Venice and Milan against Florence and Naples and their Orsini supporters in Rome. But within months he had reconciled with Ferrante I of Naples for fear of Charles VIII (r. 1484–1498) of France who, urged on by Cardinal Giuliano della Rovere, threatened to descend on Italy to make good his claim to the throne of Naples and to depose the pope for simony. Alexander tried in vain to protect Ferrante's successor, Alfonso II (r. 1494–1495), by forming a broader alliance that would have included Spain and the empire. When the victorious army of Charles VIII stopped at Rome in 1494–1495 on its way to Naples, the pope negotiated terms of peace with the French, but then joined the anti-French league once Charles's position in Naples proved untenable. As a reward to the Spanish rulers for their assistance in expelling the French, Alexander in 1494 reconfirmed their official title of "The Catholic Monarchs." The pope favored the restoration of Alfonso II's son and heir, Ferrandino II (r. 1495–1496), as king of Naples.

In a reversal of his earlier foreign policy, Alexander followed the lead of Cesare in allying with the new French king, Louis XII (r. 1498–1515), who conquered Milan and so helped Cesare to subdue the regions of Romagna and the Marches that in 1501 the pope conferred on this son the title of duke of Romagna. Although Alexander had previously favored the Neapolitan House of Aragona (indeed, two of his children had married into that royal family), he nonetheless agreed to the Treaty of Granada (1500) that called for its deposition and that assigned Sicily to Fernando II of Aragón and Naples to Louis XII of France; he sent his sons Cesare and Jofré to help drive Federico (r. 1496–1501) from the Neapolitan throne. When the French opposed Cesare's growing power in the

Papal States, Alexander drew closer to Fernando but never formally acquiesced in his conquest of the Neapolitan mainland in 1503.

Alexander did not provide effective leadership in the area of church reform, although he did support the reform efforts of others. He promoted various forms of Marian devotion, including the building and restoration of churches in honor of Mary. He also took stern measures against heretics and was particularly severe with those who feigned conversion from Judaism. But a serious reform of the Roman Curia ranked low among his priorities, for he devoted his primary energies to politics and nepotism, which led to his appointing unqualified men as cardinals and bishops. The murder of the pope's son Juan in June of 1497 led to a period of repentance during which Alexander planned a sweeping reform of the Curia. But the draft reform bull that resulted from months of careful labor was never signed, and Alexander returned to his customary concerns with family and politics.

Among the pope's primary critics was the Dominican preacher of Florence, Girolamo Savonarola (1452–1498), who attacked the Roman Curia and the pope himself as sources of corruption and helped ally Florence with France in 1494. When Alexander forbade him to preach publicly, the friar obeyed for several months but then resumed his preaching in 1496, denouncing Rome as the new Babylon. The letter Savonarola sent in March 1497 to Charles VIII urging the convocation of a council to depose Alexander VI for simony was intercepted and reported to Rome. The pope excommunicated Savonarola in May of that year, but the friar disregarded this penalty, functioning as a priest at Christmas and preaching in February 1498. When the pope in retaliation imposed an interdict on Florence, city officials sided with him and prohibited Savonarola's preaching. Finally rioting broke out after an ordeal by fire was canceled because of conditions imposed by Savonarola and his followers. The friar was arrested and interrogated, and a confession of fabricated revelations was extracted under torture, a confession he later retracted. The judges sent by the pope from Rome condemned him of heresy and schism and handed him over for execution to civil authorities on May 23, 1498.

Alexander VI's long-standing cordial relations with the rulers of Spain were invaluable to the monarchs in securing full control of the American lands found by Columbus. Because the bulls of Nicholas V (1455), Calixtus III (1456), and Sixtus IV (1481) had given Portugal exclusive possession of all lands from Cape Bojador in West Africa south to India, the Portuguese complained that Columbus's discoveries were in the region of the Indies. The Spanish monarchs thereupon sought papal confirmation of their new territorial claims. In an initial bull, *Inter caetera divinae* dated May 3, 1493, Alexander VI granted the Catholic monarchs sovereignty over the lands discovered by Columbus, provided they were not already owned by a Christian prince. Columbus suggested that in addition to the latitudinal Line of Demarcation earlier approved by the popes, a new longitudinal line be drawn one hundred leagues west of the Azores to separate the Spanish and Portuguese lands. This proposal was adopted in a new version of *Inter caetera divinae* promulgated after the arrival in Rome of a new Spanish delegation in June and backdated to May 4. The revised bull also required that, for any Christian prince other than Fernando and Isabel to retain sovereignty over lands west of that line, he would have to be in possession of them prior to Christmas of 1493.

Also backdated to May 3 was the bull *Eximiae devotionis sinceritas,* which granted to the Spanish monarchs in their new lands the same rights and privileges enjoyed by the Portuguese ruler in his African possessions. Lest any doubts arise regarding Spanish sovereignty over newly discovered lands that might lie in the region of the Indies earlier assigned to the Portuguese, Alexander VI issued on September 26, 1493, the bull *Dudum siquidem,* which allowed the Spanish to take possession of and hold in perpetuity even lands south and east of India and the Orient. Portuguese alarm over this papal grant encouraged King João II to negotiate with Fernando and Isabel the Treaty of Tordesillas of June 7, 1494, which guaranteed their monopolies in accord with a new Line of Demarcation drawn 370 leagues to the west of the Azores and Cape Verde Islands. Julius II confirmed this treaty in 1506.

Alexander VI also made provisions for the propagation of Catholicism in the new lands. The bull *Inter caetera divinae* of May 3, 1493, charged the Catholic monarchs to see that the natives in these lands were instructed in the Catholic faith. To facilitate this task, Alexander VI a month later granted special powers to Bernardo Buil, a member of the recently confirmed Minim order and the person chosen by the Spanish rulers to direct the work of evangelization. To help finance this missionary undertaking, Alexander granted to the Spanish monarchs in 1501 the right to levy and receive from the new lands' inhabitants ecclesiastical tithes to be used to build churches, maintain the clergy, and support worship services. In that same year the work of evangelization had so far progressed that negotiations were begun on establishing a hierarchy in the New World.

The pope also encouraged the Spanish rulers to continue the crusade against the Moors. In 1494 he granted to them in perpetuity the *tercias reales* (the royal portion of one-third of church tithes) to help finance this military undertaking. In addition, beginning in 1494 and renewed annually for several years, Alexander VI allowed the Catholic monarchs to levy a one-tenth tax on all ecclesiastics, both secular and religious, to support a crusade in North Africa. To eliminate any dissension between the

ALEXANDER VI. Detail from Pinturicchio's fresco of the Resurrection in the Borgia (Borja) apartments of the Vatican.

NEW YORK PUBLIC LIBRARY

Christian princes of Iberia, the pope in 1494 assigned to the Portuguese as their military area the Kingdom of Fès in Morocco and to the Spanish, Tlemcen and Oran in Algeria. But not until 1505 did the Spanish launch their first serious campaign on the Barbary coast and then with money supplied for the most part by Archbishop Francisco Jiménez de Cisneros of Toledo.

In February of 1502 Columbus drafted a letter to Alexander VI. He recalled that he had wished on the return from his first voyage of discovery in 1493 to visit the pope to tell him in person the great news. But, he said, he had been prevented from doing so because his Spanish rulers quickly sent him back to claim all the lands while the dispute over their ownership between Spain and Portugal was being settled. Columbus protested that after these nine years his desire to visit Alexander VI had not diminished; he wanted to relate to him the significance of his discoveries, which he identified with the Orient and the "Terrestrial Paradise" described by saints and theologians and which he thought lay on the Venezuelan mainland. The purpose of his voyages had been twofold: the propagation of the faith and the recovery of

Jerusalem. To further the missionary work, he asked the pope to provide him with suitable monks and friars. To advance the cause of a crusade, he promised that once he had entered the House of God and visited the Terrestrial Paradise he would contribute 100,000 infantrymen and 1,000 horsemen in two equal installments in the seventh and twelfth years thereafter to conquer the Holy Land. The quantities of gold he had already supplied to the Catholic monarchs, he said, clearly indicated that he could keep his pledge. Although he had been granted perpetual government of these lands, he had been opposed by the forces of Satan who feared he would succeed in his holy enterprise. The mariner apparently was seeking papal assistance in his struggle to regain his governorship and rights to revenues from the new lands. Alexander VI is not known to have received this letter, responded to it, or championed Columbus's cause.

The pope's death on August 18, 1503, was sudden. His son's former secretary and now cardinal, Adriano Castellesi, was accused of having poisoned him and Cesare, who became very ill. The great ambitions Alexander VI had for his family were frustrated. The new head of the House of Borja, the sickly Cesare, was taken prisoner and his control of Romagna crumbled. He fled to Naples, was shipped to Spain, and finally escaped to Navarre where he died in battle in 1507. After the month-long reign of the Sienese reformer Pius III (1503), Alexander's archrival, Giuliano della Rovere, was elected as Pope Julius II (r. 1503–1513).

BIBLIOGRAPHY

Burchard, Johannes. *At the Court of the Borgia*. Edited and translated by Geoffrey Parker. London, 1963.

Cummins, J. S. "Christopher Columbus: Crusader, Visionary, and Servus Dei." In *Medieval Hispanic Studies Presented to Rita Hamilton*, edited by Alan D. Deyermond. London, 1976.

De Roo, Peter. *Material for a History of Pope Alexander VI, His Relatives, and His Times*. 5 vols. New York, 1924.

Mallett, Michael E. *The Borgias: The Rise and Fall of a Renaissance Dynasty*. London, 1969.

Pastor, Ludwig von. *The History of the Popes from the Close of the Middle Ages*. Vols. 5–6. Translated by Frederick Ignatius Antrobus. St. Louis, 1923.

Picotti, Giovanni Battista. "Alessandro VI, papa." In vol. 2 of *Dizionario biografico degli italiani*. Rome, 1960.

Schüller-Piroli, Susanne. *Die Borgia Päpste Kalixt III. und Alexander VI*. Munich, 1980.

NELSON H. MINNICH

ALFONSO V

ALFONSO V (1396–1458), king of Aragón (1416–1458). Alfonso the Magnanimous was a shrewd ruler and skilled diplomat whose ambitions for territorial expansion resulted in the acquisition of Naples in 1435. The Aragonese presence in Naples set the stage for the prolonged military involvement in Italy of Fernando and Isabel with France, the papacy, and the Holy Roman Empire.

Son of King Fernando I of Antequera and Leonor of Albuquerque, Alfonso represented the Aragonese branch of the Trastámara family. His marriage to his cousin María, the sister of King Juan II of Castile, strengthened the familial and political connections with Castile. This intertwining of the Spanish royal families culminated in the union of the two kingdoms during the reign of Isabel of Castile and Alfonso's nephew Fernando. But close family ties did not prevent armed hostilities. When Alfonso's brothers Juan (later Juan II of Aragón) and Enrique, the infantes of Aragón, interfered in Castilian affairs in 1420, Alfonso became involved also.

Alfonso, a patron of music, literature, the arts, and education, spent the last twenty years of his reign living at his court in Naples in the manner of a Renaissance prince. He was absent from the peninsular realms of the Crown of Aragón during a period of social and economic turmoil, especially in Catalonia. Because Alfonso had no legitimate heir, he bequeathed the Kingdom of Naples to his illegitimate son Ferrante. His brother Juan inherited the realms of the Crown of Aragón.

BIBLIOGRAPHY

Ametller y Viñas, José. *Alfonso V de Aragón en Italia y la crisis religiosa del siglo XV*. 3 vols. Gerona, 1903–1928.

Driscoll, Eileen R. *Alfonso of Aragon as a Patron of Art*. New York, 1964.

Pontieri, Ernesto. *Alfonso il Magnanimo, re di Napoli (1435–1458)*. Naples, 1975.

Ryder, Alan. *The Kingdom of Naples under Alfonso the Magnanimous: The Making of a Modern State*. Oxford, 1976.

THERESA EARENFIGHT

ALFONSO X (1221–1284), king of Castile and León, known as Alfonso the Wise. Alfonso's law code, the *Siete partidas* (Seven divisions), was introduced in the sixteenth century into the New World, where it had a profound impact on the legal development of all the Spanish-speaking regions. The son of Fernando III and Beatrice of Swabia, Alfonso X was born in Toledo and succeeded to the throne in 1252. After attending to the colonization of Seville and the recently reconquered territory in Andalusia, he tried to assert his supremacy over his Christian neighbors, especially Portugal and Navarre, but without success. Elected in 1257 as Holy Roman Emperor in opposition to Richard of Cornwall, he incurred great expenses over nearly twenty years in a vain effort to win recognition.

Of greater importance was his plan to invade Morocco so as to deprive the Muslims of easy access to the Iberian peninsula. In preparation he developed a naval base at Cádiz and the nearby Puerto de Santa María, and his fleet plundered Salé on the Atlantic coast of Morocco in 1260. After conquering Niebla to the west of Seville in 1262, he demanded the surrender of Gibraltar and Tarifa. Muhammad I, king of Granada, refused and stirred up rebellion in 1264 among the Muslims subject to Castilian rule in Andalusia and Murcia. While undertaking to contain the revolt in Andalusia, Alfonso X appealed to Jaime I of Aragón, who subdued Murcia early in 1266. Jerez, the last rebel stronghold in Andalusia, capitulated in October, and the king of Granada resumed the payment of a yearly tribute to Castile in 1267. Following the rebellion, Alfonso X expelled the Muslims from the recaptured towns and brought in Christian settlers.

Although tranquillity was restored, Alfonso X soon encountered strong opposition because of his innovations in law and taxation. Intent on achieving greater juridical uniformity, he drew upon Roman law in preparing a code of law for use in the royal court, namely, the *Espéculo de las leyes* (Mirror of the laws), known in its later redaction as the *Siete partidas*. The nobles accused him of denying them the right to be judged by their peers in accordance with their customs. The townsmen, while complaining about the *Fuero real*, a new code of municipal law, were also distressed by the frequent imposition of extraordinary taxes.

When the nobles confronted the king during the Cortes of Burgos in 1272, he modified his plan for a uniform body of law by confirming their customs and those of the towns. Despite that, many nobles went into exile in Granada but were persuaded to return to royal service in 1273. With his realm at peace, Alfonso X journeyed to Beaucaire in southern France where in 1275 he vainly tried to convince Pope Gregory X to recognize him as Holy Roman Emperor.

During his absence, Abu Yusuf, the ruler of the Benimerines of Morocco, invaded Castile. Intent on repelling them, the son and heir of Alfonso X, Fernando de la Cerda, hastened to the frontier, but died suddenly at Villarreal in 1275. Soon after, the invaders routed Castilian forces in Andalusia. At that point, Alfonso X's second son, Sancho, reorganized the defense. A truce was concluded, but the Benimerines invaded again in 1277. Avoiding a battlefield encounter, Alfonso X blockaded Algeciras in 1278 but had to give it up early the next year. In spite of the Moroccan threat, Castile emerged from this crisis without loss of territory.

Meanwhile, the death of his oldest son presented Alfonso X with a serious problem. Fernando de la Cerda's oldest child, Alfonso, could claim recognition as heir to the throne, but Sancho, as Alfonso X's second son, appealed to the older custom that gave preference to a king's surviving sons. After much debate, the king in the Cortes of Burgos in 1276 acknowledged Sancho. Fearing for the safety of her two sons, Fernando de la Cerda's widow, Blanche, took them in 1278 to Aragón, where Peter III kept them in protective custody.

Philip III of France, the uncle of the two boys, pressured Alfonso X to partition his realm for the benefit of Alfonso de la Cerda. Angered by the possibility of losing any portion of the kingdom, Sancho broke with his father during the Cortes of Seville in 1281. The estates of the realm, gathered at Valladolid in April 1282, transferred royal power to Sancho, leaving Alfonso X only the title of king. Abandoned by his family and his subjects, the king turned to Abu Yusuf of Morocco, who invaded Castile again. After an abortive attempt at reconciliation, Alfonso X in his last will disinherited Sancho. The king died at Seville on April 4, 1284, and was buried in the cathedral.

Despite his unhappy end, Alfonso X was one of the greatest medieval kings of Castile, and his impact on the development of Spanish law and institutions was lasting. In collaboration with a team of scholars he published in the vernacular a series of legal, historical, literary, and scientific works without parallel in thirteenth-century Europe. The *Siete partidas*, known in its initial version as the *Espéculo de las leyes*, was an extraordinary achievement. Given its systematic and comprehensive character, the *Partidas* shaped the law in all the peninsular realms and also in the Spanish colonies overseas. The *Fuero real* was an adaptation of the *Espéculo* for the use of municipalities. Alfonso X's collaborators also composed the *Estoria de Espanna*, a history of Spain from the earliest times, and the *General estoria*, or world history. The *Cantigas de Santa María*, a collection of more than four hundred poems written in Galician in praise of the Virgin Mary, was set to music and accompanied by beautiful illuminations. Avidly interested in astronomy and astrology, the king gathered in the *Libro del saber de astronomía* the translations of several Arabic treatises as well as original works on the construction of astronomical instruments. These were used in the compilation of the Alfonsine Tables, based on astronomical observations charting the position of the planets and stars from 1262 to 1272 at Toledo. The Alfonsine Tables were widely known throughout late medieval Europe and were supplanted only in the later sixteenth century. The king's last notable work, the *Setenario*, was a book of theological and moral counsel intended for his successors. By using Castilian for all these works (save the *Cantigas*), he gave great impetus to the development of the language as a proper vehicle for the expression of serious ideas.

BIBLIOGRAPHY

Ballesteros, Antonio. *Alfonso X*. Barcelona and Madrid, 1963. Reprint, Barcelona, 1984.

Keller, John Esten. *Alfonso X, El Sabio*. New York, 1967.

O'Callaghan, Joseph F. "Image and Reality: The King Creates His Kingdom." In *Emperor of Culture: Alfonso X the Learned of Castile and His Thirteenth Century Renaissance*. Edited by Robert I. Burns. Philadelphia, 1990.

Procter, Evelyn. *Alfonso X: Patron of Literature and Learning*. Oxford, 1951.

JOSEPH F. O'CALLAGHAN

ALFRAGANUS (c. 800–861), Arab astronomer and engineer. The name Alfraganus is the Latin corruption of al-Farghani, a ninth-century astronomer-astrologer employed by the Caliph al-Ma'mun (d. 833) and his successors. Al-Farghani was born in Farghana in Transoxania—hence, his name—and died in Egypt after supervising the construction of the Great Nilometer (a canal that connected al-Ja'fariyya, a new city built near the capital city of Samarra, with the Tigris) for the caliph al-Mutawakkil. Very little is known about his life, but his works have survived both in their original Arabic and in Latin translations.

Al-Farghani was responsible for spreading the astronomical knowledge found in Ptolemy's *Almagest,* the single most important work on astronomy in the ancient and medieval worlds. His greatest and most influential work is "Elements of Astronomy," a summary of the nonmathematical portions of the *Almagest*. It is based entirely on Ptolemaic methods and was intended to be an introductory text on astronomy. The popularity of the work can be attributed to both its clarity and its brevity; since it was only thirty chapters in length it was much simpler to use than the *Almagest*. In addition to al-Farghani, al-Battani also wrote a compendium of the *Almagest*. The works of both these individuals were to have a profound impact upon European astronomy until the time of Copernicus.

Like so much of Islamic science and philosophy, the great body of eastern astronomy entered the West through Spain. John of Spain, also known as John of Seville (Johannes Hispalensis), published his translation of al-Farghani's "Elements" in 1135 and Gerard of Cremona completed his translation of the work in Toledo in 1175. Until Regiomontanus's works in the latter half of the fifteenth century, European knowledge of astronomy was derived primarily from the Latin translations of al-Farghani's "Elements." Dante relied on Gerard of Cremona's translation for the knowledge of the stars he displays in his *Vita nuova* and in the *Convivio*. Al-Farghani also wrote two treatises on the astrolabe as well as a commentary on the astronomical tables of al-Khwarizmi; however, the latter work has not survived.

It is known that Columbus, too, referred to at least one of al-Farghani's calculations in planning his voyage of discovery. Columbus the man presents a fascinating dichotomy to the historian. He was a man entrenched in the Old World. Almost everything he said, did, or wrote reflected his Old World mentality. Yet he was also a determined and self-taught man who sought out new horizons. Attesting to this dichotomy are four of his books, which still exist in the Biblioteca Colombina in Seville: Marco Polo's *Description of the World* (1485 edition), Cardinal Pierre d'Ailly's *Imago mundi* (1480 to 1483), Aeneus Sylvius's *Historia rerum ubique gestarum* (1477), and Pliny's *Natural History* (1489). These books were heavily glossed by Columbus; the *Imago mundi* alone contains several hundred marginal annotations.

Columbus, in planning his journey, underestimated the circumference of the earth while at the same time overestimating the size of the Asiatic continent he wished to reach. He rejected Ptolemy's assertion that the distance between Asia and Europe was 180 degrees of longitude. Referring to the works of d'Ailly, Marinus of Tyre, and Marco Polo, he calculated the distance at sixty degrees. Columbus then needed to translate longitude into linear distance. In the *Imago mundi* he found an estimate attributed to al-Farghani of 56⅔ miles. But he erroneously assumed these to be Italian miles of 1,480 meters each, which translates into forty nautical miles (twenty nautical miles short of the correct distance). Columbus's calculations thus reduced the actual size of the world by one-quarter. These miscalculations, however, served to encourage him in his belief that the distance between Spain and Japan was a relatively short one.

BIBLIOGRAPHY

Al-Farghani. *Alfragano (Al-Fragani) Il 'Libro dell'aggregazione delle stelle.'* Edited by Romeo Campani. Città de Castello, 1910.

Al-Farghani. *Alfragani differentie in quibusdam collectis scientie astrorum*. Edited by Francis J. Carmondy. Berkeley and Los Angeles, 1943.

Carmondy, Francis J. *Arabic Astronomical and Astrological Sciences in Latin Translation: A Critical Bibliography*. Berkeley and Los Angeles, 1956.

Perry, J. H. *The Discovery of the Sea*. Berkeley and Los Angeles, 1974.

Vernet, Juan. *La cultura hispanoárabe en Oriente y Occidente*. Barcelona, 1978.

PAUL PADILLA

ALMEIDA, FRANCISCO DE (c. 1450–1510), first viceroy of Portuguese India. Almeida, born in Lisbon, was a member of a distinguished family who belonged to the highest nobility in the land. His father was Lopo de

Almeida, first count of Abrantes, and his mother, Brites da Silva, served as lady-in-waiting to two successive queens.

He began his military career at the Battle of Toro (1476) in which Afonso V (r. 1438–1481) was routed by a Spanish army under Fernando of Aragón. At the beginning of the reign of João II (r. 1481–1495) he obtained permission to serve in the war of Granada then being fought by Fernando and Isabel of Spain against the Moors, a war in which Columbus is believed to have taken part. The successful conclusion of the campaign against Granada enabled the Catholic monarchs to turn their attention to Columbus and to grant him the ships he needed for his westward voyage.

Almeida may also have been present at court when Columbus visited João II on his return from the first voyage of discovery in 1493. The king was particularly disturbed by the sight of the Amerindians who accompanied Columbus, for they resembled what he had been told the Indians of Asia looked like, and he believed that Columbus had stumbled on land that fell within the sphere of influence granted him by the pope in 1481. As a result, the king decided to send an armada to search for and take possession of the land discovered by Columbus, and he appointed Almeida as admiral. The fleet never sailed because the Spaniards, having heard about it from their spies, convinced João to allow the matter to be settled by negotiation, which eventually led to the Treaty of Tordesillas (1494).

By 1505, after the return of the first four fleets from India, the Portuguese were convinced that it was impossible to wrest the trade monopoly from the Muslims as long as their ships were forced to return to Europe after discharging their cargo. Consequently, King Manuel I (r. 1495–1521) decided to station warships in Indian waters permanently. To initiate this plan he chose Francisco de Almeida as governor-general of Portuguese India, with a provision permitting him to assume the title of viceroy after he had discharged certain duties. On March 24, 1505, Almeida departed for India in command of a fleet of twenty-two ships, taking his only son Lourenço with him. On his way up the east coast of Africa he captured the city of Kilwa, where he built a fort; in Mombasa, he destroyed the city where the Portuguese had been ill treated; and in Malindi, he showered gifts on the sultan who had treated them well.

On September 12, 1505, he reached India and set about building fortresses in the coastal cities where the Portuguese had been well received. He successfully fought the king of Honowar, who challenged him at sea, and wreaked vengeance on the Muslims who had set the Portuguese fort of Cochin afire. He formed an alliance with the rajah of Cochin and on March 15, 1506, he captured Panane, a well-frequented port about fourteen leagues south of Calicut. He sent his son Lourenço to the Maldives and Ceylon to take prizes from the richly laden Muslim vessels that were bypassing the Malabar coast of India. From Ceylon, Lourenço returned triumphantly with a treaty of friendship and tribute in the form of cinnamon.

Early in 1507 the fleet of the sultan of Egypt started for India to expel the Portuguese interlopers from the Indian Ocean. In January 1508 the combined Egyptian and Indian fleets defeated a Portuguese squadron off Chaul in a battle in which the viceroy's son was killed. In the meantime, Afonso de Albuquerque arrived from Hormuz with orders to succeed Almeida as governor of India. Almeida refused to relinquish the command since he was bent on avenging the death of his son. The simultaneous arrival of the annual fleets of 1507 and 1508 swelled his ranks, and on December 12, Almeida set sail for the island of Diu in search of the enemy. Over a hundred Indian vessels had joined the Egyptian fleet when Almeida met them at Diu on February 3, 1509, with only nineteen ships. Nevertheless, he achieved a resounding victory that proved to be one of the decisive battles of Asiatic history. For the next hundred years the dominance of the Indian Ocean remained in Portuguese hands.

Almeida returned to Cochin where Albuquerque, who had waited patiently, now pressed him to hand over his command. Again he refused. Finally, they agreed to leave the matter up to Marshal Fernando Coutinho, who was expected in India momentarily, charged by the king with full powers to act independently. The marshal decided in favor of Albuquerque, thanked Almeida for all he had done, and sent him on his way. On November 19, 1509, Almeida reluctantly sailed for home. After rounding the Cape of Good Hope, he entered the Saldanha Bay where, at the head of 150 men, he went ashore to take on water. There he was slain by the natives, along with fifty of his troops.

His four years in office were notable for a well-run administration and for the many victories he achieved over the Muslims. The only battle he lost was the one in which his son was killed. Though he built fortresses at Kilwa, Angediva, and Cannanore, he is known to have written King Manuel that "as long as you are powerful on the sea, you will have India for Yourself, otherwise, your fortresses on land will avail you little."

BIBLIOGRAPHY

Barros, João de, and Diogo do Couto. *Da Ásia de João de Barros e de Diogo de Couto.* 24 vols. Lisbon, 1778–1788.

Castanheda, Fernão Lopes de. *História do descobrimento e conquista da Índia pelos portugueses.* Edited by M. Lopes de Almeida. 2 vols. Porto, 1979.

Correia, Gaspar. *Lendas da India.* Edited by M. Lopes de Almeida. 4 vols. Porto, 1975.

Prestage, Edgar. *The Portuguese Pioneers.* London, 1933.

REBECCA CATZ

ALTURA SAILING. Altura (height) navigation was introduced at sea by the Portuguese in the latter part of the fifteenth century, probably about 1460. It preceded latitude navigation, which came into practice after the mathematical commission appointed by King João II of Portugal had worked out the procedures and calculated the necessary tables. It is not clear how altura navigation developed, but, at least in its earliest form, sometimes known as the altitude-distance method, it is as likely to have been developed by the pilots as the astronomers. The problem with existing methods arose with the largely north-south voyages from Portugal down the west coast of Africa to Guinea; the return voyage involved a wide sweep westward into the Atlantic to cross the northeast trades and regain the variable and westerly winds in the latitude of the Azores. Some method of checking on a daily basis the north-south component of the position obtained by dead reckoning was highly desirable. The ultimate objective was to attain the parallel on which the destination lay and then steer east or west to it.

The altitude-distance method involved taking an altitude of the meridian passage of the sun or a star and comparing it with a similar observation a day or so later to get the linear distance traveled in a north-south direction. In principle, any star at meridian passage would do, but the seaman was told to use the North Star when the Guards of the Lesser Bear were in the same position in relation to the North Star and, in the case of the sun, to take the second observation not more than a day or two after the first, during which time the declination will not have changed too much. By assuming a figure for the measure of the earth's meridian, the difference between the two readings could be multiplied by this value to give linear distance traveled north or south. One degree of altitude was originally taken to equal 16⅔ leagues, or 4 miles; this was later changed to 17½ leagues.

The medieval seaman was accustomed to using the position of the Guard Stars in relation to the North Star as a form of clock; this involved memorizing their position for every fortnight of the year. To help they imagined a human figure in the sky with the North Star at his breast, the head above, feet below, and arms to right and left. Diagonal lines between the limbs completed the eightfold division of the circle, each of which represented three hours. The same kind of figure was now adopted to help the pilot correct the altitude of the North Star for its counterclockwise movement, which then described a path about the true pole with a radius of about 3½ degrees. The seaman was told initially to observe the North Star on departure when the position of the Guards indicated that it was on the meridian, but later instructions gave the height at Lisbon for all eight positions, from which the heights observed later could be subtracted to get the distance traveled north or south.

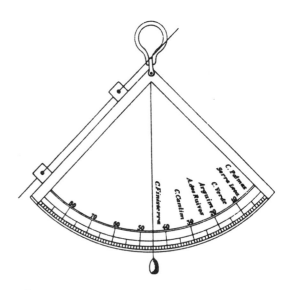

SEAMAN'S QUADRANT. This example is marked with the altitude of various capes. The first marking on the right, for example, is for Cape Palmas, in present-day Liberia.

The first observations were made with the seaman's quadrant, and in 1462 Diogo Gomes records that he marked on the instrument the altitude of the Arctic pole, by which he means the North Star, which by comparison with the altitude of the star at Lisbon gave the distance traveled better (and perhaps more reliably) than the chart. The precise meaning of the note is disputable, but it does reveal that the practice developed among Portuguese pilots of marking the instrument itself with the location at which the plumb line cut the scale when the body observed through the sights was on the meridian. It soon became clear that observations of the sun would be more convenient than observations by night, and, so as to extend the period between observations beyond the one or two days in which the change in declination would adversely affect measurements, tables were prepared giving the meridian solar altitude for each day of the year at Lisbon, Madeira, and other important seaports. Subtracting the altitude observed from, say, the Lisbon figure would give the distance required from Lisbon. In due course the mariner's astrolabe replaced the seaman's quadrant for solar observation; its earliest recorded use was on the Atlantic coast of Africa in 1481.

The mnemonic of the human figure of the sky was revised, initially to avoid ambiguity; the statement, "the Guards are in the right arm," for example, might refer to the right arm of the imaginary figure or of the observer. Later, the cardinal and intercardinal points of the compass were substituted for the eight positions of the Guards, the head becoming north, left shoulder northwest, left arm west, and so on. A yet later system dispensed with the human figure and simply showed the relative positions of the two Guards for each of eight positions of the North Star in its movement about the pole of the sky, two of which (when the Guards lay east-west) indicated the Star's meridian passage. Columbus, in his account of the third voyage, stuck to the old nomenclature and spoke several times of the North Star being elevated five degrees, or, "the Guards in the head." He was attempting to run down the latitude of Sierra Leone, which was given in the manuals at the time as eight degrees north, and it has been suggested that his quadrant must have been marked after the altura fashion, since the correction to the North Star's altitude for that position of the Guards is given as three degrees and if the plumb line on the quadrant fell at five degrees (eight minus three degrees) he would have been on the right parallel. The use of "wheels of the Pole Star," giving the altitude of the North Star for each of the rhumbs indicating the position of the Guards, became the standard method of altura sailing. Such wheels could of course be drawn up for any frequently used seaport or point of departure, but only Lisbon is referred to in the surviving documents.

[See also *Astronomy and Astrology; Dead Reckoning; Navigation.*]

BIBLIOGRAPHY

Albuquerque, Luís de. *Astronomical Navigation.* Lisbon, 1988.
Taylor, E. G. R. *The Haven Finding Art: A History of Navigation from Odysseus to Captain Cook.* London, 1956.
Waters, David W. *Reflections upon Some Navigational and Hydrographic Problems of the 16th Century Related to the Voyage of Bartolomeu Dias, 1487–1488.* Lisbon, 1988.

M. W. RICHEY

ALVARADO, PEDRO DE (1486–1541), Spanish explorer born in Badajoz, Extremadura, in the same province and just one year after Hernando Cortés. Alvarado's parents belonged to the impoverished hidalgo class. In 1510, he and his four brothers sailed to the New World and settled in Santo Domingo. The next year Alvarado took part in the conquest of Cuba. For the next eight years he had a plantation and an encomienda of Indians, but he seems to have shown little interest in them.

In 1518, he participated in the sea expedition to the Gulf of Mexico as captain of one of the ships. A year later, the expedition led by Cortés to conquer Mexico began; Alvarado served as second in command. He was left in charge when Cortés left Tenochtitlán to challenge the expedition of Pánfilo de Narváez. During the celebration of a religious festival, he feared that a rebellion was about to develop and he ordered the merciless slaughter of about four hundred Mexica nobles, an action that caused

a general uprising against the Spaniards and for which Alvarado was universally condemned. He was one of the few survivors among the rear guard during the Spanish flight from the city on June 30, an event known as the Noche Triste (Sad Night). He later led one of the three units that successfully besieged Tenochtitlán, ending the conquest of Mexico in 1521.

The second part of Alvarado's restless life as a conquistador is characterized by increasingly independent actions. On behalf of Cortés he led expeditions to subdue new territories south of Mexico City. In 1523, he conquered Guatemala and the Soconusco region, subduing the Cakchiquel, Quiche, and Tzutuhil Indians and founding the city of Santiago de los Caballeros the next year. As newly appointed captain general of Guatemala, he spent the next two years in a fierce struggle to secure control of an extensive area stretching to present-day El Salvador. In 1527 he returned to Spain to report his exploits in the court of Charles V and to contradict his enemies' accounts. His stay was successful, resulting in a knighthood and appointment as governor of Guatemala. He married Francisca de la Cueva, a woman of high nobility, who died upon arrival in New Spain in 1528.

In Guatemala he soon grew tired of office, and upon news of fabulous riches in Peru, he assembled a major fleet with five hundred men who left Guatemala City at the end of 1533. To avoid interfering with Francisco Pizarro, Alvarado went to Quito in a daring and treacherous crossing of the jungle and the Andes. The suffering proved fruitless because Diego de Almagro had secured control of the area for Pizarro, and Alvarado returned to Guatemala empty-handed after selling his armada to Pizarro for 100,000 pesos. Alvarado then resumed his duties as governor briefly but met with official opposition.

In 1536 he went back to Spain. Still under royal favor, he was confirmed as governor and married his deceased wife's sister, Beatriz. After a few years as governor, he formed yet another expedition of twelve ships to explore the Spice Islands in the Pacific, but convinced by Antonio de Mendoza, viceroy of Mexico, to join forces, he redirected his efforts to find the elusive Seven Cities of Cibola. He was about to embark by sea when he was called by New Galicia's governor, Cristóbal de Oñate, to help crush an Indian uprising. Near Nochistlán he was run over by a horse and died on June 24, 1541.

BIBLIOGRAPHY

Altolaguirre y Duvale, Antonio. *Don Pedro de Alvarado: Conquistador de Guatemala y Honduras.* Madrid, 1905.
Díaz del Castillo, Bernal. *The Discovery and Conquest of Mexico, 1517–1521.* Edited by Genaro García. Translated by A. P. Maudslay. New York, 1956.
Kelly, John Eoghan. *Pedro de Alvarado, Conquistador.* Princeton, 1932.

López Rayón, José. *Proceso de residencia contra Pedro de Alvarado.* Mexico City, 1847.

Taylor, Mark. *Impetuous Alvarado.* Dallas, 1936.

ANGEL DELGADO-GOMEZ

AMERICA, NAMING OF. News of the westward voyages and discoveries of new lands made by Christopher Columbus was slow to circulate in Europe. In the beginning only his account of the first voyage was widely distributed on the continent. His letter of February 15, 1493, describing the voyage and announcing the discovery, was written to Luis de Santángel of Aragón, and a duplicate sent to the royal treasurer Gabriel Sánchez. These letters were written in Catalán dialect and translated into Latin and German for readers throughout Europe.

Despite these many editions, the news of the discovery received little attention in Germany. Columbus's letter spoke only of islands found in the Indies, an unmapped region vaguely defined in terms that did not arouse general interest. Although *The Ship of Fools,* published by Sebastien Brandt in 1494, told of regions to the north—a country of islands he called the Pilappelande and the islands of gold discovered by the Portuguese and the Spaniards—Columbus's name was not mentioned. In contrast, Amerigo Vespucci's widely publicized letters, which appeared a short time later, had great news value and excited imagination with titillating accounts of the natives he had observed.

Upon returning from his voyage of 1501–1502, Vespucci wrote to his former employer in Florence, Lorenzo Pier Francesco de' Medici, describing his voyages. He reported that on his most recent journey he had sailed hundreds of miles along the eastern coastline of a land not yet named, from the fifth to the fifty-second parallel, in search of a passage to India. It was apparent that it was a large land mass, not an Asian island, and he described the region as a "new world" distinct from the known continents. His concept, fundamental and original with him, was that these lands were not part of Asia but a separate continent. The letter was translated from the original Italian into French and was reprinted the following year in Venice under the title *Mundus novus* (The new world). The work quickly spread to other countries and was published in at least fourteen editions between 1503 and 1505.

In September 1504, upon his return from his third voyage, Vespucci wrote another letter, to Piero Soderini, a former schoolmate and at that time chief magistrate of Florence. Vespucci expanded on his earlier account to de' Medici and vividly described the native peoples. This letter, *Quattour navigationes* (The four voyages), was published in Florence and was translated into Latin by the Dominican Giocondo of Verona in Paris and published by the Parisian printer Jean Lambert. It was reprinted immediately in France and Italy, and at least seven editions appeared in Germany. The popularity of the letters was due both to Vespucci's insistence that the newly discovered lands were a new continent, a concept that fired the imagination, and to his vivid description of cannibalism and the sex lives of the inhabitants. These letters were so widely read that as a consequence Vespucci emerged as a major figure in sixteenth-century exploration and discovery, and for more than a generation his claims overshadowed the achievements of Columbus.

It was at about the time that the Vespucci letters appeared that the hitherto dormant science of geography began to experience a renaissance, inspired by the recovery and translation of the Greek manuscript and printed editions of Claudius Ptolemy's geographical atlas. Among the first working in the field was a little group of humanists in the remote town of Saint-Dié in the Vosges Mountains of northeastern France. The current patron of Saint-Dié, Duke René II (1451–1508), did much to promote interest in geography, seeking out well-educated and talented young men to fill his court's administrative positions and diplomatic posts.

One recipient of René's support was Gauthier Lud, who had served as the duke's chaplain and later as director-general of the duchy's mining industry. He was appointed a canon at Saint-Dié and chief official of the community and of the abbey associated with the church. In 1494 he acquired a printing press, which he installed in his home for printing ordinances of the monastic order and which later was used to print books and maps.

Lud, who shared his patron's serious interests in astronomy and cosmography, had published a work on a form of stereographic projection of the terrestrial globe. To promote these interests at Saint-Dié, Lud in 1507 formed a small intellectual circle called the Gymnase Vosgien in imitation of German literary societies. He decided that their first project would be the production of a new translation and updated version of the *Geography,* Ptolemy's world atlas. In addition to Lud, the group consisted at first of his nephew, Nicolas Lud, and Jean Basin de Sandaucourt, vicar of the church of Notre-Dame de Saint-Dié and a distinguished Latinist and poet. The next members to be enlisted were Mathias Ringmann (1482–1511), who could translate Greek and Latin manuscripts, and Martin Waldseemüller (1474–1519), an accomplished draftsman skilled in designing and printing and possessed of an extensive knowledge of geography.

Born in the nearby Vosges Mountains, Ringmann had attended the University of Heidelberg and went on to study mathematics and cosmography in Paris. Although he proved to be a talented poet, Ringmann's preference was the field of geography, and in 1505 he translated Vespucci's letter to de' Medici. Of the many editions of the Vespucci letter that appeared at this time, Ringmann's version was of the greatest interest. He changed the letter's title from *Mundus novus* to *De ora antarctica per regem Portugalliae pridem inventa* (About the Antarctic coast [shore] long ago discovered through the king of Portugal). In comparing Vespucci's account to the works of Ptolemy, he discovered that the lands Vespucci described related to a new world not mentioned by Ptolemy, a world apparently lying under the Antarctic pole. He brought a copy of his publication with him when he arrived at Saint-Dié.

Work there had already begun on the projected atlas when the duke received from de' Medici a copy of the Vespucci letter describing his four voyages as well as several marine charts depicting the newly discovered lands. Excited by the Florentine merchant's accounts, Lud and his associates discontinued work on the atlas to produce a world map and a related treatise to publicize the discoveries. As part of the project, Waldseemüller in 1506 first produced a set of twelve gores, or triangular sections, for a terrestrial globe in which the new continent was named "America." These were engraved on wood, probably to save money, and are believed to be the first to have been printed from woodblocks; previously gores for globes were painted by hand.

Although the date of its production is not certain, Waldseemüller also designed a sea chart that included the name "America" for the new lands. A single copy has survived; it is possible that it was not intended for distribution and that no additional copy was made. The chart was later included in the atlas produced at Saint-Dié, but with the name "America" deleted.

Next Waldseemüller set to work on the preparation of a tract on cosmography to serve as an introduction to the map as well as to the atlas. It was entitled *Cosmographie introductio cum quibusdam geometriae ac astronomiae principiis ad eam rem necessariis. In super quattuor America Vespucci navigationes* (An introduction to cosmography with several elements of geometry and astronomy required for this science, and the four voyages of Amerigo Vespucci). Working together with Ringmann, Waldseemüller began writing the tract in the summer of 1506 and completed it the following winter. Printers were brought from Strasbourg and Basel to help print the first edition, which was issued on April 25, 1507. Four editions were printed at Saint-Dié in that year.

The *Cosmography* consists of two parts. The first contains an explanation of the world map and provides the basic principles of geometry and astronomy to assist readers in understanding the work. The second section contains Vespucci's letter translated into Latin by Basin de

Rhomes/ antidiaBorifchenes: a grǫca ꝑticula anti q̄ oppofitūvel cōtra denotat. Atꝗ in fexto climate Antarcticū verfus/& pars extrema Africǫ nuper reperta &/Zamzibar/laua minor/& Seula infulǫ & quarta orbis pars(quam quia Americus inueuit Amerigen /quafi Americi terrā / fiue Americā nun Ameri cupare licet) fitǫ funt. De quibus Auftralibns eli≠ ge matibus hǫc Pomponij Mellǫ Geographi verba in telligēda funt /vbi ait. Zonǫ habitabiles paria agūt Pōpo: anni tempora/verū nō pariter. Antichthones alte≠ Mellǫ ram/nos alteram incolimus. Illius fitus ob ardorē in tercedentis plagǫ incognitus /huius dicendus eft. Vbi animaduertendum eft quod climatū quodꝗ alios ꝗ aliud plerūꝗ fœtus ꝓducat/cū diuerfǫ fūt naturǫ/& alia atꝗ alia fyderū virtute moderentur. Vnde Virgilius.

Nec vero terrǫ ferre omnes omnia poffunt   Vergi≠
Hic fegetes/illic veniunt fœlicius vuǫ   lius
Arborei fœtus alibi/atꝗ iniuffa virefcunt
Gramia. Nōne vides croceos vt Thmolus odores
India mittit ebur: mittūt fua thura Sabǫi
At Calybes nudi ferrū: virofaꝗ pontus
Cofterea. Eliadū palmas Ep iros equarū &c.
OCTAVVM CAPVT DE VENTIS.
Quonia͂ in fuperioribus ventorū aliquando in≠ cidenter memores fuimns(cū. f. polū Boreū/ polū Nothicū/atꝗ id genus alia diximus)& ipforū co≠
a iij

WALDSEEMÜLLER'S *COSMOGRAPHIAE INTRODUCTIO*. A page from the document that first uses the name *America*. Saint-Dié, 1507.

Sandaucourt and one of Ringmann's poems. It is probable that copies were sold with the map. In this work Waldseemüller explains, "So it comes about that while we (having recently set up a printing office in the town of Saint-Dié in the Vosges) were collating Ptolemy's books from a Greek manuscript, and supplementing them from the description of Amerigo's four voyages, we have prepared a representation of the whole world in the form of a globe and in that of a map."

The *Cosmography*, the sections for a globe produced in 1506, and the world map all identified the newly discovered lands by the name "America," here used for the first time. In this volume Waldseemüller explains the reason for the selection of the name:

Now, really these [three] parts [Europe, Africa, and Asia] were more widely traveled, and another fourth part was discovered by Americus Vesputius (as will be seen in the following pages), for which reason I do not see why anyone would rightly forbid calling it (after the discoverer Americus, a man of wisdom and ingenuity) "Amerige," that is, land of Americus, or "America," since both "Europa" and "Asia" are names derived from women. Its location and the customs of its people will be easily discerned from the four voyages of Americus which follow.

The world map is entitled *Universalis cosmographia secunda Ptholemei traditionem et Americi Vespuccii aliorum que lustrationes* (A drawing of the whole earth following the tradition of Ptolemy and the travels of Amerigo Vespucci and others). The earth is depicted in a cordiform (heart-shaped) image and marked in degrees of latitude and longitude. The two parts of the recently discovered American continents are shown separated by a strait with the western coast depicted for the first time but without delineation. In a planisphere at the head of the map, however, the two are joined by land. The delineation of the Atlantic coast of South America appears to have been based on the world portolano (a medieval navigation manual) of the Portuguese cartographer Nicolo Caneiro, and the western coast is shown for the first time. The North American continent extends from the eleventh to the fifty-third degree and is labeled *Terra ulteri incognita*. The South American continent is shown to extend from the ninth degree of latitude to beyond Cape St. Vincent. Its northeastern coast is labeled *tota ista provincia inventa est per mandatum regis Castelle* (all of this province was discovered by mandate of the king of Castile). The name "America" appears approximately in midsection.

The map includes planispheres that depict the Old World and the New as well as a portrait, probably symbolizing Ptolemy, which would indicate that his work provided the source for the Old World cartography. A portrait labeled "Vespucci" next to the New World suggests that he provided the information for that part of the map. Waldseemüller also indicates in the legend that the map was based upon Ptolemy's maps, probably from the Ulm edition of 1482, and upon the published accounts of Vespucci.

The world map was designed as a large wall chart and consisted of twelve sheets, each measuring 450 mm × 500 mm (17.7 × 19.7 inches). The sides of each sheet were made to be trimmed off so that the edges of the map proper could be brought together, although the match proved to be sometimes one or two centimeters off. When assembled, the map would be 1200 mm (47.2 inches) high and 2400 mm (94.5 inches) wide. It is printed in black ink from woodcuts. Some of the place names and descriptions were cut in the woodblock itself, while others were set in printer's type and inserted into openings cut in the wood. Occasional touches of hand-applied color occur, such as red dots for cities and red and yellow coloration in the armorial crests. In the surviving copy a grid of red lines has been drawn by hand in pen and ink over the printing to mark off degrees and a number of handwritten corrections are to be found. The four corners of the map contain long introductory texts within woodcut frames. Neither the mapmaker's name nor the place or date of production appears on the map. The identity of the

printer is not known, but Johann Grüninger of Strasbourg is considered to have been the most likely. (Although a number of Strasbourg printers worked for the Gymnase at Saint-Dié, Grüninger had the longest association with the group, and in fact Ringmann had been employed by him as proofreader immediately before joining the group.)

The world map appears to have been widely distributed, for other cartographers quickly copied it and adopted the use of the name "America." Among the earliest copies made from it were maps produced in 1509 by Johann Grüninger, a map dated 1512 by Jan Stobniczy, Johannes Schöner's terrestrial globe of 1515, Peter Apian's map and *Cosmographicus* of 1520, the world map of Gerhard Mercator, and maps produced by Henricus Glareanus, Johannes Honter, Louis d'Albi Boulenger, Erhard Reysch, and others.

If one studies the surviving example of the map, it is clear that it was not part of the first edition, but printed at a later time, probably in about 1516, because it shows ample evidence that the woodblocks from which it was printed were damaged and well worn in many instances. Furthermore, the watermark of the paper on which it is printed coincides with that used for the *Carta marina* designed by Waldseemüller and dated 1516.

After completing the sections for a globe, the *Cosmography*, the sea chart, and the world map, the members of the Gymnase Vosgien resumed work on the new edition of Ptolemy's atlas, to be entitled *Claudii Ptholemei viri Alexandrini mathematicae disciplinae philosophi doctissimi geographiae opus novissima traductione e Graecorum archetypis castigatissime pressum; caereris ante lucubratorum multo praestantis* (The geographical work of Claudius Ptolemy, the man of Alexandria, a most erudite philosopher of mathematical learning, closely reprinted by reproduction of the Greek originals). In order to resolve disparities in place names and textual content the scholars turned to other manuscript and printed copies of Ptolemy's atlas. Ringmann translated place names and texts from Greek to Latin and Waldseemüller designed the maps. Then several factors interfered with the progress of the work. Ringmann died of tuberculosis in the autumn of 1511 and Gauthier Lud experienced increasing financial difficulties. Finally work on the atlas had to be abandoned. The maps, texts, and related materials were acquired by two Strasbourg lawyers who arranged to have the atlas completed and published by the Strasbourg printer Johann Schott. It is probable that Waldseemüller moved to Strasbourg for a time to work with Schott to complete the remaining maps. The atlas appeared in 1513 and was immediately popular. Two more editions were published within the next decade.

During the following years, Waldseemüller and his colleagues accumulated much additional information about the Spanish and Portuguese voyages of discovery. They revised some of their earlier misconceptions, realizing, for example, that the lands discovered by Columbus and those reported by Vespucci were the same.

In 1516 Waldseemüller completed the design of a nautical chart in the form of a large wall map entitled *Carta marina navigatoria Portugallen* (A Portuguese navigator's sea chart); it included the *Tabula terre nove* (Map of the new lands) from the 1507 world map which had also been incorporated into the atlas. The *Carta marina* contained information derived from the voyages of Columbus as well as from Vespucci's letters. The name "America" was deleted, as was the strait between the two American mainlands. The phrase "Brasilia terra sive papagalli" (Brazil, land of parrots) was added to the northeastern coast of South America, and a more complete nomenclature was provided. Cuba continued to be identified as part of Asia, however, and owing to the interruption caused by the borders, the map gave the erroneous impression that the newly discovered lands were a continuation of the east coast of Asia.

Although celebrated in its own time as a magnificent scholarly production containing the latest information about the known world and reportedly published in an edition of one thousand, for several centuries no copies of either the world map or the *Carta marina* were known to have survived. In the course of time Waldseemüller's cartographic work was superseded, and his use of the name "America" was forgotten. It did not come to notice again until 1828 when the American author Washington Irving noted in his *Life and Voyages of Columbus* that the explanation for naming the continent "America" was to be found in the *Cosmography*. Irving's work attracted little attention until 1838 when the German geographer Alexander von Humboldt commented on Irving's report in his *Examen critique de l'histoire de la géographie du nouveau continent aux XVe et XVIe siècles* (Critical examination of the history of the geography of the New Continent in the fifteenth and sixteenth centuries). This led to a search for the missing map in libraries and archives throughout Europe but without success. One explanation for the lack of surviving copies may be its size: the sheets of the world map were usually pasted onto a board or a wall; as the map became worn or damaged it was discarded.

It was not until 1901 that a copy of the world map was found. While Josef Fischer, a professor of geography, was conducting research on the Norse settlements in North America, he discovered a copy in the library of Castle Wolfegg in Wolfegg (in present-day Baden-Württemberg). Its twelve sheets had been bound into a volume together with the twelve sheets of Waldseemüller's *Carta marina*, a star chart by Albrecht Dürer, and two incomplete sets of gores, one for a terrestrial globe and another for a celestial globe. Those for the terrestrial globe had been used to reinforce the binding. The volume is bound in sixteenth-century tooled pigskin bearing the bookplate of the geographer Johannes Schöner, who presumably had them brought together and bound.

Fischer identified the world map from contemporary copies and references, and in cooperation with the German historian Franz von Weiser, he produced a work containing a facsimile of both the world map and the *Carta marina* accompanied by a historical essay published at Innsbruck and London in 1903. In 1983 the unique copy of the map left Castle Wolfegg on a temporary loan and was placed on public display in the National Museum of American History of the Smithsonian Institution in Washington, D.C.

[See also *Cartography* and biographies of Humboldt, Ptolemy, Santángel, Vespucci, and Waldseemüller.]

BIBLIOGRAPHY

Avezac-Macaya, Armand d'. *Martin Hylacomylus Waldseemüller: Ses ouvrages et ses collaborateurs.* Paris, 1867. Reprint, Amsterdam, 1980.

Fischer, Josef, and Franz von Weiser. *The Oldest Map with the Name America of the Year 1507 and the Carta Marina of the Year 1516 by M. Waldseemüller (Ilacomilus).* Innsbruck and London, 1903.

Harris, Elizabeth. "The Waldseemüller World Map: An Appraisal." *Imago Mundi* 37 (1985):30–53.

Humboldt, Alexander von. *Examen critique de l'histoire de la géographie du nouveau continent aux XVe et XVIe siècles.* Paris, 1836–1838. Vol. 4, pp. 101–111.

Laubenberger, Franz. "The Naming of America." *Sixteenth Century Journal* 13, no. 4 (1982).

Morison, Samuel Eliot. *The European Discovery of America: The Southern Voyages, 1492–1616.* New York, 1974.

Schwartz, Seymour I., and Ralph E. Ehrenberg. *The Mapping of America.* New York, 1980.

Skelton, R. A. "Bibliographical Note." In facsimile edition of *Claudius Ptolemaeus. Geographia Strassburg 1513.* Amsterdam, 1966.

SILVIO A. BEDINI

ANGHIERA, PIETRO MARTIRE D' (c. 1457–1526), humanist, author of earliest description of the New World. Pietro Martire (Peter Martyr) d'Anghiera's career began at the ducal court of Milan; from there he went to Rome to serve as the secretary to the governor, Francesco de Negri. A member of the humanist circle centered on the Roman Academy, d'Anghiera became friends with powerful patrons such as Cardinal Ascanio Sforza and the count of Tendilla, the Spanish ambassador to the papal court. When in 1487 the count of Tendilla persuaded d'Anghiera to relocate to the Spanish court, d'Anghiera

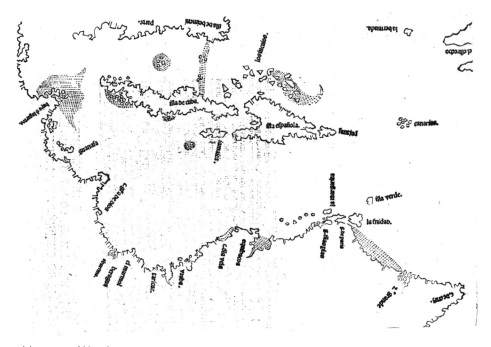

MAP OF THE WEST INDIES. From d'Anghiera's *Decades*, 1511.

promised Sforza that he would write to him regularly about events in Spain. D'Anghiera arrived in Spain in 1488. Ordained as a priest, he was appointed chaplain and humanist at the royal court, where he was well-positioned to observe the events that unfolded in the wake of Columbus's triumphant return from his first voyage. As a member of the Council of the Indies, to which he was appointed in 1518, d'Anghiera was able to supplement first-hand oral accounts from the returning explorers (including Columbus himself), conquistadores, and Indian slave-raiders with the stream of reports, petitions, and official documents related to the events he describes.

D'Anghiera's two major works consisted of letters written to patrons and friends. The *Opus epistolarum* contains eighty-three letters, the first dated 1488 and the last 1525. The *De rebus oceanis et Orbe Novo decades* consists of eight sections, or decades, containing letters written over thirty-two years (1493–1525) and addressed to six patrons, including Sforza.

Both works deal with the New World. D'Anghiera first gives news (in a letter written on September 13, 1493, included in the *Opus*) of the "new discovery" and of Columbus's return "safe and sound" with reports of the "marvelous things" including "gold" as "proof of the existence of mines" that he had found. The historiography of Columbus's *Indias occidentales* begins, however, with *De Orbe Novo*, in which d'Anghiera advances the new thesis of a homogeneous earth, which contradicted, and

ultimately replaced, the premises of classical geography. The *De Orbe Novo* popularized what J. H. Elliot calls the "myth of America" by transposing to the New World Greco-Roman ideas about a golden age and the noble savage in a state of nature. As the anthropologist Jacob Pandian notes, the factual differences of New World cultures and peoples would be seen as signs of human otherness to the "true" rational self and culture of the Europeans. New World peoples would be represented either as noble savages and temporal others who lived "without enforcement of laws" in the peaceful "goulden worlde of which Owlde writers speake so much" (from Richard Eden's translation) or as cannibals who were "savage and monstrous" (Decade 3, book 2).

These interpretations, as Richard Waswo shows in the related case of Edmund Spenser's *Faerie Queene*, would serve to shape perceptions, and therefore to legitimate the social domination of the incoming European settlers over the indigenous peoples of d'Anghiera's New World.

In 1520, d'Anghiera was appointed court historiographer in recognition of his *De Orbe Novo*. In 1524 the king named him to the abbacy of the island of Santiago (Jamaica). This abbacy had been established in 1515 in Sevilla la Nueva, the first town founded, in 1509, by Columbus's son, Diego Colón (then newly appointed viceroy of the Indies), on the site on which Columbus and his crew had been shipwrecked for a little over a year on his return from his fourth and last voyage. D'Anghiera used the tithes from his abbacy to build the first stone church in Sevilla la Nueva and managed to coax matching funds from the emperor, Charles V.

D'Anghiera never set foot in Jamaica or in any part of the New World of which he wrote. However, where his descriptive set pieces were written in terms of the preestablished themes of classical literature, they were interspersed with first-person reports taken fresh from the mouths of the returning participants and through the prism of their cultural perceptions. It is this that gives to *De Orbe Novo* its unique and irreplaceable quality, the quality of a report from the front, as seen by one of the sides in the major confrontation that took place between two worlds that had remained oblivious of each other's existence until, as d'Anghiera begins, "a certain Christopher Columbus, a Genoese, proposed to the Catholic King and Queen, Ferdinand and Isabella, to discover the islands which touch the Indies."

BIBLIOGRAPHY

Anghiera, Pietro Martire d'. *De Orbe Novo: The Eight Decades of Peter Martyr D'Anghera.* Translated by Francis A. MacNutt. New York, 1912. Reprint, 1970.

Anghiera, Pietro Martire d'. *Decades del nuevo mundo.* 2 vols. Edited by Edmundo O'Gorman. Mexico, 1964.

Elliot, J. H. *The Old World and the New, 1492 to 1650.* Cambridge, 1970.

Gerbi, Antonelli. *La natura delle Indie Nove: Da Cristoforo Colombo a Gonzalo Fernandez de Oviedo.* Milan and Naples, 1975.

O'Gorman, Edmundo. *La idea del descubrimiento de America. Historia de esa interpretación y critica de sus fundamentos.* Mexico City, 1951.

Pagden, Anthony. *The Fall of Natural Man: The American Indian and The Origins of Comparative Ethnology.* Cambridge, 1982.

Pandian, Jacob. *Anthropology and the Western Tradition: Towards an Authentic Anthropology.* Prospect Heights, Ill., 1985.

Van Sertima, I. *They Came before Columbus.* New York, 1976.

Waswo, Richard. "The History That Literature Makes." *New Literary History* 19 (1988): 541–565.

Wynter, Sylvia. *New Seville: Major Facts, Major Questions.* Kingston, Jamaica, 1984.

SYLVIA WYNTER

ANIMALS. See *Domesticated Animals; Fauna.*

ANTICHRIST. According to Christian doctrine and legend, Antichrist is a malevolent leader of evil forces who will appear on the eve of the end of time to contest Christ and the church in a final cataclysmic combat. Antichrist is mentioned but four times in scripture. These all occur in the Johannine letters: *1 John* 2:18, 2:22, and 4:3; and *2 John* 7. Other passages drawn from the Old and New Testaments, the Apocrypha, and late antique Jewish and Byzantine apocalyptic and prophetic literature have traditionally been considered to refer to Antichrist as well.

Throughout the medieval period, Antichrist figured prominently in the interweavings of prophecy and political ideology characteristic of a body of authoritative providential histories and related exegetical literature. In such writings, Antichrist and his forces frequently were identified with individuals and groups who threatened social and religious stability from within and without Europe. A number of these works, notably Joachim of Fiore's *Liber concordie Novi et Veteris Testamenti* and *Expositio in Apocalypsim,* and Roger Bacon's *Opus maius* (all written in the thirteenth century), influenced Europeans active in the early phases of the exploration and conquest of the Americas.

Christopher Columbus appears to have been acquainted with the figure of Antichrist and his eschatological role primarily through a cluster of works written in 1414 by the prominent late-medieval theologian Pierre d'Ailly (1350–1420). In these works, d'Ailly drew heavily upon sections of Bacon's *Opus maius,* itself a digest of earlier apocalyptic materials, especially the seventh-century Byzantine apocalypse of Pseudo-Methodius.

Columbus's annotations to d'Ailly's works, the materials he gathered for an unfinished work to be called "The Book of Prophecies," and several letters he wrote to Fernando and Isabel indicate that he anticipated the imminent advent of the Antichrist and the end of time. Although he sought to place his achievements and those of his regents within a historical context that was penultimate, Columbus does not appear to have identified Antichrist with any particular contemporary.

References to Antichrist also appear in a number of works composed by mendicant missionaries active in the evangelization of the indigenous peoples of Mexico subsequent to Hernando Cortés's conquest of the Aztec empire in 1521. Franciscan chroniclers in particular, heirs to the Joachimite tradition of apocalyptic conversion, believed that they were effecting the final Christianizing of the infidel that would presage the end of time. In perhaps the most well known of such chronicles, Gerónimo de Mendieta's *Historia eclesiástica indiana* (completed in 1596), Antichrist is identified with the Protestant leader Martin Luther. The many conversions of Indian souls in the New World, Mendieta argues, will offset the contemporaneous losses to this Antichrist in the Old World.

BIBLIOGRAPHY

Alexander, Paul. *The Byzantine Apocalyptic Tradition.* Berkeley, 1985.

Bossuet, Wilhelm. *The Antichrist Legend.* London, 1896.

Emmerson, Richard Kenneth. *Antichrist in the Middle Ages: A Study of Medieval Apocalypticism, Art, and Literature*. Seattle, 1981.

Phelan, John Leddy. *The Millennial Kingdom of the Franciscans in the New World*. 2d ed. Berkeley, 1970.

Reeves, Marjorie. *The Influence of Prophecy in the Later Middle Ages: A Study in Joachimism*. Oxford, 1969.

Watts, Pauline Moffitt. "Prophecy and Discovery: On the Spiritual Origins of Christopher Columbus's 'Enterprise of the Indies.'" *American Historical Review* 90 (1985): 73–102.

PAULINE MOFFITT WATTS

ARANA, BEATRIZ DE (c. 1465–1522), mistress of Christopher Columbus; mother of his son Fernando Colón. Beatriz Enríquez de Arana was born to Pedro de Torquemada and Ana Núñez de Arana in Santa María de Trassiera. After the death of Pedro de Torquemada, his widow moved to Córdoba, where she died in 1471, leaving two children: Beatriz and Pedro. Their grandmother, Eleonora Núñez, and the maternal aunt, Mayor Enríquez de Arana, took charge of the guardianship of the two orphans.

Beatriz de Arana learned to read and write, a rare achievement in a period in which most wives and daughters of noblemen did not know how to sign their own names. After the death of their grandmother, the minors continued their education in the house of their aunt until her death sometime after May 12, 1478. Thereafter, the guardianship and trusteeship of the minors fell to Rodrigo Enríquez de Arana, a cousin of Ana Núñez, who was the closest relative of the orphans.

How did Beatriz come to meet Columbus? During the first thirty months of his sojourn in Castile (1485–1487), Christopher Columbus chose Córdoba for his residence. The monarchs of Spain were living there in 1485 when Columbus arrived in Castile. It is probable that Columbus did not accompany the sovereigns to Galicia, but joined them some months later in Salamanca, where he was to participate in the council examining his project. Columbus returned to Córdoba when the court did, in the first days of March 1487. Here he resided until March 1488, when he moved to Murcia, where he would again be received by the Catholic monarchs.

During this time Córdoba was a lively place. Because of its strategic position, the monarchs were transforming it into the most important center of Andalusia. There were many Italian merchants present in Córdoba then, prominent among them the Genoese storekeepers Luciano and Leonardo Esbarroya. It was in Esbarroya's shop that Christopher Columbus met Diego de Arana and his father, Rodrigo Enríquez de Arana.

Diego, a cousin of Beatriz, brought the Genoese into his home, and it is probable that it was he who introduced Beatriz to Columbus. By the end of October 1487, their relationship was intimate. In July 1488, in Córdoba, Beatriz gave birth to a son whom Columbus recognized as his and to whom he gave the name Fernando in honor of the Spanish king.

There is no doubt that Fernando eventually became recognized as Columbus's legitimate son. He acquired all the honors of his father and participated in the inheritance. In a public act undersigned by the Admiral in Seville on October 31, 1497, Diego and Fernando were defined as "his legitimate sons," and the title of "don" conferred not only on Diego but also on Fernando. (J. Manzano Manzano gives us a detailed and well-documented analysis of the manner in which the legitimation process must have taken place.)

But at the moment of his birth Fernando was illegitimate—his father was widowed; his mother, unmarried. Bartolomé de las Casas attests that Diego was the legitimate son of the Admiral, and Fernando "his natural son." And Gonzalo Fernández de Oviedo calls don Diego the legitimate and older son, and adds, "and the other son of his, don Fernando."

Columbus never married Beatriz. When he returned from the first voyage, he was given the greatest of honors and elevated to the highest position in Spain. Because of his discovery, he became one of the most illustrious persons at the Spanish court and had to submit, like all the great persons of the time, to customary legal restrictions on matters of marriage and extramarital relations. The Alphonsine laws forbade extramarital relations of concubinage for "illustrious people" (king, princes, dukes, counts, marquis) with plebeian women, if they themselves were or their forefathers had been of inferior social condition.

This is why Columbus, in other ways so scrupulous and pious, did not regularize his relationship with Beatriz but ordered his son and heir, Diego Colón, "to take care of Beatriz Enriquez, mother of don Fernando; let my son provide the necessary means so that she may live honestly, on account of my good name. And let this be done for the relief of my conscience, because it weighs much on my soul. It is not right/lawful to record here the reason."

With these words Columbus reveals his undischarged debt to Beatriz and entrusts to his heir the reparation of his error. Just as revealing are Columbus's words, also directed to Diego in 1502, before the beginning of the fourth and last voyage to the Indies: "I recommend to you for my sake, Beatriz Enríquez, as I would your own mother."

After the discovery, however, Columbus was not very generous toward the woman to whom he owed so much. Fortunately, the revenue from real estate inherited from her own mother and from other close relatives, together with the above-mentioned pension, gave Beatriz a livelihood.

After the death of the Admiral, Beatriz complained to her son Fernando about the lack of punctuality Diego showed in paying the annual pension assigned to her by Columbus. At least, this seems to be the significance of her last known public act. On May 11, 1521, she gave a power of attorney to the Genoese Francesco Cassana, residing in Seville, so that he could collect from the Genoese Juan Francesco de Grimaldo, a Spanish banker, all the maravedis he would be willing to give to her on account of her son Fernando Colón.

Beatriz Enríquez de Arana apparently died not too long after. On September 8, 1532, Diego Colón, who was making his will on the island of Santo Domingo, wrote that the heirs of Beatriz were to be paid all the pensions left unpaid in the preceding three or four years. At her death, all the real estate she possessed in Santa María de Trassierra, consisting of a house with a workshop and a wine press, two orchards, and three vineyard plots, went to her son Fernando. The latter, on August 17, 1525, gave this property as a gift to his cousin Pedro de Arana, one of the sons of Beatriz's only brother.

These events reveal that the behavior of the Admiral and his heir, Diego, was marked sometimes by negligence and forgetfulness, and sometimes by scruples and sincere intentions, if not actual deeds, to remedy a wrongful situation.

BIBLIOGRAPHY

Ballesteros Beretta, Antonio. *Cristóbal Colón y el descubrimiento de América*. Vol. 1. Barcelona and Buenos Aires, 1945.

De la Torre, J. *Beatriz Enriquez de Harana y Cristóbal Colón*. Madrid, 1933.

Manzano Manzano, Juan. *Cristóbal Colón: Siete años decisivos de su vida, 1485–1492*. Madrid, 1964.

Taviani, Paolo Emilio. *Christopher Columbus: The Grand Design*. London, 1985.

PAOLO EMILIO TAVIANI
Translated from Italian by Rodica Diaconescu-Blumenfeld

ARANA, DIEGO DE (fl. 1490s)

ARANA, DIEGO DE (fl. 1490s), marshal of the fleet on Columbus's first voyage. A native of Córdoba, Diego de Arana was a cousin of Beatriz Enríquez de Arana, Columbus's mistress and mother of the Admiral's second son, Fernando. As marshal of Columbus's flagship, *Santa María*, in 1492, Arana was recognized as chief marshal of the fleet with overall authority over the marshals of the other ships in the fleet (each ship had a marshal responsible for maintaining order, resolving disputes among the crew, and punishing offenders).

During the build-up of mutinous feelings among some members of the crews of all three ships in the tense days before the landfall at Guanahani (San Salvador), Arana seems to have earned Columbus's trust. While exploring the north coast of the large island which he named La Española (Hispaniola), Columbus sent Arana ashore with an interpreter to present a gift to the local cacique (chieftain) and to inquire about gold. A few days later, when *Santa María* ran aground and broke up on a reef, Columbus decided to build a fort, which he named La Navidad, to be garrisoned by crew members from *Santa María* and *Niña*. He designated Arana as commander of the settlement. When the ships of the second voyage returned to La Navidad, Columbus learned that Arana's two lieutenants had formed a gang of malcontents that left the fort to maraud for gold and women. An important cacique, Caonabó, had the marauders killed and attacked the fort. Although aided by a friendly cacique, Guacanagarí, Arana and the ten men with him were killed.

BIBLIOGRAPHY

Gould, Alicia B. *Nueva lista documentada de los tripulantes de Colón en 1492*. Madrid, 1984.

Morison, Samuel Eliot. *Admiral of the Ocean Sea: A Life of Christopher Columbus*. 2 vols. Boston, 1942.

WILLIAM LEMOS

ARANA, PEDRO DE (fl. 1490s), captain of one of the ships of Columbus's third voyage. A native of Córdoba, Pedro de Arana was a cousin of Diego de Arana, commander of the garrison left at La Navidad when Columbus returned to Spain at the end of the first voyage. More significantly, perhaps, Pedro was the brother of Beatriz Enríquez de Arana, Columbus's mistress and mother of Fernando, the Admiral's second son. This kinship quite likely was a factor in his appointment by Columbus as captain of one of the eight ships of the third voyage.

There is no extant record of the name of the ship captained by Arana. It is known, however, that it was one of three caravels, *Garza*, *La Gorda*, or *La Rábida*, loaded with supplies, artisans, farmers, laborers, and *ballesteros* (crossbowmen) for the new colony, Isabela Nueva (now Santo Domingo), established in 1496 by Columbus's brother, Bartolomé Colón, on the south coast of La Española (Hispaniola). Having departed from Sanlúcar de Barrameda on May 30, 1498, as a part of the third voyage fleet, these three caravels were detached at the Canary Islands and instructed by Columbus to proceed independently to Isabela Nueva.

Unfortunately, the pilots of the three caravels lacked Columbus's skill in dead-reckoning navigation and made their landfall at Jaraguá at the western end of La Española, where Francisco Roldán and his rebels were in control. Not knowing about Roldán's rebellion, the captains of the caravels allowed their men to go ashore, where many of them were induced to desert. The captains, remaining loyal to Columbus, finally managed, despite strong headwinds and adverse current, to make their way to Isabela Nueva in their undermanned ships. There the historical record of Pedro de Arana ends.

BIBLIOGRAPHY

Gould, Alicia B. *Nueva lista documentada de los tripulantes de Colón en 1492*. Madrid, 1984.

Morison, Samuel Eliot. *Admiral of the Ocean Sea: A Life of Christopher Columbus*. 2 vols. Boston, 1942.

WILLIAM LEMOS

ARAWAKS AND CARIBS. See *Indian America*, article on *Arawaks and Caribs*.

ARCHAEOLOGY. [This entry includes two articles that introduce the techniques and results of archaeological research concerning European presence in the New World during the early years of contact and European settlement:

Land Archaeology

Underwater Archaeology

See also *Bahamas; Cuba; Cuzco; Española, La; Jamaica; Landfall Controversy; Puerto Rico; Settlements; Vinland; West Indies*. For discussion of related research, see *Disease and Demography*.]

Land Archaeology

Archaeology on sites believed to have been visited or occupied by Christopher Columbus has been carried out intermittently since the nineteenth century. The goals of this research have included the search for and verification of sites at which Columbus is known to have been, the study of the earliest settlements he founded, the recovery of relics related to his ventures, and the investigation of the immediate impacts of his arrival on the people of the Americas.

Most of the New World sites identified with Columbus, and nearly all of those outside La Española (Hispaniola), are Caribbean Indian settlements believed to have been visited by him. One of the most difficult methodological problems in the archaeology of these sites lies in recognizing a European presence (as opposed to the mere presence of European objects) in the archaeological record. European artifacts of the Columbian era in association with contact-era Amerindian remains is provoca-

tive, but could be accounted for by the very active and widespread trade networks among the native peoples of the Caribbean. European items (particularly iron, glass, and glazed ceramics, which were unknown in the Americas prior to European contact) were highly exotic and therefore widely prized by the American Indians, as is amply verified in documents of the era. Such items are likely to have been curated and traded, and they were probably hoarded by the economic elite of native Caribbean society. They are not likely to have been lost or discarded, the most common ways (along with burials) in which articles enter the archaeological record. The most successful identifications of sites occupied by Columbus, therefore, have been those that reveal and date nonartifactual European features and that closely correlate archaeological, documentary, and geomorphological evidence.

A related problem in identifying the presence of Columbus is the fact that it is not possible (except in the extraordinary cases of dated coins) to distinguish artifacts of 1492 from artifacts of 1500. This presents the obvious difficulty of isolating materials left by Columbus from materials left by the many travelers and explorers who followed him during the fifteenth century.

Most of the archaeological efforts related to the presence of Columbus have relied on a relatively limited group of artifacts that can be confidently dated to the closing decades of the fifteenth century. This dating has been based both on the contemporary accounts of Columbus and his companions and on the excavations of sites, such as La Isabela, that are known to have existed only during the Columbian era.

Trade items known to have accompanied all of the voyages include glass beads of blue, green, and yellow; combs, scissors, and mirrors; hawkbells; iron fishhooks; coins; glass bottles; and "tinklers" (brass or copper shapes with a perforation for sewing on clothes). Articles from archaeological sites have included the pottery types of Melado ware (a honey-colored glazed ware) and green bacín; the majolica types of Isabela polychrome, Columbia plain, Caparra blue, and Yayal blue on white; perforated brass crescents, circles, and triangles; tiny doughnut-shaped glass beads in yellow and green; brass finger rings set with a single, colored glass stone; horseshoes; small iron buckles; and Venetian style glassware, both plain and latticinio.

With the advances in transatlantic commerce and the radiation outward from La Española, the material world of Columbus was greatly changed after 1500. This transition has been archaeologically traced at a number of sites throughout the Caribbean.

Much of the archaeology in support of the Columbian quincentenary has been concerned with the issue of the original Bahamas landfall site of October 1492. With regard to this controversial issue, archaeology has been engaged in a supplemental role: to search for contact-period Indian sites in locations hypothesized to have been that of the landfall. Although possible sites have been located, few contain evidence of European presence, and none can definitively be said to have been the landfall site, owing to the methodological problems noted above.

The Long Bay site on San Salvador Island, excavated by Charles Hoffman of Northern Arizona University, has yielded a variety of late fifteenth-century Spanish and Italian artifacts, including glass beads, metal buckle fragments, Castilian coins of the late fifteenth century, and fragments of Spanish pottery. These occur in association with Taino Indian remains and are the kinds of objects (if not the actual objects) brought to the Americas on Columbus's voyages of exploration.

Another approach to the landfall issue has been taken by William Keegan and Steven Mitchell, who have attempted to correlate Columbus's physical descriptions of the Bahamas with geomorphological reconstructions of the islands' coastlines as they may have been in 1492. They are able in turn to correlate these results with archaeological sites.

Columbus visited and named a large number of the Caribbean islands and portions of the South and Central American coastlines during his four voyages. He and the chroniclers accompanying him often described Indian towns and chiefs they visited. Most of these encounters, however, were of a few days duration at most, and there was no long-term European occupation during the Columbian era except for La Española. Relatively little archaeological material related directly to Columbus can thus be identified elsewhere in the Caribbean, although considerable speculation about the specific locations visited has been offered by archaeologists working throughout the islands.

Cuba was briefly explored during the first and second voyages (1492 and 1494), and large Indian towns were described and visited. Cuban and North American archaeologists have identified several Indian sites containing early Spanish materials in the Banes region of northeastern Cuba, known to have been visited by Columbus on his first voyage. These sites contain glass beads; iron buckles and knife fragments; horseshoes and harness hardware; bits of chain, scissors, nails, and coins; and pieces of Spanish pottery. One of these sites, at Yayal, has been extensively excavated over the years and, as Lourdes Dominguez has shown, was apparently occupied well into the sixteenth century by the Cuban Indians.

Jamaica was first visited and described by Columbus in 1494, and he was later shipwrecked and stranded there for more than a year, during his fourth voyage. The site of the shipwreck and camp is believed to be at Saint Ann's Bay, and archaeological work in search of it has been undertaken. Columbus also visited the island's south coast, where he described a very large Indian town on a high hill that appears to correspond to the White Marl site at which John Goggin found fifteenth-century Spanish pottery.

Columbus also met difficulty during his fourth voyage in what is now Panama (then known as Veragua), near the Belen River. Storms forced the fleet into the Belen harbor in January and then silted the river mouth to the extent that Columbus could not leave until the end of April. He built a small settlement and named it Santa María de Belén. From there he and his men traded and fought with the resident Indian population. When storms finally opened the harbor, Indian hostility forced Columbus to abandon the small settlement. He was also obliged to abandon one of his vessels, Gallega, in the Belen River, owing to the considerable worm damage suffered during the stay in the river.

In the Lesser Antilles there are few sites at which European artifacts of the Columbian era have been identified, although Columbus is known to have visited a number of these islands. Neither have fifteenth-century European sites been conclusively identified in Trinidad or at the adjacent Peninsula and Gulf of Paria at the mouth of the Orinoco River (Venezuela). Both of these areas were explored by Columbus during his third voyage.

It was also during the third voyage that the "pearl coast" of northern Venezuela and its associated islands was first recorded by Columbus. This area was later to become a major focus of settlement, because of the economic interest in pearls. Much of the pearl industry was centered on Margarita and Cubagua islands, where the important site of Nueva Cádiz was located and excavated. Although Nueva Cádiz (1515–1545) was not occupied during the Columbian era, the excavation of the site by José Cruxent, Alfred Boulton, and John Goggin during the 1950s yielded a large collection of early sixteenth-century Spanish and Indian materials. These illustrate a transplanted Spanish lifestyle, supported by the exploitive, Indian-slave-based pearl fishing industry.

The earliest and only planned European settlements of the Columbian era were in La Española, primarily in that part which is today the Dominican Republic. The earliest nonintentional settlement, the fortress of La Navidad, was also located in La Española; it was established in 1492 near present-day Cap Haïtien, Haiti.

On Christmas Eve of 1492, Santa María was grounded and could not be repaired. With the assistance of the Indian chief Guacanagarí, the ship was dismantled and unloaded and a small fortress was constructed in or near Guacanagarí's town. Columbus left thirty-nine men there for nine months, during which they all died.

EXCAVATIONS AT NUEVA CÁDIZ, CUBAGUA ISLANDS, 1960.   UNIDAD DE FOTOGRAFIA CIENTÍFICA, I.V.I.C.

The site of Guacanagarí's town, and possibly of La Navidad, was located by William Hodges in 1976. It has been subsequently excavated by Kathleen Deagan, working with Hodges, and excavations have verified its date and the presence of European animal and artifact remains from the Columbian era. No structural features definitely attributable to European origin have yet been verified.

Columbus returned to La Navidad on his second voyage in 1492 with seventeen ships and nearly two thousand men (no women). He brought all the resources believed necessary to establish a formal colony, including craftsmen and artisans, animals, and plants. When they found La Navidad burned and all of the men dead, they decided to abandon that area and sail eastward along the north coast of La Española. They established the first Spanish town in the Americas at La Isabela, about seventy kilometers east of La Navidad.

La Isabela had several stone and packed-earth buildings, including a church, fortress, storehouse, and the house alleged to have been occupied by Columbus. It had a limestone quarry and kilns (recently discovered and excavated by José Cruxent) for making tiles, bricks, and possibly simple pottery. The 1,700 inhabitants lived in some two hundred thatch and wood huts.

The site of La Isabela has been known to scholars since its abandonment in 1498. Several of the stone structures have been located, excavated, and identified, as have been the quarry and kiln. The town has been investigated archaeologically a number of times since 1892.

La Isabela was plagued from its start by disease, discord among the settlers, mutinies, Indian attacks, and crop failures. By 1498 it had been largely abandoned, and other Columbus-related settlements took precedence.

Within months of founding La Isabela, Columbus established the small fortress of Santo Tomás, located about three miles from the present town of Janico. Santo Tomás was intended to guard the route between La Isabela and the allegedly gold-rich interior of the island. It was made of wood and packed earth, and had a moat on one side. The site has been located and recorded by Elpidio Ortega, and traces of the moat can still be seen. No excavations have been reported at the site.

In 1495 another fort was established in the interior (referred to as the "Cibao"). This was Concepción de la Vega, which is today, like La Isabela, a Dominican Republic national park. It was intended as a fortified center from which to trade gold, and it soon became a thriving, large town built largely of brick and tile. The site still contains substantial architectural remains, including those from the cathedral, the fort, the monastery, the water and irrigation systems, and other structures. Archaeological work has been underway intermittently since the 1950s, concentrating for the most part on the major architectural elements of the fort and monastery.

A very large and rich assemblage of artifacts reflects a very European material world. These include Spanish and Italian pottery, ornate Venetian glassware, gilded book and chest clasps, and a wide range of ornaments, tools, and domestic household items. This material has not been analyzed or published as of the time of this writing; however, much of it may be seen at the Museo de las Casas Reales in Santo Domingo. The town was destroyed by an earthquake and abandoned in 1562.

The year after the establishment of Concepción de la Vega (1496), Santo Domingo was founded on the south coast of the Dominican Republic by Bartolomé Colón, acting as governor during his brother's absence. The original settlement was on the east bank of the Ozama River, and this site was located in 1986 and has been tested by archaeologists Elpidio Ortega and Marcio Veloz-Maggiolo. Shortly after 1500 the settlement was moved across the river, to its present location. Extensive archaeological work by various agencies of the Dominican government has taken place in Santo Domingo over the years, and

EARLY SIXTEENTH-CENTURY SPANISH ARTIFACTS FROM CARIBBEAN SITES. *Clockwise, from top left:* glass lid finial, from Nueva Cádiz; twisted turquoise glass bead, from Nueva Cádiz; Spanish lustreware pottery, from Concepción de la Vega; gilded belt tip, from Concepción de la Vega; copper alloy scabbard tip, from Concepción de la Vega; gilded, enameled book hardware, from Puerto Real, La Española; *(center)* chain-mail links, from Nueva Cádiz. FLORIDA STATE MUSEUM, GAINESVILLE

many of the remains are to be found at the Museo de las Casas Reales. Although dense urban occupation has caused considerable damage to the earliest archaeological record of the city, the projects that have been undertaken have permitted the restoration of structures dating to that era, including the cathedral and the house owned by the Columbus family.

By 1500 the settlements established by Columbus were in serious difficulty. Not enough gold had been found to consider the venture an economic success, and there was resentment among the Spanish settlers over the poor living conditions, leading to uprisings and mutinies. The Indian tribute system had also collapsed by that time, owing in great part to the reduction of the Indian populations through disease. Thus in 1500 to Santo Domingo came Francisco de Bobadilla to end the Colón family governorship of the island and to send Columbus back to Spain in disgrace.

The period of Columbus's occupation of La Española (1493–1500) was a time of devastating social and demographic upheaval for the native peoples of the Caribbean. The rapid decline in population among the Caribbean Indians as a consequence of their vulnerability to European diseases is well-documented through ethnohistorical sources. Much of what we know of this period from the native perspective comes from archaeological excavations.

Archaeologists such as Manuel Garcia-Arevalo have located and excavated a number of Taino Indian sites with remains dating to the Columbian era. The earliest such sites are burials, such as the La Caleta site near Santo Domingo, in which European articles (pottery, beads, metal ornaments) were incorporated into traditional Taino burial ritual. Slightly later sites also show evidence of European influence on native craft traditions. Indian-made pottery of that period occasionally makes use of European vessel forms and functions, and aboriginal-style tools are sometimes fabricated from metal.

Columbus also introduced the institutions of Indian slavery and tribute to La Española, although neither survived his tenure as governor because of the virtual disappearance of the Indians. Archaeological work at sites of Indian slavery (such as Concepción de la Vega, Puerto Real in Haiti, Nueva Cádiz, Venezuela, and Santo Domingo), however, show that under these conditions Indian pottery became greatly simplified and lost much of its contact-period form and decorative variation. At Concepción de la Vega, in fact, excavation has revealed a remarkable Indian-made pottery combining traits of European form and South American and Hispaniolan Indian decoration. This suggests to archaeologists that there was a conscious effort very early to direct Indian crafts into directions more appealing to European tastes.

The remains of Columbus's settlements and their legacies can be seen today throughout the Dominican Republic. Archaeology has not only located many of these sites but also helped reveal the nature of life in these very earliest Columbian colonies. It is through these material remains that we get a glimpse of the beginning and the end of the medieval presence in the Americas.

BIBLIOGRAPHY

Brill, Robert. "Laboratory Studies of Some European Artifacts Excavated on San Salvador Island." In *Proceedings of the First San Salvador Conference: Columbus and His World.* Edited by D. Gerace. San Salvador, Bahamas, 1986.

Cruxent, José. "The Origins of La Isabela." In *Columbian Consequences.* Edited by D. H. Thomas. Washington, D.C., 1990.

Deagan, Kathleen. "The Archaeology of the Spanish Contact Period in the Caribbean." *Journal of World Prehistory* 2 (1988).

Dominguez, Lourdes. *Arqueología colonial cubana: Dos estudios.* Havana, 1984.

Garcia-Arevalo, Manuel. "La arqueología Indo-Hispano en Santo Domingo." In *Unidades y variedades: Ensayos en homnenaje al José M. Cruxent.* Caracas, 1978.

Goggin, John. *Spanish Majolica in the New World.* Yale University Publications in Anthropology, no. 2. New Haven, 1968.

Hoffman, Charles. "Archaeological Investigations at the Long Bay Site, San Salvador, Bahamas." In *Proceedings of the First San Salvador Conference: Columbus and His World.* Edited by D. Gerace. San Salvador, Bahamas, 1986.

Mitchell, Steven, and William Keegan. "Reconstruction of the Coastlines of the Bahamas Islands in 1492." *American Archaeology* 6 (1987).

Montas, Eugenio Perez. *Republica Dominicana: Monumentos historicos y arqueológicos.* Instituto Panamericano de Geografia y Historia, no. 380. Mexico City, 1984.

Ortega, Elpidio. *Arqueología colonial en Santo Domingo.* Santo Domingo, 1982.

Ortega, Elpidio. *La Isabela y la arqueología en la ruta de Colón.* San Pedro Macoris, Dominican Republic, 1988.

Sauer, Carl O. *The Early Spanish Main.* Berkeley, 1966.

Willis, Raymond. "The Archeology of 16th-Century Nueva Cádiz." Master's thesis, University of Florida, 1976.

KATHLEEN DEAGAN

Underwater Archaeology

Underwater archaeology is simply archaeology conducted under water. Theoretical concepts are identical to those of terrestrial archaeology, although methodology has been adapted to an aqueous environment. A relatively new branch of the discipline that has grown steadily since the inception of self-contained underwater breathing apparatus (scuba), underwater archaeology has developed techniques to deal with excavating and recording under water, and with the recovery and conservation of waterlogged materials. More specialized forms include marine archaeology, which is conducted in salt water, but which often is confused with maritime archaeology, the study of the remains of seagoing enterprises, whether shipwrecks or harbor works. Another form, nautical archaeology, studies watercraft and their evolution and functions over time.

The origins of underwater archaeology are associated with discoveries by Mediterranean fishermen and sponge divers of significant artifacts like bronze statues. These objects were brought to the attention of archaeologists, who came to realize that shipwrecks preserved an abundance of materials not normally found in terrestrial sites, except perhaps tombs and graves. Attempts to retrieve portions of shipwrecked cargoes followed, with archaeologists directing divers impeded by heavy equipment. With the advent of aqualung diving after World War II, pioneers of undersea exploration tried their hand at shipwreck excavation, followed by traditional archaeologists. In the Americas, scuba divers began to follow the leads of fishermen and explore shipwrecks, especially in the waters of Florida, Bermuda, and the Caribbean. The Smithsonian Institution's program to investigate submerged sites gave birth to underwater archaeology in the Western Hemisphere. As in the Mediterranean, emphasis initially was placed on the recovery of cargoes and armament from shipwreck sites, many of them located through historical research in European archives. Underwater archaeologists became conversant in commercial and military history to help them interpret their finds. They also became proficient in naval architecture, as the remains of ancient wooden ships were increasingly encountered.

Yet, while the sites of classical Greek, Roman, and Egyptian ships came under scrutiny, remains of vessels associated with early European expansion in the Americas still awaited investigation. Thus, the architecture of ships built thousands of years ago became familiar to students of the evolution of seafaring, but components of the ship types that carried Vasco da Gama, Christopher Columbus, and Ferdinand Magellan into distant waters remained a mystery. Of the vast number of underwater sites in the New World, only a handful have begun to shed light on the nautical technology that allowed medieval mariners to sail into the Renaissance, joining two independent worlds for the first time.

The 1554 Fleet. Discovery by beachcombers in 1964 of Spanish coins along a section of Padre Island, Texas, prompted treasure hunters to search for a source offshore. Dates and denominations of the coins led to archival documents connected with the loss of three Spanish merchantmen in 1554. Salvage of one of the wrecks began in 1967, yielding many artifacts that were removed from Texas before the operation was halted by a court order. Legislation established the Texas Antiquities

Committee, and the salvaged materials were returned to the state, where a facility for their conservation was constructed in 1971.

During the next six years, the Antiquities Committee conducted research on the 1554 fleet. Translated documents helped piece together the tragedy of *Santa María de Yciar, Espíritu Santo,* and *San Estéban.* Excavated remains of the latter vessel and its cargo were conserved for public display. Publication of the inventory of restored artifacts and the archival documentation provided the most comprehensive study to date of colonial Spanish shipwrecks.

Red Bay Wreck. In the frigid waters of Labrador, investigations of a Basque whaling station at Red Bay led to the discovery of the well-preserved remains of a vessel thought to be *San Juan,* which had lost its moorings in 1565 while preparing to return to Spain loaded with casks of whale oil. Underwater archaeologists from Parks Canada, under the direction of Robert Grenier, began in 1978 to probe the remains of the galleon, unearthing navigational equipment and portions of the vessel's running rigging. The ship's hull lay in ten meters of water, flattened by centuries of winter ice but well preserved by the cold water. Disassembly of its components revealed a ship built for work rather than warfare. Timbers were mapped, pried loose, brought to the surface for recording, and then returned to the seabed. A rubber cast of the central portion of the ship was poured under water to obtain a mirror image of the structure, and a one-tenth scale model was constructed for a three-dimensional perspective of the hull.

The Red Bay wreck represents a well-preserved example of sixteenth-century shipwrightery; reconstruction of the ship's architecture on paper suggests that it was a three-masted vessel of 250 to 300 tons, built and fitted out in the Basque region of Spain. Remains of two other vessels and a small whaling boat were also revealed in the harbor, providing additional examples for the study of early Iberian shipbuilding.

Molasses Reef Wreck. Perhaps the oldest European shipwreck to be found in the Western Hemisphere was discovered by hunters in the 1970s at the crossroads of the Windward Passage and the Old Bahama Channel. The site was situated on a remote reef at the edge of the Caicos Bank, north of Hispaniola, where the ocean floor abruptly rises to within a few feet of the water's surface. Visible wreckage of the ship consisted of a small mound of ballast stones, an anchor, and numerous pieces of artillery. The divers recognized the antiquity of the wrought-iron ordnance and took several pieces as souvenirs. Treasure seekers eventually arrived at Molasses Reef, claiming in 1980 to have found the wreck of Columbus's *Pinta,* hoping to raise funds to work the site. Their unsuccessful attempts to mount an expedition prompted the government of the Turks and Caicos Islands to invite the Institute

of Nautical Archaeology (INA) at Texas A&M University to give the wreck site the scientific attention it deserved.

Three seasons of mapping and excavation began in 1982 under the direction of Donald H. Keith, resulting in the recovery of data and artifacts. The small vessel had been heavily armed with a wide variety of weapons, from two large wrought-iron cannons, called *bombardettas,* to a battery of fifteen smaller swivel guns, or *versos,* mounted on the ship's railings. Unlike later artillery cast in a mold, each piece had been forged by hand, by welding long iron staves together to form the barrel, which was then reinforced by sleeves and rings. Ammunition consisted of cast- and wrought-iron solid shot, solid lead shot, and lead wrapped around an iron cube. The ship's crew apparently cast ammunition at sea because two-part shot molds were discovered on the wreck site. In addition, fragmentary examples of smaller arms were found: two harquebuts, which were an early form of matchlock musket, and the remains of two crossbows. Part of the ship's defensive system, these weapons would also have been carried ashore.

Disassembly of the ballast pile was accompanied by careful recording of stone sizes and stowage patterns in the hold of the ship; petrographic study of samples suggested the ship probably had taken on ballast at some point in Lisbon, England, and the Azores. Fragmentary shards of ceramic vessels collected from the ballast pile represented storage containers for the ship's provisions, basins for washing, pots for waste, and tablewares for the crew. Despite the wreck's exposed situation in the shallow fore-reef zone, fragile portions of tiny glass medicinal vials were unearthed; they may have belonged to a pharmaceutical chest carried on board.

Beneath the ballast stones, remnants of the ship's wooden hull had survived despite shipworms, storms, and centuries under the sea. A section of the bottom of the vessel had been preserved sufficiently to discern at least twenty-two frames and six hull planks. Although these wooden remnants were insufficient to obtain the exact dimensions and shape of the hull, frame spacing and fastening patterns provided clues to the size and method of construction of the ship.

The encrusted artifacts and waterlogged wood were shipped to INA's laboratory where mechanical excavation of conglomerates revealed a cross section of the ship's fittings and tools. Encrustations that once contained iron were injected with molding compounds to create casts of the original objects. Researchers spent thousands of hours to conserve the recovered components so they could be returned to the Turks and Caicos Islands to be displayed in a museum. Comparative analysis of the wreck's ordnance and ceramic and glass types with known examples from Europe and other early Spanish terrestrial sites in the Americas dates the Molasses Reef wreck to the

Molasses Reef wreck. Lifting a wrought-iron cannon (*bombardetta*) from the seabed.

Institute of Nautical Archaeology, College Station, Texas

first decades of the sixteenth century, although its identity still remains a mystery. Several slaving voyages to the islands occurred during these years, but many more probably went unrecorded. Fragments of sand-tempered native pottery and a pair of iron leg manacles recovered from the wreck site suggest the possibility that the vessel may have been involved in the slave trade.

Highborn Cay Wreck. A similar shipwreck of the same era was discovered by skin divers in 1965, some four hundred miles to the northwest, in the lee of tiny Highborn Cay, an island in the Exuma chain on the edge of the Great Bahama Bank. The site consisted of a small ballast mound with several pieces of encrusted artillery and an anchor. The discoverers obtained a salvage license, and in 1966, all visible iron materials were raised from the site. To learn more about the wreck site and to contrast its components with those at Molasses Reef, an INA research team in 1983 contacted members of the original salvage team for comparative data. From photographs and drawings they learned that the site had contained two *bombardettas* with four associated breech chambers, similar to those found on Molasses Reef. In addition, at least thirteen smaller swivel guns of two types had been found with numerous powder chambers and iron breech wedges. At least one breech block had been loaded; both powder and wooden plug were still in place. Examples of

lead-wrapped iron dice had also been found throughout the site.

As with the Molasses Reef site, a large anchor had been found in association with the two *bombardettas* atop the ballast mound. This pattern of distribution suggested that all three heavy iron objects had been stowed in the holds when the vessels sank. Rather than coincidence, it would appear that small seagoing vessels during this period normally carried heavier ordnance and anchors below decks to lower the center of gravity while underway. Two additional anchors were found some 100 to 150 meters (110 to 165 yards) from the bow portion of the wreck site, suggesting that the Highborn Cay vessel had been at anchor when it sank.

Because of the site's similarity to the wreck at Molasses Reef and the fact that the majority of the ballast had been left undisturbed by previous salvage efforts, the INA team decided in 1986 to reinvestigate the Highborn Cay wreck and examine the ship's surviving structure. The hypothetical location of the vessel's mainmast step assembly and associated structure was deduced from previous survey data compared with the original salvor's site plan. A transverse trench across the ballast pile revealed beneath the coral and stone mantle a large mast step mortice, carved into the keelson. Between bracing timbers were found limber boards designed for easy removal to clear debris from the bilge. Additional boards, called filler planks, protected the bilge area from trash and ballast, which could clog the pump. Two concave cavities had been cut into the keelson to accept cylindrical pump shafts. What may have been the pump box survived only in splinters.

Test excavations of the Highborn Cay vessel provided the kind of constructional details missing from the Molasses Reef wreck. For the first time, dimensions of each of the principal timbers and the manner in which they were joined allowed a detailed image of a discovery-period sailing vessel to be assembled. Together, the remains of both ships and their wreckage represented a major archaeological breakthrough in knowledge of how early sixteenth-century vessels had been built, provisioned, and armed.

Bahía Mujeres Wreck. Another shipwreck undergoing investigation represents the second wave of seafaring conquistadores as their routes shifted from the islands to the Mexican mainland. Entombed by coral in the shallow waters of Bahía Mujeres off the eastern coast of Yucatán, the site was discovered by local divers, who removed examples of wrought-iron ordnance and anchors in the 1950s. Initially and erroneously believed to be the remains of *La Nicolasa,* a ship used by the conquistador Francisco de Montejo in an abortive attempt to establish a colony on Yucatán's shores in 1527, the wreck site and its artifacts are being studied cooperatively by INA and Mexico's National Institute of Anthropology and History (INAH). Surviving ordnance salvaged from the Bahía Mujeres wreck is similar to that of the other sites, but also includes a *verso* of a different type than those found on the Molasses Reef and Highborn Cay wrecks. The number of artillery pieces and the size and weight of the anchor suggest that this vessel may have been smaller than the other two.

With the help of one of the original divers, the wreck site was relocated in 1984 after some twenty-three years. A low mound of ballast stones, almost covered with coral formations, marked the resting place of the ship's hull—the earliest to be discovered in Latin America. A scatter of stones trailed toward the north, where another anchor had been found in the 1960s. Ongoing investigations of the Bahía Mujeres wreck, together with information gleaned from the sites described above, constitute a steadily growing corpus of data on early sixteenth-century ships of a distinctly Atlantic type.

The Search for the Ships of Columbus

The search for remains of Columbus's ships began on the north coast of Jamaica, where the Admiral's fourth voyage to the Indies ended. Beached in a shallow bay in 1504, the sinking caravels *Capitana* and *Santiago* became a survival outpost for more than a year until the marooned mariners were rescued. The last two ships commanded by

Columbus were forgotten until 1935, when amateur archaeologist William Goodwin began to probe a secluded inlet called Don Christopher's Cove near St. Ann's Bay. After three seasons and more than 150 test holes, Goodwin gave up his search, having found only one small ceramic shard for his efforts.

Meanwhile Samuel Eliot Morison was preparing an expedition to retrace the Columbus voyages. When he sailed into St. Ann's Bay in 1940, Morison set out with the help of a local amateur, Charles Cotter, to reconstruct the surroundings of Columbus's unintentional exile. Both scholars rejected Don Christopher's Cove as a possible location for the beached ships because of the inlet's narrow shape and shallow depths. They determined that its name had been derived not from the famous Admiral but from Cristóbal Yssasi, the last Spanish governor of Jamaica, who used the cove to hide from invading seventeenth-century English troops. Morison and Cotter concurred that Columbus's ships probably were abandoned in the western section of St. Ann's Bay, where the island's first European settlement, Sevilla la Nueva, later was established. Morison published this hypothesis in *Admiral of the Ocean Sea* (1942), which contained a map of the proposed resting place of the caravels.

In 1966, while conducting excavations at the sunken city of Port Royal on the south coast of Jamaica, Robert Marx briefly visited St. Ann's Bay. Probing the muddy bottom, he encountered fragments of wood, stone, ceramics, and obsidian. Two years later, Marx returned with an engineer, Harold Edgerton, who produced sonar images of several buried targets in the area that Morison had proposed. Core sampling yielded additional materials, including glass, charcoal, flint, an iron tack, and a black bean. Examined by different laboratories, the samples were judged to be of varying dates and ambiguous origins. Yet the sonar targets raised hopes that both Columbus vessels had been found.

At Marx's urging, the Jamaican government sought international support to begin test excavations, and in 1969, the French diver Frederick Dumas was invited to investigate the site. Several days of dredging turned up ballast stones, artifacts, and glass fragments under the sloping mudbank near a colonial English wharf. Owing to the type and variety of artifacts, and because an old chart depicted two anchors at the location he had tested, Dumas concluded the site probably was an anchorage midden associated with the wharf. Recovery of eighteenth-century wine bottle bases and clay pipe fragments reinforced this hypothesis. The government was told that Columbus's caravels probably were buried elsewhere, and the mystery remained unsolved.

In 1981, INA researchers decided to resume the search for the lost caravels. They reasoned that, if known vessels of discovery could be found and studied, many questions could be answered about the nautical technology that brought Europeans to the Americas and the maritime lifestyles that accompanied them. They also hypothesized that, since the caravels had been beached in the shelter of a bay rather than wrecked on an offshore reef, their remains might be relatively well preserved. Furthermore, because the vessels had been used to house Columbus and his men for more than a year before being abandoned, they might contain archaeological evidence such as food remains and other domestic debris that might help interpret one of the earliest sustained relationships between Europeans and native Americans.

To gather data on geomorphological changes in the bay since the time of Columbus, a series of preliminary cores were undertaken at several locations in St. Ann's Bay. These suggested that portions of the shoreline had variously eroded or accreted over time owing to marine and alluvial action. Other areas had been altered by colonial and modern construction. In conjunction with the government of Jamaica, a cooperative effort to pursue the abandoned caravels began in 1982, combining traditional disciplines of archaeology and history with modern advances in electronics and marine geology. A team of archaeologists and students from the United States and Jamaica, under the direction of Roger C. Smith, assembled at the historic English plantation of Seville, once the site of Sevilla la Nueva and now a national park.

They began a systematic magnetometry survey along the present-day beach and in the shallow waters of the bay to obtain magnetic readings that might represent buried cultural material. A subbottom sonar device also was employed to penetrate marine sediments. Offshore of the old wharf where Marx and Dumas had worked, a cluster of five sonar images was discovered. Test excavations confirmed the site as an anchorage midden with two discrete layers of cultural debris deposited during periods of intense plantation activity in the eighteenth century. Nearby, readings from the instruments led to the discovery of a mid-eighteenth-century English trading vessel preserved under two meters of mud and silt. By the end of the second season, the shoreline and waters of the bay had been surveyed and tested. Additional underwater middens and several other colonial shipwreck sites were encountered, including a salt trader and a merchantman loaded with iron sugar mill apparatus, but none of these sites dated from the sixteenth century. No evidence for early Spanish maritime activities had been found.

The project team decided to return to the area around the old stone wharf where Morison believed the caravels had been beached. The location of the wharf had been well chosen by plantation planners, since a natural deep channel through the bay ran up to the shore at this point, providing ideal access for shipping. The researchers wondered whether the English wharf could have been built on top of an older Spanish structure, which, in turn, might have been constructed from the ballast piles of the abandoned caravels. Electronic sensing and probing of the ruins had proved difficult, since the stones interfered with instrument readings, and subsurface debris hampered coring. Reluctant to dismantle a portion of the historic ruin and undermine its stability, the team devised an alternate strategy for test excavation. A four-foot diameter aluminum culvert pipe was inserted alongside the wharf to form a caisson, within which excavations could be carried out without disturbing the surrounding sediments. As each section was emptied, it sank into the water-saturated soil, and another section was added.

In this manner, more than a ton of river and ballast rock intermixed with hundreds of artifacts was extracted by hand during two seasons of difficult underwater work in tight quarters with no visibility. English trade ceramics, fancy glass stemware, rum and wine bottles, beef, pork, and turtle bones, sailor's buttons and culinary implements, slave-produced pottery, and roof tile and brick fragments all attested to the variety of commerce conducted across the plantation's wharf over three centuries. Oyster shells of a nontropical variety reflected the North American colonial connection; Pacific money cowries found their way via Africa to the West Indian sugar plantations along with the slaves they helped purchase. As late-seventeenth-century materials began to emerge, the stratigraphy became less discrete and the sediments more sterile. Excavation continued as far as the caisson would allow, and then a long core was driven to a total depth of ten meters. No sixteenth-century materials were encountered; no evidence for a Spanish wharf or ship was found. After four seasons, the team discontinued its explorations, and research shifted to the study of early shipwrecks found elsewhere in the Caribbean.

The earliest recorded European shipwreck in the Americas was that of Columbus's *Santa María*, which occurred in 1492 on the north coast of Hispaniola. The remains of this famous vessel became the target of a search that began in 1949, as the pilot Don Lungwitz spotted a dark oval blur inside the barrier reef of Cap Haïtien, Haiti. The blur seemed to rise almost to the surface of the water, but unlike other coral mounds scattered throughout the reefline, this one lay at a right angle to the surf zone and was oval-shaped like a ship.

Ten years before, Morison had sailed into Cap Haïtien Harbor carefully studying the contour of the coastline to retrace the fatal course of *Santa María*. Concluding that the site of La Navidad, partially built from the flagship's timbers, was situated near the present-day fishing village of Limonade Bord-de-Mer, he hypothesized that the vessel had wrecked on one of three small shoals between the shore and the barrier reef. The underwater archaeological methods by which to test his theory had yet to evolve, however.

Some 150 years earlier, the eighteenth-century French historian Moreau de Saint-Méry had recorded the discovery of one of *Santa María*'s anchors in the muddy bottom of Grand Rivière, a mile from its mouth and two miles from Limonade Bord-de-Mer. Over the centuries, the mouth of the river had gradually accreted out into the sea. Saint-Méry conjectured that the anchor was the same one that Diego Alvarez Chanca, the physician of Columbus's second voyage, reported seeing near the burned ruins of La Navidad. This anchor is now on display at the National Museum in Port-au-Prince. In 1955, the underwater explorers Edwin and Marion Link briefly visited Cap Haïtien to search for *Santa María*. Diving far to the west of Morison's hypothesized location, they recovered an early anchor from a reef in the harbor entrance. Although the ring, part of the shank, and the palms were missing, it resembled the anchor found by Saint-Méry. Examined by Mendel Peterson of the Smithsonian Institution, both the Saint-Méry and the Link anchors were conjectured to have come from the same ship, possibly *Santa María*.

In 1967, another explorer, Fred Dickson, came to the north coast of Haiti. Knowledgeable about the Morison and Link expeditions, Dickson met Lungwitz, who offered to fly him over the reefs of Cap Haïtien. Intrigued by what he saw, Dickson organized an expedition and later that year, exploratory excavations began on a mysterious coral mound. Under twelve feet of coral and ballast rock, ship-related materials such as wood, copper and iron fastenings, lead sheathing, and ceramics were recovered. An organization called the Santa María Foundation was formed to raise funds for further investigations.

Dickson decided that more extensive survey of the immediate area was needed, but it was not until 1970 that a magnetometer was employed on the coral mound, revealing a major anomaly at one end. Test excavations produced more wood, ballast, fasteners, and ceramics, but also glass fragments, grapeshot, and two large, square iron bars of a type carried as ballast on warships. The archaeologist Carl Clausen concluded that the artifacts were consistent with an eighteenth- or nineteenth-century shipwreck. Despite frustration and lack of money, Dickson persisted in his efforts to investigate the axis of the mysterious coral mound. While continuing his search for *Santa María* in 1972, he tragically died following a diving accident.

The vagueness of the historical narrative describing the loss of *Santa María,* and dramatic changes that have occurred to the shoreline since that event took place, present serious obstacles to the eventual discovery of its grave. Surviving elements of the ship may no longer be recognizable owing to the offshore environment in which it was lost and the extensive salvage carried out by its crew with the aid of natives. Of the other recorded ship losses sustained by Columbus, the remains of the caravel called *Gallega* have a greater potential to be located and identified.

Left behind in a river on the isthmus of Panama during the first of several disasters that befell the Admiral's fourth voyage, *Gallega* became the object of a search begun in 1987 by a team of archaeologists led by Donald H. Keith. To conclusively identify the remote river that Columbus had named Belén in 1503, an aerial reconnaissance of all rivers along the northern isthmus was conducted. Only the one currently named Río Belén matched the historical descriptions; it too had been visited and identified by Morison in 1940. In conjunction with the Panamanian Institute of Culture, an expedition was organized to map the river mouth. The resulting data indicated that the river's course remained relatively unchanged. Subbottom penetrating sonar and magnetometry, deployed in the shallow riverbed from a small boat, produced several promising anomalies. Continued survey and careful testing of targets may produce evidence of buried ship's wreckage. Río Belén's remote location offers the preserving elements of fresh water and alluvial sediments that may well have protected the remains of a Columbus ship for nearly five hundred years. The discovery of *Gallega* would be a landmark in underwater archaeology.

BIBLIOGRAPHY

Arnold, J. Barto, III, and Robert S. Weddle. *The Nautical Archaeology of Padre Island: The Spanish Shipwrecks of 1554.* New York, 1978.

Frye, John. *The Search for the Santa María.* New York, 1973.

Grenier, Robert. "Excavating a 400-Year-Old Basque Galleon." *National Geographic* 168, no. 1 (1985): 58–68.

Hajovsky, Rick. "Phase II of the Search for Gallega." In *Underwater Archaeology.* Edited by J. Barto Arnold, III. Proceedings from the Society for Historical Archaeology Conference, Baltimore, Md., 1989.

Keith, D. H., and J. J. Simmons. "An Analysis of Hull Remains, Ballast and Artifact Distribution of a 16th-Century Shipwreck: Toward a Better Understanding of Wrecking and Reconstruction." *Journal of Field Archaeology* 12, no. 4 (1985): 411–424.

Keith, D. H., et al. "The Molasses Reef Wreck, Turks and Caicos Islands, B.W.I.: A Preliminary Report." *International Journal of Nautical Archaeology* 13, no. 1 (1984): 45–63.

Myers, Mark D. "An Archaeological Reconnaissance of Río Belén, Panamá." In *Underwater Archaeology.* Edited by James P. Delgado. Proceedings of the Society for Historical Archaeology Conference, Reno, Nev., 1988.

Oertling, Thomas. "The Highborn Cay Wreck: The 1986 Field Season." *International Journal of Nautical Archaeology* 18, no. 3 (1989): 244–253.

Oertling, Thomas. "The Molasses Reef Wreck Hull Analysis: Final

Report." *International Journal of Nautical Archaeology* 18, no. 3 (1989): 229–243.

Smith, Roger C., and D. H. Keith. "The Archaeology of Ships of Discovery." *Archaeology* 39, no. 2 (1986): 30–35.

Smith, Roger C., et al. "The Highborn Cay Wreck: Further Exploration of a 16th-Century Bahaman Shipwreck." *International Journal of Nautical Archaeology* 14, no. 1 (1985): 63–72.

Tuck, James, and Robert Grenier. "A 16th-Century Basque Whaling Station in Labrador." *Scientific American* 245, no. 5 (1981): 180–188.

ROGER C. SMITH

ARCHITECTURE. For discussion of European architecture in Columbus's day, see *Art and Architecture.*

ARIAS DE ÁVILA, PEDRO. See *Ávila, Pedro Arias de.*

ARMILLARY SPHERE. An armillary (from Latin, *armilla,* ring) sphere is an instrument in which the celestial sphere is represented and delineated by rings representing the polar circles, the tropics, the celestial equator, and the ecliptic circle (the apparent path of the sun through a band of constellations [the zodiac] in the course of the year). It derives from a large, fixed, observational instrument, the *astrolabos* or *astrolabon organon* (which is not to be confused with an astrolabe) used by Ptolemy of Alexandria (fl. A.D. 127–148) and employed as an observational instrument in Islamic astronomy. Although the *Libros de saber de astrología* (Burgos, c. 1276) of Alfonso X, known as Alfonso the Wise, describe an observational armillary sphere, the influence of the *Libros,* written not in Latin but in a vernacular (Castilian), appears to have been slight, and the armillary sphere in medieval Europe was primarily an instrument for demonstrational or didactic use.

A small sphere, placed at the center of the sphere, represented the earth and made the sphere a model of the Ptolemaic geocentric system. Star pointers, as on an astrolabe, attached to the constituent rings, demonstrated the apparent rotation of the stars about the celestial pole. Small medieval armillary spheres were attached at the base to vertical handles, but if the sphere were placed in a ring representing the terrestrial horizon, with its polar axis inclined at an angle corresponding to the latitude of a particular place, rotation of the sphere could demonstrate the rising, meridian transits, and setting of stars and of the sun, and could become, like an astrolabe, an analogue computer for solving simple problems in spherical trigonometry. A pair of curved dividers, as used with globes, aided measurement on the sphere. Such dividers were used by João de Castro in 1538 on a *poma* (Portuguese,

ARMILLARY SPHERE. Circa 1425, representing Ptolemaic cosmography.   MUSEUM OF THE HISTORY OF SCIENCE, OXFORD

apple), apparently a form of solid or armillary sphere used in navigation, possibly hung from an adjustable suspension ring.

During the latter half of the sixteenth century, the Arsenius instrument workshop at Louvain made armillary spheres with sights (enabling them to be used for observations) and astronomical rings, an observational simplification of the armillary sphere invented by Rainer Gemma Frisius (1508–1535) of the University of Louvain. The astronomical ring was developed by the English mathematician William Oughtred (1575–1660) into the universal equinoctial ring dial, a sundial that became one of the few useful nautical instruments. The large fixed observational armillary sphere was revived in the late sixteenth century by the Danish astronomer Tycho Brahe (1546–1601).

The armillary sphere has often been used as a symbol of astronomy and was given as a heraldic device by King João II of Portugal (1455–1495) to his cousin, Prince Manuel, later, King Manuel I (1469–1521). It thus appears on a gold coin minted for Portuguese India during the reign of Manuel I and is familiar as a motif of Manueline architecture in Coimbra and Lisbon.

[See also *Astrolabe*.]

BIBLIOGRAPHY

Alfonso X. *Libros de saber de astrología*. Edited by Manuel Rico y Sinobas. 4 vols. Madrid, 1863–1866.
Maddison, Francis. *Medieval Scientific Instruments and the Development of Navigational Instruments in the XVth and XVIth Centuries*. Agrupamento de estudos de cartografia antiga, vol. 30. Coimbra, 1969.
Nolte, Friedrich. *Die Armillarsphäre*. Abhandlungen zur Geschichte der Naturwissenschaften und der Medezin, vol. 2. Erlangen, 1922.
Turner, Anthony. *Early Scientific Instruments: Europe 1400–1800*. London, 1987.

FRANCIS MADDISON

ARMS, ARMOR, AND ARMAMENT. Within the vast body of literature devoted to Columbus and his voyages of discovery, there is little information about the armament of his ships or of the arms carried or the armor worn by the seamen and colonists. Historians either ignore the subject completely or suggest, as J. H. Parry has in *The Age of Reconnaissance*, that the explorers sailed in ships meant for the coastal trade. What arms they carried were mostly personal weapons.

Samuel Eliot Morison suggests the same in *The Great Explorers*, indicating that the ships carried a stand of swords, cutlasses, and pikes for use against attackers who might try to fight their way aboard. It is clear, however, from entries extracted by Bartolomé de Las Casas from the lost logs of Columbus's first and third voyages, and in accounts of the second and fourth voyages by Michele da Cuneo and the Admiral's son Fernando, respectively, that all Columbus's ships carried cannons as well as personal weapons of various types. Both Columbus and Cuneo refer to the cannons as lombards. Unfortunately, neither specifies the number per ship nor their size. During the first voyage it was recorded in the log that a lombard was fired as a signal that land had been sighted. Later, after *Santa María* ran aground on a reef off the north coast of La Española, all salvageable equipment, including her armament, was carried ashore. A fort was built for the protection of those members of the crew of *Santa María* who were left behind as the first colony of Europeans in these islands. Lombards were appropriately mounted in the fort, and Columbus ordered a demonstration firing in

the presence of local Indians to impress them with the Spaniards' capacity to protect themselves.

Soon after Columbus's triumphant return from his first voyage, a papal bull, issued in May 1493, granted Spain control of the lands discovered by the Admiral. Despite this, the Spanish sovereigns wanted to make certain that an armed presence was put in place there as soon as possible to guard against any incursion by Portugal. Accordingly, they ordered a large fleet of seventeen vessels to be manned and outfitted with food, arms, munitions, supplies, equipment, and tools for up to twelve hundred crewmen, artisans, farmers, miners, and workmen to establish a self-sustaining colony on La Española.

Setting sail from Cádiz on September 25, 1493, Columbus took a more southerly course than he had followed on the first voyage in order to explore an island chain southeast of La Española that had been described to him on that voyage by his Indian guides. He chose the name Dominica for the first island sighted because of the Sabbath landfall. It was in this island chain that the Spaniards had their first recorded fight with New World peoples, the fierce, hostile, and cannibalistic Caribs. One Spaniard was killed by a poisoned arrow that pierced his buckler. That he was not the first Spaniard to have been killed by native inhabitants, however, was revealed when the fleet, on November 27, reached La Navidad, where the crew of the wrecked *Santa María* had been left on the first voyage. There the entire garrison had been killed.

In March 1494, after establishing the planned colony, which he named La Isabela, at a site on the north coast of La Española to the east of La Navidad and closer to the gold-rich mountains of Cibao, Columbus decided that he must take personal charge of the mining efforts. He assembled the necessary artificers, workmen, miners, munitions, and tools. Because of past incidents of violence on the part of Indians of the Cibao region loyal to the powerful cacique (chieftain) Caonabó, reputed destroyer of the La Navidad garrison, Columbus took with him a substantial and well-armed force composed of a cavalry troop with swords and lances, men-at-arms with crossbows, and hidalgos armed with swords and arquebuses to protect the work force and deter the Indians from any further violence. Washington Irving relates that

On the 12th of March, Columbus set out at the head of about four hundred men well armed and equipped, with shining helmets and corslets; with arquebuses, lances, swords, and crossbows, and followed by a multitude of the neighboring Indians. They sallied from the city in martial array, with banners flying, and sound of drum and trumpet. When the Indians beheld this shining band of warriors, glittering in steel, emerging from the mountains with prancing steeds and flaunting banners, and heard, for the first time, their rocks and forests echoing to the din of drum and trumpet, they might well have taken such a wonderful pageant for a supernatural vision. In this way Columbus disposed of his forces whenever he approached a populous village, placing the cavalry in front, for the horses inspired a mingled terror and admiration among the natives.

Arriving in the foothills of the Cibao mountains, Columbus chose a level field within a bend of a clear stream as the site for a fort and a center for mining operations. Leaving over fifty men under the command of Pedro Margarit, as well as a few horses, which were greatly feared by the inhabitants, Columbus returned to La Isabela. The day after he arrived there, a messenger came from Margarit reporting that the friendly Indians had fled and that the dangerous cacique Caonabó was making preparations to attack. In response, Columbus sent seventy armed men with provisions and ammunition to help Margarit defend the fort and the mining operation.

With the crops planted at La Isabela already beginning to ripen, Columbus decided that it was time to resume his efforts to explore the mainland of "Asia." On April 24, he set sail once again to the west with the three smallest caravels, which he had specifically selected for the mission of exploration, Niña, San Juan, and Cardera. When he reached the eastern point of Cuba, which he believed to be the eastern extremity of the Asian mainland, Columbus decided, with the concurrence of his pilots, officers, and gentlemen volunteers, that they should explore the south coast rather than the north, 150 miles of which he had already explored on his first voyage.

Hearing reports of gold from the Indians, Columbus headed south to Jamaica, where his three caravels were surrounded by about sixty canoes loaded with apparently hostile Indians. Columbus ordered several blank shots fired from the cannons and the Indians fled ashore. Columbus had portable swivel guns mounted in the bow of each ship's boat and armed the boat crews with crossbows and shields and went ashore. They were met by a hail of stones and responded with arrows from the crossbows and shots from the swivel guns, killing a number of Indians. The following day the well-armed Spaniards again went ashore and were greeted by entirely friendly natives who offered them food and water. Comparable incidents also occurred during both the third and fourth voyages.

Recent findings by nautical archaeologists give a richer picture of the weapons and munitions used during the four voyages than the historical record does. Two shipwrecks of the discovery era have been found in the Caribbean and have yielded excellent evidence of the armament of ships of the period and of the arms carried by their crews and early colonizers. These shipwrecks were surveyed and excavated in the 1980s by a team headed by

Donald Keith of the Institute of Nautical Archaeology (INA) at College Station, Texas. One wreck is located on Molasses Reef near the Turks and Caicos Islands and the other just off the northwest shore of Highborn Cay in the northern Bahamas. The size and shape of the reasonably intact mounds of stone ballast at both sites indicates that the ships had been of the approximate tonnage of Niña or Pinta, a common size for caravels of that period and hence specifically indicative of the arms and armament of the principal type of vessel used by Columbus.

At the Molasses Reef shipwreck site the INA team recovered two authenticated fifteenth-century, wrought-iron, breech-loading cannons (bombardettas), with fifteen separate breech chambers; fourteen smaller breech-loading swivel guns, or versos, a variety of falconet, with forty separate breech chambers; two lightweight, muzzle-loading swivel guns, or harquebuts; two wrought-iron, muzzle-loading shoulder arms, or arquebuses; and a large number of various types and sizes of shot for all the weapons. Portions of two crossbows were also found.

Ordnance found at the Highborn Cay wreck included two wrought-iron, breech-loading bombardettas with compatible breech chambers and at least thirteen smaller wrought-iron breech-loading swivel guns with eighteen breech chambers and the iron wedges used to lock the chambers in the breech assemblies. Most of the swivel guns were small versos of less than 2 meters in length, but two were the larger versos dobles and measured 2.7 meters in length. Shot found was of the iron-cored, lead-wrapped variety.

Ten of the fourteen swivel guns excavated from the Molasses Reef wreck appear to have been lashed together in pairs of similar types. The remaining four were found with loaded and plugged breech chambers wedged into the breech assemblies ready to be fired. Had this wreck been the only one found, one might have assumed that the ten lashed pairs were being carried as cargo and that the four loaded swivel guns almost certainly had been mounted on the vessel as her own armament and constituted her total complement of swivel guns. But a comparable number of swivel guns were found at the Highborn Cay wreck, located at a considerable distance from and apparently unrelated to the Molasses Reef wreck. Thus it appears that a discovery-era caravel normally carried a substantial number of swivel guns in addition to a pair of bombardettas. The answer may be found in the various accounts of swivel guns being mounted in the ship's boats when explorers went ashore in the presence of natives who might not be friendly. It is also possible that spare swivel guns, the smaller ones of which weighed only about eighty pounds, may have been used to arm the several forts that were built during the period. As for personal weapons such as swords, cutlasses, halberds,

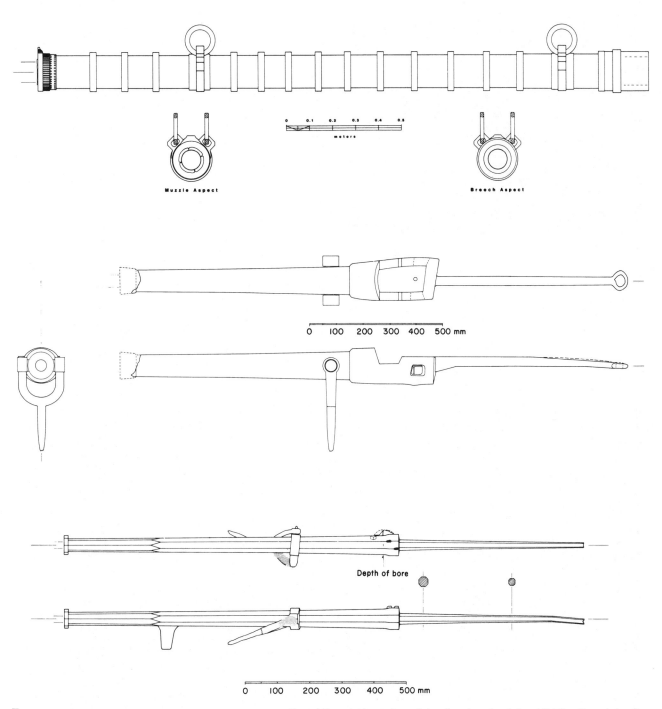

javelins, lances, and knives, none was found at either of the wreck sites. But these are items that survivors of the wrecks would have taken with them.

The heaviest cannons were identified by J. J. Simmons, INA ordnance analyst, as *bombardettas* in the catalog of the Museo del Ejercito (Army Museum) in Madrid. This term is the diminutive of "bombard," the name more commonly found in the historical record of heavier armament. Guns of this type have also been called lombards by some historians. The two *bombardettas* from

WROUGHT-IRON CANNONS FROM THE MOLASSES REEF WRECK. Being raised from conservation tanks.

INSTITUTE OF NAUTICAL ARCHAEOLOGY, COLLEGE STATION, TEXAS

the Molasses Reef wreck measured 8.7 feet in length with bore diameters of about 3.5 inches. The inner surface of the bore of each tube was made up of several iron staves reinforced by alternate abutting sleeves and hoops with their inner surfaces pressed against the inner lining of the staves. The tops of the muzzle hoop and the rear lifting ring hoop have squared-off raised surfaces to serve as gun sights. The separate breech chambers were constructed in the same manner as the gun tubes except that the butt ends were plugged and the forward ends were tapered to fit tightly into the breech end of the gun tube. Breech chambers of two lengths were found. The shorter more numerous chambers measured approximately twenty-four inches in length and the longer ones, presumably loaded with a greater amount of gunpowder for use against more distant targets, measured about thirty inches. No wooden carriages on which the *bombardettas* would have been mounted were found. Such carriages were recovered in excellent condition from the 1545 wreck of HMS *Mary Rose*, which carried a few wrought-iron bombards in addition to numerous more modern cast-bronze and cast-iron cannons.

The most common armament of discovery-period ships was the swivel gun. The types found at the Molasses Reef and Highborn Cay wrecks were called versos, characterized by some as a variety of falconet. Three types of versos were found at the Molasses Reef wreck: *versos lisos*, *versos normales*, and *versos dobles*. As the names indicate, the *versos normales* were the most common and the most numerous, with smaller numbers of the lighter *lisos* and the heavier *dobles*. The overall length of the most common verso was about 6 feet with a bore diameter of about 1.75 inches. Except for differences in size and weight, all were similar in shape and were made up of

tapering barrels, Y-shaped swivels by which they were mounted in a socket on the ship's rail, integral breech assemblies designed to hold the separate breech chambers, and a permanently attached tiller by which the gun could be swiveled from side to side and up and down. The separate breech chambers were shaped to fit tightly into the breech end of the gun barrel and had an iron handle welded near the butt end at an offset angle from the vertical so as to be clear of the touchhole by which the explosive charge in the chamber was fired with a red-hot iron poker. Each chamber had a horizontal lip fashioned into its sealed butt end slightly below its midpoint. When a retaining wedge was driven through carefully positioned slots in the breech assembly to force the chamber tightly into the gun's breech, the wedge also lay atop that protruding horizontal lip and prevented the chamber from jumping out of the breech assembly when the gun was fired.

Two types of portable wrought-iron, muzzle-loading guns were also found at the Molasses Reef site. One of these types was represented by two small wrought-iron, muzzle-loading swivel guns identified by Simmons as harquebuts. These were similar in form to the versos except that being muzzle-loading guns, they had no breech assembly. One of their distinguishing characteristics was a tang welded to the bottom of the barrel between the muzzle and the swivel. The gun, weighing only about thirty-three pounds, could either be hooked over any convenient rail aboard ship or a ship's boat with the tang acting as a recoil preventer or semipermanently mounted in a swivel socket as was done with the versos. Even more portable were two wrought-iron, muzzle-loading shoulder arms. This type of firearm, identified as an arquebus, had a barrel about 3 feet in length with a bore diameter of about 0.55 inches.

Most of the shot found at the Molasses Reef site were solid cast iron, but small numbers of wrought-iron, hollow cast-iron, iron-cored lead, and solid lead shot also were found. All the solid lead shot were for the harquebuts and arquebuses. Of the remaining shot, some were for the *bombardettas* and some for each of the three types of versos.

Except for the portions of muzzle-loading arquebuses and of crossbows found in the Molasses Reef wreck, no armor or personal arms were found at either site. Since it appears that the crews survived and made it to shore, it is reasonable to assume that they took with them whatever arms and armor they had for self-protection. On the first voyage, the sole purpose of which was exploration, it is probable that such arms as swords were available only to the ships' officers. Every crewman, of course, would have carried his own seaman's knife. It is not likely that any armor was carried on board. The nature of the subsequent

ASSORTMENT OF SHOT AND BRONZE SHOT MOLD. After restoration. From the Molasses Reef wreck.

INSTITUTE OF NAUTICAL ARCHAEOLOGY, COLLEGE STATION, TEXAS

voyages, however, was such that, particularly on the second and third voyages, which involved the establishment of colonies and subjugation of Indians, personal arms and armor would have been used extensively.

The various types of personal arms carried by caballeros and men-at-arms were mentioned above. As for armor, unfortunately Columbus historians have not addressed the subject except in passing references such as "this shining band of warriors, glittering in steel," in Washington Irving's description of the force led by Columbus into the interior of La Española during the second voyage. On the other hand, historians interested in the subject of armor have provided information about the types of armor used in Spain during the period. One can assume that such information is relevant to early forays in the New World.

It is important to note that much of the armor available in Spain during the Age of Discovery was not made there. Wealthy hidalgos, who could afford the finest equipment, purchased armor in either Germany or Italy. King Fernando, for example, had at least one fashionable suit of armor from Milan. In fact, armor made in Milan was especially popular in Spain at the end of the fifteenth century. Milanese armorers were more than willing to tailor their suits of armor to the particular tastes of their wealthy Spanish clients. The Milanese style could be distinguished by the squared-off shape of the movable sections fastened around the bottom of the solid steel breastplates of that period. For those who could not afford the most elegant styles, or preferred simpler attire, Spanish-made armor of good quality was available in the cities of Zaragoza and Calatayud. They were particularly well known for their fine helmets and a lighter version of

armor that was more popular in Spain than in other parts of Europe.

During the war against the Moors, the Spanish were forced to rely on light cavalry, or *jinetes,* for swift raids and counterraids by both sides. Spanish light cavalrymen learned to ride fast horses in the Moorish style with stirrups high and close to the saddle and their knees high against their horses' flanks, wielding a light lance overarm. Such tactics demanded that less and lighter armor be worn. Swords also became more slender and lighter. The city of Toledo, long famous for the quality of its sword, became a major producer of this new rapierlike weapon.

[See also *Archaeology,* especially the article on *Underwater Archaeology; Equipment, Clothing, and Rations.*]

BIBLIOGRAPHY

Frieder, Braden K. "Arms and Armor in the National Museum of the Viceroyalty, Tepotzotlán, Mexico." Unpublished thesis, University of New Mexico. Albuquerque, N.Mex., 1988.

Irving, Washington. *The Life and Voyages of Christopher Columbus and His Companions.* 3 vols. New York, 1849.

Morison, Samuel Eliot. *The Great Explorers.* New York, 1986.

Parry, J. H. *The Age of Reconnaissance.* London, 1963. Reprint, Berkeley, 1981.

Simmons, J. J., 3d. "Wrought-iron Ordnance: Revealing Discoveries from the New World." *International Journal of Nautical Archaeology* 17 (1987): 25–35.

WILLIAM LEMOS

ART AND ARCHITECTURE. The Age of Exploration coincided with one of the great moments of transformation in art. While Portuguese and Spanish ships were expanding the horizons of the European world, a new style, which became known as "Renaissance," was born in Italy. Innovations in optics and perspective enabled artists to construct a three-dimensional space on a flat surface, which, in turn, led to new developments in navigation and cartography. The invention of engraving allowed artists to create visual images from the written descriptions of the explorers that fired the imagination of a largely illiterate public. Subsequently, still-life painting developed in response to a desire to have a permanent record of perishable flowers and fruits from far-away places, and patrons of the arts such as the Medici began to collect Indian artifacts as both objects of curiosity and admiration.

European art and architecture in the fifteenth century can be divided into two main styles: late Gothic, dominant north of the Alps from the Iberian Peninsula to the Holy Roman Empire; and Renaissance, which originated in Italy beginning around 1400. The latter style, based on the revival and reinterpretation of classical forms deriving from ancient Rome, began to permeate northern sensibilities in a significant way only after the king of France, Francis I, returned from his invasion of Italy in 1517. He brought with him Leonardo da Vinci and a determination to decorate his palace at Fontainebleau in the new style. The Renaissance style gradually spread across Europe and was espoused by Francis's great rival, Emperor Charles V, followed by his son, Philip II of Spain.

The Gothic style had shaped European art and architecture for several centuries. Originally associated in the twelfth century with the French royal house, the style had taken on, by the fifteenth century, local characteristics and become much more florid than the understated elegance of its first manifestations. In France it was called the "style flamboyant," in England, "perpendicular," in Germany, "Spätgotik," and in Spain, "plateresque," but all used the Gothic pointed arch and stressed verticality and light. Many of the cathedrals took decades, if not centuries, to build, and the gradual evolution of the regional styles can be easily seen in them. Some of the finest examples of late Gothic churches of the fifteenth century are the Stephansdom in Vienna, Sankt Lorenz in Nuremberg, Saint-Maclou in Rouen, King's College Chapel in Cambridge, and Seville cathedral.

Late Gothic was not confined to ecclesiastical buildings. Town halls, marketplaces, and private palaces were also built in this manner. The trading town of Bruges in Flanders, one of the wealthiest cities in Europe in the fifteenth century, is virtually a monument to this showy style, which suited the nouveau-riche burghers. Nor was Gothic limited to architecture. Painting, manuscript illumination, lettering, and sculpture were all affected by the fashion for increasing decoration and embellishment. The movement was international; there was a lively exchange of ideas and works of art throughout Europe. The Netherlandish artist Hugo van der Goes was commissioned in 1474 by Tommaso Portinari, the agent for the Medici bank in Bruges, to paint a large triptych (three-part altarpiece). This work, shipped to Florence, created a sensation with its use of oil paint and its contrast to the new Renaissance style. It influenced later fifteenth-century Florentine artists, most notably Domenico Ghirlandaio, in whose workshop Michelangelo served as an apprentice. The central panel has a high vanishing point resulting in a steep angle for the foreground, animated drapery, clear colors and light, and a heavy emphasis on linearity. For all the "realism" with which the shepherds are portrayed, the overall impression is one of brittleness and stylization, characteristic features of the style that had become known as "international Gothic" because of its widespread popularity.

Sculpture had always formed an integral part of church decorations, and there are innumerable figures on late Gothic structures. In addition, by the fifteenth century, complex and enormous wooden altarpieces could be found from the Iberian Peninsula to the eastern Holy Roman Empire. No surface was left smooth or empty. Three-dimensional figures painted and gilded to make them seem more lifelike are surrounded by architectural and botanical forms. Agitated lines abound, from the cascading hair of the Virgin to often graphically explicit Crucifixion scenes. These were especially popular in Germany. One of the outstanding surviving examples is the Sankt Wolfgang altarpiece (1471–1478) by Michael Pacher in the Pilgrimage Church of Abersee.

With the marriage of Fernando and Isabel in 1469, Spanish art received new impetus. The Catholic monarchs undertook large building programs to imprint their sover-

THE PORTINARI ALTARPIECE. Triptych by Hugo van der Goes, 1474.   ALINARI/ART RESOURCE

eignty and Christianity on the newly united kingdoms. But centuries of Moorish culture had left a mark on the arts, particularly as many craftsmen were still Muslim. Spanish Christian art of the fifteenth and sixteenth centuries was an amalgam of late Gothic excess, Flemish-German expressiveness, and Moorish techniques. This latter can be seen most obviously in architectural and decorative forms such as the horseshoe arch and mudejar, the repetitive ornamentation of flat surfaces. A particularly fine example is the cloister of San Juan de Los Reyes in Toledo, built by Fernando and Isabel to celebrate their victory at the Battle of Toro in 1476.

Although in Moorish art and architecture the effect was rhythmical and balanced, the mix with Gothic could result in an overload of often incompatible images and forms. This can be clearly seen by comparing the *mocárabe*, or stalactite plaster work, of the late fifteenth-century Patio de los Leones at the Alhambra, palace of the last Moorish rulers in Spain, with the post-1492 portal of the Colegio di San Gregorio, Valladolid, built by Queen Isabel's confessor. The gentle nonrepresentational organic patterning has given way to a heavily symbolic but disconnected decorative scheme that includes the royal arms held by rampant lions in a pomegranate tree as a memorial to the reconquest of Granada ("pomegranate" in Spanish), putti playing among its branches, and warriors, pages, and wildmen occupying niches encumbered with Gothic trimmings. The name given to this style, plateresque, is derived from the Spanish *platero*, or art of the silversmith, because of its characteristic excessive and precious ornamentality.

This style was not limited to architecture. The enormous carved *retablos*, or altarpieces, of the late fifteenth century exceed even the German taste for crowded surfaces and quantity of decoration. The great *retablo* of Seville cathedral (fifty-nine feet high) has forty-five figurative scenes in addition to all its extra decoration, and the *retablo mayor* of Toledo (1498–1504) is a complete cycle of the Life and Passion of Christ with countless three-dimensional figures separated by elaborate Gothic canopies. Also in Toledo is one of the most extravagant processional *custodias* (tabernacles) ever made: ten feet high and weighing 350 pounds, it is an enormous Gothic steeple of gilded silver and jewels surmounted by a cross made from the first gold brought back by Columbus. Some of this gold was also to find its way to the Spanish pope in Rome, Alexander VI, who used it to gild the ceiling of the early Christian basilica of Santa Maria Maggiore.

Gothic had its proponents in Italy, too. In Venice it blended elegantly with the Byzantine influences on the facades of the palazzi, and in Milan, it was the style for the new cathedral (begun about 1386). In painting and sculpture, the international Gothic remained popular in Italy throughout the fifteenth century. At the same time, Italian

MILAN CATHEDRAL. Construction begun circa 1386.

ALINARI/ART RESOURCE

Renaissance art began to develop with the work and theories of three Florentine artists, the architect Filippo Brunelleschi (1377–1446), the sculptor Donatello (1386?–1466), and the painter Masaccio (1401–1428). The new style involved revived interest in classical proportions and design, increasing realism in portraiture, and closer imitation of the natural world through perspective and foreshortening.

The early Renaissance style gradually transformed to High Renaissance in the second half of the fifteenth century with such masters as the painters Andrea Mantegna (1431–1506) in northern Italy, Giovanni Bellini (c. 1430–1516) in Venice, and the Florentine sculptors-painters Andrea del Verrocchio (c. 1435–1488) and Antonio Pollaiuolo (c. 1431–1498). Of these, Mantegna was the truest to the antique revival. Much of his art contains direct quotations from ancient models and his portrayals of classical monuments are almost literal. At the same time, his work was highly innovative, with dramatic foreshortenings and daring spatial effects, as in, most notably, his oculus in the Camera degli Sposi (1474) in the ducal palace at Mantua, where he was court painter. He was also one of the first to work in the new medium of engraving, and his impact there was considerable.

Giovanni Bellini, Mantegna's brother-in-law, was the chief painter to the state of Venice until his death, despite the growing reputation of the young Titian. His paintings

MONUMENT TO BARTOLOMMEO COLLEONI. By Andrea del Verrocchio, 1483–1488.   ALINARI/ART RESOURCE

impart a monumental stillness and dignity, highly refined perspectival spaces, and a bold, clear light, all apparent in one of his greatest masterpieces, *Saint Francis in Ecstasy* (1485).

Verrocchio, Donatello's heir, worked in many media, including marble, silver, and terra-cotta. His final work was his greatest, the bronze equestrian monument (1483–1488) to the mercenary Bartolomeo Colleoni for the city of Venice. Rather than emulating the calmness of the antique Marcus Aurelius in Rome or even Donatello's own Gattamelata monument of forty years earlier, Verrocchio has made his subject a defiant and bold figure. Standing upright in the stirrups, scowling ferociously at his adversaries, Colleoni is every inch the soldier leading his troops into battle.

Although monuments of a different kind, Pollaiuolo's bronze tombs of Pope Innocent VIII (1492–1498) and Pope Sixtus IV (completed 1493) also show increasing realism in the features. They were deemed of such quality that they were the only tombs saved when the old Saint Peter's was torn down in the sixteenth century. Both were revolutionary. Innocent was given a wall tomb with the enthroned live pope represented over his effigy in death. This double portrait was to become a favorite motif of the Renaissance

and the baroque periods. The tomb of Sixtus, an even more radical departure, is a floor tomb designed to fill the entire chapel with the recumbent pope lying atop a bronze bed surrounded by images of the Liberal Arts and Virtues. The references to Christianity have been allegorized to incorporate non-Christian ideas. But the ultimate power of the monument lies in the beautifully crafted death mask of the powerful, intelligent, and crafty man who built the Sistine Chapel and reestablished the Vatican Library after twenty years of neglect.

It was Sixtus IV who brought the Renaissance to Rome, where it reached its height in the early sixteenth century under the papacy of his nephew, Julius II, patron of Raphael (1483–1520), Donato Bramante (1444?–1514), Andrea Sansovino (c. 1467/71–1529), and Michelangelo (1475–1564). Sixtus founded a museum of antiquities and brought the finest artists of his day—mostly Florentines—to Rome in 1481 to decorate his new chapel with a fresco cycle of the lives of Moses and Jesus intended as a political declaration of the primacy of the pope in the ruling hierarchy of this world. The work was shared by Pietro Perugino (1445/50–1523), Sandro Botticelli (c. 1445–1510), Domenico Ghirlandaio, Cosimo Rosselli (1439–1507), and Luca Signorelli (1445/50–1523), all leading artists of the day. Perhaps the most daring of all artists in Rome during the last quarter of the fifteenth century was Melozzo da Forli (1438–1494) whose extreme foreshortening and skillful perspective make his figures seem to start out of their background and appear three-dimensional. Unfortunately, most of his work has been lost.

But even in the forward-looking world of Italian Renaissance art, the international Gothic continued. Beautiful clear colors, elegant lines, and gilded highlights are all hallmarks of Bernardino Pinturicchio (c. 1454–1513) whose greatest works were fresco cycles for various popes. Among the most famous are the wall paintings (1492–c. 1495) for the papal apartments of Alexander VI. These combine the old style with the new: among the deep tones and gold stucco work are subtle evocations of antiquity and obscure pre-Christian iconography. The pope's daughter, Lucrezia, is depicted as Saint Catherine of Alexandria, a pun on her father's papal name, and Alexander himself kneels at the foot of the cross, his Renaissance profile offset by an extravagant international-Gothic cope heavily encrusted with gold.

While Rome was enjoying its first taste of the Renaissance, there were continuing innovations in northern Italy. In Milan, Bramante, who would become architect of the new Saint Peter's in Rome in 1506, was beginning his experiments with the monumental forms that were to translate so successfully to Rome. Here for the first time was an architect using not only the vocabulary but the scale of ancient architecture. His choir of Santa Maria

TOMB OF SIXTUS IV. By Antonio Pollauiolo, completed 1493. One of two tombs preserved when Saint Peter's was rebuilt in the sixteenth century.

delle Grazie, begun in 1493 as a memorial to the Sforza, the ruling family of Milan, stresses the great size of the space it encloses and overpowers the observer used to the more intimate spaces of Brunelleschi. When the Sforza fell in 1499, Bramante left Milan for Rome, where he found employment first from Cardinal Ascanio Sforza and then from the cardinal's archrival, the newly elected Pope Julius II. After Sforza's death Julius interred his longtime enemy in the choir of Santa Maria del Popolo, in a grand tomb by Andrea Sansovino (1505) under a monumental coffered apse attributed to Bramante.

Florentine art was also changing. By the mid-1480s, Botticelli had executed *The Birth of Venus*, the first full-length painted female nude since antiquity, and Leonardo da Vinci (1452–1519) had established his reputation. Trained in Verrocchio's workshop, Leonardo, by his early work in the 1470s, so impressed the master that Verrocchio swore he would never touch a brush again. His fascination with the natural world led Leonardo to develop the technique of sfumato, which gives a misty quality to his paintings, making it appear as if the objects exist in a real atmosphere. This is in sharp contrast to the clear light of both international Gothic and contemporary Renaissance painting. He also heightened the use of chiaroscuro, a balance between light and shadow in paintings, giving figures greater dimensionality and feeling of being in space. His portrait *Mona Lisa* (1503) is an outstanding example of both techniques. Perhaps his most famous work is *The Last Supper* for the refectory of Santa Maria

delle Grazie in Milan (1495–1498), which began deteriorating almost immediately owing to Leonardo's unfortunate propensity for experimentation with paints. Here for the first time the psychological reaction of the Apostles to Christ's announcement of impending betrayal is shown. Subsequently, movement was to be used in art to display emotion and drama. But Leonardo was also a Renaissance Man in the truest sense. He dissected human bodies to study and draw them. His anatomical drawings are not only exquisite works of art but are also highly accurate. His fascination with technology and war led him to work first for Lodovico il Moro, duke of Milan, and then, after his fall in 1499, for Cesare Borgia, son of Pope Alexander VI, in 1502–1503. Again, his sketches for war machines are sometimes fantastic, but others foreshadow much of modern warfare, such as the tank and the helicopter. He returned to Florence in 1503, where he befriended the young Raphael and competed with Michelangelo. In 1513, he went to Rome and in 1517 accompanied Francis I to France, where he died two years later.

Michelangelo was almost twenty-five years younger than Leonardo. The son of a Florentine magistrate, Michelangelo had to overcome parental opposition to get artistic training. Originally apprenticed to the painter Ghirlandaio, Michelangelo soon found sculpture a more consuming passion. He was befriended by the sculptor Bertoldo di Giovanni, who was the keeper of the Medici sculpture garden and probably an illegitimate Medici. When Lorenzo the Magnificent died in 1492, Michelangelo

Pietà. By Michelangelo Buonarroti, completed 1498.

ALINARI/ART RESOURCE

began what was to become a lifelong emotional tug-of-war between Florence and Rome. In 1498 he completed the *Pietà* in Rome. Its great beauty and extraordinary balance of design established his reputation; also impressive was his carving of two figures out of one block of marble (which was inspired by ancient writers praising artistic achievements). Upon his return to Florence he received a commission for the *David* (1501–1504), which created a sensation when it was finished. It was deemed too beautiful to be placed in the site originally planned, high up on the cathedral, and a committee decided to put it next to the entrance of the Palazzo della Signoria as a symbol of the Republic of Florence. Immediately thereafter Michelangelo and Leonardo were engaged in an artistic competition to decorate the Council Hall, but neither of their works was ever finished, and both are known today only from copies. Nonetheless, the abandoned cartoons for Leonardo's *Battle of Anghiari* and Michelangelo's *Battle of Cascina* were so famous that for centuries many artists came to study them.

In 1506 Leonardo left Florence to return to Milan and shortly thereafter Michelangelo received a summons from Pope Julius II in Rome to carve his tomb. From this stay, two of the greatest monuments of the Roman High Renaissance emerged: the statue of *Moses,* part of the never-realized Julius tomb, and the ceiling of the Sistine Chapel (1508–1512). This extraordinary work of art, restored in the 1980s to its original glorious colors, had an immediate and powerful impact. The bold brushstrokes, dramatic colors, difficult poses, and total glorification of the nude ushered in a new era in art. After the death of Julius in 1513, Michelangelo spent the rest of his life working for popes, usually against his will. For Clement VII he created the Medici Chapel in Florence (begun 1524) and for Paul III, *The Last Judgment* (1536–1541). He served as chief architect of Saint Peter's from 1546 until his death in 1564, designing the great cupola and reinforcing the piers to carry the weight. During his own lifetime he was known as "il divino Michelangelo." No other artist has had so serious or continuing an influence on Western art.

During the first decades of the sixteenth century, Italian art became better known north of the Alps, thanks to the travels of such artists as the German Albrecht Dürer (1471–1528), who first visited Venice in 1494. He was a great admirer of Giovanni Bellini and was accused in 1507 of selling pirated copies of Italian engravings in Venice. He must have seen works by Giorgione (c. 1477–1511), whose innovative atmospheric landscape paintings and mysterious subjects made him, with Leonardo, one of the inventors of the High Renaissance style. Just as Raphael followed Leonardo, so Titian (1488/90–1576) succeeded Giorgione.

But it was not such peaceful exchanges that spread Italian taste to foreign lands. As France, Spain, and the Holy Roman Empire became increasingly entangled in Italian wars, their rulers also became aware of the new art that recalled the glory of the ancient Roman Empire. Unfortunately, their artists did not always understand the delicate balance between the structures and their proportions, and there are unhappy examples of a mixture of classical and Gothic motifs. By the end of the sixteenth century this combination had successfully melded into a new international style known as the baroque, which Spanish missionaries carried to the New World.

BIBLIOGRAPHY

Beck, James. *Italian Renaissance Painting.* New York, 1981.
Hartt, Frederick. *History of Italian Renaissance Art: Painting, Sculpture, Architecture.* 3d ed. New York, 1988.
Heydenreich, Ludwig H., and Wolfgang Lotz. *Architecture in Italy, 1400 to 1600.* Translated by Mary Hottiger. Harmondsworth, England, 1974.
Pope-Hennessy, John. *Italian Renaissance Sculpture.* 2d ed. London, 1971.
Snyder, James. *Northern Renaissance Art.* New York, 1985.

Sordo, Enrique. *Moorish Spain: Cordoba, Seville, Granada.* Translated by Ian Michael. New York, 1963.

Swaan, Wim. *The Late Middle Ages: Art and Architecture from 1350 to the Advent of the Renaissance.* Ithaca, 1977.

HELEN S. ETTLINGER

ASIA. For discussion of European knowledge of Asia in the Age of Exploration and how this information compares with the modern view of Asia's history, see *China.* For discussion of Japan, see *Cipangu.*

ASTROLABE. The word *astrolabe* (from Greek, *astrolabos* or *astrolabon organon*) usually refers to the planispheric astrolabe, an instrument deriving from the *planisphaerium* described by Ptolemy of Alexandria (fl. A.D. 127–148). It was used primarily for observation not to determine accurately the position of a celestial body but by day or by night for timetelling, for astrological purposes, for surveying, and for teaching astronomy. The essential circles and star-positions of the celestial sphere, as modeled on an armillary sphere are reduced to a flat surface by the geometrical procedure of stereographic projection, which retains angular measurements undistorted from the center.

The usual form of a planispheric astrolabe consists of a thick (c. ⅛- to ½-inch) main-plate (Latin, *mater*) with a deep recess on one side, leaving only a narrow raised limb, and provided with a suspension-ring attached to the rim. In the recess are a number of separate flat plates (Latin, *tympana,* sing. *tympanum*), prevented from turning by a lug fitting into a notch. Over the plates is a plate (Latin, *rete*) of the same diameter, that can be rotated; the rete is cut away to define circles and pointers. There is a rotatable rule (usually semidiametrical) over this plate; over the flat back of the main plate, there is a rotatable sighting rule (alidade) equipped with a pair of pinhole sight-vanes. The whole is held together by a thick pin, passed through coincident central holes in the main plate, the separate plates, and the cutaway plate, and held secure by a wedge pushed into a longitudinal slot in the pin.

The limb of the front of the main plate is engraved either with a scale of 360 degrees (Islamic astrolabes) or with a scale of twenty-four equal hours in two sequences of one to twelve (European astrolabes). Around the circumference of the back of this plate is a scale of degrees disposed into four quadrants so as to permit altitude measurements and various other scales or graphs (for example, a sine/cosine grid, a shadow "square" [for elementary surveying that avoids the need to know trigonometrical methods] as well as astrological tables [terms, limits, and

faces of the planets] on Islamic instruments. Also inscribed are a horary diagram for unequal hours [constituting, with a scale engraved on the alidade, a form of sundial] and a zodiac/calendar scale [correlating the date with the sun's position in the ecliptic; e.g., ten degrees Aries might correspond to March 21] on European instruments). The separate plates are engraved on each side with a stereographic projection from the south celestial pole onto the plane of the equator of the horizon, celestial pole, zenith, circles of altitude between the horizon and the zenith (almucantars), and, below the horizon line, lines of unequal hours. The cutaway plate is a similar projection of the ecliptic circle, of part of the equatorial circle, and of the Capricorn circle (which, in this projection, forms the boundary of the separate plates and the cutaway plate), with pointers attached to the tracery, the tips of which indicate the relative positions of a selection of the brighter stars, the names of which are engraved adjacent to the appropriate pointers. The cutaway plate, or rete, is thus a star-map, similar to a modern plastic planisphere except that it is an external view of the celestial sphere (as seen when looking at a celestial globe), not the sky as seen from the earth. Rotating the rete over the plate immediately below it simulates the apparent rotation of the stars and of the sun about the celestial pole (represented by the center of the central hole) and in relation to the horizon engraved on the plate: an analogue computer, in modern terms.

For use in a particular latitude, the astrolabe was assembled with the plate most appropriate to the latitude on top of the pile of plates in the recess in the main plate, immediately underneath the rete. As an example of use, to tell the time at night, the astrolabe was held by its suspension ring and allowed to hang vertically; the alidade was used to sight one of the stars for which a pointer was provided on the rete, and its altitude above the horizon was noted from the scale of degrees on the limb (after this, it was no longer necessary to suspend the astrolabe). The rete was then turned until the tip of the pointer, representing the star observed, lay on the altitude circle engraved on the plate beneath, corresponding to the observed angular elevation. The star pointer was positioned on the circle either east or west of the meridian line (on an astrolabe of the type described, north is at the bottom, south at the top) according to whether the star, when observed, was east or west of the meridian. The rule over the rete was then turned until it crossed the position of the sun in the ecliptic (that is, the solar declination on the day in question, e.g., twenty-three degrees Leo, ascertainable from astronomical tables or, on a European astrolabe, from the zodiac/calendar on the back). The position of the rule on the hour-scale on the limb then gave the time in equal hours. (On Islamic astrolabes, the

PLANISPHERIC ASTROLABE. Front (*left*) and back (*right*) of a brass astrolabe attributed to Jean Fusoris, circa 1430.

time in unequal [planetary] hours or, sometimes, Babylonian or Italian hours, was found from hour lines engraved on the plate below the horizon line.)

The complexity of design and construction of an astrolabe made it expensive; many of the data it provided were irrelevant to navigation; the use of a solid disk in a wind or on the moving deck of a ship was not conducive to accurate observation. There is no evidence that planispheric astrolabes were ever regularly used at sea, despite the claim of the instrument maker Johann Krabbe of Munden, who described his version of a conventional planispheric astrolabe as especially suited to the needs of seamen in *Neuwes Astrolabium* (1608). Universal (that is, usable in any latitude) variants of the astrolabe described above, not requiring separate plates, and based on stereographic or orthographic projections of the celestial sphere on the colures (great circles) of the solstices, were no more useful to the mariner; the same is true of the rare spherical and linear astrolabes.

Mariner's or Sea Astrolabes. During the latter part of the fifteenth century, an altitude-measuring instrument, called an astrolabe and intended for employment at sea, came into use. In 1487–1488, Bartolomeu Dias had "astrolabes" on his voyage to the Cape of Good Hope; in 1497 at the bay of St. Helena (southern Africa), Vasco da Gama used, on land (because of the difficulties of making the necessary observations at sea), a large (c. 24-inch diameter) wooden astrolabe, suspended from a tripod. In 1519, Magellan took with him one wooden and six metal astrolabes on his circumnavigation of the earth. The exact form of these sea astrolabes is uncertain. It is not until Alessandro Zorzi's letter of 1517 that an illustration of a mariner's astrolabe of characteristic form is found, and this precedes by eight years the earliest of two drawings on charts by the cartographer Diego Ribeiro of what he called "astrolabio maritimo," but which appears to be a solid disk based on the design of the back of a conventional astrolabe, though the sight vanes on the alidade are placed in the close position characteristic of the mariner's astrolabe.

Vasco da Gama's large wooden instrument was probably nearer in form to the wheel design of the characteristic mariner's astrolabe and was perhaps derived rather from a circular wooden observational instrument, with an alidade, used by medieval astronomers. The characteristic mariner's astrolabe consists of a heavy cast body in the form of a four-spoked wheel, sometimes slightly wedge-shaped in side-view, heavier in the lower part, where part of each of the two void quadrants is symmetrically filled in. There is a suspension ring, similar to that on a conventional astrolabe, and an alidade, with two sight vanes, pierced by pinhole sights, set much farther inward along the arms of the alidade than on a conventional astrolabe. Clearly, the position near the center of the sight vanes would have made it very difficult to use a mariner's observation for stellar observations; it was intended to measure solar altitude (or zenith distances) that, with the aid of appropriate solar-declination tables, permitted the determination of the latitude at the place of observation. The method of making the observation was to hold the astrolabe by the suspension-ring, directing it sideways toward the sun, and to rotate the alidade until the sunlight passing through the pinhole in the foresight fell as a spot of light exactly on the matching pinhole on the backsight; the pointed end of the alidade on the scale on the limb then indicated the sun's elevation. Scales of ninety degrees were graduated on the limb in the upper two quadrants, either (from the horizontal) to measure altitude or, on the later sixteenth-century Portuguese instruments (from the vertical) to measure zenith distance.

Some sixty-five mariner's astrolabes have been recorded (compared with about 1,500 planispheric astrolabes), many found in wrecks. The earliest is Portuguese and dates from 1540; the series continues into the eighteenth century, by which time the mariner's astrolabe was mostly superseded, in northern Europe, at least, by the cross-staff or by the backstaff. Deficiencies of the quadrant (high wind resistance in relation to size, a swinging plumb bob, difficulties in holding it if making a solar observation by the technique described above) doubtless encouraged the development of the mariner's astrolabe, the design of which sought to overcome a seaman's practical difficulties in making an astronomical observation. Columbus's journal of his first voyage (entry for February 3, 1493) mentions that he was unable to use an "astrolabio" because of the rough seas, but what type of astrolabe this was remains unknown. Astronomical observations made with an instrument that are mentioned were made with a quadrant.

[See also *Cross-staff*; *Quadrant*.]

BIBLIOGRAPHY

North, J. D. "The Astrolabe." *Scientific American*, no. 230 (Jan. 1974), pp. 96–106. Reprint in J. D. North, *Stars, Minds and Fate:*

Essays in Ancient and Medieval Cosmology, pp. 211–220. London and Ronceverte, W.Va., 1989.

Stimson, Alan. *The Mariner's Astrolabe: A Survey of Known, Surviving Sea Astrolabes*. HES Studies in the History of Cartography and Scientific Instruments, vol. 4. Utrecht, 1988.

Turner, Anthony. *Early Scientific Instruments: Europe 1400–1800*. London, 1987.

Turner, Anthony. *The Time Museum: Catalogue of the Collection*. Vol. 1 of *Time Measuring Instruments*. Part 1, *Astrolabes. Astrolabe Related Instruments*. Rockford, Ill., 1985.

FRANCIS MADDISON

ASTROLOGY. See *Astronomy and Astrology*.

ASTRONOMY AND ASTROLOGY. Astronomy and mathematics had little direct effect on navigation until the end of the thirteenth century. However, Greek science (and in particular Ptolemaic ideas of geography), which was transmitted to the Christian West by the Arabs, was to have a profound effect on the world of learning and on cosmographical concepts in the years leading up to the Age of Discovery.

Mathematical scholarship began to flourish in Italy soon after Leonardo of Pisa's (Fibonacci) introduction to the West, in 1202, of the Hindu (Arabic) system of numerals, which replaced the awkward Roman figures that made calculations so complicated. In the Norman kingdom of Sicily, which included southern Italy, Greek texts were being translated from Arabic into Latin with the help of Arab and Jewish scholars, while in Toledo in 1252 King Alfonso X of Castile and León assembled fifty Jewish and Christian scholars to translate scientific texts, including Ptolemy, from Arabic into Castilian.

The compilation, entitled *Libros del saber de astronomia*, included all known works on astronomy and related subjects, and its twenty-four theses summarized contemporary knowledge and gave instructions for making a variety of astronomical instruments, such as the astronomer's astrolabe, the quadrant, the armillary sphere, and so on. Most of the original texts were in Arabic and most of the translators, who rendered the texts into Castilian, were Jewish. Included were the Alphonsine Tables, based on the longitude of Toledo; translated into Latin, they were later circulated widely among astronomers. The astrolabe, an instrument of great antiquity, was introduced into Europe by the Arabs during the tenth century and was used for both astronomical and astrological purposes. It displayed the positions of the stars at night for different times and latitudes and could be used for timekeeping as well as for finding the precise direction of Mecca (which the builders of mosques were required to know). It could also be used to determine the altitudes, azimuths, and amplitudes of stars and, in the armillary type described by Ptolemy in the *Almagest,* enabled the celestial latitude and longitude of a body to be read without having to convert the altitude and azimuth into ecliptic coordinates.

In the Middle Ages the distinction between astronomy and astrology was a fine one. A person's horoscope, for instance, which governed his future, could only be cast if the exact position of the heavenly bodies could be determined as they rose; the position of the heavenly bodies in relation to the zodiac must be established for an exact hour. The astrolabe was in use in Portugal before 1090, and early tables, such as the collection known as the Portuguese Almanacs of Madrid, record a wide variety of astrological, astronomical, and geographical data, including meridian heights of the sun on a given parallel, the coordinates of stars and of geographical locations, dominical letters, and other data for determining movable feasts, eclipses, and the position of the moon in the zodiac, duration of days and nights in each month, and so on. The manuscript, compiled in Coimbra during the reign of King Dinis of Portugal (1261–1325), was derived from the Latin translation of an Arabic almanac calculated for the radix year 1307. King Dinis, the grandson of Alfonso X, is said to have received from his grandfather a copy of the *Libros del saber de astronomia,* which was finished in 1256. The almanacs, for all their astrological leanings, show a level of scientific learning among the astronomers working in Portugal that bodes well for the development of a navigational science.

A small work that was to assume great importance in the history of early nautical astronomy was *De sphaera mundi,* written in the early thirteenth century by the Englishman Johannes de Sacrobosco, or John of Holywood, probably as an introduction to a more advanced course on astronomy and cosmology. It became a standard text during the Age of Discovery and in a translation into Portuguese formed an integral part of the navigation manuals produced at the end of the fifteenth century. It is based largely on the work of the great Arab astronomer Alfraganus (al-Farghani, d. 861) and presents the Ptolemaic system as put forward in the *Almagest.* The treatise gives proofs of the sphericity of the earth, defines astronomical and terrestrial terms such as the ecliptic, equator, small and great circles, meridians, astronomical coordinates, and the twelve signs of the zodiac, and explains various astronomical phenomena, such as eclipses. It was Alfraganus whose calculation of the degree of the meridian— 56⅔ miles—so misled Columbus, who failed to take into account the difference between the Arabic and the Italian mile.

The degree of the meridian is the angle subtended at the earth's center between two places on the same meridian, and the linear distance between them will depend on the figure adopted for the circumference of the earth. Early miles—Roman, Mediterranean, and Arabic—were defined in terms of other units unconnected with the size of the earth. Eratosthenes had measured the size of the earth in the third century B.C. and rounded off his findings to 252,000 stadia, so that each degree would have 700 stadia, which is 70 nautical miles. Ptolemy's *Almagest,* on the other hand, which was again in circulation in the fifteenth century, calculated the degree as 62 Roman miles. For the navigator none of this was of importance until, during the Age of Discovery, latitude on the charts became associated with distance. In what seems to be the earliest instruction to the seaman on the observation of altitude, repeated in an archaic addendum printed in the 1563 edition of Valentim Fernandes's *Reportorio dos tempos* (1518), the observer is told that for each degree marked on the scale of his quadrant he must "count 16 leagues and two thirds, which is 2 miles, reckoning 3 miles to a league." This would give a degree of only 50 miles, and later instructions to Portuguese navigators were to count 17½ leagues of 4 miles to the degree, yielding a degree of 70 miles. In *The Haven Finding Art,* E. G. R. Taylor suggests that Portuguese astronomers accepted Eratosthenes' degree of 700 stades, while Spaniards and Catalans chose Ptolemy's 500 stades, both reckoning 10 stades to the mile but each using the local league. To the seaman, however, the earth's size was of little conceptual import, for in the early days of astronomical navigation the navigator thought of his observations not in terms of latitude but rather in terms of the linear distance sailed between observations of the same body.

The first observations were of the North Star made in one of eight positions of the star's counterclockwise path around the pole as defined by the relative positions of the two Guard Stars, whether in terms of the altitude at Lisbon or as a correction to that altitude, and displayed either in terms of an imaginary human figure in the sky or in one of numerous "wheel" diagrams. The navigator was told in the manuals that, disregarding fractions of a degree less precise than those that could be observed at sea, the altitude of the North Star at Lisbon varied between thirty-six and forty-two degrees (giving a latitude of thirty-nine degrees).

There are numerous early Jewish and Islamic works translated into Latin that show how to determine latitude from the meridian altitude of the sun when the declination is known. The earliest, dating back to the ninth century, was by the astrologer Messahalla, but the rules apply only to an observer north of Cancer. The *Libros del saber de astronomia* contained a number of works derived from

Messahalla, including a set of rules that could be adapted for use south of the equator. The Portuguese astrologers who introduced latitude navigation in the Southern Hemisphere, where the North Star became invisible, would thus have had access to sources indicating, if only by analogy, the rules for the determination of latitude from the noonday altitude of the sun in positions with either northerly or southerly declination. Whether the rules set forth by the mathematical commission appointed by King João II of Portugal and set down in the earliest surviving navigation manual were in fact derived from Messahalla is not certain. The Regiment (or Rule) of the Sun in its various forms dealt with the problem of applying the declination to the altitude of the sun to obtain latitude in either hemisphere, when the sun was north or south of the observer and north or south of the equator. The relative positions of the sun and the observer were judged from the direction of shadows. Authorship of the Regiment is generally attributed to José Vizinho, the Jewish astrologer and physician to João II, who was sent on a voyage to Guinea in 1485 to test its efficacy in practice. Columbus refers to his observations.

To use the regiment of the altitude of the pole at noon, as Pedro Nunes was to term the Regiment of the Sun, the navigator needed to know the sun's declination, its angular distance north or south of the celestial equator. Medieval astrologers were accustomed to measuring the sun's position in the sky in terms of one of the twelve signs of the zodiac, each governing thirty degrees of the ecliptic. It was simple to calculate the solar declination from its position on the ecliptic, provided the precise angle between the ecliptic and the equinoctial was known, but astronomers differed on this measure, and so solar declination tables differed. The sun, furthermore, takes a little over a day to get through each degree of the zodiac, and four calendar years pass before the figures repeat themselves (even then a correction factor had to be applied to compensate for the difference between the length of the mean year in the Julian calendar and the duration of the sun's annual course). Tables of the sun's position were thus generally quadrennial, and a correction was made after the four-year period to allow for the sun having advanced 42 minutes and 56 seconds during that time. The most important ephemerides from the point of view of navigation were the tables in Abraham Zacuto's *Almanach perpetuum*. These were calculated from the year 1473 and gave the positions of the sun at noon for the quadrennial period 1473 to 1476 and the declination in degrees and minutes at any point on the ecliptic defined in whole degrees. A correction for use after the four-year period was included with the declination tables. The inclination of the ecliptic was taken to be 22°33'. In his *Tratado em defensam da carta marear*, Nu-

nes found Zacuto's value excessive and based his own tables on an obliquity of 23°30'. Vizinho had been a pupil of Zacuto at Salamanca and translated the introductory parts of the *Almanach perpetuum* into Latin and Spanish; he was no doubt also responsible for adapting the tables for inclusion in the *Regimento do astrolabio e do quadrante*. The sun's declination could of course be calculated by astronomers graphically or with the help of scientific instruments, such as the astrolabe, but few of these methods were suitable for use at sea.

[See also *Distance; Navigation; Science.*]

BIBLIOGRAPHY

Albuquerque, Luís de. *Astronomical Navigation*. Lisbon, 1988.

Cortesão, Armando. *History of Portuguese Cartography*. 2 vols. Coimbra, 1969.

Taylor, E. G. R. *The Haven Finding Art: A History of Navigation from Odysseus to Captain Cook*. London, 1956.

M. W. RICHEY

ATAHUALPA (d. 1533), Inca emperor. Atahualpa (Spanish, Francisco Atahualpa Inca) was born in Cuzco, the son of Huayna Capac and an Inca princess (Tupa Palla by one account, Tocto Coca by another, and Palla Coca by still another), and the elder brother of Huascar.

He was described as wise, cheerful, and very intelligent, of good appearance and manner, somewhat thickset. He had a large face, handsome and fierce, and his eyes were reddened with blood. He spoke gravely with the authority of a great ruler.

Huayna Capac's death left an ambiguous situation because the son he designated as his successor on his deathbed died in the same epidemic that killed him. Since the Incas had no rule of primogeniture, but settled authority on the one most able and fit to rule, struggles for succession were normal after the death of every Inca ruler. Huascar initially won with the support of the court and administration in Cuzco. Atahualpa had been left in charge of the Inca army at Quito and he probably acted as provincial governor on behalf of Huascar, for whom he was building new palaces at Tumipampa. However, Huascar suspected that Atahualpa was planning treason and sent a militia army to invade Quito; it was defeated by the Inca army, which was loyal to Atahualpa. Atahualpa entered Tumipampa triumphantly and took for himself the Inca crown, the *llautu* (a red woven headband with a fringe that covered the forehead), and title of Sapa Inca (supreme Inca).

The Inca army pursued Huascar's troops to Huanacopampa, west of Cuzco, where it defeated them and took Huascar prisoner. Atahualpa's army entered Cuzco triumphantly with much local support because Huascar had alienated many of his earlier supporters, notably the lineage Hatun ayllu. Atahualpa killed members of Huascar's family and the rival lineage, Capac ayllu. (The story of a northern-southern split of the Inca empire was a fabrication of Garcilaso de la Vega that appealed to the European mentality.)

Atahualpa, celebrating his victory, began to move south slowly with his retinue when he heard of the arrival of Francisco Pizarro's third expedition. He stopped at the hot spring baths near Cajamarca with about 80,000 troops to receive the Spaniards with intentions of capturing them. However, he seriously miscalculated the effect of the Spaniards' weapons and armor and was overconfident and drunk on November 16, 1533, when Pizarro ambushed him in the main square of Cajamarca after the priest Valverde attempted to deliver a sort of *requerimiento* (formal summons to surrender and accept the church and Spanish rule on pain of suffering war and enslavement). About seven thousand of Atahualpa's retinue were killed and his troops surrendered the next morning. Atahualpa was imprisoned but offered the Spaniards a ransom, in return for his life, of a room filled once with gold and twice with silver. He was tried for treason based on rumors that his army was preparing an attack. He was prepared for burning at the stake in the main square, but was garrotted instead when he accepted Christianity and was baptized Francisco.

BIBLIOGRAPHY

Hemming, John. *The Conquest of the Incas.* San Diego, 1970.
Rostworowski de Díez Canseco, María. "Succession, Coöption to Kingship, and Royal Incest among the Inca." *Southwestern Journal of Anthropology* 16 (1960): 417–427.
Rostworowski de Díez Canseco, María. *Historia del Tahuantinsuyu.* Lima, 1988.

JEANETTE SHERBONDY

ATLANTIC RIVALRY. As soon as European explorers ventured out into the Atlantic in search of new lands and commodities to trade, the ocean became part of international rivalries, an extension of the land-based rivalries among contending European states. What might be called the Battle of the Atlantic began several centuries before Columbus's voyages and continued for several centuries thereafter.

One of the earliest European ventures far into the Atlantic reputedly occurred in the sixth century, when an Irish monk named Brendan led a band of followers in search of a pristine land where they could worship God free from the distractions of life at home. It is not clear how far they ventured or even if the voyage occurred at all, but the legend of this monk, who later became Saint Brendan, continued to inspire European Christians in Columbus's time and beyond. At the start of the eleventh century Viking explorers began sailing westward across the north Atlantic from their Scandinavian homelands to the Shetland and Orkney Islands, and then to Iceland, Greenland, and to what would later be called North America. Neither the voyages of Saint Brendan nor the voyages of Leif Ericsson and his compatriots seem to have inspired rivals, however. They occurred before long-distance trade had developed fully enough to generate much profit, and before the population had risen enough to make the acquisition of new lands very attractive to the countries that rimmed the Atlantic.

Both European trade and population expanded considerably in the centuries after Leif Ericsson sailed, and governments rose that could tap the resources of their people and use them to pursue national goals. Among those goals were new sources of food and trade goods to enhance their countries' wealth. The scope and volume of trade in late medieval Europe had two main poles of development: the northern Atlantic and Baltic coastlines and the Mediterranean. Commercial cities in those two areas became the prime movers of late medieval trade and its main beneficiaries, although inland cities that controlled vital trade goods also played a role. In southern Europe, Portugal was ideally located to participate in both poles of medieval trade. Portugal and its late medieval monarchs identified their interests much more with the Atlantic than with the Mediterranean, however, seeking out supplies of grain and fish along the coasts of northern and western Africa as the population grew. Another powerful African lure was gold, which arrived in the ports of the Mediterranean overland from sources south of the Sahara desert. The trans-Saharan trade was controlled by Muslim merchants, but the Portuguese were quick to see the possibilities of a sea-borne approach to the sources of African gold. Castile, Portugal's neighbor and rival in the Iberian Peninsula, saw the same possibilities in African fishing and trade. Their rivalry would intensify during the fifteenth century.

Partly in pursuit of trade and partly as a continuation of its rivalry with the Islamic world of the Mediterranean, Portugal reached across the Strait of Gibraltar to conquer Ceuta in Morocco in 1415. This conquest gave the Portuguese a trading port in North Africa and a Mediterranean foothold as well. From this foothold, Portuguese merchants exported grain, textiles, and the products of the trans-Saharan caravan trade, primarily gold and slaves. From Ceuta the Portuguese explored westward and southward along the African coast, expanding their trading network and searching for a sea route around Africa toward Asia. Although local African rulers were powerful on land, they had little interest in the sea. Except for

Castile, Portugal had no serious rivals on Africa's Atlantic coast during the fifteenth century.

The situation was similar farther out to sea, although various European powers had been interested in exploring the Atlantic west of southern Europe for several centuries. The first documented voyage after Saint Brendan involved an expedition in 1291 led by two brothers from Genoa, Ugolino and Vadino Vivaldi. At that time attempts to establish overland trade with Asia were being thwarted by the breakup of Mongol authority. Moreover, the last Christian enclave in the Middle East, left from the days of the Crusades, had fallen under Muslim control again. Any future trade would depend on the changeable attitudes of whoever controlled the trade routes. In search of the markets of Asia, the Vivaldi brothers sailed southward from Europe as far as the latitude of the Canary Islands, but they were not heard about thereafter, except in legend.

The Canaries had been known to classical antiquity as the Fortunate Isles, but they and the other Atlantic islands did not engage the serious interest of southern Europeans until the fourteenth century. Sometime before 1340 a Genoese named Lancellotto Malocello explored the Canaries and gave his name to the island of Lanzarote in that chain. In 1341 the king of Portugal launched an expedition composed of Portuguese, Castilians, Florentines, and Genoese to conquer the Canaries, but it evidently failed. Also in the 1340s Clement VI, the pope in Avignon, authorized a nobleman named Luis de la Cerda, who held titles in both Spain and France, to conquer and rule various islands in the Atlantic. While he readied his expedition in France with help from Aragón, both Portugal and Castile argued that they had prior claims. Clearly, the Atlantic islands were becoming valuable prizes. De la Cerda's expedition and his claim came to nothing, however. He died, and Europe was overtaken by the Black Death in 1348. From the 1340s on, the Canaries were visited by several small expeditions, one of them a missionary effort sponsored by the king of Aragón to Christianize the islanders. Mariners from Andalusia also visited the islands regularly at the end of the fourteenth century. In 1402 the Crown of Castile began the definitive conquest of the Canaries, granting patents to captains who would claim the lands for Castile. These captains recovered their investment, first by capturing and selling slaves and later by establishing sugar plantations.

Like the Canaries, the Madeira islands attracted the interest of several rival groups of Europeans from the late thirteenth or early fourteenth century. As mariners ventured out farther into the Atlantic, the winds and currents ensured that they would eventually reach the Madeiras. By the late fourteenth and early fifteenth centuries both Portuguese and Castilian ships stopped there for wood

and for the red dye called "dragon's blood," a resin from the so-called dragon tree. The Madeiras were uninhabited, and no serious attempts were made to colonize them until Castile sent a large force to the islands in 1417. In response King João I of Portugal sponsored an expedition of about one hundred people to colonize the islands for Portugal. Grain, sugar, and other agricultural products made the islands of Madeira and Porto Santo profitable colonies from about 1450 on.

The northernmost of the Atlantic islands, the Azores, were discovered in 1427 by Portugal, which probably began to colonize them in 1432. Eventually they produced profitable exports of grain and dyestuffs, but sugar had little success. The Cape Verde Islands, close to the African coast off Senegal, were probably reached by the Portuguese in 1455 and quickly developed into a center for the growing slave trade. The islands were soon producing cotton and cotton cloth, the latter a key item in bartering for slaves on the mainland. Local seashells were also prized, and a certain variety was used as money on the mainland. In all, the Portuguese were able to turn handsome profits from their island colonies, which attracted rivals.

Through the fifteenth century regular voyaging to the Atlantic islands and tentative exploration continued. During the years that Columbus was in Portugal, he became familiar with Portuguese outposts on the African coast and the Atlantic islands and the sea lanes that served them. Undoubtedly this experience contributed to the formulation of his grand design of sailing west to reach Asia. In the meantime, the Portuguese were concentrating their efforts on exploration southward, trying to round Africa to establish a sea route to the Far East. Castilian mariners continued to challenge the Portuguese in these pursuits. Their rivalry in the Atlantic was one of the issues involved in Portugal's intervention in the Castilian civil war of 1475–79. As part of the settlement between Portugal and Castile, the Treaty of Alcáçovas-Toledo set out spheres of influence in the Atlantic for the two Iberian powers. By the terms of the treaty, Castile recognized Portugal's title to the Azores, the Madeiras, and the Cape Verdes in return for Portuguese recognition of Castile's title to the Canaries.

More important, Castile accepted a Portuguese monopoly on new discoveries in the Atlantic from the Canaries southward and toward the African coast. In 1481 the pope granted Portugal a "bull," or charter, ratifying this monopoly. The bull, called *Aeterni Regis*, was followed by four other papal grants in the wake of Columbus's first voyage. In the first two, Pope Alexander VI, fortunately for Spanish pretentions a member of the Borja (Borgia) family of Valencia, granted Castile all lands discovered or to be discovered in the area Columbus had explored. The third bull, called *Inter caetera*, drew a north-south line one hundred leagues west of the Azores and the Cape Verdes. The Portuguese sphere of influence would lie east of the line, the Castilian sphere west of the line.

To that point, Portugal could accept that its interests as well as Castile's were served by papal intervention. The fourth bull, *Dudum siquidem,* changed that perception. Because it extended Castilian control to all lands west, south, and east of India, the main focus of Portuguese efforts, João II of Portugal protested. When the pope refused to change his mind, João approached Isabel and Fernando directly and persuaded them to negotiate. The rival claims of both parties were settled in 1494 with the Treaty of Tordesillas. It redrew Pope Alexander VI's dividing line at 370 leagues west of the Azores and the Cape Verdes, ratifying Portugal's title to its outposts in Africa and its eastern route to India (plus Brazil, as it happened). The recognition was particularly important because Bartolomeu Dias had rounded the cape of southern Africa in 1487–1488, clearing the way for a Portuguese sea route to India. Castile gained an undisputed claim to what would become its empire in the western hemisphere.

Other countries in Europe, especially England and France, were also interested in Atlantic exploration, especially after Columbus's 1492 voyage proved that lands lay close enough to the west to be feasibly explored and exploited. The English sponsored several voyages across the north Atlantic before 1500, the most famous being that of John Cabot (Giovanni Caboto, a Genoese) in 1497. Cabot claimed lands in present-day Labrador and Newfoundland for England. In 1499 the Portuguese Gaspar Côrte-Real followed the same route and claimed parts of Newfoundland for Portugal. In the 1502 map known as the Cantino planisphere, commissioned by a Portuguese nobleman, the lands claimed by Côrte-Real were depicted on the Portuguese side of the demarcation line established by the Treaty of Tordesillas, presumably to avoid conflict with Castile. John Cabot's claims for England were not shown at all. By then Portugal had found another prize in the Atlantic: Brazil. The Portuguese had discovered that the best way to round the landmass of Africa lay in sailing southwestward from Iberia into the Atlantic on the prevailing winds and currents, until intersecting the winds and currents that flowed southeastward. On one of those voyages in 1500, Pedro Álvares Cabral encountered the bulge of Brazil jutting out into the Atlantic, clearly on the Portuguese side of the demarcation line. By 1500, even before Europeans realized that the lands they had found were not in Asia, various countries had staked out claims to own and exploit them and were in the process of having those claims recognized by their European rivals.

In the wakes of Columbus, Cabot, Côrte-Real, and Cabral, dozens of other European mariners obtained charters of exploration for the Atlantic. Undoubtedly many of them believed those lands were a part of Asia, if somewhat removed from the fabled temples and markets of Cipangu and Cathay. Only with the circumnavigation of the globe begun by the Portuguese Ferdinand Magellan in 1519, sailing for Castile, did the true scope and nature of the world's oceans begin to be known. When the remnant of Magellan's small fleet arrived back in Spain in 1521 (minus Magellan, who had been killed in the Philippines), it became clear that a vast expanse of ocean lay between the southern extreme of the new lands and the real Asia known to Europeans since the Middle Ages. The Atlantic Ocean was the route to a New World, rather than the route from one shore of the Old World to the other.

Through most of the sixteenth century the claims that had been warily staked out by 1500 held rivalry in the Atlantic to a minimum. Castile conquered two large empires in the central and southern portions of the Western Hemisphere and created a huge bureaucratic and commercial empire in their place. Early on, pirates from rival European countries hoped to steal Castile's profits from conquest, plunder, taxation, and trade by lying in wait in the eastern Atlantic to ambush inbound voyages. A system of armed convoys organized around 1522 generally thwarted these attempts, and Castile had no serious rivals in its empire or in the sea lanes that served it for most of the sixteenth century. Portugal maintained its claim to Brazil and extracted several items of commercial value from it but did little to colonize the vast interior during the sixteenth century, concentrating instead on its trading posts in Africa and India.

In areas north of the region being developed by Castile, France took the early lead in exploration during the sixteenth century. The Florentine Giovanni Verrazano sailed for Francis I of France in 1524–1528 in search of a passage through North America to the Pacific Ocean and Cathay. Although Verrazano hoped the French would colonize the lands and Christianize the natives of North America, the markets of Asia remained the goal of Francis I and his court. Jacques Cartier's voyages in 1534–1542 continued the fruitless search. Ironically, in the early sixteenth century European rivalry in the Atlantic centered on a battle for the Pacific. The Spanish made similar attempts to find a passage through North America, for the same reasons and with the same results. They made no attempt to colonize or hold the area they explored, although Spanish fishermen and whalers regularly visited the coasts of Newfoundland and Labrador and frequently spent the winter there.

In the late sixteenth century English mariners began to take a greater interest in exploration, and under Elizabeth I a series of expeditions interloped on the monopoly claimed by Spain in the Western Hemisphere while continuing the search for a northwest passage. As relations between England and Spain deteriorated in the 1560s, a new battle for the Atlantic ensued. At stake were control of the lands across the Atlantic and the profits Spain reaped from trade, although the Northwest Passage to Asia remained a central goal of English exploration for centuries to come. Francis Drake, Martin Frobisher, Humphrey Gilbert, and others all made the attempt. Walter Raleigh tried to establish a permanent English colony in 1585–1586 in what was called Virginia, part of the land claimed but not effectively settled by Spain, but the attempt failed. Nonetheless, English and Dutch incursions into the Caribbean intensified in the late sixteenth century, provoking a strong Spanish response.

When pressed, Spain could muster the resources to defend its colonies and its trade monopoly in the Western Hemisphere. Portugal could do likewise, ousting the Dutch from northwest Brazil after a hard-fought struggle in the 1640s. Still, neither Spain nor Portugal could satisfy all the needs of their vast American empires without products from the rest of Europe. The English, French, and Dutch realized that the best hope of profit lay in diplomatic agreements with Spain and Portugal and in founding permanent colonies of their own. By a series of treaties in the seventeenth century, the rest of Europe recognized the titles of Spain and Portugal to their American empires. In exchange, they were able to trade freely with the Spanish and Portuguese empires, either legally through the established monopolies, or clandestinely through a widespread contraband trade that was openly acknowledged by all concerned. By about 1650 rivalry in the Atlantic had established spheres of influence that closely resembled the situation in 1500, with no one power in control of trade and the sea lanes, and the lands in control of whoever could hold them effectively.

[See also *Exploration and Discovery; Trade.*]

BIBLIOGRAPHY

Andrews, Kenneth. *The Spanish Caribbean: Trade and Plunder 1530–1630.* New Haven, 1978.

Davies, K. G. *The North Atlantic World in the Seventeenth Century.* Minneapolis, 1974.

Diffie, Bailey W., and George D. Winius. *Foundations of the Portuguese Empire, 1415–1580.* Minneapolis, 1977.

Fernández-Armesto, Felipe. *Before Columbus: Exploration and Colonization from the Mediterranean to the Atlantic, 1229–1492.* Philadelphia, 1987.

McAlister, Lyle N. *The Growth of the Iberian Empires to about 1650–1700.* Minneapolis, 1974.

Morison, Samuel Eliot. *The European Discovery of America: The Northern Voyages A. D. 500–1600.* New York, 1971.

Morison, Samuel Eliot. *The European Discovery of America: The Southern Voyages A. D. 1492–1616.* New York, 1974.

Parry, J. H. *The Age of Reconnaissance: Discovery, Exploration and Settlement 1450–1650.* New York, 1969.

CARLA RAHN PHILLIPS

ÁVILA, PEDRO ARIAS DE

ÁVILA, PEDRO ARIAS DE (1440?–1530), Spanish soldier and colonial governor. Disturbing rumors coming out of Tierra Firme (in present-day Panama) in 1513 concerning the conduct of Vasco Núñez de Balboa's government there caused the Spanish king to appoint a courtier, Pedro Arias de Ávila, known as Pedrárias Dávila, governor of the colony and to authorize him to investigate Balboa's actions. Pedrárias, a native of Segovia and a minor member of the Spanish nobility, was a veteran of Spanish campaigns in North Africa. Close to the bishop of Burgos, he was an important royal adviser.

Pedrárias took with him nearly fifteen hundred people, including retainers, settlers, and adventurers. This expedition served as a testing ground for later conquests. Important among the members of the expedition were Hernando de Soto, Bernal Díaz del Castillo, and Gonzalo Fernández de Oviedo. Díaz, in his famous history of the conquest of Mexico, indicates that many members of the expedition who failed to gain wealth moved on to other, later adventures.

The government of Pedrárias in Tierra Firme was marked by cruelty and division. From the outset, the small colony was split between followers of Balboa and those of the new governor, both of whom claimed royal authority over the region. The presence of gold and the growing strategic importance of the place heightened the stakes in the conflict. Balboa opted to move to the Pacific coast, away from Pedrárias's sphere of activities. But he kept in close contact with affairs at court in Spain, sending many letters home denouncing his rival's excesses. Balboa hoped that the reform movement in Spain would eventually call Pedrárias back, allowing Balboa to regain his monopoly in power. But Pedrárias intercepted some of these communications and charged Balboa with treason. When word reached the colony that a royal investigator had been sent out to proceed against Pedrárias, he contrived the arrest of Balboa, who after a brief trial was executed.

In 1519, Pedrárias formally founded the territory of Panama, having moved northward from the original settlement of Santa María la Antigua de Darién. This new territory encompassed all of the original jurisdiction acquired by Balboa, as well as the Pacific coast granted to the latter under his title as adelantado. Although Pedrárias is noted for his ruthlessness, and especially for the execution of Balboa, he is credited with expanding the Spaniards' geographical knowledge of Central America. He organized many expeditions north and south of Panama, laying the groundwork for later conquests of

Nicaragua and eventually of Peru. The important conquistadores Gil González Dávila and Francisco Pizarro served under Pedrárias's direction. His expeditions were basically searches for slaves, gold, and precious stones. Through his exploitation of the region he was able to maintain himself and finance further explorations.

He died while serving as governor of the province of Nicaragua. His career had put his stamp on the southern sector of Central America, much of which he had controlled and explored himself. Service under him became one of the features linking the conquests of Mexico and Peru.

BIBLIOGRAPHY

Alvarez Rubiano, Pablo. *Pedrarias Dávila: Contribución al estudio de la figura del "Gran Justador."* Madrid, 1944.
Sauer, Carl Ortwin. *The Early Spanish Main.* Berkeley, 1966.

JOHN F. SCHWALLER

AYLLÓN, LUCAS VÁZQUEZ DE (1480?–1526), judge of the audiencia of Santo Domingo and colonizer of North America. Ayllón was born in Toledo, Spain, to a family whose ancestors had been leaders of the Mozarabic community (Christians who had remained in Toledo under Muslim rule). Educated in the law, he served as alcalde mayor, or superior judge, of the mining district of La Española from 1504 to 1509. While in Spain from 1509 to 1513, he obtained his licenciate and was appointed one of the judges of the audiencia of Santo Domingo when it was created in 1511 (he served in that office until his death). In 1523 he became a member of the Military Order of Santiago.

On June 24, 1521, a pilot sailing under his sponsorship made the first recorded landing on the coast of South Carolina, at the Santee River. Granted a contract to explore and settle this "new discovery," which he falsely claimed was at the latitude of Andalusia, Spain, Ayllón sent Pedro de Quejo to explore from Cumberland Island, Georgia, to the Delaware Bay in 1525. On or about September 29, 1526, Ayllón founded a Spanish colony, San Miguel de Gualdape, in the territory of the Guale Indians, in the vicinity of Sapelo Sound, Georgia, after initially landing at the Santee River–Winyah Bay area. His death at San Miguel resulted in the abandonment of the site by early November 1526.

Ayllón gained a reputation as a learned if partial judge and as an exploiter of his office for personal gain. In addition to holding properties in Spain and La Española, he engaged in the trade in Indian slaves. As a judge of the audiencia, he was a key figure in royal efforts to vitiate the powers that Diego Colón, Columbus's son and heir, won in his lawsuit over Columbus's privileges. Among other things, he carried the audiencia's complaints and charges against Colón to Spain in 1521.

Ayllón's colonial activities were part of the wave of continental explorations and settlements that began in 1514. By that date, Columbus's belief that he had found Asian islands and the Malay Peninsula had been discredited, and the early Spanish exploiters of the New World had nearly exhausted the Indian groups and gold mines he had discovered. Also, the limitation in 1511 of Diego Colón's claims of government and a right to a percentage of revenues cleared the way for the king and his officials to encourage exploration and exploitation of areas not found during the Columbian voyages.

Ayllón's claim of the discovery of a new Andalusia survived in the writings of Pietro Martire d'Anghiera (Peter Martyr) and influenced later French and English colonial ventures at Port Royal Sound and Roanoke Island, respectively. Quejo's information about the North American coast was the basis for official Spanish maps until the 1560s.

BIBLIOGRAPHY

Hoffman, Paul E. *A New Andalucia and a Way to the Orient: The American Southeast in the Sixteenth Century.* Baton Rouge, La., 1990.
Malagón Barcelo, Javier. "Un oidor conquistador." *Eme-Eme, Estudios Dominicanos,* no. 25 (July-August 1976): 3–18.

PAUL E. HOFFMAN

AYLLÓN, LUCAS VÁZQUEZ DE (1514?–1565?), contractor for colonization of North America from 1562 to 1564. Born Juan Vázquez de Ayllón at Santo Domingo, this eldest son of Licenciado Lucas Vázquez de Ayllón (1480?–1526) took his father's name after coming of age. While married to Isabel de Pasamonte, niece of his father's political ally Miguel de Pasamonte, he went to Spain in 1547 but did not press his rights, as his father's heir, to colonize North America. In 1561, however, the rediscovery of Chesapeake Bay revealed an area of more promise than those his father had explored and tried to settle. Ayllón then pressed his claim.

Ayllón the Younger was awarded a contract on February 28, 1562, to establish a small agricultural colony, probably at Chesapeake Bay. Problems of raising money and worries about the French colony at Port Royal Sound delayed his sailing until September 1563. His expedition broke up at Santo Domingo, and he fled to Santa Marta (Colombia) to escape debts. Persuaded to engage in conquest there, he was killed by Indians during a slave- and gold-seeking raid.

Ayllón the Younger's colonial venture was the last of the unsuccessful Spanish attempts to colonize North America.

The collapse of Jean Ribault's Charlesfort colony meant that his failure did not have immediate consequences for Spain's claims to the continent, although his venture did delay Spanish occupation three more years, until 1565. By then Philip II was willing once again to put royal money behind a Spanish colony, as he had with Tristan de Luna from 1559 to 1561.

BIBLIOGRAPHY

Hoffman, Paul E. *A New Andalucia and a Way to the Orient: The American Southeast in the Sixteenth Century.* Baton Rouge, La., 1990.

PAUL E. HOFFMAN

AZORES. The Azores Islands, located between latitudes 36°50'N and 39°44'N and between longitudes 25°W and 31°16'W, are about 1,450 kilometers (900 miles) west of Portugal. Between 1440 and 1470 the previously uninhabited islands were colonized by Portugal. The archipelago has nine principal islands: the western islands of Flores and Corvo, the central islands of Fayal, Pico, São Jorge, Graciosa, and Terceira, and the eastern islands of São Miguel and Santa Maria.

Because of their position nearly halfway across the Atlantic Ocean toward Newfoundland, the Azores have a mild maritime climate with plentiful rainfall, particularly from winter storms. The islands lie along the southern boundary of the prevailing westerlies, where winds can be variable but are predominantly from the west. Ocean currents in the vicinity of the Azores flow from west to east, in the region where the warm Gulf Stream broadens as it flows across the North Atlantic Ocean to form the North Atlantic Current. These winds and currents made the Azores an unfavorable place to start westward voyages of discovery.

The Azores were strategically located for sailing on northward and eastward voyages. In spite of the extra distance, it took less time for ships traveling from the west coast of Africa to return to Portugal via the Azores than to fight the northerly winds and the southward Canary Current closer to the African coast. The islands provided much-needed supplies as well as safe harbors. Columbus stopped at the island of Santa Maria after experiencing a strong winter storm on his return from the first trip to the New World.

BIBLIOGRAPHY

Duncan, T. Bentley. *Atlantic Islands: Madeira, the Azores and the Cape Verdes in Seventeenth-Century Commerce and Navigation.* Chicago, 1972.

McAlister, Lyle N. *Spain and Portugal in the New World, 1492–1700.* Minneapolis, 1984.

Morison, Samuel Eliot. *Admiral of the Ocean Sea: A Life of Christopher Columbus.* 2 vols. Boston, 1942.

Rudloff, Willy. *World-Climates.* Stuttgart, 1981.

COLLEEN A. LEARY

AZTECS. See *Indian America*, article on *Aztecs and Their Neighbors*.

B

BACON, ROGER (between 1210 and 1215–1292), philosopher and scientist. Little is known of Bacon's life save for some sparse information that Bacon himself provides in his work. He studied at Oxford University and the University of Paris, where he likely developed his lifelong interest in natural philosophy and optics. He entered the Franciscan order sometime between 1251 and 1257. All three of his major works—*Opus maius, Opus minus,* and *Opus tertium*—were completed by 1267, apparently in response to Pope Clement IV's formal request of June 22, 1266.

Opus maius is the most comprehensive and historically significant of Bacon's works, a kind of encyclopedia or compendium of the knowledge of his day. Following the introductory section, ''Causes of Error,'' the book is arranged in six sections devoted to philosophy, foreign languages, mathematics, optical science, experimental science, and moral philosophy. The work appears to have two principal purposes: to underline the role that knowledge plays in the salvation of the Christian and to demonstrate the power of knowledge as a tool in the rational (as distinct from forcible) conversion of the non-Christian.

Around 150 years after Bacon completed *Opus maius,* the influential late medieval thinker Pierre d'Ailly (1350–1420) copied substantial sections of it into a number of short interrelated works that he composed between 1410 and 1414. Christopher Columbus read and annotated an early edition of these works printed by John of Westphalia between 1480 and 1483. The section of *Opus maius* given to mathematics appears to have been a particularly important source for d'Ailly's and hence Columbus's conceptions of geography and history.

D'Ailly's discussion of the size and shape of the earth and the disposition of the land and sea draws upon important ancient and early medieval sources. In *Opus maius* Bacon had suggested (as had Aristotle before him) that it should be possible to sail from Spain to the Indies. D'Ailly copied this passage into the eighth chapter of one of his works, *Imago mundi.* This chapter, ''De quantitate terrae inhabitabilis'' (On the extent of the inhabitable earth), was heavily annotated by Columbus. His manifest interest in the contents of *Imago mundi* has led scholars generally to agree that it was a major source for Columbus's ''Enterprise of the Indies''—his conviction that the Far East could be reached by sailing west across the Atlantic.

In other parts of the section on mathematics, Bacon outlined an apocalyptic vision of history, paying particular attention to astrological and prophetic materials that he believed provided the basis for marking events that would presage the imminent end of time and the fulfillment of the providential plan. D'Ailly also incorporated these passages into other works contained in the collection used by Columbus. Columbus annotated these works and

ROGER BACON. From a French medal, 1818.

copied a number of passages for inclusion in a work he never completed, his Book of Prophecies.

In the prefatory letter to Fernando and Isabel that accompanies the Book of Prophecies, Columbus indicates that he intended to place his achievements and those of his monarchs within a framework of apocalyptic history traceable back to late antiquity through the works of Bacon and d'Ailly. Columbus was probably not aware that in reading d'Ailly he was frequently reading Bacon. But his indirect use of *Opus maius* gives its thirteenth-century author, Roger Bacon, a significant role in the genesis of the "Enterprise of the Indies."

[See also *Writings*, article on *Book of Prophecies*.]

BIBLIOGRAPHY

Bacon, Roger. *The Opus Maius of Roger Bacon.* Translated by Robert Belle Burke. Philadelphia, 1928.

Watts, Pauline Moffitt. "Prophecy and Discovery: On the Spiritual Origins of Christopher Columbus's 'Enterprise of the Indies.' " *American Historical Review* 90 (1985): 73–102.

PAULINE MOFFITT WATTS

BAHAMAS. The Bahama Islands stretch in a chain about 1,300 kilometers (800 miles) long from near the Florida coast to a point near the north coast of Hispaniola (La Española). There are about seven hundred islands, of which thirty are inhabited. The sea between them is mostly shallow, whence their Spanish name, Bajamar, or "shallow water." In the fifteenth century the Bahamas were inhabited by the Lucayans, a branch of the Arawak family of peoples. We know little about their way of life but must suppose that it resembled that of their better-studied cousins on the Greater Antilles.

After Columbus had crossed the Atlantic in October 1492 he made landfall at the Lucayan island of Guanahani, which has been traditionally identified with the island of San Salvador. Here he found the land "very green and fertile" and the Lucayans friendly, though he soon passed through the chain and into the seas around the Greater Antilles, where he thought there was more possibility of finding gold.

After this initial reconnaissance the islands were largely neglected, except for frequent slaving raids by the Spaniards during the 1490s and 1500s. It has been estimated that forty thousand Lucayans were captured and sent to work in the mines of La Española between 1492 and 1508, with the result that the islands were quite depopulated. Nor were Europeans quick to resettle them, for despite their strategic position covering the routes back to Europe from the Spanish Main, they were not as attractive as the Greater Antilles in terms of agriculture, and indeed they were easily eroded once Europeans did establish intensive agriculture there in the eighteenth century.

[See also *Indian America*, article on *Arawaks and Caribs*. See *Landfall Controversy* for discussion of the Bahamas as the scene of Columbus's first landing in the New World.]

BIBLIOGRAPHY

Craton, Michael. *A History of the Bahamas.* Waterloo, Ont., 1986.

DAVID BUISSERET

BALBOA, VASCO NÚÑEZ DE (c. 1475–1519), Spanish explorer and colonial governor. Although not a conqueror of great empires, Vasco Núñez de Balboa ranks as one of a handful of the most important participants in the discovery and conquest of the Americas. His major accomplishment was the first European sighting of the Pacific Ocean, but his career was paradigmatic of that of many conquerors and early settlers of the Americas.

Balboa came from the Extremaduran town of Jerez de los Caballeros, although some authors claim that he came from the larger nearby city of Badajoz. The exact date of his arrival in the Indies is unknown, but certainly by 1500 he was in the New World. He sailed with Rodrigo de Bastidas and Juan de la Cosa on their expedition to the Gulf of Urabá and the coast of Panama. Following that, he settled in Salvatierra de la Sábana on the island of La Española, where the conqueror of Cuba, Diego Velázquez, also resided.

Following Bastidas's explorations of the Panama coast, the region was hotly contested by two other explorers, Diego de Nicuesa and Alonso de Ojeda. By a royal concession of 1508, Tierra Firme was divided into two parcels, the easterly, called Urabá, under the leadership of Ojeda, and the westerly, Veragua, under Nicuesa. Ojeda had made several expeditions to the northern coast of South America, and by 1505 he had been given the right to explore and settle the Gulf of Urabá. The region had already been visited, not only by Bastidas but also by Cosa on his own, and by others. Cosa had joined with Ojeda, and they had established a town at San Sebastian. Subsequently, Cosa died from a poisoned arrow, and Ojeda fled back to La Española. Nicuesa had little better luck in his concession. Martín Fernández de Enciso was sent from La Española to relieve the settlement which was besieged by Indians. Balboa went with him, having, according to traditional sources, stowed away in a barrel. It was he who suggested that the survivors be resettled on the western side of the Gulf of Urabá where the Indians did not use poisoned arrows. The settlement, Santa María la Antigua del Darién, became one of the more successful of the early attempts at colonization.

Soon after arriving at Darién, Balboa was elected as a justice of the town and ultimately gained near-total control of the settlement. Nicuesa and his followers were brought to Darién, where they were tried for failure to comply with royal authority: Nicuesa had rather foolishly claimed that he had ultimate authority over Darién by virtue of his royal grants. The members of the Fernández de Enciso expedition found Nicuesa guilty, but his death sentence was commuted, pending his appeal before the governor in La Española. The ship made available to Nicuesa and his men for the return to La Española leaked badly, however, and it never reached its destination. Balboa and his supporters then ousted Fernández de Enciso and forced him to return to La Española, thereby making Balboa's control complete.

As the leader of the group, Balboa demonstrated many of the characteristics common among the later Spanish conquistadores. Although he manifested fierce opposition to idolatry and native practices, he was also able to establish an accord with indigenous groups. He maintained peace with the Indians and stipulated regular tribute from them, thereby protecting the Spanish settlers from reprisals while extracting from the Indians a modicum of food and labor.

After making several explorations of the immediate hinterland and collecting information from local inhabitants, Balboa became convinced of a source of gold overland to the west from Darién. In early 1513 he outlined his plans in a letter to the king. This news stirred such excitement that a relief expedition was put together under the leadership of the courtier Pedro Arias de Ávila (Pedrárias), who was also to serve as a judicial investigator into Balboa's rule, especially concerning the trial of Nicuesa and banishment of Fernández de Enciso.

Balboa set off on his expedition to the west around September 1, 1513. About September 27, he caught sight of the Pacific. A few days later, he strode into the surf with sword and banner and claimed the whole sea for the king of Spain. The expedition continued along the Pacific coast, finding important pearl fisheries. By New Year's Day, they were back where they had begun. He had discovered the Pacific Ocean and come across villages that crafted objects in gold, but he had not found the actual source of the gold.

Pedrárias arrived at Darién in June 1514, and thereafter conditions in the settlement worsened. Accompanying him were many Spaniards such as Hernando de Soto and Bernal Díaz del Castillo who would play important roles in further adventures. Pedrárias ruled the region with an iron hand, dispatching numerous punitive raids against what were largely peaceful Indians. Scores of Spaniards, especially among the newcomers, died as a result of Indian resistance and from tropical diseases. The tension between the two captains mounted. Balboa attempted to absent himself from Darién, choosing to occupy the western coast of Panama and begin efforts to exploit his concession as adelantado of that region. He maintained correspondence with the Spanish Crown, continually

denouncing the excesses of Pedrárias and hoping that reform efforts on the peninsula might oust his rival. Nevertheless, as a royal investigator was being sent to the colony, Pedrárias arrested Balboa on charges of treason and after a brief trial had him executed.

Balboa was typical of the explorers of his time. He was coolly pragmatic in his dealing with the Indians. He was cruel at times, but overall he recognized the importance of keeping the native peoples as allies rather than making them enemies. He never failed at any of his enterprises. His settlement of Darién and his discovery for the Spanish of the Pacific opened a new chapter in the history of exploration of the continent.

BIBLIOGRAPHY

Romoli, Kathleen. *Balboa of Darien: Discoverer of the Pacific.* Garden City, N.Y., 1953.
Sauer, Carl Ortwin. *The Early Spanish Main.* Berkeley, 1966.
Vigneras, Louis-André. *The Discovery of South America and the Andalusian Voyages.* Chicago, 1976.

JOHN F. SCHWALLER

BARCELONA. The "head and hearth" (*cap i casal*) of Catalonia, Barcelona was the major commercial, naval, and administrative center of the Crown of Aragón during the late Middle Ages. Centrally located on the Catalan coast, it possessed easy communications with the Pyrenean hinterland and a Mediterranean-wide trade network. In 1358, a decade after the Black Death, the city contained roughly thirty-five thousand inhabitants, a size it maintained for a century. Long the hub of royal administration and the depository of extensive royal archives, Barcelona also became the permanent seat of the Generalitat, the standing committee of the Catalan Cortes.

Mediterranean trade laid the foundation for Barcelona's prosperity. Its merchants first redistributed goods produced elsewhere. Fine clothes from northern France and Flanders obtained in southern French ports, Sicilian grain and cotton, North African gold, wax, and slaves, Sardinian coral, Levantine spices and alum, and local leather, pelts, and wine made up the bulk of trade. After 1300 an important textile industry developed. Low-cost cloth, Catalan saffron, glassware, and silverwork increased exports. Together with smaller Catalan ports, Barcelona vied with Genoa for economic domination of the western Mediterranean.

Although subject to royal officials, Barcelona developed independent institutions. King Jaime I established a municipal assembly in 1249, which soon evolved into the Council of a Hundred with an executive body of five magistrates. In 1359 the city gained control over all municipal taxes. To finance public debts, a municipal bank was set up in 1401. Merchants, too, carved out their own jurisdiction. The first Iberian Consulate of the Sea, a maritime guild whose court settled business disputes, was functioning by 1283. The rules established there form the core of the *Llibre del consolat de mar,* the first systematic compilation of maritime commercial law. The construction of a spacious Gothic mercantile exchange, vastly expanded royal shipyards, and an impressive town council hall provided elegant testimony to the city's fourteenth-century prosperity. An ambitious breakwater was begun in 1439; its completion took more than twenty years.

Despite challenges and temporary setbacks, Barcelona retained its preeminence in the Crown of Aragón until the disastrous civil wars of 1462–1472. The municipal leadership had split into two factions, the Busca and the Biga, which were sharply divided over trade protectionism and monetary devaluation. The resulting internal instability and bitter warfare dealt the city a devastating blow. Its population fell to twenty thousand, and its commerce foundered. Fernando of Aragón aided Barcelona by granting it trading and industrial privileges and by reforming the strident town council in 1493 and 1498. A modest recovery ensued, but the damage had been done. Sixteenth-century Barcelona became rigidly stratified and its economy stagnant, profiting only marginally and indirectly from Spain's Atlantic empire.

On April 20, 1493, Fernando and Isabel ceremoniously received Columbus at Barcelona where he arrived with news of his first voyage. Since the city had long ceased to be the preferred residence for Aragonese monarchs, the site of the reception was coincidental but perfectly appropriate. The great Atlantic explorer had come to render homage in the city that centuries earlier had pioneered Iberian Mediterranean expansion.

BIBLIOGRAPHY

Amelang, James S. *Honored Citizens of Barcelona: Patrician Culture and Class Relations, 1490–1714.* Princeton, 1986.

Batlle Gallart, Carmen. *La crisis social y económica de Barcelona a mediados del siglo XV.* 2 vols. Barcelona, 1973.

Capmany y de Monpalau, A. de. *Memorias históricas sobre la antigua ciudad de Barcelona.* 3 vols. 2d ed. Edited by E. Giralt and C. Batlle. Barcelona, 1961–1963.

Carrère, Claude. *Barcelone: Centre économique, 1380–1462.* 2 vols. Paris, 1967.

Stephen P. Bensch

BEHAIM, MARTIN (c. 1436–1507), German geographer. The problems raised by the Martin Behaim globe, the oldest extant globe, dating from around 1492, are similar to those related to the Henricus Martellus map. In both cases we are dealing with what can be regarded as "Portuguese-German" cartography of the end of the fifteenth and the beginning of the sixteenth century—that is, with cartographic objects made by Germans, but based on Portuguese prototypes and geographic knowledge.

The contributions of Martin Behaim (or Martinho of Bohemia, as he was called in Portugal) were probably much overrated in the historiography of the nineteenth century by Alexander von Humboldt and other authors (particularly Germans). Clearly, Behaim's role must have been negligible in the development of the scientific foundation for the Portuguese discoveries, particularly as regards celestial navigation. The reality of the part he played has long since been established in such studies as those of the English author Ernest Ravenstein and the Portuguese writers Joaquim Bensaude, Fontura da Costa, Luciano Pereira da Silva, and more recently, Luís de Albuquerque. Even today, however, some subscribe to the old myths, citing the German influence on Iberian navigational science and the fantastic voyages that Behaim made with the Portuguese to the Cape of Good Hope before Bartolomeu Dias, to America before Columbus, and as far as the Straits of Magellan.

Behaim, who came from Nürnberg, lived in Portugal as a commercial correspondent charged with financial responsibilities, like many other Germans and Italians (Columbus and Amerigo Vespucci are examples). His knowledge of cosmography and mathematics was certainly limited, and his knowledge of nautical and geographical science would have come from the Portuguese. Contrary to what has been suggested by João de Barros, it has been clearly shown that the development of celestial navigation in Portugal was independent of any influence from Behaim, who would have been transmitting the ideas of the German cosmographer Regiomontanus. Portuguese nautical science had its origin in the astronomy of Iberians such as Abraham Zacuto and Joseph Vizinho, not in that of Regiomontanus. The tables of the sun's declination used later in Portuguese celestial navigation, for example, came from the *Almanach perpetuum* of Zacuto, not from the *Ephemerides* or *Tabulae directionem* of Regiomontanus. And certainly there never was an institutionalized board of mathematicians at the service of the Portuguese king João II. There likely were some cosmographers and astrologers from whom the king regularly sought counsel, but they were predominantly Jewish astronomer-astrologers.

In 1492, while on a visit to his native city, Behaim constructed or first presented his famous globe. On it, Africa appears with a great extension to the south and east, in an image similar to that on the Martellus map. Did this extension correspond to the concepts actually prevalent in Portugal or rather reflect a distortion resulting from incorrect information? This is not an easy question to answer, with regard to either Behaim's globe or the Martellus map.

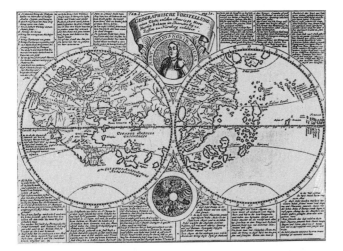

BEHAIM'S GEOGRAPHY OF THE WORLD. Based on his globe of 1492.

ELSEVIER PUBLISHING PROJECTS, AMSTERDAM

BIBLIOGRAPHY

Chillany, Friedrich Wilhelm. *Geschichte des Seefahrers Ritter Martin Behaim, nach der ältesten vorhandenen Urkunden.* Nürnberg, 1853.

Dodge, Robert. "Martin Behaim and His Globe at Nurembergh." In *Memorials of Columbus.* Maryland Historical Society. Baltimore, 1851.

"Martin Behaim and the Astrolabe." *Geographical Journal* 2, no. 2 (1893): 175.

Morris, John Gottlieb. *Martin Behaim, The German Astronomer and Cosmographer.* Maryland Historical Society. Baltimore, 1955.

Ravenstein, Ernest George. *Martin Behaim: His Life and His Globe.* London, 1908.

Ravenstein, Ernest George. "The Voyages of Diogo Cão and Bartholomew Dias, 1482–88." *Geographical Journal* 16, no. 6 (1900): 638–649.

ALFREDO PINHEIRO MARQUES
Translated from Portuguese by Rebecca Catz

There are differences between the two cartographical representations. Behaim places the extreme southern tip of Africa farther north, and he shows Dias's discoveries less clearly. Some interesting information about the Portuguese voyages along the African coast is found only on Behaim's globe, especially regarding those under the command of Diogo Cão—the placement of the first stone pillar erected by the navigator on his second voyage, for example. Behaim undoubtedly had access to Portuguese knowledge concerning the explorations south of the Gulf of Guinea. But this in no way implies that Behaim participated personally in those voyages and explorations—as he would have us believe from a passage he was certainly responsible for in the *Liber chronicarum* of Hartmann Schedel, published in Nürnberg in 1493, when Behaim was in the city. Behaim is even presented here as one of the commanders, together with Diogo Cão, of those voyages, an assertion that certainly does not correspond to reality.

Behaim was married to the daughter of a donatary-captain (grant holder) of the Portuguese islands of the Azores, and though neither a navigator nor a discoverer, he must have been familiar with the Portuguese nautical world. We owe to him the collection and transcription in Latin of an oral report made by a navigator called Diogo Gomes, who in midcentury, in the days of Henry the Navigator, had done some exploring along the African coast. This report, though enigmatic, provides priceless information about the period, for other sources are scarce. Behaim's globe, like the map of Martellus, is valuable for its documentation of the European vision of the world at the end of the Middle Ages, on the eve of the voyage of Christopher Columbus.

BENZONI, GIROLAMO (b. 1519), Italian traveler and chronicler. Born in Milan of humble parents who had been further impoverished by the wars of the time. Benzoni, aged twenty-two, left his native city to travel in France, Germany, and Spain, and in 1541 sailed from Seville for the Indies in search of fortune. During his fourteen years in America—including the West Indies, Tierra Firme (modern Venezuela and Colombia), Peru, and Central America—he probably practiced his trade as silversmith and took part in many expeditions. Having acquired a few thousand ducats, and weary of travel, he determined to return home to write a book telling of "the strange and rare things" he had seen in the New World.

Benzoni's celebrated *La historia del mondo nuovo* (History of the New World) was published in Venice in 1565, with a dedication to Pope Pius IV, and reprinted in 1572 with the addition of the author's own artless line drawings. Numerous editions of the *History* were issued in the sixteenth and seventeenth centuries. The book secured wide diffusion through its inclusion in the *Grands voyages* (Great voyages), a series of handsomely made, profusely illustrated travel accounts published by the Walloon engraver Théodor de Bry and his sons Jean Théodor and Jean Israel in Frankfurt between 1590 and 1634. In this series de Bry included two editions of Benzoni's book: first Urbain Chauveton's Latin translation, issued in three parts between 1594 and 1596, and then Nicolas Hoeniger's German version in 1597. The reasons for the book's popularity are easily explained: its simple, almost naive style; its moving descriptions of Spanish cruelty to the Indians; the numerous anecdotal details; and the general effect of candor and compassion. The impact on European minds of Benzoni's heart-rending descriptions of Spanish cruelty to the Indians was greatly enhanced by de Bry's illustrations, copperplate engravings that vested the Indian figures with classic beauty and grace. The large interest in Protestant countries in works that documented the unworthy character of Spanish Catholic colonization in America certainly contributed to the popularity of Benzoni's book. Benzoni's *History* and Las Casas's *Brevíssima relación de la destruición de las Indias* (Very brief account of the destruction of the Indies) are commonly regarded as the cornerstones of the so-called Black Legend of Spanish inhumanity to the Indians.

Beginning with Benzoni's contemporary, the French chronicler André Thevet, who claimed that Benzoni had never set foot in America, the *History* came under harsh attack from critics who charged Benzoni with a strong anti-Spanish prejudice and with padding out his own scanty historical account with wholesale borrowings without acknowledgment from such chroniclers as Peter Martyr, Gonzalo Fernández de Oviedo, and Francisco López de Gómara. The historical criticism of the nineteenth century dealt severely with Benzoni. As late as 1945 the Mexican historian Carlos Pereyra was inclined to believe that Benzoni's book was a "historical fiction" used by Spain's enemies to strengthen their case.

Most modern studies, however, have tended at least partly to rehabilitate Benzoni and his work. The notion that the *History* was a literary fiction was long ago refuted by the Chilean historian José Toribio Medina, who discovered a colonial document describing Benzoni as a Milanese silversmith living in Honduras who had been pronounced a Lutheran heretic reconciled by the Mexican Inquisition in 1555. Granted the offenses of padding and plagiarism—very common among writers of the time—the book nevertheless contains a substantial body of eyewitness testimony on Spanish dealings with the Indians in the Caribbean area. The claim that Benzoni displayed a violent hostility toward Spain and the Spaniards also appears excessive. Benzoni warmly praised the Dominicans in the Indies for their efforts in behalf of the Indians, and Emperor Charles V for promulgating the famous New Laws in favor of the native peoples. Benzoni even complimented Viceroy Antonio de Mendoza for his prudence in not attempting to enforce the New Laws against the overwhelming opposition of the Spanish colonists. The Argentine historian Rómulo Carbia, a passionate defender of Spain's work in America, compared Benzoni's balanced view of the Spanish Conquest favorably with that of Las Casas. Another champion of Spain's colonial record, the Peruvian Raúl Porras Barrenechea, concluded that Benzoni's book contains valuable data on Peruvian ethnology and the history of the conquest of Peru. After a searching examination of Benzoni's travels in Venezuela, the Venezuelan scholar

Leon Croizat found that as a reporter of what he had himself seen and done, Benzoni was worthy of faith and that there was no reason to doubt that the great majority of the events he relates actually happened.

In the first book of the *History*, Benzoni gave a detailed account of Columbus and his voyages, based almost entirely on such familiar sources as the chronicles of Oviedo and Gómara. However, he defended the Italian nationality of Columbus against the "inventions" of some Spanish historians who could not abide that "an Italian had conquered such great honor and glory, not only among the Spanish nation but among all the nations of the world." For his edition of the Latin translation of Benzoni's book, de Bry prepared a series of plates dealing with Columbus and the Discovery: they include a celebration of Columbus—a triumph with mythological figures; and, among others, scenes depicting the famous anecdote of the egg, Columbus's departure on his first voyage, and his return from the third voyage in chains. They are among the earliest and finest pictorial representations of events related with the Discovery and Columbus's life.

BIBLIOGRAPHY

Benzoni, Girolamo. *History of the New World.* Translated by W. H. Smyth. London, 1857.
Benzoni, Girolamo. *La Historia del mondo nuevo.* With an introduction by Leon Croizat. Caracas, 1967.

BENJAMIN KEEN

BERNÁLDEZ, ANDRÉS (d. 1513?), chronicler, also known as Andrés Bernal. Andrés Bernáldez was born in the town of Fuentes (modern Fuentes de León) and during the reign of Fernando and Isabel served as parish priest of the village of Los Palacios, about twenty-five kilometers (fifteen miles) south of the city of Seville. He wrote an important chronicle of the reign, in which he gives detailed information about Christopher Columbus and his voyages. Columbus and Juan Rodríguez de Fonseca were his house guests in 1496 after the second voyage to America, and the admiral left some of his papers with Bernáldez at that time. The chronicler made excellent use of these documents, particularly the *First Letter from America* and accounts by passengers, such as Diego Alvarez Chanca's letter describing the second voyage.

Bernáldez closely observed natural phenomena in his own environment. His descriptions of earthquakes, locust invasions, droughts, flooding, and epidemics make his chronicle the most vivid narrative of Spain during the reign of Fernando and Isabel. His account of the epidemic (probably typhus) that swept through southern Spain in 1507 reveals the devastation of disease before the age of antibiotics. Bernáldez and his sacristan both became ill and each was bled twice. The priest survived, but his parishioners were not so lucky; in that year Bernáldez buried one-third (160 out of 500) of the children and adults in his village, including all four of the boys who served as his acolytes.

The chronicler's identity has sometimes been disputed, in part because of confusion about his last name. In the baptismal registers from 1488 to 1513 (which disappeared sometime before 1870), Andrés signed his last name both as Bernáldez and Bernal, while the only document from Seville in which he is mentioned calls him Andrés Bernal.

BIBLIOGRAPHY

Gil, Juan. "Noticia de Andrés Bernal, cura de Los Palacios." In *Temas Colombinos*. Seville, 1986.

Carriazo, Juan de Mata, and Manuel Gómez-Moreno. Introduction to *Memorias del reinado de los Reyes Católicos*, by Andrés Bernáldez. Madrid, 1962.

Helen Nader

BIBLIOGRAPHY. The modern scholarly study of the life and writings of Christopher Columbus has four phases. The first is the discovery of the relevant written documents of an initial "discovery period" embracing Columbus's lifetime and its historical context. These have been found largely in the archives of Genoa and Spain. Except for nonwritten records like archaeological findings, portraits, and so forth, such documents provide all the available evidence. Most of the primary documents now available had been discovered by the turn of the twentieth century, although a few more have turned up since then.

The publication of these documents, frequently in large compendia, constitutes the second phase. Written records of the discovery period have appeared in various collections such as those of G. B. Spotorno, *Codice diplomatico Colombo-Americano ossia raccolta di documenti originali e inediti* (Genoa, 1823); M. F. de Navarrete, *Colección de los viajes y descubrimientos que hicieron por mar los Españoles desde fines del siglo XV . . .* (Madrid, 1825); J. F. Pacheco, et al., *Colección de documentos inéditos relativos al descubrimiento, conquista y colonización de las posesiones españolas en América y Oceania*, series 1, 42 vols. (Madrid, 1864–84), series 2, 25 vols. (Madrid, 1885–1932); and M. del Rosario Falcó y Osorio (the duchess of Berwick), *Autógrafos de Cristóbal Colón y papeles de América* (Madrid, 1892). Single documents have appeared in many and scattered publications: see Foster Provost, *Columbus: A Guide to Scholarship on His Life and Writings* (Providence, R.I., 1991), chapters 1 and 2.

The third phase of Columbus study began in the late nineteenth century. It consists of the preparation, on reliable principles, of critical editions of the primary documents. Such editions attempt to record the exact words intended by the author, with all slips of the pen corrected and all errors of transmission emended as accurately as the available evidence and the disciplines of philology and textual criticism permit. To accompany this corrected and emended, or "critical," text the editor prepares full textual notes recording all of the data on which the corrections and emendations are based, and explaining each of the editor's decisions wherever the critical text departs from the "copy text" on which the edition is based.

The copy text, as currently understood, is the manuscript that most closely represents the author's full and final intention or, if the manuscript is not extant, the earliest printed edition of it. The alternative readings that the editor must consider usually come from other manuscripts or printed editions of the same work, especially those that the author can be shown to have influenced personally. The ideal critical edition will provide the user with all the pertinent readings and make clear the reasons for every correction and every emendation of the copy text.

The primary documents include the writings from Columbus's own hand and the documents recording the context within which these were made. The first and only fully critical edition of the known writings of Columbus is Cesare de Lollis's *I scritti di Cristoforo Colombo*, in the Italian government's monumental *Raccolta di documenti e studi pubblicati dalla R. Commissione colombiana pel quarto centenario dalla scoperta dell'America*, part 1, 3 vols. in 4 tomes (Rome, 1892–1894). In the United States, the difficulty of finding and using the unwieldy and rapidly deteriorating copies of this basic edition has seriously hampered Columbus scholarship.

Since 1894, not only has the canon of Columbus's writings expanded through the discovery of previously unknown documents, but the principles of critical editing have been refined. Consequently a full re-editing has become necessary, and it is not certain that such a project is yet under way. Still, much preparatory work has been done. In recent years, Consuelo Varela's *Cristóbal Colón: Textos y documentos completos, relaciones de viajes, cartas y memoriales* (Madrid, 1982; 2d ed., rev., 1984; 3d ed., rev., 1986) has drawn together almost all the available texts (except for many of the marginal annotations in the books of Columbus's personal library and parts of the Book of Prophecies). This paperbound edition, inexpensive and highly useful, prepared by a careful and knowledgeable textual scholar, unfortunately lacks the textual notes essential to a fully critical edition and so does not answer the scholar's needs fully.

The critical editing of essential primary documents not by Columbus himself also began in the late nineteenth century and continues today. The Italian government's *Nuova raccolta colombiana* (Rome, 1988–), besides including many of the de Lollis texts from the 1892–1894 critical edition, will contain newly transcribed and edited texts of other documents, both those by Columbus that have turned up since 1894 and a large selection of the primary documents not written by Columbus.

Unfortunately, this new collection does not offer a new critical edition of Columbus's writings. A further monumental project, one sponsored by the University of California at Los Angeles, the *Repertorium Columbianum*, initiated by the late Fredi Chiappelli and continuing under Geoffrey Symcox, will present the documents (with facing-page English translations) of the Spanish explorations of the entire discovery period from 1492 to 1519, including Columbus's writings. A considerable philological effort is going into these texts and translations; it remains to be seen whether they will constitute a body of critical texts based on modern principles of copy-text and textual emendation.

In the absence of fully authenticated critical texts, the student of Columbus must have recourse to whatever texts are available. In English translation we have Cecil Jane's *Select Documents Illustrating the Four Voyages of Columbus*, 2 vols. (London, 1930–1933), including a generous selection of the most important documents, and S. E. Morison's *Journals and Other Documents on the Life and Voyages of Christopher Columbus* (New York, 1963), which to some extent supplements Jane's *Select Documents*. Morison continues the emphasis on the voyages but adds important documents from the remainder of Columbus's life. (For further information on texts in various languages, and on studies of these texts as texts, see Provost, *Columbus: A Guide*, chapters 1–3.)

The fourth phase of Columbus study attempts to establish the details of Columbus's life on the basis of the documents and relevant information from allied disciplines such as archaeology. Research has focused on such questions as where and when Columbus was born, what his family and religious backgrounds were, and when, how, and in what order he conceived his "Enterprise of the Indies." Many of these issues have been resolved with much certainty, but since the second, third, and fourth phases of the scholarship depend on the thoroughness with which the tasks of the previous phases have been carried out, historical scholarship on Columbus is still in flux and will remain so until the last relevant surviving document has been discovered, critically edited, judiciously analyzed, and examined in light of the findings of allied disciplines.

Biographical Studies

Even though the textual basis is not uniformly sound, the fourth phase has been intensively developed. Beginning with biographies, we note four basic sources among the hundreds of fifteenth-century accounts of Columbus (all the others being briefer and more fragmentary). First, the initial "decade" of Peter Martyr's *De Orbe Novo* (1511), is available in a new critical edition with copious scholarly apparatus in the *Nuova raccolta*, vol. 6, *La scoperta del Nuovo Mondo negli scritti di Pietro Martire d'Anghiera*, edited by E. Lunardi, E. Magioncalda, and R. Mazzacane (Rome, 1988). There is an English translation by F. A. MacNutt, *De Orbo Novo, the Eight Decades of Peter Martyr d'Anghera* (New York, 1912). The second essential early life is by Columbus's son Fernando, a work usually called the *Historie*, after the title of the unique surviving text, the 1571 Ulloa Italian translation of the much earlier original. There is no critical edition; the best edition is probably that by Rinaldo Caddeo, *Le historie della vita e dei fatti di Cristoforo Colombo* (Milan, 1930). This work has been translated into English by Benjamin Keen as *The Life of the Admiral Christopher Columbus by His Son Ferdinand* (New Brunswick, N.J., 1959).

The third early source of extensive information on Columbus's life is the account of his career in the first volume (1535) of G. F. de Oviedo's *Historia general y natural de las Indias*, edited by J. Amador de los Rios (Madrid, 1851); the material on Columbus will be published in a new edition as volume 10 of the *Nuova raccolta* under the title *Le scoperte di Cristoforo Colombo nei testi de Fernández de Oviedo*, edited by Francesco Giunta.

The last, and best, of the comprehensive early sources is Bartolomé de las Casas's *Historia de las Indias*, which remained in manuscript until finally published in Madrid in 1875–1876. The work is available in a modern transcription by A. Millares Carlo, with an introduction by Lewis Hanke (Mexico City and Buenos Aires, 1951; 2d ed., revised, 1972).

At least one study of each of these biographical sources should be cited. For Peter Martyr, the *Nuova raccolta* volume containing his text is comprehensive. For Fernando Colón's *Historie*, see A. Rumeu de Armas's *Hernando Colón, historiador del descubrimiento de América* (Madrid, 1973), which contains an enormously detailed analysis. For Oviedo, the best modern study is by A. Gerbi, *La natura delle Indie nove* (Milan and Naples, 1975), available in an English translation by Jeremy Moyle, *Nature in the New World* (Pittsburgh, 1986). For Las Casas, the most comprehensive reference is the forthcoming volume 9 of the *Nuova raccolta*, titled *La scoperte di Cristoforo Colombo nei testi di Bartolomeo de Las Casas*, edited by Francesca Cantù.

Modern study of Columbus's life began with William Robertson's *The History of America* (London, 1777), which contains a scholarly, straightforward account that served as the basis of the many popular biographies appearing at the end of the eighteenth century. J. B. Muñoz's *Historia del nuevo-mundo* (Madrid, 1793) and Washington Irving's *A History of the Life and Voyages of Christopher Columbus* (New York, 1828) are based on intense study of documents in the Spanish archives, although Irving's study sprinkles much sentimentality among the genuine scholarship.

The truly classic account among early- and mid-nineteenth-century biographies is that by A. F. von Humboldt in his *Examen critique de l'histoire de la géographie du nouveau continent et des progrès de l'astronomie nautique aux quinzième et seizième siècles*, 5 vols. (Paris, 1836–1839). Henry Harrisse's *Christophe Colomb* (Paris, 1884) is a model scholarly biography except that it is tinged with Harrisse's distrust of Las Casas's account, a prejudice that he later abandoned but that colored historians' views of both Las Casas's *Historia* and Fernando's associated *Historie* until at least 1950, when both works began to be credited as being full of genuine historical information about Columbus.

The new documents that became available in the last quarter of the nineteenth century, beginning with the first volume of Pacheco's *Colección* (Madrid, 1864), made possible a rush of excellent biographies at the time of the fourth centennial. As with several earlier biographies, some are only a part of larger historical studies. Noteworthy among these is John Fiske's *The Discovery of America* (Boston and New York, 1892), a detailed attempt to set Columbus's life and voyages in the context both of European history and of what was then known about aboriginal America at the time of discovery. Equally impressive in its encyclopedic vigor, though somewhat lacking in scholarly method, is J. B. Thacher's *Christopher Columbus: His Life, His Work, His Remains* (New York and London, 1903).

The 1940s brought two salient biographies: S. E. Morison's *Admiral of the Ocean Sea: A Life of Christopher Columbus*, 2 volumes (Boston, 1942) and A. Ballesteros Beretta's *Cristóbal Colón y el descubrimiento de América* (Barcelona and Buenos Aires, 1945). As a narrative, Morison's book is probably the best work on Columbus in English, and the notes in its scholarly two-volume version are thorough beyond the call of duty. Unfortunately, the success of the one-volume version—a condensed popular version stripped of its scholarly apparatus—drove the scholarly version out of print.

Ballesteros's book is a workmanlike account of what could be known of the discoverer's life in the 1940s, cautious and comprehensive. Unfortunately the annotation is limited to the listing, at the end of each chapter, of the items consulted. This approach makes the book as far inferior to Morison's in its annotation as it is superior in its thorough, judicious treatment of the scholarly issues.

The biographies since Ballesteros are generally deriva-tive, with the notable exception of Jacques Heers's *Christophe Colomb* (Paris, 1981), which opens new vistas in Columbus biography with its vigorous attention to fifteenth-century history, especially regarding Genoese activity in Spain, Portugal, and the Atlantic islands.

Concerning Columbus's birthplace and nationality, an overwhelmingly detailed case for his Genoese origin appeared in 1931 in a work so cogent that since that time no responsible scholar has proposed a birthplace outside Liguria: *Christopher Columbus: Documents and Proofs of His Genoese Origin* (Genoa, 1931). P. E. Taviani places this case in the context of the various claims for other birthplaces in *La Genovesità di Colombo* (Genoa, 1987).

Gaetano Ferro reviews Columbus's Portuguese years, 1476 to 1485, in the context of the Portuguese discoveries of the fifteenth century in *Le navigazione lusitane nell' Atlantico e Cristoforo Colombo in Portogallo* (Milan, 1984). A. M. Freitas and R. Maney, in *The Wife of Columbus* (New York, 1893), treat the marriage of Columbus to Felipa Moniz Perestrelo (mother of Columbus's first son and heir, Diego Colón) and her antecedents, Portuguese and Italian.

The Spanish years, 1485 to 1492, constitute the decisive period in Columbus's search for a sponsor. Many of the central issues of this biographical period are developed by Henry Vignaud in *Études critiques sur la vie de Colomb avant ses découvertes* (Paris, 1905). Vignaud, though frequently criticized because of his lifelong contention that Columbus did not expect to reach the Orient on his enterprise of discovery, nonetheless drew together—and commented learnedly on—more documentary evidence about Columbus than anyone else except possibly the indefatigable scholars Henry Harrisse and Alicia Bache Gould. Follow-up studies on major issues include Angel Ortega's *La Rábida: Historia documental crítica* (Seville, 1925–1926); A. Palomeque Torres's "Ambiente político y científico que rodeó al futuro Almirante de Indias d. Cristóbal Colón en la España de los Reyes Católicos," *Studi Colombiani* 2 (Genoa, 1952): 303–355; J. Manzano Manzano's *Cristóbal Colón: Siete años decisivos de su vida, 1485–1492* (Madrid, 1964); and A. Rumeu de Armas's *La Rábida y el descubrimiento de América: Colón, Marchena, y fray Juan Pérez* (Madrid, 1968).

A succinct account of Columbus's voyages, with excellent notes, can be found in S. E. Morison's *The European Discovery of America: The Southern Voyages, A.D. 1492–1616* (New York, 1974). The same material is treated in detail in Morison's *Admiral of the Ocean Sea* (Boston, 1942) and P. E. Taviani's *I viaggi di Colombo: La grande scoperta* (Novara, Italy, 1984).

Among the many questions associated with the first voyage, the dominant one has been the identity of the island in the Bahamas at which the 1492 landfall occurred.

Possibilities include Watlings Island, Grand Turk, and a good many others. The subject is treated vigorously in J. Parker's and L. De Vorsey's *In the Wake of Columbus: Islands and Controversy* (Detroit, 1985; also in *Terrae Incognitae* 15 [1985]). The volume begins with Parker's essay "The Columbus Landfall Problem: A Historical Perspective." A recent attempt to assign the landfall to Samana Cay by J. Judge, "Where Columbus Found the New World," *National Geographic* 170 (Oct. 1986): 566–599, is roundly refuted by various essays in *Columbus and His World,* edited by D. Gerace (Ft. Lauderdale, Fla., 1987).

The most notable single body of twentieth-century research focuses on the first voyage: Alicia Bache Gould's monumental *Nueva lista documentada de los tripulantes de Colón en 1492,* edited by J. de la Peña y Camara (Madrid, 1984), which contains a wealth of information about not only Columbus and his 1492 crew but also a host of related matters.

For the remaining voyages, see Provost, *Columbus: A Guide,* items 331–367. Columbus's life in Spain while not on a voyage (1493–1504) is best studied in the biographies. On his death and the disposition of his body, see C. Fernández Duro, "Noticias de la muerte de d. Cristóbal Colón y del lugar de enterramiento en Valladolid," *Boletín de la Real Academia de la Historia* (Madrid) 24 (1894): 44–46, and A. Álvarez Pedroso, "Los restos mortales del descubridor de América don Cristóbal Colón," *Studi Colombiani* 3 (Genoa, 1952): 15–23.

Other Studies

Other limited studies, addressing single aspects of Columbus's career, can be grouped under the term "Columbiana." The largest body of such works concerns his cosmology and cosmography. There is no book devoted to a survey of this extensive material.

Further examples of Columbiana can be noted briefly. The development of Columbus's project to reach the Indies is treated in three useful books: Vignaud's *Histoire critique de la grande entreprise de Christophe Colomb* (Paris, 1911); P. E. Taviani's *Cristoforo Colombo: La genesi della grande scoperta* (Novara, Italy, 1974); and E. Jos's *El Plan y la génesis del descubrimiento colombino* (Valladolid, 1980).

J. Pérez de Tudela makes a full study of the initial Spanish colonization of La Española during Columbus's lifetime in the following articles: "La negociación colombina de las Indias," "Castilla ante los comienzos de la colonización de las Indias," "La quiebra de la factoría y el nuevo poblamiento de la Española," and "Política de población y política de contratación de las Indias (1502–1505)," in *Revista de Indias* (Madrid) 14 (1954): 289–357 and 15 (1955): 11–88, 197–252, and 371–420, respectively.

A major attempt to delineate Columbus's psychology appears in J. Gil's *Mitos y utopias del descubrimiento,* vol. 1, *Colón y su tiempo* (Madrid, 1988); with its study of new documents, this is one of the most important new studies of Columbus's life in Spain after the first voyage. Treatments of Columbus's language are reviewed in O. Chiareno's "Recenti studi sulla lingua scritta di Colombo," in *Atti I convegno internazionale di studi americanistici* (Genoa, 1976), pp. 107–117.

Columbus's brother Bartolomé Colón and his sons Diego and Fernando are treated in, respectively, A. Albonico's "Bartolomeo Colombo, adelantado mayor de las Indias," *La presenza italiana in Andalusia nel basso medioevo* (Bologna, 1986); L. Arranz Márquez's *Don Diego Colón: Almirante, virrey y gobernador de las Indias* (Madrid, 1982); and A. Rumeu de Armas's *Hernando Colón: Historiador del descubrimiento de América* (Madrid, 1973). The long litigation between Columbus's descendants and the Spanish Crown over the admiral's rights and privileges are treated in Otto Schoenrich's *The Legacy of Columbus* (Glendale, Calif., 1949–1950).

Two medical matters have drawn much interest: the possible transmission of syphilis to Europe by Columbus's crew and the disease *shigella flexneri* (Reiter's syndrome), the cause of Columbus's arthritic condition and eye trouble. A recent summary of what is known appears in P. A. Gemignani's *La scoperta di Colombo e la medicina* (Genoa, 1988).

Columbus's spirituality and millennialism are treated in two recent studies: A. Milhou's *Colón y su mentalidad mesiánica en el ambiente franciscanista español* (Valladolid, 1983) and Pauline Moffitt Watt's "Prophecy and Discovery: On the Spiritual Origins of Christopher Columbus's 'Enterprise of the Indies,'" *American Historical Review* 90 (1985): 73–102. On the abortive nineteenth-century movement to canonize Columbus, see G. Odoardi's "Il processo di beatificazione di Cristoforo Colombo," *Studi Colombiani* 3 (Genoa, 1952): 261–272. On his supposed Jewishness, see Vignaud's "Columbus a Spaniard and a Jew?" *American Historical Review* 18 (1913): 505–512.

On Columbus's navigation, see S. E. Morison's "Columbus as a Navigator," *Studi Colombiani* 2 (Genoa, 1952): 39–48. On portraits of the admiral, see W. E. Curtis's *Christopher Columbus: His Portraits and His Monuments* (Chicago, 1893). On Columbus's ships, see J. M. Martínez-Hidalgo's "Las naves de los cuatro viajes de Colón al nuevo mundo," in *Temi Colombiani (Scritti in Onore del Prof. Paolo Emilio Taviani,* Genoa, 1986), pp. 201–229.

A final topic, of very active interest, concerns Columbus's marginal notes in the books from his personal library. These notes, or "postils," a prime source of biographical information, have traditionally been assigned to the years 1485 to 1492, while Columbus's project was still forming, but recent indications that some notes may have been made later have led scholars to rethink the subject. Two important treatments introduce the new speculations: I. Luzzana Caraci's "La postilla colombiana B 858 e il suo significato cronologico," *Atti del II convegno internazionale di studi colombiani, 1975* (Genoa, 1977), pp. 197–223, and the introductory essay in J. Gil's edition of *El libro de Marco Polo: Ejemplar anotado por Cristóbal Colón y que se conserva en la biblioteca capitular y colombina de Sevilla* (Madrid, 1986).

FOSTER PROVOST

BIBLIOTECA COLOMBINA. See *Library of Columbus.*

BLACK LEGEND. The term "Black Legend" was apparently coined by the Spanish writer Julián Juderías y Loyot; his book of that title, *La leyenda negra* (Barcelona, 1914), charged that foreigners had created a false, distorted image of the Spanish character, wrongly attributing to the Spanish people inherent qualities of intolerance and cruelty, and ignoring the major Spanish contributions to European civilization. He conceded that Spain had once been fanatical and intolerant, but this was at a time when all European peoples shared those traits.

Some three decades later the Argentine historian Rómulo D. Carbia published his influential *Historia de la leyenda negra hispano-americana* (Buenos Aires, 1943), a violent attack on the Black Legend that gave the phrase an even wider diffusion and focused attention on the supposed defamatory treatment of Spain's record in America. Carbia assigned particular responsibility for the creation of the anti-Hispanic Black Legend to Bartolomé de las Casas. According to Carbia, Las Casas laid the solid foundation of the Black Legend with false or exaggerated charges of Spanish cruelty to the Indians, especially in his *Brevíssima relación de la destruición de las Indias* (Very brief account of the destruction of the Indies, Seville, 1552). The charges spread far and wide by the publication of translations of his tracts in French, Dutch, German, English, Italian, and other languages, often with the addition of hair-raising engravings originally published by Jean Théodor and Jean Israel de Bry. Las Casas, according to Carbia, thereby became the instrument of Spain's commercial and political rivals, especially the Protestant powers of England and Holland, who coveted Spain's imperial possessions and sought excuses to seize them for themselves. Carbia's intemperate attacks on Las Casas provided a precedent for a lengthy diatribe by the Spanish scholar Ramón Menéndez Pidal, *El Padre Las Casas, su*

ENGRAVING FROM LAS CASAS'S *VERY BRIEF ACCOUNT*. Illustrations such as this were used by publishers Jean Théodor de Bry and Jean Israel de Bry (sons of Théodor de Bry) in their editions of this work. LIBRARY OF CONGRESS

doble personalidad (Madrid, 1963). Like Carbia, Menéndez Pidal questioned Las Casas's sanity, calling him a "delirious paranoiac."

When considering the origin and evolution of the idea of a defamatory Black Legend of Spanish cruelty and intolerance, two points need to be made. First, the substance of the idea existed centuries before Juderías coined his celebrated phrase. Its rise in Spain coincided with the beginning of Spain's decline as a great power in the second half of the sixteenth century, a decline that accelerated during the Decadencia (decadence) of the seventeenth century. Sensitivity to domestic and foreign criticism and the sense of grievance reflected in the notion of a Black Legend were absent in the heyday of Spanish power; this explains the remarkable tolerance of Emperor Charles V in permitting the publication of Las Casas's fiery tracts in Seville in 1552–1553. But Spanish sensitivity to domestic and foreign criticism of Spain's colonial record grew as the country's power in the Old and New Worlds declined. In the seventeenth century Las Casas's *Very Brief Account* was banned in Spain, and official and unofficial chroniclers harshly scolded him for his services to Spain's enemies.

Second, the notion of the existence of a defamatory, anti-Hispanic Black Legend traditionally drew its principal support in both Spain and Latin America from conservative and reactionary circles. In Spain the struggle against the Black Legend reached its climax in the twentieth century. Facing a growing threat from the forces of liberalism and radicalism, Spanish conservatives and reactionaries developed a historical defense of the traditional order that denounced both the reformist eighteenth-century Bourbon king Charles III and Las Casas as the instruments of a corrupting, debilitating liberalism. Under the dictatorship of Generalissimo Francisco Franco, the need to refute the Black Legend concerning Spain's work in America became the keystone of all teaching of the subject. Meanwhile, conservative circles in Latin America, alarmed by the growth of radical Indianism and a variety of social revolutionary movements, identified themselves more closely with a Hispanic colonial past, which they viewed through nostalgic eyes. These background conditions help explain the twentieth-century upsurge of a historical revisionism predicated on a Black Legend that falsified Spain's past and particularly its work in America.

In recent decades the major premises of the idea of a Black Legend have been questioned as a result of advances in knowledge and understanding of the Spanish colonial process. One major development has been the rehabilitation of Las Casas as a source of historical information. The reliability of his estimates of Indian pre-Conquest populations and their decline following the Conquest, for example, once regarded as the patent exaggerations of a pro-Indian enthusiast, has gained credence as a result of the important work of the so-called Berkeley school of demographic history, whose studies, based on the use of a wide array of documentary sources and sophisticated statistical methods, sometimes offer estimates larger than those of Las Casas. Evidence has also accumulated that the facts cited by Las Casas were in great part drawn from official reports submitted to the Spanish monarchs and the Council of the Indies. Meanwhile the role of Las Casas in creating the Black Legend has been reduced by evidence that Black Legend writers drew their information not only from Las Casas and the Italian traveler Girolamo Benzoni but from such unimpeachably pro-Spanish chroniclers as Francisco López de Gómara and Gonzalo Fernández de Oviedo.

The change in scholarly attitude toward the Black Legend in recent decades is suggested by remarks by the late Charles Gibson in the somber conclusion to his monumental *The Aztecs under Spanish Rule* (Stanford, 1964). Surveying the "deterioration of a native empire and civilization," Gibson went out of his way to resurrect the Black Legend that the revisionists had seemingly buried. "The Black Legend," he wrote, "provides a gross but essentially accurate interpretation of the relations between Spaniards and Indians."

Christopher Columbus's dealings with the Caribbean Indians formed the first chapter in the history of Spanish-Indian relations and provided much material for the Black Legend. Las Casas, who greatly admired Columbus, believing that God had chosen him for his providential task of opening up the New World for the conversion of the Indians, nevertheless harshly criticized the Admiral for his unjust, violent treatment of the natives. Columbus's attitude toward the Indians varied according to the occasion; he sometimes described them as "noble savages," guileless and generous with all they possessed, but when they crossed him they became "filthy dogs." No such ambiguity, however, marked Columbus's conduct with the natives. From his first contact with them, he never recognized their freedom of choice or right of self-determination, kidnapping Indian men and women to serve him as guides or interpreters. Later, on the island of La Española (Hispaniola), he loaded the Indians with intolerable tribute burdens, distributed many as slaves to appease rebellious colonists, and created a situation that Samuel Eliot Morison aptly described as "Hell on Hispaniola." Fearing that Spain's rulers would tire of supporting an unprofitable enterprise of discovery and exploration, Columbus increasingly stressed the importance of the Indian slave trade as a means of making the colonial enterprise self-supporting and a source of royal revenue. In the words of Las Casas, the Indian slave trade became "the Admiral's principal business"; he shipped several thousand Indian slaves to Spain and offered to the Spanish monarchs to send thousands more. Although Queen Isabel rebuked him for enslaving her new vassals and ordered them returned to their homes, few lived to see the islands again. When Columbus landed on La Española, the island held a dense population (Las Casas estimated three to four million, and some modern estimates are even higher) organized in chiefdoms of varying size and supported by a highly productive agriculture. By 1516, thanks to the sinister Indian slave trade and labor policies initiated by Columbus, only some twelve thousand remained.

Columbus's Indian policies reflected his background as a sea captain and trader who was familiar with the slave trade as it operated with relation to Portugal's African possessions and the prevailing European view that slavery was licit under certain conditions. A combination of modern man and medieval mystic, Columbus inflicted these miseries on the Indians not from vulgar greed for gold but from a desire to promote the universal triumph of Christianity, repeatedly urging his royal masters to use the revenue from the Indies to wrest the Holy Land from Muslim hands.

[See also *Encomienda; Exploitation of Indians; Quincentenary;* and biographies of Benzoni, Las Casas, and Oviedo.]

BIBLIOGRAPHY

Gibson, Charles, ed. *The Black Legend: Anti-Spanish Attitudes in the Old World and the New.* New York, 1971.

Keen, Benjamin. "The Black Legend Revisited: Assumptions and Realities." *Hispanic American Historical Review* 49 (November 1969): 703–719.

BENJAMIN KEEN

BOABDIL (d. 1527), sultan of Granada (Arabic, Abu Abd Allah, known as Boabdil by Christians). Boabdil, titled Muhammad XII (r. 1482–1492), was the last sultan of Granada. When Fernando and Isabel began the conquest of Granada in 1481, he revolted against his father, Sultan Abu-l-Hasan Ali (1464–1485), forcing him to flee to Málaga. Though now divided in their allegiance between father and son, the people of Granada determined to resist the Christians. When the Castilians captured Boabdil at Lucena in April 1483, he regained his freedom by pledging homage to Fernando and Isabel, and his father recovered possession of Granada.

In 1485 Boabdil's uncle, al-Zagal, seized control of the government, deposing Abu-l-Hasan Ali who died later in the year. Boabdil initially collaborated with his uncle, but renewed his vassalage to Fernando and Isabel in 1487. When the Castilians occupied the southwestern region, al-Zagal submitted and retired to Morocco, leaving Boabdil as the undisputed sultan of Granada. As Fernando and Isabel tightened the siege of the city, he secretly negotiated with them and capitulated on November 25, 1491. The Castilians took possession of the Alhambra of Granada on January 1–2, 1492, and Fernando and Isabel made their triumphal entry on January 6. The Moors were allowed to retain their property, to worship freely, and to live according to their own law. That situation was altered in 1502 when, following an uprising by the Moors, Fernando and Isabel ordered the Muslims to convert to Christianity or to leave the realm. Most chose to submit, but the problem of assimilating these moriscos, as they were called, was ultimately solved only by their expulsion in 1609–1614. Boabdil, the last of the Nasrid dynasty and the last Moorish sultan in Spain, was assigned a lordship under Castilian sovereignty in Las Alpujarras but chose to withdraw to Morocco in 1493, where he died about forty years later.

BIBLIOGRAPHY

Arié, Rachel. *L'Espagne musulmane au temps des Nasrides (1232–1492)*. Paris, 1973.

Mariéjol, Jean H. *The Spain of Ferdinand and Isabella.* Translated by Benjamin Keen. New Brunswick, N.J., 1961.

JOSEPH F. O'CALLAGHAN

BOBADILLA, BEATRIZ DE (c. 1462–1501), acting captain of Gomera. On his first voyage, Columbus's last port of call in the Old World was San Sebastián, Gomera.

During his brief stay on this island, September 3–6, 1492, Columbus was entertained by and reportedly fell in love with the beautiful ruler of Gomera, Beatriz de Bobadilla.

The figure of Beatriz de Bobadilla reveals something of Canarian society in the fifteenth century. Born in Castile of noble lineage, the seventeen-year-old Beatriz came to the Spanish court as a maid of honor to Queen Isabel. An illicit affair between King Fernando and the young maid of honor soon developed. During this time, Hernán de Peraza, governor of Gomera, came to court to explain the death of Juan Rejón, commander of a fleet that had been sent from Castile to conquer La Palma and Tenerife. Rejón had been killed by one of Peraza's vassals when he disembarked on Gomera. Isabel ordered Peraza to be brought before her. Many people, including the powerful duke of Medina Sidonia, interceded for Hernán. The queen was lenient, pardoning him on condition that he help in the conquest of the Grand Canary with some companies of Gomerans. But she imposed on him another, "less onerous penance"—that he marry the beautiful Beatriz de Bobadilla. The queen, writes Joseph Viera y Clavijo, the eighteenth-century historian of the Canaries, "seeing that the King was very fond of the girl, decided to make Hernán Peraza happy by giving him her hand. By this honorable stratagem she rid herself of a rival and secured the loyalty of the Counts of Gomera." Viera y Clavijo does not say whether, on account of the king, Beatriz was no longer a virgin. But only that would explain why marrying her would be punishment.

Immediately after the marriage the newlyweds embarked for Gomera, where their first son, Guillén, was born. The marriage did not last long. Beatriz came to Gomera as a bride in February 1482. In November 1488 her husband was killed by the Guanches, who could not endure his tyrannical government and extraordinary cruelty.

The widowed Beatriz called on the Spaniards of the Grand Canary for aid and abandoned herself to vicious vendettas. Knights, Castilians, and Guanches frequented the castle, which still dominates the beach of San Sebastián. The chroniclers of the time do not furnish details of the many adventures of this femme fatale. They do, however, say that in passing through Gomera in the summer of 1498, Alonso Fernández de Lugo, the conqueror of Tenerife (1496) and the future adelantado of the Canaries (1501), found the famous widow still young and available. People began to gossip indiscreetly about the conduct of the two. Very vocal among the gossips was Francisco Ruiz de Castañeda. Beatriz summoned him at midnight and arrested him. Confessing his imprudence and repenting did not save his life: he was hanged from a beam of the tower, and for a whole day the body hung from a palm tree in the plaza before the castle.

The hanging created a scandal in the islands. The hasty marriage of the adelantado Fernández de Lugo and Beatriz could not stop it, so the newlyweds moved to Tenerife, now controlled by the Spanish Crown, putting Fernán Muñoz in charge of Gomera. That led to new complications. The lord of Lanzarote coveted Gomera for himself, contending that it no longer belonged to Beatriz because her second marriage alienated the inheritance from her first husband, and sought Muñoz's support. When rumors of these plots reached Beatriz she did not hesitate. She and thirty men got in a launch at Los Cristianos one night and crossed from Tenerife to Gomera. At San Sebastián she had Muñoz hanged in the plaza between the tower and the beach and returned to Tenerife.

"Worthy of horror is such cruelty in a sex by nature soft and sensitive," comments Viera y Clavijo. The hanging of Muñoz was the last straw. The widows of Castañeda and Muñoz appealed to the court in Castile, and the monarchs summoned Beatriz to give an explanation. Secure in the protection of her noble relatives, not to mention that of the king, she went to court confidently. But at Medina del Campo a few days after her arrival she was found dead, apparently poisoned, in her bed. Such was the woman for whom Columbus was "touched by love" during his stay on Gomera in 1492.

BIBLIOGRAPHY

Taviani, Paolo Emilio. *I viaggi di Colombo.* Vol. 2. 2d ed. Novara, 1990. Spanish ed., Barcelona, 1989.

Viera y Clavijo, Joseph. *Noticias de la historia general de las Islas Canarias.* Vol. 2. 6th ed. Santa Cruz de Tenerife, 1967.

PAOLO EMILIO TAVIANI

BOBADILLA, FRANCISCO DE (d. 1502), royal commissioner. A member of the military order of Calatrava, Bobadilla was appointed *juez pesquisidor* of La Española on May 21, 1499. The Crown instructed Bobadilla to go to the island to inquire about Columbus's rule and the rebellion led by Francisco Roldán. Bobadilla arrived in Santo Domingo at the end of July 1500 and immediately demanded from Diego Colón, the Admiral's brother, the delivery of the fortress. Once Bobadilla realized how unpopular Columbus and his brothers were, he ordered their incarceration. Columbus resisted, but Bobadilla managed to outmaneuver him and deported him and his brothers to Spain in shackles in October 1500. As a result, Bobadilla became the de facto governor of the island until his replacement arrived on July 1502.

Bobadilla won the support of Roldán's followers, but he had to adopt further measures to maintain their allegiance. Thus, he freed those imprisoned by Columbus, lowered the tax on gold collected from one-third to

COLUMBUS AND BARTOLOMÉ COLÓN ARRESTED BY BOBADILLA. Engraving from Théodor de Bry's *Americae.* Frankfurt, 1594.

one-tenth, and ratified the system of repartimientos initiated by Columbus two years before. Having observed the lack of beasts of burden, Bobadilla allotted to Roldán's followers the horses he had found on the royal properties, which he mistakenly believed belonged to Columbus. These horses were given as indemnity to those who considered themselves to have suffered losses owing to Columbus's actions and had requested payment in this manner.

Bobadilla proceeded with the repartimientos of land and Indians as a major incentive to the Spaniards. Since there were only 360 Spaniards on the island, Bobadilla ordered them "to join together in couples, forming a partnership and sharing their profits." This measure was designed to protect them from Indian attacks and to give Bobadilla wider acceptance among the Spaniards. The chronicler Bartolomé de las Casas asserts that "because of those favors, endeavors, and advice, they adored him."

By these measures, Bobadilla was adapting himself to the difficult circumstances he encountered. His mission was to carry out the Crown's plan, which was to limit the extensive powers given to Columbus in the Santa Fe Capitulations. The Crown wished, and Bobadilla thus interpreted it, to exclude Columbus as an active partner and administrator from the venture of the Indies. Columbus's rights to the profits from expeditions financed by the Crown would be respected, but the Admiral's political interference in the government of the Indies would be ended.

Bobadilla's rule on La Española was provisional. Once Columbus was removed from La Española, the Spanish monarchs began planning for its colonization according to their own interests and designs. To this end, they appointed Nicolás de Ovando as governor in September 1501. Ovando arrived at Santo Domingo in July 1502 and immediately ordered the departure of Roldán and the main rebel leaders to Spain in the same ships that were to return Bobadilla home. But the ships were struck by a hurricane and sunk off the southeastern coast of La Española. Both Bobadilla and Roldán lost their lives.

BIBLIOGRAPHY

Incháustegui, J. Marino. *Francisco de Bobadilla*. Madrid, 1964.

Las Casas, Bartolomé de. *Historia de las Indias*. 3 vols. Mexico City, 1957.

Moya Pons, Frank. *Después de Colón: Trabajo, sociedad y política en la economía del oro*. Madrid, 1986.

FRANK MOYA PONS

BOOK OF PRIVILEGES. This work is a collection of Castilian royal documents issued to Christopher Columbus between 1492 and 1502. From the moment that King Fernando and Queen Isabel agreed to sponsor Columbus's voyage west to Asia, they began issuing contracts, decrees, privileges, and orders to implement the project. The royal secretarial staff drafted these documents; the royal legal counsel checked the language for accuracy and legality; the queen or both monarchs signed the documents; and finally the chancery clerks recorded them in their registers.

Some documents became outdated once a specific voyage had been carried out. Columbus got into the habit of archiving these by leaving them with a priest in Seville. He left some royal orders and pay vouchers relevant to the first and second voyages, for example, with the chronicler Andrés Bernáldez in 1496, after returning from his second voyage. From the third voyage until the end of his life, he sent outdated documents for safekeeping to the monastery of Las Cuevas in Seville.

Columbus needed to carry other documents with him at all times, and he soon found he needed several copies. In order to govern his growing jurisdictions and responsibilities, he delegated his authority to more and more lieutenants, some in Spain and others in the Americas. All of these deputies needed copies of the official documents in order to carry out their responsibilities. He assembled the texts over a period of ten years and had them copied in varying circumstances.

Shortly before his third voyage in 1498, Columbus commissioned notaries in the city of Seville to make copies of about thirty-five royal documents. These are of two types: warrants and commissions from 1492 through 1494 appointing him admiral and governor of the Indies,

and contracts, pay orders, and instructions dated 1497 preparatory to the third voyage. Columbus carried one copy, known later as the Veragua Codex, completed in March 1498, with him on the third voyage. (The fate of the other 1498 copies is unknown.)

In the city of Santo Domingo on the island of La Española, the Admiral commissioned notarized copies of several royal documents that he had brought with him but had not included in the Veragua Codex. His purpose may have been to leave one copy in the town of Santo Domingo with his lieutenant governor, his brother Bartolomé, while the Admiral himself continued explorations.

But the colonists had become dissatisfied with Columbus's administration, and a royal investigative judge arrested Columbus and his two brothers. Columbus was charged with irregularities in his administration of justice on La Española. Back in Spain, he was exonerated, but the monarchs stripped him of his offices as viceroy and governor-general of the Indies while authorizing other captains to make exploratory voyages. Columbus's years of residence in Spain and his career in the service of the Castilian monarchy could not counter the inherent ambiguities of his position as a foreigner ruling over Castilian citizens.

Columbus turned his energies to recovering his lost authority and status by appealing to the binding legality of the royal documents. In 1502, he updated the collection, adding about twenty-five items. The new additions include a royal mandate ordering restitution of his property, legal opinions as to Columbus's rights to a share of the royal revenues from the Indies and his rights and privileges as Admiral, and Columbus's letters and arguments about his privileges. The Seville notaries finished copying this full set of documents on March 22, 1502.

Columbus regarded the Book of Privileges as the most important document he could leave to posterity. He himself selected the royal documents to be included in the collection, commissioned several notarized copies of the collection, and sent copies to the people he trusted most. Columbus sent two parchment copies of this set, bound and cased, to the San Giorgio Bank and the city government of Genoa. These were confiscated by Napoleon during his invasion of Italy. One remains in Paris in the Bibliothèque Nationale (Paris Codex), while the other has been returned to Genoa and is on display in the Archivio di Stato (Genoa Codex). The Genoa and Paris codices have different covering letters and supplementary materials because, although he sent them to the same person in Genoa, he entrusted them to separate carriers who departed from Seville about a month apart.

Columbus deposited a third copy for safekeeping in the monastery of Las Cuevas in Seville. This is probably the copy in the Library of Congress (Washington Codex), the

FIRST PAGE. Columbus's Book of Privileges. From an 1893 facsimile edition published in London.   LIBRARY OF CONGRESS

only artifact in the United States that Columbus ever held in his hands.

All the original documents (not extant) and codices deposited at Las Cuevas, as well as the 1498 Veragua Codex (now in the Biblioteca Nacional in Madrid), Columbus bequeathed to his son Diego Colón. Most of these remained safe but unused in their Italian and Spanish depositories. The Veragua Codex, however, belonged to Diego and became a living document, the focus of nearly three centuries of litigation between the Castilian monarchy and Columbus's descendants, the dukes of Veragua.

Controversy emerged as early as 1512 in the first two lawsuits. Diego Colón entered copies of portions of the Veragua Codex as evidence in the lawsuit he brought against the monarchy to claim the revenues and offices granted to his father in 1492. The courts ruled in Diego's favor in 1511, restoring the title of viceroy and granting the full revenues and powers of the 1492 contract. The

monarchy initiated a countersuit (settled in its favor in 1512), arguing that Columbus's grant extended only to those places he discovered himself. This argument was based on a strict reading of the 1492 contract and may be the source of two fragmentary collections now in the United States. (One is in the John Carter Brown Library in Providence, Rhode Island, and the other in the Huntington Library in San Marino, California.)

As the claims and counterclaims followed one another with conflicting interpretations of portions of the Book of Privileges, the courts admitted evidence from an ever-widening range of eyewitnesses and experts to define ever-smaller segments of the text. These lawsuits, the Pleitos Colombinos, are of particular interest to scholars because they contain depositions by participants in all eight authorized voyages of discovery of North, Central, and South America between 1499 and 1503. The eyewitness descriptions of flora, fauna, people, topography, equipment, and navigation are an invaluable source of information for natural scientists, geographers, cartographers, and ethnographers.

We must keep in mind, however, that these accounts are self-interested, the witnesses attempting to claim discoveries in order to preserve for themselves a share of the revenues and positions granted in their royal authorizations. They were well aware that their own royal concessions were modeled on the monarchs' 1492 agreements with Columbus and that their rewards would depend on the court's interpretation of the Veragua Codex.

The Book of Privileges is the legal foundation upon which Spanish settlement in America rested. The royal documents instructed Columbus to colonize the Americas and authorized him to establish a system of governance. The monarchs assumed that Columbus would establish towns that would assure an orderly and productive replica of the Castilian homeland and attract the native Indians to the Christian faith. At the time, these objectives were not seen to be inherently contradictory or inappropriate for the Americas.

Almost immediately, however, tensions and conflicts erupted out of the volatile mixture of the monarchs' intentions expressed in the Book of Privileges, Columbus's personal objectives, and the self-interests of native Indians and Spanish colonists. From 1498 on, most parties to the conflicts tried to justify and explain their own actions: Columbus in his letters, memoranda, and Book of Prophesies; Bartolomé de las Casas on behalf of the Indians; Oviedo from the perspective of the Spanish colonists and officials; Andrés Bernáldez and Fernando Colón in defense of the Admiral.

The royal documents granting the discoverer governing powers and a share of the treasure in the Americas shaped the success and failure of Columbus's career in Spain and defined the profit he and his successors would receive from the Americas. During Columbus's lifetime and for 250 years after his death, the wording, intentions, and precedents of the documents in the Book of Privileges were the subjects of litigation brought by the Spanish monarchs, the Columbus family and its descendants, and Columbus's pilots, navigators, rivals, and imitators.

The Book of Privileges contains documents ranging chronologically from a grant issued in 1405 by King Juan II appointing Alfonso Enríquez as admiral of Castile to notarial certificates of the authenticity and accuracy of the copies Columbus commissioned in 1502. The most widely known documents in the collection are the Capitulations of Santa Fe and Granada (the agreements of April 17 and 30, 1492) between Columbus and King Fernando and Queen Isabel. The Washington Codex alone contains the famous papal Bull of Demarcation of 1493, dividing the still-unknown Ocean Sea into Spanish and Portuguese spheres of exploration and settlement.

There are serious historical problems in understanding the Book of Privileges. The first is the same one that the Spanish law courts took years to untangle—the meaning, intent, and precedents of the Spanish original. The documents span one of the most turbulent and innovative periods in the history of the Castilian monarchy, and the secretaries who composed and dictated them were innovating—inventing, borrowing, and adapting terminology and concepts to fit bewilderingly rapid changes in the structure and needs of the royal government. Some of the titles and offices that Fernando and Isabel granted to Columbus in 1492, for example, were their own creations: they created the first Castilian hereditary title of duke in 1475 and appointed the first governor-general in 1484 and the first captain-general in 1492.

The second problem is also historical. Columbus assembled the documents haphazardly, and the notaries copied them exactly as he handed them over. Only after we rearrange them in chronological order can we begin to see the monarchs' changes in vocabulary, their realization that Columbus's discovery was not Asia but a new world, and their hardening attitudes toward Columbus. In 1492, Fernando, Isabel, and Columbus all assumed they were negotiating terms for a relatively familiar world, Asia, made up of large cities and centralized empires and monarchies. The monarchs authorized Columbus to negotiate with the rulers he would encounter and named him their viceroy and governor-general of lands he would discover en route that were not under the jurisdiction of other rulers. The jolting realization that this was not Asia and that all of what Columbus had found might be theirs begins to appear in the 1497 documents and becomes clear in those added to the 1502 codices. The documents

in the Book of Privileges reveal Fernando and Isabel's burst of enthusiastic gratitude after the first voyage and then gradual loss of confidence in the Admiral's governing abilities.

In appearance, the Book of Privileges was only the origin of Columbus's relationship with Fernando and Isabel, but today, in reality, we can see that it shaped the encounter by defining the New World's relationships with the Castilian government. The legal interpretations of the Book of Privileges during the lawsuits were transformed by practical realities of the encounter between Spanish colonists and native cultures. Yet the Book of Privileges set the agenda for debate and provided the format for future Spanish settlements in the Americas.

[See also *Lawsuits; Santa Fe Capitulations.*]

BIBLIOGRAPHY

Christopher Columbus's Book of Privileges. Translated by Helen Nader and transcribed by Luciano Formisano. Berkeley and Los Angeles, forthcoming.

Davenport, Frances. "Texts of Columbus's Privileges." *American Historical Review* 14 (1909): 764–776.

Meisnest, Frederick W. "The Lost Book of Privileges of Columbus Located and Identified." *Huntington Library Quarterly* 12 (1949): 401–407.

Muro Orejón, Antonio. "Cristóbal Colón: El original de la capitulación de 1492 y sus copias contemporáneas." *Anuario de Estudios Americanos* 7 (1950): 505–515.

Pérez-Bustamante, Ciriaco, ed. *Libro de los privilegios del almirante don Cristóbal Colón (1498).* Madrid, 1951.

Rumeu de Armas, Antonio. *Nueva luz sobre las capitulaciones de Santa Fe de 1492 concertadas entre los Reyes Católicos y Cristóbal Colón.* Madrid, 1985.

HELEN NADER

BOOK OF PROPHECIES. For discussion of Columbus's collection of prophecies concerning his plan to find a sea route to Asia, see *Writings,* article on *Book of Prophecies.*

BRENDAN (c. 520–577 or 578), Roman Catholic saint, Irish voyager. Apart from his founding Clonfert Abbey in 561, little is known definitely of Brendan's life. He is credited with making voyages to the north and west, during one of which he visited the Scottish island of Iona. His major voyage, in a skin boat with a crew of fourteen monks, became the subject of a long and adventurous story, full of miraculous discoveries and culminating in the Land of the Blessed. This voyage appears briefly in Brendan's *Life* (c. 800) and is developed in detail in his *Navigatio* (before c. 900). Varied interpretations have been given these narratives, raising a series of questions. Did

SAINT BRENDAN ON THE BACK OF A GREAT FISH. From Caspar Plautius's *Navigatio in Novum Mundum.*

Brendan find the Canary Islands? Though this discovery seems improbable, St. Brendan's Isle appears in the Atlantic in this latitude on many marine charts in the fourteenth and fifteenth centuries. Did Brendan sail north to Iceland? The narratives appear influenced by Irish monks who lived in solitude in Iceland from perhaps A.D. 750 onward and traveled to unknown areas to do penance or find solitude for meditation.

Brendan's voyage has long given rise to the claim that he discovered North America, but this claim is grounded in concerns of religious faith, not scientific knowledge. Tim Severin, in two seasons in 1976 and 1977, sailed a skin boat from Ireland to Iceland and on to Newfoundland. His venture proved that these boats could make such long voyages but, obviously, not that Brendan made the voyage. Though thought-provoking to both scholar and student, the *Navigatio* is probably best considered a work of literature rather than a historical account.

BIBLIOGRAPHY

Ireland, John De Courcy, and David C. Sheehy, eds. *Atlantic Visions.* Dublin, 1989.
Severin, Tim. *The Brendan Voyage.* New York, 1978. *The Voyage of St. Brendan.* Translated by John J. O'Meara. Dublin, 1976.

DAVID B. QUINN

BRY, THÉODOR DE (1528–1598), Walloon engraver and publisher. Born in Liège, then under Spanish domination, de Bry, accused of sympathy with the Reformation, left Flanders in 1570 to escape the Spanish Fury and found refuge in Strasbourg, a haven for refugees from persecution and a major center of the Protestant publishing industry and book trade. A distinguished engraver, at first

de Bry worked on order for the German courts and nobility. He finally settled in Frankfurt, in the domain of the Calvinist Frederick III of the Palatinate, and there established a publishing house that specialized in handsomely made, profusely illustrated books. De Bry achieved mastery in the use of copperplate engraving, a technique of reproduction known since the fifteenth century but until recently rejected by publishers because it required twice as much work as wood-engraving, since text and illustration had to be printed separately. Copperplate engraving, however, was infinitely superior to wood-engraving in its precision of line and clarity, and it permitted the reproduction of plates over longer print runs.

In the 1580s de Bry made several business trips to England and there met Richard Hakluyt, an ardent promoter of English overseas expansion and author of a great collection of English travels, *The Principall Navigations, Voiages and Discoveries of the English Nation* (1589). Hakluyt encouraged de Bry to pursue a plan he had developed for a new travel collection in four languages. The principal result, as concerned America, was the series known as *Grands voyages* (Great voyages), published by de Bry and his successors in thirteen parts between 1590 and 1634 and comprising some thirty volumes of both large and small folio size. These volumes, published simultaneously in several languages, reached a wide public in the Protestant world and beyond, a public made not only of members of the aristocracy but also of the rising class of merchants and artisans who were fascinated by the voyages of exploration and colonization and the opportunities for enrichment that they offered.

Not unexpectedly, *Grands voyages* reveals an unmistakable anti-Spanish bias, reflected above all in the selection and editing of texts. In this series de Bry published two editions (1594–1597) of Girolamo Benzoni's *History of the New World* (1565), a major source of the so-called Black Legend of Spanish inhumanity to the Indians. To illustrate Benzoni's account of Columbus's career, de Bry attached a series of plates depicting such scenes from the Discoverer's life as the anecdote of the egg, his first departure from Spain, and his return to Spain in chains—probably the earliest attempt at a more or less detailed pictorial record of the Columbian story.

Curiously enough, de Bry omitted from his collection another major source of the Black Legend, Bartolomé de las Casas's *Brevíssima relación de la destruición de las Indias* (Very brief account of the destruction of the Indies, 1552). In 1598–1599, however, following their father's death, his sons Jean Théodor and Jean Israel de Bry published Latin and German editions of Las Casas's tract, accompanied by seventeen illustrations drawn by Iodocus a Winghe. Their beauty of line and the graceful postures struck by the almost nude Indian figures heightened the horror of the scenes of massacre and torture that they depicted. In 1599 the plates were published as a separate; a simply worded legend underneath each plate summarized the event with which it dealt. Repeatedly copied and recopied, these famous illustrations carried to every corner of Europe the message of Spanish cruelty.

Interestingly enough, however, the preface to the 1598 edition of Las Casas's tract is far from being implacably anti-Spanish in spirit. Although the brothers Jean Théodor and Jean Israel de Bry used almost the same words as Las Casas when they declared that the Spaniards in the Indies had committed such cruelties that they could more fittingly be called tigers and lions than men, they disavowed any intent to defame the whole Spanish nation. Indeed, they affirmed that "if we enjoyed the freedom and license that the Spaniards enjoyed in America, with no superior magistrate to hold them in check, we would doubtless be equal to the Spaniards in savagery, cruelty, and inhumanity." Their sole aim, proclaimed these devout Calvinists, was to make men understand the terrible fruits of that root of all evil, the love of money, and to eradicate that passion from their hearts.

Whatever the political, religious, or practical motives of Théodor de Bry and his successors in publishing a large body of illustrated works dealing with America, their work largely contributed to the development of that image of the American Indian as a Noble Savage living in a Golden Age, free from private property, greed, and kings, which the fantasy of humanists like François Rabelais and Thomas More set in the New World discovered by Columbus. The de Brys did not ignore the brutal aspects of Indian civilization. Théodor de Bry's edition of Hans Staden's narrative of his life as a captive among the Tupinambás of coastal Brazil, for example, was illustrated with skillfully elaborated versions of Staden's own small and crude woodcuts luridly depicting cannibal feasts and the surrounding ritual. More commonly, however, as in the drawings of John White depicting the Indians of Virginia or those of Jacques Le Moyne depicting the Indians of La Florida—drawings brought by Théodor de Bry from London to Frankfurt and engraved on copper, with changes in composition that enhanced their attractiveness—de Bry or his engravers not only endowed the Indians with the classic beauty and poses of Greek gods and goddesses but showed them living peaceful lives of antique simplicity before the coming of the Europeans destroyed their Eden. *Great Voyages*, widely diffused throughout Europe, provided models and sources that profoundly influenced the European artistic vision of the Indian for two centuries.

BIBLIOGRAPHY

Bucher, Benedette. *Icon and Conquest: A Structural Analysis of the Illustrations of de Bry's Great Voyages.* Translated by B. M. Gulati. Chicago, 1981.

BENJAMIN KEEN

AMERICAE, PART 4. Title page of 1594 edition.

BURIAL PLACES OF COLUMBUS.

Christopher Columbus was buried in Spain. Between the burial in 1506 and the present century, however, his physical remains were moved around quite a bit. The moves were the products of three impulses in the Columbus family and in Spanish society. First, the burials of wealthy and prominent people customarily took place in two stages: a temporary burial of the full body immediately after death and a permanent burial of the bones several years later. Second, Columbus's son Diego wanted all the family admirals to be buried on the island of La Española, and Diego's son Luis honored that wish. Third, the Spanish monarchy revered Columbus's memory; when it could no longer retain La Española centuries after the Admiral's death, the monarchy moved to keep his remains in Spanish territory.

In medieval and Renaissance Europe, it was customary for the body of a wealthy or prominent person to be interred soon after death and to remain buried for several months or years until only bones were left. Often, this preliminary burial was in a local monastery, where the monks would pray for the soul while it shed the flesh. Meanwhile, the heirs could settle the estate and commission an appropriate burial monument. When the stone monument or slab was ready, the remains were disinterred, placed in a casket, and transferred to the permanent burial site. In the Middle Ages, the permanent monuments were often in the form of statues of the dead persons lying atop their tombs. Because only bones were placed under the monument, it did not need to be life-size. If family chapels became crowded, families could save space by placing the casket of bones in a vault under the floor or a niche in the wall, commissioning smaller monuments, such as an engraved stone or metal slab, to mark the spot. This was the norm in the age of Christopher Columbus.

The fate of Columbus's remains is more complicated than the norm, however, in part because his heirs wanted him to be buried on the island of La Española in the town of Concepción. After Columbus died on May 21, 1506, the funeral ceremonies were celebrated in the parish church of Santa María la Antigua in Valladolid. Immediately afterward, he was buried in the church belonging to the Franciscan monastery in the same town. In 1509, his remains were disinterred and transferred to the Carthusian monastery of Las Cuevas in Seville, where they were buried in the Chapel of Santa Ana (later called Christ Chapel), which had been constructed by order of the prior Diego Luxán.

The next move was to America. Columbus's son, Admiral Diego Colón, made his last will and testament on September 8, 1523. He ordered his heirs to construct a convent of Poor Clare nuns in the town of Concepción, on the island of La Española, for the purpose of providing a permanent burial place in the convent chapel for his and his father's remains. He also ordered that the remains of his mother Felipa Perestrelo y Moniz should be transferred to this family chapel, as well as the body of his uncle Bartolomé Colón, whose remains had also been transferred to the monastery of Las Cuevas. Diego died in 1526 and was buried in Las Cuevas.

About 1541, the transfer from Las Cuevas to La Española was carried out by Diego's son, Luis Colón, the third admiral. The move required several steps. In 1537, Emperor Charles V granted Admiral Luis Colón the space around the main altar—the chancel—in the cathedral of

Santo Domingo for use as the family burial chapel. In 1540 the emperor issued a final decree to the bishop, dean, and chapter of the cathedral to carry out his order. The remains of the great Admiral and his son Diego were buried on the gospel side of the chancel, under the floor in front of the main altar. Soon afterward, Luis was convicted of bigamy by the royal council and sentenced to heavy fines and ten years of military service at Oran in North Africa. He died there in 1572 at the age of fifty, and his remains were later moved to the cathedral of Santo Domingo. Thus, within a century after Columbus's death, he and his male descendants were all buried in La Española in fulfillment of Diego's testamentary instructions. The Columbus dynasty in the Caribbean considered the chancel of the cathedral of Santo Domingo to be their family burial place.

The family funerary chapel was not in Concepción, as Diego had instructed in his last will and testament, because that inland settlement had never flourished. In contrast, the city of Santo Domingo, which the Admiral's brother Bartolomé had established on the south coast in 1496, thrived and became the headquarters of the Caribbean judicial district (Audiencia de Santo Domingo) and archdiocese. Even after 1537, when Luis Colón gave up the family's administrative offices in the Americas in exchange for a perpetual annuity and the noble title of duke of Veragua, Christopher Columbus occupied a place of honor in the seat of Spanish power in the Americas, the empire that he had explored and claimed for Spain.

For this very reason, the Columbus burial site was identified with Spanish rule and subject to the same vicissitudes as the Spanish Empire. In 1655, the plaque over the vault was plastered over or removed when it was feared that an English fleet under Admiral William Penn (father of William Penn, the colonizer) would capture and sack the city. By the end of the next century, Spain and the remains of Christopher Columbus were both expelled from the island of La Española. In all the earlier years of pirate attacks against Spanish ports in the Caribbean, other nations had never succeeded in actually seizing and occupying Spanish territory. But Spain's participation in wars on the European continent during the seventeenth and eighteenth centuries finally drained the monarchy's military and economic resources, and Spain began to give away pieces of its American empire in order to withdraw from the European conflict. Spain ceded part of the island of La Española—the western third now comprising the Republic of Haiti—to France in the Treaty of Ryswick in 1697. A century later, during the wars of the French Revolution, Spain ceded all the rest of the island to France in the Treaty of Basel (July 22, 1795).

Administrators based in Santo Domingo now prepared to transfer Spanish headquarters to the city of Havana. The duke of Veragua at that time did not want his ancestor's remains to fall into the hands of the French and asked the cathedral chapter to permit the remains to be moved to Havana. The commander of the Spanish fleet in the Caribbean, Gabriel de Aristizábal, took charge of disinterring the remains of Christopher Columbus and transferring them to Havana.

Excavations on the gospel side of the main altar revealed a small stone vault. Inside were some lead plates about a foot long, with bones and ashes. On December 20, 1795, Aristizábal, a committee of officials, and representatives of the duke of Veragua carefully collected these fragments and placed them in a lead casket with iron locks. The casket was carried on board the brigantine *Descubridor*, transferred to the ship *San Lorenzo*, and transported to Havana. With reverent ceremony, the casket was taken to the cathedral, where it was placed in a niche on the gospel side of the altar.

Aristizábal and the duke of Veragua were satisfied that Christopher Columbus's remains had been moved to the most honorable place in the cathedral of the headquarters city of the Spanish Caribbean. The Spanish monarchy also prided itself on having treated with respect and care the remains of the founder of the Spanish Empire.

But less than a century later, the identity of the remains in Havana cathedral were thrown into question. The confusion began in 1877, and the main character in the conflict was an Italian bishop, Roque Cocchia, serving as papal vicar to the archdiocese of Santo Domingo. At that time the chancel of Santo Domingo cathedral was being repaired, and the bishop took advantage of that situation to carry out excavations. The actual digs were supervised by a priest of the cathedral, Francisco Javier Bellini. He excavated along the wall of the gospel side of the main altar, and on September 10, 1877, he found a previously unopened vault, containing a lead casket measuring forty-two by twenty-one centimeters. Inside were bones, dust, and a small lead bullet. The casket was found to have several inscriptions on it. The letters cut into the inside lid are abbreviations of the words "Illustrious and famous gentleman Sir Christopher Columbus." Other letters on the sides, front, and top are variously interpreted as initials and "Discoverer of America First Admiral" or "Dignity of Admiralty First Admiral." This lead casket was removed from the cathedral while repairs and excavations continued.

On the other side of the chancel, the epistle side, the investigators found another lead casket with an inscription that indicated it had contained the remains of Christopher Columbus's grandson, Luis Colón. The inscription on this casket correctly identified Luis as admiral but incorrectly listed his noble titles as marquis of Veragua and duke of Jamaica.

TOMB OF COLUMBUS IN THE CATHEDRAL OF SANTO DOMINGO
DOMINICAN TOURIST INFORMATION CENTER

When repairs in the building were finished and the first casket was brought back to the cathedral in 1878, the dignitaries found a previously unnoticed small silver plate lying inside the casket. The abbreviations inscribed on this plate are interpreted to read "Last of the remains of the first admiral, Sir Christopher Columbus, discoverer." All these inscriptions, on both caskets, are problematic on several grounds. Most troubling, the abbreviations are not standard for the sixteenth century, the titles contain errors, and the workmanship is far below the standard of sixteenth-century Spanish metalworkers.

The Italian bishop nevertheless concluded that what the Spaniards had taken to Havana in 1795 were the remains of the second admiral, Christopher's son Diego Colón. He issued a pastoral letter announcing this and claiming that Christopher Columbus was still buried in the cathedral of Santo Domingo.

The indignant response from Spain came almost immediately. The government was worried, and not just about national pride. In 1795, the Spanish Empire had entered on the most convulsive period in its history. First, all the nations of Europe and America became involved in the conflicts of the French Revolution and Napoleonic Wars, and part of their strategy was to attack and seize parts of the Spanish Empire. Furthermore, the North American colonies that had rebelled against England and won independence in 1776 set an example for the Spanish colonies, which began to rebel and proclaim independence in the 1820s. By 1830, the Spanish Empire in the Americas had been reduced to just a few Caribbean islands, including Cuba and Puerto Rico. By the last quarter of the nineteenth century, many Spaniards believed that the monarchy would not be able to suppress the revolts boiling up on the islands and would surely lose the last of the Spanish Empire. If they had to withdraw from Cuba, they would once again have to make a decision about the remains in Havana cathedral.

In 1879, the Spanish Royal Academy of History submitted to the monarchy a reassuring report. The report published the relevant documents from the Spanish archives, with a historical study of them by one of the academy members, Manuel Colmeiro. It was Colmeiro who established the historical facts of Columbus's five burial places and the dates and circumstances of the Atlantic crossings. Of course, he did not have access to the inscribed lead caskets excavated by the Italian clergymen, nor could he check up on just how much Aristizábal had excavated. The Spanish government was reassured that Christopher Columbus still lay in Spanish territory.

Naturally, this situation did not continue. When Cuba and Puerto Rico rebelled late in the century, the United States decided to help them along, and at the conclusion of the Spanish-American War in 1898, Cuba became an independent country and Havana its capital. Humiliated by its utter defeat in the Caribbean and Philippines, the Spanish monarchy salvaged what dignity it could. Before finally abandoning the island of Cuba, the Spanish government decided to transfer what it still believed to be the remains of Christopher Columbus to Spain. In late 1898, the lead casket was removed from Havana cathedral, transported aboard the ship *Count of Venadito* to Cádiz, and there transferred to the royal yacht *Giralda*. The yacht carried the casket up the Guadalquivir River, flag at half-mast and flying Christopher Columbus's coat of arms, and arrived in Seville on January 19, 1899. The lead casket was placed that same day in the cathedral of Seville. As far as the Spanish government was concerned, Christopher Columbus is still buried in Seville cathedral, behind or under a marble monument sculpted by the Spanish artist Arturo Mélida.

TOMB OF COLUMBUS IN THE CATHEDRAL OF SEVILLE.
NATIONAL TOURIST OFFICE OF SPAIN, NEW YORK

The government of the Dominican Republic believes equally firmly that Christopher Columbus and his grandson Luis are buried in the cathedral of Santo Domingo, and that it is the second admiral, Diego Colón, who is buried in the cathedral of Seville. In order to honor the Admiral and accommodate the many tourists expected to visit the island in 1992, the Dominican government is building a monument to Christopher Columbus. This will be shaped like a lighthouse and will stand on the east coast of the island. The Columbus remains will be transferred to this monument as their "final" resting place. Meanwhile, Santo Domingo cathedral is once again under repair and reconstruction, and the Columbus caskets have been moved to a temporary burial site.

Despite the dignity and veneration with which Christopher Columbus's remains have actually been treated by his family and the Spanish and Dominican governments over the centuries, a great many conflicting claims and counterclaims swirl around the burial places of the Admiral and his descendants. Ironically, the motive for these claims is the very great reverence and admiration that people felt for Christopher Columbus in previous centuries; everyone wanted to claim the honor of being the guardians of the great man's burial place.

There are few prospects of ever resolving this dispute on a scholarly basis. The Spanish historian Antonio Ballesteros Beretta subscribed to Colmeiro's conclusions that Christopher Columbus's remains had been removed to Havana in 1795. Furthermore, Ballesteros published drawings of the artifacts uncovered in 1877, including the inscriptions. The American historian Samuel Eliot Morison subscribed to the Dominican argument, largely on the basis of research published by Rudolf Cronau in 1891. Morison was not troubled by the probability of forgery in the inscriptions and believed that Aristizábal had simply failed to dig far enough, that had he dug closer to the wall he would have found the "real" Christopher Columbus casket in 1795. Instead, Morison believed, the naval commander carried off to Havana the remains of the discoverer's son, Diego Colón, the second admiral, leaving Christopher Columbus buried in Santo Domingo. Ballesteros and Morison, the two giants of their day in Columbus scholarship, could not agree.

After that, a flurry of new research on this problem addressed several important issues, such as the events and decisions surrounding the transfer of the remains of the third admiral, Luis Colón, from North Africa to La Española, and the extent of earthquake and hurricane damage, repair, and relocation within the cathedral of Santo Domingo before 1877. No one has accounted for that small lead bullet.

Scholarly evidence and original documents made no impression on the participants in this paper war, however, nor did they prevent the wildest charges from the most improbable sources. National pride was at stake, and for a century the disputes aroused incredible displays of patriotic competition and ethnic anger. These patriotic and ethnic claims have subsided only in the 1980s. Now that Christopher Columbus is being blamed for starting all the evils of American society, few countries or nationalities want to be associated with him even after death. Meanwhile, we can choose: Christopher Columbus has found refuge in Spain in death, as he did in life, or he rests in his beloved La Española, scene of his grandest dreams and glories.

BIBLIOGRAPHY

Ballesteros Beretta, Antonio. *Cristóbal Colón y el descubrimiento de América.* Vol. 2. Barcelona and Buenos Aires, 1945.

Colmeiro, Manuel. *Los restos de Colón: Informe de la Real Academia de la Historia al gobierno de S. M. El supuesto hallazgo de los verdaderos restos de Cristóbal Colón en la iglesia de Santo Domingo.* Madrid, 1879.

Dozier, Thomas. "The Controversy on Whereabouts of Columbus' Body." *Smithsonian* 5, no. 7 (October 1974): 92–99. Reprinted in *Editor's Choice:* Smithsonian: *The Best of Twenty Years from* Smithsonian Magazine. Washington, D.C., 1990.

Morison, Samuel Eliot. *Admiral of the Ocean Sea: A Life of Christopher Columbus.* Vol. 2. Boston, 1942.

HELEN NADER

C

CABEZA DE VACA, ALVAR NÚÑEZ (1490?–1556?), Spanish explorer. Cabeza de Vaca made two extraordinary journeys into the interior of the North and South American continents: the first from Florida to Mexico from 1527 to 1536 and the second to Paraguay from 1540 to 1545. He was the first European to walk across the mainland of North America. His *relación,* or account, of that crossing and the years he spent among the indigenous peoples of the gulf coast and southwestern part of the continent is the most gripping narrative of first contact in American letters.

Cabeza de Vaca was born to a distinguished military family in Jerez de la Frontera, Spain. He served in the army of Fernando the Catholic at the Battle of Ravenna in 1512 and later as a steward in the service of the duke of Medina Sidonia. On June 17, 1527, Cabeza de Vaca sailed from Sanlúcar de Barrameda as treasurer or representative of the Crown and provost marshal in the expedition to Florida organized by Pánfilo de Narváez. After the expedition landed near the Bay of Tampa on April 12, 1528, Narváez decided to march overland while his ships explored by sea. As the Spanish struggled through the swamps, they perished in attacks by hostile tribes or died of starvation on the beaches of the Gulf coast where the barges they had constructed from the hides of their horses had been wrecked in storms. Of that fleet of three caravels and some 350 men, only Cabeza de Vaca, Alonso del Castillo Maldonado, Andrés Dorantes, and his black servant Estebanico managed to survive as traders and slaves among the indigenous groups they encountered in what is present-day southern Texas.

Sometime around 1533 the four were reunited at a vast prickly pear harvesting area located near the lower Guadalupe and Nueces rivers. Their successful practice of indigenous healing procedures among the numerous tribes they met earned them reverence as "Children of the Sun." Throngs of friendly Indians accompanied them as they traveled westward toward the Sonora Valley through territories occupied by Piman and Opatan groups and then southward on the middle Yaqui River through Cahitan territory. Although the precise route the party traveled has long been a topic of intense debate, it is agreed that they covered more than 18,000 kilometers (11,000 miles) on foot across the North American continent.

At the climactic moment in the account, when the survivors meet Spanish soldiers somewhere north of Culiacán in May of 1536, Cabeza de Vaca's narrating perspective of "us" includes his Indian friends, and the references to the Spaniards are couched in terms of "they," or separate and other beings. His account of North American tribes, their languages and customs, and the plants, animals, and geography of their native regions includes the first description of a Caribbean hurricane, the buffalo, and the great walled cities in the northern interior. First reported orally to the viceroy in Mexico City in 1536 and later compiled as a joint report written by the three Spanish survivors, it spurred the Crown to send Fray Marcos de Niza and the expedition of Francisco Vásquez de Coronado northward in search of the Seven Cities of Cibola in 1539 and 1540.

Cabeza de Vaca returned to Spain in 1537, where he began writing his own *La relación,* published in Zamora in 1542. It represents a vision of the indigenous peoples and geography of North America through the eyes of a Spaniard living among those societies. To survive, he acculturated to them and defended them against the Spanish abuses he witnessed on the northern frontiers of New Spain.

In 1540 Charles V named him governor and captain

general for Río de la Plata, charged with rescuing the possible survivors of the Pedro de Mendoza expedition to Paraguay. In October 1541 he and his party set out from the island of Santa Catalina off the Brazilian coast, marching more than 1,700 kilometers (1,050 miles) through the jungles of Paraguay to reach Asunción in 1542. On the way the group discovered the falls of Iguazú, and one of his party, Hernando de Ribera, reported news of El Dorado and the Amazons.

Cabeza de Vaca's tenure as governor, however, was short-lived and filled with conflict: his generous attitude toward the Indians caused resentment among his enemies. In 1544 he was taken prisoner by mutinous colonists led by his second in command, Domingo Martínez de Irala, and was sent back to Spain in chains in 1545. His account of that bitter experience was set down in *Los comentarios*, written under his supervision by his secretary, Pedro Hernández, and published together with the edited version of *La relación* in Valladolid in 1555.

BIBLIOGRAPHY

Adorno, Rolena. "The Negotiation of Fear in Cabeza de Vaca's 'Naufragios.'" *Representations* 33 (1991).

Bishop, M. *The Odyssey of Cabeza de Vaca*. New York and London, 1933.

Cabeza de Vaca, Alvar Núñez. *Cabeza de Vaca's Adventures in the Unknown Interior of America*. Translated by Cyclone Covey. New York, 1961. Albuquerque, N. Mex., 1988.

Cabeza de Vaca, Alvar Núñez. *The Narrative of Alvar Núñez Cabeza de Vaca*. Translated by Fanny Bandolier. Edited by John Francis Bannon. With Oviedo's version of the lost joint report translated by Gerald Theisen. Barre, Mass., 1972.

Cabeza de Vaca, Alvar Núñez. *La Relación o Naufragios de Alvar Núñez Cabeza de Vaca*. Edited by Martin A. Favata and Jose B. Fernandez. Potomac, Md., 1986.

Chipman, Donald E. "In Search of Cabeza de Vaca's Route across Texas: An Historiographical Survey." *Southwest Historical Quarterly* 91 (1987).

Molloy, Sylvia. "Alteridad y reconocimiento de los *Naufragios* de Alvar Núñez Cabeza de Vaca." *Nueva Revista de Filología Hispánica* 35 (1987).

MAUREEN AHERN

CABOT, JOHN (c. 1455–1498 or 1499), explorer and navigator. Cabot was born in Genoa, the son of Giulio Caboto and an unknown mother. His family moved to Venice in 1461, living on Chioggia, and Cabot was naturalized as a Venetian in 1476. He claimed to have traveled as a merchant and seaman to the eastern Mediterranean, engaging in the spice trade as he made his way possibly to Mecca. He probably moved to Spain about 1490 with his wife Mattea and their elder sons. He may well have worked as a chart maker, but if he is the same person as Juan Caboto de Montecalunya, he is found planning harbor works at Valencia in 1491–1493. He is described in 1498 as "another Genoese like Columbus, who had been in Seville and at Lisbon seeking to obtain persons to aid this discovery" after his successful voyage of 1497. This description raises the probability that Cabot had early contacts with Columbus, either as a rival or, for a time, as collaborator. He was in Valencia when Columbus passed through in 1493 on his way to report to the Catholic monarchs at Barcelona and so would have heard of Columbus's success. It is likely that this report inspired Cabot to attempt an Atlantic crossing in more northerly latitudes where the distance would be shorter.

The date of his arrival in Bristol, England, is unknown, but it is likely to have been either 1493 or 1494. From about 1491, Bristol was annually sending out exploring expeditions of two to four ships. Bristol could not possibly have afforded to send these expeditions unless profitable cargoes were being brought back. Hence, the conclusion might well be made that the men of Bristol were already fishing off Newfoundland from some time before Cabot's voyage. Cabot had to have time to convince local merchants that he was serious; it may have been in 1495 that he made his first, unsuccessful voyage to the west. This voyage failed, probably because of inclement weather. Cabot's contacts in Bristol were sufficient, however, to get him recommended to Henry VII, who on March 5, 1496, granted, by patent, permission to Cabot and his three sons, Ludovico, Sebastian, and Sancio, to discover and annex lands across the ocean for the Crown. The patent also authorized Cabot and, in succession, his sons to rule these lands in the king's name.

The first expedition under the patent took place between May and August 1497. Cabot's ship left Bristol with a crew of twenty on May 20 and reached "the land first seen" (*terra prima vista*) according to his son Sebastian, on June 24, at forty-five degrees (approximately at Cape Breton). Cabot then sailed up the east coast of Newfoundland, leaving Cape Bauld about July 18. He landed once and found only superficial signs of human occupancy, bringing home "a stick half a yard long pierced at both ends, carved and painted with brazil." (Brazil, a red dye of Asian origin, was clearly iron oxide.) The estimated distance from Bristol to America as eighteen hundred miles was not unreasonable, and the definition of the south-north distance traveled as between the latitudes of the mouth of the Garonne and Dursey Head in Ireland (forty-six to fifty-one degrees) was accurate within a hundred miles. But Cabot's claim to have traversed the coast for four hundred leagues (twelve hundred miles) is absurd; he may have traveled four hundred miles. He made a speedy crossing to Bristol on August 6 and then traveled to London, having agreed to make a world map

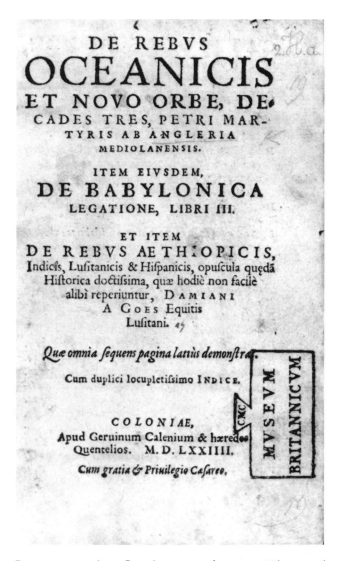

FIRST ACCOUNT OF JOHN CABOT'S VOYAGE TO LABRADOR. Title page of *De rebus oceanicis et novo orbe decades tres...*, by Pietro Martire d'Anghiera (Peter Martyr). Cologne, 1574.

and a globe for Henry VII to illustrate the location of his supposed discoveries in the land of the Great Khan. Henry responded rapidly, giving him a present of ten pounds and a smaller sum to follow (possibly in return for the cartographical evidence). This reward was followed by the generous life grant of twenty pounds a year from the Bristol customs. Cabot's discovery was clearly of an immense island or a continent, presumed by Cabot to be Asiatic.

The king equipped a ship in the Thames for another voyage, and London merchants loaded it with English woolen cloth and other English products, hoping to gain silks and spices in return. The four small Bristol ships that joined it added "slight and gross merchandises, as coarse cloth caps, laces, points and other trifles," showing a skepticism about the luxury trade and suggesting earlier contact with the primitive Newfoundland Boethuks, to whom such items would be attractive. The fleet set out in 1498, provisioned for a year. It met with unknown disasters, including a major storm. One ship, in distress, put in at Ireland. Of the rest of the fleet we know nothing definitive. One vessel may have returned; several persons who were thought to have gone on the expedition were later found alive. Cabot conceivably reached Bristol, though Polydor Vergil wrote in 1512, "he is believed to have found the new lands nowhere but on the very bottom of the ocean." If Cabot survived it was not for long. His pension terminated on September 29, 1509, as did the lease of his house. Sebastian and his mother evidently remained in Bristol; all mention of his brothers is absent.

Cabot's historical importance stems from his being the first clearly recorded discoverer of the North American continent, as was Columbus of South America in the year following the 1497 voyage. In addition, Cabot confirmed the existence of a great fishing ground off Newfoundland. The exploring and fishing expeditions of 1501–1504 followed from this confirmation and his territorial discoveries. A sketch of Cabot's alleged discoveries was sent to Columbus by John Day, a Bristol merchant, who promised later to send a map, presumably a world map. A Spanish ambassador also sent a sketch to his masters in 1498, following his attempt to convince Henry VII that Cabot had infringed the Spanish monopoly under the papal grant and the Treaty of Tordesillas. The long extent of "the sea discovrd by the English" on Juan de la Cosa's map of 1500 certainly impinged on territory that Spain could claim, but this extension could well have been the result of a stretched-out version of an unscaled drawing.

John Day had informed Columbus about John Cabot's voyage very shortly after Cabot's return. Toward the end of 1497 Day wrote to Columbus stating, "It is certain that the cape of the said land was found and discovered in the past by the men of Bristol who discovered Brazil, as your Lordship knows" ("Se presume cierto averse fallado e descubierto en otros tienpos el cabo de la dicha tierra por los de Bristol como dello teine noticia Vuestra Senoria"). This statement implies that both Cabot and Columbus knew of an earlier transatlantic discovery made from Bristol. Brazil was associated with the Island of the Seven Cities (which comprised places that Day designated as being Cabot's discoveries). The words *en otros tienpos* (in the past) have been variously interpreted. Alwyn Ruddock considered this report to be a revised old tale of some distant or supposed discovery. Samuel Eliot Morison classified the report as "Bristol gossip." I regard it as a reference to either a 1481 expedition, reported as being sent "to search for and find the Isle of Brasil," or a voyage made after 1490, conceivably as late as 1494, a date favored by early writers on Cabot.

BIBLIOGRAPHY

Morison, Samuel Eliot. *The European Discovery of America: The Northern Voyages.* New York, 1971.

Quinn, David B. *England and the Discovery of North America.* New York, 1974.

Quinn, David B., Alison M. Quinn, and Susan Hillier, eds. *New American World.* 5 vols. New York, 1979.

Ruddock, Alwyn A. "John Day of Bristol and the English Voyages across the Atlantic." *Geographical Journal* 122 (1966).

Vigneras, Louis-André. "New Light on the 1497 Cabot Voyage to America." *Hispanic-American Historical Review* 36 (1956).

Williamson, James Alexander. *The Cabot Voyages and Bristol Discovery under Henry VII.* Cambridge, 1962.

DAVID B. QUINN

CABOT, SEBASTIAN (c. 1476?–1557), explorer and cartographer. Born in Chioggia, Venice, Sebastian Cabot was the second son of Mattea and Giovanni Caboto (John Cabot). He probably accompanied his family to Spain about 1490, lived in Valencia for most of the years 1491–1493, and then migrated with his family to Bristol, England, in 1493 or 1494. As a young man he appears to have been taught, probably by his father, the art of making charts and possibly globes. At the age of about fifteen, he accompanied his father on his successful 1497 voyage, the first-known large-scale exploration of eastern North America (antedating by a year Columbus's discovery of an American landmass). If Sebastian Cabot was on the 1498 voyage, he was one of the fortunate few who survived it.

From 1501 onward, several syndicates sponsored explorations and cod-fishing expeditions. Sebastian was a leader of at least one such voyage, which in 1504 ranged from New England possibly up the coast of Labrador. For this he was to receive a royal pension for life for his work "in and aboute the fyndynge of the newe found landes." With two ships that, he reported to Pietro Martire d'Anghiera (Peter Martyr), he "equipped at his own cost in Britain" and with three hundred men, he set out in 1508 on a voyage to sail north around the recently discovered landmass to Asia. Cabot later insisted that the ships were provided and equipped by Henry VII. Neither this claim nor that regarding the size of his company appears to be true. It is even suspected that he found finance in the Netherlands. Certainly he was back in England by May 7, 1509, applying for arrears of his pension for part of the period 1506–1509. This pension was subsequently rescinded. He continued to live in Bristol, but he accompa-

nied an English force to France in 1511, where he made a map of Gascony and Guienne. Very shortly after his return, he visited Burgos where he met representatives of King Fernando of Aragón and agreed to transfer to the Spanish service. On September 13, 1512, Fernando wrote to Cabot that his service was sought because of his knowledge of "the navigation to the Indies and the Island of the Bacalaos (Newfoundland)." Cabot then moved to Spain and was in the service of the Spanish Crown until 1548. Henry VIII is not known to have objected.

Cabot had sailed in 1508 from an unknown port; he reached the Labrador coast in July and continued northward. His course thereafter has been a topic of considerable controversy. The Spanish writer Francisco López de Gómera, in 1552, put Cabot's northing as fifty-eight degrees. Cabot himself claimed that he reached some sixty-seven degrees (well up the coast of Baffin Island and north of the Arctic Circle). Given the uncertainty of latitude estimation at this time, he may have entered Hudson Strait at approximately sixty degrees, for he reported encountering numerous icebergs, which is characteristic of that channel in July. He wintered along the eastern shore, probably investigating possible entries into the interior, and finally sailed from North America be-

SEBASTIAN CABOT.   MASSACHUSETTS HISTORICAL SOCIETY

tween twenty-five and thirty-five degrees north, arriving in England shortly before May 7, 1509. Whatever the details of the voyage, it was a notable one and inspired many attempts to find a passage to the Pacific. Cabot's Spanish masters, however, did not attempt to follow him into icy latitudes, choosing rather to send Ferdinand Magellan south to make the circumnavigation, which was completed by Juan Sebastián de Elcano in 1522. Cabot did not give up his plans for a northern voyage. He secretly went to England in 1521 and ingratiated himself with the powerful Cardinal Thomas Wolsey, but failed to convince London merchants to support him. Back in Spain he opened equally fruitless negotiations with Venice.

Cabot taught pilotage and prepared charts on the expanding Spanish empire at the Casa de la Contratación in Seville, where he became head of the pilot office as pilot major in 1518, an office he retained, with one short interval, for thirty years. Holy Roman Emperor Charles V thought highly of Cabot, and, in 1526, he commissioned him to lead an expedition to examine the Río de la Plata, discovered some years before, to determine if there was a passage to the Pacific in a temperate latitude. Cabot did his best to explore the great complex of rivers that combine to create the estuary, but he found neither a trans-American route nor gold. Dissension among his crew forced him to return in 1530, after which he engaged in no further expeditions.

In 1548, he returned to England and spent some years planning a northern route for English trade to the Pacific. In 1553, a northeast passage route was attempted, though this linked trade with northern Russia, not China. Sebastian Cabot remained nominal governor of this Muscovy Company until his death. The world map of 1544 with which he was associated contained notes on early English voyages and was revised by him in 1549. When he died, his considerable achievements had been to build on the discoveries made by his father and on the exploration of eastern Spanish South America in the wake of Columbus, Juan Díaz de Solís, and Magellan.

BIBLIOGRAPHY

Almagià, Roberto. *Comemorazione di Sebastiano Caboto nel IV centenario della morte.* Venice, 1958.

Biggar, Henry P. *Precursors of Jacques Cartier.* Ottawa, 1911.

Morison, Samuel Eliot. *The European Discovery of America: The Northern Voyages.* New York, 1971.

Quinn, David B. *England and the Discovery of North America.* New York, 1974.

Quinn, David B., Alison M. Quinn, and Susan Hillier, eds. *New American World.* 5 vols. New York, 1979.

Toribio, Medina. *El veneciano Sebastián Caboto ene el servicio de España.* Santiago, 1908.

Williamson, James Alexander. *The Cabot Voyages and Bristol Discovery under Henry VII.* Cambridge, 1962.

DAVID B. QUINN

CABRAL, PEDRO ÁLVARES

CABRAL, PEDRO ÁLVARES (1467 or 1468–1520), Portuguese discoverer of Brazil. One of more than ten children, Cabral was born in Belmonte, in east central Portugal, the second son of Isabel de Gouveia and Fernão Cabral, lord of the manor of Azurara, civil governor of Belmonte and nobleman of the household of King Afonso V (r. 1438–1481). Like most of the sons of the nobility, at the age of fourteen he entered the court of King João II (r. 1481–1495) where he completed his education. Sometime later, King Manuel I (r. 1495–1521) appointed him to his privy council and offered him the habit of the Order of Christ. As a result of his marriage to Isabel de Castro, he enlarged his holdings considerably and allied himself with one of the most illustrious and powerful families of the day. He was also related by marriage to Afonso de Albuquerque, his mother-in-law's brother.

After the return of Vasco da Gama from his momentous voyage in 1499, King Manuel I decided to send a large armada to India that would impress the Asians with his power and prestige and start the spices flowing from the East. He chose Pedro Álvares Cabral as commander of a fleet of thirteen ships carrying the most experienced pilots and mariners of the day. On March 8, 1500, the day appointed for departure, the king and his court accompanied the mariners to the beach at Restelo, where mass was celebrated by Diogo Ortiz, then bishop of Ceuta, who had been a member of King João II's scientific council when it refused Columbus's request for ships.

Owing to the weather, the fleet did not sail until the following day. On March 14, five days after their departure, they reached the Canary Islands, and on the twenty-second, they touched at but did not stop at Cape Verde. It was there they noticed that Luis Peres's ship was missing, but there had been no adverse weather to account for it. They searched for two days but never found it. The remaining twelve ships of the fleet continued on their way, sailing far to the west. The advantages of following a more southerly route from the Cape Verde Islands, making use of the northeast trade winds, had been apparent during the voyage of Columbus, which is why this course seems to have been chosen. The instructions given to Cabral are supposed to have been dictated by Vasco da Gama, who described a curve after passing the Cape Verdes, the course Bartolomeu Dias had followed, only this time the curve was larger.

On Tuesday of Easter week, April 21, 1500, they saw signs of land, and on the twenty-third they anchored next to the mouth of a river. Since it was not a safe anchorage, on Saturday the twenty-fifth they moved the ships to a safer port, which Cabral named Porto Seguro. They established friendly relations with the natives who brought them a generous supply of food and fearlessly boarded the ships. Cabral decided to linger a while. On Easter Day, they heard mass ashore, which was celebrated in a tent with great solemnity while the natives looked on, enjoying the spectacle. On the first of May, a commemorative pillar was erected on top of a hill near the beach, and on the third of May they departed.

They dispatched Gaspar de Lemos in the supply ship with letters to the king, among them the famous letter of Pero Vaz de Caminha, the ship's scribe. It is a beautifully written letter giving a valuable and detailed description of the ten days they spent in Brazil. The letter is dated May 1, 1500, and is written from "Porto Seguro in your island of Vera Cruz," which proves that Caminha believed Brazil to be a great island. As early as 1501, however, the Portuguese no longer believed that it formed part of Asia.

With the departure of Lemos's caravel, the fleet was reduced to eleven ships. On May 23, as they were approaching the Cape of Good Hope, they were struck by a sudden storm that capsized four of the vessels, with the loss of all hands. One of the ships to go down was that of Bartolomeu Dias, who thus found a grave in the very waters of the cape he had discovered twelve years before. A fifth ship, that of Dias's brother Diogo, carried astray by the storm, took a wide detour into the Indian Ocean and touched the island of Madagascar. His ship, traveling on, approached the mouth of the Red Sea from where it returned around Africa alone without stopping except at Cape Verde. There, in 1501, it met up with Amerigo Vespucci, who was on board the first fleet sent by King Manuel I to explore Brazil.

The remaining six ships proceeded on their way without Diogo's ship. After running through a storm for twenty days, under bare poles and separated from one another, they met again on June 10 off the coast of Sofala. Continuing their journey along the east coast of Africa, they reached Mozambique on July 20, Kilwa on July 26, and Malindi on August 2, where Cabral strengthened the good relations that had been established with the king by Vasco da Gama. From there they departed in the direction of Calicut on August 2, with two Gujerati pilots, dropping anchor on the island of Angediva on August 23, 1500; finally, on September 11, they arrived in Calicut.

There Cabral delivered to the Hindu ruler of Calicut, or the *samuri*, as he was called, a letter from King Manuel, along with the presents he had brought, which, unlike those of Vasco da Gama before him, were deemed satisfactory. The *samuri* granted Cabral the trading rights he sought, and André Gouveia was appointed factor of Calicut. But the Muslim merchants of the city, who had

FLEET OF PEDRO ÁLVARES CABRAL. Detail, from Lizuarte de Abreu's *O sucesso dos visoreis*, mid-sixteenth century. The illustration notes the name of the captain of each vessel and its fate. A storm near the Cape of Good Hope claimed four vessels, one of them (lower right) with Bartolomeu Dias, the cape's discoverer, aboard.

THE PIERPONT MORGAN LIBRARY, NEW YORK; M.525, F.7; M.525, F.16v–17.

enjoyed a centuries-old monopoly of the Indian trade, placed a series of obstacles in their way, leading to hostilities that ended with the assassination of Aires Correia and his companions on December 17. According to the chronicler Lopes de Castanheda, Cabral ordered his captains to seize ten Muslim ships that were in port. The cargo was confiscated and the ships set afire with all hands on board. On the following day, Cabral, after bringing his ships as close to shore as possible, ordered the artillery trained on the city, killing and destroying everything and everyone in sight. Even the *samuri* was forced to flee when a cannon ball exploded near him.

A day later, since there was nothing left to destroy, Cabral sailed for Cochin where he had heard that the rajah was friendly to the Portuguese. In Cochin, where he arrived on December 24, he signed a treaty with the rajah and took on pepper. From there he went on to Canna-nore, also on the Malabar coast, to load cinnamon. In Cranganore he came across a community of Jacobite Christians. Wisely ignoring a hostile fleet of the *samuri*, which had followed him all the way, he turned homeward, departing from Cannanore on January 31, 1501. He crossed the Indian Ocean and landed in Mozambique, from where he sent Sancho de Tovar to explore the Bay of Sofala, with orders to sail home once he had done so. On his way home, Cabral ran into many storms as far as the Cape of Good Hope, where one of the ships became separated from the fleet and was not seen again on the rest of the voyage. In spite of the dangers he encountered, he eventually rounded the cape on May 21, 1501. He anchored in Cape Verde and finally entered Lisbon harbor on June 23, 1501. Sancho de Tovar arrived later.

King Manuel received Cabral solemnly and conferred various honors on him. He offered Cabral the command of another India-bound fleet of twenty ships, five of which were to form a special squadron under the command of Vicente Sodré. At the last minute, however, for some unknown reason (the chroniclers offer varying explana-tions), the king changed his mind and offered the command instead to Vasco da Gama who eventually departed on what was to be his second voyage to India. Cabral retired to Santarém and was never again called on to serve the king.

Cabral's voyage was not regarded as a success at the time, but in light of the results, it stands out as one of the greatest of the Portuguese voyages. His achievements consisted of establishing friendly relations with two minor kingdoms—Cochin and Cannanore—on the Malabar coast of India; establishing a factory at the former place, the first permanent factory in India; finding an early Christian settlement at Cranganore; visiting Sofala; and ascertaining a practical sea route to the cape. Though he exercised extreme cruelty toward the Muslims of Calicut, he showed a humanitarian and sympathetic attitude in his treatment of the Amerindians of Brazil, and—unlike Columbus—there is no suggestion that they might have been used as slaves. In the discovery of Brazil, Cabral added to his native land a country that exceeded in area, wealth, and opportunity Portugal itself. It is true that the Portuguese would have discovered America in the course of their voyages to India, probably within a decade, had Columbus not crossed the Atlantic, but this does not lessen the importance of the voyage of Cabral as the first chapter of European history in Brazil.

Just as there are those who question the fact that Columbus discovered America on October 12, 1492, so too there are those who question the fact that Cabral discovered Brazil on April 22, 1500. Was Cabral indeed the first European to discover Brazil, they ask, and if so, was it

accidental or intentional? Bailey W. Diffie, one of the doubters, asserts that after Columbus returned to Spain, many other men set out on exploring expeditions, and some of them reached Brazil before Cabral landed in 1500, notably Amerigo Vespucci, Vicente Yáñez Pinzón, and Diogo de Lepe. Many Portuguese historians have held that Cabral had secret instructions from the king to explore en route to India. If such secret instructions ever existed in any form, oral or written, no witnesses have been produced or written documents discovered. These and other questions regarding the voyage of Cabral still remain to be answered.

BIBLIOGRAPHY

Castanheda, Fernão Lopes de. *História do descobrimento e conquista da Índia pelos portugueses.* Edited by M. Lopes de Almeida. 2 vols. Porto, 1979.
Diffie, Bailey W. *Who Was the First to Discover Brazil?* Buffalo, N.Y., 1975.
Greenlee, William Brooks, ed. and trans. *The Voyage of Pedro Álvares Cabral to Brazil and India.* Hakluyt Society Publications, 2d ser., vol. 81. London, 1938.
Peres, Damião. *Pedro Alvares Cabral e o descobrimento do Brasil.* 4th ed. Porto, 1975.
Prestage, Edgar. *The Portuguese Pioneers.* London, 1933.

REBECCA CATZ

CABRILLO, JUAN RODRÍGUEZ

CABRILLO, JUAN RODRÍGUEZ (1498?–1543), soldier and explorer. Often said to be Portuguese, Juan Rod-ríguez Cabrillo is considered by most historians to be Spanish. Probably born in Seville, he was in the New World by 1510. A tough, self-sufficient boy, he became a merchant-adventurer and served with Pánfilo de Narváez in the conquest of Cuba. Rodríguez could read, write, keep accounts, and trade goods for a profit, but he could also ride a horse, use a crossbow, and handle a sailing ship.

In 1520 Rodríguez went to the mainland with Narváez, joined the army of Hernando Cortés, and served in the second siege of the Aztec capital, Tenochtitlán. Situated in the middle of a lake, Tenochtitlán was vulnerable to attack by ship. Consequently Cortés sent troops to the moun-tains to cut timber for vessels to be used in retaking the city. Rodríguez commanded a detachment to gather pine resin to mix with tallow and make pitch for waterproofing the ships. Lacking animal fat for tallow, the men used human fat, according to one story, from Indians killed in battle. True or not, the story reflects the reputation of Rodríguez as a tough conquistador.

In 1521 Rodríguez marched through Oaxaca with the soldiers of Francisco de Orozco and then went to Guate-mala with the army of Pedro de Alvarado. Fighting and marching almost constantly for the next few years, the army occupied the provinces of Vera Paz, San Salvador, and Nicaragua, finally settling in the new city of Santiago de Guatemala. With a grant of land, plus Indian laborers to work it, Rodríguez became one of the richest men in the country. By 1532 he controlled gold mines, had ships on the Pacific coast of Guatemala, and engaged in trade with the Spanish soldiers involved in the conquest of the Inca Empire.

Though he had children by an Indian woman, Rodríguez returned to Spain about the fall of 1532 to marry the daughter of a prominent family of Seville, Beatríz Sánchez de Ortega, with whom he had two sons. During the 1530s he acquired the name Cabrillo, probably as a nickname, though the meaning is unclear.

Cabrillo built a fleet for Alvarado to use in a daring plan to cross the Pacific and trade with China and the Spice Islands, the lands Columbus had tried to reach in 1492. He joined the fleet with his own ship, *San Salvador*, serving as second in command. When Alvarado died in a misadventure, Cabrillo took the *San Salvador*, a smaller vessel, and a launch and sailed north in 1542. Confident that North America was either joined to Asia or separated from it by a narrow strait, the men expected to reach China by following the coastline north and west. Instead, they found themselves confined by winds and currents to the west coast of North America, unable to sail much beyond forty degrees north latitude. The expedition spent the fall exploring the coastline of present-day California. Winter camp was established on Catalina Island, where the commander was injured in a fall while trying to extricate his men from a fight with the suddenly hostile inhabitants. He died on January 3, 1543, and was buried on the island. His fleet made a second attempt to sail north and probably reached the Oregon coast before returning to New Spain.

Cabrillo's original reports and maps have been lost, but Andrés de Urdaneta interviewed the survivors of his fleet, made a summary of the journal, and sent the coastal map to Europe, where the results appeared in a world map drawn by Andreas Homem in 1559. Urdaneta used Cabrillo's report and map in 1565 when he made the first successful trip across the Pacific to the Spice Islands and back, thus completing the project started by Columbus.

BIBLIOGRAPHY

Kelsey, Harry. *Juan Rodríguez Cabrillo.* San Marino, Calif., 1986.
Mitchell, Mairin. *Friar Andrés de Urdaneta, O.S.A. (1508–1568): Pioneer of Pacific Navigation from West to East.* London, 1964.
Wagner, Henry R. *Spanish Voyages to the Northwest Coast of America.* San Francisco, 1929.

HARRY KELSEY

CADAMOSTO, ALVISE (1432–1488), Venetian navigator, explorer, and merchant. Cadamosto (or Ca'da Mosto), who is credited with discovery of the Cape Verde Islands, was a young trading partner in the Venetian company of Andrea Barbarigo when in August 1454 he entered the service of Prince Henry the Navigator. Henry was preparing a trading expedition to explore the Atlantic coast of Africa, for the Portuguese were very interested in the region as a source of spices, slaves, ivory, gum arabic, and gold. Cadamosto departed as a trading partner in March 1455, and after landing in the Madeiras and Canaries he followed the African coast south to the Senegal River. Along with several Genoese vessels he proceeded up the Gambia River, but returned to Portugal after the crews became restless in the face of hostile natives.

In April 1456, Cadamosto set out from Lagos with the Genoese Antoniotto Usodimare and headed south a second time. Rounding Cape Blanco, they were caught in a wind shift that sent them out to sea, apparently resulting in the discovery of the Cape Verde Islands. Cadamosto explored Boa Vista and São Tiago; then, returning to the coast, he headed south and reached the Bissagos Islands. Although Cadamosto is generally credited with the discovery of the Cape Verde Islands, some, including the historian of Genoa Jacques Heers, claim that Antonio di Noli discovered them in 1460.

Cadamosto wrote an account of his voyages that was first printed at Vicenza in 1507 in the collection *Paesi nuovamenti ritrovati et Novo Mondo da Alberica Vesputio Fiorentino intitolato.* His acute and often vivid observations of the African lands, people, and trading customs are among the earliest European accounts. The cartographer Fra Mauro of Venice used either a portolan map made by Cadamosto, now lost, or his verbal descriptions in constructing his famous world map of 1460.

BIBLIOGRAPHY

Caddeo, Rinaldo. *Le navigazioni atlantiche di Alvise da Ca'da Mosto, Antoniotto Usodimare e Niccoloso da Recco.* Milan, 1928.
"The Voyages of Cadamosto." *Hakluyt Society,* 2d ser., 80 (1937).

JOSEPH P. BYRNE

CANADA. The vision of Columbus and the encounter of the New and Old Worlds evidenced by his four voyages had pronounced influence on the evolution of Canada in the years 1497 to 1550. The Columbian age of Canada's development was one characterized by English, Portuguese, and French attempts to find a Northwest Passage to the rich and profitable lands of the east, including Cipangu (Japan), Cathay, and the Moluccas. Private and government interests in both England and France sought to follow up on Columbus's discoveries and to carve out spheres of influence in the New World once they came to realize that America was not Asia and that, in any event,

America offered resources, labor, foods, and places to settle. Equally important, the English and French entered into arrangements for the first time with the native peoples of Canada. From the natives they learned techniques of survival and travel in a land characterized by long, cold winters. The Europeans introduced diseases unknown to the natives of Canada. Some of the natives they kidnapped. They settled in lands previously occupied by native peoples. Not the least of the features of this cross-cultural encounter was the European desire, chiefly on the part of the French, to expand Christian mission activities. The French were the first to plant the cross on Canadian soil and to commence proselytizing.

On May 2, 1497, John Cabot (Giovanni Caboto), a Genoese navigator who had emigrated to England, sailed in *Mathew* from Bristol on an expedition sponsored by King Henry VII. Following the example of Columbus he sailed due west, but in more northerly latitudes. Cabot made a North American landfall on June 24, possibly at Cape Breton, Nova Scotia. He made an extensive coastal exploration and sailed along the eastern coast of Newfoundland before departing for Bristol. He reported large shoals of fish, and his observation further induced many European fishermen to undertake cod fishery off Newfoundland and Labrador. Bristol merchants had already been sending ships across the North Atlantic to search for the legendary island of Brasil, and some of them may have reached the area now known as Canada before Cabot.

Cabot's discovery is shown on the world map of Juan de la Cosa (1500), now in the Museo Naval, Madrid. Though far from accurate or complete as to details, it indicates English discoveries by showing English flags marking a certain portion of North America; moreover, it verbally attributes discovery to the English. Cabot's 1497 discovery of a New-Founde-Land led Bristol to equip five vessels in 1498 to return to the landfall of the previous year and to coast southward in search of Cipangu, which was thought to lie near at hand. John Cabot and the five ships were never heard of and were presumably lost at sea.

English exploration of Canada was then taken up by Sebastian Cabot, who had sailed with his father on the 1497 voyage. His 1508–1509 expedition, which is clouded in uncertainty, brought him fame if not notoriety. By his claim, he entered a strait, which opened between latitudes sixty-one and sixty-four degrees north, in search of a Northwest Passage and continued westward for about ten degrees of longitude. Cabot claimed that he then turned south into a large sea, which he believed to be the Pacific Ocean. Possibly he had entered the body of water later called Hudson Bay. For many years thereafter, the English concentrated on finding a Northeast Passage above Siberia, a search carried out by the Muscovy Company, of which Sebastian Cabot became the nominal governor. However, in 1575 Sir Martin Frobisher was granted an English license for an expedition to discover a Northwest Passage above Canada. He returned from the Canadian north with some pyrites, thinking they might be gold, and in 1577 he went for a second time, this time to west Greenland for ore. From a third voyage he brought back pyrites, which were truly fool's gold. Meanwhile, in 1578, Sir Humphrey Gilbert had published *A New Passage to Cathaia,* and eventually, when Frobisher's schemes came to nothing, Gilbert was given a license for colonial discovery. In 1583 he sailed to settle Newfoundland and claimed it for England, but died on his return voyage.

Meanwhile the Portuguese had undertaken voyages to seek a Northwest Passage. In 1500 Gaspar Côrte-Real sailed from Lisbon in two ships sponsored by King Manuel I to find the passage and possibly establish Portuguese sovereignty over land discovered by John Cabot in 1497. Côrte-Real sighted a coast that he took for Asia, but it was probably Greenland or possibly Newfoundland. In the following year, he sailed in three ships from Lisbon on a similar expedition and made a landfall probably on the Labrador coast. Two of the ships returned to Portugal with about fifty captive Inuit. Gaspar Côrte-Real was lost at sea, and in 1502 his brother Miguel sailed to Newfoundland to find the lost mariner and reached Newfoundland, but he, too, was never heard of again. In 1520 João Alvares Fagundes visited the vicinity of Newfoundland, Nova Scotia, and St. Pierre and Miquelon, and was given rights of colonization by Manuel. Fagundes may later have tried to settle in this area, but the details are altogether unclear. Portuguese fishermen increased their fishing off Newfoundland in consequence of these voyages.

In 1504 fishing vessels from Brittany began to visit the Grand Banks, and in 1506 Jean Denys, from Honfleur, made the first Norman fishing voyages to Newfoundland. French fishing activities then ensued from Rouen. In 1524, Giovanni da Verrazano sailed from Madeira on an expedition sponsored by Francis I of France. Landing near Cape Fear, North Carolina, he sailed northward until he reached about latitude fifty degrees north off Newfoundland. Ten years later, in 1534, Jacques Cartier, a Breton mariner, who had already sailed "to Brazil and the New Land," was entrusted by Francis I to sail to Newfoundland, where gold and other riches were said to exist. He located the south shore and islands of the Gulf of St. Lawrence. At Gaspé on July 24 he erected a cross, contrary to the wishes of the local chief, Donnacona. Shortly afterwards he captured the chief's two sons and left for the north, assuring Donnacona that they would be returned. On his return to France, Cartier convinced the French court that he had discovered an inland sea. His reported alliance with the local Indians and his optimistic perspectives concerning the possibilities of the passage in those latitudes led to his being allowed to return to the St. Lawrence. In 1535 he undertook his second voyage. With the help of two native guides, he entered the St. Lawrence River. He reached Stadacona, near present-day Québec City, and then the Indian village of Hochelaga, a palisaded town of fifty houses lying below a mountain that Cartier named Mount Royal. From its heights Cartier could see the great cataract known as the Lachine Rapids, which he believed to be the sea route to China; this was to become the highway of French penetration of the continental interior. In 1541 Cartier undertook his third voyage to Canada, with a colonization party under the leadership of Jean-François de La Rocque de Roberval. At Cap Rouge, near Stadacona, Cartier built a fort and nearby Roberval founded his colony, called Charlesbourg Royal. The heavy winter took its toll on the settlers: scurvy, famine, and rebellion were the results, and the colony survived only with native assistance to combat scurvy. Cartier and Roberval did not remain in Canada. The iron pyrites they found were not gold and the mica was not diamonds. They realized too that no easy passage to China existed.

French interest in Canada lay dormant for half a century and French attempts at settlement were not resumed until Samuel de Champlain, a geographer and cartographer, established a colony in the Bay of Fundy in 1604, moving it to Québec in 1608 to plant the first permanent French settlement in the area now known as Canada. Between Cartier and Champlain the French undertook several fishing and fur-trading expeditions, depending on the Indians for help in fur trading. Champlain's 1612 map offers the first reasonably accurate representation of Canada.

In terms of international law Spain protested to France and also to Rome about Cartier's voyages, claiming that

MAP OF QUÉBEC. Showing Jacques Cartier, Indians, and European settlers. From the Vallard Atlas, 1547.

the lands west of the Line of Demarcation belonged to Spain. Francis I replied that "to pass by and to discover by eye is no title of possession." Pope Paul III did not object to France's claim, perhaps because he needed French support against Spain's dominant power, and because Cartier's third expedition was sent under a commission to extend the Christian faith in lands not already inhabited by any Christian prince. In this way France penetrated lands that Spain thought reserved for itself.

[See also *Northwest Passage.*]

BIBLIOGRAPHY

Cooke, Alan, and Clive Holland. *The Exploration of Northern Canada 500 to 1920: A Chronology.* Toronto, 1978.
The Dictionary of Canadian Biography. Vol. 1. Toronto, 1966.
Hoffman, Bernard G. *Cabot to Cartier: Sources for a Historical Ethnography of Northeastern North America.* Toronto, 1961.
Morison, Samuel Eliot. *The European Discovery of America: The Northern Voyages, A.D. 500–1600.* New York, 1971.
Oleson, Tryggvi J. *Early Voyages and Northern Approaches, 1000–1632.* Toronto, 1963.
Williamson, James A., ed. *The Cabot Voyages and Bristol Discovery under Henry VII.* Cambridge, 1962.

BARRY M. GOUGH

CANARY ISLANDS.

CANARY ISLANDS. The Canary Islands are located between latitudes 27°30'N and 29°30'N and between longitudes 13°20'W and 18°10'W. This places them between 145 and 485 kilometers (90 and 300 miles) west of the southernmost extension of the Moroccan coast, about 485 kilometers (300 miles) south of the Portuguese Madeira Islands, and about 1,695 kilometers (1,050 miles) northeast of the Cape Verde Islands. The Canaries were known to European sailors before 1300, but their conquest and colonization by Spain were not accomplished until the period 1477 to 1497. The seven larger islands that make up the archipelago are Tenerife, Gran Canaria, Fuerteventura, Lanzarote, La Palma, Gomera, and Hierro (Ferro). The smaller named islands are Alegranza, Graciosa, Lobos, Roque del Este, Roque del Oeste, and Montaña Clara. The western islands of Hierro, Gomera, La Palma, and Tenerife have the most rainfall and the most varied topography. The eastern islands of Lanzarote and Fuerteventura have low relief and are quite arid; their climate is a westward extension of the Sahara Desert.

The strategic importance of the Canary Islands for the early explorers lay in their location about six to ten days' sail from Spain. The Canaries provided a convenient stopping point to make repairs and provision ships for westward voyages to the New World. The waters between Spain and the Canary Islands are frequently rough, but the southward Canary Current speeded the passage from

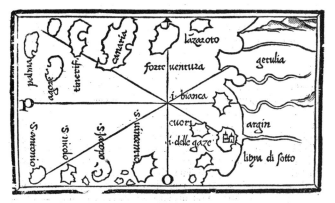

MAP OF THE CANARY ISLANDS. From Benedetto Bordone's *Isolario.* Venice, 1528. NATIONAL MARITIME MUSEUM, GREENWICH

Spain. Throughout the year, the Canary Islands lie in the northeast trade winds.

Columbus stopped at the Canary Islands on each of his four westward voyages. On his first voyage, he repaired the rudder of *Pinta* and rerigged *Niña* to a square rig for efficient westward travel.

BIBLIOGRAPHY

Hastenrath, Stefan, and Peter J. Lamb. *Climatic Atlas of the Tropical Atlantic and Eastern Pacific Oceans.* Madison, Wis., 1977.
McAlister, Lyle N. *Spain and Portugal in the New World, 1492–1700.* Minneapolis, 1984.
Morison, Samuel Eliot. *Admiral of the Ocean Sea: A Life of Christopher Columbus.* 2 vols. Boston, 1942.

COLLEEN A. LEARY

CANNIBALISM.

CANNIBALISM. Cannibals were reported by Columbus during his first two voyages. He claimed that the Taíno Indians spoke of *canibales, caribales, caniba, canima, cariba, caribe, cariby,* and *carib.* These words, their European derivatives (French, *Caraïbe;* English, *cannibal* and *Caribbean* as well as Shakespeare's *Caliban;* among others) and the tribal or language names *Kalina, Calinago,* and *Galibí* are based on related Indian words that evidently implied ferocity and perhaps enmity. Columbus understood that the Indians of the Greater Antilles applied this name to their enemies in the Lesser Antilles, whom they accused of being eaters of human flesh. The accusation confirmed a common European preconception about savages and barbarians. Spanish law soon, in 1503, adopted the principle that cannibalism of itself justified war against its practitioners and, moreover, that cannibals were the only Indians who could be enslaved. In light of these functions, as well as the common human tendency to accuse strangers and enemies of atrocities, accounts of cannibalism require careful evaluation.

It is doubtful that any human society has ever engaged in customary cannibalism for purely dietary or subsistence reasons. But it is, on the other hand, certain that many societies, including some in Europe in the sixteenth and even the eighteenth centuries, have engaged in customary cannibalism within narrowly defined limits as to victims, body parts and amounts eaten, and occasions or motives.

The customary cannibalism in the Americas that is best understood, because of the quality and number of qualified observers, is that of the Tupinambás of coastal Brazil during the sixteenth century. Each Tupinambá province or territorial group of villages was engaged in continual warfare with its neighbors, most of whom shared the same language and customs. The purpose of warfare was the capture of prisoners, all of whom were eventually sacrificed and eaten. The treatment of captured enemies was governed by heavily theatrical ritual, which was also certainly full of religious significance, though only hints of the latter are preserved in the documentary sources. There were two principal occasions for the ceremonies: when the captive first arrived at the captors' village, and when he was finally killed and eaten. The two occasions were separated by a period of months and often years. The length of his captivity was the only element of his fate that was not known to the captive, and surely it was psychologically important that this should be so, enabling the captive to play out his role properly until the end came. Only at the beginning and end of the captivity was the victim displayed, taunted, and forcefully reminded of his future. The women undertook particularly important parts in these ceremonies, and the contrasting ritual duties of the sexes is so prominent that it is likely that the treatment of the occasional female captives was also quite different, although the sources say little about these captives except that they too were eaten.

On his arrival at the captor's village, the captive was made to clean the grave of the person whose death his own was now to avenge. He announced to the women met on the path, "I, your future food, have arrived." The men and the women chose the parts of his body each would eat, and often thereafter taunted him with reminders. After his initial reception, the captive was incorporated almost completely into the daily life of the village. He was in effect adopted, replacing the one whose grave he had cleaned. The hammock, weapons, and other property of the deceased were given him, and as wife he was assigned the widow, or else a sister or daughter of his captor or a woman the latter requested for him. Such a marriage was considered prestigious and was not refused. Although it is said that this wife was to keep him from escaping, there was little need for such a guardian. His

own people would not have accepted him should he have returned. Considering him cowardly and believing that his escape implied that they were not strong enough to avenge him, they would probably have killed him. If the captive's wife bore him any children, these too were considered enemies in this patrilineal society, and they were killed and eaten before their father was.

The final ceremonies lasted from three to five days. They included a symbolic recapture and a mock battle in which the captive's movements were constrained by ropes while he shot blunt arrows and threw rocks, potsherds, and hard fruits. At the execution, the victim, the executioner, and even the sacrificial club were heavily decorated. The victim and the executioner engaged in a formalized dialogue emphasizing revenge and threats of revenge. The executioner finally killed him with a blow to the nape of the neck, despite the prisoner's dodging and resisting while he was held by a cord around his waist. The body was then butchered, and the women cooked it, grilling the flesh on a barbecue frame and boiling the entrails. The entire body was eaten, with the possible exception of the brain. Everyone present, guests and villagers, from the oldest to the youngest, had to eat some of the captive. Nursing babies were fed by smearing the victim's blood on their mothers' nipples. If there was insufficient meat to feed everyone, a broth was made so all had at least a taste. There were a few restrictions: the genitalia could be eaten only by someone of the opposite sex, and the executioner had to disgorge what he ate.

The key to understanding Tupinambá cannibalism is their need for vengeance, as they often explained to European inquirers. As Michel de Montaigne wrote in his essay "Of Cannibals" (1580), after interviewing French observers and some Tupinambás brought to Normandy, "it is not, as some think, for nourishment, as it was among the ancient Scythians; it is to carry out the most extreme revenge." The dead had to be avenged, whether they had died in combat or otherwise. The sacrifice was thus a funerary rite, required to appease the spirits of the dead. Ingesting the enemy may also have been a way of regaining and reincorporating the substance and qualities of one's relatives whom the captive had previously eaten. The religious nature of the custom is also shown by the severe restrictions placed on the executioner. He changed his name; he was isolated as though he were ill or in mourning; and he underwent a long period of rigorous fasting. Upon completion of his task, he gained prestige and authority.

Whether or not the Island Caribs accused of cannibalism by their Taíno enemies were in fact eaters of human flesh is a topic of debate. Very likely they practiced endocannibalism, that is, the ingestion of parts of deceased relatives as part of funerary rites. Many South

EUROPEAN DEPICTION OF CANNIBALISM IN THE AMERICAS. The sensational appeal of such images can be supposed from the number produced and their graphic intensitv. This engraving is from Caspar Plautius's *Navigatio in Novum Mundum*. Many similar images were published by Théodor de Bry.   LIBRARY OF CONGRESS, RARE BOOK DIVISION

American peoples are documented as ingesting the ground-up bones or ashes of cremated relatives, and some, such as the Guayakí of Paraguay, ate the roasted and boiled flesh of their deceased relatives in order to prevent the souls of the dead from entering their surviving relatives and causing illness and death. The material evidence of funerary endocannibalism and other non-European funerary practices may well have been misinterpreted by Columbus and others as evidence for exocannibalism, the eating of enemies and the hunting of humans in order to eat them. But there does seem to be good evidence for Island Caribs, mainland Caribs, and perhaps Arawaks and others in Venezuela and the Guianas practicing ritualized cannibalism with selected body parts of war captives in a manner and with motives not greatly dissimil   to those of the Tupinambás.

Customary cannibalism is also documented as a minor part of the elaborate sacrificial complex of the Aztecs. The victims were war captives or slaves who were ritually constituted as gods. When they were sacrificed, their bodies were sacred objects and their arms and legs were often eaten. The gods' flesh was thereby consumed as a sort of communion.

Among North American Indians, there is good evidence for the practice of cannibalism as a part of the ritual of the torture of war captives by the Iroquois and Hurons in what is now New York and Ontario in the seventeenth century and before. Here the principal motive seems to have been the incorporation of some of the good qualities of the enemy. It is probable that only particular parts of the body were ingested, rather than essentially the whole body as in Tupinambá practice.

BIBLIOGRAPHY

Abler, Thomas S. "Iroquois Cannibalism: Fact not Fiction." *Ethnohistory* 27, no. 4 (1980): 309–316.

Forsyth, Donald W. "The Beginnings of Brazilian Anthropology: Jesuits and Tupinamba Cannibalism." *Journal of Anthropological Research* 39, no. 2 (1983): 147–178.

Friederici, Georg. "Caribe." In *Amerikanistisches Wörterbuch*. University of Hamburg; Abhandlungen aus dem Gebiet der Auslandskunde, vol. 53. Series B: Völkerkunde, Kulturgeschichte und Sprachen, vol. 29. Hamburg, 1947.

Henríquez Ureña, Pedro. "Caribe." In *Para la historia de los indigenismos*. Biblioteca de dialectología Hispanoamericano, supp. 3. Buenos Aires, 1938.

Métraux, Alfred. "L'anthropophagie rituelle des Tupinamba." In *Religions et magies indiennes d'Amérique du Sud*, pp. 45–78. Paris, 1967.

Sahlins, Marshall. "Culture as Protein and Profit." *New York Review of Books* 25, no. 18 (November 23, 1978).

Sahlins, Marshall. "Cannibalism: An Exchange." *New York Review of Books* 26, no. 4 (March 22, 1979).

Whitehead, Neil L. "Carib Cannibalism, the Historical Evidence." *Journal de la Société des Américanistes* 70 (1984): 69–88.

WILLIAM C. STURTEVANT

CÃO, DIOGO

CÃO, DIOGO (fl. 1480–1486), Portuguese navigator. From 1480 on, the *mare clausum* (closed sea) policy in the Gulf of Guinea was reinforced by Prince João of Portugal with coast guard squadrons. Diogo Cão appears for the first time in the historical record as a naval captain in one of these missions. These squadrons had orders to execute summarily any intruders found south of the parallel of the Canary Islands as far as a place called Mina, where gold was being extracted.

In 1481, the "perfect prince" ascended the throne as João II and immediately issued orders to Diogo de Azambuja to construct a castle in Mina, in order to exercise control over the gold trade. The castle of São Jorge da Mina (St. George of Elmina), which was finished in about 1482, became the principal source of the precious metal in the fifteenth century, thereby giving Portugal supremacy in this profitable trade. As part of the same strategy, João II ordered the first voyage of geographical exploration commanded by Diogo Cão (1482–1484) to sail beyond the then known limits of the African coast, south of the Gulf of Guinea, below the equator.

Sailing in caravels, Diogo Cão ventured along the coast and reached the Rio Zaire and, farther south, a place called Cape Lobo, located on the coast of Angola. Although this was the farthest point he reached on his first voyage, he thought he had discovered the southern tip of Africa and reached the waters of the Indian Ocean. On the way he made contact with the Kingdom of the Kongo; he established friendly relations with the Kongo people and brought back to Portugal some of the local inhabitants. As a sign that he had passed through these lands, he left some impressive inscriptions engraved on the rocks of Ielala, on the banks of the Rio Zaire, and set up stone pillars at the mouth of the river and at Cape Lobo.

In the meantime, while the first voyage of Diogo Cão was under way, a Portuguese adventurer, João Afonso de Aveiro, was sent overland to explore the interior of Africa, starting from the coasts of Benin and present-day Nigeria. He returned in 1485 with the news that "Ogané" was near. This was an African potentate whom the Portuguese identified possibly with the legendary Prester John of the Indies.

The combined results of the explorations of Diogo Cão and João Afonso de Aveiro may have led the Portuguese to believe that they were about to reach India. In the same year, the Portuguese ambassador Vasco Fernandes de Lucena, in a speech given before the pope in Rome, stated that Portuguese ships had sailed beyond the Promonto-rium Prassum of Ptolemaic geography and discovered the southern tip of Africa.

This must certainly have been one of the reasons the Portuguese king at that time rejected Columbus's proposal to sail west to India. The Portuguese knew that the estimate of the size of the globe on which Columbus based his figures (in accordance with Ptolemy and other written sources) was wrong, and they were above all interested in an African route to the Indies.

During the years 1485–1486, by order of the king, Diogo Cão undertook his second voyage of exploration. Still sailing in caravels, he passed beyond the limit of his first voyage, returned the Kongo people to their homeland, and reached a point on the African coast called Serra Parda. Here he realized he had been mistaken, and that the coastline continued farther south—India was not yet near. Nevertheless, he placed a stone pillar at a point on the coast called Cabo do Padrão (Cape Cross, in present-day Namibia). It is not known whether he died there (as

MONUMENT (*PADRÃO*) OF CAPE CROSS. Placed by Diogo Cão at latitude 21 degrees, 47 minutes south, on the Namibian coast. Such stone monuments were carried on board by Portuguese navigators and were erected to indicate Portuguese claims of dominion. MUSEUM FÜR DEUTSCHE GESCHICHTE, BERLIN

some authors say, basing their judgment on a doubtful reading of a legend on the map of Henricus Martellus) or returned to Portugal. In any case, there is no further reference to him. If he did return to Portugal, it is probable that the king did not forgive him for the high expectations raised by the first voyage but dashed by the second.

In the meantime, in 1488, João II sent Columbus (who was in Spain at the time) an enigmatic letter, assuring him of a safe return to Portugal where his services would be appreciated. This may have reflected the king's disappointment over the results of Diogo Cão's voyages and a subsequent decision to consider the alternate route proposed by Columbus. Or it could have been a diversionary maneuver—to show interest in the western route and thus induce his Castilian rivals to support Columbus's project, leaving the southern route free for the Portuguese to explore at their own pace.

In any case, the Portuguese expedition headed by Bartolomeu Dias departed in 1487. It followed immediately upon Diogo Cão's voyages and finally succeeded in going beyond the southern tip of Africa. When in December 1488 Dias returned to Portugal with the news of his discovery, either Columbus or his brother Bartolomé was probably present when the results of the voyage were announced to the king. With this news, the Portuguese Crown may well have lost any continuing interest in Columbus's plan, for it was then that Columbus last departed for Castile, where he finally found royal support for his westward project.

The voyages of Diogo Cão were consequently of great importance. They brought Portuguese explorations to a new phase and resulted in João II's decision to pursue an African route to India. They also instigated the manufacture of cartographic charts, some of which have survived to this day. The oldest extant signed Portuguese map is the chart of Peter Reinel (c. 1485). It is a direct representation of the explorations of Diogo Cão. Other important cartographic charts reflecting his voyages were prepared in those years, namely the map of Henricus Martellus (c. 1490) and the globe of Martin Behaim (c. 1492), the latter containing specific information about Cão's explorations, including the location of the first stone pillar set up by the navigator on his second voyage.

BIBLIOGRAPHY

Barros, João de, and Diogo do Couto. *Da Asia de João de Barros e de Diogo do Couto.* 24 vols. Lisbon, 1778–1788.
Campos, Viraiato. *Viagem de Diogo Cão e de Bartolomeu Dias.* Lisbon, 1966.
Cordeiro, Luciano. "Descobertas e descobridores: Diogo Cão." *Boletim da Sociedade de Geographia de Lisboa* (1892).
Cordeiro, Luciano. *Diogo Cão.* Lisbon, 1971.
Lewis, Thomas. "The Old Kingdom of Kongo." *Geographical Journal* 31 (1908): 589–615.
Pina, Rui de. *Chronica d'elrey D. João II.* Edited by M. Lopes de Almeida. Porto, 1977.
Prestage, Edgar. *The Portuguese Pioneers.* Pp. 206–211. London, 1933.
Ravenstein, E. G. "The Voyage of Diogo Cão and Bartolomeu Dias, 1482–88." *Geographical Journal* 16 (1890): 625–655.

ALFREDO PINHEIRO MARQUES
Translated from Portuguese by Rebecca Catz

CAPE OF GOOD HOPE. The Cape of Good Hope, located on the southwest coast of Africa at 34°21′S, 18°29′E near Cape Town in the Republic of South Africa, was first rounded by Bartolomeu Dias in 1488. This voyage was the culmination of over one hundred years of voyages of exploration by Portuguese sailors south along the west coast of Africa. It confirmed hopes that India could be reached by sailing around Africa. Vasco da Gama rounded the Cape of Good Hope in 1497 on the first sea voyage to India from Europe.

Rounding the Cape of Good Hope on a sailing ship was a practical as well as a symbolic victory. A ship sailing southward and eastward had to fight not only adverse head winds but currents as well. The cool Benguela Current flows northward along the west coast of southern Africa, and the warm Agulhas Current flows westward around the southern coast of Africa. Storms with gale force winds in the prevailing westerlies off the Cape of Good Hope can generate waves of twenty feet or higher. In fact, Dias originally named the cape Cabo Tormentoso (Cape of Storms). When no storms are present, the coastal region can experience frequent heavy fog.

Columbus was in Lisbon when Dias returned from the first rounding of the Cape of Good Hope. The success of Dias ended King João II's interest in Columbus's plan to sail westward and resulted in Columbus's return to Spain.

BIBLIOGRAPHY

Bowditch, Nathaniel. *American Practical Navigator.* Washington, D.C., 1966.
Morison, Samuel Eliot. *Admiral of the Ocean Sea: A Life of Christopher Columbus.* 2 vols. Boston, 1942.
Rudloff, Willy. *World-Climates.* Stuttgart, 1981.

COLLEEN A. LEARY

CAPE VERDE ISLANDS. The Cape Verde Islands, known officially as the República de Cabo Verde, are located between latitudes 14°48′N and 17°13′N and longitudes 22°41′W and 25°22′W, about 640 kilometers (400 miles) west of the bulge of the African coast at northern

Senegal. Between 1455 and 1462, the first Europeans to discover the Cape Verdes claimed the uninhabited islands for Portugal. The first settlers arrived in 1462, and the Cape Verde Islands remained part of Portugal until the republic was founded in 1975.

Located about 1,700 kilometers (1,050 miles) southwest of the Canary Islands, the Cape Verdes provided a safe anchorage for ships traveling to the New World, as well as to and around Africa. The islands lie near the equatorward edge of the northeasterly trade winds, in a region where the ocean current flows southwestward. In spite of their name, the Cape Verdes have a dry desertlike climate similar to that of western Africa.

The ten principal islands of the archipelago are oriented in a rough V shape with the point facing toward Africa. The islands are, in order of decreasing size, São Tiago, Santo Antão, Boa Vista, Fogo, São Nicolão, Maio, São Vicente, Sal, Brava, and Santa Luzia. Although the average elevation of the islands is only 800 meters (2,600 feet) above sea level, the islands are actually the tops of undersea mountains. Fogo has an active volcano, and the adjacent island, Brava, experienced tremors and exhibited signs of volcanic activity in the recent past.

On his third voyage of discovery to the New World, Columbus traveled from the Canary Islands to the Cape Verde Islands before crossing the Atlantic to land on the coast of South America.

BIBLIOGRAPHY

Duncan, T. Bentley. *Atlantic Islands: Madeira, the Azores and the Cape Verdes in Seventeenth-Century Commerce and Navigation.* Chicago, 1972.

Morison, Samuel Eliot. *Admiral of the Ocean Sea: A Life of Christopher Columbus.* 2 vols. Boston, 1942.

COLLEEN A. LEARY

CAPITULATIONS OF SANTA FE. See *Santa Fe Capitulations.*

CARIBS. See *Indian America,* articles on *Island Caribs* and *Arawaks and Caribs.*

CARLOS I. For discussion of the Spanish king Carlos I, see *Charles V.*

CARPINI, GIOVANNI DA PIAN DEL (c. 1180–1252), Franciscan friar and papal envoy to the Mongol khan. Carpini was among the first Westerners to visit the Mongol leader in his home territory. A contemporary of

Saint Francis of Assisi and a native of Umbria, Carpini had become a Franciscan by about 1220. For twenty-five years he served in Franciscan provincial offices in Germany, Spain, and perhaps Barbary. Pope Innocent IV chose Carpini, then about sixty years old, to lead the first of several official missions to the khan, whose fierce armies had invaded Christian eastern Europe, resulting in widespread fear and destruction. Carpini and two other friars were to observe the nature of the Mongol territories, reach the Grand Khan, and register protests against his invasions; they also hoped to gain his aid against Islam.

After leaving Lyons in April 1245, the friars reached Kiev early in 1246 and Karakorum in Mongolia, near the khan's camp, on July 22, 1246. They witnessed the enthronement of a new khan on August 24 and were presented to him formally. In November the khan drafted an imperious reply in Mongol, Arabic, and Latin and sent the Westerners on their way. Their winter journey was filled with hardship, but they reached Kiev in June 1247 and Lyons, where the pope was waiting, seventeen months later. For his services, the pontiff rewarded Carpini with an archbishopric in Dalmatia.

Carpini's formal report, contained in his treatise *Historia Mongolorum,* or *Liber Tartarorum,* contains observations on the territories they traveled through, and the customs, religions, history, and character of the East. He comments on the policies and tactics of the Mongol leadership and suggests ways to oppose them. His work is a solid report, largely devoid of fantasy, on lands that had been closed to Europeans for centuries.

Western leaders regarded the Mongol empire not only as a threat but also as a field for evangelization, a possible trading partner, and a powerful counterweight to Islam. Carpini's perceptive observations were widely circulated; they were abstracted in Vincent of Beauvais's popular *Speculum historiale* (c. 1260; printed in 1473) and alluded to in Roger Bacon's *Opus maius* (c. 1266). The complete work was not published, however, until the nineteenth century.

BIBLIOGRAPHY

Dawson, Christopher, ed. *The Mission to Asia.* Toronto, 1986.

Guzman, G. G. "The Encyclopaedist Vincent of Beauvais and His Mongol Extracts from John of Piano Carpino and Simon of Saint-Quentin." *Speculum* 49 (1974).

Phillips, J. R. S. *The Medieval Expansion of Europe.* Oxford and New York, 1988.

Rachewiltz, I. de. *Papal Envoys to the Great Khans.* London, 1971.

Spuler, Bertold. *History of the Mongols, Based on Eastern and Western Accounts of the 13th and 14th Centuries.* Translated by Helen and Stuart Drummond. Berkeley, 1972.

JOSEPH P. BYRNE

CARTIER, JACQUES (1491–1557), French navigator and explorer. Little is known of Cartier's youth and early career. He was born in Saint-Malo (Brittany) where he rose to the position of master pilot, in part because of his marriage to Catherine Des Granges, daughter of the high constable of the city, in 1520. When King Francis I in 1532 expressed an interest in furthering the exploration of North America begun by Giovanni da Verrazano, the bishop of Saint-Malo, Jean Le Veneur, recommended Cartier, who, he said, had already visited Brazil and the Newfoundland fishery. Of Cartier's navigational skills there is no doubt, having begun his career as a *mousse* (ship's boy) when only thirteen, rising soon to the rank of novice and then sailor. The recommendation was confirmed the following year when Le Veneur obtained from Rome an interpretation of the papal bull of 1493 allowing France to move into territories not already occupied by Spain or Portugal.

Cartier was familiar with the New World that he would be commissioned to explore. There can be little doubt he had contacts with Breton and Norman fishermen who had been coming to Newfoundland waters since at least the late fifteenth century. His accounts also included accurate observations on Brazil. In 1534 he sailed directly to Cape Bonavista and the Strait of Belle Isle as if to a familiar rendezvous.

The royal commission granted him in 1534 ordered him "to discover certain islands and lands where it is said that a great quantity of gold, and other precious things, are to be found." The French Crown obviously hoped to gain access to American treasure and a sea route to the Orient while leaving the costs of initial investigation to private maritime interests. The first expedition, consisting of two sixty-ton ships and a sixty-one-member crew, left Saint-Malo on April 20, 1534, and crossed the Atlantic in twenty days, a remarkably short transatlantic voyage. Cartier's account of his entry into the Gulf of St. Lawrence makes clear that the northern bays and islands were known, frequented, and assigned Breton and Norman names. He even met a fishing vessel returning to La Rochelle. Cartier had taken the route of western European fishermen and marine hunters who in turn probably followed the route beyond Icelandic fishing grounds first navigated by the Vikings. Since the north shore of the gulf, apart from offering havens to vessels in case of storms and supplies of fresh water, seemed uninhabitable, Cartier called it "the land God gave to Cain" (it was popularly believed that Cain was condemned to wander everlastingly in the desolate regions of the earth until the end of the world).

Cartier then headed southward along the west coast of Newfoundland, then westward to the Magdalen Islands and the mainland coastline, searching for a passageway to the Orient. At Chaleur Bay he met some Micmacs with whom he engaged in some brisk trading. Farther north, at Gaspé, he encountered a summer fishing encampment of friendly Laurentian Iroquois with whom he bartered goods sailors normally stocked for such encounters—beads, mirrors, red caps, needles, knives—in return for well-worn beaver cloaks. It was obvious that the natives who came brandishing furs on the end of staves to attract European attention were not novices to such exchanges. His accounts mention at least eleven crosses erected on headlands to serve as navigational aids, but the ten-meter cross erected at Penouille Point, Québec, bearing the arms of the king, appears to have been intended as a formal *prise de possession*. The Iroquoian headman Donnacona so interpreted the ceremony of the erection of the cross and gestured that he wanted it removed as the territory belonged to his people. The chief's sons, Domagaya and Taignoagny, were forcibly taken aboard Cartier's vessel, which headed northward to Anticosti Island but missed the entrance to the St. Lawrence River. These young men subsequently served as interpreters and guides to their permanent base at Stadacona on the St. Lawrence River. By mid-August Cartier thought it advisable to return to France, but he was convinced that a second expedition would enable him to penetrate far to the west to discover fabulous riches.

He was back in Saint-Malo on September 5 and within two months his optimism was shared by Francis I, who granted him a second commission, a promotion, and a subsidy of three thousand livres for the undertaking. The second expedition set out with 110 men and three vessels—*Grande Hermine* commanded by Cartier himself, *Petite Hermine* commanded by a brother-in-law, and *Emérillon* by a compatriot. On board were Domagaya and Taignoagny, who had learned some French during their almost nine-month sojourn in France. This crossing took fifty days, and it was mid-August when the Iroquois captives guided Cartier along "the route toward Canada." He noted passing the "very deep and rapid" Saguenay River and the Ile d'Orléans "where the territory of Canada begins." Donnacona, happy to see his sons again, received the French hospitably. Cartier anchored his ships below the village of Stadacona. He was determined to go farther upstream, though his hosts tried to dissuade him by gifts and then by a display of sorcery. But Cartier would not be deterred from his search for the western passage. With thirty men on long boats he reached the Island of Montréal. Here he was received at the fortified village of Hochelaga, which was surrounded by cornfields near a mountain which he named Mont-Royal. From its summit he could see the widening of the Ottawa River where it joined the St. Lawrence. He was told it led to a "freshwater sea" and to the kingdom of Saguenay where all manner of exotic goods could be had.

When Cartier returned to his base camp he found his men building a fort to defend themselves against increasingly hostile Stadaconans. A harsh winter set in by mid-November bringing scurvy in its wake, which killed twenty-five of Cartier's men. Fortunately Cartier was able to learn the Iroquoian remedy of making an infusion from the bark and needles of the *annedda*, probably white cedar. When spring came, Cartier captured Donnacona and his sons and sailed off to France with seven additional captives. He reached France on July 16, 1536, after an absence of fourteen months.

In October 1540 Cartier was named captain general of a third expedition, but in January 1541 the commission was annulled in favor of a Protestant nobleman, Jean-François de La Rocque de Roberval, who was named commander of a colonization venture with the commoner Cartier as his subaltern. Roberval authorized Cartier to proceed ahead of him with a first contingent of settlers, which he did on May 23, 1541. None of the Iroquois captives survived to return to Canada. Although initially well received at Stadacona, Cartier thought it wise to establish his fortified base upstream at Rivière du Cap-Rouge, which he called Charlesbourg-Royal. In September Cartier made a second trip to the island of Montréal and visited the Lachine Rapids in anticipation of venturing into the upper country the following year. He never realized this objective because relations at Stadacona deteriorated. Charlesbourg-Royal was under constant attack from the natives, who were now decimated by an epidemic, probably of French origin. No fewer than thirty-five Frenchmen had been killed by June 1542, and it was decided to abandon the settlement.

Cartier met the inbound Roberval contingent at St. John's, Newfoundland, but with his vessels loaded with precious metals and having no desire to face the Laurentian Iroquois again, he slipped away under cover of darkness for France. His gold proved to be iron pyrites and his diamonds only quartz. Though he was not punished for having abandoned the Roberval colony, he was never entrusted with another major undertaking. He lived in bourgeois comfort on his country estate at Limoilou during the next fifteen years, until his death at the age of sixty-six during an outbreak of the plague. His widow survived him by eighteen years and as they had no children his papers and charts went to his nephews.

The accounts of Cartier's voyages were published piecemeal: the account of the first voyage was first published in Italian by Ramusio in 1565; the account of the second was published anonymously in French in 1545; and the account of the third was published in a fragmentary English version by Hakluyt in 1600. The Franciscan André Thévet obtained much information about the continent and its native peoples directly from Cartier;

Sebastian Cabot also visited him at Saint-Malo; Rabelais made use of information about Canada in the writing of *Pantagruel*.

Cartier's enduring contribution is the inauguration of the St. Lawrence approach to French exploitation and colonization in North America. The geographical information he provided was soon reproduced on contemporary maps. He also extended the territories of the fishermen, whalers, walrus hunters, and eventually the fur traders.

BIBLIOGRAPHY

Biggar, H. P. *A Collection of Documents Relating to Jacques Cartier and the Sieur de Roberval*. Ottawa, 1930.

Braudel, Fernand, ed. *Le monde de Jacques Cartier*. Montréal, 1984.

Hoffman, Bernard G. *Cabot to Cartier: Sources for a Historical Ethnography of Northeastern North America, 1497–1550*. Toronto, 1961.

Trudel, Marcel. *Les vaines tentatives, 1524–1603*. Vol. 1 of *Histoire de la Nouvelle-France*. Montréal, 1963.

CORNELIUS J. JAENEN

CARTOGRAPHY. Maps were a nearly indispensable part of the process by which the Europeans settled what they called the New World. Not only were they necessary for navigators, who used them to negotiate the new seas, with their many islands and reef-protected shores, but they also became an important part of the process by which, back in the Old World, kings and queens and statesmen decided where next to send their ships, sailors, and colonists.

Nor were the newcomers the only ones to use maps, for throughout most of what became known as America the indigenous peoples had cartographic skills. In the north they drew maps on such materials as deerskins and walrus tusks, and they made sketches in sand to give cartographic information to the Europeans. Similar mapping traditions existed throughout Central and South America. They were most developed in the Aztec kingdom of Mexico, where maps were drawn showing not only space, but also time, in the form of accompanying genealogical tables. The only area from which no maps have survived seems to be the Caribbean. It may be, though, that some of the region's numerous surviving rock carvings will one day be shown to be maps, and it is highly likely that the Caribbean Amerindians, like those on the rest of the continent, sketched rough maps in the sand.

The Cartographic Tradition in Europe

By the middle of the fifteenth century, three quite separate cartographic traditions had developed in Europe, and these were beginning to influence one another. First, there was the tradition of the medieval *mappamundi* (pl., *mappaemundi*), which went back at least to the eighth century. These became quite numerous from the twelfth century onward. Then, there were the portolan charts, highly accurate delineations of the Mediterranean coastline that emerged about 1300. Finally, there were the maps based on the geographical ideas of Ptolemy (Claudius Ptolemaeus), who lived about A.D. 200 and whose writings began to win new popularity in the early fifteenth century.

When Columbus began to study maps he was able to rely on these three traditions, each of which added something to his vision of the world. Curiously, he probably embarked in 1492 without having seen a globe, since the earliest European example seems to date from that very year, when an "Earth-apple" (as the Germans called it) was constructed in Nuremberg by Martin Behaim. Thereafter, many such globes were built, and they became an ornament of princely courts and libraries.

Mappaemundi. The *mappaemundi* varied greatly in style and detail, but they were nearly always roughly circular and oriented toward the east. The simplest fifteenth-century types are versions of a map that goes back to the eighth century. In these simple versions, the Ocean Sea, or "Mare Oceanum," surrounds the three continents, Asia, Europe, and Africa. Beneath the names of the continents are the names of the sons of Noah whose descendants peopled them: Sem for Asia, Jafeth for Europe, and Cham for Africa. A T-shaped body of water separates the continents, labelled "Great Sea" or "Mediterranean." In other maps of this kind, the stem of the T alone is the Mediterranean, while the left-hand branch is the Black Sea, and the right-hand branch the Red Sea. Obviously a map of this kind is highly schematic and is simply a way of keeping a general outline in one's head. Some historians of cartography compare these maps to modern maps of subway systems, which similarly try to give a general image of the system without pretending to offer accuracy in every part.

One such map is marked with the four cardinal points, "Oriens," "Occidens," "Meridies," and "Septentrio," and may be interpreted either as a flat disk or as a hemisphere. Most commentators agree that people of some learning in the Middle Ages considered the earth round, so these "T–O" maps, as they are called, should probably be envisaged as showing a hemisphere, which they would have called the *oikoumene*, or known world, as opposed to the unknown world, which presumably lay on the other side of it.

Some *mappaemundi* were much more elaborate. The map by Giovanni Leardo of Venice, drawn in 1452, shows the known world surrounded by the Ocean Sea. Jerusalem is in the center, with the Mediterranean Sea stretching away to the west (left) of it. The coastline of the countries

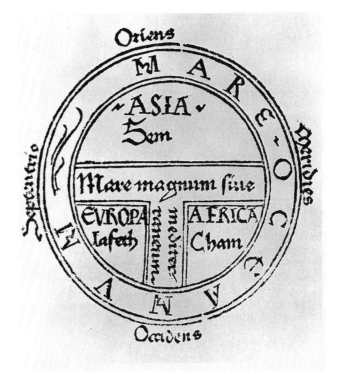

T-O MAP. Fifteenth-century printed version. From *Etymologiarum sive originum libri xx* by Isidore of Seville. Augsburg, 1472.

THE NEWBERRY LIBRARY, CHICAGO

bordering the Mediterranean is well delineated, as are the Black Sea and Red Sea. Outside the Mediterranean, to the west, the cartographer's knowledge becomes very sketchy; he has some idea of the West African coast but very little of the British Isles and none of Scandinavia. In the east, beyond the Red Sea, Arabia is well shown, but knowledge fades well before India is reached.

This remains a geography very strongly influenced by Christian traditions. The four Evangelists occupy the four corners of the Leardo parchment, with the lion for Mark, the bull for Luke, the angel for Matthew, and the eagle for John. In the extreme east of the map is the terrestrial paradise, named, in red capitals, the Paradixo Teresto. We can also identify Noah's Ark resting on Mount Ararat, the site of Mount Sinai, and the River Jordan. There are also elements that represent ideas from the classical world: to the north is a desert so cold that none could cross it ("Dixerte dexabitado per fredo"), and to the south another desert, this so hot as to defy entry ("Dixerto dexabitado per caldo"). This work by Leardo not only is a summary of the *mappamundi* tradition but also introduces elements from the other two strands of medieval cartographic tradition, the portolan charts and Ptolemaic geography.

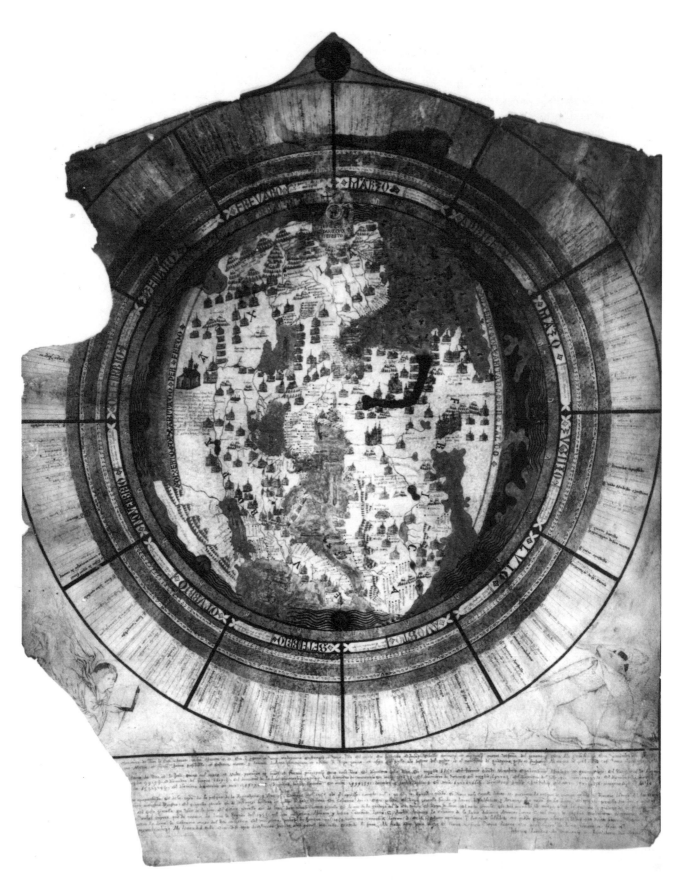

Portolan charts. The portolan chart is a cartographic type that, unlike most, seems to have appeared quite suddenly in almost perfect form. The first such chart known is called the Carte Pisane, because it seems to have originated at Pisa. It dates from about 1300. Its delineation of the Mediterranean Sea is a vast improvement on anything earlier that is known. Scholars have debated a good deal on how such perfection of outline was achieved so suddenly, and the best opinion seems to be that these charts resulted from a combination of established sailing directions (or portolanos) and use of the marine compass, which was beginning to appear in the Mediterranean. Putting these two elements together, the argument goes, allowed the chartmakers to achieve at once something like a perfect outline of the coasts with which they were most familiar.

In the 1456 portolan chart by Petrus Roselli not only the Mediterranean is shown with accuracy, but also the Atlantic coasts of France and Spain as well as the Black Sea. It also includes some Atlantic islands and a summary delineation of the British Isles, but the cartographer's knowledge comes to an abrupt end at the North Sea and at the western coast of Africa. There is very little internal detail—these are, after all, marine charts—and the place-names are written at right angles to the coast. Many islands are shown with a deep, opaque color. Flags fly over territories to indicate their sovereigns, and here and there important cities are shown in profile. These maps

GIOVANNI LEARDO'S WORLD MAP (facing page). From a manuscript of 1452. On the schematic representation (above), north is at top. On the original (facing page), north is at left. The schematic maps accompanying originals in this article are by Tom Willcockson of the Newberry Library, Chicago.

AMERICAN GEOGRAPHICAL SOCIETY COLLECTION, UNIVERSITY OF WISCONSIN, MILWAUKEE

often have scale bars and are covered with a latticework of lines. Originally they were designed to be rolled up on a wooden spindle, which would have been fixed to the right-hand edge of the piece of vellum.

Ptolemaic Maps. The geographical and cartographic knowledge of the ancient world was summarized in the works of Ptolemy, who lived at Alexandria. Ptolemy seems to have been the compiler of a work known as *Geography*, which is essentially a very large listing of the geographical coordinates (latitude and longitude) of many places in the world known to Greece and Rome; it also gives instructions as to how these listings can be used to make maps.

The very idea that any place on the earth's surface could be represented by two sets of figures gives Ptolemy his extraordinary importance. Maps do not have to be constructed in this way—neither the *mappamundi* nor the portolan chart was—but if the coordinates are known, then it is possible to set about recording the shape of the round earth on flat paper in accordance not merely with pragmatic observations but with some kind of mathematical theory. Of course, there is an almost infinite number of possible "projections," but the significance of Ptolemy's system is that his coordinates make it possible to apply the same basic information to any one of these projections.

After the fall of the Roman Empire the ideas of Ptolemy fell into obscurity. Some of his ideas were taken up by Muslim cartographers, for there was a thriving cartography within the empire of Islam. From the twelfth century onward, however, the people of western Europe, and especially of Italy, proved more and more open to ancient learning, which they set about to recover in all its aspects. Roman law was among the first disciplines to be rediscovered; then followed the poetry of Virgil, the physics of Aristotle, the medicine of Galen, and so forth. The geography of Ptolemy was another branch of antique learning recovered during the Renaissance; the process began early in the fifteenth century, when manuscripts of his geography began to circulate among the learned.

One of these Ptolemaic manuscripts, composed about 1460, shows a segment of the world floating, as it were, in space, while angelic heads blow winds upon it. Around the top and bottom edges are the figures of longitude, running from zero at the left to 180 degrees at the extreme right; this is thus meant to represent half the world in longitude. Figures of latitude climb up and down the right-hand edge of the map, beginning at the sharp bend that marks the equator.

Ptolemy's outline of the Mediterranean is markedly less perfect than on the portolan charts. But he shows Europe rather convincingly; indeed, it is hard to imagine how a person living in Alexandria in the second century could have had so accurate a knowledge of the British Isles. Asia Minor and Arabia are also well delineated, as we should

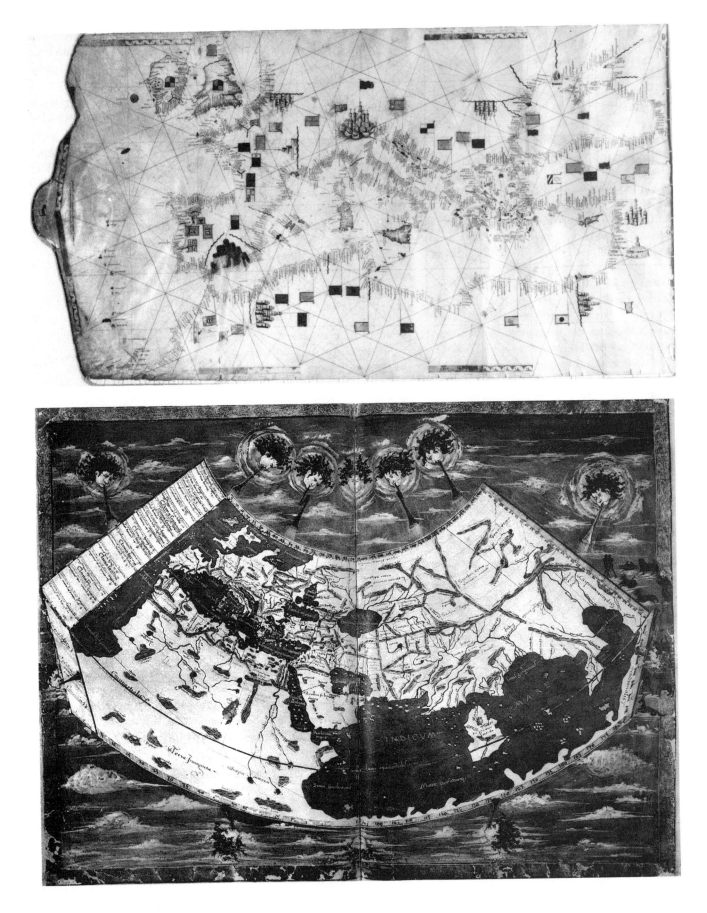

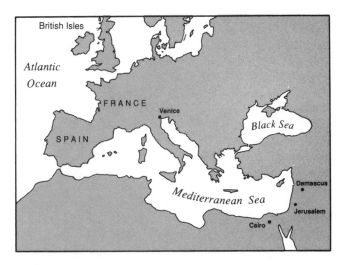

PORTOLAN CHART (*facing page, top*). By Petrus Roselli, 1456. Delineation of the coastline approaches the accuracy of modern maps, as shown in the schematic representation (*above*) of the original.   THE NEWBERRY LIBRARY, CHICAGO

expect, and so is the north coast of Africa. However, the southern half of the hemisphere is, as Ptolemy notes, "Terra Incognita," unknown land, and his knowledge of the lands bordering the Indian Ocean is very defective. In particular, he showed a very large island, called Taprobana, in the Indian Ocean; this perhaps represents some distorted notion of the island of Sumatra.

The Ptolemaic vision of the world was very important in the formation of Columbus's own. Note that for Ptolemy the distance between the western tip of Spain and the eastern edge of Asia was something like 200 degrees, leaving 160 degrees for the land "round the back." Columbus in fact carried this error further, but Ptolemy's estimate was already hopelessly optimistic, since in fact

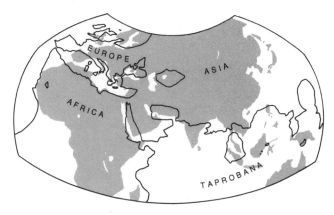

PTOLEMAIC WORLD MAP (*facing page, bottom*). From a manuscript of circa 1460. The shading on the schematic map (*above*) shows the true outlines of landmasses.   NEW YORK PUBLIC LIBRARY

the distance from eastern Asia to the western seaboard of Europe is not 160 degrees but about 220 degrees. If the mariners of the late fifteenth century had realized the immense distances involved, they surely would never have set sail—but then they did not know, either, that a New World lay between western Europe and eastern Asia.

After having circulated in manuscript during much of the fifteenth century, Ptolemy's geography was eventually printed and soon ran through many editions. The first edition with maps was printed at Bologna in 1477, and by the middle of the sixteenth century more than twenty other editions in various languages had emerged. It was no doubt this work, more than any other, that made educated Europeans familiar with the idea of having a book—an "atlas," as it would be called—within which was a collection of maps that would give the reader some idea of the outline of the world.

Use of Maps in Early European Exploration

During the reign of Henry the Navigator, the Portuguese were pushing their explorations ever southward down the West African coast. They drew maps as they went, using the techniques of the portolan chart. These techniques were also beginning to be applied in the early fifteenth century to the charting of the Atlantic Ocean. A chart drawn in 1424 by the Venetian Zuane Pizzigano on a single sheet of vellum has the usual latticework of lines radiating from a set of wind-roses. The coasts of western Europe and northern Africa are shown in typical portolan chart style, with an accurate delineation and the names of the towns at right angles to the coast.

The Mediterranean islands are shown with a rich, opaque color, in the usual way, and so are the islands of the eastern Atlantic, the Azores (shown too close to the European coast), Madeiras, Canaries, and two large islands in midocean, Antilia and Satanazes. These last are of course imaginary in the sense that they do not exist where they are shown. But some historians believe that they represent an interpretation of reports by sailors who had in fact crossed the Atlantic; certainly such ideas were in the air for decades before the epic voyage of Columbus.

Early Maps of the New World. The earliest surviving European map to show the New World is the one by Juan de la Cosa, now preserved at the Museo Naval in Madrid. This map strikingly demonstrates the way in which cartographic techniques developed in the Old World were used to map the New, for the Mediterranean region is drawn exactly in the portolan chart style, which is then applied also to the area of the Caribbean and South America that had been explored.

The same stylistic transmission can be seen on the second great manuscript world map surviving from this earliest period, the Cantino planisphere. This large and

Pizzigano chart. Nautical chart of the Atlantic Ocean by Zuane Pizzigano, 1424.

beautiful map was obtained at Lisbon in 1502 by Alberto Cantino, diplomatic agent of the duke of Ferrara; it was sent back to the ducal library in Modena, where it remains. The Cantino map was almost certainly a copy from the Portuguese *padrão real,* the master map that was kept at Lisbon by the royal chartmakers and constantly updated. The information contained therein was not to be divulged under pain of death.

This is the first map to show the Line of Demarcation fixed by the Treaty of Tordesillas, which was signed by Spain and Portugal in 1494. Spain was to have the territory to the west of the line, and Portugal that to the east. The Portuguese land is marked, as on a portolan chart, with flags flying over what is now Brazil and Newfoundland, which the Portuguese probably claimed because of its rich fisheries. To the west of the line are isolated patches of land, floating in the Western Ocean or "Oceanus Occidentalis." The West Indies are the "Antilles of the King of Castille," but the area to the west of them is left blank. The map reflects growing Portuguese knowledge of the East, for Taprobana has disappeared, the Indian subcontinent has taken on something like its correct form, and the Malaysian peninsula is beginning to emerge.

In the early sixteenth century, the Spaniards and Portuguese did not have printing presses capable of reproducing large and complicated maps. Such maps were printed in Italy and especially Germany. One such map, printed in Rome in 1507 but showing the latest cartographic knowledge from Spain and Portugal, was engraved by Johan Ruysch, with the aim of showing "the known world, drawn from recent discoveries." This type of projection makes it possible to show the whole northern part of the globe; the degrees of longitude run

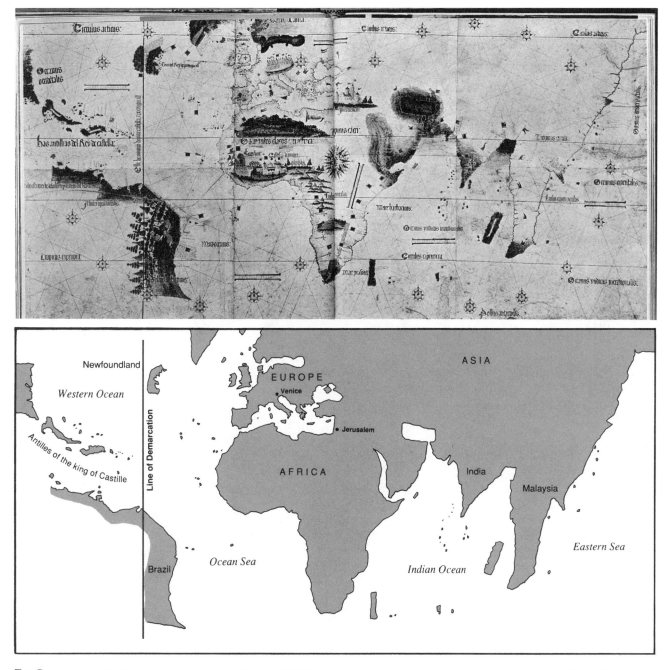

THE CANTINO MAP. Portuguese manuscript world map of 1502.

around the semicircle, with two sets from 0 to 180 degrees; the degrees of latitude end at 38 degrees in the Southern Hemisphere.

Ruysch has a fair notion of the shape of the northeastern part of South America, though he has to cover the west coast with a scroll. He also knows the West Indian islands east of Cuba. But he draws in the eastern end of Asia a little way north of Cuba, having absolutely no idea of the existence of North America. Indeed, he writes that "what the Spaniards call Hispaniola is really Japan." At this time

the New World is South America, described here as the "Terra sancte crucis, sive Mundus Novus" (the land of the holy cross, or New World).

All this would change in 1513, when Vasco Núñez de Balboa became the first European to sight the Pacific Ocean, and still more after 1522, when the fleet of Ferdinand Magellan had completed its circumnavigation of the globe. By then the vastness of the ocean one day to be known as the Pacific had become evident. It was plotted particularly well on the charts produced at the

Casa de la Contratación in Seville. Here pilots and cosmographers interrogated ships' masters as they came in from their voyages, plotting accurate information about sites and their latitude and longitude onto the master map, or *padrón real*.

This master map was the Spanish equivalent of the one kept by the Portuguese. The most famous map to emerge from the Casa was no doubt the one drawn by Diogo Ribeiro in 1529, but the previous decades had seen similar efforts, of which about a dozen survive. These are scattered about the archives of Europe, for the only ones that remain are those sent as gifts to foreign princes; seemingly, none survived in Spain itself.

The Salviati world map was probably a gift from the Emperor Charles V (in part of whose huge empire Seville lay) to Cardinal Giovanni Salviati. The Old World is still shown in portolan-chart style, as is the New World. Now

the northeast coast of North America is quite accurately known, ending at the "Tierra de Labrador," and so is the eastern coast of South America, right down to the Strait of Magellan. Very little of the west coast is known, apart from the part bounding Mesoamerica; here two labels distinguish between "Tierra Firme" and the "Mar del Sur," or Pacific. The extent of this great ocean has now been realistically conceived; although there are no figures of latitude and longitude, there are marks at ten-degree intervals along the equator, and similar marks at ten-degree intervals along the lines of latitude.

The Salviati map and the other products of the Casa represent the culmination of the first phase of European world cartography; from this time onward the general extent of the world was known; it was now simply a matter of filling in the various areas with more or less accuracy. The world of the *mappamundi* had exploded outward to

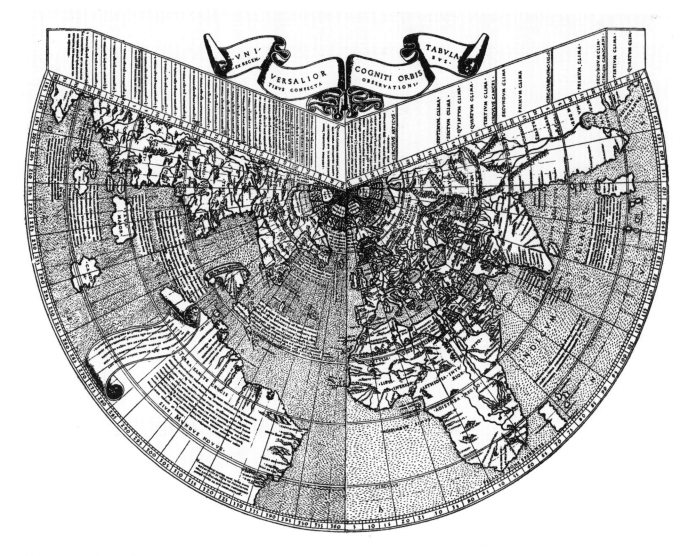

WORLD MAP OF JOHAN RUYSCH. *Universalior cogniti orbis tabula.* Rome, 1507.

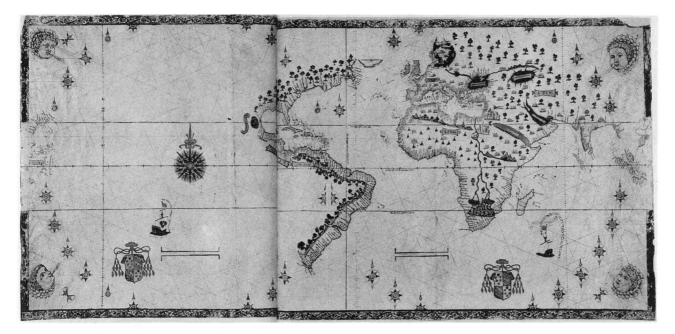

THE SALVIATI MAP. Spanish manuscript world map, circa 1526.

THE VALLEY OF TEPETLAOZTOC, MEXICO. Manuscript map of 1583.

<small>THE HACIENDA OF SANTA INES, MEXICO. Manuscript map of 1569.</small>

give a radically new image of the globe. But this image was constructed using medieval methods. For a long time the style and technique of the portolan chart would still pervade these maps, and they would continue to be constructed according to projections known to Ptolemy, using his system of coordinates. This would not change until after the middle of the sixteenth century, with the adoption of Mercator's projection.

Detailed Land Maps of the New World. When the Europeans came to map the internal regions of the Americas, they often called upon the cartographic expertise of the indigenous peoples. Sometimes this knowledge was transmitted verbally or in transient images like drawings in the sand. At other times the native peoples made drawings on hides or tusks. In Central America, the Aztecs in particular had a rich tradition of portraying places and events in pictorial form. When, for instance, the Aztec ruler Motecuhzoma II (Moctezuma) heard that strangers (the Spaniards) had been seen landing on his coast, he sent artists to make drawings of these people and the localities through which they were passing. An Aztec map dating from 1583 shows the valley of Tepetlaoztoc, through which a road, marked with footprints, runs. There is a river (though lacking the usual fish symbols) at the top and right, a forest, and low hills jutting into the plain. The inverted shields bear place-names, and the area at the bottom of the image perhaps represents fields, with boundaries between them. Many such maps survive at the Archivo de la Nación in Mexico City, testimony to a lively and widespread cartographic tradition.

When the Spaniards occupied much of the New World, they had maps drawn of the areas under their control; these were often sent back to Spain, to help in the planning of imperial policy. These maps are often an interesting conflation of the European and Amerindian styles, plainly showing elements from each culture. One such map, drawn in 1569 in the course of a dispute over water-rights, delineates the hacienda of Santa Ines, to the north of Mexico City in the Valley of Mexico. Here the Jesuits eventually had a great plantation, the proceeds from which supported their Colegio de Tepotzotlán. We see a church (on the right) and four chapels, outlined on the original in red. The Indians live in the blockish houses scattered more or less at random; care is taken to show the sheep-pens (*corrales*). All these buildings are in a more or less European style. In the fields, however, are New World plants, and on the roads footsteps are shown, in the Aztec style. Such a map obviously cannot give a precise indication of acreage, but it does give a good idea of the layout of the hacienda.

Maps were very important in establishing the power of the European peoples, whether they showed the Saint Lawrence Valley or the Valley of Mexico or the coast of Virginia. Some of the early English maps, indeed, speak very tellingly to this idea of the map as an emblem of power, for they show large English ships approaching a virtually empty continent in which a few small Indian figures can be detected. The reality, of course, was that the invaders approached a vast continent that in places was heavily peopled. True, the European technology, of which the map was an important part, was in some ways superior to that of the Amerindians, but their most potent weapons were those they carried unknowingly: the germs of various diseases until then unknown in the New World.

Eventually, maps would also come to be used to sustain the rights of the Indians, infrequently during the seventeenth century and more often in the modern era. They were a powerful tool for visualizing and, so to speak, "capturing" the vast extent of land that had opened up to peoples used to much narrower horizons. From the beginning, cartography played a central role in the encounter between these different worlds.

[See also *Nautical Charts; Sailing Directions.*]

BIBLIOGRAPHY

Bagrow, L., and R. A. Skelton. *History of Cartography.* Cambridge, 1964.

Cortesão, Armando, and Avelino Teixeira da Mota. *Portugaliae monumenta cartographica.* 6 vols. Lisbon, 1960. New edition, Lisbon, 1987.

Cumming, W. P., R. A. Skelton, and D. B. Quinn. *The Discovery of North America.* London, 1971.

Hale, John K. *The Age of Exploration.* New York, 1966.

Harley, J. B., and David Woodward. *Cartography in Prehistoric, Ancient and Medieval Europe and the Mediterranean.* Vol. 1 of *The History of Cartography.* Chicago, 1987.

Mollat du Jourdin, Michel de La Roncière, and Monique de La Roncière. *Sea Charts of the Early Explorers.* London, 1984.

Morison, Samuel Eliot. *The European Discovery of America: The Southern Voyages, A.D. 1492–1616.* New York, 1974.

Nebenzahl, Kenneth. *Atlas of Columbus and the Great Discoveries.* Chicago, 1990.

Organization of American States and the Instituto Panamericano de Geografía e História. *Precedentes cartográficos del descubrimiento de América.* Mexico City, 1989.

Parry, J. H. *The Age of Reconnaissance.* Berkeley, 1981.

Putnam, R. *Early Sea Charts.* New York, 1983.

Sauer, Carl Ortwin. *The Early Spanish Main.* Berkeley, 1966.

DAVID BUISSERET

CASA DE LA CONTRATACIÓN. The Casa, or House of Trade, was set up by a decree of Queen Juana, dated February 14, 1503. The officials named were a treasurer, a contador (notary), and a factor (i.e., business manager). The establishment of this body signified the change from exploration and discovery to royal commercial enterprise in the Indies. A clearinghouse for the trade, the Casa was also a center for the development of an *artes y oficios de navegar,* or an institute for licensing, controlling, and teaching all aspects of navigation. A pilot major was appointed in 1508, and the Casa was charged with maintaining a *padron real* (mastery map) to instruct pilots in the art of navigation.

Starting to function on January 20, 1503, in the *ataranza* (arsenal) of Seville, the officials of the Casa were to put the relationship of the colonists to the metropolis on a par with the regulation of commerce in other parts of Castile. They collected data on the demand and supplies of the markets and supervised the fleets operating between Seville and the Indies. The assembly and licensing of ships and cargoes resulted in a roster of manifests that were controlled at both terminals of the Indies trade (*carrera de Indias*). Two early problems of the system involved the casas set up in the Indies, which soon became mere customs houses, and the rivalry between the harbors of Seville and Cádiz. After 1504, incoming tribute, treasure, goods, and people had to be cleared through the Casa in Seville, even if they had arrived in Cádiz.

The special needs of the mercantile and the nautical groups engaged in the Indies trade led to the development of a special branch of the judiciary at the Casa in 1539. The relation of the judges to the local system and the course of appeal of cases before them were gradually defined.

Rounding out the mature institution was a variety of activities: the examination and licensing of pilots and nautical instruments (astrolabes, jacob staffs, compasses, almanacs), the supervision of construction of ships for the trade, instruction in gunnery, and keeping of chronicles.

BIBLIOGRAPHY

Haring, Clarence Henry. *Trade and Navigation between Spain and the Indies in the Time of the Habsburgs.* Cambridge, Mass., 1918.

Haring, Clarence Henry. "Trade and Navigation between Spain and the Indies: A Re-View, 1918–1958." *Hispanic American Historical Review* 40 (1960): 53–62.

Lamb, Ursula. "Science by Litigation: A Cosmographic Feud." *Terrae Incognitae* 1 (1969): 40–57.

Veitia Linaje, José de. *Norte de la contratación de las Indias Occidentales.* Seville, 1672; new ed., Buenos Aires, 1945.

URSULA LAMB

CASAS, BARTOLOMÉ DE LAS. See *Las Casas, Bartolomé de.*

CATHERINE OF ARAGÓN

CATHERINE OF ARAGÓN (1485–1536), princess of Castile; queen of England. Born Catalina, the youngest child of Isabel and Fernando, Catherine was married to Arthur, prince of Wales, in 1501. The alliance was the centerpiece of Anglo-Castilian diplomacy, but it was threatened when Arthur died only months after the wedding. Catherine's subsequent marriage in 1509 to Arthur's brother, King Henry VIII, ended in the infamous divorce proceedings that led to the English Reformation.

Catherine spent most of her early childhood as witness to the momentous events of late-fifteenth-century Castile: the conquest of Granada, the Inquisition, the expulsion of Jews and Muslims, and Columbus's reception in Barcelona following his return from the New World. Like her mother, Catherine was deeply pious. She spoke fluent Latin and was schooled in classical literature as well as theology.

Her marriage to Henry appears to have been happy, but unfortunately for Catherine their sons were stillborn or died shortly after birth. Only their daughter, Mary, born in 1516, survived to adulthood. By 1525 there was no hope for a male heir. Desperate to secure the succession, Henry questioned the validity of his marriage to Catherine, basing his argument on the canon law prohibition against marrying the widow of one's brother. Catherine fought the divorce action and marshaled powerful allies, among them her nephew, Emperor Charles V, and Pope Clement VII. The pope ruled in Catherine's favor, but by then Henry had severed ties with Rome and declared himself head of the Church of England. Henry married his mistress, Anne Boleyn, shortly before Catherine's death in 1536.

BIBLIOGRAPHY

Claremont, Francesca. *Catherine of Aragon.* London, 1939.
Mattingly, Garrett. *Catherine of Aragon.* New York, 1941.

THERESA EARENFIGHT

CELEBRATIONS

CELEBRATIONS. Although the momentous arrival of Christopher Columbus in the Western Hemisphere was recognized in the first two hundred years after his exploit, there is no evidence of any large public celebrations during that time. It was not until the three-hundredth commemoration that public recognition of the event occurred in the United States. In 1792 celebrations were held in New York City, Boston, Baltimore, Providence, and Richmond to commemorate the voyage. In Boston, Jeremy Belknap presented "A Discourse Intended to Commemorate the Discovery of America by Christopher Columbus" to the Historical Society of Massachusetts on October 23, 1792. During the dinner the memory of Columbus was toasted and Belknap's ode was sung by a choir. Also that year the New York Tammany Society unveiled an obelisk dedicated to Columbus and provided entertainment in celebration of the event.

On the four-hundredth anniversary, in 1892–1893, the celebratory activities increased markedly in contrast to the earlier centennials. Interest stirred in a number of cities to commemorate the Columbian legacy in a broad manner. Columbus had become the embodiment of the United States and inspired strong nationalistic fervor. The *Youth's Companion* magazine introduced the Pledge of Allegiance specifically to mark the four-hundredth anniversary.

Following months of spirited competition among a number of cities, including Chicago, Washington, New York, and St. Louis, Chicago was named as the site of the first major public event in honor of Columbus. The World's Columbian Exposition opened amid great excitement on May 1, 1893. Located on 664 acres on the shore of Lake Michigan, the fair featured forty buildings for main exhibitions, forty-two structures for state exhibitions, and eighty buildings and walkways to accommodate foreign nations, colonies, districts, and corporations. The fair cost over $30 million and attracted 24 million visitors, the largest crowds for any single event in the history of the world to that point. Four times as much money was spent on the Columbian Exposition in 1893 than on the 1876 Centennial Exposition in Philadelphia, which commemorated the independence of the United States.

The fair exhibited statues of Columbus, facsimiles of his letters, a reproduction of the monastery of La Rábida, and full-sized replicas of *Niña*, *Pinta*, and *Santa María*. The Chicago fair was opened officially by President Grover Cleveland accompanied by Thomas Palmer, president of the U.S. National Commission, and Harlow Higinbotham of the Exposition Company. Among the dignitaries who attended the opening ceremony were the vice president of the United States Adlai Stevenson, the secretaries of state, treasury, navy, interior, and agriculture, various world's fair directors and officers, the governor of Illinois, the duke and duchess of Veragua, and other Spanish notables. The World's Columbian Exposition was consid-

TWO VIEWS OF THE WORLD'S COLUMBIAN EXPOSITION, CHICAGO, 1893. *Top:* The lagoon and the Palace of Mechanic Arts. *Bottom:* The main basin looking toward the Administration Building, with a statue of Liberty, or Columbia, representing the Republic, in the foreground.

LIBRARY OF CONGRESS; PHOTOGRAPHS BY FRANCES BENJAMIN JOHNSTON

ered the greatest international fair of its time. It was seen as expressing the continuity of the progress of American civilization and opening a new period in humankind's effort to master the environment.

Earlier, in 1892, Columbus-related activities were celebrated in New York City. In October there were five days of parades, floats, fireworks, speeches, marches, naval pageants, statue unveilings, and opera performances. The highlight occurred on October 12, 1892, with the opening of the Columbus memorial corner of Central Park, called Columbus Circle. The federal government, through a congressional joint resolution and a declaration by President Benjamin Harrison, called upon citizens to observe Columbus Day at home, at work, and in school. Congress proposed October 23 as the day of observance, but October 12 remained the popular celebration date. Coins and stamps were issued in honor of the anniversary in the United States and other countries. And in Spain that year, a special event, the Columbian Historical Exhibition, was held in Madrid.

In addition to these world-class spectaculars, a number of complementary activities related to the centennial have occurred over the past century. In many respects, though not as spectacular as a world's fair, some of these events have had an international impact related to Columbus. In the United States the annual Columbus Day celebration has received the strong support of Italians and Hispanics as well as the Knights of Columbus since 1892. Angelo Noce of Denver, Colorado, lobbied for the first official noncentennial Columbus Day in 1905, and its annual observance became state law in 1907. By 1910 Columbus Day had become an official holiday in fifteen states, and in 1938 it became a national holiday, following a proclamation in April 1934 by President Franklin D. Roosevelt. In Latin America, the recognition of the landfall date took a different meaning as the observance of El Dia de la Raza (Day of the Spanish Race) emerged following the 1892 commemoration. By 1938 El Dia de la Raza was celebrated in twenty-two countries in South, Central, and Caribbean America.

For the quincentenary in 1992, Spain plays host to Expo '92, the Universal Exposition, from April 20 to October 12, in Seville. The theme of the exposition, "The Age of Discovery," refers to human discoveries through the ages in every field of activity. The site of the fair, the island La Cartuja in the Guadalquivir River, is the location of the fifteenth-century monastery where Columbus was first buried. Spanish planners hope that Expo '92 will project the modern image of today's Spain, contribute to international unity, and provide an opportunity to improve the environment around the fair area in Seville.

In Genoa, Italy, a specialized exhibition to be held in the summer of 1992 will be devoted to maritime explorations and the technical means and instruments of navigation from Columbus's age to the present day.

A variety of other activities are also planned as the five-hundredth anniversary of Columbus's first voyage to America approaches. By 1990 thirty-two nations and over thirty states and entities of the United States had formed official quincentenary commissions. The National Christopher Columbus Quincentenary Jubilee Commission (United States) was established by law in 1984, and many other countries, including Spain, Mexico, Portugal, Italy, the Dominican Republic, Colombia, and Argentina, also established commissions, some of them functioning several years before that of the United States.

Interpretations of Columbus as representative of one nation's skill or another's genius and the portrayals of him as the agent of capitalist ingenuity and persistence are being challenged by international conferences addressing issues related to the impact of the Columbian voyage on America, Europe, and elsewhere. Planned for the period around October 12, 1992, are conferences on history, law, medicine, music, literature, geography, space exploration, cartography, pre-Columbian studies, library science, and social studies related to the Columbian legacy. Although the directions of these conferences have expanded thematically, they continue to use the opportunity provided by the quincentenary as the occasion for meeting. Out of these activities a new and richer understanding of the consequences of the Columbian voyage and those that followed is emerging.

Throughout the Atlantic world, a wide array of programs has been planned to commemorate, to understand, to debate, and to study the enduring relationship between America and Europe that was set into motion by Columbus's voyage of 1492. Among them are An Ongoing Voyage of the Library of Congress, The Seeds of Change of the Natural History Museum of the Smithsonian Institution, and The Encounter of Two Worlds of the Organization of American States. Unlike the celebrations of 1892, these initiatives seek to establish a broader view of the consequences of the Columbian landfall, although they retain some elements of the nationalistic fervor of a hundred years ago.

[See also *Columbianism*; *Iconography*, articles on *Numismatics* and *Philately*; *Quincentenary*.]

BIBLIOGRAPHY

Badger, Reid. *The Great American Fair: The World's Columbian Exposition and American Culture.* Chicago, 1979.

Quinto Centenario del Descubrimiento de America Commission: 500 Years, 500 Programs. Madrid, 1985.

Sale, Kirkpatrick. *The Conquest of Paradise: Christopher Columbus and the Columbian Legacy.* New York, 1990.

JOHN R. HÉBERT

CHANCA, DIEGO ALVAREZ (c. 1463–c. 1515), royal physician; accompanied Columbus on his second voyage to America. Little is known about Diego Alvarez Chanca's early years. He was born in Seville around 1463, but we have no information about his schooling or his training as a physician prior to 1492. His knowledge of Latin, his references to classical literary motifs in his account of Columbus's second voyage, and his medical texts reveal, however, an erudite and solid grounding in the classical and humanistic culture of the late medieval world. Documentary evidence from July 1492 reveals that he held the prestigious post of royal physician, accompanying Fernando and Isabel during the final siege of Granada. As a sign of royal trust, Chanca was named physician to the Infanta Juana, the eventual heir to the throne of Castile and mother of Charles V. On July 7, 1492, Isabel ordered her accounts to pay Chanca 68,750 maravedis in compensation for his services; he retained his position as royal physician until at least 1501. There is some evidence that he may have held this position from a much earlier period and that he may have also served in the retinue of the Infanta Isabel at the Portuguese court between 1481 and 1483.

The Catholic monarchs by a royal letter of May 23, 1493, requested that Chanca accompany Columbus on his second voyage to the New World and ordered the royal accounts to pay him a salary and *ración* (allowance) while in the Indies. The 1493 expedition was not the adventurous sailing into the unknown of Columbus's first voyage. Instead, seventeen ships and more than one thousand men revealed the commitment of the Castilian Crown to the enterprise of the Ocean Sea. Chanca's nomination as physician to the fleet also reflected the interest of the monarchs in the scientific and medical aspects of the voyage.

The best sources for this second voyage are Chanca's letter to the city council of Seville and sections of Andrés Bernáldez's *History of the Catholic Monarchs*. Chanca's letter took the form of a report to the city council of his native city. A copy of the manuscript, now at the Real Academia de la Historia in Madrid, was published by Martín Fernández de Navarrete in his *Colección de los viages y descubrimientos*. Chanca's letter relates Columbus's uneventful second crossing and the discovery and exploration of the Lesser Antilles. Although his account never gained the celebrity bestowed upon some of the contemporary histories of the first age of discovery, such as those of Las Casas, Pietro Martire d'Anghiera (Peter Martyr), and others, it deserves recognition.

His letter, albeit written in a confused and often grammatically incorrect Castilian, is the first "scientific" description of the New World, revealing the awe of Europeans at the sights of these new lands. His was the first attempt at depicting the natural beauty of the Caribbean islands and the diversity and uniqueness of their flora and fauna. Chanca's letter was also the first of what eventually would become a long list of "ethnographic" descriptions of the inhabitants of the New World. His letter contains lyrical descriptions of peaceful and beautiful Indians without clothing, weapons, or visible political organization. His image of a "natural man," when used by more eloquent writers, would become one of the central themes of European thought and a source of utopian ideals in early modern Europe. But Chanca also described, in horrified tones, the warlike and aggressive Caribs and their proclivity toward anthropophagy. His gruesome stories of the Castilians' discovery of dismembered bodies and of emasculated children being fattened for the Caribs' feasts also became part of the European imagination. Scholars currently debate what the Spaniards really did find in the Caribbean and whether their reports transposed the image of the other from classical and medieval literary sources (such as those of Pliny, John Mandeville, and others) or reflected reality. Chanca knew his classics well, but his letter also breathes a feeling of authenticity and of somber adherence to observed reality: the meek and friendly Indians on the one hand and the fierce Caribs on the other.

Chanca's voyage ended at La Española where his services were required to treat the myriad tropical diseases affecting the new colonists. In this sense, he was the first European doctor to come face to face with a host of new illnesses. How he dealt with them is not known. There is no evidence in his later writings that he reflected at all on the medical conditions or problems he faced in the New World. Moreover, he remained in the Americas only for a short period before returning to Seville in 1495.

Married twice without issue, Chanca enjoyed a successful career as a noted scholar on medical matters. In 1499 he published his *Tractatus de fascinatione* and seven years later a treatise, written in the vernacular and printed by Jacob Kronberg, on the afflictions to the sides of the body caused by pestilence, *Tratado nuevo . . . en que se declara de que manera se ha de curar el mal de costado pestilencial*. His last known work, *Commentum novum in parabolis divi Arnaldi de villa nova*, a commentary on the enigmatic medieval physician and philosopher Arnau de Vilanova, was also printed in Seville by Kronberg in 1514. There is an extant will of Chanca from 1510; he probably died around 1515.

BIBLIOGRAPHY

Cecil, Jane, ed. *The Four Voyages of Columbus.* Reprint. New York, 1988.

Morison, Samuel Eliot. *Admiral of the Ocean Sea: A Life of Christopher Columbus.* 2 vols. Boston, 1942.

Paniagua, Juán Antonio. *El doctor Chanca y su obra médica.* Madrid, 1977.

TEOFILO F. RUIZ

CHARLES V (1500–1558), Holy Roman emperor (1519–1556); Carlos I, king of Spain (1516–1556). Charles ruled a vast and far-flung empire that encompassed both the Old World and the New. He dominated European politics through a combination of military prowess, diplomacy, administrative acumen, and overseas exploration. His was a turbulent age: it witnessed the divorce of Henry VIII of England from Charles's aunt Catherine of Aragón, the growth of the Protestant Reformation, the abduction of Pope Clement VII, the conquest and colonization of the New World, and the circumnavigation of the globe by Ferdinand Magellan's fleet in 1522.

Charles was born in Ghent in 1500, the year of Pedro Álvares Cabral's discovery of Brazil. Son of Juana I (Juana la Loca) and Philip the Handsome, archduke of Austria, Charles was the first king to rule a united Spain, which included Castile, Aragón, Naples, Sicily, Mallorca, and territories in the New World. He inherited the Burgundian Netherlands from his father, and upon his election as Holy Roman Emperor (1519) he acquired the hereditary Habsburg estates in Germany and Austria.

He remained in Flanders when his parents went to Castile to claim the Spanish Crown and was raised by his aunt Margaret, regent of the Netherlands. He was educated as a Renaissance prince in the opulent Burgundian court. His tutors included Guillaume de Croy and Adrian of Utrecht, the future Pope Adrian VI.

To solidify the Castilian inheritance Charles married Isabel, infanta of Portugal, daughter of Manuel I and Isabel of Castile, in 1526. Their son Philip II (1527–1598) would inherit the Spanish and Burgundian realms, but the German territories and the title of emperor were granted to Charles's brother Ferdinand.

SHIELD OF CHARLES V. Depicting an allegory of the discovery of the New World.

CHARLES V. The style of dress depicted on this coin makes reference to the rulers of the Roman empire of the ancient world. Minted in Milan.

The demands of his extensive realms required Charles to rule his territories, both in the New World and in Europe, through lieutenants. He spent more time in Spain than elsewhere in his realms, especially in the early years of his reign. He ruthlessly quelled civil unrest in Castile (1521), Navarre (1521), and Valencia (1519–1523). With order restored, Charles appointed Spanish nobles and prelates to serve as his lieutenants and ruled Castile as an absolute monarch.

As king of Spain, Charles supervised the settlement of colonies, established systems of government, and enacted legislation to abolish slavery in the Americas. Early in his reign Hernando Cortés claimed Mexico (1522) and California (1536) for Castile, and Francisco Pizarro explored Peru (1521), territories that brought considerable prestige and wealth to Spain. Charles's treasury was the envy of Europe, but the influx of gold and silver fueled inflation and contributed to a serious economic crisis.

Charles was extraordinarily successful in his military exploits. The Spanish army formed the backbone of the imperial army, which sacked Rome in 1527 and defeated the French at Pavia (1525), the Turks at the Danube (1546), and the German Protestants at Mühlenberg (1547).

In 1554 Charles began to cede territories to Philip, and by the time of his death in 1558, he had abdicated all of his realms. He went into retirement on the estates of the Convent of San Jeronimo de Yuste and was buried in a tomb prepared by his son Philip at San Lorenzo in the Escorial.

BIBLIOGRAPHY

Fernández Álvarez, Manuel. *Charles V: Elected Emperor and Hereditary Ruler.* Translated by J. A. Lalaguna. London, 1975.

Fernández Álvarez, Manuel. *La España del Emperador Carlos V.* Vol. 18 of *Historia de España.* Edited by Ramón Menéndez Pidal. Madrid, 1966.

Rassow, Peter. *Karl V: Der letze Kaiser des Mittelalters.* Göttingen, 1957.

Terlinden, Charles de. *Charles Quint, empereur des deux mondes.* Brussels, 1965.

Tyler, Royall. *The Emperor Charles the Fifth.* London, 1956.

THERESA EARENFIGHT

CHARLES VIII (1470–1498), king of France. The only son of Louis XI, Charles succeeded him at age thirteen in 1483. Because of his youth his older sister Anne of Beaujeu governed for him. Much of the nobility, led by Louis of Orléans and Francis of Brittany, rebelled. In July 1488 Louis was defeated and imprisoned for three years. Francis died shortly after the defeat, leaving his duchy to his daughter Anne, who was persuaded to marry Charles, ending Brittany's autonomy.

By 1491 Charles had begun to govern for himself and set about planning the first French invasion of Italy to make good the Valois claim to Naples, ruled by Ferrante of Aragón. He won the temporary neutrality of Fernando of Aragón by returning Roussillon and Cerdagne in the Pyrenees to him. (In his preoccupation with Naples, Charles passed up the opportunity to fund Columbus's first voyage, when Columbus's brother Bartolomé came to France seeking royal support.) With an army of thirty thousand men and the most powerful artillery train yet seen, Charles invaded Italy in September 1494. Brushing aside limited Italian resistance, Charles marched to Naples and proclaimed himself king. But Fernando of Aragón joined with the major Italian states in an anti-French league. In July 1495 Charles, returning to France, was confronted by an allied force as he crossed the Appenines. The ensuing Battle of Fornova was enough of a French victory to allow him to complete his return to France.

Shortly after, Charles's only child died, which made Louis of Orléans his heir. Three years later, on April 10, 1498, Charles struck his head on a doorway in the Château of Blois on his way to watch a tennis game. Within ten hours he had died, passing the throne to his second cousin Louis XII.

CHARLES VIII OF FRANCE. From Aliprando Capriolo's *Ritratti de cento capitani illustri.* Rome, 1596.

BIBLIOGRAPHY

Bridge, John. *A History of France from the Death of Louis XI.* 5 vols. New York, 1929.

Febvre, Lucien. *Life in Renaissance France.* Translated by Marian Rothstein. Cambridge, Mass., 1977.

Labande-Mailfert, Yvonne. *Charles VIII et son milieu.* Paris, 1975.

FREDERIC J. BAUMGARTNER

CHIBCHAS. See *Indian America*, article on *Chibchas*.

CHINA. Apart from a handful of medieval travelers who left accounts of their wanderings in the East, little was known about China in the West until early in the fourteenth century when Marco Polo's book appeared. During the Renaissance, it was the chief Western source of information on the East, and its influence on Columbus and the European Age of Discovery has never been fully assessed. [See also *Polo, Marco.*]

When Columbus and his contemporaries spoke of China, they were referring to Marco Polo's Cathay, which they did not connect with China; it was not until nearly a century after Columbus discovered America that the mysterious Cathay was located. Later, Europe learned that from 907 to 1125, North China had been ruled by the non-Chinese Liao dynasty, an ethnic group known to the Chinese as Ch'itan or Khitan, and to their Central Asian neighbors as Khitai, from which the word *Cathay* was derived. Since the Arabs who traded at Canton had never used the term *Cathay*, European geographers were confused by the existence of what they took to be two entities, China and Cathay. As for the name China, it is commonly accepted that the word was derived from the Ch'in or Ts'in dynasty that flourished in the third century B.C. and became widely known in India, Persia, and other Asian countries. Confirmation that China and Cathay were one came in 1607 when the Portuguese Jesuit, Bento Goes, reached Cathay by the northern overland route and sent word to Matteo Ricci (1552–1610), who had reached Peking (Beijing) by way of Canton and Macao.

The Cathay described by Marco Polo was the Mongol China of Kublai (or Khubilai) Khan. The Mongol Yüan dynasty ruled over all of China from 1279 to 1368. Mongol rule extended over Korea, but attempts to invade Japan in 1274 and 1281 ended in failure. However, Mongol troops under Batu Khan, a grandson of Genghis (Chingis) Khan, got as far west as Hungary, turning back to Karakorum, the Mongol capital, only because of the death of the Grand Khan Ögödai in 1241.

Of all the medieval accounts of European contacts with the Mongol dynasty, the most famous and the most influential was that of Marco Polo. The effect of his account on Columbus is well known, for in his great enterprise, Columbus let it be known that he was seeking, not a new continent, but a shorter route to the Cathay of Marco Polo.

Kublai Khan died in 1294 at the age of eighty. His nine successors were not outstanding rulers, and the dynasty fell in 1367 after many years of rebellions and internal warfare, to be succeeded by the Ming dynasty (1368–1644), which began reluctantly to open China to the West. The Ming was the last imperial dynasty whose ruling family was of Chinese origin. The major problems facing the early Ming rulers were consolidation of control in China, acceptance of Ming suzerainty by such tributary states as Korea and Vietnam, and the military security of the northern border. The first Ming emperor (r. 1368–1398) was interested in the political aspects of the tribute system, but wanted to restrict trade to a very low level, a policy that struck at the economic livelihood of both Chinese and foreign traders and led to smuggling and piracy.

The second emperor was not a military man, and he proved no match for his uncle, the prince of Yen, who

rebelled and seized the throne, reigning as Yung-lo (1402–1424). A successful soldier, he transferred the capital from Nanking to the former Mongol capital in the north, which he renamed Peking. Not long after the beginning of his reign he decided to expand China's contacts. In 1405 he sent Cheng Ho (c. 1371–c. 1433), eunuch commander of the Ming fleet, on a series of expeditions by which China's ships ultimately reached the east coast of Africa and Arabia. The most famous navigator in Chinese history, Cheng sailed the greatest distance of any ship captain up to his time. Yung-lo sent Cheng on a first expedition to southeast Asia, Ceylon, and India, with a fleet of sixty-two ships and nearly twenty-eight thousand men. Later expeditions visited several ports on the Persian Gulf. Cheng's fifth and sixth expeditions (1417–1419 and 1421–1422) explored the Arab and African coasts, and much of Chinese geographical knowledge, prior to the arrival of the Jesuits in the late sixteenth century, was based on Cheng's reports. The Chinese now had some general knowledge of the shape of Africa and heard details about countries of the Mediterranean.

Cheng's expeditions, while endorsed by the emperor, were strongly criticized by a segment of the scholar bureaucracy, who based their opposition on the Confucian concept that China produced all that was necessary for its needs and that foreign expeditions introduced exotic luxuries, which were unnecessary if not harmful.

After Yung-lo's death in 1424, further voyages were banned by his successor, Hung-hsi (d. 1425), who was determined to reverse those of his father's policies that did not conform to Confucian ideas; he put a sudden stop to the expeditions, and issued a decree—that was often ignored—forbidding his nationals from leaving the country. His son, Hsüan-te (r. 1425–1435) permitted Cheng to lead one last expedition (1431–1433) before he retired as military commander of Nanking. However, the Confucian opposition was finally victorious, and even plans for Cheng's ships were later destroyed.

Silk was the major Chinese export to the West in the sixteenth century, despite the fact that trade along the Silk Road was severely limited by the reclusive nature of the Ming. But it was not the only trade route to the West. There were Arab ships trading at Canton and other Chinese ports that continued to call until the Portuguese seized Malacca in 1511, giving them a dominant position in the sea trade of Southeast Asia.

The population of the country is estimated to have been 53,280,000 about the year 1500. In the Yangtze Valley, commerce and industry developed most quickly. Grain transportation to the frontiers came to an end in early Ming time. The rich inland merchants, whose cities bordered on the provinces of Anhui and Chekiang and who had first specialized in the silver trade, spread their activities all over China in the Ming period. They often monopolized the salt, silver, rice, cotton, silk, or tea businesses. In the sixteenth century they had well-established contacts with smugglers on the Fukien coast and brought foreign goods into the interior. Their home was also close to the main centers of porcelain production in Kiangsi, which was exported overseas and to the urban centers. With the development of printing, the paper industry was greatly stimulated, and with the application of block printing to textiles, another new field of commercial activity was opened. There was a growing specialization and division of labor, so that cloth was no longer produced from the raw cotton to the finished product by one worker, but spinning, weaving, and dyeing were done by different specialists, often in different cities.

The growth of the small gentry, which had its stronghold in the provincial towns and cities, as well as the rise of the merchant class and the liberation of the artisans, are reflected in the new literature of the Ming period. While the Mongols had developed the theater, the novel may be regarded as the typical Ming creation. Together with the development of drama (or, rather, opera) went the modernization of music. Woodcut and block printing developed largely as a cheap substitute for real paintings.

The most widely spoken version of Chinese was—and is—Mandarin, the language spoken by the upper classes and based on the Peking dialect. There were many other dialects, some of which were mutually incomprehensible. More nonstandard dialects existed in the south than in other parts of the country, due to the physical difficulties of communication in mountainous areas. Cantonese and related dialects were spoken in Kwantung province. The written language was never a transcription of the spoken language, and with the passage of time the separation between the two increased.

Ten years after Yung-lo sent Cheng on his Asian expeditions, Prince Henry the Navigator (1394–1460), the third son of King João I of Portugal, took part in the campaign in which Portugal captured the North African port of Ceuta from the Moors. This was the beginning of the period of European expansion that was eventually to see Portuguese ships sail into the Pearl River estuary of Canton. The expedition to Ceuta aroused Henry's interest in Africa and exploration. From 1419 onward he dispatched a series of expeditions down the western coast of Africa, each reaching a bit farther into the unknown. The relentless step-by-step exploration of the West African coast proceeded although commercial rewards were meager.

Prince Henry's death caused only a brief hiatus in the exploration of the West African coast. In 1469 King Afonso V, Prince Henry's nephew, made an agreement with a wealthy Lisbon merchant, Diogo Gomes, who committed himself to discover at least one hundred leagues (about 485 kilometers [300 miles]) of the African coast each year for the next five years. The Gomes contract produced an impressive annual series of African discoveries southward across the equator. When Gomes's contract expired, the king gave the trading rights to his own son, who became King João II in 1481. This was the king who rejected Columbus's appeal in 1484 for support for his projected voyage across the western ocean to what he thought would be Cathay. Nevertheless, one of the voyages João sponsored was that of Bartolomeu Dias who, in 1488, rounded the Cape of Good Hope. Christopher Columbus, who was in Lisbon making another effort to persuade João II to subsidize his projected seaborne expedition, witnessed Dias's return.

Ten years after Dias's rounding of the Cape, Vasco da Gama dropped anchor in Calicut, on the west coast of India. In 1508, King Manuel I, who had succeeded João II in 1495, instructed the commander of one of the subsequent fleets he sent to India to find out all he could about China, which was not yet identified with Marco Polo's Cathay. Between 1513 and 1515, the first contacts with China were made by individual merchant-adventurers who sailed from Malacca for the South China coast in native junks. In 1517, a Portuguese squadron commanded by Fernão Peres de Andrade, the first European ships to appear in Chinese waters, anchored in the Pearl River of Canton. With Peres de Andrade was Tomé Pires, the first European ambassador to China. After some hesitation on the part of the Chinese, Pires was allowed to proceed to Peking and Peres de Andrade established peaceful and profitable relations with the local officials of Canton. But the good impression made by the Portuguese was ruined by Simão Peres de Andrade, brother of Fernão, who visited the Pearl River estuary with a squadron of four ships in 1519 and whose piratical behavior caused a rupture in official Sino-Portuguese relations that lasted for thirty years. However, during the third and fourth decades of the sixteenth century, the Portuguese carried on a clandestine trade with local smugglers in various isolated places in the coastal provinces of China.

About the year 1550, with the development of their trade with Japan—with whom the Chinese were forbidden to trade—it became increasingly urgent for the Portuguese to establish a firm base on the South China coast within easy reach of Canton, where the silk fairs were held. This was secured in 1554 by Leonel de Sousa who, after prolonged negotiations, concluded an agreement with Wang Ho, the acting commander of the coast guard fleet, whereby the Portuguese were allowed to trade in Kwangtung on the same terms as the Siamese. The arrangement was an oral one, and it also seems that the Portuguese were admitted as Siamese, or as foreigners belonging to some other of the Chinese tributary states. This agreement made between Sousa and the provincial authorities at Canton was not reported to the court at Peking, which was not aware of the establishment of the Portuguese at Macao until long afterwards.

Between 1580 and 1615 the lucrative Macao-Japan trade was carried on chiefly by the annual carrack that voyaged from Goa to Macao to the island of Kyushu. Since the Ming court prohibited all direct trade between China and Japan, the Portuguese had the distinct advantage of serving as intermediaries.

The year 1600 may be said to mark a turning point in the history of the Far East. First and most important, it is the date of the decisive battle of Sekigahara (the tenth of October), which gave Tokugawa Ieyasu the mastery of Japan and went far to settle the fate of that country for the next 250 years. Second, it saw the appearance of the first Dutch ship in Japanese waters, whose pilot was the Englishman Will Adams. Third, in December 1600, Queen Elizabeth of England granted a charter to the merchant adventurers who formed the John Company, as the subsequently famous East India Company came to be called. The voluntary dissolution of the English factory at Hirado (Japan) in the year 1624, and the consequent withdrawal of Richard Cocks and his countrymen from Japan, left the Macaonese with only one European competitor in this market, the Dutch. It was the Dutch who were eventually responsible for the dismemberment of the Portuguese empire in the East—with the exception of Macao.

BIBLIOGRAPHY

Boxer, Charles R. *Fidalgos in the Far East.* The Hague, 1948.
Boxer, Charles R. *The Great Ship from Amacon.* Lisbon, 1963.
Boxer, Charles R. *South China in the Sixteenth Century.* London, 1953.
Eberhard, Wolfram. *History of China.* Rev. ed. Berkeley and Los Angeles, 1977.
Prestage, Edgar. *The Portuguese Pioneers.* London, 1933.

REBECCA CATZ

CIPANGU (JAPAN). Europe first heard about Japan from Marco Polo, whose book, *The Description of the World* (Italian title, *Il Milione*) enjoyed widespread popularity in the fourteenth century. Polo had never been to Japan but he described it from hearsay as an island rich in pearls, precious stones, and palaces covered with gold. Of course, he was mistaken, but his book captured the imagination of Columbus, who set out across the Atlantic in an effort to find Cathay and Cipangu—as Polo called Japan—which, he said, was located some fifteen hundred miles east of the Asian continent.

Sometime in the year 1470, a contemporary and compa-

triot of Columbus, the astronomer Paolo dal Pozzo Toscanelli, suggested to King Afonso V of Portugal (r. 1438–1481) that Cathay, Cipangu, and the Spice Islands could be reached more quickly by sailing due west from Portugal than by attempting to find a sea route to Asia around Africa, as the Portuguese were then trying to do. Toscanelli illustrated his proposal with a map on which the island of Cipangu was marked. This map, like his proposal, was obviously based on his reading of Marco Polo. Though Afonso rejected the proposal, there is no doubt that it was later adopted and elaborated by Columbus, who eventually persuaded Fernando and Isabel to sponsor his plan for reaching the east by sailing west.

The name *Japan* entered European history in this form for the first time in the *Suma oriental* of Tomé Pires, which was written between the years 1512 and 1515. It is generally agreed that it is derived through the Malay *Japun* or *Japang* from the Chinese *Jih-pen-kuo* in one or another of its coastal dialect forms, meaning literally "origin of the sun." But Pires's report, which mentions the name *Japan* only briefly, was not published in full for more than four centuries, and the Portuguese chroniclers who used his manuscript did not appreciate the significance of his reference to Japan, still less in connection with Polo's Cipangu.

Columbus failed in his attempt to reach Japan, and a century and a half was to elapse before the first Europeans arrived in that island nation. They were a group of three Portuguese who were caught in a typhoon and blown to Japan aboard a Chinese junk. The merchant adventurer Fernão Mendes Pinto laid claim to being one of them. Although his claim is much disputed, it is certain that he was one of the earliest Portuguese travelers to that country, which he visited four times between 1544 and 1556. As such he had plenty of opportunity to know the real discoverers, whose version of the actual contact in 1542 or 1543 he may have adopted as his own and incorporated into his pseudo-autobiography, *Peregrination* (1614).

The earliest European accounts of Japan that conflict with Pinto's are those of Garcia de Escalante and Jorge Álvares, both of which date from about 1548. Escalante's account is pure hearsay, based on what he was told by a Galician sailor named Pero Diez, who said he had been there in 1544. Although Escalante's account contains some errors, it is of interest as the oldest known report on Japan by a European who had actually visited that country.

The report of the Portuguese captain Jorge Álvares is of greater interest because he was a much better educated and more observant man than the Galician sailor. It is also noteworthy for being the last European report written by a layman for fifty years, since after the arrival of Francis Xavier in 1549, Japan was seen only through the eyes of Christian missionaries until the coming of the Dutch. On his return voyage from Japan in December of 1547, Álvares was accompanied by a Japanese fugitive named Yajiro, whom he presented to Francis Xavier in Malacca.

The most important Japanese account of the European contact is to be found in the *Teppo-Ki* (History of the introduction of firearms into Japan). It was first printed in 1649 but was written during the Keicho period (1596–1614). The author places the arrival of the Portuguese in Tanegashima on the Japanese date corresponding to September 23, 1543, and offers a remarkably accurate description of the Europeans as seen through the eyes of a native.

But all accounts agree that the Portuguese owed their cordial reception in Japan primarily to the novelty of their firearms. The civil strife then endemic in Japan supplied a ready market for their guns and for many years all firearms of this type were known as "Tanegashima," which was the name of the island where the Portuguese first landed and where the firearms were first manufactured.

Not long after Jorge Álvares had presented Yajiro to Francis Xavier, Yajiro, a servant of his, and another compatriot were converted to the Catholic faith. In Goa, where Xavier had enrolled them at the Jesuit College of Saint Paul, they made rapid progress in studying Portuguese. In April 1549 Xavier, accompanied by the three Japanese, two Spanish Jesuits, and two servants, left Goa for Malacca on the first stage of a voyage to Japan. At Malacca they transferred to a Chinese pirate junk, and on August 15, 1549, dropped anchor in Yajiro's home port of Kagoshima, where Xavier stepped ashore for the first time on the south coast of the Japanese island of Kyushu.

The land where Xavier began to preach—with the full permission of the lord of Satsuma—was a land of strife and turmoil. Satsuma itself was not involved in the civil wars, but chaotic feudal anarchy prevailed throughout most of Kyushu and on two of the other main islands, Honshu and Shikoku. Ever since the collapse of the imperial authority and later of the Minamoto shogunate (1200), the provincial war lords had been fighting among themselves in a bewildering series of ever-changing combinations. These endemic civil wars had ceased only for brief spans under the strongest of the Ashikaga shoguns, as when the whole nation combined to repel the Mongol invasions of 1276 to 1281. At the time of the Portuguese contact, Japan was in the middle of the Sengoku-jidai (country at war) period (c. 1460–1600), during which the transition from a patrician to a feudal social and economic order, begun under the Kamakura shogunate (1185–1338), was completed. The emperor at Kyoto still had much of his former moral prestige, but none of his former temporal power.

The condition of the emperor's deputy, the shogun, was not much better. The powerful military dictatorship established in 1192 by Minamoto Yoritomo, after his defeat of the rival Taira clan, had by now shrunk to an empty shell. The Ashikaga shogun, whom the Jesuits usually referred to by his popular title, *kubosama*, exercised only a tenuous authority throughout the *gokinai*, or five home provinces around Kyoto, and none at all elsewhere. However, in one respect the shogunate was better off than the imperial house, since the Ashikagas still possessed considerable landed property from which they derived a fairly substantial income, though they spent it freely on their lavish patronage of the arts. They had delegated many of their administrative duties to provincial constables (*shugo*), who had either become practically autonomous or had delegated their authority to others. The warring daimyo (feudal barons) whether owing a nominal allegiance to the shogun or not, were thus virtually independent of both him and the emperor, ruling their own fiefs as they saw fit.

Another important factor in the political and cultural life of the country was the Buddhist priesthood. Commerce and war lured many of the monks from leading an austerely devout and holy life, but the Buddhist clergy kept the torch of culture alight during this time, in a manner similar to that of the Christian clergy in Europe after the disappearance of the Roman Empire. The fortunes of the Shinto tradition throughout the sixteenth century were completely overshadowed by Buddhism. Nevertheless, the ancient cult was preserved in relatively pristine purity at the great national shrines of Ise and Idzumo. It was some time before the Jesuits grasped the difference between Shinto and Buddhism.

By 1569, the civil wars had reached a point at which there were fewer than half a dozen principal contestants for political supremacy, of whom the most centrally placed was Oda Nobunaga, who in that year had occupied Kyoto on behalf of his puppet, Yoshiaki, the nominal Ashikaga shogun. Nobunaga continued his campaigns to consolidate and extend his dominion and by 1582 he was a master of more than half the provinces of Japan. His career of conquest was cut short by the rebellion of Akechi Mitsuhide, who treacherously attacked and killed him at Kyoto on June 21, 1582.

The discovery of Japan opened a new and most welcome market to the Portuguese, for despite the ravages of civil war, there was a keen demand for foreign goods, and particularly for the Chinese silk yarn, which the daimyo and samurai preferred to the native product.

Because Japanese pirates (*wako*) terrorized the maritime provinces of China and Korea in the fifteenth and sixteenth centuries, the Ming emperor had closed his coasts to them and forbade all intercourse with the Japanese. The Portuguese profited from this situation, since they became not only the carriers but the intermediaries in Japan's trade with China. An agreement made by Leonel de Sousa with the Chinese of Kwangtung in 1554, followed by the acquisition of Macao three years later, virtually placed Portuguese-Chinese relations on an official basis. Within a few years, the Portuguese ships had visited all the harbors on the coast of Kyushu, and not long afterwards the traders were followed by Jesuit priests from the missions at Macao and Goa.

Desire for foreign trade was the primary impulse that accounts for the early success of Christianity in Japan. Some of the daimyo in Kyushu, having noticed the deference the Portuguese traders paid to the priests, favored the Jesuits in hopes of attracting merchant ships to harbors in their own fiefs. After a while, the Jesuits were acting as interpreters and intermediaries, and at times, as brokers, for a fee. The Portuguese annual black ship (kurofune) came to Nagasaki, which had been ceded to them by the local baron, for the first time in 1571. The Jesuits retained the virtual overlordship of Nagasaki until Toyotomi Hideyoshi brought them under the direct control of the central government in 1578 as part of his successful campaign to unify the country.

The rivalry between the various Roman Catholic orders in Japan—Portuguese Jesuits and Spanish Franciscans—was one of the prime causes of the ruin of their missions, and as time went by many things, among them the close connection between politics and religion exemplified by the Portuguese and Spanish in their respective colonial empires, confirmed Hideyoshi's view that Christianity was a political threat. In 1587 he issued an anti-Christian edict, which was not enforced in the Christian fiefs of Kyushu, where the Jesuits were allowed to propagate their faith openly. This proved that Christianity in Japan depended on the annual ship from Macao, and the presence of the Jesuits was thought to be essential to the smooth conduct of the Macao trade at Nagasaki. Hideyoshi's tolerance of Christian propaganda was in direct proportion to the profits he hoped to gain from the Iberian traders. In 1597, Christianity was proscribed and persecution began, but Hideyoshi did not enforce his edict of 1587 because he was occupied with other matters; he died in 1598.

Hideyoshi's successor, Ieyasu, at first displayed a similar tolerance and for similar reasons, hoping to encourage the growth of Japan's merchant marine, while maintaining the country's foreign trade. He offered to open the ports of eastern Japan to Spanish ships, while making it clear that he would not enforce the edicts against Christianity. A Dutch ship arrived in Bungo in 1600; the pilot major of the squadron, an Englishman named Will Adams became a favorite of Ieyasu, advising him on matters of trade and navigation and informing him of the attitude of the Protestant countries of Europe toward the Church of Rome. Ieyasu began to think it preferable and possible to have foreign trade without foreign priests.

In August 1602 the Dutch founded a trading post at Hirado. Although the English tried and failed to establish themselves in Japan, there is no doubt that the presence of the Dutch and English had a decisive influence on the course of Japan's foreign relations at a critical moment in her history.

By 1612 Ieyasu thought that he had little reason to fear the loss of foreign trade, because the Dutch and English were eager to visit his ports, and although there was still no authorized traffic with China, Japanese junks had brought Chinese products from entrepôts in Cochin China and elsewhere. In 1612 and 1613 some Christians were banished, some sanctuaries were destroyed, and fifty Christians were executed. Persecution became more intense in some districts in 1614 and, after Hidetada succeeded Ieyasu in 1616, it became widespread throughout the country, especially after 1617. Hidetada feared that stability and order in his realm would be upset by the presence and the infighting of the Portuguese, the Spanish, the Dutch, and the English. Toward 1622 the shogun Hidetada, suspecting the complicity of the Roman Catholic Church in Spanish plots to invade Japan, began to treat the priests more harshly. In 1624, the cruel and capricious Iemitsu, who succeeded his father, Hidetada, on his retirement in 1623, ordered the deportation of all Spaniards, priests and laymen, and decreed that no Japanese Christian should travel overseas. In 1637, rebellion broke out among the Christians of the island of Amakusa and the Shimabara peninsula, which attracted Christians from neighboring districts. Early in 1638 several thousand of them took possession of a dilapidated feudal castle in Shimabara, where they held out for more than two months. Nearly all were put to the sword and with this massacre, Christianity was virtually exterminated in Japan.

Dread of such uprisings gave the last impulse to the exclusionist sentiment that had been gradually gaining strength in Japan. The English and the Dutch did not come within the scope of the policy of exclusion (the English trading station had been closed in 1623), but after 1640 there were no foreigners in Japan except certain authorized Chinese and a handful of Dutch, who were confined in a small settlement at Nagasaki, to which a few trading ships, strictly limited and closely watched, came annually. Japan had otherwise shut its gates to all foreigners and lapsed into an isolation that lasted for over two hundred years, until July 8, 1853, when an American naval officer, Commodore Matthew C. Perry, forced them open at gunpoint.

BIBLIOGRAPHY

Boxer, Charles Ralph. The Christian Century in Japan, 1549–1650. 2d ed. Berkeley and Los Angeles, 1967.

Boxer, Charles Ralph. Fidalgos in the Far East, 1550–1770. The Hague, 1948.

Boxer, Charles Ralph. *The Great Ship from Amacon: Annals of Macao and the Old Japan Trade, 1555–1640.* 2d ed. Lisbon, 1963.

Dahlgren, Erik Wilhelm. "A Contribution to the History of the Discovery of Japan." *Transactions and Proceedings of the Japan Society* (London) 2 (1912–1913): 239–260.

Sansom, G. B. *Japan, a Short Cultural History.* Rev. ed. New York, 1943.

Schurhammer, Georg. "O descobrimento do Japão pelos portugueses no ano de 1543." *Anais da Academia Portuguesa da História.* 2d ser., 1 (1946): 9–172.

Schurhammer, Georg. *Francis Xavier: His Life, His Times.* Translated by M. Joseph Costelloe. 4 vols. Rome, 1973–1982.

REBECCA CATZ

CIRCUMFERENCE. Christopher Columbus's views as to the size and shape of the earth came through both study and practical experience. His geographic and geodetic views were formed primarily during the period 1472 to 1484, when he gained his initial experience as a seaman and navigator. But we know, too, that throughout his life, whenever the opportunity arose, he drew, modified, and sold sea charts. (His younger brother Bartolomé had preceded him as a cartographer.) Columbus's convictions as to the earth's dimensions, the distribution of its lands and seas, and the relationship of the earth to the heavenly bodies (collectively and loosely termed "cosmography" in his day) developed through his study of four works: three cosmographical treatises, *Tractatus de sphaera* by Sacrobosco (d. 1256; also known as John of Holywood) and *Tractatus de imagine mundi (Imago mundi)* and *Cosmographiae tractatus duo* by Pierre d'Ailly (d. 1420), and a sensationalist travelogue, *The Book of Ser Marco Polo* (c. 1299).

From Sacrobosco and d'Ailly, Columbus learned that the size of a spherical earth had been estimated, and in some cases measured, by various philosophers, astronomers, and geographers, from Aristotle (384–322 B.C.) to Alfraganus (al-Farghani), a ninth-century Arab astronomer. He also learned that the estimates of the earth's circumference, including those based on attempted measurements, varied widely, although the methods employed were basically similar. The objective in each case was to determine the length, on the surface of the earth along a meridian, of a degree of latitude. Three hundred sixty such degrees would give the circumference of a great circle of the earth's surface. The trace on the earth's surface of a plane intersecting the earth and passing through its center is a great circle; the equator is a great circle, and the meridians, stretching between the North Pole and South Pole, are each one-half of a great circle.

Through the works of Sacrobosco and d'Ailly, Columbus was indirectly introduced to the great geographical, astronomical, philosophical, and natural history writings of Strabo (c. 63 B.C.–after A.D. 23), Pliny (A.D. 23–79), Ptolemy (fl. middle of second century A.D.), Macrobius (Theodosius; fl. A.D. 395–423), Isidore of Seville (fl. c. 560–636), Alfraganus, al-Biruni (973–1048), and Roger Bacon (between 1210 and 1215–1292). Their ideas were covered in sufficient detail to reveal three interesting geographic propositions: one relating to the size of the earth, the second to the length of the Eurasian continent, and the third to the width of the sea that separated Spain and Portugal from the Orient. (There was no knowledge, no inkling, of the existence of the American continents lying between Europe and Asia.)

Columbus learned of Aristotle's arguments for a spherical earth and his estimate of its size: 400,000 stades for the circumference, or 1,111.11 stades for the length of a degree. He learned that Archimedes (d. 212 B.C.), or possibly Dicaearchus of Messana (d. 285 B.C.), had made a measurement (of sorts) of the earth's circumference in which the result obtained was 300,000 stades. He was impressed by the "double-measurement" of the length of a degree carried out between Alexandria and Syene (present-day Aswan), Egypt, by Eratosthenes (c. 276–c. 194 B.C.). Columbus drew some strength from the fact that Eratosthenes' result, 250,000 stades for the earth's circumference, arbitrarily enlarged to 252,000 (so that the length of a degree would be 700 stades), was accorded different equivalent lengths in Roman miles (R.M.) by Strabo, Pliny, and Isidore of Seville, who set Eratosthenes' degree at 87.5 R.M., and by Macrobius and Sacrobosco, who set the degree at 70 R.M. Columbus was pleased to learn that Posidonius (135–51 B.C.), a Greek astronomer and geographer, had made a measurement of a degree between Rhodes and Alexandria and had obtained a degree smaller than that of Eratosthenes. Cleomedes, Posidonius's pupil, reported the result as 666⅔ stades, which, using a stade length of 148.15 to 148.8 meters, or 10 stades to the Roman mile, yields a 66⅔ R.M. degree and a figure for the earth's circumference of 24,000 R.M. Strabo, however, reported that Posidonius's degree measured 500 stades and the earth's circumference 180,000 stades. Using his equivalency of 8 stades per R.M., the degree and the earth's circumference were reduced still further, to 62.5 R.M. and 22,500 R.M., respectively.

There is nothing to indicate that either Marinus of Tyre, a first-century geographer, or Ptolemy ever attempted to measure a degree of latitude. Rather, it appears that both accepted Strabo's interpretation of Posidonius. Columbus was not particularly interested in their views of the size of the earth, because he had come across a reference to Alfraganus's 56⅔-mile degree in both Sacrobosco and d'Ailly. In his *Chronologica et astronomica elementa*, Alfraganus described the measurement of a degree of

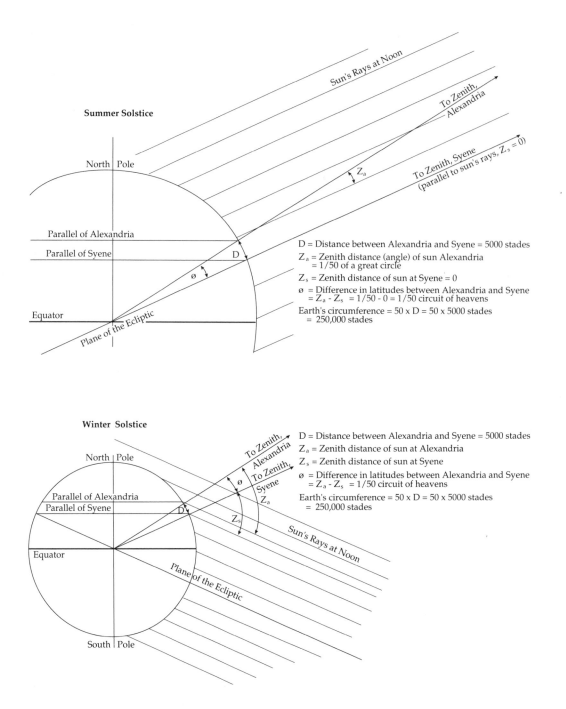

ERATOSTHENES' DETERMINATION OF THE CIRCUMFERENCE OF THE EARTH AT SUMMER AND WINTER SOLSTICES. Eratosthenes chose Syene for its proximity to the Tropic of Cancer: at noon on the summer solstice the sun is directly overhead (*top*). This makes its zenith distance zero. One need only measure the zenith distance at Alexandria, therefore, to obtain the difference in latitudes between the two sites, 1/50 the circuit of the heavens (7°12′). Hence the earth's circumference must be fifty times the distance between the two sites, measured (paced) to be 5,000 stades (circumference = 50 × 5,000 = 250,000 stades). Eratosthenes determined the zenith distance of the sun at Alexandria by means of a skiothern, a hemispherical bowl with a radius equal to the height of a vertical gnomon set in its center. The interior of the bowl was so inscribed with concentric rings around the gnomon that the gnomon's shadow gave a direct measurement of the sun's zenith distance. When Eratosthenes repeated the measurement at noon on the winter solstice (*bottom*), he used skiotherns at both points.

AFTER FRED. F. KRAVATH, *CHRISTOPHER COLUMBUS, COSMOGRAPHER*, RANCHO CORDOVA, CALIF., 1987, P. 80.

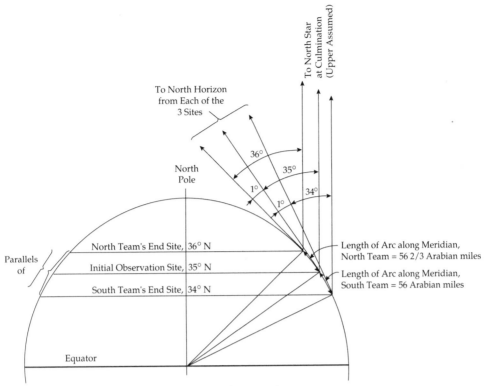

To North Star at Culmination (Upper Assumed)

To North Horizon from Each of the 3 Sites

North Pole

36°
35°
1°
34°
1°

Parallels of

North Team's End Site, 36° N

Initial Observation Site, 35° N

South Team's End Site, 34° N

Length of Arc along Meridian, North Team = 56 2/3 Arabian miles

Length of Arc along Meridian, South Team = 56 Arabian miles

Equator

Section of Earth through Longitude 39° E (and 141° W)

PROBABLE METHOD USED BY AL-MA'MUN TO MEASURE THE LENGTH OF ONE DEGREE OF LATITUDE (CIRCA A.D. 830). First, the altitude of the North Star (at its upper culmination) was determined at an initial site at approximately 39° E and 35° N in the desert of Sinjar (Syria). Then, two teams proceeded along the meridian of the initial site, one to the north and one to the south, until they obtained readings of altitude for the North Star one degree greater (for the north team) and one degree less (for the south team) than the altitudes taken at the initial site. One of the teams measured 56⅔ Arabian miles for the surface distance corresponding to one degree of arc; the other measured 56 Arabian miles. The former was selected as the more valid measurement of the length of one degree of latitude. In this illustration, end observation site parallels have been drawn with exaggerated differences in latitude from the initial observation site. AFTER FRED F. KRAVATH, *CHRISTOPHER COLUMBUS, COSMOGRAPHER*, RANCHO CORDOVA, CALIF., 1987, P. 121.

latitude by the astronomers of the caliph al-Ma'mun in the Syrian desert near Sinjar in A.D. 830. Not only was the result, 56⅔ miles, the smallest numerically of any of the measurements Columbus encountered in the works of Sacrobosco and d'Ailly, but Alfraganus stated that Ptolemy had made his degree too large, in the ratio of 66⅔ to 56⅔. The Arabs' result was stated in Arabian miles. Columbus assumed the Arabian and Roman miles to be identical and adopted the standard of 56⅔ R.M. for the length of a degree of latitude, 20,400 R.M. for the earth's circumference. He claimed to have verified this standard by a measurement at sea, en route from Spain to Guinea, sometime in the period 1482–1484.

In reading Sacrobosco and d'Ailly, Columbus came across a statement from Ptolemy's *Geographic Syntaxis* (Atlas of the world) to the effect that Marinus had given

the habitable world a length of 225 degrees of longitude, stretching from the Fortunate (Canary) Islands, the zero meridian, to Sera, the capital of the Seres and the most easterly inland city of which he had knowledge. Ptolemy arbitrarily reduced this length to 180 degrees. The implication in both cases was that there was an unknown additional stretch of land between Sera and the Atlantic Ocean. Eleven hundred years after Marinus, essential confirmation of his estimate came from Marco Polo, whose book provided details as to the entire continent of Asia and indicated further that 1,500 miles east of the China coast lay the fabulously wealthy island of Cipangu (Japan).

For each of these early geographers, longitudinal distances were determined from the descriptions of travelers' reports, troop movements, caravan operations over reasonably well-known routes, and, where feasible, data

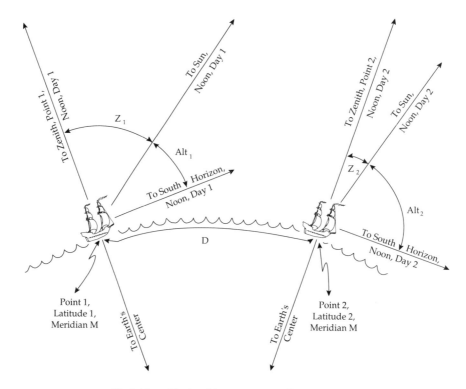

Alt$_1$ & Alt$_2$ = altitudes of the sun at noon on Days 1 & 2

Z$_1$ & Z$_2$ = zenith distances (angles) of the sun at noon
on Days 1 & 2 (zenith distance = 90° - Alt)

Latitude 1 - Latitude 2
= (Z$_1$ + declination$_1$) - (Z$_2$ + declination$_2$)
= (Alt$_2$ - declination$_2$) - (Alt$_1$ - declination$_1$)

D = surface distance between Points 1 & 2 on Meridian M
= distance traveled due south between noon on Days 1 & 2

Length of 1 Degree of Latitude
$$= \frac{D}{(\text{Alt}_2 - \text{declination}_2) - (\text{Alt}_1 - \text{declination}_1)}$$
= 56 2/3 Roman miles, according to Columbus
= 75 Roman miles (111,111 meters), actually

A RATIONALIZATION OF COLUMBUS'S "MEASUREMENT" OF THE LENGTH OF ONE DEGREE OF LATITUDE AT SEA.
The length of one degree of latitude is equal to the distance traveled divided by the change in
latitude. To use the sun's noontime altitude to determine latitude, one must correct for
declination (the sun's zenith distance or angle at the equator). Declination changes day to day.
With this change, the end points of the measurement may have been as many as nine degrees
of latitude apart, or 675 Roman miles (1,000 kilometers), a four- to eight-day sail in Columbus's
time. Whether Columbus even considered declination in his measurement is moot considering
the extremely difficult task of taking the sun's altitude aboard a moving ship.
AFTER FRED F. KRAVATH, *CHRISTOPHER COLUMBUS, COSMOGRAPHER*, RANCHO CORDOVA, CALIF., 1987, P. 182.

from the logs of ships engaged in trade. Such data were
highly unreliable, for rarely were itinerary reports anything more than a series of estimates of course direction
and speed of travel, and they were invariably inflated and
inaccurate. In Marinus's use of such reports, and in the
interpretations by Columbus and several contemporary
geographers of Marco Polo's book, the east-west length of
the Eurasian continent was greatly overestimated.

Columbus used Marinus and Marco Polo together to
estimate the east-west length of the Eurasian continent,

plus offshore islands, somewhere between 280 and 300 degrees. The westward sea voyage from the Canary Islands to Cipangu was allotted 60 to 80 degrees (depending upon the reporting historian). Since this voyage would likely be made at latitudes between 28° N and 36° N, there was involved a sea journey of from 3,000 to 4,000 R.M. at 28° N and possibly as little as 2,750 to 3,670 R.M. at 36° N. Further, the voyage could be broken up by a stop at the island of Antilia (a fictitious place shown on many fourteenth and fifteenth-century portolan charts).

Columbus had heard of correspondence between the Italian astronomer and physician Paolo dal Pozzo Toscanelli (1397–1482) and the Portuguese monarch Afonso V pertaining to the feasibility of a voyage westward from Lisbon to the Indies. It was said that Toscanelli had attached a map to his response. Columbus wrote Toscanelli, giving his own views as to how such a voyage could be made. In return, sometime before his death Toscanelli wrote Columbus, expressing warm approval of his enterprise and attaching a copy of the map he had sent the Portuguese monarch.

Certain of the more prominent biographers of Christopher Columbus, unaware of the extent of Marco Polo's influence over geographers from the time of Columbus to as late as the middle of the sixteenth century, have ridiculed the Great Navigator's enormous extension of the Eurasian continent. The work of the German geographer Henricus Martellus, for example, shows a Eurasian continent with an estimated length of 255 to 265 degrees of longitude. A globe produced by Martin Behaim, a Nürnberg cosmographer and cartographer, in 1492 shows features similar to the Martellus map and a cosmography similar to that of Columbus. J. C. Dopplemayer reproduced Behaim's globe in map form with two hemispheres in 1730.

One of the more interesting maps showing an elongated Eurasian continent is Martin Waldseemüller's world map of 1507, which was responsible for the New World being named after the Florentine Amerigo Vespucci. Despite the necessity of finding room on his map for an American continent and the Greater and several of the Lesser Antilles, Waldseemüller allots a full 270 degrees of longitude for Eurasia, including the Canary Islands (zero meridian), Japan, and the other islands east of China and Southeast Asia.

[See also Cartography; Compass, article on Declination of the Compass; Distance, Measurement of.]

BIBLIOGRAPHY

Bunbury, E. H. A History of Ancient Geography. 2d ed. 2 vols. London, 1883. New edition, New York, 1959.

Dreyer, J. L. E. History of Planetary Systems from Thales to Kepler. Cambridge, 1906. Revised by W. H. Stahl and reissued as History of Astronomy from Thales to Kepler. New York, 1953.

Kimble, George H. T. Geography in the Middle Ages. London, 1938.

Kravath, Fred F. Christopher Columbus, Cosmographer. Rancho Cordova, Calif., 1987.

Morison, Samuel Eliot. Admiral of the Ocean Sea: A Life of Christopher Columbus. 2 vols. Boston, 1942.

Nordenskjold, A. E. Facsimile Atlas to the Early History of Cartography with Reproductions of the Most Important Maps Printed in the XV and XVI Centuries. Stockholm, 1889. Reprint, New York, 1973.

Skelton, R. A. "The Cartography of the First Voyage." Appendix to The Journal of Christopher Columbus, translated by Cecil Jane. New York, 1960.

Skelton, R. A. Explorers' Maps. New York, 1958.

Vignaud, Henry. Toscanelli and Columbus: The Letter and Chart of Toscanelli. First English edition, 1902. Reprint, New York, 1971.

Fred F. Kravath

CISNEROS, FRANCISCO JIMÉNEZ DE. See Jiménez de Cisneros, Francisco.

CLOTHING. See Equipment, Clothing, and Rations.

COAT OF ARMS. As a newly created nobleman, Columbus required the grant of a coat of arms to provide a visible indication of his rank. It is not known when Columbus first conceived of acquiring nobility status, with a title and a coat of arms, as a reward for his achievement—but probably not before 1491. His wish for this status and its accoutrements undoubtedly was based in several factors, including his resentment for having wasted six and a half frustrating years in Spain awaiting royal approval, the summary treatment he had received, and a desire to perpetuate in his family the glory of his achievements.

The coat of arms assigned to him contained the royal arms of the castle and the lion, quartered with his proper bearings, which were a group of islands surrounded by waves. These were specified in a letter patent issued by the Catholic sovereigns on May 20, 1493, confirming his right and that of his descendants to bear arms and declaring:

> You may place above your arms a castle and a lion that we grant you for arms, viz., the gold castle on a green field in the upper quarter of the shield of your arms on the dexter hand and in the other upper quarter on the sinister hand a purple lion rampant with green tongue on a white field, and in the other quarter below on the dexter hand some gold islands in waves of the sea, and in the other quarter below on the sinister hand your own arms which you are accustomed to bear.

It was a singular honor for the sovereigns to allow Columbus to augment his arms with the gold castle of

COLUMBUS'S COAT OF ARMS. A facsimile from a modern edition of Columbus's Book of Privileges, published in London, 1893.

the said ocean sea in the said region of the Indies . . . we do by these presents confirm to you and to your children, descendants and successors, one after the other, now and forever, the said office of Admiral of the Ocean Sea, Viceroy and Governor of the said islands and mainland that you have found and discovered, and of the other islands and mainland that shall by you or your industry be found and discovered henceforward in the same region of the Indies.

No exact description of the coat of arms as quoted in the granting documents has survived, although they are represented in the document of the sovereigns dated June 20, 1493, granting them to Columbus. Undoubtedly each of the vessels that set forth on Columbus's second voyage featured the Admiral's arms emblazoned on their banners and waistcloths.

By the time Columbus had compiled his Book of Privileges in 1502 for the benefit of his descendants, he had made some important alterations in the blazon. He made the chief identical with the royal arms by placing the gold castle on a red field and bringing the lion rampant in accord with the lion of León. Because by this time he had discovered Tierra Firma, he changed the lower dexter quarter so that it now featured an emerging continent as well as a cluster of islands. He added a new sinister quarter to represent the office of the Admiral of the Ocean Sea. This consisted of a group of five golden anchors arranged horizontally on a blue field. The family arms, blazoned as a blue bend on a gold field with a red chief, were now situated in the base between the third and fourth quarters in an arched point.

According to Continental usage, Columbus was within his rights to make the alterations, which had no particular significance. In that period England was the only country having a heralds' college; in all other countries people frequently altered and augmented their escutcheons, few adhering strictly to their original blazon.

If Columbus had pretended to a noble origin, an origin proposed but with no basis in fact by his son Fernando Colón, he would in all likelihood have selected pretentious symbols, like a flock of doves, appropriate to such a claim. A dove, for which the word in Italian is *colombo*, is generally featured in all known arms of patrician families bearing the Columbus name, including the Colombo families of Italy and the Colóns of Castile and Aragón.

The colors of Columbus's arms, consisting of a blue bend on a gold field with red chief, which he afterward quartered with the arms of Castile, probably were derived from the arms of the local guild of clothiers in Genoa, of which his father was a member and occasionally its representative. It is even probable that Columbus's father, a political activist, may have himself used this coat of arms. In European communities during the fifteenth century, members of a trade guild often bore arms, as indeed did

Castile and the purple lion of León, but inasmuch as a difference of the fields was specified, these were not, strictly speaking, the royal arms. No provisions were made, however, for a crest, a motto, or a blazon in the original document assigning the arms to Columbus, which is now among the manuscripts of the duke of Veragua in the Archivo General de Indias in Seville.

These rights and privileges had been conferred conditionally upon Columbus at Granada on April 30, 1492, prior to his departure on his first voyage. After the conditions had been fulfilled with the successful discovery of new lands on the first voyage, it became necessary that the title and arms be officially expressed and formalized. Accordingly, confirmation was issued on May 28, 1493, which repeated the text of the Granada document given above and then went on:

> And now, forasmuch as it has pleased Our Lord that you discover many of the said islands, and as we hope with His aid that you will find and discover other islands and mainland in

other ordinary citizens, for any freeman had a right to assume simple arms. Many of the surviving arms in Continental countries originally were borne by middle-class families. It is to be noted that none of the ingenious promoters of the "real Columbus," whether of Portuguese, Jewish, Catalan, French, or Polish origin, has been able to show that his contender had a coat of arms bearing a blue bend on a gold field under a red chief.

To the family arms as enhanced by Columbus was later added a motto, rendered by Fernando as:

A Castilla y á León
Nuevo Mundo dió Colón

(To Castile and León
Columbus has given a New World)

In the first edition of his *Historia general de las Indias,* Gonzalo Fernández de Oviedo compounded confusion about the coat of arms with an illustration in which the Columbus arms are further enhanced by the addition of a crest representing a globe surmounted by a red cross and featuring a white ribband containing the motto, which encircled the shield. It is possible that the crest and motto had been added by Columbus's son, Diego Colón, the second admiral.

Much effort has been expended over the years by heraldic experts and others on studies of the "family arms" of the 1502 shield to resolve some of the numerous legends that nineteenth-century writers created around the figure of Columbus. These efforts have not met with much success.

BIBLIOGRAPHY

Colón, Fernando. *Historia del S. D. Fernando Colombo, nella quale s'ha particulare e vera relatione dell'Ammiraglio D. Cristoforo Colombo, suo padre, nuovamente di lingua Spanuola tradotte nell'Italiana dal S. Alfonso Ulloa.* Reprint, Venice, 1571.

Morison, Samuel Eliot. *Admiral of the Ocean Sea: A Life of Christopher Columbus.* 2 vols. Boston, 1942.

Navarette, Martín Fernández de. *Collección de los viajes y descubrimientos que hicieron por mar los Españoles.* Vol. 2. Madrid, 1825–1837.

Oviedo, Gonzalo Fernández de. *Historia general de las Indias.* Vol. 1. Seville, 1535. Reprint, Salamanca, 1851.

Stevens, Benjamin F. *Christopher Columbus: His Own Book of Privileges.* London, 1893.

SILVIO A. BEDINI

COINS. See *Iconography,* article on *Numismatics.*

COLOMBO. Members of the Columbus family whose lives centered in Italy can be found under *Colombo.* For those whose lives centered in Spain or in Spanish America, see *Colón.* See *Columbus, Christopher,* for several articles detailing the life and achievements of Christopher Columbus.

COLOMBO, DOMENICO (1418–1495/1499), father of Christopher Columbus. Domenico Colombo, the son of Giovanni Colombo from Mocónesi, was born in Quinto. At the age of eleven, he became an apprentice to Guglielmo de Brabante, a Brabant weaver in Quinto. Ten years later, in 1439, he was a master craftsman.

From 1439 to 1447, Domenico Colombo practiced his trade in Genoa. He was one of many Genoese who became involved in the political rivalry between the Adorno and Fregoso parties in Genoa. He took the side of the Fregosos, acquiring moderate political influence. He was undoubtedly a loyal party member, for in 1447 the new doge Giano appointed him warden of the Olivella gate, a position that customarily lasted thirteen months. Pietro Fregoso had been named captain general of the city on February 3, 1447, the day before Domenico Colombo's appointment, and it is probable that he suggested the appointment to the doge. When Pietro Fregoso became doge, the custody of the Olivella gate was again entrusted to Domenico (October 1, 1450). Domenico Colombo apparently lived comfortably during this period, for he invested money in the purchase of land in Quarto.

Domenico married Susanna Fontanarossa around 1445. Cristoforo Colombo (Christopher Columbus), their eldest son, was born in 1451. From 1452 to 1455, Domenico Colombo resided in Genoa, probably in a house in Vico Olivella. In 1455 he went to live in a house in Vico Diritto. The same building contained both his dwelling and his shop. In February 1470 he was no longer in Genoa, having moved to Savona, where he practiced the trades of weaver and tavern keeper.

Six months later he was back in Genoa with his son Christopher to appear in court, as attested to by the earliest document (September 22, 1470) naming Christopher Columbus. On that day, Domenico was arrested, only to be released a few hours later by a criminal judge who declared that he did not find him *culpabilem.* The reasons for the arrest and for the trip to Genoa were the same: a legal question of a debt that Domenico and his son Christopher owed to a Girolamo del Porto. According to a document dated September 28, 1470, the judge imposed a fine of thirty-five lira on Domenico. In order to raise that sum he sold to a Caprile family some lands "in Ginestreto, potestacie Bisannis," which had been his wife's dowry.

In a document of the Savona weavers' guild dated March 12, 1473, the name Domenico Colombo appears again. On September 24 of the same year, he sold his house on dell'Olivella Street in Genoa. At the beginning of 1477, when he bought land with a house in Légino, near Savona, he sold his house in Vico Diritto, in the Sant'Andrea district. On August 17, 1481, he leased his house in Légino in order to return to Genoa.

In a document dated January 27, 1483, he is cited as a former weaver (*olim textor pannorum*). He was around sixty-five years old, and his wife was probably dead. Of his sons, none had remained by his side. Giovanni Pellegrino, his second son, apparently died young. Christopher and Bartolomé were in Lisbon. Giacomo was also far from home. His daughter Bianchinetta was about to be married to Giacomo Bavarello, son of a cheese maker, who would take his father-in-law's place at the house in Vico Diritto, outside Porta Sant'Andrea. On November 17, 1491, Domenico was in Savona, where he received a sum of money from a debtor, and in 1494, on September 30, he acted as a witness for a notarized document affirming that his sons were "*quondam Dominici.*"

All in all, he is named in seventy-seven notarial acts, attesting to his long and apparently eventful life.

BIBLIOGRAPHY

"Albero genealogico della famiglia Colombo." In part 2, vol. 1 of *Raccolta di documenti e studi pubblicati dalla R. Commissione Colombiana pel quarto centenario dalla scoperta dell'America.* Rome, 1896.
Genoa, City of. *Christopher Columbus: Documents and Proofs of His Genoese Origin.* English-German edition. Bergamo, 1932.
Taviani, Paolo Emilio. *Cristoforo Colombo: Genius of the Sea.* Rome, 1990.

PAOLO EMILIO TAVIANI

COLOMBO, GIOVANNI

COLOMBO, GIOVANNI (d. around 1442), grandfather of Christopher Columbus. Giovanni Colombo, the son of Antonio Colombo, was born in Mocónesi, a village in the interior of Liguria. Mocónesi had long been the destination of mule teams carrying grain from Piacenza. Here, and in neighboring villages, mills would grind the grain, using the waters of the Lavagna River. The sacks of flour would then be sent, again by means of mules, to Genoa, or more exactly, Quinto. This road from Piacenza to Quinto thus came to be called "the bread road." This was the well-worn route Giovanni Colombo followed as he traveled from Mocónesi to Quinto.

A document preserved in the State Archives of Genoa, dated February 21, 1429, states that Giovanni Colombo of Mocónesi, a resident of Quinto, gave as apprentice his son Domenico, eleven years old, to Guglielmo di Brabante, a Brabant textile weaver. Giovanni Colombo, like his ancestors of Mocónesi, was a peasant, and he wanted his son to become a good artisan. From two documents

preserved in the Columbian Hall of the State Archives of Genoa, Giovanni Colombo appears to have died between September 1440 and January 1444.

BIBLIOGRAPHY

"Albero genealogico della famiglia Colombo." In part 2, vol. 1 of *Raccolta di documenti e studi pubblicati dalla R. Commissione Colombiana pel quarto centenario dalla scoperta dell'America.* Rome, 1896.
Genoa, City of. *Christopher Columbus: Documents and Proofs of His Genoese Origin.* English-German edition. Bergamo, 1932.
Taviani, Paolo Emilio. *Cristoforo Colombo: Genius of the Sea.* Rome, 1990.

PAOLO EMILIO TAVIANI
Translated from Italian by Rodica Diaconescu-Blumenfeld

COLOMBO, GIOVANNI ANTONIO

COLOMBO, GIOVANNI ANTONIO (c. 1475–c. 1540), cousin of Christopher Columbus and participant in voyages of discovery. During his third voyage Columbus named three captains: Pedro de Arana, brother of Beatriz de Arana, who bore Columbus's son Fernando; Alonso Sánchez de Carvajal, a dignitary of the city of Baeza; and Giovanni Antonio Colombo of Genoa. Thus another relative, another Genoese, makes his appearance, one who did not Hispanicize his surname to Colón, preserving the Italian name Colombo. He had participated earlier in the Columbian enterprise; at the end of 1497 and the beginning of 1498 he was the Admiral's majordomo. Later he was one of the faithful supporters of Columbus during the Roldán rebellion on La Isabela in 1498. Columbus mentions him and his brother Andrea twice in an autograph document for the sale of some gold in Spain sometime between July 1502 and March 1504 and in a letter of January 4, 1505.

When the Admiral died, Giovanni Antonio remained in the service of Columbus's son Diego, who, in his will of February 19, 1515, left him one hundred gold pesos. His brother Andrea, nicknamed "André Ginovés" (Andrew the Genoese), took part in Columbus's fourth voyage as a groom aboard *Santiago* and was in charge of obtaining some provisions on La Española. As procurator to Diego in San Salvador, he testified in an action brought by Diego in 1515 against the treasury. Bartolomé de las Casas says that Giovanni Antonio was "a man of great ability, prudent and authoritative, with whom I held frequent conversations." Las Casas was certain that the brothers, Giovanni Antonio and Andrea, belonged to the Admiral's family. They were probably second or third cousins.

Giovanni Antonio may have been the Johannes de Columbo of Quinto mentioned in a notary's document of October 11, 1496, reproduced in the *Raccolta Colombiana.* The text (from Latin) reads as follows:

Giovanni Columbus of Quinto, Matteo Columbus, and Amighetto Columbus, brothers of the late Antonio, knowing that Giovanni must go to Spain to visit Christopher Columbus, Admiral to the King of Spain, and that whatever expenses are to be borne by the said Giovanni in order to find the said Christopher should be borne by all three of the brothers named above, each of them is paying a third . . . and so they are agreed.

It is not clear whether this is the same Giovanni Antonio or another. Nevertheless, one cannot help but think that when news of the surprising fortune of Domenico's eldest son spread among the Columbuses of Liguria, not a few of them sought him out in quest of some benefit. The Admiral accepted them all—brothers, nephews, and cousins of Liguria and in-laws of Córdoba—placing them in positions of responsibility and command, showing trust for relatives and suspicion of strangers.

BIBLIOGRAPHY

Ballesteros Beretta, Antonio. *Cristóbal Colón y el descubrimiento de América*. Vol. 2. Barcelona and Buenos Aires, 1945.

Columbus, Ferdinand. *The Life of the Admiral Christopher Columbus by His Son, Ferdinand.* Translated by Benjamin Keen. New Brunswick, N.J., 1959.

PAOLO EMILIO TAVIANI

COLÓN, BARTOLOMÉ (1461–1514 or 1515), brother of Christopher Columbus. Bartolomé Colón, the third son of Domenico Colombo, was born in Genoa and, like his brother Christopher, lived there and in Savona.

The Genoese chronicler Antonio Gallo writes that Bartolomé was probably already in Lisbon when Columbus arrived there. Gallo, a neighbor, was a friend of the Colombo family and, at the time he wrote his book, chancellor of the San Giorgio Bank, with which the Admiral had many dealings. Agostino Giustiniani, who cites Gallo in his *Annali della Repubblica di Genova* (1537), adds that Christopher "dedicated himself to the art of navigation and arrived in Lisbon, Portugal, where he learned cosmography . . . [from] a brother who made maritime maps." Although Gallo and Giustiniani were well informed on the subject of Columbus's Ligurian period, neither was familiar with his Portuguese years.

When Christopher Columbus arrived in Portugal in 1476, he was twenty-five years old, and Bartolomé was only fifteen. Thus the latter could not yet have been an expert in cosmography, nor is it clear how he could have gotten to Lisbon. It is more probable that Bartolomé was not yet in Portugal in 1476, but that Christopher himself called him there around 1480.

Bartolomé de las Casas says that Bartolomé was no less an expert in cosmography than was his brother. He adds that Bartolomé used to compile and draw maps and design nautical instruments. Las Casas also attests that Bartolomé was a better calligrapher than the Admiral. This comparison has led to numerous arguments regarding the attribution to the brothers of various annotations found in the books of the Biblioteca Colombina, Seville.

Above all, however, Bartolomé was a sailor. Before 1492, he sailed to England and probably to Guinea. After the great discovery, he sailed to the New World, becoming an "adelantado de mar," or governor of a region across the sea. And it was Bartolomé who saved the caravel *Bermuda* from shipwreck against a treacherous reef in a terrible storm during the fourth voyage.

From 1480 until the Admiral's death, Bartolomé was close to his older brother. When he was not with him in person, he was helping and promoting his brother's projects. That said, it should be understood that no contribution may be attributed to him for Columbus's project of sailing westward in order to reach the East. Bartolomé was only nineteen when he joined his brother in 1480. Christopher Columbus had already arrived at this notion by himself, with the aid only of the sea and his creative intuition regarding its currents, its winds, and its mysteries.

Although Bartolomé had nothing to do with the genesis of the great design, he was nevertheless present and of immense help during the difficult years that brought the design to fruition. He was a devoted, diligent, and intelligent collaborator. His collaboration was particularly important in times of grave difficulty.

In the winter of 1487–1488, for example, when Columbus had all but abandoned hope of receiving funds from Castile for his proposed voyage, he sent Bartolomé to England to solicit the support of King Henry VII. Bartolomé, however, was captured by pirates before he arrived and endured a long period of captivity before being set free. He arrived finally in England, but was not successful. So he went on to France to enlist the aid of Charles VIII. Here the news reached him that his brother in the meantime had received the help of the Spanish monarchs and had made the great discovery on the other side of the Atlantic.

Bartolomé returned immediately to Seville and, taking with him his nephews Diego and Fernando, went to the court. He then took command of a supply fleet with which he sailed for La Española, where he arrived on June 24, 1493. From this time on he was united with his brother and embarked on enterprises as explorer, colonizer, administrator, and warrior.

As administrator of La Española in Columbus's absence, Bartolomé governed the unruly settlers justly but severely and was feared by them. When the brothers, after the third voyage, were returned to Spain in chains by Fran-

SKETCH MAP OF THE COASTS OF CENTRAL AND SOUTH AMERICA.   Drawn by Alessandro Zorzi, based on a map by Bartolomé Colón.

cisco de Bobadilla, Bartolomé helped the Admiral reclaim his rights. Bartolomé went to Rome in 1506, the year of Columbus's death, to solicit from Pope Julius II a recommendation to King Fernando to entrust to him an expedition of discovery. He obtained it three years later and returned to the Indies in 1509 with his nephew Diego. There he held office in the government of Santo Domingo.

Bartolomé died, probably toward the end of 1514 or in the first days of January 1515, in the city of Concepción and was buried in Santo Domingo. He left his estate to Diego.

Two episodes in the eventful life of Bartolomé Colón deserve particular note: the founding of the city of Santo Domingo and the battle he fought during his year at Santa Gloria in Jamaica at the end of the fourth voyage of discovery. The founding of Santo Domingo took place in 1496. Columbus had departed for Europe, leaving to Bartolomé the establishment of a new capital. Bartolomé explored the southern coast of La Española, where he found an excellent natural harbor at the mouth of the Ozama River in an exceptionally fertile region. He named the new colony Santo Domingo in memory of his father, Domenico. In order to confer more solemnity upon his choice of name, Bartolomé led the settlers to the chosen site on a Sunday (*domenica*, in Italian), which that year coincided with the day dedicated by the church to Saint Dominic. Santo Domingo flourished from the beginning. Philip II called it the "escala, puerto y clave de todas las Indias" (stopover, port, and key of all the Indies).

Santa Gloria was a northern beach in Jamaica where

Christopher Columbus and his crew were marooned from June 26, 1503, to June 29, 1504. Among the stormy events of that year was the revolt of the Porras brothers, who in 1504 succeeded in convincing the crew to revolt against Columbus. On May 19 they marched on Santa Gloria, where Columbus had entrusted the defense to Bartolomé. Once the armed groups were in position, Francisco de Porras ran to the attack. The boldest of his men surrounded Bartolomé, but with one stroke Bartolomé killed an adversary and then swiftly felled the other five. Francisco de Porras advanced and struck Bartolomé with his sword so violently that he broke Bartolomé's shield and wounded him in the hand. But Porras's sword had penetrated to the hilt, and he could not retrieve it. At this point, Bartolomé could have killed him, but instead he knocked him down, disarmed him, and took him prisoner. Thus, Las Casas recounts, Bartolomé set the rebels to flight. This episode demonstrates that Bartolomé Colón was not only a good cosmographer, as he is usually remembered, but a courageous and able soldier.

BIBLIOGRAPHY

Ballesteros Beretta, Antonio. *Cristóbal Colón y el descubrimiento de América.* Vol. 1. Barcelona and Buenos Aires, 1945.

Columbus, Ferdinand. *The Life of the Admiral Christopher Columbus by His Son, Ferdinand.* Translated by Benjamin Keen. New Brunswick, N.J., 1959.

Las Casas, Bartolomé de. *Historie de las Indias.* Vol. 2. Mexico City, 1951.

Morison, Samuel Eliot. *Admiral of the Ocean Sea: A Life of Christopher Columbus.* 2 vols. Boston, 1942.

Oviedo, Gonzalo Fernández de. *Historia general y natural de las Indias.* 5 vols. Madrid, 1959.

Rubio, V. *Datos para las historia de los origenes de la ciudad de Santo Domingo.* Santo Domingo, 1978.

Taviani, Paolo Emilio. *Christopher Columbus: The Grand Design.* London, 1985.

Taviani, Paolo Emilio. *I viaggi di Colombo.* 2d ed. Vol. 2. Novara, 1990. Spanish ed., Barcelona, 1989.

PAOLO EMILIO TAVIANI
Translated from Italian by Rodica Diaconescu-Blumenfeld

COLÓN, DIEGO (c. 1462–1515), brother of Christopher Columbus. Giacomo Colombo (Spanish, Diego Colón), the second brother of Christopher Columbus, was the son of Domenico Colombo and Susanna Fontanarossa. His name first appears in a document dated September 10, 1485, in which he agrees to become the apprentice of a weaver, Luchino Cadermatori, of Savona, Italy. The will of Susanna Fontanarossa, dated July 21, 1489, lists Giacomo among her heirs.

After Christopher Columbus's return from the first voyage, Giacomo Colombo moved to Spain, where he was called Diego Colón. He became a Spanish subject in 1504; his naturalization documents refer to ecclesiastical honors and benefits, which indicate that he was a cleric. According to Bartolomé de las Casas, Diego Colón was seeking to become a bishop in La Española at this time. Further evidence that he was a cleric is a draft of Columbus's will, dated February 22, 1498, which settles the modest annual income of 100,000 maravedis on him because he was a member of the clergy.

BIBLIOGRAPHY

"Albero genealogico della famiglia Colombo." In part 2, vol. 1 of *Raccolta di documenti e studi pubblicati dalla R. Commissione Colombiana pel quarto centenario dalla scoperta dell'America.* Rome, 1896.

Genoa, City of. *Christopher Columbus: Documents and Proofs of His Genoese Origin.* English-German edition. Bergamo, 1932.

Taviani, Paolo Emilio. *Christopher Columbus: The Grand Design.* London, 1985.

Taviani, Paolo Emilio. *I viaggi di Colombo.* 2d ed. Vol. 2. Novara, 1990. Spanish ed., Barcelona, 1989.

PAOLO EMILIO TAVIANI
Translated from Italian by Rodica Diaconescu-Blumenfeld

COLÓN, DIEGO (c. 1480–1526), Christopher Columbus's son and second Admiral of the Indies. Christopher Columbus's son by his marriage of 1479 to Felipa Perestrelo y Moniz, Diego Colón was born either on Porto Santo in the Madeira Islands or in Lisbon. His mother having died by the time he was four years old, Diego accompanied his father from Lisbon to Spain in the summer of 1485. During the next seven years, he lived at the Franciscan house of La Rábida, or possibly in Moguer with Violante (or Brigulaga, according to Diego's will of 1509) Moniz, his mother's sister, and her husband, Miguel Moliarte.

On May 8, 1492, Diego was appointed a page in the household of Juan, King Fernando and Queen Isabel's only son, but did not go to court until 1494. During the next dozen years, Diego served in a variety of positions in the royal court. He was a page from 1494 to 1497 in Juan's household, and from 1498 to 1503 in Isabel's. On November 15, 1503, he was appointed a *contino* (member of the household guard), a capacity in which he served until Isabel's death the following year. He remained at court until July 1507, but was with his father when he died on May 20, 1506.

Philip I acknowledged Diego as heir to his father's titles and heritable privileges on June 2, 1506, but failed to clarify the geographic area where they applied or the extent of Diego's powers as viceroy, admiral, and governor-general.

In July 1507, Diego obtained permission to take his household to meet Fernando the Catholic, who was returning from Italy to Castile to assume control over its government following the sudden death of Philip I and Queen Juana's mental and emotional retreat from reality (she is known to history as Juana, la Loca [the mad]). By late August, Diego had joined Fernando in Valencia. He followed the court to Burgos where, in October and November 1507, he had an affair with Constanza Rosa, who was said to have borne him a child the following year. Early in 1508 he had a second affair, with Isabel Samba, who bore him a son, Cristóbal Colón, in October 1508.

During the next eighteen months, Colón established himself as his father's successor. Now of age, he sued the Crown to obtain the offices and privileges he believed had been granted to his father; this and subsequent lawsuits are known as the Pleitos Colombinos. Promised that if he would marry he would be named governor-general of the Indies, in the summer of 1508 he married María de Toledo y Rojas, daughter of Fernando de Toledo, brother of the second duke of Alba, thus allying the highest-ranking noble of the Indies with the highest-ranking noble in Castile. They eventually had seven children: Felipa, María, Juana, Isabel, Luís (third admiral of the Indies), Cristóbal, and Diego.

Although his claims had not been satisfied, Colón went to Santo Domingo with his wife to take up his office, arriving on July 10, 1509. Their court and palace gave new life to the capital.

Granted only limited powers by the Crown and subject

DIEGO AND FERNANDO COLÓN. Depicted with their father, Christopher Columbus, and Fernando's mother, Beatriz Enríquez de Harana. Engraving.

to the watchful eye of Miguel de Pasamonte, the royal treasurer—and after 1512 subject to the audiencia judges—Colón managed to use his first period of personal rule at Santo Domingo (1509–1514) to build an extensive base of political support not only on La Española but on Puerto Rico, Cuba, and Jamaica as each was occupied. His judicial and other appointees, often men who had served his father or who were longtime residents of the Antilles, were only a few of those who looked to him for protection and reward. Equally important were the locally resident encomenderos. Granted the right to distribute Indians, Colón seems to have worked out an unofficial arrangement whereby vacant encomiendas were not reported to Spain, but quietly granted (or redistributed) by him to local residents. On a few occasions he even evaded Fernando's orders to grant Indians to absentee courtiers, which, along with his role in the naming of alcaldes (municipal judges) and regidores (municipal councilors) in the municipalities of La Española, eventually came to Fernando's attention and were important reasons for Colón's recall to Spain in 1514.

His political achievement seems to have been only partially matched by financial gain. La Española was in a period of economic and demographic decline. Both the mines and the Indians who were compelled to work them had begun to give out well before Colón arrived. The decline continued in spite of ongoing resettlement of the remaining Indians, the importation of Indian slaves from other parts of the Caribbean, and Fernando's repeated orders to find more gold. Unable to make a living on La Española, Spaniards left for the new colonies or returned to Spain. Nor did the new colonies generate much royal income, of which Colón was entitled to a tenth. Only a little gold was found on Puerto Rico; gold was found on Cuba late in 1514, but proved to be limited as well. Colón did bestow Indians, mines, and farms and ranches on himself, but the extent of his incomes from these sources—as from the tenth of royal income—is not known aside from what can be inferred from some sizable bequests in his will of 1523. And set against these revenues were the heavy expenses of maintaining a court and of patronage on a scale befitting so great a noble.

Although in many respects a victory for Colón, the decision of 1511 in the Pleitos Colombinos proved to be the opening round in the undermining of Colón's quasi-seignorial power in the Caribbean colonies. The court restricted Colón's powers to the Greater Antilles and the eastern part of Venezuela and allowed the Crown to appoint appeals and residencia judges to review the actions of Colón's judicial appointees. Fernando immediately did so, creating the audiencia of Santo Domingo on August 5, 1511, and then appointing residencia judges. In the fall of 1513, Fernando appointed judges to carry out a new distribution of the remaining encomienda Indians, thereby removing Colón's most important tool of patronage. Colón was recalled for discussions in the fall of 1514. He sailed for Spain, which he had visited in 1511 and 1513, in April 1515.

Colón's stay in Spain lasted four and a half years because of Fernando's death and Charles V's succession to the throne in 1516 and because of his own efforts to acquire additional privileges once he had the new king's favor. Ever the courtier, Colón managed to charm the young king and, by late 1518, his restoration to his offices and privileges in the Indies seemed well advanced, only to be further delayed when he demanded observance of other privileges he believed had been granted by the Santa Fe Capitulations. He was also delayed because his enemy, Cardinal Juan Rodríguez de Fonseca, was again the virtual minister of colonial affairs. In the end, by a decree of May 17, 1520, the second lawsuit was settled, largely in Colón's favor. Still unsatisfied, he instituted an appeal that made even more sweeping claims than he had made in the previous suits.

Once Charles left Spain, Colón hastened to Santo

Domingo, sailing from Seville in the fall of 1520. He arrived at his capital on November 12, to find a vastly changed situation from the one he had left. His revenues continued to fall with the economic fortunes of the Antilles and each tax reduction the Crown granted to the islands in hopes of stimulating a reversal of their economic decline. To compensate, Colón arbitrarily, and without clear legal authority, raised taxes and fees. He also invested in a sugar plantation with forty black slaves (making it one of the larger of the nineteen plantations then in existence) and in slaving enterprises on the Venezuelan coast. The latter brought him into conflict with Bartolomé de las Casas and the Dominican reformers, who were attempting to demonstrate there that missions and Spanish farmers could peacefully convert the local Indians into good Spanish Christians. These powerful enemies quickly joined the audiencia's judges in denouncing Colón's actions. And since this was happening during the period of the Comunero Rebellion in Spain—which directly challenged royal power—Colón soon received a royal reprimand and an order to return to Spain, dated March 1523, not long after Charles landed in Spain to reassert his authority. Diego's "Indian summer of political feudalism," as Troy Floyd has so aptly called these three years, was at an end. In September 1523 he set out again for Spain on what proved to be his final journey.

Colón's experience in Spain was similar to his previous visit, but without obtaining what he wanted. After joining the court at Vitoria in late January 1524, he continued to follow it for the next two years and to explain away the charges against him. During this time, Charles treated him with great respect, but Colón's claims never received definitive handling. Twenty years later, Hernando Cortés would receive similar treatment.

When Charles left Toledo for Seville and the celebration of his marriage to Isabel of Portugal, Colón was too ill to travel with the court. Improving somewhat, on February 21, 1526, he left Toledo in a litter, but was forced by his illness to halt at Montalbín, six leagues from Toledo. There he lodged in Alonso Tellez Pacheco's house, where he died on February 23, 1526. Some years later his bones and those of his father were taken to Santo Domingo and buried in the cathedral.

In his will, Colón acknowledged debts totaling 1.6 million maravedis (about 4,253 ducats) in Spain and more than 3,000 pesos de oro (3,600 ducats) in La Española. He claimed that at least 14,350 ducats were due to him (10,000 of which were loaned to Charles V in 1520), as well as the eighth and tenth of the royal revenues from the colonies, none of which had been paid since his father's time. In addition, he had extensive properties on La Española.

Las Casas, who knew Colón well, described him as being tall, large framed, and well proportioned like his father. He had a long face and a dignified bearing and knew how to please as well as how to try to get his way through quiet negotiation and political action. His faults—a tendency to authoritarianism and grasping—seem to have been those of nobles of his rank.

[See also Lawsuits; Santa Fe Capitulations.]

BIBLIOGRAPHY

Floyd, Troy S. *The Columbus Dynasty in the Caribbean, 1492–1526.* Albuquerque, N. Mex., 1973.

Nieto y Cortadellas, Rafael. *Los descendientes de Cristóbal Colón: Obra genealógica.* Havana, 1952.

Schoenrich, Otto. *The Legacy of Christopher Columbus.* 2 vols. Glendale, Calif., 1949.

Thacher, John Boyd. *Christopher Columbus, His Life, His Work, His Remains.* 3 vols. 1903–1904. Reprint, New York, 1967.

Winsor, Justin. *Christopher Columbus and How He Received and Imparted the Spirit of Discovery.* Boston, 1891.

PAUL E. HOFFMAN

COLÓN, FERNANDO (1488–1539), historian and bibliophile; son of Christopher Columbus. Fernando Colón was born in Córdoba on August 15, 1488, the son of the Admiral and Beatriz Enriquez de Arana, Columbus's companion during many difficult years of his life.

In 1494 Fernando was received with his older brother, Diego, among the pages of the Infante Juan. After the death of the prince in 1497, Fernando and his brother entered the service of Queen Isabel. He was educated at her court and remained there until May 9, 1502, when with his father and his uncle Bartolomé, he embarked from Cádiz in the small fleet that undertook the fourth voyage of Columbus.

The presence of the fourteen-year-old boy on this voyage was not a mere formality. Fernando and his uncle played an important role in the explorations of the mountain ranges of Veragua (northwestern Panama) beyond Santa María de Belén, a colony that had been founded by Columbus but had failed to prosper because of floods and Indian attacks. In the course of these explorations, in 1503, the Europeans discovered cocaine. Fernando himself wrote about this discovery: "The colonial chief and his dignitaries never neglected to put in their mouths a dry herb and to chew it, and sometimes they would use a certain powder, which they carried with the herb mentioned. Which [custom] seems a very ugly thing."

After returning to Spain, the young Fernando remained with his infirm father. Contrary to legend, Christopher Columbus was not poor. In fact, he was fairly rich, but he had by now become politically marginal. When he died in Valladolid, on May 20, 1506, Fernando was closest at his side among the relatives, friends, and servants who had gathered to catch his last words of faith.

After Christopher Columbus's death, Fernando became actively involved in defending the rights to the titles and revenues that had been granted to Columbus and his descendants in the Santa Fe Capitulations, an agreement signed on the eve of his first voyage, and which the monarchs of Spain no longer acknowledged. These rights were argued in the Pleitos Colombinos, a series of lawsuits with varied outcomes, which started in 1508 and did not end until 1536. To defend his brother in these trials, Fernando elaborated a number of petitions in which he maintained that the Crown should keep all promises made to Columbus, since Columbus had kept his promise—he had presented the monarchs with lands and riches. This intransigent position turned out to be, perhaps, more damaging than useful to his family, even though it was consistent with the position his father had taken all his life.

In July 1509, Fernando made his second and last voyage to America, accompanying his brother, Diego, who had been named governor of the Indies. But two months later, in September, Fernando returned to Spain in order to follow closely the developments of the Pleitos.

In 1512–1513, again on behalf of Diego, he made his first trip to Italy, visiting Rome and his father's native city, Genoa. He had begun by now to accumulate a library, and in the course of this trip and subsequent ones, he purchased books in each city he visited.

With Carlos I's (Charles V) accession to the throne, a new phase began in Fernando's life. Accompanying the king, who went to take possession of the lands he had inherited from the House of Austria and from the Imperial Crown, Fernando Colón undertook a long journey in 1520–1522 to Brussels, Ghent, Louvain, and Worms. Then he went again to Genoa, Milan, Venice, and other Italian cities. From Italy he traveled to Switzerland, Germany, the Netherlands, and London.

In the meantime, his reputation as a cosmographer was growing. In 1524, he was called to join a group of experts that constituted the Committee of Badajoz, which was instituted for the purpose of resolving the problem of delimiting the antimeridian (180 degrees from the Line of Demarcation). In March of 1526 he was entrusted with the task of putting together another group of experts in order to create a general nautical map, which was to serve as a model for maps used by ships going to the New World.

That same year, Diego died, and his wife, María de Toledo, as guardian of her son, Luis, took over the complicated legal and patrimonial affairs of the family. From that time on, Fernando increasingly limited his participation in the business of the Pleitos, which allowed him to devote greater attention to his library.

Containing now more than fifteen thousand volumes, the library had become one of the richest of its time. A part of it, called the Biblioteca Colombina, still exists. He began to build in Seville an edifice to house it and devoted his last years to book collecting. He died in Seville on July 12, 1539.

Fernando Colón wrote several works that have remained, for the most part, in manuscript form. Among them were a politico-historical treatise entitled *Colón de concordia*, which is lost, and *Descripción y cosmographia de España*, which remained unfinished. The most famous text attributed to him is *Le historie della vita e dei fatti dell'Ammiraglio Don Cristoforo Colombo*, a biography of his father. Precisely because it was attributed to Fernando, this biography was long considered the most authoritative source on Columbus, notwithstanding many obvious incongruities and inexactitudes.

The *Historie* has survived only through an Italian translation by Alfonso de Ulloa, which was published in Venice in 1571, more than thirty years after the death of its presumed author. Doubts about its authenticity, raised since the beginning of the nineteenth century, seem confirmed by recent scholarship. The *Historie* is apparently a posthumous compilation, based on a writing of Fernando's, but substantially changed by the insertion of false or imprecise statements made with the purpose of exalting the figure of Columbus and bringing glory to his descendants.

Although such reservations diminish the value of the *Historie*, it remains a fundamental text in Columbian historiography, especially with regard to the narrative of the four voyages, the fourth of which is derived directly from a text whose authenticity is not in doubt.

[See also *Lawsuits*; *Library of Columbus*; *Santa Fe Capitulations*.]

BIBLIOGRAPHY

Belgrano, L. T., and Marcello Staglieno. "Documenti relativi a Christoforo Colombo e alla sua famiglia." In part 2, vol. 1 of *Raccolta di documenti e studi pubblicati dalla R. Commissione Colombiana pel quarto centenario dalla scoperta dell'America*. Rome, 1896.

Colombo, Fernando. *Le historie della vita e dei fatti dell'Ammiraglio Don Cristoforo Colombo*. Vol. 8 of *Nuova Raccolta Colombiana*, edited by Paolo Emilio Taviani and Francesca Cantù. Rome, 1991.

Columbus, Ferdinand. *The Life of the Admiral Christopher Columbus by His Son, Ferdinand*. Translated by Benjamin Keen. New Brunswick, N.J., 1959.

Harrisse, Henry. *Fernand Columb: Sa vie, ses oeuvres*. Paris, 1873.

Luzzana Caraci, Ilaria. *Colombo vero e falso: La costruzione delle historie fernandine*. Genoa, 1989.

Marín Martínez, T. *Memoria de las obras y libros de don Hernando Colón*. Madrid, 1970.

Rumeu de Armas, Antonio. *Hernando Colón: Historiador del descubrimiento de América*. Madrid, 1973.

Taviani, Paolo Emilio. *Christopher Columbus: The Grand Design*. London, 1985.

PAOLO EMILIO TAVIANI
Translated from Italian by Rodica Diaconescu-Blumenfeld

COLÓN, LUÍS (1521–1572), Christopher Columbus's grandson and third Admiral of the Indies. The eldest son of Diego Colón and María de Toledo y Rojas, Luís Colón y Toledo was born in Santo Domingo and apparently resided there for several years after his mother returned to Spain in 1529 to pursue the privileges she claimed on behalf of her son as his father's heir. Nominally viceroy and governor-general, Luís is not known to have actually exercised any power prior to 1540, even though some royal orders were addressed to him. His mother, as his legal tutor, exercised the powers of his offices.

The final lawsuit in the Pleitos Colombinos was decided by the sentences of June 28, 1536, and the decrees of September 8, 1536, and March 24, 1537. Under terms of these agreements, Colón renounced his claim to 10 percent of royal revenues from the Americas, the title of viceroy, and his right to appoint officials in the colonies. In return, he received a perpetual annuity of ten thousand ducats drawn on the revenues of La Española, fiefs embracing Jamaica and a square of land twenty-five leagues on a side in Veragua (Panama), the titles of duke of Veragua and marquis de la Vega, the title of Admiral of the Indies with all its privileges, and a few minor benefits connected with the island of La Española and his properties there. By separate decrees, his two unmarried sisters, María and Juana (another was a nun), were given lifetime pensions. The fourth sister, Isabel, already seems to have been married to a Castilian nobleman. His youngest brother, Diego, was given an income-producing membership in the Order of Santiago. His other brother, Cristóbal, apparently received nothing. His mother received a grant of four thousand ducats to help repay the costs of litigation and a lifetime income of one thousand ducats a year (she later gave this to her daughter María).

Subsequently, Luís sued to clarify which ports owed dues to him as admiral (1537–1541) and what powers he had in them (1554). His final lawsuit resulted in a new settlement in 1556 under which he gave up his fief in Veragua but retained the title of duke of Veragua, lost all revenues and power associated with the title of admiral (which became honorary), became duke de la Vega, and had his annuity increased to seventeen thousand ducats, seven thousand of which were payable during his lifetime from the customs receipts at Seville. The balance was to be paid from the treasury at Santo Domingo; later, the source of this money was changed to the treasuries of Panama. Settlement of his claims for back payments was made in the form of slave licenses. He received other slave licenses and twenty thousand head of cattle from the royal herds on La Española as royal grants, marks of the king's favor.

These settlements indicate not only that the Crown was determined to recover complete control over the empire, but also to protect Luís Colón's (and his mother's) basic interests: prestige and money. A third interest—love and marriage—became evident during his years as captain general of La Española and during a subsequent period in Spain.

Colón was appointed captain general in 1540, while he was probably in Spain. Returning to Santo Domingo, he soon fathered an illegitimate daughter, Juana Colón de Toledo. In 1542 he and María de Orozco exchanged marriage vows but because of his mother's opposition Orozco was forced to continue on her way to Honduras as part of Pedro de Alvarado's party. Although a legal marriage, according to Spanish common law, the union never received ecclesiastical blessing or consummation. Four years later Luís married María de Mosquera in an elaborate church ceremonial, even though María de Orozco was still alive. Mosquera was the daughter of Juan de Mosquera, a wealthy resident and member of the city council of Santo Domingo. Their honeymoon was spent on the Isthmus of Panama as Colón unsuccessfully attempted to settle his land grant in Veragua. Luís and María de Mosquera had two daughters: María (ca. 1548–1605), who became a nun, and Felipa (1549–1577). The marriage was not a happy one.

When the news of the Pizarro rebellion in Peru reached Panama in 1547, Luís Colón immediately prepared a force to go to the aid of the royal officials in Peru. However, he prudently asked Pedro de la Gasca (the chief royal official in Peru) if he needed help and requested royal permission to leave his post as governor of La Española. The permission was denied. Seven years later he was rewarded with a grant-in-aid of fifteen thousand pesos de oro because of the expenses he had incurred.

Colón returned to Spain in 1551 to seek papal annulment of his marriage to María de Mosquera on the grounds that he had been married to María de Orozco all along. While waiting for action on his petition, he contracted an engagement with Ana de Castro Osorio, daughter of the countess of Lemos. He also pursued his claims and lived extravagantly. In 1555 he obtained a preliminary annulment of his marriages (made final in 1558) and not long afterwards married Ana. Their only child died at birth. Hearing of this marriage, María de Mosquera returned to Spain and filed bigamy charges against Luís. He was arrested in January 1559. He was confined for the next five years in the castles of Arévalo, La Mota (Medina del Campo), Simancas, and Villaverde and at Madrid while his case and appeal were heard. While in Madrid in 1564, he contracted another verbal (but not ecclesiastical) marriage with Luisa de Carvajal; they repeated their marriage contract, also without church sanction, on May 26, 1565, the day that she gave birth to a son, Cristóbal Colón y Carvajal. Luís Colón's sentence to ten years of exile at Oran, North Africa, for bigamy, originally issued in 1563, was upheld by decrees of November 1565 and August 1566. He died in Oran on February 3, 1572. His remains were later taken to the monastery of Las Cuevas, at Seville, and then to Santo Domingo, to lie with his father and grandfather in the cathedral.

According to John Boyd Thacher's account, Luís Colón's will provided that his son Cristóbal would inherit his titles and revenues should his daughter Felipa fail to marry her cousin, Diego Colón y Pravia, the son of his younger brother, Cristóbal Colón y Toledo. (Other accounts suggest that the marriage was a way of compromising competing claims to the succession.) When Felipa did marry Diego, on May 15, 1573, another clause in the will bestowed some money on Cristóbal but Diego refused to pay it. In the end Cristóbal's half sister, the nun María Colón y Mosquera, gave him an annuity of four hundred ducats. Felipa died without heirs in 1577; her husband died two months later, without having remarried. Cristóbal died in 1601, without an heir. The succession then passed through several of Luís Colón's cousins to other families.

BIBLIOGRAPHY

Enciclopedia universal ilustrada. Vol. 14, p. 246. Madrid, 1907?–1930.

Nieto y Cortadellas, Rafael. Los descendientes de Cristóbal Colón: Obra genealógica. Havana, 1952.

Schoenrich, Otto. The Legacy of Christopher Columbus. Vol. 1, pp. 251–307. Glendale, Calif., 1949.

Thacher, John Boyd. Christopher Columbus, His Life, His Work, His Remains. 3 vols. 1903–1904. Reprint, New York, 1967.

Winsor, Justin. Christopher Columbus and How He Received and Imparted The Spirit of Discovery. Boston, 1891.

PAUL E. HOFFMAN

COLÓN. Members of the Columbus family whose lives centered in Spain or in Spanish America can be found under Colón. For those whose lives centered in Italy, see Colombo. See Columbus, Christopher, for several articles detailing the life and achievements of Christopher Columbus.

COLONIZATION. [This entry surveys European overseas colonization of the New World, focusing on the sixteenth century. It includes the following five articles:

An Overview
Spanish Colonization
Portuguese Colonization of Brazil
French Colonization
English Colonization

See also Exploration and Discovery.]

An Overview

The idea of founding colonies was not a new one in the fifteenth century. The Greeks had established colonies on the shores of the Mediterranean Sea, and the Romans had extended theirs as far north as Hadrian's Wall in Britain. During the Middle Ages, the series of Crusades to the Holy Land had resulted in the establishment for a while of a European military colony there. Moreover, these various ventures had raised issues met in the fifteenth century and after, such as debates about how to treat subjugated peoples, problems arising from novel patterns of trade, and examples of syncretism, in which the mixing of two ideologies and techniques produced something new. However, the colonizing activity that began in the late fifteenth century soon reached a scale that dwarfed anything that had gone before, and eventually changed the lives of everybody living in European countries and in their colonies.

Fundamental differences in the societies and economies of the countries of western Europe ensured that their colonies would be very different. Spain and Portugal were relatively poor countries, in which the peasants often eked out a precarious existence. The lot of many Spanish peasants became even more difficult during the sixteenth century, with the loss of huge areas of arable land to sheep-farming; there was consequently considerable pressure toward emigration in many parts of the peninsula. In France and England the economic pressures were not so severe. There were, it is true, periodic famines, but nothing to compare with, say, the Great Famine of the 1840s in Ireland, which drove so many Irish people across the Atlantic. In France and England, though, there was religious dissent of a type not found in Spain or Portugal, which played a considerable part in encouraging emigration from those countries.

The extensive transfer of people across the Atlantic was not technically possible before the fifteenth century, when the European peoples, particularly the Portuguese and Spaniards, had developed ships capable of sailing for long periods out of sight of land. These ships could make headway even against contrary winds, could carry supplies to last for many months, and could be defended. Moreover, European sailors could navigate using the sun and stars and use maps to describe the lands to which they went so that others could follow.

The early reception of the Europeans by the American peoples varied widely. Columbus was fortunate in that his first landfall came among a singularly friendly group of "Indians." Other American peoples were often hostile, and the Europeans were able to establish themselves only by taking advantage of existing rivalries; in this way the Spaniards humbled the Aztecs, and the French managed to hold out against the Iroquois. In physical terms, the Americans were often apparently superior to the Europeans; the French in particular were struck by the strength and stature of the peoples they met in northern Florida. However, this outward appearance was deceptive, for the Americans were in fact highly vulnerable to the diseases carried by the Europeans, whereas the Europeans, exposed over the centuries to the great variety of diseases prevalent in the Eurasian landmass, were protected against a wider range of pathogens.

The pace of settlement varied widely. In Central and South America, the Spaniards conquered vast empires in a few decades; in the north, the English and French slowly built up their numbers in the face of Indian hostility. The Spanish conquest was not merely territorial, but also genetic, for, like the Portuguese, they had no qualms about marrying, or at any rate breeding with, native American women. Consequently, in areas that they conquered, a large mixed-blood population soon developed.

This mixing of blood was paralleled by other kinds of "creolization," whether in music, cooking, legal systems, architecture, or any other field of human activity. Astonishingly soon after the Spaniards arrived in Central America, for example, a liturgy developed that was new in music—a mixture of Aztec and Spanish styles. In the same way, the French began adapting their patterns of land settlement to the requirements of Canada, developing a system of "long-lots" without parallel in the Old World, but which still marks the areas of French settlement in North America. The process of "creolization" was much slower in the English colonies, whose inhabitants kept their distance from the Indians and tried as far as possible to duplicate the conditions of life in the old country. But even they were in the end overcome by the new necessities, and in New England as elsewhere new forms of material culture came into existence.

The European governments did their best to retain some sort of control over the colonies, establishing bodies like the English Council of Trade and Plantations or the Spanish Council of the Indies to oversee their affairs. These councils, and the crowns that they represented, were often concerned to regulate what came to be seen as the exploitation of the Americans. However, in every case the interests of the colonists prevailed over the humanitarian sentiments expressed in the European courts; the brute pressures involved in taming a vast continent and its peoples were too much for royal legislation to contend

with. The Spanish Crown was probably the most successful in imposing some degree of control over its burgeoning colonies, often in collaboration with the church. One way in which this was done was to regulate the foundation and growth of towns, which came to be planned in accordance with the Laws of the Indies; this contrasted sharply with the incoherent development of the towns in the areas of English influence.

This was, indeed, a major difference between the colonizing activities of the Spaniards and those of the northern European peoples. As part of Mediterranean civilization, the Spanish culture was primarily urban, and Spanish colonies tended to be organized around the foundation of cities, from Santo Domingo to Lima. The English colonies, on the other hand, were primarily agricultural ventures, allowing cities to form more or less haphazardly where economic activity gave rise to them. In Canada, too, the French colonies remained rural, so that Québec and Montréal were for a long time the only sizeable towns in the St. Lawrence Valley.

The French towns remained small, and dominated to a remarkable degree by the buildings of church and state: the churches, hospitals, and schools run by the church, and the fortifications, magazines, and storehouses erected by the state. The contrast with the more commercially oriented English cities eventually became very striking. They were primarily colonies directed by merchants and planters; the Anglican church played a muted role in the English colonies. It could boast nothing like the Jesuits who labored far out in the wilderness among the Hurons or the Franciscans who founded the distant missions of Mexico.

In fact, until late in the seventeenth century the scale of the Spanish colonizing effort dwarfed that of the other Europeans, even including the Portuguese. The Spaniards had been first in the field, and the combination of royal encouragement and economic necessity had given them an irresistible impetus. Moreover, they had no doubts about what they were doing; from the start, cities like Santo Domingo or Mexico City replicated the institutional framework of Iberian towns, with churches, palaces, and even, sometimes, universities. The stupendous effort needed to sustain this colonizing activity cost Spain dearly, as its own institutions slowly collapsed under the imperial burden, until it was unable even to maintain its position in Europe. But for two centuries Spain led the colonial process, leaving an indelible mark throughout the Americas.

BIBLIOGRAPHY

Bitterli, Urs. *Cultures in Conflict: Encounters between European and Non-European Cultures, 1492–1800.* Stanford, 1989.
Parry, J. H. *The Establishment of the European Hegemony, 1415–1715.* New York, 1966.

Phillips, J. R. S. *The Medieval Expansion of Europe*. Oxford and New York, 1988.

DAVID BUISSERET

Spanish Colonization

Spanish colonization of the Americas went through four phases during the sixteenth century. The initial phase, 1492 to about 1519, involved the Antilles with secondary activity, mostly looting, on the Isthmus of Panama and the northern coast of South America. Attempts to fit Columbus's "another world" (Amerigo Vespucci more accurately called it a "new world") to what was known of Asian geography dictated a primary emphasis on explorations along the Atlantic face of South America, with secondary emphasis on colonization of the Antilles and exploration of the Caribbean Basin from the Antillian centers of colonization. Hernando Cortés's founding of Veracruz and Pedro Arias de Ávila's (Pedrárias) building of Panama City in 1519 marked the beginning of a second, thirty-year phase during which the Spaniards conquered and occupied most of the rest of the areas that are today Spanish America. Explorations north and west of the Antilles and the Magellan-Elcano circumnavigation of the world indicated by 1525 that the Americas were a true New World that stood at a great distance from Asia. Accordingly, Spaniards concentrated on the exploration and colonization of the Americas while still trying to reach Asia by crossing the Pacific Ocean. The third phase embraced the decades of the 1550s and 1560s and was marked by the settlement of such peripheral areas as Florida, western and central Venezuela, and northwestern Argentina. The final phase began about 1570 and ran into the next century. Settlement advanced very slowly in peripheral areas, except for a few leaps such as the settlement of New Mexico.

During the first three phases, the administrative, judicial, ecclesiastical, and economic institutions of the Spanish colonies developed forms that did not significantly change until the late seventeenth century. This institutional history followed a slightly different periodization than did conquest and colonization, with 1524 marking the completion of the initial phase of institution building. By 1573, Spanish colonial institutions and policies had become established in laws that lasted until the reforms of the eighteenth century.

Settlement

Formal settlement on La Española began not with La Navidad, which was an accident, but with La Isabela, founded in 1493 as a typical Spanish city. Discovery of gold placers in the interior of La Española and a subsistence crisis caused the dispersal of the Spanish across the island.

By 1505, when Santo Domingo was moved to its present location, the island was being organized into municipal districts. By that date, too, the Crown had approved the first contract for settlement of another island, Puerto Rico, and slavers and men who bartered with Indians for pearls and gold were operating in the other Antilles, the Bahamas, and along parts of the Venezuelan, Colombian, and Panamanian coasts. In general, Spanish settlements in this period appeared wherever gold was found, although secondary economic activities, such as ranching, expanded colonization beyond the immediate area of the gold mines.

Occupation of the rest of the Antilles and the first Spanish settlements on the mainland occurred between 1509 and 1515. In the former year, Juan de Esquivel began the settlement of Jamaica, and Puerto Rico was invaded by Juan Ponce de León, who completed his conquest with the founding of San Juan in 1511. That same year, Diego Velázquez de León began the conquest of Cuba. After defeating the Indians, he founded Santiago de Cuba in 1514 and Havana the following year. Santa María la Antigua del Darién (Panama), the first Spanish settlement on the mainland, was founded in 1509. For most of the next decade it served as a base from which Spaniards, led by Vasco Núñez de Balboa, explored and raided on the Isthmus of Panama, along the way (1513) discovering the Pacific Ocean and conducting preliminary explorations of the Gulf of Panama. As in the Antilles, the search for gold mines drove this expansion.

At the highest levels of the Spanish government, these years saw much interest in deciphering the geographic mystery that the new discoveries presented while colonizing and exploiting the gold-bearing Antillian and Panamanian discoveries. Variously interpreted as a large island off the coast of Asia (c. 1498–1520) or as a peninsula of Asia (post-1503), South America and its northward extension into Central America continued to be seen in Spain as an obstacle to be gotten around on the way to the spices of the Indian Ocean. In the New World, Spaniards were concerned mostly with exploiting native peoples and resources in an effort to re-create familiar ways of life and acquire wealth that might improve their status in the Indies, as they called Columbus's discoveries, or at home, should they return there after their stay in the colonies.

The settlement of the Antilles was largely the work of men (there were few women) drawn from Andalusia and its seaports, although persons from nearby areas of Spain also took part. The scant available information suggests that by 1519 the society of La Española had many of the hierarchical characteristics of Spanish society, but with the notable differences that Indians had taken the place of the commoners required to pay tribute (no Spaniard in the New World paid the head tax [*pecho*] commoners paid in

Spain) and that social distance among Spaniards seems to have been reduced compared to norms at home. This was the embryo of the society of castes (*castas*) that emerged fully in the mainland colonies. There, social status became a function of racial ancestry.

Hernando Cortés's founding of Veracruz and Pedrárias's building of Panama City in 1519 marked the beginning of the second, thirty-year phase of colonization during which the Spaniards conquered and occupied most of the rest of the areas that are today Spanish America. This continental colonization embraced Mexico (1519–1526) and Central America (1523–1542); outposts along the northern coast of South America at Cumaná (1520), Santa Marta (1525), Coro (1528), and Cartagena (1533); the conquest and settlement of Peru (1532–1535), Ecuador (1533–1537), central Colombia (called New Granada, 1538–1541), and Chile (1541–1550); the short-lived occupation of Buenos Aires (1535–1541); and the permanent occupation of Asunción, Paraguay (1536). Ponce de León's attempt to settle on the west coast of Florida in 1521 and Lucas Vázquez de Ayllón's colony on the east coast of North America (in Georgia) in 1526 were failed attempts to establish a presence in North America.

Many areas, such as central Guatemala, eastern Central America, and parts of modern Colombia and (western) Venezuela, were not brought under Spanish control during these years. Even larger areas in northern Mexico, southeastern and southwestern United States, the western edges of the Amazon Basin, and northern Argentina were explored without any effort being made to settle Spaniards permanently among native inhabitants. In general, the Spanish military style of conquest failed (outside of the Antilles and Panama) wherever the Spaniards encountered Indians living in chiefdoms rather than more highly organized polities. Where the Spanish had outposts in such areas (e.g., coastal Venezuela and Colombia) they were content to loot native cultures for food, gold, and slaves rather than to try to dominate the hinterland. Only later, when Old World diseases, feral cattle, and the destructive effects of raiding on native societies had reduced their abilities to resist did Spanish settlers move into such areas.

In the more densely inhabited highland areas of the Americas, Spanish conquest was followed by the development of a mixed monetary and subsistence economy in which mining was the leading sector. Columbus's efforts to introduce the domesticated plants and animals of Europe into La Española were repeated in each new colony, often with more success (with plants) than had been the case in the Antilles. Cattle, which had overrun the Antilles, multiplied prodigiously on virgin grasslands on the continents, sometimes destroying that environment in drier areas. Vast numbers made beef a cheap staple food and their hides the major bulk export of

colonies all around the Caribbean. Although the consumption of European foods retained a high status value, combinations of American and European foods rapidly developed—the origins of the distinctive national cuisines of today. Alongside native weavers and potters, the Spanish built their own textile factories and pottery works. By the 1570s, a monetarized Hispanic economy existed in all but the more remote areas of the empire. Government officials and merchants used tribute demands, the market, and such devices as the *repartimiento de bienes* (forced sale to Indians of goods needed for "civilized" living) to further expand that economy.

The initial years of this phase produced a final answer to the question of the extent of the discoveries and their relationship to Asia. Explorations to the northwest of Cuba in 1508 (Díaz de Solís and Peralonso Niño) and from 1517 to 1519 (Juan de Grijalba, Francisco Fernández de Córdoba, Alonso Alvarez de Pineda) revealed the continent that rings the Gulf of Mexico. Other explorations by Ponce de León (1513), Esteban Gómez (1523), and Pedro de Quejo (1525) completed the map of the Atlantic face of North America as far as Newfoundland. The Magellan-Elcano voyage of 1519–1523 showed that the Columbian discoveries were separated from Asia by the vastness of the Pacific Ocean. In sum, the Indies truly were a New World, as Amerigo Vespucci had said. Although some Spaniards (e.g., Hernando Cortés) continued to pursue sailing routes to Asia, most turned to exploring and colonizing the vast expanses of the Americas and conquering their various native peoples.

In general, the conquests and settlements of 1519 to 1533 were the work of persons who had survived the difficult early years in the Antilles, although large numbers of persons drawn from Spain came out in 1514 (with Pedrárias) and after 1521 when first Mexico and then Peru offered prospects of quick improvements in economic and social standing. After 1526, royal policy required the organizers of expeditions to supply their manpower needs from Spain, not the rapidly depopulating Antilles, but this policy was not at first effective. By the time of Hernando de Soto's expedition to Florida (1538–1543), however, most new ventures were staffed with persons from Spain.

Limited data indicate that most of the men who participated in these continental conquests were semiskilled youths who were in their early twenties at the time of immigration. They came from landowning peasant backgrounds or were craftsmen and professionals such as notaries. Except for a group sent in 1498, few were criminals nor were many of them veterans of the Italian wars, although some veterans accompanied Pedrárias in 1514. More than 45 percent of the first settlers came from the Spanish provinces of Andalusia and Extremadura. A corridor stretching from León in the north through

Badajoz in the west to Seville in the south supplied about 85 percent of all documented persons. Probably more African slaves (drawn from southern Spain, not directly from Africa) than Spanish women and children came to the colonies prior to the founding of the cities that governed the mainland colonies. One result of the lack of Spanish women was the birth of a large first generation of mestizo children, the fruits of Spanish cohabitation with Indian women. The African slave trade began to grow in the late 1510s as La Española shifted to sugar cultivation. Africans added yet another "caste" to the emerging Latin American society.

By 1548 and the end of the Peruvian civil wars—sparked by personal rivalries and the question of who would control the Indians and under what terms—and of the great epidemic of 1546–1548 in Mexico, the rapid expansion of Spanish conquest and settlement had spent itself. But expansion of the area of settlement continued in response to economic, religious, and military needs. Two periods may be distinguished, the 1550s and 1560s, and the last thirty years of the century.

The expansion of Spanish settlement during the 1550s and 1560s took place in Venezuela, northern Mexico, Florida, and Chile. In western Venezuela the founding of the Spanish towns of Pamplona (1549), Ibagué (1551), Barquisimeto (1552), Trujillo (1556), and Mérida (1558) built a line of settlements based on mining and agriculture in the southwestward curving valleys of the Cordillera de Mérida. To the east, the founding of Valencia in 1555 marked a first step toward settlement of central Venezuela's lush mountain valleys. That progression was completed with the founding of Caracas (1568) and the extension of Spanish agriculture throughout the central highlands. Only the lack of a good port retarded the economic and demographic growth of central Venezuela.

In Mexico, the discovery of the silver deposits at Zacatecas (1548) and elsewhere in the northern interior basin produced a period of frontier expansion into the progressively drier (as one goes north) region of seminomadic peoples whom the sedentary agricultural Indians of Mexico called Chichimecs (sons of dogs). By 1570 Spanish mining centers employing wage laborers and slaves (rather than coerced Indians) reached to within a few hundred miles of the present U.S.-Mexican border. Ranches (haciendas) developed along the roads to the mines to supply them with draft animals, meat, tallow (for illumination), and hides and to provide security for travelers against nomadic raiders. Missions, too, began to be founded in this area after 1560 as the mendicant orders sought to save souls and the government sought a way to end the rapidly escalating costs of defending Spanish interests against the nomads.

In North America the Spaniards finally—in the face of French attempts to occupy ports near the mouth of the Bahama Channel (Port Royal, 1562; the St. Johns River, 1564)—founded a permanent town, St. Augustine (1565), and another, Santa Elena (on Parris Island in Port Royal Sound), that lasted from 1566 to 1586. These settlements never developed into the self-sustaining agricultural communities that their founders envisioned. Instead, they became garrisons dependent on Mexico and Cuba for their sustenance. They were valued primarily for their strategic locations near the Bahama Channel. Hegemony over the inland Indian polities, established in 1566, collapsed in the early 1570s. Spanish control along the coast between their towns increased during the 1580s and 1590s as the Franciscans built missions in coastal Georgia. These survived the abandonment of Santa Elena and the Indian revolt of 1597 and anchored weak Spanish control of the area until the 1670s.

The final area of expansion in the 1550s and 1560s was in Chile. Along its southern frontier, a bitter war with the Araucanian Indians that began in 1553 had come to a temporary end in 1557. The troops thus freed were used in 1562 to found the cities of Mendoza and San Juan east of the Andes in present-day Argentina. Thereafter, Spanish settlement slowly filled in the territories surrounding their initial towns.

The persons who carried out this third phase of colonial expansion have not been studied, but were probably similar in age and occupations, if not in regional origins, to the persons who carried out exploration, conquest, and colonization during the pre-1548 period. Elsewhere in the Spanish empire, immigrants came from a wider cross section of Spanish provinces, especially in Old Castile, and were more likely to be servants of officials or minor nobles going out to serve in the colonies or to try to remake their fortunes there.

After the expansive activities of the 1550s and 1560s, the pace of new settlement slowed. The occupations of New Mexico in the 1590s and of Buenos Aires in 1580 stand out in an era when the Crown was generally unwilling to provide either permission or resources for new frontier settlements. Private interests, moreover, found it more profitable to exploit the existing colonial economy rather than to seek resources speculatively in areas offering mostly agricultural possibilities and usually at a great remove from access to world and even regional markets.

Institutional Development

Spanish colonization of the New World began under mixed signals so far as governmental and economic institutions were concerned. In his contract with the Catholic monarchs, Columbus secured the titles of viceroy (vice-king), admiral, and governor, indicating that he expected eventually to rule a large free population with an extensive maritime commerce, rather like the Kingdom of

Catalonia. Yet the expedition of 1493 was organized as a royal monopoly company, although not everyone in the colony was an employee. To compound the confusion, La Isabela, in La Española, was organized as a standard Spanish municipality, although its officers were also key employees of the royal company.

This mixture of institutional forms quickly broke down because of the Columbus brothers' inability to govern, the desires of the unemployed Spaniards to exploit the natives and the gold mines, and the determination of King Fernando and Bishop Juan Rodríguez de Fonseca, Fernando's unofficial minister of colonial affairs, to void the terms of Columbus's contract so that licensed private interests could take over the expense and risk of colonization and, to a lesser degree, exploration. In 1499, Francisco de Bobadilla was sent to investigate conditions on La Española, and licenses were issued for voyages in which Columbus had no part. Bobadilla's *visita,* or ad hoc investigation, was the first of a long series by which the Crown attempted to restrain independent-minded officials and to check abuses. In this case, it quickly turned into a residencia, a formal inquiry into an official's conduct in office made at the time that he left office. This device, too, was a means through which the Crown tried to maintain control over its officials during the centuries that followed.

Nicolás de Ovando, who began to serve as royal governor of La Española in 1502, carried out a complete reorganization of the government of the colony so that it conformed to an idealized peninsular province. Fifteen municipalities were organized, each with a council and its local justices (alcaldes ordinarios) and minor officials such as notaries. Judicial appeals and certain felony cases were placed under two superior judges (alcaldes mayores). Treasury officials, present since 1493, became more concerned with collecting taxes on commerce and mining, both now freed from the earlier monopoly, than with administering the royal mines and property. In Spain, the House of Trade (Casa de la Contratación) was created in 1503 to administer navigation acts that opened the discoveries to all Spaniards. Finally, the Crown sent out additional secular as well as regular clergy and pressed the papacy for the creation of two bishoprics and rights of patronage *(patronato)* to those sees. A bull of 1508 granted royal control over the church in the colonies. In short, by 1509, when Ovando was removed from office and colonization was beginning to move to other islands, Spanish society on La Española had been given the political, economic, and religious institutions of those areas of the peninsular kingdoms under direct royal rule. In addition, the Crown had control over the Catholic church to an extent that it did not have in most of Spain.

Ovando's other great work was to settle the question of the place of the native Americans in the new colonial society. Drawing on the experience of his military order in Andalusia and orders from the Crown, he systematically conquered the native polities of the island and distributed them (by caciques or chiefs) as encomiendas to be administered by selected Spaniards. Under this system, the Indians were required to work for the Spaniards, in part to earn money to pay their tribute (head tax) but mostly because they were a subject people and because their labor was essential to the colonies. Spaniards were required to care for their charges' spiritual and physical welfare in accordance with decrees that the Crown issued at frequent intervals. Ovando's method of incorporating the native Americans remained standard Spanish practice down to the end of the continental conquests.

Ovando's government was followed by a brief period, 1509–1523, during which the Crown prevented the reestablishment of the seigneural power of the Columbus family, which had won a lawsuit over the terms of Columbus's contract. The institutional means used were treasury officials and their taxing authority and the audiencia, an appeals court instituted in 1511 to oversee the work of the judges whom Diego Colón, Columbus's son and successor, was allowed to appoint (judicial authority was, with control of economic resources, the basis of most seigneural power in Europe). In addition, since all royal orders had the force of law and were thus subject to judicial interpretation, the audiencia had ample grounds for interfering with Colón's administration of the Antillian colonies. An uncommon institution in Spain (there were only two in the sixteenth century), the audiencia here became, as it later remained elsewhere in the empire, the keystone in the arch of royal control over viceroys (Colón's title) and all lesser officials. Hernando Cortés and Hernando Pizarro discovered in turn the power of these two royal institutions to prevent the development of quasi-seigneural power in the colonies. Audiencias were subsequently created in Mexico City (1528), Panama (1538), Lima (1542), Guatemala (1542), New Galicia (northwestern Mexico, 1548), and Bogotá (1549). The office of viceroy, which was ended when Colón returned to Spain (1523), was revived for the government of Mexico (1535) and Peru (1544) with powers similar to those it had in Catalonia.

The final step in creating the political-administrative-judicial system of the empire was the founding of the Council of the Indies in 1524, patterned on the Council of Aragón (1494). Its founding was a recognition that, given their numbers, the Spanish colonies, and in particular the populous "kingdom" of New Spain, had outgrown administration by one man or by other royal councils as their secondary business. The Council of the Indies advised the Crown on appointments and policy matters and served as the court of appeal from the audiencias in capital offense cases and in civil suits involving large sums. In the beginning it supervised the final auditing of the accounts of treasury officials in the Indies, but this function was delegated to special accounting tribunals in the New World in the early seventeenth century.

In the years between 1524 and 1573, the institutions established prior to 1524 were transferred to each new Spanish colony in turn, but with certain modifications to fit changing circumstances. Whether acting under royal authority or independently of it (as at Veracruz in 1519), the first formal act of the Spanish in a new territory was the creation of municipalities to divide and govern the land. Treasury officials usually accompanied each new, royally licensed expedition. Conquest and periods of personal rule by expedition leaders (who had varying titles) regularly gave way to rule by royally appointed alcaldes mayores, governors, viceroys (for Mexico and Peru), and audiencias. Encomiendas were distributed, often without regard to the intricate sociopolitical systems of native societies. Mendicant (regular) clergy and secular priests accompanied new expeditions, ministering to the Spanish and trying to convert native Americans. The establishment of bishoprics followed. Increasingly, the secular and religious institutions of each new colony were fully elaborated and staffed when the first soldier began the conquest. Of the institutions and practices established prior to 1524, three underwent significant modification by 1574: the operational structure of the Roman Catholic church, trade practices, and, most important, the systems for using Indian labor.

In Europe, the secular or parish clergy of the Catholic church dominated church operations, with the mendicant orders performing mostly acts of charity and prayer. In the early Spanish colonies, however, the shortage of established churches and "livings" meant a shortage of secular priests. The mendicants, especially the Franciscans and Dominicans, and after 1560 the Jesuits (who were not mendicants), filled the void. Using authority granted to them in 1521–1522 to administer the sacraments in areas where there was no secular priesthood, they became the principal, often the only church presence in most Indian communities and many Spanish ones as well. In time, however, the growth of the number and power of the secular clergy produced demands that the friars relinquish parishes in nonfrontier areas to the seculars. A decree of 1574 settled this quarrel in favor of the seculars. Thereafter the mendicants could administer parishes only on the frontiers of the empire and only until the secular clergy were ready to take over the new parishes.

Like the operations of the Catholic church, so the trading system underwent change in this era. European wars and their attendant raids on Spanish shipping caused the abandonment of the original "sail when ready" system of commerce with the Indies. Group sailings, even in

SKETCH OF THE SPANISH PORT NOMBRE DE DIOS. On the Caribbean coast of present-day Panama. A port used by the Spaniards to transship gold from Peru. This sketch is from *Histoire Naturelle des Indes*, often called the Drake Manuscript, and could be from the hand of Sir Francis Drake himself, who raided Spanish shipping here.   THE PIERPONT MORGAN LIBRARY, NEW YORK; M.3900, F.97

peacetime (1521), and then convoying that reached to the Canary and Azores islands (1520s onward) and then into and back from the Caribbean (1543–1545, 1552–1559) restricted competition among merchants and led to a system of fairs at Nombre de Dios (Panama) and Veracruz and to the establishment of the merchant guild (*consulado*) of Seville (1543). Thus granted corporate advantages during the wars of Charles V, the *consulado* merchants obtained their continuation during the official European peace after 1559. Resumption of the convoys (1561) and the legal exclusion from the Indies trades of non-Spanish but naturalized merchants during the 1560s were among the means they used to solidify their monopoly in a form that became infamous throughout Europe.

The third institution to be modified during the years

before 1573 was the encomienda. Prior to 1530, the Crown pursued a policy of issuing increasingly more detailed regulations concerning the treatment of the Indians, many of them responses to the Dominicans' complaints of continuing abuses. Then, in 1530, the Crown put all Indians not already in private encomiendas under the supervision of royally appointed corregidores de indios and began to claim encomiendas upon the deaths of their owners. The New Laws of 1542 carried this process to its logical conclusion by ending Indian slavery, all unpaid Indian service to individuals (but not to the church or the community), and all encomiendas upon the deaths of their holders. All Indian labor would thenceforth be obtained by request from a corregidor de indios under a system of fixed-term labor drafts generally referred to under its Peruvian name, the mita.

Because these laws challenged the labor basis of the Spanish colonies and provoked threats (carried out in Peru) of Spanish rebellion if enforced, the Crown had to give up trying to end the encomienda immediately. It was able, however, to insist that the encomienda was a sinecure administered by royal officials rather than the encomenderos themselves. Continuing depopulation and the development of a pool of wage laborers eventually made the encomienda and the mita less important as sources of wealth and labor except in the mines of Bolivia.

Parallel with the emergence of the so-called tamed encomienda was the development in the continental colonies of separate republics of Indians and Spaniards. The origins of this development lay in the initial residential and cultural separation of the two communities (although members of each group could be found in the other's towns), Indian unwillingness to give up their cultures, royal laws restricting Spanish residence in the native communities in order to protect them from abusive, direct exploitation, and the desire of many of the early mendicant missionaries to keep the Indians separate from the vices of European society. Additionally, there were several notorious "failures" to convert Indians into "Spaniards" during naive experiments in Mexico in the 1530s. The process was completed by the pragmatic recognition that the Indians required special legal "privileges" if they were to receive justice from the unfamiliar political and juridical world the conquest had forced upon them. For example, they were granted unlimited, free access to the audiencias' judicial processes. Special courts, the juzgados de Indios, were also created. At the same time, the governments of many Indian communities were forced into the mold of Spanish municipal government, and the role of chief (or headman) was transformed from its preconquest norms into ones that fit the demands of the Spanish republic, especially for labor through the mita. Indian towns that lost large parts of their populations to disease

were occasionally "congregated" into new towns organized along Spanish lines and controlled by friars and royal officials. This also helped to segregate Indians into their own so-called republics.

Finally, out of the struggle for justice that swirled around the problem of Indian labor, there emerged a new royal policy on future additions to the empire. As early as the 1560s, but definitively in the laws of colonization of 1573, Spanish activity in new areas was limited to the exercise of their rights under the law of nations (jus gentium) to create their own settlements in areas not used by the Indians, to peaceful trade, and to missionary activity. In general these strictures seem to have been obeyed.

In addition to the three major institutional developments from the 1524 to 1574 era, others produced the forms and customs that remained common until the reforms of the eighteenth century. Examples are the repartimiento de bienes system for distributing goods to the Indians, procedures for annual audits of treasury accounts, the regular use of the residencia, and the development of elaborate processes of consultation in decision making.

The issuance of the laws for new colonization in 1573 and the decree of 1574 laying down the jurisdictional rules for the regular and secular clergy marked the end not only of the second phase of institutional development in the Spanish colonies but also of the major institutional innovations that accompanied Spanish colonization in the Americas. Institutionally, as territorially, the Spanish empire had attained the essential form it would hold for the next two centuries.

[See also Cuba; Encomienda; Española, La; Jamaica; Puerto Rico; Settlements; West Indies.]

BIBLIOGRAPHY

Burkholder, Mark A., and Lyman L. Johnson. Colonial Latin America. New York, 1990.

Crosby, Alfred W. The Columbian Exchange: Biological and Cultural Consequences of 1492. Westport, Conn., 1972.

Floyd, Troy. The Columbus Dynasty in the Caribbean, 1492–1526. Albuquerque, 1973.

Hanke, Lewis. The Spanish Struggle for Justice in the Conquest of America. Philadelphia, 1949.

McAlister, Lyle N. Spain and Portugal in the New World, 1492–1700. Minneapolis, 1984.

Parry, J. H. The Discovery of South America. New York, 1979.

Sauer, Carl O. The Early Spanish Main. Berkeley, 1966.

Simpson, Lesley B. The Encomienda in New Spain: The Beginnings of Spanish Mexico. Rev. ed. Berkeley, 1966.

Super, John C. Food, Conquest and Colonization in Sixteenth Century Spanish America. Albuquerque, 1988.

PAUL E. HOFFMAN

Portuguese Colonization of Brazil

For Brazil, the relationship between history and geography is of the utmost importance: the country's size and tropical environment to a great extent determined its history. The discovery and claim of the land of Brazil by Pedro Álvares Cabral in 1500, part of the Portuguese explorations of the fifteenth and sixteenth centuries, took place against the background of the international diplomatic problems entailed by the division of the newly discovered lands. The importance of the Treaty of Tordesillas (1494), in which Portugal and Castile divided the planet between them, was only beginning to be realized. Determining a strict demarcation of the line was very difficult. No agreement as to the Line of Demarcation had ever been reached *in loco,* creating diplomatic and economic problems regarding spheres of influence from the New World to the Moluccas. In South America, these persisted until the eighteenth century. This was the context within which Brazil was formed. It was constantly expanded and defended by the Portuguese, in moves later recognized by the Spaniards, far beyond the limits of the Line of Demarcation. Thus, a country-continent was created, a giant occupying nearly half the space of South America.

Some historians have hypothesized that there were precursors to Cabral. Among Portuguese explorers, Duarte Pacheco Pereira and Bartolomeu Dias (1498) have been mentioned, and among the Spanish, Alonso de Ojeda (who took Amerigo Vespucci with him), Vicente Yáñez Pinzón, and Diego de Lepe, who navigated along the northern coast of South America in 1499, some months before Cabral, Gonçalo Coelho, and Amerigo Vespucci touched at Porto Seguro. The fact remains, however, that it was with Cabral that the effective exploration and development of Brazil began. Spanish explorations of the northern coast, even if they took place (which is debatable) had no significant impact.

During the early years of the century, after Cabral took official possession of Brazil in 1500, the exploration of the coastline was undertaken. The exploratory voyages were related to the trade in brazilwood, the first material wealth from the new land traded commercially. Coelho and Vespucci participated in this process in important ways. The commerce of the new land had been leased to the merchant Fernão de Loronha.

The French and the Spanish also began to appear along the coast at this time. The former traded sporadically in brazilwood (the first Frenchman to touch the coast of Brazil must have been the trader Goneville, in 1504). The latter hoped to procure a passage to the "Southern Sea"; this was the motivation for the Spanish expedition commanded by Juan Díaz de Solís, who arrived in Río de la Plata (the Plate River) in 1516 (note that the Plate estuary

LETTER TO KING MANUEL I GIVING NOTICE OF THE DISCOVERY OF BRAZIL. Dated May 1, 1500, this letter is one of three surviving documents relating to the India-bound voyage of Pedro Álvares Cabral that landed on the Brazilian coast.

ARQUIVO NACIONAL DA TORRE DO TOMBO, LISBON

had already been visited by Portuguese ships), and that commanded by Ferdinand Magellan in 1520.

With the expeditions and coastal armadas under the command of Christopher Jacques in 1516–1519 and 1526–1528, and with the establishment of a permanent trading post in 1516, further steps were taken by Portugal to keep other Europeans at a distance. The repression of the French and the exploration of the southern and northern territorial boundaries took on fresh energy with the expedition of Martim Afonso de Sousa in 1530–1533. The initial steps toward a systematic colonization were undertaken: the founding of São Vincente and the first town in the interior (the future São Paulo), the establishment of an embryonic administrative organization, the settling of colonists, and the first expeditions into the backlands. The Portuguese were also preoccupied with the idea of expanding their zone of influence in the direction of the

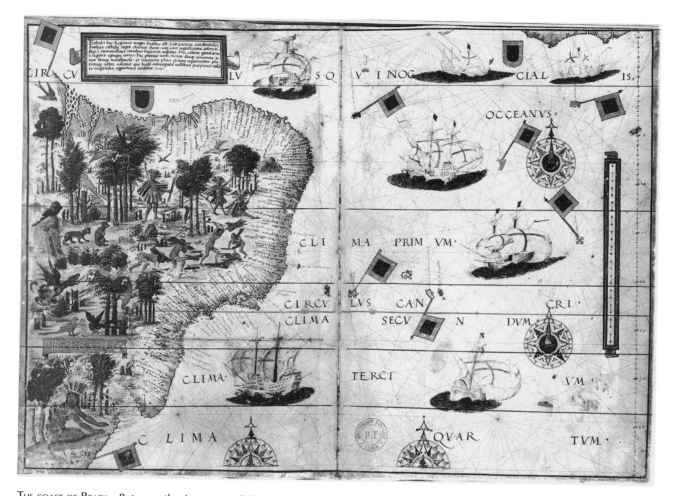

THE COAST OF BRAZIL. Between the Amazon and Río de la Plata. From Pedro Reinel's Miller Atlas.

Río de la Plata estuary (Pero Lopes de Sousa reached the region in 1531), and up the north coast to the Amazon region. The exploration was carried out as far as the mouth of the Amazon.

Soon after the expedition of the Sousa brothers, the Portuguese Crown ordered the division of the territory into hereditary captaincies. Although this regime failed in most of the regions, it allowed for the maintenance—and in some cases, the reinforcement—of the Portuguese presence, especially in the regions of Pernambuco in the northeast and São Paulo in the south. The foundation was thereby laid for the transformation of these areas into two great centers of Portuguese Brazil. On the northern coast, however, the failure of colonization efforts was overwhelming. At the end of the century these territories were not effectively controlled by the Portuguese. Not until the period of the union between the Crowns of Portugal and Castile during the seventeenth century were the territories secured and the Indians and foreign intruders driven out.

The administrative and economic characteristics of these hereditary captaincies in the sixteenth century are still debated: were they remnants of a feudal economy or nascent capitalist enterprises? Old words can hide new realities. Consequently, it is useful to distinguish institutions and ideologies, however archaic and medieval they might be, from economic structures that were developing in the direction of a modern market—a monoculture of exportation and colonial commerce in capitalist terms.

Between the two geographic poles of development in sixteenth-century Brazil—the Pernambuco and São Vincente regions—were extensive coastal territories. Here the captaincies failed and foreigners continued to trade sporadically with the natives.

This situation changed during the second half of the century, owing to the introduction of a central government by the Portuguese Crown and that government's establishment of a new administrative center in Bahia. From this new center, which was eventually transformed into an administrative, military, and religious capital, the successors of the first governor, Tomé de Sousa (1549), oversaw the consolidation of control of the entire eastern coast, the establishment of Portuguese population centers, and the expulsion of foreigners. Tomé de Sousa, in cooperation with the natives, created a true administrative, economic, and military apparatus in the new city. His successor, Mem de Sá, soon attacked and expelled the French of Villegaignon, who were trying to install themselves in Guanabara Bay. Once victorious, the Portuguese founded the city of Rio de Janeiro. The Jesuits began to arrive in the middle of the century, instituting an almost exclusively missionary program and establishing ascendancy over the Indians.

The sixteenth century, then, was a period of occupation and defense of the coast; the next two centuries were devoted to an expansion into the interior. By the end of the sixteenth century the Portuguese presence in Brazil had been consolidated along the eastern coast, where there were two principal centers: the northeastern region of Pernambuco and Bahia and the southeastern region of São Vincente and São Paulo.

The Brazilian northeast, that "most ancient of all the Brazils," began in the last three decades of the century to build its prosperity as a "sugar civilization." New Brazils would be joined to it, born of a multifaceted, decentralized, and continuous geographic expansion. But this region would remain as the historic "cradle" of Brazil.

The economic and social structures of the northeast were based on sugar as the dominant product, with brazilwood, cotton, tobacco, and rum of lesser importance. Thus arose a culture of estates and a laboring class whose continuance was assured by an influx of slaves (already being imported from Africa in the last decades of the sixteenth century). The sociologist Gilberto Freyre characterized this system as a patriarchal society and an economy of "mansions and shanties." But a mestizo class and a generalized acculturation of the three basic components of Brazilian society began to emerge. The Portuguese element was omnipresent, but an African culture predominated on the coast and an Indian culture in the interior.

The indigenous population was of major importance in the sixteenth century; only later, with the arrival of massive numbers of Africans, was it superseded. There were numerous tribes in the Brazilian territory, especially those of the two great linguistic families of the Tupi and Tapuiya. Their social organization and material culture corresponded in a general way to that of hunter-gatherers everywhere. Among the Tupi, however, there was an incipient agriculture. Cannibalism was practiced.

The native peoples moved into the new societies created by the Europeans and even became integrated with them, though the process involved a kind of devolution of the once powerful native peoples into dependents and slaves even as their demographic destruction was taking place. But their heritage persisted, especially in regions where miscegenation and mutual acculturation were common.

To northeastern Brazil was joined, in the late sixteenth and early seventeenth centuries, all of Brazil of the northern coast. This expansion occurred because of military conquest by the Portuguese-Spanish Crown from 1584 to 1616, during which foreign intruders were expelled and enemy tribes repressed. In 1614 the French were ousted from the Maranhão, where they had tried to establish themselves as "Equinoctial France," and in 1616 Francisco Caldeira de Castelo Branco arrived at the mouth of the Grão Pará River and founded the fortress that became the city of Belém. From this city the Portuguese during the next two centuries defended, explored, and finally occupied all the immense regions not only of the Pará but also of the Río Negro as far as Peru. Thus was born northern Brazil, which in the second half of the eighteenth century would achieve prosperity.

In the meantime the growing colony suffered attacks by the Dutch in the "sugar wars" of the first half of the seventeenth century. Taking advantage of the weakness of the Portuguese in the final period of the Iberian union, they attacked the heart of the northeast and in 1630 conquered Pernambuco. The Dutch remained there for nearly twenty-five years and were expelled by the Portuguese-Brazilian forces only after the independence of Portugal had been regained. The regaining of Portuguese independence from Spain was, in part, motivated by the difficulties in which Brazil found itself during the period of its alliance with Spain because it was attacked by the enemies of the Spanish monarchy. Brazil was already the "crown jewel" of the overseas Portuguese empire. Since India had in great part been lost, Portuguese interests now centered on the South Atlantic with its Euro-Afro-American trade.

But while the colony was experiencing these difficulties in the northeast, it was developing a notable vitality in its remote territories farther south. A great expansion took place in the center and the south, stimulated by the São Vincente and São Paulo population centers. From the city of São Paulo the great movement of the Paulist (as those from São Paulo are known) *bandeiras* arose—expeditions of backlanders into the interior in search of Indian slaves and mineral wealth. By promoting the capture of Indians and the destruction of the Spanish Jesuits who were trying to advance to the east, energizing the search for alluvial gold and the advance to the south, penetrating into the interior, and surpassing the limits defined by the Treaty of Tordesillas, the Paulist expansion created central and east central Brazil.

It was the Paulist *bandeirantes* who, in the final years of the seventeenth century, found gold in the region of

Minas Gerais. From this time, the region was linked to the northeastern sugar bowl by the colonization (encouraged also by a flourishing cattle industry) along the São Francisco River, which came to be called the "river of national unity." Thus finally were joined two economic activities—sugar and gold mining—creating a unified Brazil from the northeast to the southeast. Beginning with the gold economy and the settlement of Minas Gerais, the prosperity of this interior colony was developed. A great demographic density was created, and local agriculture continued the development initiated by the gold rush.

The gold rush extended to the far west, to the lowlands of Mato Grosso, Goiás, and the borders shared with Brazil's Hispanic neighbors. The "Monsoons" were regular voyages by river that gave continuity to the movement of the *bandeirantes* and expanded the fluvial highways of the Mato Grosso in the direction of the Amazon. Thus were set the limits of Brazilian territory along its western boundaries.

As for the actual occupation of the Amazon region, the Portuguese always had the advantage over their Hispanic neighbors (though the Spaniards had made the earliest explorations). From the city of Belém in the Pará region, after 1616 the *entradas* (raids) of the *tropas de resgate* (liberation troops) began. The Portuguese controlled the Amazon basin for some two centuries, exploiting it for its vegetable products such as cocoa. In 1669 São José do Rio Negro, precursor of Manaus, was founded.

The advance to the south continued at the instigation of the Portuguese Crown, which created after 1680 the colony of Sacramento, an isolated fortress on the Río de la Plata, directly in front of the Spanish city of Buenos Aires. This Portuguese entrepôt eventually depended for its livelihood on trade and contraband with its adversary on the other side of the river, appropriating part of the flow of silver exported from there. This solitary outpost—at times a thorn in the side of the Spanish, at times a go-between in diplomatic affairs—allowed the Portuguese-Brazilian rear guard to advance, thereby colonizing the entire south over the next hundred years. The Portuguese-Brazilians took possession of the regions of Santa Catarina, Paraná, and Rio Grande do Sul, where by the beginning of the eighteenth century had developed that great source of wealth: cattle.

Thus the Paulist expansion was probably primarily responsible for the creation of the central and west-central parts of Brazil and for the early reclamation of the south. The official expansion instigated by the Portuguese Crown led to the rise of the northeast, the southeast, and the north and the defense and settlement of the south. But the distinction between the two formative influences should not be too closely drawn. As historian Jaime Cortesão has pointed out, both factors were at work in each region. For example, António Raposo Tavares was without doubt one of the most important of the Paulist *bandeirantes*, but his connection with the Portuguese Crown was obvious. Raposo Tavares undertook the *bandeira* of 1649, covering a great territory, from the Río de la Plata to the Amazon, across the upper Paraguay River, and from the Guaporé to the Madeira rivers. This circuit defined a unity that would later be consolidated as the Brazilian national territory. In contrast to other European colonies in America, Brazil, when it became an independent state, was already fully formed.

[See also *Portugal.*]

BIBLIOGRAPHY

Boxer, Charles Ralph. *The Dutch in Brazil, 1624–1654.* Oxford, 1957.
Boxer, Charles Ralph. *The Golden Age of Brazil, 1695–1750: Growing Pains of a Colonial Society.* Berkeley, 1962. Reprints, 1969, 1975, 1984.
Boxer, Charles Ralph. *Salvador de Sá and the Struggle for Brazil and Angola, 1602–1686.* London, 1952. Reprint, Westport, Conn., 1975.
Marchant, Alexander. *From Barter to Slavery: The Economic Relations of Portuguese and Indians in the Settlement of Brazil, 1500–1580.* Baltimore, 1942.
Morse, Richard McGee. *The Bandeirantes: The Historical Role of the Brazilian Pathfinder.* New York, 1965.
Sanceau, Elaine. *Captains of Brazil.* Porto, 1965.
Schwartz, Stuart B. *Sovereignty and Society in Colonial Brazil: The Judges of the High Court of Bahia, 1586–1750.* Berkeley and Los Angeles, 1974.
Tomlinson, Regina Johnson. *The Struggle for Brazil: Portugal and "The French Interloper," 1500–1550.* New York, 1970.

ALFREDO PINHEIRO MARQUES
Translated from Portuguese by Rebecca Catz

French Colonization

Breton, Norman, and Basque fishermen from France were active off the Atlantic coast of northeastern North America as early as the closing decades of the fifteenth century. After European Atlantic fishermen were closed out of Icelandic fishing grounds in 1478, they looked for other sources of "sea silver" to meet the demand in Europe, where the religious calendar indicated over 150 days of abstinence from meat and dairy products in a year. The first official record of annual cod-fishing expeditions from French ports is dated 1504. By 1510 Breton and Norman fishermen kept the market at Rouen supplied with "Terreneufve" cod. In 1520, Jean and Raoul Parmentier combined their fishing with loading furs in Cape Breton. There followed a marked increase in the size of the fishing fleets, especially after 1540 as the fishermen selected a favorite beach for landing and later for drying fish. Although some men wintered in Cape Breton, there was as yet no true colonization. By 1578 an eye-witness report confirmed that the French were the most numerous in spite of the Wars of Religion at home.

In addition to cod, fishermen became interested in the walrus of morse, the "beast of the great teeth." The French began hunting them sometime after 1510 for their "white gold," or ivory, their fat oils, which were used as sealant on ships, and their tough hides, which were used for shields and armor as well as for ropes and rigging. The islands of the Gulf of St. Lawrence provided the most profitable rookeries for exploitation. Jacques Cartier's nephews had an interest in the Magdalen Islands establishments and by the end of the century the French had succeeded in driving out the Portuguese and the English, with the help of Micmac warriors, from the gulf. Exploitation of the walrus rookeries led to the first French colonization venture on the coastal islands. In 1598, a Breton nobleman, Marquis Troilus de la Roche, was granted letters patent to found a colony on Sable Island and was authorized to recruit hardened criminals "chosen by the best judges in France." Sable Island, however, failed to attract immigrants and the colony was eventually abandoned.

The slow development of the fur trade out of the cod fishery led to more permanent colonization. When the explorer Jacques Cartier visited Chaleur Bay in 1534, he was approached by Micmacs who "set up a great clamor and made frequent signs to us to come to shore, holding up to us some furs on sticks." His crew frightened the Micmacs off, but, when they returned the following day, bartering ensued at a brisk pace. Obviously, this was not the first trading encounter for the Micmacs, nor were the French caught without appropriate goods to exchange. The lasting consequence of Cartier's second voyage in 1535 was the discovery of the St. Lawrence River entrance to the continent, although he did not realize at the time that the river led to the Great Lakes basin in the heart of North America. France decided to pursue exploration in this region and to found a colony to establish its sovereignty. In 1541 Cartier was commissioned to undertake a third voyage, as part of a colonization scheme to be headed by a nobleman from southern France, Jean-François de La Rocque de Roberval, to "enter deeper into these lands, to converse with the peoples found there and live among them, if need be." Cartier arrived near the Laurentian Iroquois village of Stadacona (Québec) with a first contingent of settlers and established a base camp that he called Charlesbourg-Royal (Cap Rouge), then proceeded to explore upstream as far as the Iroquoian villages of Hochelaga and Tutonaguy (Montréal Island). A combination of a particularly harsh winter, shortage of

food, scurvy, and increasing native hostilities as an epidemic swept the Laurentian Iroquois villages, together with the discovery of what were believed to be gold and diamonds, convinced Cartier and the colonists to return to France in June 1542. Putting in at the natural harbor of St. John's (Newfoundland), he met the Roberval contingent with its settlers, cattle, and equipment. Cartier slipped away under cover of darkness, leaving Roberval and the second contingent to face the rigors of a Canadian winter and native hostility before it too abandoned the settlement scheme.

Settlements were not seriously attempted again until 1603, when Henry IV granted Pierre de Monts, a distinguished Calvinist soldier and administrator, a trade monopoly in North America with the obligation to establish sixty colonists a year and promote Catholic missionary work among the native peoples. De Monts organized an association of merchants from several cities and named the Dutchman Cornelis de Bellois as chief shareholder to finance a joint Catholic-Protestant expedition to explore and colonize Acadie. (Most of the sixteenth-century French overseas ventures had involved Protestants and there was even a proposal to solve the religious problem in France by sending all the Protestants to the colonies.) Three vessels carrying artisans, soldiers, vagabonds, two Catholic priests, and a Huguenot pastor sailed into the Bay of Fundy, where a first settlement called Sainte-Croix was laid out on Dochet Island. The following year it was decided to move the settlement across the Bay of Fundy to the Annapolis valley at Port Royal. In 1611 the marquise de Guercheville bought out the merchant association's interest in Port Royal and sent out Jesuit missionaries to work

Map of New France. With representations of Indians. From Ramusio's *Navigatoni e viaggi*. Venice, 1556.

among the Micmacs. The colony in Acadie survived but was subject to raids by interlopers in the fur trade monopoly, to corsairs, and to attacks from the English colonies established along the Atlantic littoral.

Since de Mont's trade monopoly extended to the St. Lawrence valley, in 1608 he named Samuel de Champlain, an experienced geographer, his lieutenant charged with establishing a beachhead at "the point of Québec" where a century earlier the Laurentian Iroquois village of Stadacona had stood. The French were aware that the northern Algonquian bands and the Hurons were at war with the Five Nations Iroquois to the south; Champlain therefore fortified his "habitation" at Québec in 1608. In July 1609, Champlain and a party of Frenchmen joined a raiding party into Iroquois country; the ensuing encounter resulted in a century of Iroquois hostility that at times threatened the very survival of the French colony. The French had little choice but to join with their fur-trading partners in this intertribal war. Exploration of the "upper country" of Canada progressed well, but there were few colonists who came out from France. Champlain sent out young men to live among the Hurons and Algonquians to learn their languages and ways and in return received a few native children to be given a French education. In 1615 missionaries of the Recollet order, a branch of the Franciscans, arrived to undertake missionary work; they soon chose the sedentary agricultural Huron tribes along Georgian Bay as their main center of activity. The Hurons lived at the northern limits of corn culture, were noted traders with neighboring tribes, had established themselves as middlemen in the French trade, and were strategically located in the Great Lakes basin, which gave access by waterways to the Mississippi valley, the Far West, Hudson's Bay, and the St. Lawrence entrance from the Atlantic. However, they were still engaged in sporadic but interminable warfare with the Five Nations Iroquois to the south.

In 1627 Cardinal Richelieu intervened to set the colony on a firm financial foundation. A monopoly company known as the Company of New France (popularly the Hundred Associates) was charged with the administration of Canada, its settlement, and its social organization in return for a fifteen-year monopoly of commerce and perpetual control of the fur exports. The company undertook to bring out four thousand settlers within fifteen years, but a three-year occupation of Québec by the English, constant harassment by Iroquois war parties, and the general unattractiveness of the region to persons not involved in the fur trade rendered the company's mandate unrealizable. In 1645 the company ceded its fur-trade monopoly to a small group of local merchants, known as the Community of Habitants, in return for assuming the administrative costs of the struggling colony.

The charter of the Company of New France had stipulated that no foreigners or Protestants were to be permitted to settle permanently in the Laurentian outpost. What measure of success there was in this period was achieved largely by religious organizations. The Jesuits joined the Recollets as missionaries in 1625 and by 1634 were the sole evangelizers in Canada. They had their headquarters at Québec but sent out missionaries in pairs to the nomadic Algonquian bands and to some Iroquois villages and established a large mission among the Hurons with a regional headquarters in 1639 at Sainte-Marie-des-Hurons (Midland, Ontario). Shortly before his death, Champlain had established a second settlement at Trois-Rivières. In 1642, a lay religious millenarian group known as the Société de Notre-Dame, an off-shoot of extensive revivalistic activity in France associated with the Catholic Reformation, founded Ville-Marie (Montréal) on the island of Montréal. This third settlement was ideally located in good agricultural land, at the confluence of trading and communications routes, and at a strategic point for dealing with native peoples.

In 1639 two women's religious communities arrived to inaugurate important hospitals, schools, and houses of charity. The colony could even boast of a Jesuit college, founded in 1635. These extraordinary advances in the social and cultural fields masked a slow progress in settlement and in the development of an agricultural base.

The inability of private entrepreneurs to attract a significant number of immigrants and of the French fur traders to provide a base for commercial and artisanal development convinced King Louis XIV to extend his personal rule to the colony under the system known as royal government. Canada, from its earliest stage of development, required centralized public direction and initiative and state intervention in the economy to ensure its survival and progress. Tasks first undertaken by private entrepreneurs, merchant associations, and religious zealots were now taken up by the bureaucratic, military, and ecclesiastical establishments within the French state. Each created its own dominant elite and clientele and each assumed responsibility for a sector of public affairs under the Crown. Settlement proceeded along lines of the native strategy of territorial occupation—for example, penetrating the waterways of the continent or establishing settlements at strategic points of communication, trade, and defense. As early as 1665, the French government decided that the strategy of extending French sovereignty over a vast hinterland also required restriction of French settlement to the narrow ribbon of the St. Lawrence valley and recognition of native independence and self government in all regions beyond the riverine colony. In native ancestral lands the French might with permission establish mission stations, trading posts, and military garrisons, following the native tradition of sharing resources and offering hospitality.

Under the system of royal government introduced by stages in 1663, New France came under the jurisdiction of the Ministry of Marine and Colonies in Versailles. The colonial administration consisted of a governor-general at Québec, who was the king's representative with responsibility for military matters and relations with native peoples; an intendant who was responsible for justice, commerce, and public order; a bishop, who as the chief ecclesiastical official supervised the church's mandate in education, social welfare, hospitalization, and missionary work; and an appointed sovereign council at Québec, made up of local notables who sat as a court of appeal and acted as a chancery registering all royal edicts and colonial legislation to give them colonial application. In the eighteenth century, under the Regency and during the reign of Louis XV, the sovereign council was enlarged and its legislative role greatly restricted; it retained its judicial role and was renamed superior council. While the governor held the most prominent position in the power structure, it was the intendant who wielded the greatest influence over daily affairs through control of financial affairs, the justice system, and correspondence with Versailles, as well as the presidency of the Superior Council. The bishops found their role increasingly relegated to purely spiritual matters, especially in the eighteenth century, in keeping with the Gallican maxim that "the church is in the state" and so was subject to the temporal power.

The colony reflected the social distinctions and ranking that prevailed in France itself, although in the early decades of settlement the pioneer environment imposed some social leveling and stimulated a spirit of independence. There was less upward social mobility in the eighteenth century as the class structure became more entrenched. Nevertheless, when faced with unwilling immigration, pioneer hardships, and external threats from the English colonies, the administration adopted a sense of social responsibility to all classes—an attitude that has been called paternalism. Royal instructions in 1663 said that "the general spirit of government ought to lean in the direction of gentleness, it being dangerous to employ severity against transplanted peoples, far removed from their prince...." Religion was important in inculcating a kind of social conscience, a sense of just price and reasonable labor, and respect for authority. Though there were no parliamentary institutions, there were periodic consultative assemblies called by the governor and intendant dealing with matters of general concern such as brandy trafficking, price controls, statute labor, and parish boundaries. The general rule remained, however, that "each should speak for himself, and none for all."

Government could consult but mass petitioning would not be tolerated.

The Custom of Paris became the customary Canadian legal code regulating property rights, inheritance, contracts, and marriage and family relations. Its inheritance rules, for example, provided for all the children "male and female, living and not in holy orders" and protected the right of women to property. The royal courts were located in the three principal towns and provided rapid and relatively cheap justice to those living nearby. Fees were fixed and there was little litigation about seigniorial dues, which were fixed in the contracts, or about tithing, whose rate was set by the state officials. Criminal law was harsh and the punishments barbaric, as in Europe, but only crimes against God and the king were brutally punished. Proceedings were adversarial and inquisitorial, with judicial torture provided for in extreme cases; the accused had to prove his innocence to the judges. Capital punishment was meted out publicly, as were lesser punishments that used such instruments as the stocks, the pillory, and the wooden horse, or *amende honorable* (judicial penance) in nightshirt and candle at the door of the parish church.

The population of New France was largely rural, and it was not until the end of the French regime that villages emerged as markets and service centers. Outside the three towns—Québec, Montréal, and Trois-Rivières—the people were for the most part settled on seigneuries. In theory all the land belonged to the Crown, which made grants of estates to the privileged orders, the clergy, and the nobility. At the beginning of royal government, the religious owned about 11 percent of cultivated lands, but by the end of the French regime almost one-quarter of the land was in their hands. Initially it appeared that the lay seigneuries would be restricted to the nobility but this never became the rule. There was little speculation in land because land was readily available and required time and labor to become productive as an investment. The traditional French seigniorial system underwent a few changes in Canada. The estates were surveyed as trapezoidal parallelograms running back from the St. Lawrence River in such a way that each *censitaire* (landholder) had access to the river as the transportation axis and the source of water, fish, and marine animals. Each farm cut across the grain of the land affording a variety of soils and vegetation—wet fodder lands, heavy soils for cereals, upland meadows for grazing, and wood lots for fuel and lumber at the upper reaches of the property. The *habitants,* as the peasants preferred to be called, enjoyed privacy on their individual farms of about 150 meters frontage, yet were not too distant from neighbors. Besides retarding the emergence of villages, this pattern of settlement also shielded the rural population from the constant supervision of the seigneur or parish priest. As the seigneuries became populated and all arable land was brought into production, seigneurs began to exact all the customary dues and to exercise their traditional privileges and honors.

The population generally practiced its religion out of conformity and social convention and loved the ritual and ceremonial aspects, but was not excessively zealous. The state found it necessary to legislate observance of Sunday rest and attendance at mass, the closing of taverns during divine office, the payment of tithes, the maintenance of church property, and even respectful behavior in church. The church did succeed in exercising effective censorship, in controlling education, and in offering adequate hospitalization and welfare services in the major centers. It did not stamp out popular superstitions, eliminate the brandy traffic, or convert the majority of the native peoples. Recruitment of the parish clergy never kept pace with population growth, so that at the end of the French regime there were about 240 seigneuries but only 114 parishes served by a mere 169 priests, including seminary, missionary, and chaplaincy personnel. Instead of a priest-ridden colony, there was a crisis of religious vocations.

Though population growth outstripped religious vocations, immigration never reached the levels experienced in other European colonies. At the introduction of royal government in 1663 there were less than four thousand colonists. By 1700 there were still only about 15,000 colonists in spite of state-supported schemes to settle soldiers, brides, artisans, and professionals. Over more than a century an estimated 11,000 French remained permanently in the colony and founded families.

Québec remained the chief port, administrative center, and fortified capital of the colony. From here a threefold colonial strategy had been elaborated during the final years of the reign of Louis XIV. First, peace was concluded with the Iroquois Confederacy in 1701 and its neutrality in international wars was guaranteed. Second, a settlement was permitted at Detroit in the upper country and a plan evolved for settlements in the Illinois country, a colony at the mouth of the Mississippi river, and a chain of forts linking these distant places to the Laurentian colony. By 1713 it was clear that Canada should be held not for its economic value but for geopolitical reasons, as a strategic outpost capable of containing the English colonies along their Atlantic seaboard and forcing Britain to maintain overseas garrisons and a navy. Third, the native peoples had to be supplied with the goods they desired and conciliated to French sovereignty in order to retain their support against the British.

During the Seven Years' War large contingents of French regulars, *troupes de terre* from the Ministry of War, under their own commanders arrived to assume the brunt of the fighting against British land and naval invaders, resulting in the adoption of European formation fighting supported by artillery when the British attacked using traditional siege tactics. Since the seventeenth century engagements against the Iroquois, the Canadian militia had adopted the guerilla tactics of the native auxiliary forces in raids on English settlements and in thwarting invading forces. The colonial strategy championed by the Governor Vaudreuil was jettisoned, causing him to complain, "Now war is established here on the European basis . . . . It is no longer a matter of making a raid, but of conquering or being conquered. What a revolution! What a change!" The colonial militia and the native auxiliaries became marginal to the conflict and New France fell finally to British forces with the capitulation of Montréal in September 1760. Military occupation and martial law were imposed until the definitive treaty of peace, the Treaty of Paris, was signed in 1763 bringing the French regime to an end.

BIBLIOGRAPHY

Eccles, W. J. *Canada under Louis XIV, 1663–1701.* Toronto, 1964.
Jaenen, Cornelius J. *The French Relationship with the Native Peoples of New France.* Ottawa, 1984.
Miquelon, Dale. *New France, 1701–1744: A Supplement to Europe.* Toronto, 1968.
Stanley, George F. G. *New France: The Last Phase, 1744–1760.* Toronto, 1968.
Trudel, Marcel. *The Beginnings of New France, 1504–1663.* Toronto, 1973.

CORNELIUS J. JAENEN

English Colonization

There was little coherence in the initiatives of the English Crown in regard to North America in the sixteenth century aside from the fact that all derived directly from it. John Cabot in 1496 was given wide-ranging powers to rule the non-Christian lands that he might annex to the English Crown, much as Columbus was given in Spain, but nothing came of this or subsequent patents in the years following. After 1505, no English activity was formally authorized until 1553, when what later became the Muscovy Company was given a monopoly on trade with the northeast and northwest, including that part of North America north of about fifty degrees. This authorization was superseded in 1577 by the patent creating the Company of Cathay, which was authorized to exploit the (nonexistent) gold reserves of Baffin Island and to control English access to the supposed Northwest Passage. These powers collapsed with the company in 1578. The patents of 1553 and 1577 created companies that were operated by their subscribers and a governor and council. From 1578 onward, patents relating to North America were normally granted to individuals or small syndicates; these patents granted very wide powers to the recipients if they succeeded in their objectives.

Early English Colonies and Explorations of North America

A new interest in North America followed the collapse of the Company of Cathay. On June 15, 1578, Sir Humphrey Gilbert was given a patent that authorized him to annex and colonize all lands that were not yet occupied by a Christian power (though only eastern North America was intended). Gilbert interpreted his authority widely and drew up plans by which vast feudal estates were to be conferred on associates and subscribers under a code of laws drawn up by Gilbert himself. His ideas often outran his practical capacity, however. He ultimately conceded some rights to form a consultative council by the larger proprietors, although this council remained under his control. In August 1583, he formally annexed Newfoundland to the Crown and assumed control of its inshore fishery. This annexation, however, came to nothing, as Gilbert was drowned at sea on a return voyage.

Roanoke Island. Gilbert's patent (excluding Newfoundland) was regranted to his half brother, Walter Raleigh, on March 25, 1584, but Queen Elizabeth would not let Raleigh take part in the subsequent voyages in person. His reconnaissance vessels of 1584 located a possible site for a colony on Roanoke Island, and in July 1585, Governor Ralph Lane and 108 colonists maintained the first English colony until mid-June 1586. Among its discoveries was the deep-water harbor of Chesapeake Bay. The colony produced little economic return and was brought back to England in July 1586.

Raleigh lost interest in direct participation in the colony for a time and surrendered his rights over the Chesapeake Bay area to a syndicate. John White and his twelve assistants were given authority to settle a colony of families on lands that were not fully occupied by Indians. By chance, the expedition landed on Roanoke Island and was forced to make its way overland to the Elizabeth River in present-day Virginia. White returned to England for supplies, leaving a party on Roanoke Island to guide him to the colony when he came back. The Spanish war, however, delayed his return. Indeed, in 1588, Raleigh planned a new venture on the shores of Chesapeake Bay as an advance base against the Spanish fleet, but his ships were countermanded to help fight the Armada that year. In 1590, White made a brief call at Roanoke Island only to find the island deserted. The lost colonists remained out of contact with England, though they were assumed to be still alive, at least until 1603. Raleigh authorized minor searches around 1600–1602 and some exploration of New

England in 1602–1603, but his patent lapsed in the latter year. These colonists were finally killed about 1606 by Powhatan, the Algonquian ruler of southern Virginia.

Jamestown. A new period of English colonization started in 1606. Thus far, no known English colonies had been established in North America. The Virginia Company Charter of April 10, 1606, created a commercial company drawn mainly from London merchants, with a parallel company based at Plymouth. Both enterprises were to be controlled by a royal council, as was the Consejo de Indias in Spain. The Plymouth Company settled a small colony on the Kennebec (Sagadahoc) River in 1607, but it was underfinanced and its members unfamiliar with the fur trade. In the autumn of 1608, it was abandoned.

Attention then focused on the Chesapeake Bay area. Christopher Newport conveyed a group of about one hundred colonists, all servants of the company, to the James River in 1607. The first settlement was on Jamestown Island, which offered the advantage that ships could moor close to its shore. The site's superficial attractions soon faded, however, because the environment was extremely unhealthy. The company had nominated Edward Maria Wingfield as the first governor and named his councillors. While a fort, church, and houses were being built, Newport proceeded to explore the James River valley until he was stopped at the river's fall line in the vicinity of modern Richmond, beyond which navigation was not possible. (Only brief reconnaissance beyond the falls was attempted.) Newport was able to bring home only a few samples of indigenous products.

Among the remaining 104 persons in the colony, division and illness (more than half the original settlers died from drinking brackish water or from typhoid or other diseases) led to the deposition of Wingfield in September. Powhatan, who ruled most of the Indian tribes in the area from Weromacomoco on the York River, welcomed the Jamestown settlement as a source of copper and iron, and of knives, tools, and other European goods. Capt. John Smith, however, was captured by Indians in December 1607 and was formally adopted as a leader under Powhatan, who henceforth regarded Jamestown as a subordinate unit in his domain.

When Newport returned in January 1608 with fifty additional colonists, he was shocked at the condition of the settlement. Smith was released in time to meet him, but the village was burned down a few days later. Newport had brought insignia from King James in order to make Powhatan a vassal of the English Crown, which he did in February. (Neither Smith in December 1607 nor Powhatan in 1608 understood the implications of the ceremonies in which they were involved.) Newport was once again dissatisfied with what had been produced in the colony, especially as reports in 1607 of a possible gold deposit had

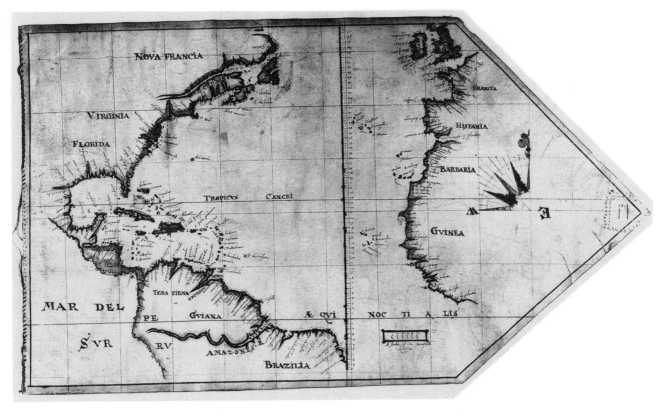

THE VIRGINIA COMPANY CHART. Circa 1607–1609. Manuscript map on vellum.   NEW YORK PUBLIC LIBRARY

been shown to be false. In June, Smith set out on his exploration of the Chesapeake basin and its rivers. He found that the fall line everywhere obstructed further navigation. The Potomac River was especially disappointing, as the obstructions above the site of present-day Washington were formidable barriers to further penetration. His pioneer work in mapping the area and locating Indian settlements, however, has proved invaluable to modern scholars.

Newport made a third visit, with yet another group of colonists. Smith had been made governor and had set the colonists to clearing land, growing crops, and lading processed timber. The colony's death rate had slowed, but it still remained high. Crops that were grown in comparable latitudes in Europe (37 to 38 degrees), such as olives and sugar cane, could not thrive in the misunderstood continental climate of North America.

A complete reorganization of the company was then undertaken. It was relaunched under a second charter of May 25, 1609, which expanded the membership to over six hundred subscribers, abandoned the Royal Council, and entrusted the company's council with some royal authority. The Royal Council, as its last act, appointed Sir Thomas Gates as governor, naming his council and providing him

with extensive instructions. Of the eight ships sent out from England, six reached Virginia. The flagship carrying Gates, his council, and his instructions went aground on Bermuda. Gates and Sir George Somers organized their men to maintain themselves and salvage enough from the ship to equip two pinnaces, which, with a cargo of wild pigs and pork, reached Jamestown in May 1610. There they found disaster had almost destroyed the colony. The addition of some five hundred settlers was impossible for Smith to assimilate. His credentials as governor were challenged amid severe dissension. He did succeed in getting the bulk of the newcomers to create a major new settlement, Henrico, near the falls, but he himself had to leave for England, owing to injuries incurred in an accident.

Under George Percy and Francis West, the colony had deteriorated. Powhatan, in effect, had declared war on these intruders who had overthrown the arrangements he considered he had made with the Jamestown colony. Supplies of corn from most of the Indian villages ceased, and, in return, vicious and brutal raids were made on a number of those villages. In the winter, the colonists had died in great numbers. When Gates and Somers appeared, only some sixty remained alive. They could give

Nova Britannia.
OFFERING MOST
Excellent fruites by Planting in VIRGINIA.

Exciting all fuch as be well affected to further the fame.

LONDON
Printed for SAMVEL MACHAM, and are to befold at
his Shop in Pauls Church-yard, at the
Signe of the Bul-head.
1 6 0 9.

ENGLISH PROMOTIONAL TRACT ADVERTISING OPPORTUNITIES IN VIRGINIA. Printed in London, 1609. The text promises "a most comfortable subsistence" to those who would make the voyage and settle in the New World.   NEW YORK PUBLIC LIBRARY, RARE BOOK DIVISION

them first aid, but they could not restore the colony. They were in the process of evacuating the colonists when Lord De La Warr, a new governor, intercepted them. From June 1610, the colony, which remained at war with Powhatan until 1614, was governed by a strict body of laws. In effect, Sir Thomas Dale governed the small colony like a military garrison between 1612 and 1616, gradually weakening Indian power and slowly leading the colony toward self-sufficiency. During this period, John Rolfe experimented with Trinidad tobacco (*Nicotiana tabacum*) as a possible export crop. A final reorganization of the company took place in 1612. The charter of March 12, 1612, extended membership and authorized participation in quarterly courts to which the treasurer and council were elected. In 1614, Powhatan made peace with the colonists,

allowing his daughter Pocahontas to become a Christian and to marry the colonist John Rolfe.

In 1616, earlier promises that land would be distributed to subscribers and settlers of seven years' seniority came due, but it was 1618 before final arrangements were made. Sir George Yeardley was authorized to begin the process of distribution and to initiate grants of extensive blocks of land to individuals or syndicates for "particular plantations." He arrived on April 19, 1619, and a period of hectic colony building began (the Indians now appearing too weak to resist). Among other innovations was permission to create a general assembly. Yeardley incorporated a number of towns, and from them and "particular plantations" a body was elected, which formed, with the governor and council, a legislative body that modified the strict legal code of 1610 and dealt with local matters. This was an important precedent for local self-government, though it did not become a continuing part of Virginia government until 1639.

Under the direction of the treasurer of the company, Sir Edwin Sandys, some five thousand colonists had been sent out by 1624; the colony expanded over most of the James-York peninsula. The death rate remained high, but the production of glass, soapash, and, above all, the new tobacco, together with plans for a major ironworks, gave hope of a varied and prosperous community. The process, however, was abruptly checked by an Indian uprising. Opechancanough had succeeded Powhatan in 1618, and his forces were strong enough on March 22, 1622, to sweep through the colony, destroying many new settlements (though not taking Jamestown) and killing some 150 colonists.

This uprising led to a retraction of the colony to a relatively small area; many colonists died of starvation and epidemics, even though extensive help came from England. The company went bankrupt, and the king was obliged to step in, declaring the Virginia Company dissolved in 1624. The new king, Charles I, promptly reestablished Virginia as a royal colony in 1625, with a governor and council appointed by him and under government control. This act may be said to have created the basis for a continuing expansion of royal authority over increasing areas of eastern North America.

The Pilgrims at Plymouth Harbor. In 1620, the Pilgrims landed at Cape Cod and soon moved to Plymouth Harbor where they established the first autonomous colony that owed nothing to royal authority. Nonconforming Congregationalists had been driven into the Netherlands in 1607, but they had retained English contacts. In 1619–1620, they obtained backing from London merchants and other Congregationalists in England who were being persecuted. They had a grant for a "particular plantation" from the Virginia Company when they sailed from Plymouth on

September 26, 1620, for the northern fringe of the company's territory. But they put ashore on the first land they came to, Provincetown Harbor, on November 31, and drew up the famous Mayflower Compact, forming a civil society of their own. Their move to Plymouth Harbor was completed on December 16. More than half of the Pilgrims died that winter, but under the guidance of William Bradford they proceeded with remarkable skill and endurance to establish a settlement that was to be a singular and lasting one on the site of a former Indian village. They remained for a long time a unique religious and political grouping with no formal recognition of royal authority.

Bermuda. Because Bermuda had seemed so attractive to Gates and Somers, the Virginia Company set up a subsidiary body to colonize it in 1611. A master carpenter and builder, Richard More, was chosen as governor. With a party of colonists, he landed at St. George's Harbor on July 11, 1612. For three years he concentrated on building fortifications to protect from a possible Spanish attack.

Colonists flooded into Bermuda, especially when it obtained a separate charter in 1614. Early conditions were chaotic, but the island was surveyed and divided into parishes, most of which were allocated to major investors. It took some time to establish that tobacco was the easiest and most profitable crop, but under the governors Daniel Tucker and Nathaniel Butler the colony gradually found a balanced existence, though it never became the paradise for growing subtropical fruits and other products that Somers had envisaged in 1610.

Newfoundland. From 1583 to 1608 only occasional plans were made for the colonization of Newfoundland. In the latter year John Guy of Bristol explored its eastern shores, where a fishery, operating between May and September, had become a major industry. As a result of cooperation between London and Bristol capitalists, a patent was obtained on May 2, 1610, for a company to colonize Newfoundland. A treasurer and council were to govern the company and to appoint a governor for any colony it should establish.

John Guy accepted the post of first governor, and an expedition of thirty-nine men landed at Conception Bay in August 1611, creating the colony of Cupids Cove. Their remit was to explore and engage in fur trading as well as cod fishing and drying. Guy, who directed the planting of root crops, the construction of a warehouse large enough for building boats in the winter, and the exploration of territories while the snow was still on the ground, was an able commander. Additional settlers, including women, came out in 1612, and the first two years yielded good fishing returns and some furs, which were sent back to England. Before returning to Bristol to report progress in 1611, however, Guy unwisely imposed regulations on the inshore fishermen, who had a long-standing stake in the

summer fishery. These regulations led to a campaign against the colony that was ultimately fatal to its expansion, without which it could not pay its way. In 1612, the pirate Peter Easton disrupted the fishery, though he did not attack the colony. Plans for a second settlement were abandoned, and in 1613 colonists began to drift homeward. Guy and the treasurer John Slany quarreled, and after Guy's departure in 1613 the colony declined to a handful of people.

By 1616 the colony was bankrupt and kept going only by selling concessions to other interested parties, five in all, covering most of southeastern Newfoundland. Several parties never took up their grants, but others made interesting, though ultimately unsuccessful, experiments in the 1620s. The company survived until 1631, but as early as 1621, the fishing interests began a campaign against colonization. This campaign hampered and, in the end, virtually destroyed opportunities for colonization until much later.

Quest for the Northwest Passage. The search for a Northwest Passage, in which the English were leaders, affected the exploration of the whole of northern North American waters. Under a patent granted in February 1584, John Davis explored and defined the shorelines of Greenland, Baffin Island, and northern Labrador (1585–1587), paving the way for later explorations but finding no passages that were not blocked with ice. In 1600, the East India Company was constituted and given, among many other things, rights over any northern passages. It financed an expedition in 1602 under George Waymouth, which appears to have entered Hudson Strait but which was unable—as a result of both ice and crew problems—to establish any hopeful prospect of finding a passage.

An unofficial syndicate of London merchants in 1610 financed the voyage of Henry Hudson during which he discovered Hudson Bay. While Hudson wintered in James Bay, he was cast off in a shallop by a mutinous crew, a few of whom survived to tell the tale. In 1612, Thomas Button explored the main outline of Hudson Bay and brought back indications that a passage might be found. An explosion of interest ensued, and a patent was granted to the powerful North-West Passage Company on July 26, 1612. A resulting 1613 voyage was a fiasco. In 1615, Robert Bylot and William Baffin extended the range of exploration north of the bay, but they too failed to find a passage. In 1616, a final attempt was made by the English north of Davis's exploration of 1587, which brought the expedition into new high latitudes before being checked by ice. Though valued for its explorations, the company collapsed and exploration by the English ceased for some fifteen years. The various ventures had revealed much of northern North America, but from the perspective of imperial expansion, they were a waste of money that might otherwise have been used to establish effective colonies farther south.

The English Record of the Early Years

It can scarcely be argued that by the end of 1620 England had anything that resembled an empire in North America. A single colony, Virginia, had showed promise, only to be shortly checked by indigenous resistance. Many experiments in planning and governing colonies had been made, but almost all were unsuccessful. Nevertheless, with the creation of its general assembly in 1619, the Virginia Company by the next year was showing indications of a process that was to differentiate English colonization from that of other powers. The Pilgrim venture, not yet defined by the end of 1620, revealed that collective initiatives impelled by noneconomic forces could be promising. Direct royal authority remained the source of all other colonial activity, mediated through chartered companies or powers entrusted to individuals, without any supervisory body. (The experimental Royal Council of 1606–1609 was not repeated.)

Religion, theoretically, played a part in most ventures. There was extensive writing about converting native peoples. One goal of these writings was to remove the perception by Roman Catholics that the Church of England was merely a narrow sectarian heresy with no influence outside England. In practice, however, little was done, except to provide colonists with clergy. In Virginia, church building, compulsory church attendance, and an unbroken supply of clergy to carry on the work of maintaining Anglicanism were permanent features. In the years 1620–1622 a serious attempt was made to raise money to found a missionary college for Indians, but the 1622 uprising put an end to this effort.

Although a fishery might flourish in the summer, misunderstandings about climate and the failure to ensure the self-support of the colonies at an early stage led to the repeated failure to find a staple crop with which to provide profits for those who supplied the capital for the colonies. (From 1618 onward, tobacco at last provided such a staple.) The self-supporting efforts of the lost colonists and the Pilgrims composed a distinct strand in colonization, but they had produced no substantive results by the end of 1620. There was, indeed, no effective English imperial achievement of any consequence down to this date, only a series of experiments that provided guidelines for later ventures on what not to do.

BIBLIOGRAPHY

Andrews, Charles McLean. *The Colonial Period of American History.* 4 vols. New Haven, 1934.
Andrews, Kenneth R., Nicholas P. Canny, and E. H. Hair, eds. *The Western Enterprise.* Detroit, 1978.
Axtell, James. *After Columbus.* New York, 1988.
Barbour, Phillip, ed. *The Complete Works of Captain John Smith.* 3 vols. Chapel Hill, 1987.
Madden, Frederick, and David Fieldhouse, eds. *The Empire of the Britaignes, 1175–1688.* Westport, 1985.
Quinn, David B. *England and the Discovery of America.* New York, 1974.
Rose, J. Holland, Alfred Percival Newton, and Edward A. Benians, eds. *The Cambridge History of the British Empire.* 8 vols. Cambridge, 1929.
Williamson, James Alexander. *A Short History of the British Empire.* 2 vols. London, 1930.

DAVID B. QUINN

COLUMBIAN EXCHANGE. For discussion of the transfer of plants, animals, and technologies between the Old World and the New World that resulted from the encounter of European and American cultures, see *Agriculture; Disease and Demography; Domesticated Animals; Fauna; Flora; Metal; Syphilis.*

COLUMBIANISM. As the people of the thirteen colonies that became the United States were shifting from colonial to national identity, they harked back to the origins of the New World and adopted "Columbia," the feminine adjectival form of "Columbus," a name that became the poetic identity for the new nation. Infused into the romantic nationalism of the early Republic, Columbia first entered the American ethos in literary discourse.

Two anonymous poets first referred to Columbia, but such references were prior to the political movements of the 1770s. Mrs. Mercy Warren, wife of Gen. James Warren and sister of James Otis, Jr., colonial patriots in the War for Independence, was the first to place Columbia in the context of the American Revolution. Published in the *Boston Gazette* of February 13, 1775, her poem identifies Columbia as a land "where Liberty, a happy Goddess reigned / where no proud Despot rules with lawless sway / Nor orphans spoils became the Minion's prey."

Albert J. Hoyt, the scholar who traced this poem, was responding to George H. Moore's claim that Phillis Wheatley, a freed slave, coined the literary form "Columbia." Hoyt's discovery was first published in 1886, but because little is known of his research, Phillis Wheatley is still identified as the name's original source. Though she may not have minted the name, her poetry popularized the term, thereby infusing the coinage into the general parlance.

Wheatley, the first known African American poet, was born in Africa and was the slave of a Boston businessman who granted her manumission in 1773. With a background in Latin and a command of contemporary English and

American literature, Wheatley manifested an awareness of the latinized name for Great Britain, "Britannia," in a poem in 1773. After she received her freedom Wheatley visited England where she published her first book of poetry. Benjamin Franklin and other notables visited her, and Voltaire expressed his approval of her poetry.

Wheatley's "Columbia" was included in her poem "His Excellency General Washington": "Fixed are the eyes of Natives on the scales, / for in their hope Columbia's arm prevails." Washington was so gratified by the poem he invited Wheatley to his headquarters in Cambridge, Massachusetts. The poem became widely known when Thomas Paine published it in his *Pennsylvania Gazette*. In a 1776 poem Wheatley placed Columbia on an Olympus of mythicized figures representing European nationalities: Britannia, Gallia, Germania, Scotia, and Hibernia.

The direct link between Columbus and Columbia is found in a 1778 poem by Joel Barlow. Apparently familiar with the Wheatley poem, Barlow recited his "The Prospect of Peace" as a commencement piece at Yale College. A year later he stated, "The discovery of America made an important revolution in the history of mankind. It served the purpose of displaying knowledge, liberty and religion."

Barlow's 1787 epic poem of nine books, *The Vision of Columbus*, identified Columbia as the land of liberty; he rendered the American Republic as the culmination of a new era inaugurated by Columbus. The poem was replete with biases imbedded in the Black Legend, which portrays Spain in terms of the cruelties of the Inquisition and perceives Columbus as a man who transcended the Catholic superstition of his era. The identification of Columbia with liberty had already achieved some popularity prior to Barlow's poem when New York's Kings College was renamed Columbia in 1784.

Thomas Jefferson, James Madison, and the three commissioners charged with responsibility for the capital informed Pierre L'Enfant, its first architect, that the home of the federal government would be called Washington and would be located in the federal territory of Columbia. Without any evidence concerning the commission's rationale, one may infer that the commissioners' decision intended to give the capital the aura of liberty rather than authority. Perhaps the commissioners' rationale included this idea: Columbia had severed itself from Britannia; hope had guided Columbus to the New World; Columbia symbolized the hope of the new nation.

These early manifestations of Columbianism illustrate Robert Bellah's notion of a civil religion (or, as Martin E. Marty prefers, public religion): creed, code, and cult unite diverse people into a common sense of their American nationality identified with sacred texts—the Declaration of Independence, the Constitution, the Bill of Rights, the Gettysburg Address; with special feast days—Thanksgiving, the Fourth of July; with hymns; with flag-raising rituals; and with the nation's particular place in God's providential design.

The first monument to Columbus reflected the early phase of civil religion. According to oral tradition, the idea for the monument originated at a dinner party in early 1792 hosted by the French consul in Baltimore, Chevalier Charles-François Adrien Le Paulmier d'Annemours. A guest lamented the absence of a monument to Columbus as a suitable site for commemorating the tricentennial of the landing on San Salvador. The chevalier d'Annemours, the story goes, decided then and there to erect such a monument on his property about a mile north of the city boundary. Designed as a simple obelisk, the monument, inscribed "sacred to the Memory of Christopher Columbus," was erected in a grove of cedar and ash trees about one hundred yards from Le Paulmier d'Annemours's home. Though it was nearly fifty feet in height, this first monument was a private tribute remote from the people of the city. To the French absorbed in the independence movement the monument represented loyalty to Columbus and to the land "Columbia," so symbolic of the American ethos of liberty.

The Saint Tammany Society of New York, which changed its name to the Society of Tammany, or the Columbian Order, in 1789, was one of several patriotic fraternal societies of the day. Named after Saint Tammany, a native American convert and martyr for Christianity, the society chose Christopher Columbus as a patron, and it was the first to celebrate Columbus Day, in 1790. Its observation of the tricentennial of Columbus's landing included a parade, patriotic oratory, and a grand banquet. A twelve-foot portable obelisk was erected for the occasion, one that was intended to be displayed each Columbus Day.

Jeremy Belknap's *Ode to Columbus and Columbia* that was sung by a soloist and choir in a Boston celebration of Columbus Day, 1792, resounded with discordant notes on the themes of the Black Legend and anti-Catholicism:

> Black *Superstition's* dismal night
> Extinguished *Reason's* golden ray;
> And *Science*, driven from the light
> Beneath monastic rubbish lay
> The *Crown* and *Mitre*, close allied
> Trampled whole nations to the dust
> Whilst *Freedom*, wandering far and wide
> And pure *Religion*, quite was lost.
> Then, guided by th' Almighty Hand
> *Columbus* spread his daring sail,
> *Ocean* received a new command
> And Zephyrs breathed a gentle gale.
> . . . Sweet Peace and heavenly truth shall shine
> on Fair Columbia's ground
> There Freedom and Religion join
> And Spread their influence all around.

A hundred years later, at the Chicago World's Columbian Exposition, dedicated in October 1892 and opened in the spring of 1893, Columbianism's role in the tradition of civil religion dominated the festive atmosphere. Professor John Knowles Paine of Harvard College wrote the following lyrics to accompany his Columbian march, composed for the dedication of the main exposition building:

> All hail and welcome, nations of the earth
> Columbia's greeting comes from every state.
> Proclaim to all mankind the world's new birth . . .
> Let war and enmity forever cease
> Let glorious art and commerce banish among
> The universal brotherhood of peace
> Shall be Columbia's high inspiring song.

The twentieth century, so profoundly affected by two world wars, by economic recessions, and by periods of social conflict, has witnessed the decline of romantic nationalism associated with Columbianism, and devotion to Columbia has lost its hold on the public's poetic self-understanding.

BIBLIOGRAPHY

Belknap, Jeremy. Intended to Commemorate as Discourse the Discovery of America by Christopher Columbus. Boston, 1792.

Dickey, J. M. Christopher Columbus and the Monument Columbia. Chicago, 1892.

Hoyt, Albert J. "The Name Columbia." New England Historical and Genealogical Register, July 1886.

Kilroe, Edwin Patrick. Saint Tammany and the Origin of Tammany of Columbian Order in the City of New York. New York, 1913.

Williams, John Alexander. "The First American Hero: Columbus in Columbia, 1775–1792." Typescript, 1986.

CHRISTOPHER J. KAUFFMAN

COLUMBIAN SOCIETIES. In the latter quarter of the nineteenth century many second-generation Catholic immigrants assimilated into American culture through societies that blended patriotism with a religious devotion to the Catholic "origins" of the New World, with particular focus on the great navigator, Christopher Columbus. These Columbian societies include the Knights of Columbus (founded in 1882) and two sororal societies, originally formed in association with the Knights, the Daughters of Isabella (1897) and the Catholic Daughters of the Americas (1903).

A unique blend of faith and fraternalism, the Knights of Columbus is the largest organization of Catholic laity in the world. Over its history it has responded to the myriad needs of local churches and societies in the United States, Canada, Mexico, Cuba, Puerto Rico, and the Philippines.

Michael J. McGivney, the New Haven priest who founded the Knights of Columbus in 1882, implicitly fostered an American Catholic apologetic, one that promoted harmony between religious liberty and Catholicism. Concerned with the strong appeal of the prohibited secret societies among Catholic youth and with the plight of widows and children who had suffered the loss of their breadwinner, he was eager to form a fraternal insurance society imbued with deep loyalties to Catholicism and to the American experience.

The Knights' Columbianism was born on February 6, 1882, when a small group of New Haven laymen chose Columbus as the patron of their fraternal society. One of those present at this meeting invoked the cause of Catholic civil liberty when he asserted that, as Catholic descendants of Columbus, they "were entitled to all rights and privileges due to such a discovery by one of our faith." In short, the founders perceived Columbus as a source of identity for Catholics of all ethnic groups, a cultural symbol infused into their sense of American Catholic peoplehood. Just as the ship *Mayflower* was a sign of Protestant identity, so *Santa María* was a symbol of Catholic legitimacy. The term *knight* conveyed a commitment to struggle against the forces of nativism and anti-Catholicism that periodically erupted into hysteria among groups eager for scapegoats.

Besides establishing a united front in defense of the church, the Knights cultivated patriotic sentiments based on the Catholic component in the American heritage. The initiation ceremonies were dramatic renditions of the heroic faith of Columbus, of the "Catholic baptism" of the American continent, and of the nobility of religious liberty and American democracy. In a sense, the ceremonials provided the candidates for Knighthood with a rite of passage—from Old World ties to loyalty to the Republic. Though the leaders were all second-generation Irish-Americans, they were realists on the ethnic issue. Hence, in Boston they allowed the establishment of the Teutonia Council for German-American Knights and the Ansonia Council for Italian Americans.

Thomas Cummings, one of the most impassioned proponents of Columbianism, wrote of the order's idealism. He predicted that if the Knights "honorably practiced their beliefs," then it would mean "the creation of a new type of Catholic manhood," a new spirit of lay activism in the church:

> Under the inspiration of Him whose name we bear, and with the story of Columbus's life, as exemplified in our beautiful ritual, we have the broadest kind of basis for patriotism and true love of country. . . . [B]y drawing close the bonds of brotherhood, we make for the best type of American citizenship. For the best American is he who best exemplifies in his own life, that this is not a Protestant country, nor a Catholic country, nor a Hebrew country, any more than it is an Anglo-Saxon or Latin country, but a country of all races and all creeds, with one great, broad, unmolterable [sic] creed of fair play and equal rights for all.

For the first ten years the order was primarily a Connecticut organization, but it expanded from New England throughout the nation. By 1905 the Knights were in every state in the Union, five of the nine provinces in Canada, Mexico, and the Philippines, and were poised to enter Cuba and Puerto Rico. The Knights' expansion during this period owed much to the strong sense of Catholic Columbianism it had exhibited during the celebration of the quadricentennial. Catholics in every diocese throughout the nation had manifested their loyalty to the nation and the faith by parades and religious liturgies.

Originally a women's auxiliary of Russell Council of the Knights, the Daughters of Isabella was founded in New Haven in 1897. The Columbian motif was represented in its initiation rites, which featured Isabella's role in sponsoring Columbus's first voyage. The Catholic Daughters of America (CDA) was also originally entitled Daughters of Isabella. Founded in Utica, New York, in 1903 in association with the Knights, it too ritualized Columbianism. As a result of a 1921 court case, however, the Utica society lost its right to the Daughters name and became the CDA.

Each of the three Columbian societies through the years has engaged in extensive work in projects for the Roman Catholic church as well as community and volunteer services for the handicapped, the homeless, and the aged. All three have also provided insurance benefits for their memberships, which by 1990 had reached 96,000 in the Daughters of Isabella, 145,000 in the CDA, and 1.5 million in the Knights of Columbus. Though the vast majority of Catholics have been assimilated into American society, these organizations still foster the Columbian bonds of unity and charity; they still render Columbus and Isabella as models of dedication to religion and culture.

BIBLIOGRAPHY

Kauffman, Christopher J. *Faith and Fraternalism: The History of the Knights of Columbus, 1882–1982.* New York, 1982.
Kerwin, P. K. "Catholic Daughters of America." In *New Catholic Encyclopedia.* Vol. 3. Washington, D.C., 1967.
Maguire, J. F. "Daughters of Isabella." In *New Catholic Encyclopedia.* Vol. 4. Washington, D.C., 1967.

CHRISTOPHER J. KAUFFMAN

COLUMBUS, CHRISTOPHER. [This entry provides a biography of Columbus in six articles:

Birth and Origins
Adolescence and Youth
Early Maritime Experience
Columbus in Portugal
Columbus in Spain
The Final Years, Illness, and Death

For detailed discussion of the events of Columbus's four voyages to the Western Hemisphere, see *Voyages of Columbus.* See also biographies of numerous figures mentioned herein. Biographies of several members of the Columbus family can be found under *Colombo* (for those whose lives centered in Italy) or under *Colón* (for those whose lives centered in Spain or in Spanish America). For discussion of Columbus's literary remains, see *Writings.* For analysis of Columbus's legacy in scholarship, art, and literature, see *Bibliography; Celebrations; Columbianism; Columbian Societies; Iconography; Literature; Monuments and Memorials; Museums and Archives.*]

Birth and Origins

Christopher Columbus (1451–1506) was Genoese by birth and culture. The roots of his genius and his enterprise lie in the flowering of the Italian Renaissance and in the cultural, naval, and cartographic traditions of Genoa. The term *Genoese* must, however, be broadly defined, for a fifteenth-century Genoese could be from Corsica or even Chios.

Columbus's Genoese origins are confirmed by numerous documents. One principal document is a *majorat* (entail) in which Columbus designates the heir to his titles and privileges. In this *majorat,* which played an important part in the two centuries of legal proceedings involving the claimants to the Admiral's estate, Columbus states: "that, having been born in Genoa, I came to serve them [the Spanish monarchs] in Castile, and discovered for them the Indies and the aforesaid islands to the west of terra firma."

A copy of this document, which dates back to the early seventeenth century and had been officially sent from Spain to the Republic of Genoa, is conserved in the State Archives of Genoa. The supposed original is in the Archive General de Indias in Seville.

Cesare de Lollis observes that "the history of this important document is so clear that there is no doubt about its authenticity." Both Rinaldo Caddeo and Antonio Ballesteros Beretta maintain that it is authentic. Henry Harrisse, however, considers it a forgery from a later period. Even if the document is on the whole authentic, the suspicion of interpolation cannot be excluded. This suspicion, however, has no effect on the basic fact of the Genoese birth and cultural background of Columbus. This claim is confirmed by many other documents and by recorded testimony.

There is, for example, an important letter sent by the Admiral to the San Giorgio Bank in Genoa. This letter, the authenticity of which is beyond question, begins, "Although my body may be here, my heart is there constantly." "There" is Genoa. Similarly, there exist two other letters, addressed to Nicoló Oderico, ambassador of the Republic of Genoa to the court of Spain. In these letters, Columbus states that he has assigned 10 percent of his

The Columbus Family

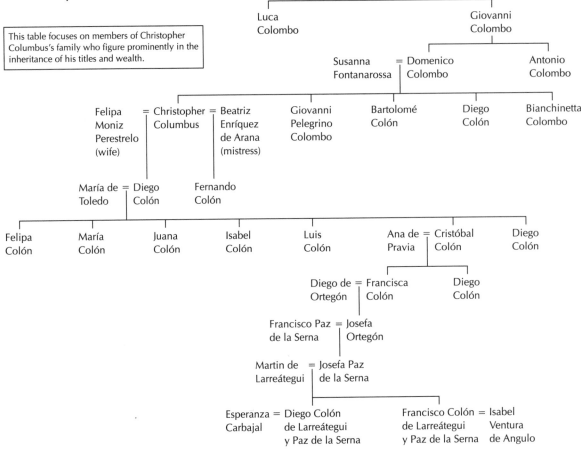

This table focuses on members of Christopher Columbus's family who figure prominently in the inheritance of his titles and wealth.

bequest to the San Giorgio Bank in order to alleviate the taxes on grain, wine, and other foodstuffs for the poor of Genoa.

Even more definitive are the public and notarial acts—original copies of which are conserved in the archives of Genoa and Savona—regarding Columbus himself, his father, his grandfather, and other relatives. There are more than a hundred such documents, clearly indicating that Columbus was from a Ligurian family. His great-grandfather lived in Mocónesi, where his grandfather, Giovanni, was born. His father, Domenico, who was born in Quinto, lived for a long period of time in Genoa and then in Savona. Today, Quinto is part of Genoa's urban complex, but in the fifteenth century it was a village a short way from the city. Christopher Columbus spent his childhood and the first years of his youth in Vico Diritto, under the gate of Sant'Andrea.

According to documents that we are certain are authentic, the date of his birth is usually set between August 25 and October 31, 1451. In a document dated October 31, 1470, Columbus declares himself *major annis decemnovem* (nineteen years old); in another document, dated August 25, 1479, which will be discussed below, he declares himself *annorum vigintiseptem vel circa* (about twenty-seven). Between August 25 and October 31, 1451, Domenico Colombo, Christopher's father, was the keeper of the Olivella gate and thus lived next to the gate itself. This, therefore, is where Christopher would have been born.

Another doubt remains to be settled: can we be sure that all the documents cited concern the Christopher Columbus who was later to become the Admiral of the Ocean Sea? In a legal document dated September 22, 1470, a judge convicts Domenico Colombo. The conviction concerns a debt owed by Domenico—*together with his son Christopher* (explicitly stated in the document)—to a certain Girolamo del Porto. In the will dictated by Columbus in Valladolid, the dying navigator remembers this old debt, which had evidently not been paid.

Still more important is an act drawn in Genoa on August 25, 1479, by a notary, Girolamo Ventimiglia (series 2a, 1474–1504, n. 266). This act is known as the Assereto Document, after the scholar who found it in the State Archives in Genoa in 1904. Following is the part in which Columbus is cited:

Lodovico Centurione, appearing by law and in the presence of the venerable Office of Merchandise, says and states that which he will or hopes or doubts to have with Paolo Di Negro, son of the late Luca, he himself or his brother Cazano with the aforementioned Paolo, and since he has some witnesses who are informed of the rights of said Lodovico, who must shortly leave this city of Genoa and depart on a long journey, thus requests that said witnesses, in eternal memory of the fact and for as long as the belief in truth does not perish, be received and examined.

First he intends to prove and to attest to the truth of the fact that was and is that other times in the past year, during the time in which the witnesses ... will say, Paolo Di Negro, commissioned by him Lodovico and by the aforesaid Cazano or one of them to the island of Madeira in order to purchase a certain quantity of sugar, and Lodovico having sent 1,290 ducats therefore, that is to say 1,290 "grossati" or their value to said Paolo, who was supposed to purchase 2,400 and more rubbi of sugar, Christopher Columbus, on the order of said Paolo, was sent to the island of Madeira and here he secured and purchased the aforementioned amount of sugar.

Witnesses in favor of Lodovico Centurione.

In nomine Domini amen. May all who see the present public testimonial document know that, having appeared in the presence of myself, the notary and the undersigned witnesses, summoned and requested for the express purpose, Christopher Columbus, citizen of Genoa, summoned here as a witness, must be received and examined as such.

When asked if he has to depart soon, he answered: yes, tomorrow morning for Lisbon. When asked how old he is, he answered that he was about twenty-seven years of age.

In addition, several notarial acts confirm the identification of the Genoese Christopher Columbus, son of Domenico, with the Admiral of Spain. For example, an act dated October 11, 1496, says: "Giovanni Colombo of Quinto, Matteo Colombo and Amighetto Colombo, brothers of the late Antonio, in full understanding and knowledge that said Giovanni must go to Spain to see M. Christopher Columbus, Admiral of the King of Spain, and that any expenses that said Giovanni must make in order to see said M. Christopher must be paid by all three of the aforementioned brothers, each one to pay a third . . . and to this they hereby agree."

In an act drawn in Savona on April 8, 1500, Sebastiano Cuneo requested that Christopher and Giacomo (called Diego), the sons and heirs of Domenico Colombo, be summoned to court and sentenced to pay the price for two lands located in Légino. This document confirms the brothers' absence from the Republic of Genoa with the words: "dicti conventi sunt absentes ultra Pisas et Niciam" (the summoned parties are absent and beyond Pisa and Nice).

Another notarial act, drawn in Savona on January 26, 1501, is more explicit. A group of Genoese citizens, under oath, "said and say, together and separately and in every more valid manner and guise, that the Christopher, Bartholomew, and Giacomo Colombo, sons and heirs of the aforementioned Domenico, their father, have for a long time been absent from the city and the jurisdiction of Savona, as well as Pisa and Nice in Provence, and that they reside in the area of Spain, as was and is well known."

Finally, there is a very important document from the notary Bartolomeo Oddino, drawn in Savona on March 30, 1515. With this act, Leon Pancaldo, the well-known Savonese who would become one of the pilots for Ferdinand Magellan's voyage, sends his own father-in-law in his place as procurator for Diego Colón, son of the Admiral. The document demonstrates how the ties, in part economic, of the discoverer's family with Savona survived even his death.

These documents, along with some seventy other Genoese and Savonese documents, irrefutably demonstrate that Christopher Columbus, the discoverer of America, was Cristoforo Colombo, son of Domenico.

BIBLIOGRAPHY

Ballesteros Beretta, Antonio. *Cristóbal Colón y el descubrimiento de América*. Vol. 1. Barcelona and Buenos Aires, 1945.

Genoa, City of. *Christopher Columbus: Documents and Proofs of his Genoese Origin*. English-German edition. Bergamo, 1932.

Morison, Samuel Eliot. *Admiral of the Ocean Sea: A Life of Christopher Columbus*. 2 vols. Boston, 1942.

Sammartino, Peter. *Columbus*. Rome, 1988.

Taviani, Paolo Emilio. *Christopher Columbus: The Grand Design*. London, 1985.

Taviani, Paolo Emilio. *Cristoforo Colombo: Genius of the Sea*. Rome, 1990.

Thacher, J. B. *Christopher Columbus: His Life, His Work, His Remains*. New York, 1903.

PAOLO EMILIO TAVIANI

Adolescence and Youth

In 1502, at the height of his fame and power, Admiral Christopher Columbus was in Spain writing with fond sentiment to the directors of the San Giorgio Bank in his native city of Genoa: "Though my body is here, my heart is always with you." His love of Genoa is one part of the abundant evidence that Christopher's youth in Genoa was happy and that he grew up in a loving and prosperous family.

Two aspects of his youth were significant in preparing him for a career: his education and his family life. Ambition and the desire for education had been behind the Colombo family's move from the mountain village of Mocónesi to the city of Genoa. Christopher and his brothers received the type of education that would carry the family even further—to foreign countries.

Italians in the fifteenth century believed that all family

members, including the children, were part of the family work force. The work of boys was to study, and for that purpose, the wool guild of Genoa maintained a school on Pavia Street. It was here that young Christopher learned to read and write and do basic arithmetic. His son Fernando later confused this grammar school with the famous University of Pavia, and so mistakenly introduced the idea that Christopher Columbus had a university education. The curriculum in the grammar school was much more humble. Children entered grammar school between the ages of five and seven. First, they learned to write using chalk on a slate or a stylus on waxed boards. By the time they left the school at age eleven or twelve, they knew how to read and write in Latin and do basic addition and subtraction. Only when they came to write their own letters did they write on paper, mixing the ink, sharpening a quill to form a pen point, folding a sheet of paper to form its own envelope, and sealing it with string and hot wax.

The usual method for teaching Latin was memorization of whole sentences chosen from the Bible and ancient classics to teach grammatical rules and inculcate morality and manners. They were not intended to give students a love of literature or make them proficient in writing beautiful Latin. Rather, the sentences Columbus learned in his grammar school were functional tools for a business career. Italian businessmen needed to be able to read contracts and political documents in Latin because it was the language of church and government records throughout Italy. As an adult, Columbus read the Latin language with ease; he bought Latin books about geography and cosmography as soon as they came off the new printing presses and wrote Latin notes (often containing errors) in their margins commenting on the texts.

After grammar school, some boys learned a profession by serving a six- or seven-year apprenticeship. That is what Columbus's father, Domenico Colombo, had done. Domenico had been apprenticed at the age of eleven to a cloth weaver for six years. In exchange for the boy's labor in his shop, the master taught his apprentice all aspects of the weaver's trade, from purchasing and processing the raw materials, through weaving several patterns, to selling the finished products. By the age of twenty-one, Domenico was a master weaver and he, in turn, brought apprentices into his household.

Domenico taught his sons the weaver's trade at home to prepare them to enter the wool guild, but he had ambitions for his family. The city of Genoa had rigid status divisions, even under the new constitution adopted in 1418, which divided the seats in the city council half and half between nobles and guildsmen, with half the guildsmen merchants and the other half artisans. In Genoa the highest-status occupation was international merchant; the

doges during the fifteenth century came from the merchant guilds. Domenico Colombo made sure that his sons received the appropriate education for the merchant profession.

The next stage of education for a future merchant was the study of mathematics. In the fifteenth century, mathematical computations were undergoing a drastic change in Italian cities. Medieval Europeans did not write down numbers to do computations. Instead they drew an abacus on a table top (or, in England, covered a table with a checkered cloth), performed computations by moving counters on this counting table, and recorded the sums in Roman numerals in their ledgers. Now this old system was being challenged by a system adopted from Arab merchants. The Arabs computed as we do today; they used algorithms, writing out their computations as they went along in Hindu-Arabic numerals. Computation involving large numbers was more rapid and sophisticated, and the change created a great demand for teachers of the new mathematics. Merchants in northern Europe sent their sons to study with Italian teachers, but Christopher had to walk only a few blocks to a local teacher.

In a city like Genoa, international commerce depended on mastery of the sea, so that the mathematical basis of navigation was an essential part of a businessman's education. Computations were performed in Arabic numerals, although sums and dates were still recorded in Roman numerals: most city governments considered the new numerals easier to counterfeit than Roman numerals and so did not accept them as evidence in litigation.

Young Christopher must have learned these lessons well, for he calculated interest income and currency exchange rates with great facility throughout his life. During his voyages he handled navigational computations with confidence and accuracy; his miscalculations of the earth's circumference were due to incorrect geographical assumptions, not computational errors. He followed the custom of using Roman numerals in business documents, but in personal letters he sometimes used Arabic numerals to record large numbers, such as the year.

The next stage of a boy's education for international commerce was accounting. Italian businessmen used double-entry bookkeeping. In this method, each transaction is recorded twice, on one page under a debit heading and on the opposite page under a credit heading. Double entry enabled a businessman to draw up a balance sheet showing his personal worth—an exercise the prudent Italian merchant carried out in private at the end of every month. Drawing up a balance also was used to distribute profits and losses among partners or to close an account no longer active. Near the end of his life, Columbus advised his son Diego: "I order you under penalty of being found disobedient to personally draw up a balance of your household expenses every month and sign it with your name, because otherwise all your employees and money will be lost, and enmities will develop."

Christopher's mathematical and accounting education indicates that his family intended him to follow a career on a larger stage than the ones his father and grandfather had occupied. The family was moving up in the world, from Giovanni's small-town farming career, to Domenico's big-city manufacturing and commerce, and now to Christopher's intended international career of import and export merchant.

Domenico's economic ventures wrought many changes in his family's life and provided a model of entrepreneurship for Christopher. In 1440 Domenico, while still a bachelor practicing his wool-weaving trade in Genoa, leased a house and land, situated in dell'Olivella Street, from the monks of the Benedictine monastery of Santo Stefano. He became involved in city politics and joined the Fregoso party, whose policy was alliance with France against Aragón. Their opponents, the pro-Aragonese Adorno party, gained power on January 4, 1447, when Barnaba Adorno was elected doge, but Barnaba was overthrown at the end of the month in an assault led by Giano da Campo Fregoso. Giano brought eighty-five men by galley to the city at night and attacked the doge's palace, which was defended by six hundred soldiers sent by King Alfonso of Aragón, uncle of the future King Fernando.

The victors appointed their supporters to all the political and military offices of the city. On February 4, 1447, Domenico was appointed warden of the Olivella city gate and tower near his house, and his brother Antonio was appointed warden of the lighthouse (Capo di Faro) at the entrance to the harbor. The usual term of appointment was thirteen months, so that by April 1448, Domenico was no longer warden of the tower, and he and his brother were living in Quinto. During the next two years, the Fregoso party ruled the city. Giano died and was eventually replaced as doge by Pietro Fregoso, who had been captain general of the city since February 3, 1447, and probably was Domenico Colombo's political sponsor. On October 1, 1450, Domenico was again appointed warden of the Olivella tower and gate for another thirteen months. Domenico's anti-Aragonese politics was probably the reason Christopher never talked about his Genoese past after he moved to Spain.

Clearly, Domenico was prospering. He married Susanna Fontanarossa. As dowry, her parents gave her land in the village of Ginestreto. In 1451, Domenico bought farmland in Quarto, the village next to Quinto, for five hundred Genoese lire and leased it to the seller on the same day. The two oldest sons, Christopher and Giovanni Pelegrino, were probably born in the house in Quinto that Domenico

and his brother Antonio inherited from their father. From 1452 to 1455 Domenico and his family lived in Genoa, probably in their house on dell'Olivella Street.

With a growing family and prospering business, Domenico and Susanna needed more space and resources. In 1455, the family moved to their permanent home—a substantial house and garden that Domenico leased from the monastery of Santo Stefano, on Diritto di Ponticello Street, near the Soprana city gate. Two younger boys, Bartolomeo and Giacomo, and a daughter, Bianchinetta, were probably born in this house. It is likely that Susanna gave birth to several more children, but this was an age when 25 percent of newborns died before the age of five, and only five of their children survived into adulthood. Diritto Street where Christopher and his brothers and sister grew up was in a new section of the city, called Borgo Santo Stefano, that had been in the countryside before being enclosed by city walls built a century earlier. The new house had everything necessary for a comfortable city home. At the front on the ground floor was the shop, where Domenico and his sons and apprentices

THE COLOMBO FAMILY HOUSE ON DIRITTO DI PONTICELLO. Near the Soprano gate. The plaque attests to Columbus having spent his boyhood and early youth in the house.   ALINARI/ART RESOURCE

manufactured cloth on large looms and sold it. At the back of the ground floor was a kitchen with its well, fireplace, and storage rooms, and upstairs were the bedrooms. Behind the house was an enclosed garden that reached to the old city wall. The neighbors on either side were Giovanni de Paravania and Antonio Bondi and their families.

Satisfying the family's growing food needs was the responsibility of Susanna and her servants and daughters. The staple of the Italian diet was wheat bread. (Pasta was eaten occasionally but did not become daily fare in Italy until late in the nineteenth century.) The Genoese had to import their wheat because most of the local countryside was too steep to plow. Fish was the principal source of complete protein, but, curiously, the waters around Genoa do not have much fish, so the Genoese imported preserved fish: herring from Flanders, salted fish from Provence or eastern Spain, tuna preserved in oil from Andalusia, and caviar from Asia. Susanna made large cash outlays for these imported staples.

Domenico and Susanna could supply most of their other food needs from their own land. Most city people depended on butcher shops, where they bought daily portions of fresh veal and pork, but families like Domenico's that owned farmland could also butcher whole hogs in the countryside to make a year's supply of sausages and hams. All of this preserving of food required enormous amounts of salt, which was one of Genoa's biggest imports and an important part of the import-export trade. Olive oil also served as a preservative, as well as the principal cooking fat; much of it came from the villages around the city, whose terraced hills were planted with perennials, such as the olive trees on the land Domenico owned in Quarto.

Susanna provided the rest of the family's food needs from her garden at the back of the house. Here on the traditional planting day, Easter Sunday, she would plant vegetables to supplement and diversify the family diet. Her principal crops were peas and broad beans to be dried for the winter, lettuce and other salad greens, onions, garlic, carrots, parsley, and basil. Tomatoes and potatoes, indigenous to the Americas, were not yet known in Europe. Susanna's new garlic would have been sprouting by Easter, and her perennials showing their spring renewal, with the fruit trees and rosemary bush in bloom, and the sage plant putting out new leaves.

Using table and garden scraps for feed, Susanna probably raised chickens to supply the family with eggs, an important source of protein. There would not have been enough feed in the city garden to raise a milk animal, so she would buy cheese in the village. Susanna was responsible for the health of the family, and she would have raised herbs in her garden for medicinal purposes.

Christopher learned these remedies and resorted to them for himself and his men in the Americas; for example, he wrote marginal notes about parsley as a diuretic.

Domenico began to branch out and diversify his business activities, adding commerce to manufacturing. He described himself as a cheese merchant during the 1460s, perhaps buying cheeses from farm housewives in the countryside around Quarto and Quinto to sell wholesale to the many cheese shops in the city. Throughout the same decade, he was also buying and selling wool cloth. He must have prospered in this venture, because he bought wool cloth from several men on credit, an indication that he was considered creditworthy. By late 1469, he was diversifying again, now describing himself in business documents as wool weaver and taverner.

From this fact of having become a wine dealer, some authors about a century ago concluded that Domenico was a drunkard. But this accusation reflects an ignorance of the role that wine played in the European diet. Wine and water were the daily beverages, for little else was available. The Asian drinks of coffee and tea had not yet been incorporated into the European diet, and hot chocolate was unknown because its basic ingredient, cocoa, is indigenous to the Americas.

Country people drank the wine that they produced themselves. After the harvest, farm families stored a year's supply of wine for their own use and sold the rest. Each region had its own preferences; in Genoa the favorite grape varieties were muscadet and grenache, which were a specialty of the region. Because of the city's large population, there was a great demand for wine, and in the local countryside grapes were an important commercial crop. Wholesale merchants bought the wine and transported it by pack train from villages in the mountain valleys or brought it by ship from villages along the Riviera, like Savona, one of the most important of these wine-exporting towns.

Prosperous city people owned vineyards in the country as close to the city as possible. Domenico and Susanna had their land in Quarto and Ginestreto. Traditionally, the whole family went out to prune, tie up, and weed the vines in March and April and to help the hired hands harvest the ripe grapes and make the wine in October. City people who owned no land in the country depended on the local wine merchant—the taverner—for their wine. Every day as part of her food purchases, the city housewife took the family's large flask to the taverner, who filled it from the wineskins he decanted from the casks in his cellar.

The family's life in the city lasted throughout Christopher's adolescence. But just when he was old enough to start a career himself, Domenico and Susanna moved to the smaller city of Savona on the Riviera coast east of

COLUMBUS, CHRISTOPHER: Early Maritime Experience 167

Genoa. Scholars have proposed several reasons for this move, although the destruction of much of Genoa's notarial archives in a bombardment of the city by the forces of Louis XIV in 1684 makes any firm conclusion difficult. The move could have been inspired by a political reversal; the city's government was taken over by the dukes of Milan in 1464. In Italian politics, such reversals usually resulted in exile for members of the losing party, and even if Domenico was not important enough to be banished from the city outright, the Fregoso supporters would have lost favorable treatment in official and political affairs.

Another reason for moving might have been Domenico's increasing involvement in the lucrative wine trade. He and Susanna bought a farm with vineyard in Légino, just outside Savona. Their house in Savona, on San Giuliano Street, was also a tavern, so Domenico had acquired the cellars necessary for business as a wine dealer.

Savona may also have represented an improvement in the family's living conditions. Domenico had represented the Genoa wool guild in negotiating an agreement of mutual membership with the wool guild of Savona. This made it possible for Domenico to move his family to the calmer and less crowded Savona and join the guild there without losing his membership in the Genoa guild. Savona may also have been attractive because many of its wool weavers came from the Fontanabuona Valley, where the Colombo family originated. Susanna and Domenico both had several cousins living in Savona.

Family solidarity was as important as political connections in the life of the Italian businessman. Domenico had a close relationship with his older brother, Antonio, who, after a brief venture in Genoese politics, remained in Quinto the rest of his life. In 1460, when Antonio apprenticed his son Giannetto to a tailor for six years, it was Domenico who acted as surety for the contract. Christopher often acted as the dutiful oldest son and conscientious big brother. After he became Admiral of the Ocean Seas, he brought his brothers and cousins from Genoa, Savona, and Quinto to command his ships and fill the offices in his admiralty.

By the time the Colombo family moved to Savona, Christopher was almost twenty years old and ready to launch his business career. Domenico had trained his son well. Every aspect of Domenico's business life had a profound and lasting impression on Christopher: the disciplined training in technical, mathematical, and linguistic skills, the constant striving for economic and social improvement, the restless moves from one place to another, and the constant involvement with family. All through his life he would follow his father's example, daringly taking the initiative in international trade to further the fortunes of the whole family.

BIBLIOGRAPHY

Airaldi, Gabriella, et al. *Cristoforo Colombo nella Genova del suo tempo.* Genoa, 1985.

Belgrano, Luigi Tommaso, and M. Staglieno, eds. "Documenti relativi a Cristoforo Colombo e alla sua famiglia." In part 2, vol. 1 of *Raccolta di documenti e studi pubblicati dalla R. commissione Colombiana pel quarto centenario dalla scoperta dell'America.* Rome, 1892.

Genoa, City of. *Colombo.* Genoa, 1931.

Heers, Jacques. *Gênes au XVe siècle: Activité économique et problèmes sociaux.* Paris, 1961.

Swetz, Frank J. *Capitalism and Arithmetic: The New Math of the 15th Century.* La Salle, Ill., 1987.

Taviani, Paolo Emilio. *Christopher Columbus: The Grand Design.* London, 1985.

HELEN NADER

Early Maritime Experience

By the time Christopher Columbus settled in Spain, he was an experienced and astute import-export merchant who understood the commercial value of a new route to Asia and had developed his navigational skills during years at sea. Like other Genoese seagoing merchants, his early career had developed in the family import-export business, which was both promoted by the city government and threatened by the city's turbulent politics. The city's power to protect Genoese commerce declined during Columbus's youth, with the result that Genoa lost most of its share of Asian commerce in the eastern Mediterranean while Venice increased its share. It is some indication of Columbus's genius that he conceived a daring new solution for this problem out of the common knowledge and everyday experiences of an Italian merchant's life at sea.

The city of Genoa gave birth to Columbus's earliest maritime experience long before he went to sea. Genoa's busy harbor would have attracted any boy. The city's economy was shaped by its strategic location on a strip of coast just where the mountains came down closest to the sea. Since ancient times, the major highway between Italy and France had snaked along this narrow coastal route. Genoa's advantage over its neighbors on this coastal highway was its splendid harbor, which was deep and protected. The city government constantly maintained and improved these natural advantages. Year after year, young Christopher would have seen city work crews building and expanding wharves, docks, sea walls, a customs house, lighthouses, shipyards, and an arsenal. The harbor of Genoa was one of the maritime wonders of Europe, bustling with the coming and going of merchant ships. Columbus and his brothers must have spent hours watching the dock workers load and unload cargoes, observing the repair and refitting of merchant vessels at the arsenal, and tracing the emergent forms of new ships as they were built in the city shipyards.

Antonio Gallo, a friend of the Colombo family and official chronicler of Genoa, wrote that the brothers Christopher and Bartolomeo went to sea when they were barely teenagers. Boys from poor families would have gone at a younger age; in the western Mediterranean, boys who planned to be sailors went to sea as cabin boys or ships' apprentices as early as age ten. But Columbus's family intended him to go to sea as an international merchant, not as a sailor. So when he was ten, he was still in school finishing his study of Latin and mathematics and beginning his study of navigation and accounting.

After completing his formal education, he would have learned international commerce by practicing it. We may suppose that Columbus first went to sea as a merchant's assistant at about the age of thirteen or fourteen. Every merchant needed help on his business trips, someone to pack merchandise for the voyage, find lodging when they landed in a new port, count pieces, weigh loads, accompany him while he invested his profits in local loans or merchandise, record these sums in the ledgers, and transport the new merchandise back to the ship.

After working with an international merchant, Columbus joined his father, Domenico, who transformed the family business from manufacturing wool cloth to exporting it. In the Italian city-states, business was family business and involved every family member. Fathers held absolute control over their children's career, education, and marriage choices. Sons were an important source of skilled labor for the family's business. Traditionally, teenage sons went abroad to learn the export business by practicing it in a friend's employ and then as young adults traveling the known world to buy and sell merchandise for their father's business. They did not return to take up permanent residence at home until they married in their late twenties or thirties.

Because they were away so much, Italian businessmen in the fifteenth century wrote letters almost constantly, producing a volume of correspondence that is unique in Europe. They wrote home to report on business, currency exchange, and political developments that might affect prices and markets. Every prudent businessman kept a travel journal recording his routes, transactions, expenses, and receipts to be posted later to the ledgers in the home office. Wherever he did business he paid notaries to record even the most trivial business contracts and credit operations. Unfortunately, many Genoese legal and notarial records perished in 1684 in a fire that started when the ships of King Louis XIV bombarded the city. French artillery made direct hits on the College of Notaries and city hall, where the historical documents were kept,

as well as inflicting serious damage on the Borgo Santo Stefano, including the house of the Colombo family. None of their private letters or ledgers survived, but a Genoese author interested in the history of the Colombo family had copied many of the legal and notarial documents in 1602. These copies, together with Columbus's own reminiscences, documents from Savona, Quarto, and Quinto, and the documents that survived the 1684 fire, enable us to piece together Columbus's travels for the family business.

Where he sailed is not difficult to discover. Columbus boasted that he had sailed all the seas of the world before he went to the court of Fernando and Isabel. In his journals of his voyages to America he mentioned the Genoese-controlled island of Chios in the Aegean and the Portuguese trading post of São Jorge da Mina on the Guinea coast of West Africa. At various times he claimed that he had commanded a ship during an attack on Tunis carried out by King René of Anjou, that he was shipwrecked in a battle off the coast of Portugal and was taken in by Genoese merchants in Lisbon, and that he sailed as far north as England, Ireland, and Iceland.

Scholars once thought that these claims were exaggerated, that he had only heard about these distant places from other mariners, but most of these stories now are accepted as true to at least some degree. We know that Genoese merchants traveled everywhere it was possible for Europeans to go by sea. Genoese merchants for centuries had sailed from the Black Sea to England and Flanders. They had established trading posts with powers of self-government on the shores of the Black Sea, on islands in the Aegean Sea, outside the walls of Constantinople, and on the island of Corsica. Colonies of Genoese merchants flourished in the port cities of Trebizond, Beirut, Alexandria, Tunis, Naples, Málaga, Seville, Lisbon, Bristol, London, Paris, and Bruges. Columbus's travels fit the model of a young Genoese merchant traveling for his father's import-export business.

His travels for the family business began in 1470 and ended when he moved to Portugal and married in 1479. These were difficult and tumultuous years in Genoa's political and economic history. When Domenico Colombo set up his wool cloth manufacturing shop in the 1440s, economic opportunities seemed vast. Since the Middle Ages, citizens of Genoa had participated in lucrative commerce with Asia. Genoese businessmen traveled overland through the Middle East and Central Asia to buy high-profit spices and aromatics and brought them back to Genoese trading stations on the shores of the Black Sea, and from there through Genoese colonies in Constantinople and the Aegean islands. Other Genoese merchants in Beirut and Alexandria bought spices and aromatics directly from Arab merchants who had transported them overland from the Red Sea and Indian Ocean countries.

But by the time Columbus was a young man, Genoese possibilities in the East were shrinking drastically. The Ottoman Turks were expanding, conquering Genoese colonies and cutting off Genoa's direct access to Asian trade. The list of losses during Columbus's lifetime is sobering. The Ottoman Turks conquered Constantinople and its Genoese merchant colony of Pera in 1453; Focea in Asia Minor, whose loss had grave consequences for Genoese alum merchants, in 1455; the Aegean islands of Enos, Imbros, Samothrace, and Lemnos (whose lordship had belonged to the Genoese Gattilusio family) in 1456; Trebizond, a seaport on the Asian shores of the Black Sea with its flourishing Genoese colony, in 1461; Lesbos, the last Aegean island possessed by the Gattilusio family, in 1462; and Caffa, a Genoese colony on the Crimean Peninsula in the Black Sea, in 1475.

To compensate for these losses, western routes became all-important to Genoese shipping. Genoese merchants increased their trade with Muslim and Christian Spain, and in 1452, they formed a corporation of shareholders, the Granada Company, to do business in Málaga, the principal port of the Muslim Kingdom of Granada. Genoese merchants had been established, with their own stock exchange and chapel, in the Christian city of Seville since 1261, and by the end of the fifteenth century their numbers had swelled to about three hundred merchants, representing three hundred Genoese companies.

Political upheaval in the city of Genoa, however, moved Columbus and many other Genoese merchants away from traditional routes and products. In 1458, the Fregoso doge of Genoa invited France to take control of the city in exchange for helping Genoa attack Naples in order to wrest Sardinia from the Aragonese. The French took over the city, but their policy of imposing taxes and forced loans to finance the Neapolitan expedition sparked a reaction, and Genoa expelled the French in 1461. The Fregoso party's inability to protect Genoese colonies and trading stations in the East discredited their government and threw the city into political turbulence.

Internal strife became so disruptive that the pro-Aragonese Adorno party asked the duke of Milan to impose order. Genoa was a tempting target for the Sforza dukes of Milan, always in need of seaports for their landlocked territory. In 1464, Duke Francesco Sforza took control of Genoa's government, but he died in 1466, leaving his widow to govern for their minor son. When Duke Galeazzo Maria Sforza came of age in 1468, he began to administer Genoa with the same administrative skill and authority he exercised in Milan.

This loss of political autonomy affected the status and safety of Genoese citizens active in pro-French politics. It drove Domenico Colombo and his Fregoso allies out of the city and cut them off from the shipping facilities of Genoa's harbor. In 1470, the Colombo family moved to Savona, an independent port city federated with Genoa. In March Domenico was doing business there, describing himself as a wool weaver and taverner and participating in the Savona wool guild. For the next few years, Domenico and his wife, Susanna, described themselves as residents of Savona, not Genoa.

With Domenico virtually exiled from Genoa, Columbus began traveling as his father's agent. From 1470 through 1476, he appears in notarial documents in Savona acting in concert with his father or in Genoa acting alone. While Domenico in Savona bought and stored merchandise, his son leased cargo space and transported the merchandise to sell in foreign ports.

Because we have no direct documentary evidence of Christopher Columbus's early maritime experience, it has been a matter of much speculation. It is possible, however, to reconstruct these "lost years" by placing other surviving documents in the context of an Italian family business.

In Savona on October 25, Domenico sold the note that he held from Bartolomeo de Castagneli to Antonio Rollero for a load of cloth worth twelve lire. In Genoa, on October 31, 1470, Columbus bought a load of wine from Pietro Bellesio, paying part of the sale price in cash and signing a note for the remainder, a significant sum of more than forty-eight lire. Because Columbus was not old enough to contract debts, his father cosigned for him.

This, the first appearance of Christopher Columbus in a document, has special significance. First, it attests that he and his father were considered creditworthy by the wine vendor. Second, Columbus was the principal merchant in the transaction and owner of the wine, thus protecting the merchandise from confiscation in case his father's property were at risk. Third, Columbus was going to export this Italian wine; he swore that he would be liable for the debt in law courts in several countries including England and France. He was taking a cargo of wine to sell abroad, and he probably laid over in England or Flanders that winter. Later, he displayed a sure knowledge of the leasing arrangements for the North Atlantic; in 1494, during his second voyage to America, he advised Fernando and Isabel that the most profitable and least expensive way to lease the resupply ships for La Española was by tonnage, the same way that merchants leased ships for Flanders.

The merchant's year followed a seasonal pattern, determined by the weather, winds, and current. Traditionally, May 20 to September 24 was considered a safe period for sailing; September 24 to November 22, risky; November 22 to March 20, dangerous; and March 20 to May 20 risky. The harbor would be busy with ships coming and going from the end of February to late November; then traffic slowed during the winter layover. Traffic revived in February when merchants returned from their layovers abroad and rushed to reembark in order to take full advantage of the safe season. August saw another flurry of activity in preparation for a short round-trip voyage, probably to the western Mediterranean islands.

Seafaring merchants had a great deal of paperwork to dispatch just before a voyage; they cleared their accounts, were called by litigants to depose in legal matters, signed powers of attorney, wrote their wills, and signed for goods they had bought on consignment or on credit. Columbus signed nearly all his documents in the months of February and March, before embarking on the long voyages to the eastern Mediterranean or northern Europe, and in August before the last short trip of the sailing season. The short trips would have included trade in the famous triangle of the western Mediterranean: Genoese wool cloth to Sicily, Sicilian wheat to Ibiza or Barcelona, Spanish salt to Genoa.

Columbus was back home by March 20, 1472, when he acted as witness to a neighbor's testamentary deed in Savona, describing himself as a wool dealer in Genoa. He and Domenico began acquiring new merchandise to sell abroad. The most common Genoese export was wool cloth—thousands of bolts of it every year. Domenico in Savona began to purchase wool cloth in wholesale quantities, purchases that can be correlated with his son's voyages. Columbus would take the cloth to sell in Spain, North Africa, or the Middle East, and with the profits buy local products, especially wheat, to sell in Genoa. Domenico used the profits from each voyage to buy more wool cloth for export.

In June 1472 Domenico bought 316 pounds of wool cloth on credit from Giovanni de Signorio for forty lire. Columbus probably sold these in Sicily or another western Mediterranean port just in time to buy the new grain harvested and threshed during the summer. In late summer, he was back in Savona, probably with a cargo of wheat to sell at a good profit.

On August 26, 1472, Columbus and Domenico together bought another 736 pounds of wool cloth from Giovanni de Signorio, for 140 lire payable in six months. Columbus could have made another round trip during these six months and returned with enough profit to enable Domenico to buy 418 pounds of Savona wool cloth on credit from Andrea Drago on February 12, 1473.

On June 4, 1473, Domenico bought seven white wool cloths on consignment from Ludovico Multedo, citizen of Savona, to be paid for within five months, with Domenico keeping the profits or incurring the loss. Two months later, in Domenico's shop in Savona, Columbus and his brother Giovanni Pelegrino agreed to their parents' sale of their house on dell'Olivella Street in Genoa to the Genoese wool weaver Petro de Cella. Giovanni Pelegrino

was now old enough to share with Christopher the burden of owning legal title to their parents' property in Genoa.

The most profitable Genoese imports were spices and aromatics from the eastern Mediterranean. Although Ottoman expansion had deprived the Genoese of their traditional markets and sources, they were still able to participate indirectly in the Levant trade because Genoa held Chios, an island in the middle of the sea lanes through the Aegean Sea. A consortium of Genoese shipowners, who called themselves the Giustiniani family, controlled all trade and shipping on Chios. By the last half of the fifteenth century, Genoese shippers were using very large ships that carried high-value cargo directly from Chios to winter over in England and Flanders, without stopping to trade in Mediterranean ports.

While Chios was an important entrepôt for goods in transit from the Muslim East to the Christian West, its importance to the story of Christopher Columbus revolves around a local product, gum mastic. Gum mastic is the sap of certain kinds of acacia trees that grow mostly in East Africa and Asia. Because the substance is slightly soluble and eventually dissolves when chewed, it was used in early medicine as a carrier that would release drugs slowly. It is also known as gum arabic, because the first sugar traders, the Arabs, got the idea of mixing gum with sugar as a thickening agent in candies and sweets (it is the basis of jujube, marshmallow, and licorice paste). Gum mastic and related resins fetched a very high price per ounce, and since the only place in Europe where that variety of acacia grows is in Chios, the Giustiniani were able to control the price by spacing the harvest of sap from the trees and by limiting the number of fleets that sailed from Genoa to Chios to just one or two every decade.

Columbus was obviously familiar with this lucrative trade; he mistakenly reported finding the Chios variety of acacia trees on more than one Caribbean island. This seems conclusive evidence that Christopher Columbus traveled to Chios as a young man. This trip could have taken place only on Genoese fleets, and that fact places the voyage in 1474 or 1475, the only years during Columbus's youth when Genoese fleets went to Chios. The first of these, Gian Antonio di Negro's fleet, left from Savona for Chios in May 1474. The second, Goffredo de Spinola's fleet, left from Genoa in September 1475. Two of the ships in the 1475 voyage were owned by Paolo di Negro and Nicolò Spinola. Although Columbus's name does not appear on the passenger or crew lists, he probably sailed on the ships of one or both of these men; he named them and their heirs among his creditors in the codicil to his will. While in Chios, the fleet would have learned of another disaster; in the summer of 1475, the Ottoman Turks captured Caffa, the last Genoese trading post on the Black Sea.

Meanwhile, the Colombo family business flourished.

Father and son bought merchandise on a large scale, obtaining credit for sums of money equal to one-half the price of a farm or city house. Domenico's status in Savona continued to rise, and he changed his self-description from wool weaver (*textor pannorum*) to wool dealer (*lanerius*). On April 14, 1474, Domenico acknowledged receipt of 250 lire in full payment for his farm in Ginestreto. Six months later, he bought a farm in Legino, a village in Savona's territory, for a total price of 250 lire. Domenico agreed to pay 50 lire in wool cloths every year on Saint Michael's Day (September 25) as payment for the farm, which included a vineyard, grain fields, an orchard, woods, and a farmhouse. This farm was next to that of the vendor, Corrado da Cuneo, whose son Michele would accompany Columbus on his second voyage to America.

While the family at home was prospering, Columbus was exposed to all the dangers and novelties of the sea, from the vagaries of weather, shifting currents, and high winds to pirate attacks. Piracy was part of warfare and a constant menace to shipping in the western Mediterranean. The richest shipowners hired military professionals to defend their ships from pirates and sailed together in fleets in order to help one another in case of attack. Because Genoa was under French domination and at war with Aragón during most of Columbus's youth, the most dangerous routes for Genoese ships were the Straits of Gibraltar and the western Mediterranean routes from Sardinia to Sicily.

From 1468 to November 1476, when Genoa was under the rule of pro-Aragón Milan, the danger came in Atlantic waters from French pirates. On August 13, 1476, Columbus was involved in a battle off the coast of Portugal. A fleet of five Genoese ships (probably including ships returning from Chios) embarked in Noli and passed through the Straits of Gibraltar headed for England. The Genoese convoy included one galleass belonging to Goffredo Spinola, one whaler belonging to Nicolò Spinola, one galleass belonging to Terano Squarcifico, one galleass commanded by Gian Antonio di Negro, and one "bechalla" (a ship of Flemish construction) commanded by Cristoforo Salvago, which had many Savonese aboard, probably including Christopher Columbus. This fleet was attacked by a French squadron commanded by the vice admiral Guillaume Casenove (Coulon). Only two Genoese ships survived—those of Goffredo Spinola and Gian Antonio di Negro. The others sank, along with four French ships. The bechalla caught fire, everyone jumped overboard, and Columbus saved himself by grabbing a floating oar and swimming. He told his son Fernando a garbled story of swimming about two leagues (seven to eight miles) to the coast and coming ashore not far from Lisbon, where he was taken in by Genoese merchants.

Although Columbus survived, he lost a great deal in this shipwreck. His merchandise in the cargo hold, now at the bottom of the sea, was probably covered by marine insurance. His personal possessions in his sea chest, however, would have been a total loss. Inventories of sailors' chests show that he would have taken on board enough clothing, liquid assets, and personal possessions to last the voyage and a winter in the North.

In 1493, Genoa was suffering an outbreak of bubonic plague, which was believed to be transmitted on merchandise, especially cloth. When ships whose crews had experienced deaths at sea from the illness came into port, the government confiscated the sea chests of the deceased sailors, inventoried their contents, and had them purified as a public health measure. (Health officials sprinkled the goods with vinegar or exposed them to dry air to purify them.) The inventories of two of these chests (on p. 172) suggest what the contents of Columbus's sea chest would have been, although his would have contained more clothing and property than the common sailor's and less military equipment than the soldier's. Also, Columbus would have been carrying account ledgers and probably more paper, ink, and books than either of the two men who died in 1493.

Columbus did not remain in Lisbon long following his shipwreck in 1476. On September 12, a new fleet left Genoa to pick up the remnants of the shipwrecked fleet in Lisbon and go on to England. Financed cooperatively by the Genoese merchant colony in London, the fleet may have continued from London to winter over in Bristol. This voyage would have a lasting effect on Columbus's imagination and ambition. He told his son Fernando that in February 1477 he had been to an island called Thule that was as large as England and lay seventy-three degrees north of the equator. The winter of 1476–1477 was an exceptionally mild one in the North Atlantic, and some scholars speculate that it was Iceland he visited.

While Columbus traveled on this, the most far-reaching of his early maritime experiences, the political situation back home in Genoa once again turned in favor of the Colombo family. The loss of Caffa and Milanese inability to protect Genoese shipping in the western Mediterranean weakened the Sforza position in Genoa. Domenico Colombo dared to reenter the city and conduct some business there on November 5, 1476. A few days later, Duke Galeazzo María Sforza died in Milan at the hands of assassins. Genoa allied again with France. Still, the city had lost much of its attraction for Domenico and Susanna, and in January 1477 they transferred title on their first Genoa house, on dell'Olivella Street, having received payment of the final installment.

By this time, Columbus was twenty-five or twenty-six years old, legally an adult and able to contract debts and marriage without his parents' consent. In 1478, he was back in Lisbon. At that time, he was the agent of a Genoese merchant, Paolo di Negro, who was buying and

Inventories of Two Sailors' Chests (Genoa, September 27, 1493)

Inventory, compiled by order of the Health Office of the Commune of Genoa, of the objects and property retrieved from the chest of the deceased Valarano Frastaria, seaman on the ship of the noble Giovanni Jacopo Spinola. The objects and property listed below were consigned by orders of the Office to Melchione Marenco to be purified with the chest.

A gilded silver ring in a small, light leather purse.

A long sword with scabbard.

A large basket full of dates weighing about 35 lbs.

Three pairs of stockings, two made of black wool and the third of white wool.

A round basket of Morisco palm.

Two vests of turquoise wool with sleeves and another without sleeves.

A man's garment of green wool.

A wool tunic.

Two shirts.

Wool underpants.

A black cap.

Four linen handkerchiefs.

Two small hampers, empty.

A lead bullet.

A pair of scissors.

Iron tongs with wood handles.

A long sheet of parchment, written on and erased.

Inventory, compiled by order of the Health Office of the Commune of Genoa, of the objects and property found in the chest of the deceased Paulino, artilleryman on the ship of the noble Giovanni Jacopo Spinola. The objects and property listed below were consigned by orders of the Office to Melchione Marenco to be purified with the chest.

A Morisco purse containing 7 coins from Ebosa and two handkerchiefs, one larger than the other.

A pair of short swords with hilts and scabbard decorated with silver.

A spherical pearl that must be worth about 40 soldi, wrapped in a sheet of paper and piece of black silk cloth.

A piece of jasper and a piece of rock for touching gold and silver, in a little sack.

An open pin.

A heavy black cap.

A *scarsella* (?) of light colored leather.

A wool *pappafico* (?).

Another black cap, used.

A man's garment of red wool, another of green wool, and a very old one of fustian.

Three pairs of lined stockings of red wool, one of them almost new.

A man's garment in linen.

Two black wool vests.

A man's black wool tunic.

A piece of heavy black wool cloth.

A bundle of various scraps and pieces of wool cloth.

A man's garment of black wool, not finished.

Nine men's shirts.

Six towels, some in good condition, others in bad shape.

A long sack about six palms in length.

One blanket.

Three handkerchiefs.

A small piece of wool cloth.

A hemmed towel about five palms in length.

Two hides.

A pair of long, fine knee boots.

One shirt sleeve.

A piece of white wool cloth.

A red fur hood.

Some scraps of velvet tied up.

A piece of red wool cloth.

Two shoes.

A prayer book written on paper with leather-bound covers.

A printed book with covers.

A pair of linen stockings.

A long sword with scabbard.

A short sword with scabbard.

Two shoes.

One pickax.

One inkwell made of cypress wood.

A small box with a few odds and ends.

A hemp sack containing some squid bones (? *ossa sepiarum*)

A lump of iron weighing about 10 pounds.

A *verrina* (?)

A small basket, about one palm in diameter and pretty, with its cover.

Two bunches of string.

shipping sugar from Madeira to Genoa with the money and instructions of Luigi Centurione in Genoa. With the money that Centurione had forwarded to Paolo, Columbus went to Madeira in June and bought twenty-one tons of sugar ready to be loaded on the ship of Fernando Palencia, then in the harbor.

Many years later, Columbus referred to the Atlantic sugar trade in knowledgeable detail. In the letter to the Spanish monarchs in which he advised them to lease ships for America the same way ships were leased for the Flanders trade, Columbus also offered advice on purchasing sugar from Madeira. In 1494, the Spaniards on La Española were suffering an epidemic, and sugar was one of the most recommended foods for the ill. Columbus wrote:

> For the sustenance of the healthy as well as for the sick, it would be very good to have 50 pipes of sugar syrup from the island of Madeira, because it is the best and most healthful sustenance in the world. It usually does not cost more than 2 ducats without the cask. If Their Highnesses would order a caravel to stop over there on the way back here, it could buy the syrup and also 10 boxes of sugar, which are desperately needed. This is the best time of year, between now [January 30] and the month of April, to find it available and get a good price on it.

Columbus now had enough experience and stature to command a ship. He told his son Fernando that he had once tried to attack an Aragonese ship while commanding a ship in a French attack on Tunis. The details have never been clear, which is not surprising; the story would have been an embarrassing admission that Columbus had fought against King Fernando's father, King Juan II of Aragón. The events must have taken place while the Angevins were at war with the Aragonese from 1472 to 1479. Columbus claimed that King René of Anjou sent him to Tunis to capture the Aragonese galleass *Fernandina*. Near the island of San Pietro off Sardinia they found the ship with three others. His crew wanted to go back to Marseille for reinforcements. Columbus agreed, only to fake the ship's course by night, so that the next morning, when the crew expected to be off Marseille, they found themselves off Cape Carthage in North Africa.

In August 1479, Columbus was in Genoa and ready to embark on another voyage. Either Luigi Centurione had not received the sugar shipment or Paolo's efforts did not satisfy him, because now, more than a year after the fact, he called Columbus to depose about the matter. On August 25, Columbus testified that he had received the money in Lisbon from Paolo di Negro and had used it on Madeira to purchase the sugar for Centurione. Considerable doubt is cast on this statement by the fact that, just before he died, he ordered his son Diego to pay thirty thousand Portuguese reales to the heirs of Luigi Centurione. In 1479, however, his deposition pictured him as a prosperous young man with many possibilities. He described himself as twenty-seven years old and possessing more than a hundred florins in cash, and stated that he was embarking the next morning. It was his last visit to his native city and probably his final voyage in the Mediterranean.

The shift from the Mediterranean to the Atlantic had been gradual. Columbus may well have found Lisbon a more congenial setting for his future than Genoa, with its precarious political and economic situation.

His maritime experience had encompassed both the Mediterranean and the Atlantic, often on the same voyages. For years, he moved back and forth from Genoa to Lisbon, where he was part of the colony of foreign businessmen. He formed lifelong connections with the Genoese merchants in Lisbon; on his deathbed, Columbus ordered his son to pay twenty-five hundred Portuguese reales to "Antonio Vazo, a Genoese merchant who used to live in Lisbon," and the equivalent of a half mark of silver to a Jew who used to live at the entrance to the Jewish quarter in Lisbon, though he did not recall this man's name.

Portuguese merchants, in turn, were also moving back and forth between the Atlantic and the Mediterranean. One example alone indicates the degree to which ships, merchants, and merchandise that we traditionally associate with the Atlantic where equally part of Mediterranean commerce. If Columbus had been in Genoa during the winter layover of 1474–1475, he could have met a Portuguese ship's captain named Bartolomeu Dias, who on January 3, 1475, received a safe-conduct from the city government of Genoa. Dias was the future discoverer of the Cape of Good Hope, carrying on trade in sugar and slaves between the Atlantic and the western Mediterranean. He was also engaged in piracy and the slave trade in the Mediterranean. In 1478, Dias, captain of the ship *Charachone*, again arrived in an Italian port city, Porto Pisano, with a cargo of sugar on the account of a Florentine company, the Cambini. The same ship probably unloaded sardines sent from Lisbon by the merchant-banker Bartolomeu Marchionni. On his return from Porto Pisano, Dias stopped in Genoa to buy slaves and continued from there to Lisbon, indulging along the way in a bit of piracy on behalf of King João II, who was at war with Castile. In Lisbon on June 21, 1478, King João issued an acknowledgment of debt granting Dias one-fifth of the prisoners he had captured at sea in payment of the twelve thousand reals that Dias had spent on the slave he had bought for the king in Genoa.

Columbus married a Portuguese woman, Felipa Moniz y Perestrelo, probably in 1479, and from then on used

Lisbon, already familiar to him, at his home port. Now Columbus was no longer a foreigner. By virtue of his marriage, he acquired Portuguese citizenship and therefore the right to trade in all Portuguese overseas possessions. He probably had not participated in the Africa trade earlier, because the Portuguese monarchy tried to reserve it for Portuguese citizens and ships, just as Genoa reserved trade with Chios for its own citizens and ships. What does seem certain is that, after 1479, Columbus made his living navigating the Atlantic and doing business in Atlantic ports. The most lucrative Portuguese trade formed a triangle: Portuguese slavers loaded slaves from sub-Saharan Africa, sold them to sugar plantations on the Portuguese island of Madeira, and used the profits to buy sugar, which they would sell in Europe.

Columbus, through his Portuguese citizenship, acquired the opportunity to participate in this trade, which placed him in the midst of the Atlantic currents and winds that would eventually carry him to America. Through observation, he made those winds and waters his own. He also gained access to the nautical lore and wisdom of Portuguese mariners and shipbuilders, who were at that time making many subtle and ingenious improvements in ship design, sails, and navigational equipment to cope with Atlantic conditions.

These years in the Mediterranean and the Atlantic were a crucial period in Columbus's life. In the Mediterranean, he became accustomed to the piracy, violent storms, and warfare that were constant dangers for merchant shipping. In Genoa's slave market he learned to see humans from Asia and Africa as commodities. In Genoa's eastern trade with Asia, he learned the financial and military risks associated with trading posts and colonies financed and governed by merchant companies without a government to protect them.

In the Atlantic voyages he traveled farther north and south than the Mediterranean allowed and encountered oceanic conditions that existed nowhere else. In the mid-Atlantic, counterclockwise ocean currents and winds made sailing straight north from sub-Saharan Africa difficult without first going west. Coping with these conditions had driven Portuguese and Spanish merchant ships far out into the Atlantic, and there they had discovered the Madeiras, the Azores, and the Canary and Cape Verde islands. King João II sent a heavily manned and armed fleet to build a fortified trading post, São Jorge da Mina, on the West African coast south of Cape Bojador in 1482.

Columbus traveled these same Atlantic routes and integrated their lessons into a scheme for reestablishing direct trade with Asia by sailing west. He learned the currents and winds for both the outward and homeward passages to Africa. He calculated the latitudes of Atlantic locations as far north (Thule) and south (Mina) as Europeans had ever sailed in order to calculate the circumference

of the earth. His writing is full of Atlantic Ocean vocabulary and Atlantic nautical terms; it is nearly devoid of such terms from the Mediterranean. He knew the flora and fauna of the Atlantic—its birds, seaweed, and marine life. He knew the Portuguese slave trade in Africa and its importance to sugar production on Madeira. He knew the only Portuguese site on the African mainland, São Jorge da Mina, whose survival depended on royal financing and protection.

Columbus's maritime expertise was the product of long experience in the import-export trade of the Atlantic and Mediterranean. He knew that the king of Portugal acted as a partner in the commercial voyages of Portuguese ships, and that, though Portuguese merchants sacrificed a fifth of their profits to the king, they received royal financial and military backing. Everything in Christopher Columbus's early maritime experience had taught him that partnership with the monarchy provided a level of protection unknown in the precarious and high-risk world of the Genoese merchant companies.

BIBLIOGRAPHY

Ballesteros Beretta, Antonio. *Cristóbal Colón y el descubrimiento de América.* 2 vols. Barcelona, 1945.

Borghesi, Vilma. *Il Mediterraneo tra due rivoluzioni nautiche (secoli XIV–XVII).* Florence, 1976.

Columbus, Ferdinand. *The Life of the Admiral Christopher Columbus.* Translated by Benjamin Keen. New Brunswick, N.J., 1959.

Documenti relativi a Cristoforo Colombo e alla sua famiglia. Compiled and edited by L. T. Belgrano and M. Staglieno. In *Raccolta Colombiana.* Part 2, vol. 1.

Fonseca, Luis A. *O essencial sobre Bartolomeu Dias.* Lisbon, 1987.

Genoa, City of. *Colombo.* Bergamo, 1932.

Grendi, E. "Traffico portuale, naviglio mercantile e consolati genovesi nel Cinquecento." *Revista Storica Italiana* 80 (1968): 593–629.

Heers, Jacques. *Gênes au XVe siècle: Activités économiques et problèmes sociaux.* Paris, 1961.

Heers, Jacques. "Le royaume de Grenade et la politique marchande de Gênes en Occident (XVe siècle)." *Moyen Âge* 63 (1957): 87–121.

Lane, F. C. "The Mediterranean Spice Trade: Evidence of Its Revival in the Sixteenth Century." *American Historical Review* 45 (1940): 581–590.

Martini, Dario G. *Cristoforo Colombo tra ragione e fantasia.* Genoa, 1987.

Morison, Samuel Eliot. *Admiral of the Ocean Sea: A Life of Christopher Columbus.* 2 vols. Boston, 1942.

Phillips, Carla, and William D. Phillips, Jr. *The Worlds of Christopher Columbus.* Cambridge, forthcoming.

Pryor, John H. *Commerce, Shipping, and Naval Warfare in the Medieval Mediterranean.* London, 1987.

Pryor, John H. *Geography, Technology, and War: Studies in the Mediterranean, 649–1571.* Cambridge, 1988.

Salinero, Giulio. *Annotationes Julii Salinerii iureconsulti savonensis ad Cornelium Tacitum.* Genoa, 1602.

HELEN NADER

Columbus in Portugal

Christopher Columbus first arrived in Portugal in May 1476 during a naval battle in which the ship he was serving on was destroyed. Forced to swim for his life, he landed on the beach at Lagos, near Cape St. Vincent, where Prince Henry the Navigator had first set in motion the systematic exploration of the West African coast that was eventually to lead the Portuguese to India.

Columbus's Experience as a Merchant. After recovering from his wounds and the long swim, Columbus went to Lisbon and soon joined a second fleet sent from Genoa to pick up the survivors of the battle of Cape St. Vincent; at the end of December 1476, the Genoese fleet continued the voyage interrupted five months before.

One of the organizers of the second Genoese fleet was Paolo di Negro (or di Negri), who was well known for his trading activities in the route from Lisbon to the Netherlands by way of England. His fleet would have brought Columbus to England about February 1477. He probably arrived at Southampton and he may have gone to London; two prominent Genoese trading families, the Spinola and di Negro, maintained establishments in both cities. It is most probable that Columbus visited Bristol, where he was introduced to English commerce with Iceland. The return route of the Bristol trading vessels was by the west coast of Ireland, their first objective there being the port of Galway. At that time the English merchants had a virtual monopoly of the Iceland fish trade. They brought the fish from Iceland along the western coast of Ireland, making landfall at Galway, and transferring the fish to Portuguese vessels to meet the insatiable Portuguese demand for bacalao, or cod.

The little that is known about Columbus's voyage to Iceland comes on the authority of his son Fernando, quoting from a now lost memorandum from his father:

In the month of February 1477 I sailed one hundred leagues beyond the island of Tile [Iceland]. Its southern part is seventy-three degrees north and not sixty-three degrees as some say. Furthermore, it does not lie on the meridian where Ptolemy says the West begins, but a great deal farther west. To this island, which is as big as England, the English merchants go, especially those from Bristol. And at the time when I was there the sea was not frozen, but there were vast tides, so great that they rose and fell as much as twenty-six fathoms [about fifty feet] in depth.

This passage, which was intended to prove that the Arctic zones were habitable, contains so many improbabilities that some critics refuse to believe that Columbus ever went to Iceland. His report of the height of the tides is wrong; the maximum range at Reykjavík is less than fifteen feet. His statement that the southern coastline of Iceland is at seventy-three degrees is wrong; it is in fact at sixty-three degrees, sixty minutes. There seems little doubt, however, that Columbus did visit Iceland in 1477 because of an annotation in the margin of his personal copy of the *Historia rerum ubique gestarum* (*History of memorable things that have happened in my time*) by Enea Silvio Piccolomini (Pius II): "Men of Cathay, which is toward the Orient, have come hither. We have seen many remarkable things, especially in Galway, in Ireland, a man and a woman of most unusual appearance have come to land in two boats."

The Iceland voyage appears to be the only occasion on which he could have visited Galway. His assumption that the two bodies he saw came from the Orient suggest that he was already obsessed with the idea of Marco Polo's Cathay. The unusual appearance of the two dead bodies strongly suggests that they were Inuit (Eskimos) who were probably caught in an Atlantic storm off Labrador and eventually dashed lifeless against the Irish coast. These elements do fit together with the trade route pioneered by the Bristol men, and the Portuguese vessel to which Columbus transferred would have brought him back in the autumn of 1477 to Portugal, where he was to stay for nearly a decade.

It is not known how much time he spent at sea or in Lisbon, where his younger brother Bartolomé was living. Antonio Gallo (d. 1510), who was the official chronicler of the republic of Genoa from 1477 until his death, says that Bartolomé had settled in Lisbon before Christopher arrived, opened a chart-making business, took his elder brother into partnership, and imparted to him the ideas that led to his voyage to the New World. Andrés Bernáldez of Seville, in whose house Columbus lived when he returned from the second voyage to America, describes him in his contemporary history of the reign of the Catholic monarchs as a "hawker of printed books . . . very skilled in the art of cosmography and the mapping of the world." Samuel Eliot Morison (1942) believed that Columbus was a skilled chart maker, and that the two brothers became partners in providing articles for which the Portuguese maritime expansion created a great demand. Like every sailor in other centuries, he may have worked at several trades, as a mapmaker and bookseller in the winter months and as a merchant seaman at other times. It is possible that he may have had a commercial career as factor or agent for the rich Genoese merchants in Lisbon. Some Columbus scholars, for example, David B. Quinn, believe that for the first twenty-five years of his life Columbus was primarily a trader, part of the widespread network of Genoese traders who had outposts in the Iberian lands, and who were active in the later fifteenth century as far afield as Chios in the east, England and France in the north, and Madeira and Guinea in the west and south. One family, the Spinolas, appears to have been prolific enough to have had members or even trading concerns in most if not all of these places; a Spinola is named in Columbus's will. But most of the Genoese trade at that time was between Genoa and Portugal, England, and Flanders, a new pattern of trade that was established about 1466 due to the loss of most of the Genoese colonies in the eastern Mediterranean, as well as to political strife at home that increased the flow of emigration from Genoa to the west.

Of all the voyages that Columbus may have made during his early Portuguese years, his voyage to Madeira in 1478 and 1479 is fairly well documented. In 1478, Paolo di Negro, a Genoese living in Lisbon who had organized the fleet in 1477, commissioned Columbus to go to Madeira to purchase sugar on behalf of Luigi Centurione, a resident of Genoa. Columbus chartered a Portuguese vessel and sailed from Lisbon for Madeira in July 1478, but without having received 1,290 ducats that Centurione had sent to di Negro. In Madeira, Columbus placed an order for the sugar with Erogio Catalão, expecting any day to receive the money from Lisbon with which to pay for it. But when he received from di Negro only 103 ducats and woolen goods that found no buyers, he was able to load only a small portion of the sugar he had ordered. When Columbus finally reached Genoa, it was only natural that protests were lodged by the ship captain, who wanted payment for the entire amount of the freight even though he had not carried all the merchandise stipulated in the contract, and by Centurione, who wanted to know why Columbus had only delivered a fraction of the merchandise he had ordered and paid for in advance.

Both protests were heard and duly recorded by a notary public, Gerolamo Ventimiglia, who signed the notarial documents in Genoa on August 21, 1479, in the presence of Columbus as both witness and concerned party. In his sworn statement before the notary, Columbus declared that he was a citizen of Genoa, that he was about twenty-seven years old, that he had one hundred florins on his person, and that he intended to depart for Lisbon the following day. (This record, the "Asseretto document," was discovered in 1904 by Hugo Asseretto; it is held in the notarial archives of the government of Genoa.)

Columbus's Marriage to Felipa Perestrelo y Moniz. It was probably in the year 1479 that the twenty-eight-year-old Columbus took a decisive step in his private life and one that was to prove equally important to his future career. He married Felipa Perestrelo y Moniz, the daughter of Isabel Moniz and Bartolomeu Perestrelo, the first governor of the island of Porto Santo in the Madeiras. Practically all that we know of this marriage is derived from the writings of the principal biographers of Columbus, namely, Fernando Colón, youngest son of the Admiral, and Bartolomé de las Casas, his friend and admirer.

Much has been written about how and why Christopher Columbus, the son of a humble weaver, a part-time seaman and trader, and dealer in books and maps, came to meet, woo, and marry a woman of aristocratic birth on both sides of her family. According to Fernando, they met at the Convento dos Santos in Lisbon where Columbus used to attend mass. The convent belonged to the nuns of the military order of Santiago; its purpose was to provide a home for the wives and daughters of the knights of the order while the knights were at war. For an ambitious young man eager to marry into upper-class society, there could have been no better place to choose for his churchgoing, since only in church was it possible for the men and women of different social strata to meet.

Nothing is known about the appearance of Felipa, but whether she was attractive or not, she was undoubtedly a good catch. As for Columbus himself, Gonzalo Fernández de Oviedo, who first saw him in Barcelona in 1492, fourteen years after Felipa met him, describes him

> as a man of fine appearance, well built, taller than most, and with strong limbs. His eyes were lively and his features in good proportion. . . . His hair was very red and his face ruddy and freckled. He spoke well, was tactful in his manner and was extremely talented. He was a good Latinist and a very learned cosmographer, gracious when he wished, but hot tempered if he was crossed.

Fernando explains the attraction that Felipa had for him in the following manner: "Inasmuch as he behaved very honorably, and was a man of such fine presence, and withal so honest, that she held such conversation with him and enjoyed such friendship with him that she became his wife." As far as Columbus was concerned, whether or not he was deeply attracted to Felipa, the advantages of the match were immense. She was to prove the key that opened the way for his acceptance into a world where power and influence could be courted and obtained. Though very little is known about Felipa herself, a great deal is known about her family.

The Moniz and Perestrelo families. On her mother's side, Felipa came from the powerful family of Moniz, which had been in close contact with the Portuguese royal family since the twelfth century, when its founder, Egas Moniz, became governor under Afonso Henriques, the first king of Portugal. One of the gates in the Castle of St. George, an enormous fortress overlooking Lisbon and the Tagus River, still bears the name of Egas Moniz, who defended the gate by himself during a battle against the Moors in 1147, preventing them from penetrating the walls. The grandfather of Felipa, Gil Ayres Moniz, ruled one of the richest seigniories of the Algarve, the last of the lands conquered from the Moors, and accompanied Henry the Navigator when he took part in the conquest of Ceuta in 1415.

On her father's side, the family was no less illustrious and perhaps more powerful. Felipa's father, Bartolomeu, descended from the Italian Pelestrellos or Pallastrellis of Piacenza, one of whom, Filippo or Filippone Palestrelli, moved to Portugal in the year 1385; he established himself first in Porto and later in Lisbon and dedicated himself to commerce. With him when he left Italy was his wife, Catarina Sforza. On January 8, 1399, Filippo obtained a tax exemption from King João I, after proving that he was descended from an aristocratic line (in those days, the nobility did not pay taxes). Filippo had four children— Richarte, Isabel, Branca, and Bartolomeu; the last was the father-in-law of Columbus. The oldest son, Richarte, sometimes called Rafael, took holy orders and rose to become prior of the parish of Santa Marinha of Lisbon. He fathered two children whom he legitimized in 1423. Later, his descendants played outstanding roles in the enterprise of India; one of his grandsons was among the first Portuguese to visit China. Isabel and Branca became the mistresses of the great churchman and powerful political figure, Pedro de Noronha, archbishop of Lisbon, who was related to the reigning families of both Castile and Portugal.

Noronha's mother was the daughter of King Fernando of Portugal (r. 1367–1383) and his father was related to the royal family of Castile. One of his brothers was count of Vila Real; another, Sancho, was count of Odemira; his sister Constanza married Afonso, count of Barcelos, later duke of Braganza, bastard son of King João I. In 1424, when Pedro de Noronha was barely twenty-eight years old, he was elected archbishop of Lisbon. With Isabel Perestrelo he had a son, João. With the younger sister Branca he had three children—Isabel, Diogo, and Pedro. Despite his position as head of the Portuguese church, he had all his offspring officially legitimized in 1444 and saw to it that Isabel married into the royal house of Braganza and his two sons rapidly reached the highest posts in the state and in the church. Branca Perestrelo, the younger sister, was eventually abandoned by Noronha and retired to a convent until her marriage to Eanes de Beja.

Bartolomeu Perestrelo, Captain Donatário of Porto Santo. On the basis of Columbus's two earliest biographies, by his son Fernando and by Las Casas, the view has been traditionally held that Bartolomeu Perestrelo, Columbus's father-in-law, had been given the hereditary captaincy of the island of Porto Santo because of his seamanship and valorous deeds. Both Fernando Colón and Las Casas elaborate a story about papers and instruments and hints about islands to be discovered that

Perestrelo's widow was supposed to have given her son-in-law, Columbus. The part played by Columbus's father-in-law in the discovery of Porto Santo is described by Las Casas in the following manner:

> As days went by, the mother-in-law realized how bent on the things of the sea and of cosmography was Cristóbal Colón . . . so that . . . she told him how her husband, Perestrelo, had also been a person leaning to affairs of the sea, and how, by order of Prince Henry, he had gone in company with two other gentlemen to the island of Porto Santo, recently discovered, and soon after, he alone was entrusted with the task of populating the island; and the Prince [Henry the Navigator] granted him properties in it; and as in those days there was a great boiling over of the practice and exercise of discoveries on the coast of Guinea and on the islands of the Ocean Sea and the said Bartolomeu Perestrelo had the hope of discovering other islands from his, as indeed they were discovered . . . he probably had instruments and papers and pictures on navigation which the mother-in-law gave Colón, from seeing and reading which, he received much pleasure. . . ."

It is plain that Las Casas himself suggests that the existence of "instruments, papers, and pictures" belonging to Perestrelo is a mere conjecture. Salvador de Madariaga, a twentieth-century biographer of Columbus, believes that it was the connection of the Perestrelo family with Archbishop Noronha that supplies the key to the reputation of Bartolomeu Perestrelo as a discoverer and populator.

Perestrelo's name is not included among the discoverers of Porto Santo by the chronicler João de Barros, who entitled a chapter in his *Décadas da Ásia* (1552) "How João Gonçalvez and Tristão Vaz discovered the island of Porto Santo, owing to a tempest which took them there." Barros claims to have gotten his information from the chronicler Gomes Eanes de Zurara, who wrote about a hundred years before him. Referring to João Gonçalvez and Tristão Vaz, Barros writes that the two knights, who were sent on a discovery voyage by Prince Henry the Navigator, accidentally discovered the island of Porto Santo. Henry was extremely pleased to hear about the discovery and even more pleased when the two discoverers told him that they wanted to return to colonize it. Many others who had heard about the discovery also offered to settle there, among them Bartolomeu Perestrelo, who was a "gentleman of the household of Prince João," Prince Henry's brother. Henry then had three ships outfitted, one of which he gave to Bartolomeu Perestrelo and the two others to Gonçalvez and Vaz, the original discoverers. In the two years that they lived on Porto Santo, it was impossible to sow or plant anything because of the overpopulation of the rabbits that Perestrelo had brought there, and so the colonizers began to hate the work and their way of life, and Bartolomeu Perestrelo decided to return to Lisbon.

From Barros we also learn that the knights who discovered the island of Porto Santo, even if much against their will, were definitely Gonçalvez and Vaz; Perestrelo was a hanger-on of Prince João who was attracted by the prospect of profit and was given a ship through favoritism; and his efforts toward populating the island that his widow, in Las Casas's version, says was entrusted to him alone were limited to breeding rabbits.

Nevertheless, his influence at court convinced Prince Henry in 1425 to entrust him with another expedition to populate Porto Santo. His lack of success does not seem to have warranted a long stay, for in 1431 he was given a house in Lisbon, where in 1437 he was registered as a municipal councilor. In 1446, over twenty years after his two unsuccessful attempts and two years after the legitimization of his sisters' children had demonstrated the power of Pedro de Noronha, Perestrelo was granted by Prince Henry the title of *capitão donatário* (grant-holder) of Porto Santo.

The Perestrelo family, then, enjoyed power and social standing and a well-known permanent connection with the island of Porto Santo, the captaincy of which was hereditary. And since Bartolomeu Perestrelo lacked a talent for seafaring and competence as a colonizer, it is obvious, though it was not to Las Casas, that his supposed "papers and instruments" could not have been the cause or the inspiration of Columbus's design. This fact strengthens the argument that the scheme or "urge" toward discovery was active in Columbus's mind before he ever married Felipa Perestrelo and therefore that he probably married into the Perestrelo family because it was so powerful in Porto Santo, which was an admirable base for exploring the western seas.

The marriage of Bartolomeu Perestrelo with Isabel Moniz—Columbus's mother-in-law—must have taken place in 1449 or 1450. It seems that Isabel was his second or third wife. With his first wife, Perestrelo had had three children; and he had three children with Isabel Moniz: Bartolomeu, Felipa, who married Columbus, and Violante or Briolanja, with whom Columbus maintained good relations long after the death of his wife.

Bartolomeu Perestrelo lived in Porto Santo from 1446 probably until his death in 1457, when Isabel Moniz moved back to Lisbon. She had looked for someone capable of taking charge of the captaincy of Porto Santo and found no one more apt than Pedro Correia da Cunha, who was married to a daughter from her husband's first marriage. He belonged to the highest nobility and was a gentleman of the court of the infante, Prince Henry, who made him *donatário* of the Azorean island of Graciosa. Isabel Moniz had sold the captaincy of Porto Santo for three hundred thousand reis in 1458, when the young

Bartolomeu Perestrelo was only eight years old. When he was old enough, he served in Africa and, on his return, he reclaimed the captaincy of Porto Santo, which he obtained when the king annulled the previous grant with the obligation on the part of Perestrelo of returning to his relative Pedro Correia the 300,000 reis.

It is interesting that Columbus never mentions the name of his wife in any of his papers that have survived, though he does refer to her twice: once in a letter of 1500, and the second time in his testament of August 25, 1505, when he recommends to his son Diego that he should have mass said for "the souls of my father, my mother, and my wife."

The island of Porto Santo was, and still is, not as prosperous as the island of Madeira, and many of Columbus's biographers believe that not long after his marriage, Columbus moved to Madeira, where he probably engaged in trade and went on a number of voyages. There he probably met with and listened to the tales of mariners who, long before him, had sailed into the Atlantic, and where signs of land to the west were constantly being washed ashore.

Portuguese Knowledge of Western Islands. During the years that he lived in Portugal and its island territories, Columbus amassed considerable evidence of exotic lands to the west. From what Las Casas tells us, he either heard of or saw definite physical clues of transatlantic lands with exotic flora, as well as indefinite rumors of islands. One day he was told by a pilot of the king of Portugal, Martim Vicente, that at about 450 leagues west of Cape St. Vincent, he had picked up from the sea a piece of carved wood that, as far as he could see, was not cut by iron. Since the wind had been fixed in the west for many days, he came to the conclusion that this piece of wood had come from some island or islands lying further west.

Another pilot, Pedro Correia da Cunha, who was married to the sister or half-sister of Columbus's wife, told him that he had picked up a similar piece of driftwood in the harbor of Porto Santo. He also told him that he had seen some very thick reeds or canes that would easily hold three large measures of wine or water. Columbus himself says that he heard the king of Portugal say the same thing and that the king had these reeds shown to him. The king thought, as Columbus says, that they had come from some island, not very far off, or had been brought from India by the strong winds and swift currents, since no such reeds were known to exist in Europe. Columbus thought that these reeds must be the bamboo of India described by Ptolemy. Morison determined that though large pieces of driftwood rarely come ashore on the outer Azores, Central American treetrunks—probably of the light cuipo tree—did wash ashore on the island of São Miguel in a storm in 1869 (the Azores are about 1,100 kilometers [700 miles] northwest of Madeira).

According to Las Casas, Columbus was also informed by

some of the people who lived in the Azores that when strong westerly and northwesterly winds blew, the sea carried pine trees that washed up on the shore, especially on the islands of Graciosa and Faial, although there were no pine trees growing in the Azores. Others told him that on Flores Island, also in the Azores, two corpses had come aground, with very broad faces and features quite unlike those of European men. On another occasion, near Cape Verga on the west coast of Guinea, long, narrow canoes with moveable deckhouses ran aground; they may have been sailing from one West Indian island to another when strong winds or currents drove them off course, their crews died, and their boats drifted to Africa. Antonio Leme, a resident of Madeira, assured Columbus that he once had caught sight of three islands far in the west. Whether this was true or not, it is common for sailors from the Azores and from Gomera and Hierro islands in the Canaries to report that they have seen islands lying toward the west. But Columbus says that in 1484 he knew of a resident of Madeira who went to ask the king for a caravel to discover a certain land that he swore he caught sight of every year and always in the same way, which agreed on this point with what the Azoreans maintained.

The tale of the unknown pilot. Though it appears, then, that Columbus had definite physical clues as well as indefinite rumors of lands in the west, it was also rumored that he had definite information about them. Not long after he returned from his first voyage of discovery in 1493, it was said that he had known all along exactly where he was going and when he would get there because of what he had learned from an unknown pilot who died in his arms.

Almost all the chronicles of the West Indies mention the pilot, about whom nobody seemed to know anything definite. Las Casas relates that he first heard about him in 1500 when he was living in La Española. But it was not until 1535 that the tale of the unknown pilot first appeared in print in the first part of the *General and Natural History of the Indies, Islands and Mainland of the Ocean Sea* by Gonzalo Fernández de Oviedo (1478–1557). According to Oviedo

some say that a caravel that was sailing from Spain to England, charged with merchandise and provisions, such as wine and other things which are usually shipped to that island . . . was subjected to such mighty and violent tempests and foul winds that she was forced to run westward for so many days that she picked up one or more of the islands of these regions and Indies; and [the pilot] went ashore and saw naked people . . . and when the winds moderated which had driven him thither against his will, he took on water and wood to return to his first course. They also say that the better part of the cargo which this vessel carried consisted of provisions and things to eat and wines, whereof they were able to sustain life on so long a voyage.

But since it took four or five months to return, everyone except three or four mariners and the pilot died en route, and all save he arrived in such bad condition that they died shortly after.

Moreover it is said that this pilot was a very intimate friend of Christopher Columbus, and that he understood somewhat of the latitudes, and marked the land which he found, and in great secrecy shared it with Columbus, whom he asked to make a chart and indicate on it the land which he had seen. It is said that Columbus received him in his house as a friend and sought to cure him, as he too landed very weak; but that he died like the rest, and thus Columbus was informed of the land and navigation of those regions, and he alone knew the secret. Some say that this master or pilot was Andalusian, others have him Portuguese, others Basque; some say that Columbus was then living on the island of Madeira and others in the Cape Verde Islands; and that there the aforesaid caravel came to harbor, and in this way Columbus learned of the land. Whether this was so or not, nobody can truly affirm; but so the story ran among the common people. As for me, I hold it to be false."

In his *History of the Indies* (1552), Francisco López de Gómara (1512–1572) attributes the discovery of the Indies to the unknown pilot and describes his voyage in a manner similar to that of Oviedo:

There are also some who say that the caravel reached Portugal, others say Madeira or one of the islands of the Azores; but no one affirms anything. Only that they all agree that that pilot died in Columbus's house, in whose hands he left the log of the caravel and the relation of that whole long voyage, with the mark and latitude of the lands newly seen and found. . . . Columbus lived on the island of Madeira where I think he resided at the time that the said caravel arrived there. Columbus took him into his house and he told him about the voyage he had undertaken and the new lands he had seen, so that he could copy it onto a chart. In the meantime, the pilot died and left him the relation, sketch, and latitude of the new lands and that is how Columbus found out about the Indies [for] he had never thought of such a thing until he came across the pilot who found them by fortunes of the sea.

Las Casas devotes Book 1, chapter 14, of his *History* to the pilot. Las Casas, who was living in La Española at the time the story was current, gives us more or less the same version as Oviedo except that he advances an argument in favor of the unknown pilot's existence by relating the tradition among the Indians of the bearded white man who had visited the islands not long before the arrival of Columbus. However, Las Casas concludes that since there were so many other reasons to inspire Columbus to make the voyage of discovery, the story of the unknown pilot may well be ignored. He adds it is certain that Columbus "was so sure of discovering what he discovered and of finding what he found, that it was as though he had it all locked up in a room under lock and key." But he does not come out for or against the tale of the unknown pilot.

Morison summarizes the different versions of the story of the unknown pilot:

> Some name the unknown pilot as Alonso Sánchez and give his home as Palos, Huelva, Galicia, or Portugal; some say the ill-fated caravel was engaged in commerce between the peninsula and Madeira or the Canaries or the Gold Coast; she is "blown across" in 28 or 29 days by an "east wind of great fury and relentlessness" in 1484; in the different versions she returns to Graciosa, Terceira, Madeira, Porto Santo, or the Canaries, in each of which Columbus performs his well-rewarded act of charity.

For twenty years, writes Ballesteros Beretta in his *Christopher Columbus and the Discovery of America* (1945), he believed in the truth of the tale since it offered a plausible explanation for Columbus's tenacity. "Today," says Ballesteros,

> we no longer believe in the fairy tale. It is a sailor's tale in which Oviedo does not believe and which Las Casas doubts. Some other data, document, or indication, would be needed to incline the balance in favor of the fantastic pilot. Until the present time everything is up in the air and covered with clouds.

Morison suggests that the story appeared credible to people in the sixteenth century because the winds in the Atlantic had not been charted. Perhaps a seaman did die in Columbus's house and people later believed that he had told Columbus his tale. Most probably, the story was concocted by someone in La Española to cast doubt on Columbus's originality.

The westward voyages of the Portuguese. It was inevitable that Columbus should learn from both his own activities at sea as well as his work in his brother's chart- and mapmaking business of the voyages that were taking place almost every year along the African coast and in the Atlantic. These voyages must have been the common talk of the waterfront.

Columbus mentions some of the voyages that contributed to his training in his own notes, as excerpted by Las Casas. He says that in 1452 Diogo de Teive, one of Prince Henry's captains, discovered the two westernmost islands of the Azores, Flores and Corvo. Teive was a well-known Madeiran who, in 1452, was ordered by Prince Henry to build the first sugar mill on that island. Sailing southwesterly from Faial in the Azores, Teive had run into the Sargasso Sea, the sea of weeds that forty years later, Pedro de Velasco, the Spanish pilot who accompanied Teive on the 1452 voyage, told Columbus not to fear. On the second half of that voyage, Teive continued on a northeast course in search of the mythical island of Brazil and reached the latitude of Cape Clear, Ireland. Unequipped for the cold weather he ran into, and quite unprepared for so long a voyage, he turned back to Portugal, where Teive

put it on record that he was convinced that there was land to the northwest. Not only is it certain that Columbus heard about Teive's voyage, but in the year 1492, when Columbus was hiring the crew that was to sail with him to America, Velasco, who was living in Palos at the time, proved to be of invaluable assistance. He came forward and volunteered the information about "the land of the Indies." Moreover, he publicly encouraged the people, urging them to sign on board with Columbus, assuring them that "they would find a very rich land." Las Casas says that the Portuguese pilot Vicente Dias, on a voyage from Guinea to the Azores, thought that he had seen an island, which he later sought in vain.

The general belief that there were lands lying farther west in the Atlantic found support in several official Portuguese documents. They show that under a royal charter of February 19, 1462, João Vogado was granted the nonexistent islands of Lovo and Capraria that often appeared on charts of the period. They were islands derived from the legend of Saint Brendan, the seagoing Irish saint of the sixth century whose saga of ocean voyaging was one of the most popular stories of the Middle Ages. Much as Columbus stumbled on a New World when in search of the Indies, so the captains of Prince Henry, when searching for the mythical Saint Brendan isles, found the Azores. Seven of them had been discovered by 1439, and in 1452, as mentioned above, Teive came upon far-flung Flores and Corvo.

On October 29, 1462, King Afonso V granted to his brother Fernando a nonexistent island that Gonçalo Fernandes claimed to have sighted west-northwest of the Canaries and Madeira, on his return from the fisheries off the African bay known as the "River of Gold," not far from Cape Bojador. The king, on the ground that Fernando had frequently and unsuccessfully sought an island "that appears over against the island of São Tiago" in the Cape Verdes, conferred the island on his sister Brites, wife of the duke of Viseu. The duchess made no profit on that grant, for the Cape Verde Islands were already known and no more islands were to be found in those waters.

A charter of June 21, 1473, granted João Gonçalves da Câmara, for his service in Africa, an island that he hoped to discover. Another royal document, dated January 28, 1474, granted to Fernão Teles any islands he might discover, a grant that was extended to the Island of the Seven Cities (Antilia) or other inhabited islands, by a charter of November 10, 1474, provided they were not in the region of Guinea. It was in this same year that the Florentine cosmographer Paolo dal Pozzo Toscanelli wrote to Fernão Martins, encouraging the Portuguese to seek Asia by sailing westward and not by sailing around Africa. Ten years later, a royal charter of June 30, 1484, granted Fernão Domingos do Arco an island that he intended to discover; this was the year that Columbus laid his "Great Enterprise" before King João II.

These charters show that a growing number of people in Portugal believed in the existence of islands or a mainland to the west, and that some believed they had caught sight of them. These beliefs in turn prove that sailing on the high seas, far from the African coast and even west of the known archipelagoes, had become frequent and that the Portuguese felt no apprehension in doing so. On the other hand, these lands are never identified with Asia in Portuguese documents, nor is there any talk of crossing the Atlantic to seek out the Far East. Thus, there are no signs that anyone wanted to follow Toscanelli's advice until Columbus came along.

In 1474 Fernão Teles had sought Antilia in vain. But the story of its existence would not die, and Columbus's certainty that he could find it en route to the Indies, if properly equipped and suitably rewarded, probably had something to do with the detailed and significant letters patent of donation issued in 1486 by King João to Ferdinand van Olm, or Fernão Dulmo as he was known in Portugal. Dulmo was a Fleming and a gentleman of the royal household who had settled in the Azores. He established himself on the north coast of Terceira and was appointed captain of that part of the island. The terms of Dulmo's grant betray a new and livelier interest on the part of the king in Atlantic discovery. According to a long entry in the registry of the royal chancellery, Dulmo declared that he proposed "to seek and find a great island or coast of a mainland, which is presumed to be the island of the Seven Cities (or Antilia), and all this at his own proper cost and expense." He prays that he may have a royal donation of any such islands or mainland, populated or unpopulated, as he or anyone acting under his orders may "have discovered or found," together with civil and criminal jurisdiction over the same, these rights with their fees and incomes to be hereditary. The king granted his request and on March 3, 1486, issued letters patent accordingly, and further promised that he would confer upon Dulmo if he were successful "such titles of honor as would appear to us to be reasonable"—a reflection of Columbus's ambition to be viceroy and admiral. One clause in particular shows a keener interest in the generation-old search for islands:

In the event that he cannot conquer the said islands and mainland, We shall send with the said Fernão Dulmo men and fleets of ships with Our power to effect the same, and the said Fernão Dulmo shall always be Captain General of the said fleets, and is acknowledged by Us always for his King as Our subject.

Dulmo evidently found the enterprise too much to accomplish alone. Three months later he brought in João

Afonso do Estreito of Madeira as a partner, praying that the king admit him to a share of the enterprise and the profits, on certain conditions. Estreito was required to provide two good caravels fully equipped and provisions for six months, to be ready to sail on March 1, 1487, while Dulmo would engage pilots and mariners for the fleet and pay their wages. Estreito would command one caravel and Dulmo the other, and for forty days after their departure, Dulmo was to be captain general and set the course for both caravels and possess all lands discovered in that space of time, after which Estreito was to be captain general and possess all other lands discovered thereafter and until their return to Portugal. The king confirmed all this, and much more in the way of detail, on July 24 and August 4, 1486, promising that Estreito would enjoy all such privileges, liberties, and franchises in his share of the discoveries as Dulmo had been granted originally. Perhaps for this voyage the king congratulated himself on driving a much better bargain than he could have concluded with Columbus, who demanded so much more.

Whether Dulmo and Estreito ever undertook their expedition is not known. The only further mention of it is one oblique reference in Las Casas, who says that the pilot Pedro de Velasco told Columbus that on the voyage he took with Diogo de Teive in 1452, they saw land to the west of Ireland that they believed was the land that "Hernan Delinos" sought to discover, "as shall presently be told." Hernan Dolinos is most likely a Spanish form of Fernão Dulmo. Unfortunately, Las Casas neglects to tell more, and Dulinos's story has perished. It is not difficult to imagine why Dulmo and Estreito did not succeed if they did sail. The month of March, in which they proposed to sail, is a bad one for sailing westward from the Azores, for it is the month of tempestuous west to northwest winds.

The Dulmo-Estreito expedition was the last effort of the Portuguese, of which we have any record, to discover new lands in the west before the first voyage of Columbus. And there may well be some connection between their failure and the cordiality of King João's letter of March 20, 1488, to Columbus, who by that time was already living in Spain.

There is no doubt that the westward voyages of the Portuguese were made possible by contemporary technical advances. Improvements in shipbuilding, progress in the pilot's art culminating in navigation by the stars, development of chart making leading to the introduction of the scale of latitudes, study of weather and ocean current conditions, and the consequent tracing of the best routes taking into account the winds and currents of each area—all these factors made it possible to create a real system of high-seas navigation in the Atlantic, while the old system of sailing characteristic of coastal navigation, by dead reckoning only, continued to be used in the Mediterranean. Columbus came on the scene precisely when half a century of progress in these spheres was leading to spectacular practical results, at the outset of what has been described as the period of great sea discoveries.

Columbus's Appeals for Royal Support. Not long after the birth of Columbus's first son, Diego, in Porto Santo, his wife died and Columbus returned to Lisbon. It was during this period that Columbus sailed one or more times to the west coast of Africa, which the Portuguese called Guinea, where they were engaged in trade and in building a fortified factory or trading post at São Jorge da Mina. It was on his voyages to West Africa with the Portuguese that he observed that the winds in this area blew predominantly from the northeast, which is ideal for running down a latitude in a westerly direction. He, as well as the Portuguese who had preceded him, had discovered that phenomenon, the northeast trade winds, upon which the economy of Europe was to depend for centuries to come. At any rate, it must have been on these voyages under the Portuguese flag, if not before, that he became a proficient navigator.

No one can say for certain at what moment Columbus conceived the idea of sailing westward across the Atlantic to reach the Indies. But it must have been on his mind during the early years he spent in Lisbon. The best evidence of this is to be found in the correspondence he is known to have had with a Florentine physician, Paolo dal Pozzo Toscanelli. In 1474, Toscanelli corresponded with a canon of Lisbon cathedral, Fernão Martins, who had been trying to convince King Afonso V that there was a quicker way to the Indies than around the southernmost point of Africa. Toscanelli, who took the writings of Marco Polo very seriously, believed that the earth was a great deal smaller than it actually is. Some time later, perhaps in 1481, Columbus wrote to Toscanelli, enclosing a sphere with his letter, in which he expressed a desire to open communications with the East by a direct voyage west across the Atlantic. Toscanelli sent him a chart based on his conception of the earth, largely derived from Marco Polo's account of the Far East, and enclosed with it a copy of the letter he had earlier sent to Fernão Martins. In that letter, Toscanelli had maintained that a course west out of Lisbon would bring the navigator to the Chinese province of Mangi (Man-tzu, a territory south of the Yellow River conquered by the Mongols in 1276) after about 8,000 kilometers (5,000 miles)—though 18,000 kilometers (11,000 miles) would have been nearer the mark—and "passing by the island of Antilia, after only two thousand miles [thirty-two hundred kilometers] he would reach 'Cipangu,'" the Japan that Marco Polo had described, an island rich in all precious metals and stones, which stirred Columbus's imagination.

But the important thing that Columbus obtained from Toscanelli, apart from the prestige of having an eminent scholar approve his enterprise, was the Florentine's approval of Marco Polo. Columbus, however, thought that the ocean was even narrower than Toscanelli supposed. At any rate, by the time that Columbus returned from his voyage to Africa, probably in 1484, he was ready to make an amazing proposition to King João II of Portugal.

Columbus's proposal to João II. João, who succeeded his father Afonso V in 1481, was undoubtedly the right man for Columbus to approach with his project of a great voyage to the west. Known in history as João the Perfect, he was as ambitious for his country overseas as he was determined to ensure Portugal's stability by curbing the power of the nobles at home. Unfortunately, the state of the kingdom of Portugal was such that João was far too preoccupied in the 1480s with potential civil war and disputes with Spain to devote much time to the extension of Portuguese sea exploration. But it is evidence enough of his eagerness to promote such adventures that he agreed in 1484 to consider the plan of the importunate Genoese.

Apparently, Columbus experienced none of the difficulties in obtaining an audience with King João that he was later to encounter in meeting with Isabel and Fernando. He may have used the influence and connections of his powerful in-laws, for he knew that without the backing of the king there could be no hope of his securing the ships and men he needed for the voyage.

Armed with all the information he had been collecting over the years, Columbus appeared at court. He was now thirty-one years old. He proposed to João II an expedition that would sail west into the Atlantic, rather than following the current Portuguese practice of attempting the circumnavigation of Africa. He would thus reach the desired lands and "the kingdom of the Great Khan" by the direct westward route. Actually, there is no direct evidence concerning the exact nature of his proposal. But that he presented his proposal to João of Portugal is confirmed by his son Fernando and by Las Casas, as well as by the Portuguese chroniclers Rui de Pina, García de Resende, and João de Barros who, years later, after Columbus's return from his first voyage, alluded to it.

According to Las Casas's account of that momentous meeting, Columbus held out a promise of rich rewards: "He proposed the project to the King, which was as follows: that going by way of the west toward the south he would discover great lands, islands and terra firma, all very prosperous, rich in gold and silver, pearls, and precious stones, and an infinite number of people."

Columbus's own demands in return for the vast fortune that he was offering King João were in keeping with the grandiosity of his ideas. First he thought that he should be granted nobility, which carried with it the right for him and his descendants to be called "Dom" and to be armed as a knight with golden spurs. He asked that he be granted the title of Grand Admiral of the Ocean Sea with all the same honors, privileges, rights, and dues enjoyed by the grand admiral of Castile. He wanted to be appointed the "perpetual viceroy and governor of all the islands and lands which he might discover or which might be discovered by anyone else under his command." He also demanded "a tenth of all the income accruing to the king from all the gold, silver, pearls, precious stones, metals, spices, and other valuable things, and from every kind of goods bought, exchanged, discovered, or acquired within the region of his admiralty." He concluded by stipulating that in any future expeditions he should have the right to put up one-eighth of the expenses in return for receiving one-eighth of the profit.

These demands were the same as those he presented years later to the Catholic monarchs and are not confirmed in the Portuguese sources. Some critics have even accused Las Casas of merely copying these demands as they appear in the Santa Fe Capitulations made to the Catholic monarchs. But Antonio Ballesteros Beretta, a modern Columbus scholar, believes they are authentic because if Columbus could have made the same demands in Castile, when he was weary and disconsolate after years of waiting, without giving up one of his points, he must have been even firmer in Portugal, where his situation was clearer and he was not worn out or disillusioned. Ballesteros cannot explain why Columbus asked for the same rights as an admiral of Castile, a demand that certainly would have offended the Portuguese.

Columbus's demands and overbearing manner were so outrageous that the king had his doubts about having anything further to do with him. Nevertheless, João showed him special consideration by referring his proposal to a scientific council. The council returned an unfavorable report. However, it appears that the king remained interested in the project and determined to put it to the test himself. It was said that he secretly chartered two caravels and ordered their masters to sail westward from the Azores to find the great Island of the Seven Cities, the legendary Antilia. The caravels returned after being heavily buffeted by head winds and the project was abandoned. The Portuguese who rejected Columbus's project did only what might have been expected of any well-ordered government dealing with an adventurer of vast pretensions but meager attainments.

Charles E. Nowell, in his penetrating article, "The Rejection of Columbus by John of Portugal," examines the possible reasons for the rejection. First, Columbus failed to give the king's advisers a convincing demonstration that a westward route to the Indies existed. Since Columbus lacked the requisite intellectual background to impress the king's learned councilors, he could offer them no respectable calculation regarding the westward distance to Cipangu. Second, João made it his policy to distinguish between national and private enterprise. His treasury financed the explorations down the African coast that year by year were bringing him closer to his goal of rounding Africa. This constituted a national enterprise. The men whom he sent on these expeditions, like Diogo Cão or Bartolomeu Dias, were royal agents, sent to do a particular task; none of these discoverers acquired private rights in the regions they explored. Columbus wanted to be the king's agent, but he also wanted to make his terms in advance, contrary to established policy. His projected voyage fell rather within the category of private initiative, the Portuguese pattern of discovery in the Atlantic and its islands. Without money and financial backing, Columbus proposed to enter a field hitherto dominated by private entrepreneurs, and, even more, he claimed rewards far greater than any other entrepreneurs had thought of demanding. In keeping with João's policy, the private speculator had to finance himself. On successful completion of the type of discovery voyage proposed by Columbus, he would generally have received proprietary rights and some economic privileges, but nothing like the noble title of Dom that Columbus demanded, or the rank of an admiral, or ships supplied by the Crown. Private discovery missions cost the Crown nothing; hence permission for them was easily granted. But for the Crown to outfit an adventurer and then to step into the background in that adventurer's favor was out of the question.

Although Columbus remained on friendly terms with the king, he knew that it was time to look elsewhere for a patron. With his dreams of financial success in ruins, and with his even greater dream of discovering the Indies dismissed by the king's advisers, Columbus left for Spain, clandestinely, it was said, to avoid his creditors. Interestingly enough, Fernando attributes the reason for his father's departure from Portugal to the fact that King João had secretly sent an expedition to where his father had proposed to sail, and as a result, he "formed such a hatred for that city and nation that he resolved to depart for Castile with his little son Diogo . . . ," his wife having died in the meantime. He took ship for Palos, not far from Huelva, where his wife's sister Violante lived, intending, it is believed, to leave the child with her.

Second approach to João II. But Columbus was not finished with Portugal. Near the end of 1487, he contacted King João again. Writing from Seville, he asked João to be allowed to return to Portugal under a safe conduct that would protect him—it is presumed from his creditors, though there is no mention of them in the king's letter. Columbus's letter to the king is lost, but it is obvious from the king's reply that it was the future Admiral who had initiated the correspondence. Writing from Avis on March 20, 1488, João urged him to return to Portugal in an extremely cordial letter.

On the outside the letter is addressed to "Christovam Collon [sic], our special friend in Seville." Inside it reads:

Christoval Colon [sic]: We, Dom Joham, by the grace of God King of Portugal, the Algarves on this side and beyond the sea in Africa, and lord of Guinea, send you warm greetings:

We have seen the letter you wrote us and we thank you very much for the good will and affection expressed therein for our service.

As for your coming here, we not only desire you to come, for the reasons you give, but for other reasons as well, for we will have great need of your ability and fine talent. Therefore, we would be very pleased if you would come. Moreover, all matters concerning you will be taken care of in such a way that you must needs be content.

And if by chance you are in fear of our justice officials owing to some obligation you have incurred, we, by means of this letter, can assure you that during your coming, your stay, and departure, you will not be arrested, detained, accused, summoned, or prosecuted, for any reason whatsoever, under the civil and criminal code. By virtue of this selfsame letter, we hereby command all our justice officials to comply with these orders as set forth herein. Therefore, we beg you and urge you to come soon and not to be reluctant to do so for any reason whatsoever. Moreover, we will be grateful to you for doing so and will regard it as being of great importance to our service.

Written at Avis, on the xx day of March in the year 1488. The King.

Columbus did not know at the time that he wrote to the king that two years before, in 1486, João had sent another expedition down the coast of Africa. This one was led by Bartolomeu Dias, who had been dispatched from Lisbon with three caravels to continue the southward exploration of Africa beyond the limits that had already been reached by Diogo Cão. At the time that Columbus wrote to the king, Dias had been away for many months; he had rounded the Cape of Good Hope and discovered the dream of Henry the Navigator—the sea route to the Indies. Columbus was in Lisbon in December 1488 when Dias returned triumphant. It must have been a moment of intolerable bitterness for him, for the prospect of reaching Asia by way of Africa meant the end of any chance he might have had of arousing the king's interest in his own project for a westward route. Once again, Columbus left Lisbon for Spain, a disappointed man.

Perhaps it was for his own good fortune that he was rejected by the king of Portugal. Had his project been accepted, he probably would have set out in high latitudes from the Azores, as earlier Portuguese explorers before him had done. In that event, he would have been forced to buck the westerlies and we would have heard no more

of him. But sailing for Spain, as he did in 1492, he had no choice but to depart from the Canaries, a Spanish possession, where he picked up the trade winds that blew him, on an almost perfect course, to America.

Unexpected Return to Portugal. Columbus returned to Portugal on an unexpected visit that put his life and the success of the 1492 voyage in jeopardy. In February 1493, on the first homeward-bound voyage from America, Columbus was forced to make two unscheduled stops in Portuguese territory before returning to his home port in Spain.

The island of Santa Maria in the Azores. Overtaken by a storm as he was approaching the Azores, he put in on the island of Santa Maria in the Azores. Another storm, a few days after his departure from the Azores, forced him to land at Lisbon.

The Portuguese chroniclers of the period have described the stopover in Lisbon in great detail, but they have nothing to say about Columbus's brief stop in the Azores during the ten days from February 18 to 28, 1493, which Columbus himself describes in his log. On February 10, Columbus reckoned that his two ships were about on the latitude of Flores in the Azores. Two days later a gale blew up and *Pinta* and *Niña* ran before the wind under bare poles. On the night of February 13, the two ships lost contact with each other. Battered by the storm and drenched by the sea, the crew of *Niña* prayed and three times drew lots to see which of them should make pilgrimages of devotion to Santa María de Guadalupe, to the shrine of Santa María de Loreto, and to Santa Clara de Moguer, not far from their home port of Palos. Finally, all hands vowed to make a pilgrimage, clad only in their shirts, to the nearest church of Our Lady at whatever place they should first make land.

The island of Santa Maria was sighted shortly after sunrise on Friday, February 15, and an unsuccessful

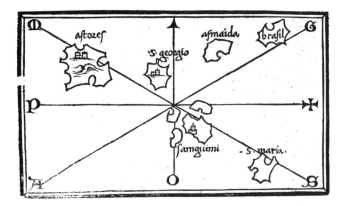

MAP OF THE AZORES. From Benedetto Bordone's *Isolario*. Venice, 1528.

attempt to anchor was made on February 15. It had never been Columbus's intention to call at the Azores and he had carefully avoided all the Portuguese islands, but ship and seamen had taken such a beating that he decided to take a chance in the hope of obtaining wood, water, fresh provisions, and a bit of rest.

After sunrise on Monday, February 18, Columbus anchored on the northern side of the island and sent the boat ashore. The local people told his sailors that they were on the island of Santa Maria in the Azores and showed them where they could find a safer anchorage for the caravel on the other side of a high rocky cape called Punta dos Frades. After sunset on Monday, February 19, three islanders visited the ship. Since the next day was Shrove Tuesday, they brought, according to Columbus's log,

> fowls and fresh bread, and other things that were sent by the captain of the island, who was called Juan de Castañeda [João de Castanheira in Portuguese], saying that he knew me very well, and that as it was night he did not come to call, but at daybreak he would come and bring more refreshments with the three men of the caravel who remained there, whom he did not send back because of the great pleasure that he had with them, hearing about events of the voyage.

Informed that there was a little shrine near the sea dedicated to Our Lady, Columbus decided to fulfill the third vow that had been made at the height of the storm. At daybreak on Tuesday, February 19, he sent half the crew ashore in *Niña*'s one boat, asking the messengers who returned with them to seek out the village priest to say mass, after which the men were to return to the ship while Columbus with the other half of the crew went ashore to hear mass. As the first group was at mass, clad only in their shirts, they were taken prisoner by the villagers, acting under Castanheira's orders.

About eleven in the morning, Columbus, anxiously awaiting the return of his boat from the village that he was unable to see, decided that either the boat had been wrecked on the rocks or the crewmen detained. Weighing anchor, he sailed *Niña* around Punta dos Frades and came upon a troop of well-armed men commanded by Castanheira. They came out to the ship with the obvious intention of arresting Columbus. Columbus attempted to lure Castanheira aboard *Niña* in order to hold him hostage, while Castanheira tried to lure Columbus into the boat in order to take him prisoner along with the men who had been captured at prayer. Columbus said that he was "the Admiral of the Ocean Sea and Viceroy of the Indies which belong to their Highnesses," and that he would return to Castile with half his crew if the others were not released and see to it that the offending Portuguese were suitably punished. Castanheira replied

that "they did not recognize the King and Queen of Castile here, nor their letters, nor were they afraid; rather, they would have us understand that this is Portugal, and they said this in a threatening way." Rash and angry words were exchanged before Columbus returned to anchor in the harbor where he had first arrived, the anchorage that the villagers had warned him about.

On February 20, *Niña*'s cables broke and Columbus made sail for the island of São Miguel, which is usually visible from Santa Maria in fair weather; because of foul weather *Niña* was unable to reach the island by nightfall. Also, it was very difficult to handle the ship because only three of the crew left aboard were seamen; the rest—soldiers, landsmen, and Indians—were not very useful for navigating the ship. At sunrise on February 21, Columbus decided to return to Santa Maria and see whether he could negotiate the release of his crewmen. As *Niña* lay at anchor in the bay east of Punta dos Frades, the *Niña*'s boat appeared, carrying five of the captured seamen, two priests, and a notary public. The priests and the scribe scrutinized the Admiral's credentials, expressed themselves satisfied, and granted him free entry. Castanheira released the rest of *Niña*'s crew, who said that the real reason for their release was Castanheira's failure to capture Columbus; the seamen alone were too unimportant for him, they said.

With its full crew restored, *Niña* left this uneasy anchorage for the last time on February 23, and sailed around Santa Maria to the west, in search of a good place to take on wood and stone ballast. However, since the weather was favorable for going to Castile, Columbus gave up the idea of taking on ballast and ordered the course to the east. Before daylight, *Niña* was well beyond the inhospitable island. A few days later he ran into another, more violent storm that carried *Niña* to the mouth of the Tagus River. On the night of March 2 and 3, the fifth day of the storm, a violent squall split the sails and placed *Niña* in grave danger because, as Columbus knew by dead reckoning and the look of things, he was very near the coast of Portugal. At 7:00 P.M. on March 3, the seamen sighted land dead ahead by the light of a full moon. At daybreak on March 4, Columbus recognized the Rock of Sintra, north of the mouth of the Tagus River. He decided to enter the Tagus because, as he says in his logbook, he could do nothing else. This stopover in Portugal was to cause him some difficulties on his return to Spain where he was unfairly accused of having visited Lisbon for the express purpose of betraying the Catholic monarchs, a charge repeated by a number of modern writers.

The court of João II. Shortly after sunrise, *Niña* entered the Tagus estuary and came to anchor at 9:00 A.M. on Monday, March 4, off the beach of Restelo. Learning that the king was in the country, Columbus requested permission to proceed upstream to Lisbon. He cited his credentials from Fernando and Isabel, and informed King João that he was coming from the Indies and not from Guinea. Having written to King João, Columbus added a postscript to the letter to Fernando and Isabel announcing his discovery that he had composed at sea and dated at Santa Maria on February 15, and sent it off to Spain.

Moored near *Niña* was a great Portuguese warship whose master was Bartolomeu Dias, discoverer of the Cape of Good Hope. Dias came aboard *Niña* and ordered Columbus to return with him and give an account of himself to the captain of the warship, Álvaro Damão. Columbus stood on his dignity as Admiral of the Ocean Sea and replied that he could not come unless by force of arms; he also refused to allow Vicente Yáñez Pinzón, captain of *Niña*, to convey the ship's papers to Damão. Dias then asked to see his papers, which Columbus was only too glad to show him. After Dias made his report to Damão, Damão then came aboard *Niña* himself to pay a visit of courtesy to the new Admiral of the Ocean Sea and offered to do all he commanded.

On Friday, March 8, 1493, Martim de Noronha, a gentleman of the king's court, delivered a letter from King João himself inviting the Admiral to visit him. The king ordered his agents to supply *Niña* with provisions and with whatever stores she needed at his expense. Mules were provided by Noronha, and Columbus, on starting out, probably took with him some of the gold and a few other souvenirs he had found in the Caribbean, as well as some of the captive Indians, to exhibit at court. He found the king at the monastery of Santa Maria das Virtudes (Saint Mary of the Virtues), situated in a pinewood at the foot of the Vale do Paraíso (Paradise Valley), a rich farming region about fifty kilometers (thirty miles) from Lisbon, where the court had gone to escape an outbreak of the plague. The meeting of the king and the Admiral, both men of high courage and inflexible will, must have been dramatic. Columbus was then forty-two years old, King João thirty-eight. Columbus had seen him as a petitioner in 1484 or 1485 and had been rejected; he had been summoned by him to court in 1488 and had again been dismissed.

Columbus gave an account of their meeting in his log for March 9:

> The King ordered that I should be received with great honor by the principal personages of his household, and he himself received me with great honor and showed me much respect, asking me to sit down and talking very freely with me. He told me that he would order everything done which would be of use to your Highnesses [the Catholic monarchs] even more fully than if it were for his own service. He indicated that he was greatly pleased that the voyage had been accomplished successfully, although he understood that in the capitulation

between the Sovereigns and himself the conquest belonged to him. I told him that I had not seen the capitulation and did not know anything other than that the Sovereigns had commanded me not to go to La Mina [São Jorge da Mina] nor to any part of Guinea, and that this had been proclaimed in all of the ports of Andalusia before I started on the voyage. The King graciously responded that he was certain that there would be no need for mediators in this matter. He made me the guest of the Prior of Crato, who was the most important person there, and from whom I received many honors and favors.

There are several other accounts of his interview with King João written by three Portuguese chroniclers that give a somewhat different version of what took place at court that day. The first was written by Rui de Pina (1440?–1533?), who not only was present at court when Columbus arrived, but also took part in the diplomatic negotiations between Spain and Portugal over the boundaries of their respective discoveries. In his *Chronicle of King John II*, Pina reports that on March 6, 1493, an Italian by the name of Christovam Colombo dropped anchor in the port of Lisbon, inbound from a voyage of discovery to the islands of Cipangu and Antilia. He had with him a few natives of those lands as well as gold and some other things he had found there. He had been given the title of admiral of those islands. The king summoned him to Vale do Paraíso. Pina claims that João II was both dismayed and chagrined by Columbus's visit, not only because he believed that the discovery fell within his sphere of influence, but also because the Admiral's attitude was arrogant and the account of his discovery greatly exaggerated. Columbus upbraided the king for having refused to accept his enterprise of the Indies when first proposed. Pina reports that the courtiers were so outraged by his behavior that they suggested that he be secretly murdered, which would put an end to his discovery, but the king would not hear of it; on the contrary, he dismissed the Admiral with honor and favor.

Garcia de Resende (c. 1470–1536) also describes the king's interview with Columbus in his chronicle of the reign of King João II (1533). Much of what he wrote was copied from Rui de Pina, except for an addition that extolls the role of the king in directing the negotiations of the Treaty of Tordesillas from afar, and in wisely distributing his bribes in order to obtain the favorable terms he sought for the treaty.

The best description of Columbus's visit to Portugal in 1493 was written by João de Barros (c. 1496–1570). The first volume of his *Decades of Asia*, published in 1552, contains the most detailed account of the visit. Barros repeats much of the same information found in the works of Pina and Garcia de Resende. He describes Christóvão Colom not as an Italian, as do his two predecessors, but as a Genoese (which is important in view of the later polemics over the nationality of Columbus), and claims that the reason King João sent for him was that he knew him personally and he was aware of the fact that King Fernando of Castile had sent Columbus on a voyage of discovery about which he wanted to hear. Columbus came to court, according to Barros, not so much to please the king as to spite him. He adds that the king was quite perturbed when he saw the natives who accompanied Columbus because they fit the description he had been given of the Indians of Asia. He explains that Columbus had "imagined," as he told the king in 1484 or 1485, that he could reach Cipangu by sailing west because of his reading of Marco Polo, what he had heard of the western discoveries made in the days of Prince Henry the Navigator, the discussions he had had with the Portuguese mariners about their past discoveries, and his reliance on the experience of foreign navigators. Barros goes on to speak of King João's thwarted attempt to send an armada in search of Columbus's discovery, the disputes that arose between Spain and Portugal over the location of the discovery, and the dispatching of embassies from one kingdom to the other. After more than a year of procrastination on the part of the Spanish sovereigns who were waiting for Columbus to return from his second voyage with more specific information about the location of his discovery, the Treaty of Tordesillas, which divided the non-Christian world into two zones of influence, was finally signed, on June 7, 1494. In principle, the treaty followed the papal bull issued in 1493 by Pope Alexander VI, which fixed the demarcation line along a circle passing 100 leagues west of the Cape Verde Islands and through the two poles. This division gave the entire New World to Spain, but Africa and India to Portugal. However, at the objection of the Portuguese, the Treaty of Tordesillas, as it was finally signed, shifted the demarcation line to a circle passing 370 leagues west of the Cape Verde Islands, thus giving Portugal a shadowy claim to Brazil.

From these three Portuguese accounts, it is apparent that it must have been with smoldering anger that King João heard a firsthand relation of Columbus's voyage.

A stopover in Madeira. Columbus visited Portuguese territory one last time, again unexpectedly, in Madeira in 1498, on his third voyage to America. Spain was at war with France and it was rumored that a French armada was lying in wait for him and his six ships off Cape St. Vincent. The Admiral sailed south, passing near the African coast, instead of following a direct course for Porto Santo. Eight days later, on June 7, 1498, his fleet arrived in Porto Santo, after having sailed at least 1,050 kilometers (650 miles). When Columbus decided to take on wood, water, and provisions, and to hear mass, the inhabitants confused his fleet with that of the French corsairs and fled inland with their flocks. Finding no one in Porto Santo, Columbus sailed for Madeira that same night, reaching Funchal, no more than sixty kilometers (forty miles) from Porto Santo,

on June 10. Las Casas writes that Columbus "was given a very fine reception and much entertainment, for he was well known there, having been a resident thereof for some time."

That was the last known time that Columbus set foot on Portuguese soil.

BIBLIOGRAPHY

Ballesteros Beretta, Antonio. *Cristóbal Colón y el descubrimiento de América.* Barcelona and Buenos Aires, 1945.

Bradford, Ernle. *Christopher Columbus.* New York, 1973.

Columbus, Ferdinand. *The Life of the Admiral Christopher Columbus by His Son Ferdinand.* Translated by Benjamin Keen. New Brunswick, N.J., 1959.

Fuson, Robert H. *The Log of Christopher Columbus.* Camden, Me., 1987.

Las Casas, Bartolomé de. *Historia de las Indias.* 3 vols. Edited by Agustín Millares Carlo. Mexico and Buenos Aires, 1951.

Madariaga, Salvador de. *Christopher Columbus: Being the Life of the Very Magnificent Lord Don Cristobal Colon.* 3d ed. New York, 1967.

Morison, Samuel Eliot. *Admiral of the Ocean Sea: A Life of Christopher Columbus.* 2 vols. Boston, 1942.

Morison, Samuel Eliot. "Christophe Colomb et le Portugal." *Boletim da Sociedade de Geografia* (July–September 1956): 269–278.

Morison, Samuel Eliot. *Portuguese Voyages to America in the Fifteenth Century.* Cambridge, Mass., 1940.

Mota, Avelino Teixeira da. "Christopher Columbus and the Portuguese." *Journal of the American Portuguese Cultural Society* 2, nos. 1, 2, 3 (Winter, Spring, Summer 1968): 1–22.

Nowell, Charles E. "The Rejection of Columbus by John of Portugal." *University of Michigan Historical Essays* (1937): 25–44.

Quinn, David B. "Columbus and the North." Paper delivered at University of California, Los Angeles, June 6, 1989.

Ruddock, Alwyn A. "Columbus and Iceland: New Light on an Old Problem." *Geographical Journal* 132, part 2 (June 1970): 177–189.

Sale, Kirkpatrick. *The Conquest of Paradise: Christopher Columbus and the Columbian Legacy.* New York, 1990.

Taviani, Paolo Emilio. *Christopher Columbus: The Grand Design.* Translated by William Weaver. Edited by John Gilbert. London, 1985.

Vigneras, L. A. "Columbus in Portugal." Paper presented at the first annual meeting of the Society for the History of Discoveries, Washington, D.C., December 28, 1961.

REBECCA CATZ

Columbus in Spain

Columbus was a Genoese businessman living in exile most of his adult life. His ideas and hopes had been shaped by his Italian background, but circumstances in the eastern Mediterranean dictated that he could not realize these hopes in the city of Genoa. During his early maritime experience, Columbus had witnessed in the Black and Aegean seas the ending of two centuries of Genoese trade with Asia. He kept the hope of Asian trade alive by transferring the Italian dream to Castile, the most dynamic and prosperous monarchy in Europe. In Spain he found employment at the highest levels possible to a foreigner, royal interest in his Asian trade proposal, government officials with the expertise to expedite such a venture, and experienced seamen to carry it to completion. These resources and benefits impelled Columbus to spend more of his adult life in Spain than in any other country—most of the twenty years from late 1485 until his death in 1506.

A Move to Spain. Settling in Spain was not his original intent. Genoese businessmen lived in constant motion, moving by sea from one country to another in order to buy low and sell high. Even after a merchant married and established a permanent household, home for him was a base of operations, not a place of continuous residence. Columbus had many reasons to base himself in Portugal; by the early 1480s he was a family man, with Portuguese wife, children, household, and business based in Lisbon, and he was a Portuguese citizen by virtue of his marriage. Yet he transferred his base of business operations from Portugal to Spain in late 1485. The move was more than the usual business trip. Things were not going well in Portugal for his wife's family, who were friends and followers of the duke of Braganza. In May 1483, King João II had had the duke of Braganza executed for treason, and in August 1484, the king personally executed the duke of Viseu, the queen's brother. Portuguese politics may well have been a factor in Columbus's decision to move to Spain.

His years there were very long for an international merchant, but conditions in Castile were particularly favorable for an experienced trader. King Fernando and Queen Isabel needed supplies and provisions for two great projects. The royal children were growing up, and all five of them married between 1490 and 1500. Their parents wanted to supply luxury gifts, clothing, and furnishings of premium quality for trousseaus and wedding festivities on an unprecedented scale. At the same time, the monarchs were carrying on a war of conquest against the Kingdom of Granada. From 1482 to 1492, Castilian armies commanded by Fernando were conquering one Muslim city after another, and they needed to sell their war booty. For the Genoese, the war required an adjustment because their traditional trade with Muslim Málaga dropped off sharply. Increasingly, the Italians dealt with the monarchy, basing themselves principally in the city of Seville.

Columbus had traded in Spanish ports since he first went to sea in the early 1470s. The most logical place to set himself up in Spain was the city of Cádiz. It was well known to him as the traditional stopover on Genoese voyages from Chios to northern Europe, and there was at hand an advantageous person to work with, a Castilian businessman with influence at the royal court. On the north shore of Cádiz Bay lay the town of Puerto de Santa María, which belonged to the duke of Medinaceli. The duke had developed the shipping business in this port, and in the 1480s he was developing the village of Rota, on the peninsula opposite Cádiz, into another important port. He put Columbus on his staff, presumably employed in his shipping business.

Columbus became much more than just a member of the duke's staff, because he had a startling proposal to make. The idea had developed in response to events he had observed at the Portuguese royal court in Lisbon. In May 1485 he witnessed an important event in the Portuguese search for a way to Asia. A land navigator, José Vizinho, returned from an epic trek across Africa and gave King João a report on the distance across Africa at the equator. (The Portuguese had earlier sought an opinion on this subject from an Italian scientist in Florence, Paolo dal Pozzo Toscanelli.) Vizinho's information led João to the conclusion that the distance and obstacles across Africa were so great that an overland route linking the Atlantic and the Indian oceans was not commercially feasible. The Portuguese turned their efforts once again to finding a sea route south and east around Africa.

Columbus, however, drew a startlingly different conclusion from this same information because, as usual, he underestimated the size of the globe. If Asia extended as far into the ocean as Toscanelli believed, then the Ocean Sea must not be very wide. If Africa turned out to be as long from north to south as it was wide from west to east, the shortest and fastest route to Asia would not be around Africa; it would be directly west across the Ocean Sea. By taking the western route ships could avoid both the long detour around Africa and the trip across the Indian Ocean, going directly to the rich market cities of Cathay. He proposed such a voyage to the duke of Medinaceli. The duke was responsive to the idea and calculated that three or four caravels would be sufficient for a one-year voyage. But then the duke realized that the project was more suitable as a royal enterprise and wrote to his uncle, Cardinal Pedro González de Mendoza, introducing Columbus to the court.

Columbus Enters Royal Service. The year when Columbus left the duke's staff and entered Castilian royal service has been a matter of fierce debate in Columbus scholarship. On January 14, 1493, Columbus wrote in his Diario that he had entered the service of the Spanish monarchs "seven years ago on January 20, this very month." That seems to be a direct statement, but it is problematic. If we count back in the modern way by subtracting 7 from 1493, he would have entered royal service on January 20, 1486, in

Alcalá de Henares, where the monarchs were spending a few days in late January that year. But if Columbus counted both the first and last of the seven years (the method he apparently used in calculating his age in a Genoese document of 1470), then the first service was on January 20, 1487, in the city of Salamanca, where the monarchs were spending the winter. By then, he had been in the duke's service long enough to win the confidence of this important person who could provide him with an introduction to the royal court. The year 1487 is further supported by contemporary documents.

Columbus went to court to propose that the monarchs sponsor an exploratory commercial voyage west to Asia. He must have been very persuasive, because King Fernando and Queen Isabel took him seriously. Spanish monarchs followed a standard procedure with proposals; they appointed a subcommittee of the royal council to make a feasibility study. The chairman of the committee was one of the queen's confessors, Hernando de Talavera, bishop of Ávila. The rest of the committee were royal councillors, experts in subjects important to the success of such a proposal: royal finances, law, and foreign affairs. A Franciscan friar, Antonio de Marchena, who had a reputation as an astronomer, may have been brought in as a scientific expert.

The committee began its deliberations in Salamanca and continued as the royal court resumed its incessant travels around the realms of Fernando and Isabel. On January 30, the monarchs began traveling south on their way to resume the war against Granada. They arrived in the city of Córdoba on March 2, and Isabel established the court there for the duration while Fernando mobilized municipal militias and royal forces for the campaign. Córdoba was the heart of the war effort, the place where supplies and equipment were collected, where administrators planned strategy and dispatched armies to carry it out, and where the royal treasury disbursed payments to suppliers and employees.

In Córdoba, Columbus appeared on the royal payroll, reporting to Bishop Talavera in some activity administered by the queen's comptroller of finances, Alfonso de Quintanilla. On May 5 Columbus received his first payment from the royal treasury—three thousand maravedis—probably for the months of February, March, and April, because royal employees were paid quarterly for services rendered. The payments continued through June 16, 1488, for a total of seventeen thousand maravedis in five payments. This was a small amount of money—about equal to a seaman's annual wages.

Payments from the monarchy provided only part of his income. He was still in business, and in the time-honored Italian tradition, he employed his younger brother, Bartolomé, as his agent in northern Europe. The chronicler

COLUMBUS AT THE COUNCIL OF SALAMANCA. Bronze relief, detail from the Rogers Doors (sculpted by Randolph Rogers, 1858) in the Rotunda of the U.S. Capitol. The doors depict various scenes from the life of Columbus.   ARCHITECT OF THE CAPITOL

Andrés Bernáldez reports that Columbus was selling printed books—a growth industry at that time—in several cities in southern Spain. He probably also sent books to Bartolomé, who was based in Lisbon and trading with France and England.

The nature of Columbus's employment with the Castilian monarchy was never divulged. The journal entries written by the royal accounting clerks give only the vaguest sense of what his service to the monarchy was: "On this day I gave 3,000 maravedis to Christopher Columbus, foreigner, who is here on Her Majesty's secret service." This means not that he was a spy but that the project was still too sensitive to be made public. Several possibilities concerning his activities have been suggested, among them that Columbus had already started some preparations for the momentous voyage west, and that the secrecy was necessary to prevent Portuguese spies from finding out about the project. But this is unlikely because, as Columbus himself complained, the monarchs did not approve the project immediately.

Another suggestion, more credible, is that Columbus was involved in selling war booty for the royal treasury. The monarchs during 1487 and 1488 were following a new strategy, attacking the coast in order to outflank the Muslim capital in Granada and cut it off from trade and assistance from the sea. On May 7, the king set siege to the city of Málaga, which, contrary to the monarchs' expectations, refused to surrender and put up the most stubborn resistance of the entire war. On May 23, Isabel left Córdoba to join Fernando in the royal encampment outside Málaga while the siege dragged on, costing more time and money than the monarchs had anticipated and arousing their determination to deal harshly with the Malagueños once they were defeated. On August 18, the monarchs launched a massive assault against the city and its fortress and then returned to the royal encampment while their troops destroyed the defeated city and enslaved its inhabitants. Ten days after taking this potentially lucrative prize, the queen sent Columbus four thousand maravedis from the royal treasury "so that he could go to the royal encampment at Málaga." The coincidence is probably significant.

In this world of war booty and government contracts, the Genoese were the most famous but by no means the only operators. In Spain Columbus did business with Italians from Florence, Milan, and Naples, and with Castilian, Aragonese, and Portuguese merchants, nobles, and monarchs. Although Columbus was traveling almost constantly, moving merchandise from one city or country to another, his years in Spain are the best-documented period of his life, for wherever Italian businessmen went they left a paper trail. Several hundred Spanish documents by and about Columbus and his business associates, only recently discovered and examined by historians, yield a fairly full picture of Columbus's career during this period. They reveal that Columbus studies published before 1980 were romantic fictions and show that he was, first and foremost, interested in commerce and profit.

If Columbus was involved with the war at all, it may have concerned the transport and sale of enslaved Muslim war captives. He formed a business association with a Florentine merchant in Seville, Juanoto Berardi, who had been engaged in slave trading in Portugal and then moved to Spain about 1485. Berardi would later finance Columbus's huge investment in the momentous 1492 voyage, and the two Italians maintained their association until Berardi's bankruptcy and death in 1495.

A more attractive explanation of Columbus's employment by the Castilian monarchy centers around the queen's primary concern at the time—preparations for the marriage of her eldest daughter, Princess Isabel. A marriage between the Castilian and Portuguese royal families had been anticipated in the Treaty of Alcáçovas that the two monarchies had signed in 1479 ending Portuguese participation in the Castilian succession war. Princess Isabel (born October 7, 1470) was now of marriageable age, and her parents began negotiations for a marriage with the crown prince of Portugal, Afonso. Queen Isabel threw herself into the arrangements with all the force of her personality.

The marriage alliance with Portugal fulfilled Castilian objectives at the highest level, resolving foreign policy issues of overwhelming significance. Negotiations, appropriately, were carried out by high-level diplomats in secrecy. But at another level, the marriage posed an embarrassing dilemma involving Castilian prestige and the queen's personal pride. The Portuguese court prided itself on being the most elegant in Europe. Members of the royal family wore the latest hat fashions from Flanders when having their portraits painted, and they furnished their palaces with luxurious tapestries and tableware.

The Spanish royal family lived in utter simplicity compared to the Portuguese. The Castilian royal court was ambulatory, moving all year except for the coldest winter months. The royal family did not have a residence, except for a couple of hunting lodges and castles, such as the Alcázar in the city walls of Segovia and the fourteenth-century Alcázar Palace that had been built by King Pedro in Seville. In every other place to which they traveled, Fernando and Isabel borrowed someone's house, usually a bishop's palace. When they were on campaign, as they frequently were from 1474 until 1492, they set up camp and lived in tents. If any housewifely impulses stirred in Queen Isabel, she satisfied them with needle and thread; she made and embroidered all King Fernando's shirts.

This level of personal and domestic simplicity would not do for the marriages of her children, and no one could have been more aware of it than the queen; she herself had not had a trousseau because she and Fernando had eloped. Queen Isabel's personal pride was at stake in every aspect of her daughter's wedding, clothing, and future household. Requiring samples of the latest Lisbon fashions and furnishings, she may well have turned to someone like Columbus, who had access to the Portuguese royal court and moved between the two societies at a certain practical level.

In early 1488, he wrote to King João II, asking for permission to return to Portugal under a safe conduct. Columbus and Berardi may also have been offering to sell Muslim slaves to the Portuguese. On March 20, João replied to Columbus's letter, addressing him as "our special friend in Seville," assuring him of royal protection, and urging him to return to Portugal where his services would be appreciated.

Columbus also had powerful personal reasons to return to Portugal; his wife had died during his absence. (Columbus once reminded Queen Isabel that in order to enter her service he had left behind "wife and children whom I never saw again.") But now that he worked for the Castilian queen, he needed guarantees from arrest by the suspicious Portuguese king so that he could settle his wife's estate and pick up his one remaining child in Portugal, Diego.

Although Columbus stayed in Portugal for about two

years, there is no record of his activities in that country either for then or for any other period. Nevertheless, the overall timing and tenor of Spanish documents indicate that he was probably working at least part time on the project that preoccupied Isabel during this period, arrangements for the royal wedding.

On May 12, 1489, Queen Isabel sent a letter to the city council of Seville instructing the city to give free lodging and provisions to Columbus, whom she expected to return to Seville soon. But Columbus did not come, and so he missed the most spectacular Spanish event of the year 1490. The Portuguese envoy arrived in Seville to finalize the marriage contract, and Queen Isabel personally supervised preparations for the wedding festivities, gifts, and bride's trousseau. The bride's table service alone, all of gold and silver, cost 3,277,227 maravedis. Princess Isabel signed the contract in Seville on April 18, 1490, and the festivities were elaborate. The bride's brother, Prince Juan, organized processions, plays and masques, jousts, sports competitions, and banquets. The expenses of costumes, gifts, horse trappings, and food were so great that the monarchs had to borrow money to pay for them.

By the time the contracts were carried to Portugal for Afonso to sign there, the hot summer of southern Spain made travel dangerous. Fernando and Isabel, justifiably as it turned out, could not bring themselves to bid good-bye to their firstborn child until November. The doomed bridegroom and his splendidly costumed entourage met her at the Portuguese border, and the bridal procession moved slowly through an elaborate series of wedding festivities that outshone even the spectacles in Seville. But by July 1491, Prince Afonso was dead, trampled after a fall from his horse during a racing competition. Princess Isabel returned to Castile in widow's garb and was met by her grieving parents in Íllora, just outside Granada.

The Portuguese marriage, in which Castile had invested so much money and hope, had failed, and that failure coincided with Columbus's return to Spain later that year. He was deeply depressed and in desperate financial straits. Despite King João's cordial invitation to him in 1488, the stay in Portugal had left him destitute. He reentered Spain through the port of Huelva, intending to leave his son with his wife's sister Violante (or Briolanja) Moniz and her husband, Miguel Molyart, only to find that the couple had moved. Columbus was now a stranger; no one in the towns of Huelva or nearby Moguer or Palos remembered having seen him before. And his years away apparently affected his ability to speak Castilian; years later, witnesses recalled that he spoke with a heavy foreign accent.

The father and his twelve-year-old son now set out on foot in the direction of Seville. They got as far as the Franciscan monastery of La Rábida and there made friends

La Rábida Monastery.

Patronato Provincial de Tourismo de Huelva.

with the friar Juan Pérez. Columbus's talent for winning the loyalty of expert and well-connected supporters once again served him well; Pérez had trained as a clerk in the queen's treasury office. Pérez sent a letter to the queen, informing her of Columbus's arrival and asking her to permit Pérez to come to court as Columbus's agent and representative.

Receiving a favorable reply two weeks later, Pérez rented a mule from a citizen of the town of Moguer and went to join the court in Santa Fe, where he told the queen that Columbus and his son were ragged, without connections, and without funds. Pérez worked miracles with his old colleagues on the queen's accounting staff. The monarchs sent twenty thousand maravedis in gold coins to Columbus—payment for his two years of service in Portugal.

Proposal for a Western Voyage Revived. Pérez must have also told the monarchs what the Portuguese had learned about Africa. Events in Lisbon had once again stirred Columbus's ambition to find a western route to Asia. He was present at the Portuguese court in December 1488 when Bartolomeu Dias returned from a nearly two-year voyage and announced his discovery of the route around the Cape of Good Hope. Now that Africa had been rounded, the southern route to the Indian Ocean became available to Portuguese shippers. But Columbus drew his own conclusions. Africa extended much farther south than the Portuguese had hoped. They would have direct access to Asian trade, but the new route was not going to be shorter and more profitable than going through the Venetian trading stations in the eastern Mediterranean. The Portuguese king had entered the competition, but he had not won it. The field was still open for the Spaniards.

Now everything seemed in place for Castile to venture forth on a western voyage to Asia. King Fernando had conquered every Muslim city remaining in Spain except the capital itself, Granada. Because this city was completely cut off from supplies and allies, it agreed to capitulate without a fight. Once the Castilian diplomats had established surrender terms with the king of Granada, negotiations between the monarchs and Columbus began in earnest.

Fernando and Isabel were represented in these negotiations by the king's secretary Juan de Coloma, and Friar Juan Pérez acted as agent for Columbus. Coloma and Pérez worked out terms (capitulations) for a business partnership in which the monarchs would venture capital and Columbus would risk his life. Once the negotiators agreed on the terms, Pérez informed Columbus, who left Diego with the friars in La Rábida and traveled to the court on a rented mule. He arrived to see Castilian flags flying over the conquered city's fortresses.

Although he could now enjoy the wonders of one of Europe's largest and most sophisticated consumer societies, Columbus still faced obstacles. The monarchs once again placed the proposal and the new information about Africa before a subcommittee of the royal council. The proposal was the talk of Santa Fe that season; years later a witness named Miguel Toro testified that he had heard many people in the royal encampment discuss the question. The Castilian scientists, lawyers, and mariners were aware that Columbus's assumptions about the size of the globe were incorrect, and they pointed this out again to the subcommittee. The royal council confirmed the judgment of the earlier subcommittee; Columbus was wrong about the distance that a voyage from Spain to Asia would have to cover.

Columbus left the court in discouragement, but at this point King Fernando stepped in and turned the proceedings around. The capture of the city of Granada had changed Castilian perspectives on the possibilities of Asian trade. What the Spaniards found in Granada when they entered the city on January 2, 1492, could only have whetted their appetites for exotic goods. The marketplaces for silk, ceramics, and spices, as well as stunning palaces and mosques, had survived intact because the city had been spared a bombardment. If this was any indication of what Asia's cities held, it was worth the risk of failure. After all, the monarchs themselves would not be in any danger, and Castilian seamen were experienced and competent enough to take care of themselves.

The king, Bishop Talavera, and Bishop Diego de Deza therefore decided to explore the possibilities for financing the voyage as an experiment. Fernando's pensions clerk, Luis de Santángel, found the right argument to persuade the queen. His reasoning was economic: a relatively small investment by the king and queen held the potential for returning great profits. The journey, if it succeeded, could

solve an urgent financial dilemma. The royal treasury faced the continuing expense of further weddings, and within a year the monarchs would need an additional 24,250,000 maravedis, which they had agreed to pay the Muslim king as indemnity for Granada.

Royal officials who had thought there was no money to spare for a risky voyage now began a serious search of the accounts for any overlooked fund. The royal council, in its capacity as supreme court of law, had recently handed down a decision in a case brought by the king of Portugal. João accused seamen from the town of Palos of having violated Portuguese fishing territory off the west coast of Africa. The Castilian royal council found the defendants guilty and sentenced the town council of Palos to provide two caravels for royal service for one year. Queen Isabel thus had two ships available for which she would not have to pay leases.

Still, the voyage would require a cash outlay to charter a third ship and to outfit the ships, buy provisions and equipment, and pay the crews' wages. The monarchs did not have cash on hand, nor did they have any collateral available for a loan. The war had strapped royal finances so seriously that the queen had pawned her jewels to pay for the siege of the city of Baza two years earlier. But Santángel, who was familiar with every intricacy of court finance, pointed out that there was now a peace dividend. The federation (Santa Hermandad) of Castilian cities and towns whose funds had previously been allocated for the war effort had a surplus balance. Santángel advanced 1.4 million maravedis from the Hermandad's treasury to finance the voyage.

For the Spanish monarchs, the venture was purely and simply economic. They were at this point not trying to convert souls or reclaim the Holy Land, as later papal bulls (decrees) made politically necessary; rather, they sought pearls, gold, silver, spices, and other merchandise and resources of any sort. Even Bartolomé de las Casas, himself a fervent missionary to the Indians, reports Santángel's speech to Isabel without the missionary motive that weighed so heavily later. On behalf of the monarchs, Coloma had negotiated a strictly commercial agreement forming a business partnership between the monarchs and Columbus.

Columbus's prime vocation, of course, was international commerce, and his major preoccupation at this point was to secure royal partnership, on the Portuguese model, for a major voyage of commerce to Asia. Columbus, however, wanted more than the usual business partnership. Perhaps inspired by the example of his Portuguese in-laws on Porto Santo, he demanded military and governing authority over any islands or mainland he might discover in the Atlantic, and he wanted these as hereditary offices, not just as lifetime appointments. The granting of hereditary offices, especially to foreigners, went against royal policy, and at first the monarchs refused. On the other hand, Fernando and Isabel wanted to gain legal possession of any islands Columbus might find in the Atlantic. The monarchs intended to settle and develop them as entrepôts and supply stations on the way to Asia. Castile's claims to legal possession would be strongest if Columbus were a royal official, not just the monarchs' business partner.

On April 17, 1492, the monarchs signed the partnership terms known as the Santa Fe Capitulations. The partners agreed that Fernando and Isabel would supply two fully outfitted ships, their crews, and provisions and receive nine-tenths of any revenues. Columbus would provide his management and expertise and receive one-tenth of the revenues. If he wanted to invest money in the enterprise, he could supply up to one-eighth of the cost of outfitting the voyage and receive one-eighth of the profits.

In Granada on April 30, 1492, the monarchs issued a letter patent giving him title to everything he had asked, a document now known as the Capitulations of Granada. They decreed that, once he discovered and took possession of any islands or continent, he would be their hereditary admiral of the Ocean Sea and viceroy and governor of what he discovered, and he and his descendants would be addressed as "sir."

Throughout the negotiations and preparations, the purpose and the destination of the voyage were state secrets. Fernando and Isabel imposed strict security, issuing only sketchy orders to the fleet's outfitters and officers. If the Spanish monarchs had made public their intention of sailing west to Asia, spies would have reported the news immediately to Portugal. Thus the monarchs described the fleet's destination in the vaguest possible terms—"certain parts of the Ocean Sea."

The First Voyage. Columbus and Juan Pérez returned to the monastery on the night of May 22. For the next two months, Columbus worked to equip and man his little fleet in Palos. Fernando and Isabel issued orders implementing their part of the contract, instructing the town council of Palos to provide Columbus with two ships for a year. The town council probably used municipal funds to lease two caravels, *Niña* and *Pinta*, from members of the Pinzón family, who may have been involved in committing the trespass in the first place.

Columbus chartered a third ship, the cargo carrier *Santa María*, which he found in the port of Sanlúcar de Barrameda and leased from its owner, Juan de la Cosa. Columbus apparently did this as his share of financing the voyage, using money from his business partner, Juanoto Berardi. Berardi must have had an enormous amount of cash on hand, or he and Columbus borrowed from investors; Columbus's share of the expedition's total cost

of 4 million maravedis has been estimated at 500,000 maravedis.

Columbus persuaded members of the Pinzón family, a highly regarded shipping dynasty in Palos and Moguer, to serve as captains of two ships, and the Pinzóns then helped persuade other seamen from Palos, Huelva, and Moguer to sign on as crew. The monarchs guaranteed that during their service on the voyage the seamen's private property would not be seized and sold to pay any court-ordered damages and fines. Juan de la Cosa also agreed to go on the voyage, and he may have persuaded *Santa María*'s crew, who were mostly from the Basque lands, to sign on. Columbus himself hired two translators, whom he expected to need in the Indian Ocean where the long-distance shippers and pilots were Arabs.

During the spring and summer, Fernando and Isabel ordered merchants and outfitters to sell supplies and equipment to Columbus at reasonable prices. They instructed government officials not to collect royal taxes on the sales, extending these exemptions to Columbus's purchases for his personal needs. The monarchs issued a total of 1.4 million maravedis to Columbus as reimbursement for the money he spent to buy equipment and provisions.

These preparations for the first voyage were begun at the worst possible time of year for provisioning a fleet. By the time Columbus left Granada on May 12, 1492, the previous year's wheat supplies would have been almost depleted, and the new crop would not be harvested until June and threshed until July. Until the end of the summer, wheat would be scarce for making the ship's biscuit (unsalted twice-baked bread) that would be the staple food during the journey. Columbus had calculated that it would take six weeks to reach Asia. He expected to find islands all along the way but could not count on finding food on them; experience had shown that most Atlantic islands were not inhabited. He had to provision the ships on the assumption that the fleet would not get fresh supplies before reaching its destination. Well aware that Dias had taken almost two years to explore around the tip of Africa and back, Columbus had outfitters and provisioners load enough supplies for a year. The amount of wheat required to prepare ship's biscuit for almost one hundred men for so long must have strained the resources of the countryside around Palos that summer. Fernando and Isabel sent a royal agent, Juan de Peñalosa, to the coast to supervise the collection of supplies and equipment.

Preparations reached a peak of activity in July. Dockworkers loaded carefully packed supplies and merchandise in the holds. Able seamen rigged the sails, tested the lines, and brought their own sea chests on board. Columbus secured a home and revenues for his son

Diego. At his request, the monarchs had appointed Diego a page in the household of Prince Juan, with a yearly allowance for clothing and expenses. But Diego did not go to court yet; he went to live with Columbus's mistress, Beatriz de Arana, for whom Columbus had probably bought a house in Seville.

All was ready in time to take advantage of the safe sailing season at the beginning of August, but the departure had to be postponed for the benefit of the crew. The region around Huelva and Palos celebrated the Feast of the Virgin on August 2, and this was the traditional day to settle accounts, pay annual rents, and sign contracts for the coming year. Columbus paid the crew four months' wages in advance. The crewmen made their final arrangements for their families and property; they gave powers of attorney to their wives, deposed testimony in pending litigation, or became engaged to marry. The fleet left the port of Palos just before dawn on August 3, 1492, put in to the Canary Islands for repairs, fresh water, and additional provisions on August 9, and sailed from the last Spanish port on September 9.

After making landfall in the Bahamas at dawn on October 12, Columbus explored the coasts and named a large number of islands, including Cuba and La Española. He landed and spoke with the islanders in several languages, including Arabic, but without finding a common tongue. Most disappointing of all, he found no cities,

DEPARTURE OF COLUMBUS FROM PALOS. Bronze relief, detail from the Rogers Doors (1858) in the U.S. Capitol.

ARCHITECT OF THE CAPITOL

much less luxury consumer goods. Columbus's imagination did not fail him now; he concluded that these must be offshore islands close to the Asian continent. Since he could find no Great Khan or any other ruler with sovereignty over all of any one island, he felt justified in claiming each as Castilian territory. With the act of possession, he became an officer of the Kingdom of Castile—Admiral of the Ocean Sea and viceroy and governor of whatever he claimed for Castile. He would not prove equal to the challenge.

On the island of La Española Columbus had his first opportunity to act as governor of a Spanish territory. The results were not happy. On Christmas Day, *Santa María* ran aground, and there was insufficient space on the remaining ships for all the crews. Columbus salvaged timbers and planking from *Santa María* to construct a palisaded trading post, which he named La Navidad. Here he left behind thirty-eight unfortunate men under the command of the fleet's marshal, Diego de Arana, cousin of Beatriz. He sailed for Spain on January 4, 1493.

Columbus returned to Palos on March 15, 1493, and began a new style of life in Spain as a noble and honored hero. He could not know how brief this moment of glory would be. The monarchs, who were visiting Fernando's Aragonese domains, immediately summoned him to the royal court in Barcelona. According to the Capitulations, as soon as he had encountered and taken possession of an island, he was transformed from plain Christopher Columbus to Sir Christopher Columbus. In the royal letter, the rulers addressed him as Admiral of the Ocean Sea, viceroy and governor of the islands, and "sir."

Leaving most of the crew in Palos to happy reunions with family and friends, weddings, and years of tale-telling, the Admiral went to Seville with his Indian captives, exotic souvenirs, and some of the crew and then traveled by land to the court. Years later, Bartolomé de las Casas recalled what a deep impression this little entourage had made on his boyhood imagination; he had been fascinated by the large balls the Indians carried, which, when thrown to the ground, bounced back up as high as they started. These were the first samples of rubber Europeans had seen. Las Casas did not mention what he learned later—that throughout the Caribbean basin Indians played a deadly game with these rubber balls, a form of basketball in which the captain of the losing team lost his life.

Fernando and Isabel received Columbus with joy when he finally arrived in Barcelona. Now that the enterprise had become a reality and Columbus had fulfilled the terms of the contract by actually discovering and taking possession of islands, the monarchs and the Admiral rushed to formalize their agreements and prepare a return voyage. In a confirmation drawn up in Barcelona in March 1493, the royal secretaries made public for the first time the partnership contract and privileges of the Capitulations.

A Return Voyage. The first concern of Columbus and the monarchs was a return voyage to resupply the unfortunate crew left behind at La Navidad. Despite Columbus's assurances that the native people were meek and peaceful, no one could expect good relations to continue when the Europeans' provisions ran low. And indeed the crew had to barter for food by offering European goods of little value to Caribbean islanders; most of the European merchandise was wool cloth. The metal tools and equipment were highly desirable to the island people who had none, but European coins had no value in the local barter economy.

Thus, within a month of Columbus's return to Spain, he was instructed to organize another transatlantic crossing. In addition to relieving La Navidad, the monarchs, in the time-honored tradition of Castilian expansion in the Iberian Peninsula, wanted to lay effective claim to the islands by having Castilian citizens settle and cultivate the land. They appointed Juan Rodríguez de Fonseca as their agent to supply and organize the fleets to America. Columbus and Fonseca traveled from Barcelona to Seville together and, in these early stages, cooperated amicably to prepare a massive second voyage. Fonseca proved to be a superb administrator and soon was supervising all government contracts, fleet outfitting, emigration, and navigational matters concerned with America.

Because of Fonseca's amazing endurance and capabilities, the second voyage assumed a scale unimagined for the first. Over twelve hundred men were on board when the ships departed during September 1493. Hundreds of Spanish farmers and artisans, carrying tools, seeds, seedlings, and livestock, went as settlers to the new Castilian territory, and dozens of Italian and Spanish merchants now clamored to invest in contracts with Columbus. His boyhood friend Michele da Cuneo and his youngest brother Diego came from Italy to embark on the voyage. Five or six baptized islanders whom Columbus had brought to Spain six months earlier returned to the Caribbean with him to act as translators. The monarchs insisted that Columbus take a military force of cavalry, and sent the first Christian priests to America, a team of clergy led by Friar Bernardo Buil, to minister to the spiritual needs of the new colony and convert the natives. Other passengers who would later play distinguished roles in the American venture were the Seville physician Diego Alvarez Chanca; the cartographer Juan de la Cosa; Francisco de las Casas, father of Bartolomé; and Juan Ponce de León and Alonso de Ojeda, businessmen turned explorers.

Seventeen vessels of various types and capacities made the journey, Fonseca and Columbus having chartered them from private owners. Several probably belonged to

LETTER FROM QUEEN ISABEL TO COLUMBUS. Dated Barcelona, September 5, 1493. Isabel, with this letter, is returning a book Columbus had lent her and asks that he send her a certain navigation chart, if finished. She further requests that he not delay the departure of his voyage.

ARCHIVO GENERAL DE INDIAS, SEVILLE

the duke of Medinaceli, who had wasted not a minute in asking the monarchs to use his town of Puerto de Santa María as the port for future trade with America.

Everything we know about the preparations for the second voyage indicates a close and harmonious understanding between the Spanish monarchs and the Admiral of the Ocean Sea. Columbus and Fonseca together selected the settlers and merchants who were allowed to embark. Columbus himself drafted the specifications for the voyage, which the monarchs issued in Barcelona on May 29. The instructions covered the conduct of the voyage, the order of departure, the organization of the fleet, the course, and the procedure to be followed on arrival.

Isabel, Fernando, and Columbus all had the same hopes for the second voyage: to establish a permanent Castilian town on the island of La Española. The townspeople would supply food and textiles for sale to colonists, merchants, and natives. With this base, the Admiral could create a royal trading post through which all commerce with Asia would be conducted, collect or mine gold, and provide manpower for further exploration. Optimistic, but sadly mistaken hopes prevailed for the future of Spanish trade with Asia.

The monarchy's second concern was to gain public acknowledgment of Castilian sovereignty over the islands and western Ocean Sea. Publicity was essential. For this, Fernando's secretaries made extracts from the journal Columbus had kept of the first voyage and from a letter he had sent from Lisbon. The king published this Castilian extract, known as the *First Letter from America*, in Barcelona and then commissioned a Latin translation for publication in Rome and other cities throughout Europe. This publicity was intended as groundwork for gaining clear legal title to the islands.

Rather than reopen old disputes with Portugal, the monarchs turned to the only international court of appeals

DEPICTION OF ISLANDS DISCOVERED BY COLUMBUS. Woodcut from the Basel edition of the *First Letter from America*, 1493.

in Christendom, the papacy. Pope Alexander VI issued a series of bulls, dividing the Ocean Sea into Spanish and Portuguese spheres of exploration and settlement and rested legal title to islands and continents squarely on conversion of the native people to Christianity. Fernando and Isabel, by seeking legitimation from the church, transformed the nature of European government in America from its purely commercial Spanish and Italian origins to an enterprise infused with religious objectives. The Admiral, who had now arrived in America, did not yet know about the papal conditions imposed on the enterprise, though he would have approved of them heartily. Instead, he had his hands full coping with the natives and settlers of these islands from which he had promised so much.

By the time the Admiral returned to Seville in June 1496, the hard realities of the Caribbean had become apparent. He could not know that these realities would continue to decimate every Spanish expedition and settlement that followed for the next century, but he certainly knew that the signs were ominous for his own reputation and fortune. Despite his first glowing reports to the monarchs in 1493, the experience of the second voyage showed that the Caribbean environment could not support a European society without major compromises. The native peoples, the soil, and the climate were hostile. All the Admiral's expectations from the islands were disappointed: he found no cities, no money economy, no metal tools, manufactures, or ores.

Meanwhile, his new city—La Isabela—and trading post were floundering. The city council of La Isabela, which convened its first meeting on April 24, 1494, was helpless to avert the impending collapse of the colony. The European crops the Castilian farmers planted—wheat, barley, grapes, olives, cotton, fruits, legumes, and vegetables—failed in the tropical climate, and the food and feed supplies brought from Seville suffered an alarming rate of spoilage. Columbus refused to issue provisions from the stock he kept in the fortified royal warehouse, the only stone structure he built in La Isabela. Desperately hungry, Spaniards moved to island villages and "went native."

The demographic consequences for this and future Spanish colonies were appallingly apparent to the royal court in Castile. The modern popular notion that only Indians suffered from the bacterial and viral infections Europeans brought with them, that Europeans were immune to disease, is both biologically and historically incorrect. The monarchs could see that Europeans in the Americas died in large numbers from disease as well as warfare and shipwreck. Of the ninety crew and officers on the first voyage, thirty-nine died in La Navidad during 1493. Of the twelve hundred crew, staff, and passengers on the second voyage, three hundred died of disease in La Isabela during 1494, despite the heroic care of Dr. Chanca. Columbus himself almost died in this epidemic, and he suffered serious aftereffects for the rest of his life. He also reported to the monarchs that every contingent of Spaniards who went into the interior of the island returned with yellow complexions and seriously ill.

The weather was also hostile. A hurricane in 1495 destroyed all the ships in the harbor of La Isabela, including those that Columbus's financial backer Berardi had leased and loaded with merchandise. Columbus was able to return to Spain only by patching together two ships from the wreckage. He rounded up twelve hundred captured native Americans and selected five hundred for sale in Spain.

Columbus's Reputation Fades. Columbus's report to the monarchs when he arrived in Seville in June 1496 confirmed rumors they had already heard from the resupply ships that had crossed the ocean during 1494 and 1495. Fernando and Isabel gave the Admiral a distracted if not cool reception. They were busy with another royal wedding, even more spectacular and fateful than the first; this one—between Prince Juan and Margaret of Burgundy—would link their family to the Habsburg rulers of the Netherlands, Austria, and the Holy Roman Empire. They were also negotiating a second Portuguese marriage for the widowed Princess Isabel, to Prince Manuel, brother of her deceased husband Afonso. In April, the court celebrated the wedding of Juan and Margaret of Burgundy. Columbus played no part in these crucial negotiations and events.

Instead, the royal government kept him waiting in Seville, where he told his story to Andrés Bernáldez and Juan Rodríguez de Fonseca and tried to sell his American captives in the Seville slave market. Las Casas believed that the monarchs' neglect of the Admiral was based on a positive coolness to his slaving activities. Queen Isabel had developed a neat legal distinction between trading in slaves from other countries and enslaving her own subjects, a distinction that would later be adopted by the English colonists of North America. She suspended the sale of American natives and chastised the slavers.

By the time the monarchs summoned Columbus to court in Burgos and held an audience with him in April 1497, relations were decidedly cool. Furthermore, the royal treasury was once again empty. The monarchs approved a third voyage and granted Columbus some personal favors, but their funding and paperwork for the voyage moved at a glacially slow pace. No American-bound ships embarked from Spain that year, and since there were no sailing ships left in the islands, 1497 was the only year after 1492 that ships have not crossed between Spain and the Americas. Furthermore, when the monarchs

issued orders for the new crossing, they did so with such a profusion of details as to indicate a lack of confidence in the Admiral's judgment and reliability.

In this threatening atmosphere, Columbus returned to the Andalusian coast to organize and launch his third voyage, which left Spain on May 30, 1498, and explored the coast of Venezuela. There the Spaniards encountered rivers whose force and volume emptying into the sea constituted clear evidence that they drained a very large continent, not just an island. No one knew how far north and south this continent might extend or how wide it was.

The only good news came in La Española, where the Spaniards had found gold nuggets, which they were collecting through placer mining. The news started a gold rush. In 1498, for the first time, Columbus had good reason to believe he would realize a profit on his Asian venture. Nevertheless, when he and his brothers returned to Spain in 1500, they were under arrest and accused of mismanaging their responsibilities as royal governors of the Spanish colonies. They had persisted in refusing to distribute provisions from the royal warehouse; their continued denial of self-government to Spaniards who moved out of La Isabela to establish new towns and grow their own food had inspired a rebellion among the colonists. The royal government no longer trusted the Admiral as administrator of Spanish law and justice.

Fernando and Isabel also reconsidered their Asian policy. The monarchs had come to grips with new realities. Columbus had not arrived at the Spice Islands; he had been wrong about the extent of the Ocean Sea, and apparently a continent stood between them and Asia. In the five years from 1492 through 1497, they had invested millions of maravedis and received no profit. In fact, they had lost ships, men, and cargo on an appalling scale for peacetime voyages. They did not necessarily blame Columbus for these losses, but they did decide to develop a new policy. They would no longer send all their ships to one island under the command of one admiral. Instead, they authorized Fonseca to commission one or two voyages each year, financed by corporations of stockholders and commanded by experienced merchant shippers. Between May 1499 and June 1505, eleven of these "Andalusian voyages" systematically explored the coast and islands of South and Central America.

The monarchs permitted Columbus to make a final voyage in 1502, this time as a private venture without their partnership. They continued to address him as Admiral, but they forbade him to exercise any governing powers on the islands he had brought under their sovereignty. His administrative failures in America had diminished his reputation in Spain, and the disastrous fourth voyage damaged public opinion of his seamanship. The heady days of 1493, when all ahead seemed promising and everyone praised his acumen, had come to earth in just ten years. He spent his last years in a shadowy existence in Spain—a distrusted foreigner of faded glory and tarnished reputation.

[See also *Española, La; Granada; Isabel and Fernando; Rábida, La; Reconquista; Settlements*, articles on *La Navidad* and *La Isabela; Spain; Treaty of Alcáçovas; Voyages of Columbus*.]

BIBLIOGRAPHY

Ayala, Juan de. *A Letter to Ferdinand and Isabella, 1503.* Translated by Charles E. Nowell. Minneapolis, 1965.

Ballesteros Beretta, Antonio. *Cristóbal Colón y el descubrimiento de América.* 2 vols. Barcelona and Buenos Aires, 1945.

Cartas de particulares a Colón y relaciones coetáneas. Edited by Juan Gil and Consuelo Varela. Madrid, 1984.

Casas, Bartolomé de las. *Historia de las Indias.* Edited by André Saint-Lu. Vol. 1. Caracas, 1986.

Columbus, Christopher. *Los cuatro viajes: Testamento.* Edited by Consuelo Varela. Madrid, 1986.

Columbus, Christopher. *Textos y documentos completos: Relaciones de viajes, cartas y memoriales.* Edited by Consuelo Varela. Madrid, 1984.

Columbus, Christopher. *The Diario of Christopher Columbus's First Voyage to America, 1492–1493.* Edited and translated by Oliver Dunn and James E. Kelley, Jr. Norman, Okla., 1989.

Columbus, Ferdinand. *The Life of the Admiral Christopher Columbus by His Son Ferdinand.* Translated and annotated by Benjamin Keen. New Brunswick, N.J., 1959.

Fernández-Armesto, Felipe. *The Canary Islands after the Conquest: The Making of a Colonial Society in the Early Sixteenth Century.* Oxford, 1982.

First Images of America: The Impact of the New World on the Old. Edited by Fredi Chiappelli. Berkeley, 1976.

Floyd, Troy S. *The Columbus Dynasty in the Caribbean, 1492–1526.* Albuquerque, 1973.

Gil, Juan, and Consuelo Varela. *Temas colombinos.* Seville, 1986.

Giménez Fernández, Manuel. *Bartolomé de las Casas.* 2 vols. Seville, 1953, 1960.

Ladero Quesada, Miguel Angel. *Spain in 1492.* Translated by Helen Nader and Roland Pearson. Bloomington, Ind., forthcoming.

Manzano Manzano, Juan. *Cristóbal Colón: Siete años decisivos de su vida, 1485–1492.* Madrid, 1964.

Manzano Manzano, Juan. *Los Pinzones y el descubrimiento de América.* 3 vols. Madrid, 1988.

Morison, Samuel Eliot. *Admiral of the Ocean Sea: A Life of Christopher Columbus.* 2 vols. Boston, 1942.

Phillips, Carla, and William D. Phillips, Jr. *The Worlds of Christopher Columbus.* Cambridge, forthcoming.

Ramos, Demetrio. *Audacia, negocios y política en los viajes españoles de "descubrimiento y rescate."* Valladolid, 1981.

Roberts, David. *Great Exploration Hoaxes.* San Francisco, 1982.

Rumeu de Armas, Antonio. *El "Portugués" Cristóbal Colón en Castilla.* Madrid, 1982.

Rumeu de Armas, Antonio. *Hernando Colón, historiador del descubrimiento de América.* Madrid, 1973.

Rumeu de Armas, Antonio. *Itinerario de los Reyes Católicos, 1474–1516.* Madrid, 1974.

Rumeu de Armas, Antonio. *La Rábida y el descubrimiento de América: Colón, Marchena y Fray Juan Pérez.* Madrid, 1968.

Torre, José de la. *Beatriz Enríquez de Harana y Cristóbal Colón.* Madrid, 1933.

Varela, Consuelo. *Colón y los florentinos.* Madrid, 1988.

HELEN NADER

The Final Years, Illness, and Death

In 1506, Columbus could have looked back on his career and felt satisfied that he had accomplished what he had wanted to achieve when he came to Spain. At age fifty-five he was rich, famous, and honored. But Columbus was not satisfied with these achievements; he wanted more. And when he did not get more, he complained bitterly. Hence, paradoxes once again emerge in the story of Columbus. The Admiral died rich, but he complained about poverty. King Fernando and Queen Isabel showered him with honors and favors, but the letters that Columbus wrote in his final years are full of grievances.

The explanation for these paradoxes lies in several complicated changes that occurred in the final years of Columbus's life. Most of these changes, both administrative and personal, resulted from a growing awareness of the realities of America, realities that Columbus refused to acknowledge. A disparity between the Crown's accommodation and the Admiral's inflexibility surfaced during Columbus's third voyage (1498–1500), leading to disastrous results for the Admiral's prestige and authority.

Colonization of La Española was one of the principal objectives of the third voyage, but Columbus was unable to work harmoniously with the Spanish colonists. This conflict was not inevitable, nor was it strictly the result of hostility between Spaniards and Italians. Columbus remained on good terms with Spanish mariners, especially with the seamen of Palos. He did not expect to control these Spanish mariners; they had sailed the high seas before his 1492 voyage, and they continued to go on independent voyages. Yet Columbus failed to realize that Spanish farmers and artisans were equally independent and experienced. When he sought to control the actions of Spanish colonists, the consequence was revolt.

Spanish settlers in La Española found his government oppressive. The first Spanish city he had established on the island suffered a devastating epidemic and crop failure in 1494; most of the settlers died or returned to Spain. Those who remained on La Española claimed that Columbus's brothers, whom he left in charge while he explored other islands, did not understand the Spanish form of self-government through town councils.

If Columbus had any understanding of the settler's expectations, he had no intention of allowing them to live in the traditional Castilian way. He managed his city of La Isabela as if it were a Genoese trading station, or factory, in the Black Sea. Such a factory was simply a mercantile exchange, where businessmen could collect and store their merchandise and engage in currency exchanges until the fleet returned to Genoa.

The monarchs had agreed to Columbus's form of municipal governance in La Isabela, and, of course, they expected to make a substantial profit on their partnership with the Admiral. But they also assumed that the Spanish farmers of La Isabela would be able to provide enough food for the whole colony.

The settler's European crops failed to mature in the tropical climate, but Columbus remained inflexible. He refused to distribute supplies from the royal storehouse and forbade the colonists to farm elsewhere on the island. The ships that returned to Spain for resupply in 1494 carried may disillusioned settlers. Their disgruntled reports shattered the euphoria that had prevailed in the preparations for the second voyage.

Queen Isabel was very sensitive to the complaints from the returned settlers and understood the relationship between agricultural production and local self-government. In preparation for the third voyage, she gave the Admiral explicit instructions for establishing towns and distributing farm land. Such instructions had not previously been issued for the Americas; they were such an integral part of Castilian life that there had seemed no need to write them down.

Columbus accepted these instructions, but he did not implement them. Consequently, he had great difficulty recruiting farmers and other colonists for the third voyage. A comparison of his projected recruits in 1497 and the fleet's actual musters in 1498 show a serious shortage of colonists in all professions except the military.

When Columbus reached La Española, he found the entire island in turmoil. The Spanish crops had once again failed to mature, and Bartolomé and Diego Colón had

COLUMBUS IN CHAINS. Bronze relief, detail from the Rogers Doors (1858) in the U.S. Capitol. An interpretation of the events surrounding Columbus's arrest on La Española.

ARCHITECT OF THE CAPITOL

Occupations of Recruits for the Third Voyage

PARTIAL LISTING	PROJECTED RECRUITS (1497)	EMBARKED RECRUITS (1498)
Military officers	40	20
Enlisted men	0	57
Able seamen	30	15
Ship's apprentices	30	6
Gold miners	20	1
Unskilled workmen	100	50
Artisans	20	18
Farmers and gardeners	60	28
Women	30	6

refused the colonists' demands for seed and supplies from the royal storehouse. The colonists had gradually left La Isabela and followed the traditional methods of starting new towns. The man whom Columbus had appointed as appellate judge for the island, Francisco Roldán, led nearly one hundred Spaniards to the southwestern peninsula, where they established the town of Jaraguá. They started clearing fields, elected a town council, established a town marketplace, and petitioned Columbus for recognition of their town.

Though the settlers of Jaraguá had acted in accordance with Queen Isabel's instructions to Columbus, the Admiral called their actions rebellion. He refused to grant the Spaniards authority to live autonomously and declared the squatters rebels. In response to the rebels' complaints, the monarchs sent a royal judge, Francisco de Bobadilla, to investigate. By the time Bobadilla arrived in Santo Domingo, disputes between the Columbus brothers and the colonists had reached a stage of open rebellion and repression. Bobadilla sent Columbus and his brothers back to Spain under arrest.

King Fernando and Queen Isabel released Columbus immediately, but they took the complaints of the colonists very seriously and initiated some reforms. They stripped Columbus and his brothers of governing authority over Spanish settlers, appointed Nicolás de Ovando royal governor of La Española, and banished Columbus and his brothers from the island.

Failures in governing the colonists did not alienate the monarchs from their Admiral. They apparently agreed with the colonists' assessment that Columbus was acting out of ignorance because he was a foreigner. Far from rejecting him, the monarchs continued to support him and treat him as a respected business partner. Columbus had come full circle to his original role in the Santa Fe Capitulations, that is, as business partner to the monarchs. Money and commerce again dominated his career, and Genoese merchants in Seville again became his business associates.

His failures at governing had serious but not disastrous consequences for his financial affairs. Leaving a rich inheritance for his son Diego became the obsession of the Admiral's final years. Columbus expended much of his declining energy from 1498 to 1506 making sure that his financial privileges would remain intact and that his son Diego would inherit a rich estate.

Despite the disastrous financial losses the royal monopoly suffered on the first and second voyages, Fernando and Isabel treated Columbus with as much generosity as their treasury would allow. According to the Capitulations, Columbus's revenue from the Americas was to be one-tenth of the net royal income and one-eighth of the profits on voyages he helped to finance. But for the first five years of Spanish presence in the Americas, the monarchy received no income at all. Consequently, neither Columbus nor his financial backers received any profits.

Once the commercial difficulties began to emerge, the monarchs began modifying the original terms of commerce with the Americas. In order to compensate Columbus for his efforts and investments, the monarchs changed the partnership terms. On June 2, 1497, they ordered that Columbus, without having to invest anything at all, would receive one-eighth of the royal gross for the next three years and, thereafter, one-tenth of the royal net income.

By 1500, Columbus's income from America would have been considerable. Settlers from La Isabela had moved to the south shore of the island after they had found gold nuggets in the streams feeding into the Ozama River. By 1496, this gold rush to the south coast created a squatter settlement, Santo Domingo, to which Columbus's brother Bartolomé transferred his headquarters. The amount of wealth that passed through the city of Santo Domingo during the next few years made it the hub of Spanish government and trade in the Caribbean for the next three centuries. The Admiral appointed Alonso Sánchez de Carvajal, a former member of Queen Isabel's staff, as his business agent in Santo Domingo. Carvajal collected

240,000 maravedis as Columbus's share of the royal profits for 1494 through 1498, and 1500. (The account book for 1499 does not survive.) His income increased every year until the end of his life.

Though Columbus was rich, he was having trouble transferring his wealth from his agent in Santo Domingo to his financial backers in Seville, and this embittered Columbus against the royal treasurers in Seville. Small discrepancies between the Admiral's accounts and the treasury's audits turned into serious obstacles. At the time that he organized the third voyage, Columbus's accounts were being handled by his cousin Juan Antonio Colón. Juan Antonio's failure to balance his accounts prompted the royal treasurers to monitor the Admiral's accounts with extraordinary care. For example, while Columbus was still in Burgos in 1497, Pedro de Terreros signed on as his butler for the third voyage and received pay in advance from King Fernando's treasurer. Since he should have waited and received payment in Seville from the fleet treasurer, Bernardo Pinelo, the king's treasurer asked Pinelo for reimbursement and debited his accounts. Though all drafts associated with the voyage required Columbus's signature, Columbus never signed the voucher. Finally, Pinelo stopped all payments to the Admiral, pending the necessary transfer. Thus, even though Carvajal in Santo Domingo credited the correct amount of gold to the Admiral's account, the royal treasurer in Seville would not allow the Admiral or his creditors to withdraw the gold delivered to Seville.

The Admiral became frustrated. The monarchy's three-year grant to Columbus was drawing to a close. He wanted the grant extended or made permanent, but he also wanted to change some of its terms. He did not want to be dependent on the royal treasurers for an accounting of how much gold was being shipped from the Americas, and he wanted his own agents on both sides of the Atlantic free to draw from his accounts.

By September 1500, Carvajal was in Burgos, lobbying the monarchs for Columbus's demands. He stayed at the court until Juan Antonio Colón arrived in February 1501, apparently bringing Columbus's gold with him; during March and April, the two of them commissioned a silversmith to make a seal and a gold chain of forty-seven links for the Admiral. Clearly, the abrupt end of his governorship had not prevented Columbus from receiving gold in large amounts from the Americas.

Carvajal's tireless campaigning at court led to Columbus's regaining of some of his privileges. On December 27, 1501, the monarchs drafted a declaration of new procedures that permitted Columbus to have his own agent on La Española receive his share of the gold. He appointed Carvajal. According to the new regulations, both the Admiral's agent and the monarchy's inspector,

Diego Márques, had to be present when gold was minted and marked in Santo Domingo. Carvajal received the one-tenth of the minted gold for Columbus, as well as the one-eighth of the net profits on his investments. Carvajal remained in Santo Domingo, managing Columbus's business affairs in the islands and collecting the Admiral's share of the wealth of the Americas until 1502.

While in Spain Columbus made another commercial investment in the Americas. Ironically, this involved him in the voyage that transported to Santo Domingo his replacement as governor, Nicolás de Ovando. This investment also brought into the open serious conflicts between Columbus's profit motives and the colonists' consumer needs. The monarchs instructed fleet comptroller Jimeno de Briviesca to permit Columbus to invest one-eighth of the cost of the voyage. Columbus did not hesitate to make arrangements for a huge investment in merchandise.

The Admiral's associates for the Ovando fleet were four Genoese businessmen in Seville: Francisco de Riberol, Francisco Doria, Francisco Cataño, and Gaspar de Spínola. These merchants had so much faith in the profitability of the Americas that they loaned Columbus more than 188,000 maravadis to pay his expenses in Spain in exchange for the privilege of selling their merchandise in America. Their one-eighth of the commercial cargo consisted of the usual Genoese merchandise—woolen cloth. When the merchandise reached Santo Domingo in 1501, the monarchy's business agent, Fernando de Monroy, refused to accept the goods. He claimed that they were "not things that could be sold here very quickly and were priced higher than their worth." Monroy's response reflects the fact that the royal treasurers in Seville suspected the investors of falsifying their accounts by recording higher prices than they had actually paid for the goods.

The queen needed to take emergency measures to preserve the colony. She broke the Admiral's monopoly and allowed other merchants to engage in commerce in the Indies. In September 1502, she contracted two Spanish merchants, Juan Sánchez de la Tesorería and Alonso Bravo, to send six caravels to the Americas. The terms of the contract made clear that this was a commercial voyage. The two merchants had to deliver only limited supplies to the royal agent in Santo Domingo—no more than 3,600 bushels of wheat and flour, six horses, and 1,200 bushels of barley as feed for the horses. Beyond this, they were free to sell on their own any amounts they wanted of food, clothing, cloth, merchandise, African slaves, and mares. The monarchs again allowed Columbus to invest one-eighth in the voyage, but he and his agents appear not to have done so (though Carvajal and the Admiral later tried to claim one-eighth of the profits).

The Admiral's failure to invest in this very lucrative voyage was not because of lack of funds. His share of the gold was still coming to Seville. While Columbus was in the Caribbean on his fourth voyage (1502–1504), his business agent in Spain, Luis de Soria, invested 130,000 maravedis of Columbus's money in another commercial voyage to Santo Domingo and received one-eighth of the royal profit for the Admiral's accounts. In Santo Domingo in September 1504, after his rescue from Jamaica, Columbus had enough gold waiting for him to pay his crew two years of back pay and living expenses in cash and to pay a quarter of a million maravedis in gold to charter and supply ships for a return voyage to Seville, where he had accumulated fifteen million maravedis in gold in his accounts.

This period of enormous profits for Columbus from the Americas was soon tarnished. During early 1503, Fernando and Isabel held discussions with a colonial delegation from Santo Domingo. The delegates reported that the colonists could not buy the manufactured goods they needed from the royal storehouse. Instead of supplying necessities, such as metal tools, lightweight clothing for the tropical climate, paper, and medicines, the royal storehouse stocked overpriced merchandise that was not useful to the colony. For example, the colonists charged that Columbus had sent thick woolen broadcloth from England, which was suitable for northern European or central Asian climates but not for tropical islands.

For the monarchs, the problem seemed clear: the colonists could not flourish without supplies from Spain, and Columbus and his investors would never send the right supplies. As the colonial delegates pointed out, the royal treasury could not make a profit on undesirable merchandise; the unwanted goods rotted in the storehouse, even though the colonists had money to spend and needed European goods.

The monarchs solved this problem in mid-1503 by opening trade in the Americas to all Spaniards. Beginning in early 1504, any Spanish subject of the crowns of Castile or Aragón could export anything to La Española, except slaves, horses, arms, gold, and silver, and they could import anything from the Americas, except brazilwood.

For Columbus, this action by Fernando and Isabel was a cruel rebuff. Though he was seriously ill and crippled after the fourth voyage, he again took charge of his business affairs as soon as he got back to Spain, and he never stopped complaining about the free trade. In a letter to his son Diego in 1504, he criticized the new policy: "The privilege of the one-eighth is worthless because anyone can send merchandise to sell, without investing in outfitting the fleet and without having an account or partnership with anyone." He urged Diego, who had recently joined the queen's staff, to persuade the monarchs to reverse this policy. When this produced no results, he sent his other son, Fernando, his brother Bartolomé, and the tireless Carvajal to help Diego pressure the monarchs.

Columbus wanted desperately to be at the royal court, which was spending the winter of 1504–1505 in northern Castile, in the town of Medina del Campo. Queen Isabel was terminally ill, and Columbus wanted to see her one more time. He wanted the queen to promise on her deathbed that the monarchy would permit his son Diego to inherit his wealth, offices, and privileges.

The Admiral's gold from America had not made him happy. Columbus was a millionaire by any standard and expected his income to grow in the coming years. Although he complained that free trade had reduced his income by ten million maravedis, he had much to bequeath to his son. It was, however, this very wealth that made him anxious. He could not be sure that Diego would inherit it.

He could have solved this problem by becoming a Castilian citizen. Throughout Europe, only citizens enjoyed the protection of the law; foreigners did not have the right to dispose of their property by testament nor did the usual laws of inheritance apply to their property. The monarchs could simply seize a foreigner's property after his death and leave his heirs with nothing. Other Genoese in Spain, including the Admiral's brother Diego and his business associates Juanoto Berardi and Francisco de Riberol, became naturalized citizens of Castile. But Columbus remained a foreigner, and that left him in a tenuous position.

Columbus had already employed a device to avoid the terrible inheritance consequences of noncitizenship. He asked for and received from the monarchs the privilege of establishing a perpetual trust, and he placed all his offices, privileges, and income in that trust. But the monarchs whittled away at the contents of the trust, and Columbus could not be sure that the process would stop when he died. The possibility that the monarchy might reclaim more of his offices or continue to reduce his privileges haunted Columbus during his final years.

If he had been well, he might have fought and won this battle at court. But he could not travel because he was sick and crippled. His health problems had begun on the second voyage, when he, along with hundreds of other Europeans, fell seriously ill. Most of those who survived recovered fully. Columbus, in contrast, suffered crippling aftereffects for the rest of his life. During the third voyage, just after exploring the delta of the Orinoco River and realizing that he had reached a continent, Columbus became seriously ill. He ran a high fever and was in severe pain. His eyes became so inflamed that they bled, and he became temporarily blind. These symptoms recurred during the fourth voyage with such severity that, during the shipwreck on Jamaica, he could not walk without

assistance, and his vision was so bad that his teenage son Fernando had to act as his secretary, reading and writing for him. By the time he returned to Spain in the fall of 1504, he was dangerously ill.

The cause of Columbus's symptoms is unknown. Retrospective diagnoses are always guesswork, especially after nearly five hundred years. The most common diagnosis is that Columbus suffered from Reiter's syndrome, a genetic disorder. This syndrome produces a cluster of ailments that include crippling arthritis and inflammation of the eyes and the urinary tract. In persons with a genetic predisposition to Reiter's, onset is triggered by a severe illness, such as viral dysentery or the epidemic that occurred on La Española during Columbus's second voyage.

Whatever the disease, Columbus could travel and write only with great pain and difficulty during his final months. Though he spent several restful weeks in Santo Domingo before his last transatlantic crossing in 1504, he was dangerously ill by the time he arrived in Seville. He wrote often to his son Diego, but he explains, he could not write to his friend Diego Méndez "because of my illness, which does not permit me to write except at night, because during the day my hands are too weak."

Columbus wanted to go north to the court, but he could not even ride a horse. Carriages were unknown in Spain, and he could not have stood the roughness of a cart. In desperation, he made arrangements to borrow from Seville Cathedral an enclosed litter that had brought the body of the late cardinal archbishop to Seville. But he was advised against attempting the trip, for, he writes, "my illness is so severe, and the weather is so cold for someone in my condition, that I could end up in a dangerous state in some roadside inn."

Finally, after he had recovered somewhat and the coldest part of the winter had passed, Columbus decided to ride a mule to court. For this, he needed royal permission, because in 1494 Queen Isabel had issued a decree forbidding anyone except clergy and pregnant women to ride mules. (The breeding of mules reduced the production of horses, which were needed by the military.) After the victory of Granada, the monarchy attempted to replenish the supply of horses by depressing the desirability and price of mules. Being forbidden to ride mules was a hardship for everyone; the mule's smooth and surefooted gait made it the preferred means of travel in Castile. Nevertheless, the monarchy's need for war horses took precedence over custom. King Fernando and Queen Isabel set the example by riding horses, and all classes of society, from nobles to farmers, conformed to the royal decree.

Columbus apparently was so crippled that he could not have sat a horse on the steep roads of Castile. The journey

DEATH OF COLUMBUS. Bronze relief, detail from the Rogers Doors (1858) in the U.S. Capitol. In this depiction, the last rites are administered, as friends and attendants surround the ailing Columbus. The humble setting is meant to indicate the circumstances of Columbus's final years. ARCHITECT OF THE CAPITOL

were Spaniards. A local notary and witnesses were called, and Columbus dictated final instructions for Diego and confirmed the perpetual trust he had established. He died during the night of May 20, 1506.

Columbus performed amazing feats of world importance in Spain. Spain, especially Castile, welcomed and nurtured his talents and rewarded his deeds. With the labor and expertise of Spanish seamen Columbus had made a western voyage and claimed for Castile many islands in the Ocean Sea, just as he had predicted. On Castilian ships he had explored and claimed a continent, which he called a "New World," whose existence no European had ever imagined. Spanish seamen had risked their lives to rescue him and his brother and son from Jamaica.

He never became a citizen of Castile. The Admiral trusted few outside his circle of family and Italian friends. He expressed regret that his son Diego did not have more brothers: "Ten brothers would not be too many for you, because I myself never found in the whole world any better friend than my own brothers." He sent his most precious documents, the Book of Privileges, to Genoa and his gold and jewels to an Italian priest in Seville, Gaspar Gorricio, for safekeeping. And he recommended to the Castilian monarchs that his successor be the Italian navigator Amerigo Vespucci, who had been his original contact with the slave dealer Berardi in Seville.

from Seville to the royal court in Valladolid was over five hundred miles, and it crossed Spain's deepest river valleys and highest mountain ranges. He left Seville in May 1505 and made the journey in agonizing stages. When he reached his sons and brothers in the city of Segovia, where the widowed King Fernando and his court were residing during the summer, he confirmed his perpetual trust—an indication that he felt near death.

By the time he followed the royal court to the town of Valladolid, Columbus could go no further. He never succeeded in regaining his governing privileges from the king, but Fernando did begin discussions for Diego to marry a Castilian woman, which would give him citizenship in Castile. With these negotiations in early stages, Columbus sent his sons and brothers to give the oath of vassalage to the new queen, Juana, and her husband, who were expected soon to arrive on the north coast. When the new monarchs landed at La Coruña on April 26, however, they made no promises.

The Admiral could wait no more. His devoted employees stood watch during his final moments: Bartolomeo Fieschi, Alvaro Pérez, Juan de Espinosa, Andrea and Fernando Vargas, Francisco Manual, and Fernán Martínez. Most of them had been his mates at sea, and all but one

CASKET IN THE CATHEDRAL OF SANTO DOMINGO, DOMINICAN REPUBLIC. Said to contain remains of Columbus. Columbus was first buried in Spain, but his remains were moved several times. His son Diego wanted all the family admirals buried on La Española, and Diego's son Luis honored that wish. When the Spanish monarchy, which revered Columbus's memory, lost control of the island, the Crown acted to keep the remains within Spanish territory. The ultimate destiny of the remains, however, is the subject of much controversy. PHOTOGRAPH © WALTER R. AGUIAR

BIBLIOGRAPHY

Ballesteros Beretta, Antonio. *Christóbal Colón y el descubrimiento de América.* Vol. 2. Barcelona and Buenos Aires, 1945.

Gil, Juan. "Las cuentas de Colón." In *Temas Colombinas,* edited by Juan Gil and Consuelo Varela. Seville, 1986.

Morison, Samuel Eliot. *Admiral of the Ocean Sea: A Life of Christopher Columbus.* Vol. 2. Boston, 1942.

Weissman, Gerald. *They All Laughed at Christopher Columbus: Tales of Medicine and the Art of Discovery.* New York, 1987.

HELEN NADER

COLUMBUS THE NAVIGATOR. One of the difficulties in assessing Columbus's skill as navigator lies in reconciling the legends about his early life with the few established facts. In his journal of the first voyage to America, in the entry for December 21, 1492, he writes: "I have spent twenty-three years at sea without coming off it for any length of time worth mentioning, and I have seen all the east and west . . . and I have gone to Guinea." This alludes to 1469; yet, in signing a deed in 1472, Columbus describes himself as a "woolworker from Genoa." In 1474 he was in Chios, then a Genoese outpost, trading for the firm of Spinola and Di Negri. In 1477 he was in England, whence he claims to have visited Iceland and one hundred leagues beyond. The following year he was in Lisbon, and from there he sailed to Madeira to buy sugar for the same Genoese firm. He claims to have sailed to Guinea in the same ship as José Vizinho, the astronomer sent by King João II of Portugal to work out the procedures for determining latitude through observation of the sun. On these voyages, Columbus tells us, he would watch the work of the pilots and occasionally attempt to duplicate their observations.

In all this there is no evidence that Columbus sailed as a professional seaman. More probably, he traveled in the capacity of a ship's factor, a post that nevertheless demanded a knowledge of geography and familiarity with the port books. What he knew of navigation he had acquired through the nautical circles he frequented in Lisbon. He had read widely, but his cosmology was gravely at fault. The force of this viewpoint is not so much to detract from the legend of the great navigator as to suggest that his genius and considerable gifts lay elsewhere. As commander of an expedition, he would have conferred frequently with the pilots and masters on matters of navigation, but he would not have been expected to navigate the expedition, nor is there any hard evidence that he was equipped to do so.

The practice in navigation at the end of the fifteenth century was to establish the latitude (or *altura*) of the destination and sail along it east or west until familiar landmarks were sighted. The oldest extant Portuguese manual of navigation, the so-called Munich Regiment for the Astrolabe and Quadrant, was probably first printed in 1494, but it can be dated to before 1485, when the rules for observing the sun for latitude were drawn up. There is evidence in Columbus's journal that he had access to and possibly possessed a hand-copy of an early version of the manual, which contains a list of latitudes of the principal land features on the Atlantic coast, from the equator to Cape Finisterre, including all the reference points mentioned by Columbus and to an accuracy well beyond that achieved by Columbus in his own observations. E. G. R. Taylor has shown that while Columbus had studied the rules and procedures for observing the North Star and sun, he had failed to understand them properly and in particular misapplied the declination of the sun. His method for establishing the measure of the degree, for instance, was to compare the ship's run with successive altitudes of the sun, irrespective of any change in solar declination, a procedure probably suggested by the out-of-date version of the manual he had studied. He had trouble too with the precise conventional nomenclature used to describe the position of the Guard Stars in relation to the North Star, a technique used to find the correction to the North Star's altitude; in his letter describing the third voyage he uses an ambiguous phraseology long since abandoned by the Portuguese. Again, in a passage referring to the Guinea voyage, Columbus records that in the island of Los Idolos, off Sierra Leone, he found himself five minutes of latitude from the equinoctial. In fact the island lies 9° N, and the five minutes recorded was the sun's northerly declination for that day, for the date was March 11, the day of the spring equinox in the Julian calendar. Two weeks later he found the noonday sun directly overhead at Elmina and assumed that the fort thus lay on the equinoctial; in fact its latitude is 5½° N and the sun's declination for that day was 5°37' N. Other of his gross errors in measurement of latitude can be pointed up, as for example on October 30, 1492, off the coast of Cuba, where "in the opinion of the Admiral, he was distant from the equinoctial line forty-two degrees to the north." The sun's declination for the day was 17° N, which subtracted from 42° would have given the more reasonable figure of 25° N.

The good navigator is of course not necessarily the one who obtains the most accurate information, but rather he who makes the best use of the information available to him. Here Columbus may have been on surer ground. For all his adoption of too small a measure for the degree, his convoluted juggling of the day's run, and his occasionally lame explanations of his disagreements with the pilots, he does seem to have been possessed of a sea-sense that enabled him, in uncharted waters and with imprecise methods of navigation, to find his way about the ocean with a degree of caution that ensured success. His navigational achievements were probably due more to his seamanship than to his occasional observations and cosmological small talk.

[See also *Myth of Columbus.*]

BIBLIOGRAPHY

Morison, Samuel Eliot. *The European Discovery of America: The Southern Voyages.* New York, 1974.

Taylor, E. G. R. "The Navigating Manual of Columbus." *Journal of the Institute of Navigation* 5, no. 1 (1952): 42–54.

M. W. RICHEY

COMPASS. [This entry includes two articles, *Marine Compass,* focusing on the development of the compass's use at sea, and *Declination of the Compass,* focusing on the phenomenon of compass variation, which European navigators experienced the farther they traveled in unknown waters.]

Marine Compass

In Latin the compass is called *pixis,* in German, *Kompas,* in Italian, *bussola,* and in French, *boussole.* An early (mid-thirteenth-century) use of the word *compasso* meant sailing directions, comprising the portolano (strictly speaking, the written guide) and the nautical chart. The development of the magnetic compass as a marine instrument is poorly documented, but is probably no earlier than the first use of a magnetized needle pushed into a straw and floated on water in a bowl. There are serious practical difficulties in the use even of this improvement upon the floated lodestone (i.e., a piece of natural magnetic ore) described by Petrus Peregrinus (Pierre le Pèlerin) de Maricourt in his *Epistola de magnete* (1269). The introduction of a pivot to support the magnetized needle in a dry bowl was essential to the further development of the compass, and the pivot seems, like the magnetic compass itself, to have derived from China. Petrus Peregrinus had already described a pivoted compass needle: two pivots, above and below a vertical arbor carrying the needle. The earliest surviving instrument with a compass-needle pivot is the small astronomical *compendium* (a simple astrolabe and sundial for finding Muslim prayer-times and the direction of Mecca from various places) made in A.H. 767 (A.D. 1366/1367) by the important astronomer, 'Ali b. al-Shatir. There are no other surviving magnetic compasses that can be dated before those incorporated toward the end of the fifteenth century in sundials and a globe, and none of these instruments was intended for nautical use.

Transmission of the magnetic compass from China to Europe would suggest Islamic culture as a vector, and the earliest-cited reference to use of the lodestone in a portable nautical context seems to be in a mid-ninth-century Arabic poem. However, the first known mention of the use of a compass at sea is Alexander Neckam's (1157–1217) reference in his *De utensilibus* to mariners' finding their course when sun or stars were invisible by means of a north-pointing needle, and in his *De naturis rerum,* he describes the needle as being placed on a pivot; both treatises belong to the last quarter of the twelfth century. Neckam's priority has led some historians to seek a northern European origin for the magnetic compass. Between 1204 and 1208, Guyot de Provins wrote in his poem *La Bible* some verses concerning a needle *(aiguille)* that had touched a lodestone *(magnette,* "an ugly and brownish stone") and then been inserted in a straw *(festu)* and placed in water; this needle pointed to the polestar. Before about 1218, Jacques de Vitry, bishop of Acre, had written that the compass was "very necessary" to those navigating on the sea, and by 1225 the navigational use of the compass was apparently a commonplace in Iceland. Petrus Peregrinus, in his *Epistola,* envisaged navigation that was astronomical when he said that his compass would enable the traveler to reach all places, on land or at sea, as long as he knew his longitudes and latitudes. By the second half of the thirteenth century, use of the magnetic compass at sea must have become general in European and North African waters: the *Siete partidas,* a legal encyclopaedia edited between 1256 and 1263 under the supervision of King Alfonso X of Castile, uses a simile that refers to sailors finding their way on a dark night with "the needle which is a mediator between the star [the polestar] and the stone [the lodestone]." Likewise, the Egyptian scientist, Baylak al-Qipjaqi, wrote that the captains of ships on the sea route between Syria and Egypt, when the night was too dark for stellar observation, would take a vessel filled with water and place it inside the ship, protected from the wind; they would then take a needle and insert it in a reed (or the like) such that the latter formed a cross (perhaps to keep the needle central in the vessel), and when this was floated on the surface of the water, magnetize the needle by bringing a large lodestone over the needle, twisting the lodestone to the right (thereby turning the floating needle) and then removing the lodestone rapidly. Baylak says that he saw this procedure with his own eyes during his voyage from Tripoli to Alexandria in A.H. 640 (A.D. 1242/1243).

It might be assumed that the use of a pivot for the compass needle was common by the end of the fourteenth century or at the beginning of the fifteenth. No descriptions, illustrations, or artifacts document the history of the marine compass until the illustration of a compass box and, possibly, compass rose drawn in the margin of a manuscript of *La sfera*, a cosmological poem by Gregorio Dati (1363–1436) or by Leonardo Dati written in the first half of the fifteenth century, but it is not absolutely clear that the "star" in the picture represents a compass rose on a fly rather than just the Stella Maris on the lid of the box. Crude illustrations of mariner's compasses drawn on fifteenth-century charts show a round box and a pivoted fly, similar to those of later marine compasses, of which the earliest good illustration is perhaps in the 1562 portrait of the lord high admiral Edward Fiennes, Lord Clinton and Saye (in the Ashmolean Museum, Oxford University). There is, however, an allegorical drawing by Leonardo da Vinci, dated about 1515 to 1516, in which a wolf, seated in a sailing boat, is looking at a fixed compass that clearly has a fly.

Fiennes's compass is probably not far removed in design from the Genoese and Flemish compasses used by Columbus. It is contained in a round wooden box, slightly less than a handsbreadth in diameter. There is a fly bearing a compass rose (that is, the pivoted magnetized needle, or wire frame, is attached underneath a disk of paper-covered pasteboard on which are drawn the cardinal points separating the eight "winds" of 45 degrees each, subdivided into four "quarters" of 11¼ degrees, instead of having a simple needle pivoted within a fixed scale of divisions). The fly may derive from a cross or disk used to keep a floating needle central in its bowl, and its invention is probably not much later than the introduction of charts drawn with rhumb lines. Conceptually, it is easier to set a ship's course along a rhumb if the compass has a graduated fly, rather than a simple needle that points to a surrounding scale. For example, given that the meridian axis of the compass box is aligned on the longitudinal axis of the ship, sailing on a course a quarter west with a fly requires only the quarter west division on the fly to be kept opposite the meridian axis of the compass, whereas a simple needle has to point on the surrounding scale to the quarter east division. Fiennes's compass shows no sign of any gimbal mounting (Cardan suspension), though the idea of such a mounting was known to medieval technology (e.g., in the Sketchbook of Villard de Honnecourt, c. 1235), and its use for a compass was envisaged by Leonardo da Vinci around 1500. Compasses were kept in a box or cupboard (*gisola*, binnacle/bittacle); the inventory of a ship sold in Genoa early in 1495 includes "four needles for navigating . . . two binnacles." A marine compass, made in Lisbon in 1711 by Josep' da Costa Miranda (Whipple Science Museum, Cambridge), may be further rare evidence for the form of Columbus's compasses, though it may be slightly more elaborate.

MARINE COMPASS. This Portuguese compass, although eighteenth-century, is close to that used by Columbus in that it has no gimbals. Opposite sides of the painted wooden box containing the fly are fitted with sights for taking solar bearings.

WHIPPLE MUSEUM OF THE HISTORY OF SCIENCE, CAMBRIDGE

Some of the problems that Columbus encountered in using his compasses may have arisen because the Genoese compass makers may have placed the magnetic needle under the fly, aligned with true north, whereas the Flemish makers allowed for the declination. It is clear from A. Crichton Mitchell that Columbus did not discover, as has been claimed, the magnetic declination. From the evidence of the German roadmaps (c. 1492 or 1500) of Erhard Etzlaub of Nürnberg and the less certain evidence of portable sundials with compasses, it seems that an easterly declination of about 11¼ degrees had been observed in northwestern Europe before Columbus sailed on his first voyage. Columbus's observations on September 13–14, 1492, suggest that he was close to the agonic line (i.e., line of zero declination), but he deduced no general space variation of declination from these observations.

[See also *Lodestone.*]

BIBLIOGRAPHY

Gouk, Penelope. *The Ivory Sundials of Nuremberg 1500–1700*, pp. 73–74 and 84–88. Cambridge, 1988.

Grant, Edward, ed. *A Source Book in Medieval Science.* Cambridge, Mass., 1974.

Körber, Hans-Günther. *Zur Geschichte der Konstruktion von Sonnenuhren und Kompassen.* Veröffentlichungen des Staatlichen Mathematisch-Physikalischen Salons—Forschungsstelle—Dresden-Zwinger, vol. 3. Berlin, 1965.

Maddison, Francis. *Medieval Scientific Instruments and the Development of Navigational Instruments in the XVth and*

XVIth Centuries. Agrupamento de estudos de cartografia antiga, vol. 30. Coimbra, 1969.

Mitchell, A. Crichton. "Chapters in the History of Terrestrial Magnetism. Chapter I—On the Directive Property of a Magnet in the Earth's Field and the Origin of the Nautical Compass." *Terrestrial Magnetism and Atmospheric Electricity* 37 (1932): 105–146.

Mitchell, A. Crichton. "Chapters in the History of Terrestrial Magnetism. Chapter II—The Discovery of the Magnetic Declination." *Terrestrial Magnetism and Atmospheric Electricity* 42 (1937): 241–280.

Needham, Joseph, Wang Ling, and Kenneth Girdwood Robinson. "Physics." Part 1 of vol. 4 of *Science and Civilisation in China.* Cambridge, 1962.

Radelet de Grave, P., and D. Speiser. "Le *De magnete* de Pierre de Maricourt. Traduction et commentaire." *Revue d'histoire des sciences et de leurs applications* 28, pt. 3 (1975): 193–234.

Taylor, E. G. R. "The South-Pointing Needle." *Imago Mundi* 8 (1951): 1–7.

Francis Maddison

Declination of the Compass

The declination, or variation, of the compass at any point on the earth's surface is the difference in angular degrees between the direction to magnetic North and geographic North. Although the phenomenon had become apparent from the time that compass steering was generally practiced, it was not until the sixteenth century that its cause became known. Mediterranean pilots usually blamed the needle's variation either on careless shipboard use of the lodestone to magnetize the needle or, more frequently, on faulty workmanship by the compass maker. Later, as pilots began to keep careful logs and compared notes with other pilots, they became aware that declination, or variation, existed and also that declination varied from place to place.

It was not until navigation of the "Western Ocean" was first attempted that the strange behavior of the compass needle from place to place became a matter of serious concern. It was Christopher Columbus who made the earliest record of the phenomenon. In his journal of the first voyage westward he noted that for most of the time the compass rarely pointed true north, although it had done so at a point 2½ degrees east of Corvo in the Azores. The needle's erratic behavior caused considerable consternation among the superstitious crew and almost led to mutiny.

Columbus's entry in his journal for September 13, 1492, noted, "This day at night fall, the needles deviated to the North-West, and on the morrow they deviated slightly in the same direction." Four days later he recorded,

The pilots took an observation of the north, and found that the needles deviated a good quarter to the north west, and the mariners were afraid and were dismayed and did not say why. And the Admiral observed it and bade them repeat the observations of the north at dawn, and they found that the needles were correct: the reason was that the star, which they saw, moved, and not the needles. (Dunn and Kelly, eds., *The Diario* of Christopher Columbus's First Voyage to America, *1492–1493*)

Although Mediterranean pilots had long been aware of the occasional variation of the compass needle, magnetic variation in the Mediterranean was practically negligible until the mid-seventeenth century, and it was not an important factor in navigation. The phenomenon observed by Spanish seamen obviously was new to them, however; if it had been generally known among European navigators and seamen prior to Columbus's first voyage, there would have been no reason for the fear expressed by the sailors.

In his diary of the second voyage, Columbus noted that he was equipped with both Genoese and Flemish compasses. This was a combination that substantially multiplied the navigator's confusion because in addition to noting the needle's variation in some locations and not in others, he also observed differences in the readings between the two types of compasses. This discrepancy was due to the fact that the Genoese needle pointed to true north while the needle or wire of the Flemish compass was oriented to point east.

A significant passage in Fernando Colón's biography of his father relates to the return voyage on Coumbus's second visit to the Indies:

This morning the Dutch [Flemish] compasses vary'd as they used to do, a point; and those of Genoa, that used to agree with them, vary'd but a little, but afterwards sailing east vary more, which is a sign we are a 100 leagues, or somewhat more, west of the Azores. . . . and the Dutch needles vary'd a point, those of Genoa cutting the north point; and when we are somewhat farther E.N.E. they will alter again; which was verified on Sunday following being the 22nd day of May; by which and the exactness of his account, he found he was 100 leagues from the islands Azores, which he was somewhat surpriz'd at, and assigned this difference to the several sorts of load-stones the needles are made by; for till they come to that longitude they all vary a point, and there some held it; and those of Genoa exactly cut the north star. (Churchill and Churchill, *Collection of Voyages*, vol. 2.)

With growing awareness of variation, it had become the practice for navigators to set the needle beneath the card slightly askew to compensate for the amount of variation that occurred in a particular region. This shipboard modification became so common that compass makers eventually began to mark the variation in compasses they sold. Compasses produced in Italy—Genoa, Sicily, and Venice—generally had the needles set three-quarters of a point eastward, while the needles of compasses produced in Spain, Portugal, France, and England were set one-half of a point eastward. One point, *una quarta,* was equal to 11¼ degrees. This was only a temporary solution, however, practical for short cruises but not for longer voyages.

Although Columbus was the first to record the compass's variation, he failed to recognize its true cause. The first recorded scientific observation was made by Felipe Guillén of Seville in 1525, and a decade later Francisco Faleiro published a navigational manual containing directions for determining declination by means of an instrument similar to that devised by Guillén. In his *History of the Indies* the Spanish historiographer Gonzalo Fernández de Oviedo dealt at some length with northeasting and northwesting of the compass needle, but he neglected to mention that Columbus had reported it.

Columbus's report of the phenomenon was noted in his journal edited by Bartolomé de las Casas as well as in Fernando Colón's biography of his father, but the report did not become known to subsequent transoceanic voyagers until 1571 when the translation of Fernando's biography into Italian by Alfonso de Ulloa became available. Little note was made of it even then, for the work had limited distribution and it was not translated into other languages until more than a century later. It was, in fact, not until 1789 when Martín Fernández de Navarrete discovered the Las Casas manuscript that Colombus's observations of the phenomenon became known, long after the phenomenon of magnetic variation had become common knowledge.

On voyages undertaken during the years 1538–1541, João de Castro compiled the most complete set of observations of compass variation to that time. Pedro Nuñez, in his *De arte atque ratione navigandi* (1546), promoted the use of the compass's variation as a means of determining longitude. And it was in a preface by Giovanni Maria Negri in a book by Niccola Negri published in 1574 that for the first time magnetic variation of the compass was mentioned in a manner indicating that by then it had become general knowledge among Spanish navigators.

It is believed that compass makers in Flanders and Germany may have had some knowledge of magnetic declination prior to Columbus's voyages, and that variation for those regions were marked on Flemish compasses by their makers. The increasing growth of sea trade resulted in the rapid development of the manufacture of compasses and lodestones in Flanders from the fourteenth century on, and it is possible that by the second half of the fifteenth century, compass makers had begun to correct their compasses for variation observed in northwestern Europe. This was first achieved by mounting the compass card on the needle where it indicated magnetic north instead of where it indicated true or geographic north. The practice was copied by other compass makers in Nürnberg and elsewhere in northern Europe. Such instruments were sold widely throughout the continent by itinerant salesmen.

The earliest confirmed evidence that German compass makers and mapmakers had knowledge of magnetic variation is to be found in the work of Erhard Etzlaub, a Nürnberg physician who drew maps and made compasses. He marked the magnetic variation for Nürnberg first on a horizontal dial drawn upon a 1501 map of Germany, and he also produced and sold rectangular, wooden, folding sundials with the same feature. Magnetic variation also appears in the figure of a sundial drawn as part of the *Carta itineraria Europae,* a map of Europe produced in 1511 by Martin Waldseemüller and Mathias Ringmann. On the basis of these maps, there is no doubt that magnetic variation had become known to German mapmakers and compass makers by the beginning of the sixteenth century, if not before.

BIBLIOGRAPHY

Churchill, A., and J. Churchill. *The History of the Life and Actions of Adm. Christopher Columbus and His Discovery of the West-Indies.* In vol. 2 of *Collection of Voyages.* 3d edition. London, 1744.

Denne, W. *Magnetic Compass Deviation and Correction.* 3d edition. New York, 1979.

Dunn, Oliver, and James E. Kelly, Jr. *The Diario of Christopher Columbus's First Voyage to America, 1492–1493.* Norman, Okla., 1989.

Heathcote, N. H. de Vaudrey. "Christopher Columbus and the Discovery of Magnetic Variation." *Scientific Progress,* no. 105 (July 1932): 82–103.

Mitchell, A. Crichton. "Chapters on the History of Terrestrial Magnetism." In *Terrestrial Magnetism and Atmospheric Electricity* 38 (1932): 105–146; 42 (1937): 241–280; 44 (1939): 77–80.

Waters, David W. *The Art of Navigation in England in Elizabethan and Early Stuart Times.* London, 1958.

SILVIO A. BEDINI

CONCEPCIÓN DE LA VEGA. See *Settlements,* article on *Concepción de la Vega.*

CONQUEST. For general discussion of European expansion in the New World, see *Pacification, Conquest, and Genocide.* For discussion of particular European efforts, see *Colonization; Exploration and Discovery.*

CONTI, NICCOLÒ DE' (c. 1395–1469), Venetian merchant-adventurer. Probably born in Chioggia, Conti set out in 1414 on a trading expedition along the eastern spice trade routes that would last some twenty-five years. Having learned Arabic in Damascus, he followed the caravan routes to Baghdad and thence along the Tigris and Euphrates to Basra. He sailed down the Persian Gulf to Hormuz and then to Kalhat (present-day Qalhat, Oman), where he learned some Persian. Over the ensuing years he explored and traded along the coasts of India, Burma, and Sumatra, the origins and transit points of the spices for which Europeans were so eager. Apparently he worked out of a trading base on the western coast of India, and he may have even reached China. About 1439 Conti returned to Europe via Socotra, the Red Sea, Mount Sinai, and Cairo.

Two contemporary accounts of his travels survive. One of these Conti related in 1448 to the humanist papal secretary Poggio Bracciolini, and the second was recorded by the Spanish merchant Pedro Tafur, whom Conti met while trading in the Mediterranean. The narration to Poggio was a form of penance imposed by Pope Eugenius IV for Conti's having reportedly abjured the Christian faith while in the lands of the "infidel." Poggio included this in his *De varietate fortunae* (On the diversity of fortune), of which some thirty-one manuscript copies, mostly from the fifteenth century, survive from Italy, Germany, France, and England. The first printed Latin edition came out in 1492. This narrative contains a good deal of information about the peoples among whom Conti traveled, although there is speculation that Poggio took some of this, especially in the second half of the narrative, from sources other than Conti. The extent of Conti's exposure to the sources of Egyptian and Syrian transit trade was perhaps unique, and his account certainly was. The bounty of contemporary, pre-Columbian texts of his story attests to both Mediterranean and northern interest in this mysterious world.

BIBLIOGRAPHY

Longhena, M. *Viaggi in Persia: India e Giava di Niccolò de Conti.* Milan, 1929.

Major, R. H., ed. *India in the Fifteenth Century.* London, 1857. Reprint, New York, 1971.

JOSEPH P. BYRNE

CONVERSOS. See *Jews,* article on *Conversos.*

CÓRDOBA.   Located on the Guadalquivir River in the southern Spanish region of Andalusia, Córdoba was settled in prehistoric times. During the Roman period it was the capital of Hispania Ulterior and, later, Baetica.

After the Muslim conquest, Córdoba became capital of Umayyad Spain (756–1031). During the Umayyad dynasty, the city attained the general plan it would retain into modern times, and the mosque and other Islamic architectural monuments were constructed. Twelfth-century Córdoba was the home of the distinguished philosophers Averroës (Ibn Rushd) and Maimonides (Moses ben Maimon). In 1236 King Fernando III conquered the city from the Muslims and began its Christian resettlement.

By the late fifteenth century, Córdoba was a prominent Andalusian city with an urban population of some 25,000; another 125,000 people lived in surrounding towns and villages under the city's jurisdiction. It was a royal city whose representatives sat in the Castilian Cortes (parliament). Its municipal government was dominated by local nobles, whose bands controlled the political scene. As the seat of a bishop, it was also a center of ecclesiastical jurisdiction.

Córdoba served as a commercial transshipping point for agricultural and mining products produced in the surrounding territory. The city was located in the center of a large agrarian region whose varied topography supported fields of wheat and barley, olive groves and vineyards, and irrigated plots for fruit and vegetables. Livestock raised on extensive pastures produced meat for local consumption and hides and wool for export. Local entrepreneurs and workers manufactured leather goods (Cordovan leather), soap, and woolen textiles. The wool clipped locally or purchased from neighboring regions was exported or woven into cloth.

Christopher Columbus often visited Córdoba between 1485 and 1492, while seeking Castilian support for his enterprise of the Indies. In Córdoba Columbus also established a romantic liaison with Beatriz de Arana, an orphan living under the care of her cousin, Rodrigo Enríquez de Arana, whose wife, Lucía Núñez, owned looms and employed weavers of linen and woolen cloth. Some writers suggest that Columbus, a weaver's son, could have met Beatriz there or through the Genoese pharmacists Lucián and Leonardo de Esbarroya, whose shop was a popular meeting place. Whatever the circumstances, in June 1488, Beatriz bore a son named Fernando.

BIBLIOGRAPHY

Edwards, John. *Christian Córdoba: The City and Its Region in the Late Middle Ages.* Cambridge, 1982.

La Torre y del Cerro, José de. *Beatriz Enríquez de Harana y Cristóbal Colón.* Madrid, 1933.

WILLIAM D. PHILLIPS, JR.

CÓRDOBA, GONZALO FERNÁNDEZ DE. See *Fernández de Córdoba, Gonzalo.*

CORONADO, FRANCISCO VÁZQUEZ DE (1510–1554), Spanish explorer.

Coronado's expedition in search of the Seven Cities of Cíbola provided the first relatively accurate geographical knowledge of western North America and the indigenous peoples of the greater Southwest.

Coronado was born in Burgos, Spain, and came to New Spain in 1535 in the service of the first viceroy, Antonio de Mendoza. In August 1538 he was named governor of New Galicia, the northernmost Spanish frontier outpost. In 1536 Alvar Núñez Cabeza de Vaca had brought news of large cities in the far north, and in 1539 the viceroy commissioned Coronado commander of the army that was being assembled to explore the Kingdom of Cíbola and its Seven Cities that Fray Marcos de Niza had sighted beyond the Great Sonoran Desert.

On February 22, 1540, Mendoza personally reviewed the army at Compostela in Guadalajara and received the muster call of some 336 Spaniards of whom 225 were mounted horsemen, hundreds of Indian guides and bearers, and more than 1,500 horses, mules, and livestock. On April 22, 1540, Coronado set on ahead from Culiacán toward Cíbola with a small vanguard of eighty horsemen and twenty-five to thirty foot soldiers; the main army with the livestock and baggage train followed later. On May 9, 1540, two ships commanded by Hernando de Alarcón sailed up the northwestern coast of Mexico with supplies for the army. Although he never established direct contact with the main expedition, Alarcón navigated the Colorado River 250 miles to its confluence with the Gila River, established alliances with the Cocopas and other Yuman peoples, and observed that Baja California was not an island.

Coronado's advance guard reached northern Sonora in late May. From there it pushed through southern Arizona, finally reaching the Colorado Plateau and the outskirts of the walled Zuni city of Hawikuh on July 7, 1540. When Coronado led the assault on the adobe terraces, he was knocked senseless by a barrage of heavy stones, narrowly escaping death when two of his captains, García López de Cárdenas and Hernando de Alvarado, threw themselves over his body to protect him. "Everything was the reverse of what Fray Marcos de Niza had said," the commander wrote to Mendoza.

In the final quarter of 1540 Coronado sent his captains on a great circle of inland exploration: Pedro de Tovar to the Hopi villages; Cárdenas west to the brim of the Grand Canyon and the Colorado River; Melchior Díaz southwest to the lower Colorado River and into California. Alvarado swung east on a long reconnaissance mission with two chiefs from Cicuye (Pecos) to Acoma, the Tiguex villages along the Rio Grande valley, north to the pueblos of Santo Domingo, San Felipe, and Cochiti, finally reaching Pecos on the eastern edge of the Pueblo world and the buffalo country.

The main army had reached Hawikuh in late November and moved eastward into the Rio Grande valley in late December 1540, forcing the Tiguex to vacate one of their pueblos and provide food and blankets for the Spanish army. After Indian prisoners were burned alive at Arenal, Coronado led a winter-long siege that ended with two hundred dead Indians, ten or more slain Spaniards, and twelve Tiguex pueblos burned or abandoned.

A third phase of exploration began on April 22, 1541, when Coronado set out with guides from Pecos onto the plains, "so vast that I did not find their limit anywhere I went." The army swung east to Tucumcari, to the Texas Panhandle along the Canadian River, and then southward into the Staked Plains where they explored the Tule and Palo Duro canyons. A Plains Indian guide given them at Pecos, whom they called "the Turk," had told them of a rich province to the north whose rulers used golden vessels. Coronado sent the main army back to Tiguex and with a detachment of thirty horsemen rode north, meeting vast buffalo herds and the nomadic Querechos, probably Apaches, and the Teyas. In July 1541 the horsemen reached Quivira at the bend of the Arkansas River. It turned out to be a series of Wichita Indian villages of grass huts set in fine country for a Spanish settlement, near present-day Lyons, Kansas. After nearly a month of exploration that uncovered no gold, the Turk confessed that he had led the Spaniards astray on the plains on orders of the people of Cicuye who hoped to rid themselves of the invaders. Their return to the Rio Grande valley followed an Indian route that would become in the future the Santa Fe Trail.

Just after Christmas in 1541 Coronado was thrown under the hooves of another horse in a riding accident that nearly killed him. A strong minority of sixty men wanted to stay and hold the country; others wanted to return to Quivira. But the ailing Coronado was determined not to divide his command, and his army began the return march to Mexico City in early April 1542.

The Crown conducted a full inquiry into Coronado's conduct of the Cíbola expedition, from which he was exonerated of charges of incompetence and ill treatment of the natives. He died at age forty-two in 1554. In two short years his explorations had produced the information that transformed the geography of North America from the medieval island imagery of Columbus to that of a new continent.

BIBLIOGRAPHY

Works by Members of the Coronado Expedition

Castañeda de Náçera, Pedro de. *La relación de la jornada de Cíbola.* 1563? MS. 1596, New York Public Library.

The Coronado Expedition. Transcribed, translated, and edited by George Parker Winship. Washington, D.C., 1896. Reprint, Chicago, 1964.

Narratives of the Coronado Expedition, 1540–1541. Edited and translated by George P. Hammond and Agapito Rey. Vol. 2 of Coronado Cuatro Centennial Publications. Albuquerque, 1940.

Works about the Coronado Expedition

Bolton, Herbert Eugene. *Coronado: Knight of Pueblos and Plains.* Albuquerque, 1949. Also published as vol. 1 of Coronado Cuatro Centennial Publications.

Day, Arthur Grove. *Coronado's Quest: The Discovery of the Southwestern States.* Berkeley, 1942.

"In Coronado's Footsteps." *Arizona Highways* 60, no. 4 (1984).

Lecompte, Janet. "Coronado and Conquest." *New Mexico Historical Review* 64 (1989).

Mora, Carmen. "*La relación de la jornada de Cíbola* de Pedro Castañeda Nájera, ¿un texto censurado?" *Insula* 522 (1990).

Sauer, Carl P. *The Road to Cibola.* Berkeley, 1932.

Spanish Explorers in the Southern United States, 1528–1542. Edited by Frederick W. Hodge and Theodore H. Lewis. New York, 1907. Reprint, New York, 1965.

Udall, Stewart L. *To the Inland Empire: Coronado and Our Spanish Legacy.* Photographs by Jerry Jacka. New York, 1987.

Weber, David J. "Coronado and the Myth of Quivira." *Southwest Review* 70 (1985).

MAUREEN AHERN

CORTÉS, HERNANDO (1485–1547), Spanish explorer born in Medellín, a small town in Extremadura in the Spanish southwest. Cortés's parents were both of the hidalgo class, a lower nobility with little income. At the age of fourteen, he was sent to Salamanca where he received some formal education; two years later he returned home tired of studying and without the law degree his parents wanted him to pursue.

In 1504, Cortés sailed for La Española, attracted like many in his class by the expected but as yet unrealized riches of the New World. He was soon appointed notary of the new town of Azúa. He remained there until 1511, when he participated in the conquest of Cuba under Diego Velázquez, who as the first governor of Cuba appointed Cortés his secretary. In the following years, he prospered in his farming and mining activities as an encomendero and in his administrative career as mayor of Santiago de Baracoa, then the capital of the island. He married Catalina Juárez in 1515 and lived an uneventful life as a settler for the next three years, showing no interest in the expeditions of Francisco Hernández de Córdoba (1517) and Juan de Grijalba (1518), which were launched from Cuba to explore the mainland. On news that there were significant riches in Mexico, he maneuvered to obtain from Velázquez the command of the next expedition to explore the Yucatán and northern coast.

Velázquez seems to have had doubts about Cortés's loyalty, owing to rumors that Cortés intended to gain wealth for himself, but in February 1519 a fleet of some twelve ships with five hundred Spaniards, some Caribbean Indians, and sixteen horses left hastily for Yucatán. After some reconnaissance of the coast they disembarked at Tabasco, where Cortés quickly proved Velázquez's fears to be well founded. In a skillful political maneuver, he convinced his troops that news about a fabulous empire nearby demanded a new course of action, namely a military campaign to subdue the territory to the west in the name of the king of Spain, its rightful owner according to the papal donation. With the boldness and determination that would make him famous, he sank his ships to avoid retreat and proceeded to the interior from Veracruz, a city he had just founded in April of 1519.

The long march to Tenochtitlán took five months. His message to the Indians consisted of just one option, that of accepting immediate servitude to the Spanish Crown or being declared rebels and suffer the consequences. This ultimatum was naturally met with opposition, sometimes violent, but Cortés, an inexperienced soldier, proved an effective military leader whose able and disciplined army quickly overcame any resistance. He also was, however, a skillful diplomat, ready to make new alliances founded upon sweet promise and fierce intimidation. He took early notice that many communities such as the Cempoallans were disgruntled subjects of Motecuhzoma II (Moctezuma), the powerful leader of a triple alliance based in Mexico whose vast territories constituted a large empire, and he accordingly offered them political and financial liberation. On the other hand, he found independent republics like Tlaxcala that lived in a state of permanent war with the Mexicans, and to them he offered a solid alliance against the Mexica power. His strategy worked, and the march progressed as the confused Motecuhzoma, who may have thought the Spaniards to be deities, had strong doubts about the proper course of action. He tried to avoid the impending peril by offering rich presents and gold, but the effort was in vain.

On November 8, 1519, Cortés and his men entered Tenochtitlán, the magnificent city on the water, and were received as guests of Motecuhzoma. Soon after Cortés arrested the ruler under a feeble pretext and made him sign a pledge of allegiance to Charles V. Cortés then spent a few months strengthening his control of the city and the Mexican territories, but in May of 1520 a powerful fleet under the command of Pánfilo de Narváez was sent by Governor Velázquez to punish Cortés. In a shrewd commando-style night operation Cortés managed to overcome Narváez near the coast, but in the meantime Tenochtitlán had rebelled because of the unruly behavior of Pedro de Alvarado who had been left in charge. Cortés rushed back to the city, but after a brief pause in the conflict the general rebellion resumed, and he was forced to flee the night of June 30, the so-called Noche Triste (Sad Night) in which he lost half of his troops and most of

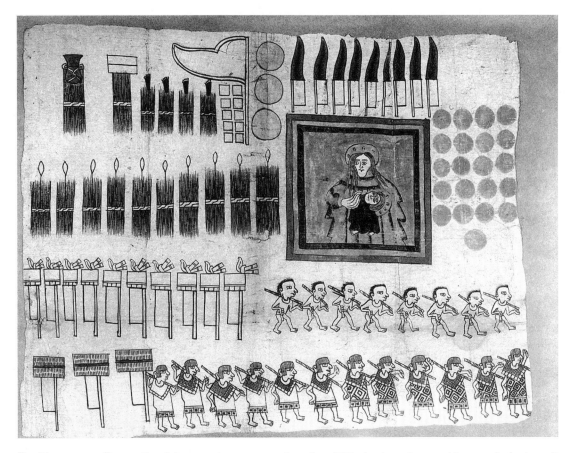

THE HUEJOTZINGO CODEX. Detail from an Aztec manuscript, circa 1531, that is a pictographic record of a lawsuit brought by Aztecs against Spanish colonial authorities to recover costs of Aztec aid to Cortés.

Motecuhzoma's treasure. After fending off an attack in Otumba, the army retreated to the allied republic of Tlaxcala. Undeterred by the costly setback, Cortés had no thoughts of abandoning his goal. He spent the winter of 1520 preparing the siege of Tenochtitlán, which lasted from late May until August 13, 1521, when Cuauhtemoc, the new lord of the Mexica who had led a heroic resistance, was captured and his people surrendered.

Cortés now controlled a vast territory, larger than Motecuhzoma's, that stretched from Veracruz to the Pacific coast; Cortés named it New Spain. Charles V, acknowledging the importance of this expansion over the objections of Velázquez, appointed Cortés governor and captain general of New Spain. Cortés then tried to combine his military role with a civilian one by expanding his control of the country to the south, founding new cities, and promoting agriculture and mining. He also organized the reconstruction of Tenochtitlán (later called Mexico City), which had been destroyed by the war and decimated by new diseases introduced by Europeans. In October 1524, he led an unsuccessful land expedition to

Honduras, during which he almost died. In his absence, chaos erupted in Mexico City, and upon his return he was stripped of his office and subjected to an official enquiry that lasted for many years.

In 1528 Cortés sailed back to Spain for the first time. He was received with honors, and Emperor Charles knighted him with the title Marquis of the Valley, a nobility status with vast territories and a huge encomienda of Indians. Although he was never to recover his governorship, he was granted permission to explore the Pacific coast, an activity to which he dedicated his best efforts in the 1530s, with mixed results. In January 1540 he left New Spain never to return. His last years in Spain remain clouded in mystery. Little is known apart from his ongoing writing of claims and demands to the Crown. He participated in an unsuccessful sea expedition to Tunisia, but otherwise he seems to have lived a life of quiet retirement with Juana de Zúñiga, his second wife, first in Valladolid and then in Seville, where he died on December 2, 1547.

The legacy of Cortés can hardly be overstated, and unlike other conquistadores, he seems to have had a good grasp of the complex issues surrounding his actions. His ideas are clearly stated in his *Cartas de relación*, the five long dispatches he sent to Charles V between 1519 and 1526. He thought of his enterprise in both political and religious terms, as a universal expansion of Charles's empire as well as a providential crusade for the Christian religion. He was also aware of the abuses committed against the Caribbean Indians, and although he supported the encomienda system, he encouraged humanitarian efforts. By expanding the Spanish possessions into the American continent, Cortés created a new perception of the New World—hitherto perceived by many in Europe as little more than some exotic islands of primitive people—as a land endowed with resources and populated by civilizations akin to those in the Old World. As such, he was able to describe with admiration the urban and artistic accomplishments of the Aztecs, but as a man of his time he understood their future only in terms of political and cultural assimilation to the European mode of life.

Cortés quickly achieved legendary status as one of the best known figures of modern times. In his own day, the spectrum of opinion about him knew the extremes of praise and blame, even in Spain. On the one hand, his official biographer, Francisco López de Gómara, hailed him as a hero whose exploits surpassed those of Caesar, and this was the prevalent view of Europeans of his time; on the other hand, Bartolomé de las Casas, protector of the Indians, accused him of exemplifying the evils of the forceful conquest of the New World. In the West, a generally favorable view of Cortés prevailed until the twentieth century, when frequent criticism of his actions reflected a reassessment of European imperial expansion overseas.

BIBLIOGRAPHY

Cortés, Hernán. *Letters from Mexico*. New York. 1971. Translated and edited by Anthony R. Pagden. Reprint, New Haven, 1986.

Díaz del Castillo, Bernal. *The Discovery and Conquest of Mexico, 1517–1521*. Edited by Genaro García. Translated by A. P. Maudslay. New York, 1956.

Gómara, Francisco López de. *Historia de la conquista de México*. 2 vols. Mexico City, 1943.

Guzmán, Eulalia. *Relaciones de Hernán Cortés a Carlos V sobre la invasión de Anáhuac*. Mexico City, 1958.

León-Portilla, Miguel. *Cortés y la Mar del Sur*. Madrid, 1985.

Madariaga, Salvador de. *Hernán Cortés, Conqueror of Mexico*. London, 1942.

Martínez, José Luis. *Hernán Cortés*. Mexico City, 1990.

Navarro González, Alberto, ed. *Hernán Cortés*. Salamanca, 1986.

Orozco y Berra, Manuel. *Historia antigua y de la conquista de México*. Vol. 4. Mexico City, 1880. Reprint, Mexico City, 1960.

Wagner, Henry R. *The Rise of Fernando Cortés*. Berkeley, 1944.

ANGEL DELGADO-GOMEZ

COSA, JUAN DE LA (d. 1510), master of *Santa María*, cartographer, explorer. Little is known of Juan de la Cosa's early life, but by the end of the fifteenth century he was one of Spain's most respected navigators and cartographers. Controversy surrounds his life and career, including his birthplace. Late-fifteenth-century documents have been variously interpreted to suggest that he was born either at Puerto de Santa María, a city on the bay of Cádiz, or at Puerto de Santoña, a small village on the coast of Cantabria. Several theories attempt to reconcile this discrepancy (Ballesteros Beretta, 1987, and Berreiro-Meiro, 1970) including one, now discredited, that suggests that there were two Juan de la Cosas (Morison, 1942).

As owner and master of Columbus's flagship, *Santa María*, Cosa took part in the famous first voyage, but his ship sank off the coast of La Española on Christmas Eve, 1492. In his log entry for December 25, 1492, Columbus blamed the wreck on the ship's master, accusing him of negligence and cowardice; however, Columbus later helped him receive restitution from the Crown for the loss of his ship, calling this accusation into question. On Columbus's second voyage to America, Cosa is listed as a master chart maker and seaman and upon his return he remained in Spain until 1499, when he made the first of several voyages to Tierra Firme (South America). In mid-May, he signed on as chief pilot for Alonso de Ojeda and explored the north coast from the Boca de la Sierpe (Serpent's Mouth, the southern entrance to the Gulf of Paria) to Cabo de la Vela on the Guajira Peninsula.

Cosa's historic manuscript map—the earliest surviving European map to show part of America—was compiled upon his return to Spain in mid-June 1500. The date of the map has been debated, though recent research using X-ray, reflection-ray, and ultraviolet-ray analysis suggests that the inscribed date of 1500 is accurate. Drawn on parchment, the original map, in the Museo Naval in Madrid, measures 183 by 96 centimeters (72 by 38 inches). It shows both the Old and New Worlds. Recording the voyages of Columbus, Ojeda, Amerigo Vespucci, Martín Alonso Pinzón, and John Cabot, among others, it is given special authority by Cosa's participation in some of the voyages. The map, in the portolano style, shows the equator, both tropics, and a meridian apparently corresponding to the Line of Demarcation established by the Treaty of Tordesillas of 1494. At the west end of the map, occupying unknown lands, is an image of Saint Christopher carrying the Christ Child on his shoulders, said by some to symbolize Columbus carrying Christianity to the shores of the New World. Beneath this image is an inscription: "This map was made by Juan de la Cosa at Puerto de Santa María in the year 1500."

In February 1501, Cosa again sailed to Tierra Firme, as a pilot for Rodrigo de Bastidas. They coasted south from

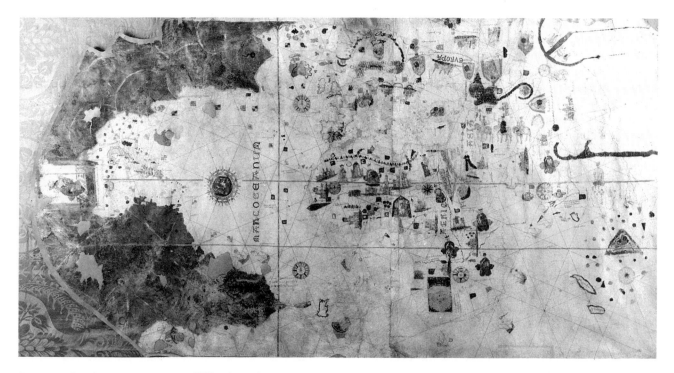

JUAN DE LA COSA'S MANUSCRIPT MAP OF 1500. The earliest surviving world map to show both the Old and New Worlds. The Old World (at right, faintly visible) is represented in white on the original, the New World (at left), in green. The two halves are in different scales, with the American portion greatly enlarged. At center left is a portrait of Saint Christopher, said to be an allusion to Columbus. The dark patches are holes in the original.   MUSEO NAVAL, MADRID

Cabo de la Vela exploring Caramairi and Urabá (the northwest coast of Columbia) and then headed north along the east coast of Panama to near Puerto del Retrete. Here they turned back after trading with the Indians, returning to Spain in September 1502.

Cosa was held in high regard by the Spanish Crown. It was perhaps due to his influence that Isabel changed her opposition to slavery; in 1503 she excluded the natives of Cartagena and Urabá from royal protection. Her decision offered the prospect of riches for Cosa, who had recently been appointed alguacil mayor (chief constable) of Urabá, granting him a share of a potentially lucrative slave trade. Perhaps in return for such favors, he undertook a secret mission to Portugal in 1503 to investigate suspected Portuguese infringements on Spanish territorial claims to Tierra Firme. His mission was discovered and he was imprisoned for a short period of time.

Following his release, Cosa prepared to claim his appointment as alguacil mayor of Urabá, though he did not reach the north coast of South America until late 1504. There he joined the Cristóbal Guerrera expedition, which had left Spain a few months earlier, and carried out a series of brutal raids that even their contemporaries condemned. Referring to Cosa and Guerrera, the sixteenth-century chronicler Gonzalo Fernández de Oviedo

states, "It seems to me this manner of exploring and bartering should be better called laying waste." But the Spaniards were repaid in kind. Death, disease, and combat took a heavy toll, and in March 1506 Cosa returned to Spain with only a handful of men. Oviedo saw a moral in these events: "See, those of you who can read, how few of the many Christians remained . . . so that you understand how much this gold costs."

In 1508, Cosa's status as the most experienced navigator in the West Indies was acknowledged by his participation (along with Vespucci, Pinzón, and Juan Díaz de Solís) in the Junta de Burgos. He contributed not only his geographical knowledge but also his technical skill as a pilot and cartographer. Both the office of pilot major in the Casa de la Contratación and the proposal for the creation of a master map of the Spanish discoveries (the Padrón Real) were initiated at this meeting.

The Junta also decided to impose Spanish authority over Tierra Firme. To this end, an expedition under the direction of Alonso Ojeda, with Cosa as second-in-command, was sent to occupy Urabá in late 1509. Shortly after landing on February 28, 1510, Cosa led a slaving raid inland, taking a village named Turbaco. The Indians counterattacked, killing seventy Spaniards including Cosa, whose body was riddled with poison arrows.

According to Oviedo, this was retribution for his previous transgressions. He left a widow and at least one daughter.

Juan de la Cosa sought wealth and found death in the New World. He was recognized by his contemporaries for his skill but condemned for his cruelty. Las Casas claims that he was the most experienced navigator in the West Indies. Pietro Martire d'Anghiera states that his maps were the most valued of their day. The world map of 1500 survives as one of the foundation documents in the early history of America.

BIBLIOGRAPHY

Anghiera, Pietro Martire d'. *Decadas del nuevo mundo*. Translated by Agustín Millares Carlo. 2 vols. Mexico, 1964.

Ballesteros Beretta, Antonio. *El cantabro Juan de la Cosa y el descubrimiento de America*, 2d ed. Cantabria, 1987.

Barreiro-Meiro, Roberto. *Juan de la Cosa y su doble personalidad*. Madrid, 1970.

Campbell, Tony. "Portolan Charts from the Late Thirteenth Century to 1500." In *The History of Cartography*. Vol. 1: *Cartography in Prehistoric, Ancient, and Medieval Europe and the Mediterranean*. Edited by J. B. Harley and David Woodward. Chicago, 1987.

Cerezo Martínez, Ricardo. "Aportación al estudio de la carta de Juan de la Cosa." In *Géographie du monde au moyen âge et à la Renaissance*. Edited by Monique Pelletier. Paris, 1989.

Morison, Samuel Eliot. *Admiral of the Ocean Sea: A Life of Christopher Columbus*. 2 vols. Boston, 1942.

Puente y Olea, Manuel de la. *Los trabajos geográficos de la Casa de Contratación*. Seville, 1900.

Vigneras, Louis-André. *The Discovery of South America and the Andalusian Voyages*. Chicago, 1976.

Watts, Pauline Moffitt. "Prophecy and Discovery: On the Spiritual Origins of Christopher Columbus's 'Enterprise of the Indies.'" *American Historical Review* 90 (1985): 73–102.

J. B. Harley and David W. Tilton

CREW. See *Ships and Crews.*

CROSS-STAFF. An angle-measuring instrument (usable vertically or horizontally), the cross-staff consisted of a bar or rod (the staff), with a sliding transversal bar, the transversary. The cross-staff was also called the sea staff or Jacob's staff (Latin, *baculus Jacobi*, perhaps from the staff of the pilgrim to Santiago de Compostela). In other languages it was called *baculus geometricus* or *radius astronomicus* (Latin), *bâton de Jacob* (French), *balestilha* or *balestinha* (Portuguese), *ballestilla* (Spanish, perhaps from the word for crossbow). These terms were applied to the astronomer's, surveyor's, and seaman's cross-staves, and theoretical distinctions in their application were not consistently maintained. The transversary was called in Latin *tabula* or *transversarius*.

In nautical use, the cross-staff was similar in principle to the *kamal*, and it has been suggested that the Portuguese navigators' acquaintance with the *kamal* led to their interest in the cross-staff. An observer held the end of the staff to his eye and moved the transversary along the staff until the upper edge of the transversary, viewed from the end of the staff, appeared to cut through the celestial body being observed, and the lower edge appeared to lie on the horizon (or similarly between any two objects, celestial or otherwise, of which the angular separation was to be measured). A scale engraved on the staff enabled the angle (or a function of it) to be read off from the position of the transversary. The problem of the position of the eye in relation to the axis of the staff (parallax error) and consequential inaccuracies in the observations were recognized from the outset and discussed in the literature. Improvements to the cross-staff included the attachment of sight vanes at the ends of the transversary, a lockable

Use of the cross-staff. For determining the altitude of the polestar, when the Guard Stars are in a particular position. Reproduced from Pedro de Medina's *Regimiento de navegación*. Seville, 1563. National Maritime Museum, Greenwich

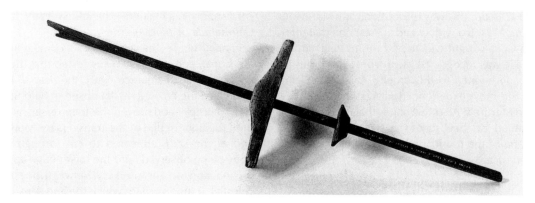

NAUTICAL CROSS-STAFF. Of wood, dating from circa 1596.   RIJKSMUSEUM, AMSTERDAM

sliding sleeve holding the transversary on the staff, changes in the proportions of the staff to the transversary (of which several of different sizes were provided), and changes in the nature of the scales. Because a cross-staff required the user to look directly at the observed object, it could not be conveniently used to make solar observations. João de Lisboa, writing of solar observations with the cross-staff made "from above" so that the sun's disk was covered by the transversary, says that a quarter degree of the measured altitude should be deducted, corresponding to the approximate apparent diameter of the sun. The back staff (or Davis quadrant), devised toward the end of the sixteenth century, obviated this difficulty.

The cross-staff was usually of hardwood, but sometimes of brass with a central wooden core. It was probably invented by the Jewish Provençal philosopher and scientist, Levi ben Gershom (1288–1344), who described it in his *Sefer tekunah;* the part of this treatise describing the cross-staff was translated from Hebrew into Latin by Peter of Alexandria in 1342. Regiomontanus and his patron, Bernhard Walther, knew of Levi's treatise, and Walther used a cross-staff *(radius astronomicus)* for many of his astronomical observations at Nürnberg from 1476 to 1504. Large and elaborate cross-staves were used by astronomers until well into the seventeenth century. The average size of the cross-staff may be judged from the woodcut in Pedro de Medina's *Regimiento de navegación* (1563).

Although the cross-staff was in principle available to Columbus, or any other fifteenth-century navigator, there is no evidence that it was used by seamen before the sixteenth century; the first navigational work to mention it is the *Livro de marinharia* of João de Lisboa, but parts of this work date from the middle of the sixteenth century. It is certain, however, the cross-staff was in use at sea by João Gomes before 1524. The type of cross-staff described by Levi ben Gershom had scale divisions that could not be read directly in degrees of arc, and seamen would have required a table to convert to degrees the readings obtained. The scale on the seaman's cross-staff, therefore, read directly in degrees. The earliest surviving cross-staves are probably those made at Louvain in 1563 and 1571 by Gualterus Arsenius, nephew of Rainer Gemma Frisius, who had published, at Antwerp and Louvain in 1545, a comprehensive book on the cross-staff; but these brass instruments were presumably not for nautical use. The earliest surviving nautical cross-staff is probably that left at Novaya Zemlya in 1596 or 1597 by the Dutch explorers Jacob van Heemskerck and Willem Barents.

[See also *Kamal.*]

BIBLIOGRAPHY

Albuquerque, Luís de. *Curso de História da náutica.* 2d ed. Coimbra, 1972.

Maddison, Francis. *Medieval Scientific Instruments and the Development of Navigational Instruments in the XVth and XVIth Centuries.* Agrupamento de estudos de cartografia antiga, vol. 30. Coimbra, 1969.

Roche, John J. "The Radius Astronomicus in England." *Annals of Science* 38 (1981): 1–32.

Waters, David W. *The Art of Navigation in Elizabethan and Early Stuart Times.* London, 1958.

FRANCIS MADDISON

CUAUHTEMOC (c. 1495–1525), the last Mexica (or Aztec) king. Cuauhtemoc, whose name means "descending eagle," ascended to the rulership of the Aztec Triple Alliance in 1520. As ruler, Cuauhtemoc tried to defeat the Spaniards who had arrived in Central Mexico in 1519. The Aztec ruler Motecuhzoma II (Moctezuma), unsure how to deal with the invaders, was captured and later killed, and the Spaniards were forced to abandon the Aztec capital of Tenochtitlan (now Mexico City). Cuitlahuac succeeded

Motecuhzoma, ruling for only eighty days; in that time he organized the first active resistance to the Spaniards. After Cuitlahuac's death from smallpox, Cuauhtemoc continued the resistance. From April through August 1521, Tenochtitlan was besieged by the Spaniards. During the siege, Cuauhtemoc called a council to decide whether to continue resistance or sue for peace. His concern was that the people of Tenochtitlan were suffering from the lack of food and water and from disease. Native priests argued for war to the death, advice which Cuauhtemoc followed. War continued until August 13, 1521, when Tenochtitlan fell. Cuauhtemoc sought to escape in a canoe, but the Spaniards captured him, later torturing him to learn where gold was hidden. Though he continued as king, Cuauhtemoc was no longer a sovereign monarch, but an instrument of Spanish rule. In 1525 he was compelled to accompany Hernando Cortés on his expedition to Honduras. En route Cuauhtemoc was allegedly involved in a conspiracy and was executed. In modern Mexico, Cuauhtemoc is a national hero, a symbol of resistance to the Conquest.

BIBLIOGRAPHY

Cortés, Hernando. *Letters from Mexico.* Translated and edited by A. R. Pagden. New York, 1971.

Díaz del Castillo, Bernal. *Historia verdadera de la conquista de México.* Mexico City, 1980.

Sahagún, Bernardino de. *The Conquest of New Spain, 1585 Revision.* Translated by Howard F. Cline. Edited by S. L. Cline. Salt Lake City, 1989.

S. L. CLINE

CUBA. Almost 1,300 kilometers (800 miles) long and over 160 kilometers (100 miles) broad in places, Cuba is by far the largest of the West Indian islands. It is generally hilly, with three well-defined groups of mountains in the east, center, and west. The eastern range, known as the Sierra Maestra, is the largest. Along the coast are river valleys and plains where intensive agriculture is possible. Two of the most fertile of these plains are in the southeast, at Santiago de Cuba and Guantánamo.

"Guantánamo," with its distinctive initial letters *(gua),* is characteristic of the place-names given by the original inhabitants. The oldest aboriginal groups were the Ciboney and Guanahatabey, who by the fifteenth century were largely confined to the western end of the island. The rest of the island was occupied by the more recently arrived Tainos, a subgroup of the Arawaks, who made up perhaps 90 percent of the population of about 100,000 people.

The Amerindian peoples of the northern West Indies seem to have shared much in terms of culture and

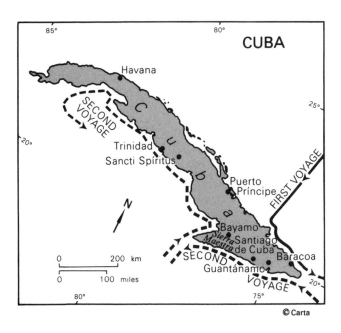

© Carta

economy. They all relied heavily on fish, which was supplemented by the cassava root, which will grow in very unpromising conditions. They lived in villages under headmen known as caciques and were peaceable, without territorial ambitions. They had animistic religious beliefs and held various sports in high esteem. Some of their artifacts are remarkable: they wove fine hammocks, crafted superb canoes from huge trees, and created distinctive pottery.

Columbus reached Cuba during his first voyage, on October 28, 1492. He named the island Juana, after the daughter of Fernando and Isabel, but the native name of Cuba eventually prevailed. On the first voyage Columbus sailed along the northeast coast of the island before heading eastward. He returned during his second voyage, in the spring of 1494, and this time sailed along the south coast, visiting Taino villages and exchanging goods with the residents.

After the voyages of Columbus there was a considerable interval before the Spaniards came back to Cuba. Further efforts were undertaken from their base in La Española. In 1510 Diego Velásquez was commissioned to settle the island, and in 1511 he established himself at Baracoa. During the next few years seven towns were founded on the island, which was thus taken over by the Spaniards. The Tainos rather quickly died out, partly through conflict with the newcomers, but more through the ravages of European diseases.

Despite its size, Cuba was not an important part of the Spanish empire. In the early sixteenth century the settlement of La Española engaged the Spaniards, and after 1521 and the conquest of Mexico they were wholly preoccupied by the conquest of the mainland. So Cuba became a sort of backwater, a land of cattle ranches and a few sugar plantations whose main importance was as a staging post for the homeward-bound fleets, which would stop over at Havana.

[See also *Indian America*, articles on *Island Caribs* and *Tainos*.]

BIBLIOGRAPHY

Portuondo, Fernando. *Curso de historia de Cuba*. Havana, 1945.
Suchlicki, Jaime. *Historical Dictionary of Cuba*. Metuchen, N.J., 1988.

DAVID BUISSERET

CUNEO, MICHELE DA (c. 1450–c. 1511), gentleman explorer and a friend of Columbus. Born into a noble family of Savona, Michele da Cuneo was the son of Corrado da Cuneo who, in 1474, sold to Domenico Colombo, father of Christopher, a house with two pieces of land in Légino. Michele da Cuneo was an educated man, who spoke not only Genoese and Latin but also Castilian and Tuscan, the latter being the Italian language of the learned. Columbus, on the other hand, being a plebeian, knew only Genoese and Latin at the time of his departure from Genoa.

Cuneo was a participant in Columbus's second voyage. Although the reason for his accompanying Columbus is not known, the fact that he did not stop at La Isabela with the Castilian noblemen who also made the journey gives support to the claim that for him scientific curiosity exceeded the economic and military interests of the expedition.

Cuneo, after his return from the voyage, wrote a letter dated December 15, 1495, which is preserved at the University Library in Bologna. Addressed to another Savonese nobleman, Gerolamo Annari, the letter is the first European document, after Columbus's journal, to give extensive details on the flora and fauna of America. Cuneo was also something of a gossip. It was he who wrote of a flirtation between Columbus and Beatriz de Bobadilla of Gomera, who was as beautiful as she was sensual and cruel.

Cuneo and Columbus seem to have been good friends. The Admiral presented him with an island, southeast of La Española, which to this day bears, in his honor, the name of Saona.

Apart from being a friend, Cuneo was also a great admirer of Columbus. He wrote about the Admiral: "I want you to know well, that in my humble opinion, since Genoa is Genoa, there is no born man as magnanimous and as expert in navigation as the said Admiral." These praises refer not only to Columbus as expert sailor, but also to the tenacity with which he faced difficult situations and his sparing the members of his crew onerous tasks: "as soon as the storm was gone, he would raise the sails while the others slept."

BIBLIOGRAPHY

Morison, Samuel Eliot. *Admiral of the Ocean Sea: A Life of Christopher Columbus*. 2 vols. Boston, 1942.
Taviani, Paolo Emilio. *I viaggi di Colombo*. 2d ed. Vol. 2. Novara, 1990. Spanish ed., Barcelona, 1989.
Vannini, Marisa de Gerulewicz. "Traducción y notas de novitatibus insularum occeani hersperii repertarum a Don Christoforo Columbo genuensi por Michael de Cuneo." Special issue of *Revista de Historia*. Caracas, 1965.

PAOLO EMILIO TAVIANI
Translated from Italian by Rodica Diaconescu-Blumenfeld

CUNHA, TRISTÃO DA (c. 1460–1539), Portuguese leader of 1506 expedition to India; discoverer of the island of Tristan da Cunha. Tristão da Cunha was the son of Nuno da Cunha, chamberlain of Prince Fernando, nephew and heir of Prince Henry the Navigator and the younger brother of King Afonso V (r. 1438–1481). Cunha himself was chamberlain of Prince Fernando's son, the ill-fated Dom Diogo, duke of Viseu, older brother of the future King Manuel I. After Dom Diogo was stabbed to death by King João II in 1484, Cunha became a member of João's household. When Manuel became king in 1495, Cunha served as councilor and trusted adviser to the monarch, accompanying him to Castile in 1498 so that they could be acclaimed heirs to the Castilian and Aragonese thrones.

In 1505 Cunha was named to be *capitão-mor* (commander) of the seventh armada to India and governor of Portuguese Asia for three years. However, illness prevented him from going to India and Dom Francisco de Almeida took his place. By 1506 Cunha had been restored to health and was named *capitão-mor* of the expedition of fourteen to sixteen ships that left Lisbon in the spring of that year and included the famed Afonso de Albuquerque. His instructions were to establish a fortress on the island of Socotra in the Arabian Sea the better to control non-Portuguese shipping through the Red Sea, and then to continue to India to take on a cargo of spices.

En route, probably in October 1506, Cunha discovered an archipelago of three small uninhabited islands and two islets in the south Atlantic about 1,900 kilometers (1,200 miles) south of the island of Saint Helena, 2,400 kilometers (1,500 miles) west of the Cape of Good Hope, and about 2,900 kilometers (1,800 miles) east of Uruguay (37°6′ S latitude and 12°15′ W longitude). The largest island (with an area of approximately 100 square kilometers [40 square miles] and reaching about 2,080 meters [6,760 feet] above sea level) and the archipelago itself now bears an anglicized version of his name (Tristan da Cunha). The smaller islands (later named Inaccessible and Nightingale) are about 16 kilometers (10 miles) apart. All three islands, because of their precipitous cliffs, were not easily accessible to shipping and Cunha did not land there. Since the region is subject to dangerous squalls, it was avoided by most seafarers during the Age of Discovery.

Arriving in Mozambique too late to catch the favorable wind to India, Cunha explored the island of Madagascar and attacked several East African Muslim strongholds. After leaving the African coast, the forces led by Albuquerque and Cunha captured Socotra after a bitter fight. In August 1507, while Albuquerque remained on the island to supervise the building of a fortress, Cunha sailed to India where he helped lift the Muslim siege of Cannanore. He also aided Viceroy Almeida in the struggle against the ruler of Calicut. In early December 1508, Cunha embarked for Portugal in command of five ships loaded with spices, pearls, and precious stones. After an absence from the Portuguese capital of almost twenty-six months, Cunha arrived in Lisbon on June 1, 1508. Four of the five ships reached Portugal safely, the fifth having been captured by the French corsair Mondragon.

In 1513 Cunha was named to head the Portuguese embassy sent to Rome to pledge King Manuel's obedience to the newly elected pope, Leo X. The embassy included three of Cunha's sons as well as Manuel's delegates to the Fifth Lateran Council. On March 12, 1514, the Portuguese embassy made its triumphal entrance into Rome accompanied by musicians, an elephant from Malabar, India, and its mahout, and a Persian on horseback accompanied by a cheetah on a leash, the latter animal a gift to King Manuel by the ruler of Ormuz. In a letter to António Carneiro, Portugal's secretary of state, Cunha wrote that "all said it was the most honored and richest embassy that ever entered Rome." Cunha later presented the animals to the pope, along with richly decorated vestments and altar cloths.

Little is known of the last two-and-a-half decades of Cunha's life. His oldest son, Nuno da Cunha, served as governor of India from 1529 to 1538 and died on the return voyage to Portugal early in 1539, predeceasing his father, who died sometime before September 6 of the same year.

BIBLIOGRAPHY

Andrade, António Alberto Banha de. *História de um fidalgo quinhentista português: Tristão da Cunha.* Lisbon, 1974.
Brander, Jan. *Tristan da Cunha, 1506–1902.* London, 1940.

FRANCIS A. DUTRA

CURRENTS. See *Tides and Currents.*

CUZCO. Cuzco was the capital of the Inca state Tahuantinsuyu until its capture by Spaniards in 1533. It is located in the easternmost range of the Andes of Peru, at fourteen degrees south latitude. It was built in a wide, well-watered valley on the Huatanay River, a tributary of the Vilcanota. At 3,250 meters above sea level, it has a semiarid climate with high daytime and low nighttime temperatures and a short rainy season.

Inca oral tradition states that Manco Capac, the original Inca, founded Cuzco at an undetermined date. By the mid-fifteenth century, when the city had attained considerable size, Pachacuti Inca rebuilt it as an elite administrative and ceremonial center. On the outskirts and scattered throughout the valley were the villages of the common people. The only eyewitness estimate of the population for the Cuzco valley gave 40,000 residences, which may have housed 100,000 to 200,000 inhabitants. Three major languages were spoken: Quechua, Aymara, and Puquina. People of different ethnic groups were required to wear distinctive clothing and hairstyles.

Cuzco impressed the Spanish conquerors as large, rich, clean, and well ordered. It was constructed of stone buildings with gabled thatched roofs along narrow, straight stone-paved streets. The river and streams were lined with stone. Palaces and temples were built as *cancha*, several rooms around an enclosed courtyard. Some included *kallanka*, long halls for ceremonies in inclement weather. The most distinguishing stylistic feature was the trapezoidal aperture for doorways, windows, and niches. Sheets of gold covered the walls of important temples.

The city was divided socially and geographically in two. In the upper half were two large open squares separated by the Huatanay River. Life-sized gold figures of people, maize, llamas, and alpacas were embedded in the fine gravel that paved one of the squares, Haucaypata. Facing it were the temple to Viracocha, the creator deity, three palaces (Cassana, CoraCora, and Amarucancha), and the Acllahuasi, the palace for the *aclla*, the women chosen to weave the enormous quantities of textiles the Incas needed and to brew the corn beer for their festivals. Coricancha, the temple to the sun, where the mummies of the Incas were kept, also had gold figures planted in its garden. Above Cuzco was the fortress-temple, Sacsahuaman.

Inca religion was based on reverence for the earth, sky, and the ancestors. The fertile, cultivated earth was revered in the form of the feminine deity Pachamama; earthquakes as the masculine deity, Pachacamac; and the largest mountains as lords. In the Cuzco area there were many official sacred places that were significant landscape features, such as springs, lakes, hills, and rock outcroppings. Of them, 329 were encoded onto a system of imaginary lines that radiated from Coricancha like spokes of a wheel; their care and worship was the responsibility of the major *ayllus* (lineages) of Inca Cuzco. The thunderbolt (Illapa) and the sun (Inti) were worshiped primarily by men and the moon (Mamaquilla) by women. Most importantly, the Incas revered their ancestors, whose mummies had extensive lands and large retinues dedicated to their care. The Incas also considered themselves children of the sun, thereby incorporating that deity as one of their ancestors.

The surrounding hillsides were terraced and watered by an extensive network of irrigation canals. Maize was grown on the lower slopes and potatoes on the higher, and at the highest elevations were pastures for herds of llamas and alpacas, used for transportation, sacrifices, wool, and meat. Cuzco and the entire Inca state were divided into four quarters connected by four major highways that originated at the two central squares, Haucaypata and Cusipata. The road to the northern province, Chinchaysuyu, reached present-day Ecuador; the road to the western province, Cuntisuyu, went to the southern coast of present-day Peru and into Chile; the road to the southern province, Collasuyu, went to present-day Bolivia; and the road to the eastern province, Antisuyu, went to the slopes of the Andes that descend into the Amazonian lowlands of Peru.

The Spaniards under Francisco Pizarro conquered Cuzco in November 1533 and refounded it as a Spanish city on March 23, 1534. Manco Inca presented himself as an ally to the Spaniards, who crowned him as a puppet Inca in December 1533. However, in 1536 Manco Inca organized a rebellion and burned Cuzco, which was rebuilt with tile roofs. Manco Inca retreated to Vilcabamba, where he set up an Inca government-in-exile until his assassination in 1544.

The colonial city became a major provider of supplies on the route from Lima to the silver mines at Potosi. Francisco, Gonzalo, and Hernando Pizarro and Diego de Almagro fought over their respective shares of the former Inca empire, which resulted in a factional war and the execution of Almagro in 1538. Almagrist forces, however, had Hernando Pizarro imprisoned in Spain (1540) and murdered Francisco (1541, in Lima) and Gonzalo Pizarro (1548). Almagrist and Pizarrist forces continued to struggle against each other and against the increasing power of the Spanish colonial state, as did the Incas from their exile state in Vilcabamba. The last claimant to the Inca throne, Tupac Amaru, a descendant of Manco Inca, led an unsuccessful rebellion against the Spaniards. He was captured and executed in Cuzco in 1572, thus ending Inca resistance to Spanish conquest. The indigenous population was reorganized into parish towns by the Viceroy Francisco de Toledo, marking the beginning of an era of strong control by the Spanish Crown over the viceroyalty of Peru.

BIBLIOGRAPHY

Hemming, John. *The Conquest of the Incas.* New York, 1970.

Hemming, John, and Edward Ranney. *Monuments of the Incas.* Boston, 1982.

Gasparini, Graziano, and Luise Margolies. *Inca Architecture.* Bloomington, Ind., 1980.

Porras Barrenechea, Raúl. *Antología del Cuzco.* Lima, Peru, 1961.

Rowe, John Howland. "What Kind of a Settlement Was Inca Cuzco?" *Ñawpa Pacha* 5 (1967): 59–76.

Jeanette E. Sherbondy

D

DA GAMA, VASCO. See *Gama, Vasco da.*

DEAD RECKONING. The dead reckoning position, as opposed to a navigational fix, is determined by advancing the course and distance made good since the last known position. The art of dead reckoning was perfected during the late medieval period in the Mediterranean, where the tideless environment enabled the magnetic compass, the nautical chart, the sandglass, and the *toleta de marteloio* (a form of traverse table) to be used to produce a purely mathematical solution to the problem of position at sea. Conditions on the Atlantic coasts of Europe, where the ebb and flow of the tide so largely dominated passage making, were not so favorable, but during the fifteenth century the traditional skills of pilots schooled in such conditions were combined with Mediterranean practices to produce the method of navigation characteristic of the Age of Discovery. Toward the end of the century, when the long ocean voyages began, a form of astronomical navigation emerged that verified one element of the dead reckoning, but, until the problem of fixing longitude was finally solved some three hundred years later, dead reckoning remained the basis of all navigation.

A vivid, if somewhat colorful, picture of Mediterranean methods is painted by the German monk Felix Faber who went on pilgrimage to the Holy Land in a three-masted galley in 1483. His account is nonetheless instructive for being that of a landsman. The pilot (or "pirate," as Faber mistakenly calls him) is described as a powerful officer who knew the shortest and safest ways across the sea but who would hand over to local officers (local pilots, one must assume) in any area he did not himself know. "Besides the pilot," Faber writes,

there were other learned men, astrologers and watchers of omens who considered the signs of the stars and sky, judged the winds and gave directions to the pilot himself. And they were all expert in judging from the sky whether the weather would be stormy or fair, taking into account besides such signs as the colour of the sea, the movement of dolphins and of fish, the smoke from the fire and the scintillations when the oars were dipped in the water. At night they knew the time by the inspection of the stars.

Faber then goes on to talk of the magnetic compass (calling it a Stella Maris), of which the ship had two, one near the mast and a second on the upper poop deck:

And beside it all night long a lantern burns, and they never take their eyes off it and there is always a man watching the star [i.e., the compass rose]. Nor does the helmsman dare move the tiller in the slightest degree except at the order of the one watching the Stella Maris from which he sees whether the ship ought to go straight on or curve or turn sideways.

The narrator then goes on to describe the nautical chart,

on which is a scale of inches showing length and breadth, and on which thousands of lines are drawn across the sea and on which regions are marked by dots and numbers of miles. Over this chart they hang, and can see where they are even when the stars are hidden.

He ends up with a passage about how the navigation of the vessel is organized, saying that the captain does not interfere in matters of navigation, nor does he know the art, but he orders the ship to go this way or that.

Though the account is impressionistic, it clearly points to the care with which navigation was conducted, both as to the course steered and in the observation of natural phenomena that might reflect on the ship's position. The "thousands of lines" drawn across the sea of course refers to the rhumbs emanating from the wind roses on the chart by means of which the pilot, using two pairs of dividers, "pricked off" his position on the chart and then laid off the new course.

Although Faber makes no mention of it, a sandglass would be turned, probably by the helmsman, every half hour, both to regulate the watchkeeping duties and to keep up the dead reckoning, for out of sight of land the measurement of (intervals of) time, in conjunction with an assessment of speed by the pilot was the only way of calculating distance run. Mediterranean books of sailing directions, such as the late thirteenth-century *Compasso da navigare* gave precise distances to be run on given courses over hundreds of miles, instructions that could be followed only by accurate steering, plotting, and estimation of distance run. Further, the *toleta de marteloio*, the form of traverse table used when the ship was forced off her intended track by headwinds, would have been useless without an accurate assessment of the distance run. The glass, whether half-hour or hour, was reset each noon, when the sun bore due south.

Although there is no documentary evidence of the *toleta de marteloio* being used outside the Mediterranean, it seems highly probable that it was and that it was adapted early in the fifteenth century to make it more suitable for use in an open ocean with currents of unknown velocity. It formed an essential part of Mediterranean dead-reckoning navigation. First referred to by the Catalan mathematician and scholar Ramon Lull (1233–1315), the tables, or in another form, as on Andrea Bianco's atlas of 1436, the diagram, resolved the problem of the "traverse" caused by the necessity in headwinds to tack on either side of the mean line of advance. What was important to the medieval navigator, before there was any indication of latitude and longitude on the chart, was the angle between the course he wanted to make good and the course he actually had to steer. Essentially, the *toleta de marteloio* in two tables told the pilot how far he had sailed away from his desired course, the distance he had made good in the intended direction, and how to get back to the intended track. Chartwork, in the sense of resolving such problems graphically, was of course impossible on the portolan chart. The tables solved the problem geometrically, that is to say, without accounting for any drift or set. They were replaced, when altura navigation was introduced, by the Rule, or Regiment, of Leagues, which used the measured change of altitude (in effect, latitude) in place of the estimated distance sailed. The rule told the seaman how far he had to sail along a given rhumb to alter the altura by one degree, which was taken to equal 16⅔ leagues. David W. Waters in *Reflections upon Some Navigational and Hydrographic Problems of the XVth Century Related to the Voyage of Bartolomeu Dias, 1487–1488* contends that the Rule of Leagues was used long before latitude (as opposed

to altura) navigation was practiced and probably dates from the first rather than the last quarter of the fifteenth century. The successive attempts to estimate the length of a degree of the meridian and to fix the value of the league and of the mile are not relevant to the subject of dead reckoning.

[See also *Altura Sailing; Navigation.*]

BIBLIOGRAPHY

Crone, Ernst. *How Did the Navigator Determine the Speed of His Ship and the Distance Run?* Coimbra, 1969.

Lane, F. C. *The Invention of the Compass.* London, 1969.

Waters, David W. "Early Time and Distance Measurements at Sea." *Journal of the Institute of Navigation* 8, no. 2 (1955): 153–173.

Waters, David W. *Reflections upon Some Navigational and Hydrographic Problems of the XVth Century Related to the Voyage of Bartolomeu Dias, 1487–1488.* Lisbon, 1988.

M. W. Richey

DEATH OF COLUMBUS. See *Burial Places of Columbus; Columbus, Christopher,* article on *The Final Years, Illness, and Death; Writings,* article on *Last Will and Testament.*

DECLINATION OF THE COMPASS. See *Compass,* article on *Declination of the Compass.*

DE LA COSA, JUAN. See *Cosa, Juan de la.*

DEMARCATION, LINE OF. See *Line of Demarcation.*

DEMOGRAPHY. See *Disease and Demography.*

DEZA, DIEGO DE (1443–1523), friend of Columbus, archbishop of Seville. A Dominican priest, Deza was the tutor of the crown prince, Juan. In the summer of 1486, Queen Isabel appointed him to the commission of experts she asked to evaluate Columbus's ideas. Deza rose quickly in the church hierarchy, becoming successively bishop of Zamora, Salamanca, Jaén, and Palencia and finally archbishop of Seville from 1505 until his death in 1523, while serving as King Fernando's confessor in 1492 and inquisitor general from 1498 to 1507. He gained a reputation for strict censorship among the humanists editing the texts of the Polyglot Bible. But Columbus remembered Deza as a warm supporter of his ideas and, after his disastrous fourth voyage, chose the archbishop as arbiter in his disputes with the king.

Deza's nephew, the Dominican priest Pedro Suárez de Deza, was appointed bishop of Concepción de la Vega on the island of La Española in 1513 and allied himself with Bartolomé de las Casas as a defender of the Indians. In December 1515, nine Indians—six women and three men—who had been captured and survived the voyage to Spain, were sent to Seville, where Diego de Deza was expected to teach them Spanish and convert them to Christianity, so that they could return to convert their own people on La Española. In 1516, Deza founded and endowed the Colegio de Santo Tomás in Valladolid, which became a haven for Las Casas and other Dominicans engaged in the great debate over the nature and status of the Indians.

BIBLIOGRAPHY

Azcona, Tarsicio de. *La elección y reforma del episcopado español en tiempo de los Reyes Católicos.* Madrid, 1960.

Bataillon, Marcel. *Erasmo y España.* 2 vols. Mexico City, 1950.

Gams, Pius Bonifatius. *Die Kirchengeschichte von Spanien.* Vol. 3. Regensburg, 1879.

Giménez Fernández, Manuel. *Delegado de Cisneros para la reformación de las Indias.* Vol. 1 of *Bartolomé de las Casas.* Seville, 1953.

HELEN NADER

DIARIO. For discussion of Columbus's journal of his first voyage, see *Writings,* article on *Journal.*

DIAS, BARTOLOMEU (c. 1450–1500), Portuguese navigator. In voyages made in the years 1487 and 1488, Dias was the first European to go from the Atlantic Ocean to the Indian Ocean. His fleet, which sailed from Lisbon in August 1487, consisted of three ships under the command of Dias himself, his brother Diogo Dias, and the infante João.

The flotilla traveled safely, using the new astronomical procedures applied to navigation in the second half of the fifteenth century. Knowledge of these new procedures are the subject of an annotation made by Christopher Columbus in one of his books. Columbus reports that he attended an interview between Dias and King João II soon after Dias's return. Dias had assessed latitudes by means of an astrolabe, surely taking account of the position of the sun. He states that he traveled to a promontory that he named the Cape of Good Hope and that he had determined with an astrolabe that the cape was forty-five degrees from the equator. This figure is ten degrees farther south than the approximate latitude of the cape, although it may be the latitude of the southernmost point

reached by Dias, since it is known that he went farther south than the southernmost point of Africa.

King João apparently made no public recognition of Dias's voyage, even though it meant the realization of the king's dream of reaching the Indies and its spices by a direct sea route. The discovery of this route had radical repercussions on European geographical concepts, which were derived primarily from Ptolemy's *Geography.* The planispheres reproduced in this work showed the Indian Ocean as an inland sea and the African continent as exceedingly wide to the south, thus giving the impression that the Atlantic was also a landlocked sea. Though maps by less prestigious authors, such as Fra Mauro, presented Africa as circumnavigable, the predominant geographical image was derivated from Ptolemaic cartography. For example, Duarte Pacheco Pereira in his *Esmeraldo de situ orbis* (Emerald of the earth), written between 1505 and 1508, states that the seas are landlocked (*medi terrani*).

Bartolomeu Dias's trip, therefore, was a revelation to Europe: it was possible to reach the Indian Ocean from the Atlantic by ship. A map drawn by Henricus Martellus Germanus in 1489 or 1490 spread this novel idea throughout Europe. In 1490 the publication of Ptolemy's *Geography* was suspended until new data about the world could be collected. The book was republished in 1507 with new tables that sought to give a new and realistic configuration of lands and seas.

Little is known about the life of Bartolomeu Dias, except that he navigated the Atlantic in order to determine current and wind conditions. João Barros writes that he experienced many "dangers at sea" during the voyage that made him famous. He was responsible for numerous activities related to navigation in the city of Lisbon and was a member of the fleet of Pedro Álvares Cabral as the commander of a caravel. Caught in a sudden storm on May 23, 1500, he and all his crew were drowned at sea.

BIBLIOGRAPHY

De Lery, Jean. *History of a Voyage to the Land of Brazil Otherwise Called America.* Translated by Janet Whatley. Berkeley, 1990.

Diffey, Bailey W. *Prelude to Empire: Portugal Overseas before Henry the Navigator.* Lincoln, Neb., 1960.

Diffey, Bailey W., and George D. Winius. *Foundations of the Portuguese Empire, 1414–1850.* Edited by Boyd C. Shafer. Minneapolis, 1977.

Morison, Samuel Eliot. *Portuguese Voyages to America in the Fifteenth Century.* New York, 1965.

LUÍS DE ALBUQUERQUE
Translated from Portuguese by Paola Carù

DÍAZ DEL CASTILLO, BERNAL (1495?–1584), Spanish soldier and chronicler born in Medina del Campo, in northern Castille. Díaz sailed for Tierra Firme, Panama, in 1514 to join the recently appointed governor, Pedro Arias de Ávila (called Pedrárias Dávila). He then moved to Cuba and participated as a soldier in three expeditions launched by its governor, Diego Velázquez, to the Mexican coast: the first led by Francisco Fernández de Córdoba (1517), the second by Juan de Grijalba (1518), and the third by Hernando Cortés, which resulted in the long campaign of conquest of Mexico (1519–1521). In 1523 Díaz accompanied Captain Luis Marín in the conquest of Chiapa and a year later he accompanied Cortés in his expedition to Honduras. Upon his return to Mexico City in 1526, he was granted an encomienda of Indians in Chamula and later was appointed regidor of Coatzacoalcos. After a brief trip to Spain in 1540, he settled in Guatemala in 1541, where he married Teresa Becerra in 1544, with whom he had several children. During another trip to Spain in 1550 he was appointed regidor of Guatemala City. He spent the rest of his long life there, active in local politics and as a landholder.

Unlike other famous conquistadores, Díaz never distinguished himself in military deeds. His fame rests solely on his *True History of the Conquest of New Spain,* an account of his participation in the campaign, designed to inform the royal officials of his service to the Crown. Such accounts were often written by conquistadores, but Díaz's is distinguished as a comprehensive history that reacts vigorously against Francisco López de Gómara's *Conquest of Mexico* (1552), which praises Hernando Cortés while making little mention of his soldiers. Díaz was fully aware of his technical inability as a historian, since, unlike Gómara, he did not have the training to write in the appropriately high literary style. But he believed his personal account of the facts more than compensated for his poor rhetoric. Díaz admired Cortés no less than Gómara, but the *True History* provides a wider perspective than Gómara's account. The book also rebuts Bartolomé de las Casas's negative view of the conquest. Like Cortés, Díaz believed he was participating in the advance of Christianity. Endowed with a prodigious memory, Díaz identified the names of all persons and places of the conquest and provided memorable descriptions of Tenochtitlán, powerful portraits of Cortés, Alvarado, Motecuhzoma II, Cuauhtemoc, and others, and enriched his account with innumerable personal anecdotes. His major success lies in his ability to recreate and evaluate his own perceptions and feelings as a conquistador, which he conveys in a sincere and almost conversational style.

BIBLIOGRAPHY

Alvar, Manuel. "Bernal Díaz del Castillo." In vol. 1 of *Historia de la literatura hispanoamericana.* Edited by Luis Iñigo Madrigal. Madrid, 1982.

Cerwin, Herbert. *Bernal Díaz: Historian of the Conquest.* Norman, Okla., 1970.

Díaz del Castillo, Bernal. *The Discovery and Conquest of Mexico, 1517–1521.* Edited by Genaro García. Translated by A. P. Maudslay. New York, 1956.

Díaz del Castillo, Bernal. *Historia verdadera de la conquista de la Nueva España.* Edited by Carmelo Sáenz de Santamaría. Madrid, 1982.

Graham, R. B. Cunninghame. *Bernal Díaz del Castillo.* New York, 1915.

ANGEL DELGADO-GOMEZ

DÍAZ DE SOLÍS, JUAN (?–1516), pilot and explorer.

Born in Lebrija near Seville in the last half of the fifteenth century, Díaz de Solís's career prior to 1508 is obscure. According to one story, before 1495 he was involved with French commerce raiders in an attack on a Portuguese royal caravel, but this account appears improbable in light of Díaz de Solís's claim of service as a pilot in Portugal's Asian trades after 1498. Whatever his previous experience, by 1508 he was known as an experienced and apparently accurate pilot.

Díaz de Solís's fame rests on two voyages he undertook in search of a way to Asia around the New World. In 1508, Fernando V commissioned Díaz de Solís and Vicente Yáñez Pinzón to sail north and west from Honduras, which Columbus had reached in 1503, to see if they could round the "island" of the New World and cross the supposed Great Gulf to India. Although the chronicler Antonio Herrera y Tordesillas raises doubts about whether and where this voyage went, more contemporary sources indicate that it resulted in the discovery of Yucatán and may have sailed as far north in the Gulf of Mexico as twenty-three degrees north. The voyage of 1508–1509 was marked by a disagreement between its leaders. Diego Colón, Columbus's son and heir, later sued, probably because he believed that Díaz de Solís and Pinzón had trespassed the area of his father's discovery.

These legal problems did not prevent Díaz de Solís's selection as chief pilot of the Casa de la Contratación in 1512 and his commission to sail to India for the purpose of determining the Line of Demarcation in the Eastern Hemisphere. However, Portuguese protests and doubts by members of the Casa de la Contratación regarding Díaz de Solís's fitness for command caused the suspension of preparations for this voyage. New preparations in 1513 were also suspended because of an investigation of unknown charges against the chief pilot.

Díaz de Solís's second attempt to round the New World took place in 1515 to 1516. He sailed from Sanlúcar de Barrameda on October 8, 1515. On February 2, 1516, he sailed his ships into the Río de la Plata, which he explored to a point on the Uruguayan shore where he landed to lay claim to the region for Spain. He and most of his party were killed by Charrúa Indian archers. Survivors of the expedition returned to Seville and spread Díaz de Solís's belief that the Río de la Plata was the beginning of a strait through the continent.

BIBLIOGRAPHY

Parry, John H. *The Discovery of South America.* New York, 1979.
Morison, Samuel Eliot. *The European Discovery of America: The Southern Voyages, A.D. 1492–1616.* New York, 1971.

PAUL E. HOFFMAN

DISEASE AND DEMOGRAPHY. When Christopher Columbus ventured into the Americas in 1492, he encountered a large, diverse population that spoke many languages and displayed many different customs. Just how many American Indians were present at that time was unknown to Columbus and Europeans immediately following. Estimates of population size of the Americas have perplexed scholars ever since. Clearly, Europeans brought new diseases to the Americas that ultimately combined with cultural changes to reduce dramatically the size of the population after 1492. The magnitude and timing of this population reduction as well as which diseases were brought by Europeans and which were already in the Americas continue to fuel scholarly debate.

Information on the size of the American Indian population in 1492 can be obtained from many sources, but none offers exact figures. Much information about population size originates from the writings of early European explorers like Christopher Columbus, Capt. John Smith, Samuel de Champlain, and Bénard de La Harpe. Many of these Europeans in early contact with American Indians were concerned about population size and related their estimates. In some cases, these estimates include direct counts, but mostly they consist of impressions and information the explorers had gathered from other Europeans or the Indians themselves. To use this information, scholars must interpret how well the Europeans knew the particular Indian group, whether the information was based on firsthand observation or on hearsay, the political context of the estimate (whether the Europeans had reason to exaggerate or minimize the estimate), and the date of the information.

A special problem in estimating the size of the American Indian population prior to European contact from European accounts is the likelihood that population size may have previously shifted. The first European to estimate population size usually postdated by many years the first European contact with most groups. The researcher hopes that early information on population size includes evidence of past declines or increases, but it is difficult, if not impossible, to be certain. The problem is compounded by the likelihood that European-introduced disease may have spread among American Indian populations even prior to the initial European contact in a given area. Although many American Indian groups were isolated from one another by language and geographical barriers, others were linked through trade networks, economic activity, and various aspects of their culture.

To supplement the information available from ethnohistorical sources, archaeologists have attempted to estimate population size from excavations. This work involves assessing the amount of village refuse (garbage) and the number of people-years needed to produce it. Excavations can reveal the size and number of houses occupied, the size and distribution of villages, and the approximate number of years a village was occupied. To interpret such archaeological data, scholars must estimate how long it would take a person to accumulate refuse and how many persons lived together in one house. Were all houses in a village occupied simultaneously by a large population, or did a smaller population move to new houses several times?

In recent years, scholars have attempted computer simulations and theoretical arguments to focus on population size. For example, by assuming that epidemics of new diseases like smallpox and measles would have caused a particular mortality in the population, scholars can work backward in time to estimate what the population must have been originally to result in a known figure for a later date. Obviously, such approaches make many assumptions about the accuracy of the recent estimate and the impact of epidemics that may not be justified.

Even bones can offer information about population size. For example, in the mid-Atlantic area of the United States, American Indian ossuaries have been found archaeologically that contain a large number of skeletons. Such deposits apparently represent a custom whereby every few years the remains of all who had died during that time were brought together for communal burial. Analysis of skeletons after excavations can reveal the ages at death of individuals, and these ages can be grouped to reconstruct mortality curves, survivorship curves, and even life tables that characterize the populations they represent. Such research tells us that people living in the mid-Atlantic area in the fifteenth century experienced a very high infant mortality rate, so that life expectancy at birth was only about twenty-three years. Although this figure seems very low, it actually is close to that estimated for cities of Europe at that time.

If the number of years represented by a skeletal sample is known, then population size can be estimated directly from the reconstructed life table. This technique can be highly accurate if the number of years represented by the sample is known and if the sample contains all of the deceased from the population.

Given the probable inaccuracy and incompleteness of the information available, and the difficulty in interpreting all the variables involved, it is not surprising that scholarly estimates of American Indian population size in 1492 vary greatly. Estimates of the size of the population of the U.S. region in 1492 range from 294,000 to 5 million. Estimates for North America for the same period range from 900,000 to 7 million and for the Western Hemisphere from 8.4 million to 72 million. For the most part, the variation in these estimates reflects the different methods used and the assumptions made by the scholars involved. But it also reflects differences in the definition of geographic areas and dates in question. For example, some scholars define North America as north of Mexico or north of the Rio Grande; for others, North America is north of "civilized" Mesoamerica. The date focused on varies from A.D. 1200 to the middle of the seventeenth century. All these problems complicate the comparison of estimates.

A 1988 study at the Smithsonian Institution in Washington, D.C., synthesized estimates made of each North American tribe by experts on each tribe. These estimates for North America (north of the urban civilizations of central Mexico) at about 1492 ranged between 1,213,475 and 2,638,900 with the "best estimate" of 1,894,350. These figures suggest a population density (number per 100 square kilometers) between 7 and 15. The area showing greatest density was California (75), followed by the northwestern coast (54) and the Southwest (18). Areas of sparse occupation were the subarctic (2), arctic (3), and Great Basin (4).

Most scholars agree that the size of the population of the Americas in 1492 culminated from a long period of population growth originating with the first migrations of people from Asia. There is some evidence that between A.D. 1000 and 1492 in some areas, population size was already declining or at least oscillating owing to disease and climatological or cultural factors.

Disease in the Americas prior to 1492

Many of the Europeans in early contact with American Indians were impressed with their good health and vitality. Such impressions have led some scholars to suggest that prior to European contact, American Indians were living in a largely disease-free environment that made them especially susceptible to the pathogens introduced from Europe.

American Indian vulnerability to many European diseases is well documented and was a major factor leading to depopulation in the sixteenth through the nineteenth centuries. But rapidly accumulating evidence suggests

that morbidity was high in many areas of the New World prior to European contact. This evidence largely originates from analysis of samples of human remains recovered in archaeological contexts.

Techniques of paleodemography, as mentioned above, enable mortality curves, survivorship curves, life tables, and other demographic statistics to be computed from the study of skeletons. But these computations require accurate estimates of age at death for each skeleton in the sample.

For infants and children, age at death can best be estimated by examining the stage of dental formation as revealed in X rays. Observations on the development of the crowns and roots of the teeth provide the most accurate estimates, and observations on the eruption of the teeth, the length and size of the bones, and the appearance and fusion of epiphyses, or small bony caps, on the ends of the bones offer other useful information, although they are less accurate than dental formation data. To estimate age at death in adults, scientists examine the extent of arthritic change, metamorphosis of the pubic symphyseal face (area where two pubic bones come together in the front), fusion of the bones of the skull, and microscopic changes in bones and teeth. These techniques have been developed from the study of skeletons of individuals whose age at death is known.

The sex of the individual can be determined accurately from the appearance of the bones of the pelvis. Sex differences are also marked in the size of most other bones of the skeleton; bones of males are slightly larger than those of females. These differences are not well marked in the bones of children; thus sex is usually estimated in skeletal samples only for adults.

Demographic analyses of samples of human remains dating prior to European contact indicate that mortality rates were increasing through time and were at relatively high levels in most areas of the New World immediately prior to 1492. The studies suggest that in many areas, as American Indians developed agriculture, they shifted their settlement pattern to a more sedentary lifestyle and began living in larger, more densely populated villages. This pattern probably resulted in sanitation problems, polluted water sources, and increased levels of infectious disease. The demographic consequence was a temporal increase in infant and child mortality, which created a decrease in life expectancy at birth.

Paleopathology is the science of interpreting diseases of past populations. Mostly this involves assessing lesions or abnormalities on archaeologically recovered human bones or preserved soft tissue on the bones. Other evidence derives from depictions on artifacts or from the study of coprolites (preserved feces). Unfortunately, few environments allow preservation of soft tissue or coprolites; thus most interpretation must focus on bone. The field is limited further in that relatively few diseases affect bone, and some diseases affect bone in similar ways. In recent years, technological advances and improvements in research design have greatly facilitated the capability to diagnose disease. Current researchers hope to identify immunoglobulins (defense proteins of the body that respond to disease) in ancient bones, which would enable them to detect specific diseases.

Artistic representations of disease have been found on ceramic vessels bearing images of deformed and diseased persons, although these have been limited largely to certain cultures in Peru and Mexico. The best such evidence comes from the Moche culture of northern coastal Peru, which dates from about A.D. 100 to 750. Missing limbs, skin diseases, blindness, cleft palate, clubfoot, and various mutilations have been recognized in the artistic depictions on these vessels.

Studies of preserved coprolites in archaeological contexts document the pre-Columbian New World presence of several parasites that previously were thought to be of Old World origin. These parasites include the hookworm (*Ancylostoma duodenale*), the whipworm (*Trichuris trichura*), the common roundworm (*Ascaris lumbricoides*), the broad fish tapeworm (*Diphyllobothrium spp.*), the pinworm (*Enterobius vermicularis*), the hairworm (*Strongyloides spp.*), the louse (*Pediculus humanus*), and Zoonoses, or diseases originating in nonhuman animals (*Moniliformis clarki*, *Trichinella spiralis*, and *Echinococcus granulosis*).

In 1973, examination of a pre-Columbian Peruvian mummy of the Nasca culture revealed not only bony changes indicative of tuberculosis but also soft tissue containing the acid-fast bacilli, which indicate terminal miliary tuberculosis. Numerous other examples of skeletal changes consistent with those documented for tuberculosis have been found in archaeologically recovered samples, all dating from the pre-Columbian period. The temporal-geographic occurrence of remains with tuberculosis indicates an association with large, dense populations living in the last few centuries prior to European contact.

For many years, scholars have debated the origin of syphilis. After 1492, the disease was a problem in both the Old and New World. To date, pre-1492 examples suggestive of syphilis have been found only in the New World. This suggests that syphilis originated in the Americas and was transported to Europe after 1492. The problem is complicated in that other diseases (yaws, pinta) produce lesions similar to those produced by syphilis and are difficult to distinguish.

Other disease conditions present in the New World prior to 1492 were bacillary and amoebic dysentery, viral influenza and pneumonia, arthritis, dental disease, and various congenital disorders and nutritional deficiencies. Research indicates that most of these health problems were increasing in frequency prior to 1492. Certainly, the increase in frequency of these infectious diseases correlates with increasing population size, density, and sedentism. These problems probably were major factors in the increasing infant mortality rate also apparent in the samples. Changes in agriculture that resulted in a less varied diet with a higher starch component apparently produced nutritional problems in some areas, as well as increases in dental caries. Samples from many areas of the New World show temporal increases in evidence of anemia, reflecting both dietary reliance on low-iron foodstuffs and the effects of dysentery and parasitism. All these problems seem to correlate with high population density and sedentism, since earlier samples from populations with more mobility, less population density, and a more varied diet seem to show less evidence of disease.

Impact of European-Introduced Disease

Columbus's arrival in La Española in 1492 marked the beginning of the end to thousands of years of isolation between the Old World and the New World. This isolation applied not only to human populations but to microbes as well. Movements of peoples throughout Europe, Asia, and Africa had created a large pool of disease microbes maintained by the large human population densities. In contrast, the comparatively smaller population density in the New World and its long isolation from the Old World allowed fewer major diseases. Although, as mentioned above, some evidence suggests that syphilis may have moved from the New World to the Old World, most other major epidemic diseases traveled in the other direction, with devastating results.

The first major epidemic following Columbus's arrival occurred in about 1520. This epidemic was smallpox, a disease that struck American Indian populations repeatedly and ultimately caused the greatest mortality of all introduced diseases. Smallpox was followed by measles, bubonic plague, cholera, typhoid, pleurisy, scarlet fever, diphtheria, mumps, whooping cough, and gonorrhea. Malaria and yellow fever probably were introduced from Africa.

The spread of the diseases and the magnitude of their impact were affected by the density of the American Indian populations, their geographic location, extent of contact with one another, and the extent of their contact with Europeans. In general, the epidemics moved from east to west, loosely following the extent of European–American Indian contact. Clearly, in some areas, disease spread in advance of actual European contact, facilitated by Indian trade networks. The timing of the first major outbreaks of disease in the New World populations was roughly as follows: smallpox, 1520–1524; measles, 1531–1533; influenza, 1559; bubonic plague, 1545–1548; diphtheria, 1601–1602; typhus, 1586; cholera, 1832–1834; scarlet fever, 1637; typhoid, 1528; and malaria, 1830–1833. Many of these diseases struck American Indian groups consecutively and repeatedly, causing great mortality.

Other factors causing population reduction among American Indians were alcoholism, warfare, genocide, cultural disruption, and declines in fertility. Beginning shortly after 1492, Europeans introduced disease and cultural disruption that dramatically reduced the size of the Indian population. In North America, the total dropped to about 1.8 million by 1600, 1.4 million by 1700, 1 million by 1800, 770,000 by 1850, and a low of below 500,000 in the early twentieth century. The rate of reduction ranged from about 95 percent in California to about 53 percent in the arctic, or an overall reduction of about 73 percent. After reaching their lowest number in the early 1900s, populations of native North America began a slow but steady recovery, reaching over 600,000 by 1925, nearly 800,000 by 1950, and over 1 million again by 1970.

Estimates of the contemporary population size of American Indians in the United States are complicated by different definitions of Indian membership. For example, the 1980 U.S. Census estimated that 1,478,523 citizens considered themselves to be American Indians (excluding Eskimos and Aleuts). A total of 1,120,245 of these identified themselves as from particular tribes. The remaining 358,278 listed themselves as "American Indian" or "tribe not reported." Note that these figures represent self-declaration; and the large increase in the total from similar estimates in 1970 probably includes incorporation of formerly non-Indians into the Indian sample and changes in census procedures. In 1970, ethnic categories from rural western areas were determined from observation by census workers. In 1980, such data were collected entirely by self-declaration.

In contrast, in 1980 only 339,475 American Indians were living on U.S. reservations (excluding Alaska). Most of them were concentrated in the Southwest, the Great Plains, and the Northeast. Official government records of tribal enrollment totaled 891,208 in 1981. Including estimates of Indian population size in northern Mexico and Canada, the North American Indian population size in 1980 would have been about 1,921,182, using the U.S. Census data; 1,390,990, using tribal enrollment data; or 872,257, using reservation data. In 1980, the census suggested that just over 232,000 citizens considered themselves to be Cherokee. In contrast, over 55,000 were enrolled in one of the Cherokee groups (North Carolina, Shawnee, or Tahlequah), and just under 5,000 were living on reservations.

However one counts the size of the contemporary population of the United States, it is clear that a remarkable population recovery is underway. By some counts, the number of Indians in North America in recent years may have reached or exceeded their numbers in 1492. As health conditions and medical care continue to improve, the demographic recovery is likely to continue.

[See also *Syphilis*.]

BIBLIOGRAPHY

Baker, Brenda J., and George J. Armelagos. "The Origin and Antiquity of Syphilis: Paleopathological Diagnosis and Interpretation." *Current Anthropology* 29 (1988): 703–737.

Cohen, Mark N., and George J. Armelagos, eds. *Paleopathology at the Origins of Agriculture.* Orlando, Fla., 1984.

Denevan, William M., ed. *The Native Population of the Americas.* Madison, Wis., 1976.

Dobyns, Henry F. *Their Number Became Thinned: Native American Population Dynamics in Eastern North America.* Knoxville, Tenn., 1983.

Johansson, S. Ryan. "The Demographic History of the Native Peoples of North America: A Selective Biography." *Yearbook of Physical Anthropology* 25 (1982): 133–152.

Snow, Dean R., ed. *Foundations of Northeast Archaeology.* New York, 1981.

Thornton, Russell. *American Indian Holocaust and Survival: A Population History since 1492.* Norman, Okla., 1987.

Ubelaker, Douglas H. "North American Indian Population Size, A.D. 1500 to 1985." *American Journal of Physical Anthropology* 77 (1988): 289–294.

Douglas B. Ubelaker

DISTANCE, MEASUREMENT OF.

While Columbus adopted in principle what he believed to be Alfraganus's measure of a degree of latitude, 56⅔ Roman miles (R.M.) to the degree, in practice he employed the seamen's standard of his era, 60 R.M. to the degree, or 1 mile to the minute of latitude.

In fifteenth-century practice, *distance* was determined by estimating the speed of the ship and recording the length of time the ship remained on the same course at the same estimated speed. *Speed* was determined by estimating the rapidity with which bubbles in the wake of a ship recede, a frustrating operation, for the wake disappears rapidly. *Time* that a ship remained on a specific course or at a specific estimated speed was determined from the *ampoletta*, or "hourglass," which required reversing every half-hour. Rough seas tended to slow the rate at which sand passed from the upper portion of the instrument to the lower. This factor, together with forgetfulness on the part of the ship's boy tending the *ampoletta* in recording each reversal or tardiness in making the reversal, worked to yield a shorter time on course than actual, which tended to offset the invariably inflated estimates of ship's speed made by the navigator or mate. Finally, *course* was determined from the mariner's compass whose needle pointed to the north magnetic pole. The direction of the ship's travel was shown by the lubber line drawn on the forward edge of the bowl containing the floating or gimballed compass card.

The magnetic compass, however, is subject to variation, that is, the angle between true north and magnetic north. Variation differs from place to place on the surface of the earth and from day to day in any particular locality. In Columbus's day nothing had been published on variation in the Atlantic Ocean. Columbus encountered it and coped with it by usual navigator's practices. At night, he took "readings" of the position of the North Star, Polaris, by the "pilot's blessing method," in which an observer in close proximity to the compass faces the North Star. Raising his arm and pointing to the star, he lowers his arm to the level of the compass, attempting to include in a single plane both star and compass. It is readily apparent if there is a significant angular difference between compass north and North Star. Repeated trials might point to variation and result in course corrections if the navigator became convinced that this was necessary.

The technique by which Portuguese and Spanish seamen navigated was known as *dead reckoning*. Employed

was a mariners' chart, essentially blank except for the delineation of known features of coastline, home and other ports, and islands (known, such as Azores, Canaries, and Cape Verde; or mythical, such as Antilia and St. Brendan's). Sometimes the only horizontal line shown would be the Tropic of Cancer, approximately 23 degrees 30 minutes north latitude. There might also be entered a series of vertical lines spaced at anywhere from one to five degrees of longitude. The proposed course to be followed on a sea voyage would be plotted before embarking. Then, as the ship proceeded, with the navigator and pilot attempting to follow the proposed course, estimates of the course actually followed would be entered upon the chart.

Columbus attempted on many occasions to take readings of the altitude of the North Star. (The altitude of the Celestial North Pole gives a direct reading of the latitude of the observer.) Such readings were inaccurate for several reasons: for one, the North Star in Columbus's time (and today as well) was not identical with the Celestial North Pole but described a path with a radius of 3 degrees 27 minutes around the pole; for another, it was extremely difficult to get a reasonably accurate reading of altitude of a not very bright star from the deck of a ship undergoing various and varying degrees of heave, surge,

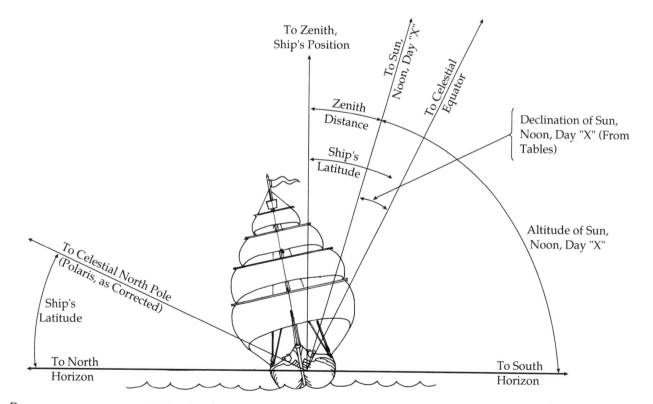

DETERMINING LATITUDE AT SEA. Relationships between ship's position and the heavenly bodies available for determining latitude.

AFTER FRED F. KRAVATH, *CHRISTOPHER COLUMBUS, COSMOGRAPHER*, RANCHO CORDOVA, CALIF., 1987.

sideslip, yaw, roll, and pitch while using a mariner's astrolabe or a marine quadrant hung from a tripod or bracket on the ship. Still, repeated attempts, all recorded, together with the plot of the estimated actual course followed, in which the north-south component of the Roman miles traversed could be converted to degrees of latitude and the east-west component to degrees of longitude, provided a number of checks. Unusually sensitive and resourceful navigators like Columbus appeared rarely to be greatly off course or in a position from which they could not return to their home ports or continue on to other explorations.

The correction for Polaris's circumpolarity was not known prior to Columbus's crossing. Columbus discovered that Polaris was circumpolar through the practice of comparing Polaris's bearing with magnetic north as given by the mariners' compass. Thus, he was at least alerted to the unreliability of a single reading of Polaris's altitude. Taking readings, however, as was the practice, at dusk and dawn (approximately twelve hours apart during the greater part of his first voyage) provided a set of altitudes and azimuthal differences between Polaris and compass magnetic north that could be averaged. Even though Polaris had a circumpolarity of 3.5 degrees, averaging

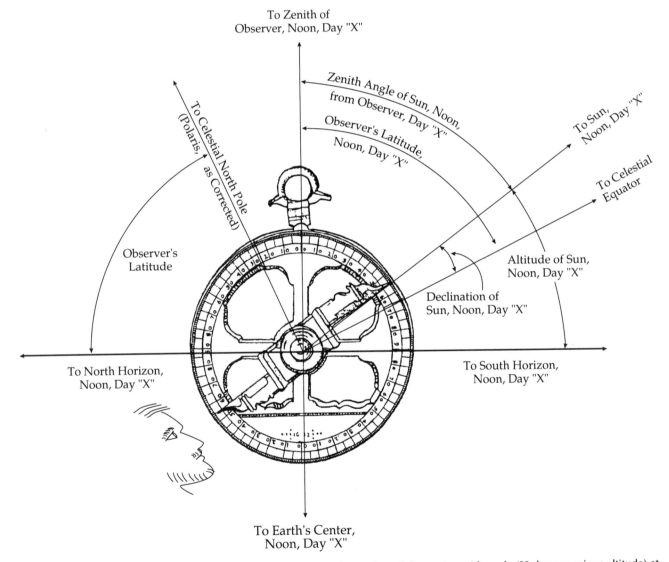

USE OF THE MARINER'S ASTROLABE. To obtain the latitude of a ship by observation of the sun's zenith angle (90 degrees minus altitude) at noon, between March 21 and September 22: If the ship is north of the equator, add the sun's declination (from tables) to the zenith angle of the sun at noon; if the ship is south of the equator, subtract this value. Between September 23 and March 21: If the ship is north of the equator, subtract the sun's declination from the zenith angle of the sun at noon; if the ship is south of the equator, add this value.

AFTER FRED. F. KRAVATH, *CHRISTOPHER COLUMBUS, COSMOGRAPHER*, RANCHO CORDOVA, CALIF., 1987.

reduced error in determining azimuth and altitude to 0.75 degree or less.

Correction for declination was required in order to utilize the sun's altitude at noon to determine latitude. Latitude, at noon, is equal to the zenith distance (or zenith angle) plus declination. Since altitude of any heavenly body is equal to 90 degrees minus the zenith distance, latitude of the observer's position is also given by 90 degrees minus altitude plus declination. While declination of the sun at noon on specific days of the year was not yet available in published charts or ephemerides in Columbus's day, it was not difficult for a navigator to construct his own set of approximate declinations. Declination is simply the zenith distance of the heavenly body (in this case the sun) with reference to the equator. All professional navigators knew that the declination of the sun at noon on the days of the vernal and autumnal equinoxes was zero, on the day of the summer solstice declination was approximately plus 23.5 degrees, and on the day of the winter solstice, minus 23.5 degrees. Ptolemy had indicated how the declination varied from day to day in his *Geographic Syntaxis*. Pilots had various methods of approximating declination. During the spring, for example, one simple method was to add 23 degrees for each of the first 31 days after the vernal equinox, 17 degrees for each of the next 31 days, and 5.5 degrees for each of the last 31 days. These measurements would then be accurate to within 6.5 nautical miles, 8.12 Roman (Italian) miles, or (in 1492) 2.03 Spanish *leguas* (leagues)—a tolerable error.

The Roman Mile and the League. The earliest linear measurement units were anatomical, or body-related. The thumb, fingers, palm, hand, forearm, upper arm, full arm, and foot were favorite appendages for indicating lengths—singly, in multiples, and in combinations. The Roman system was an outgrowth of the ancient Greek system, just as the Greek system was an outgrowth of the

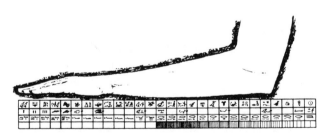

THE CUBIT. The twenty-four-digit small cubit, commonly measured from elbow to fingertips, compared to the twenty-eight-digit royal cubit, represented here by a hieroglyphics-covered royal-cubit rod from approximately 1550 B.C.

FROM MISCELLANEOUS PUBLICATION NUMBER 272, NATIONAL BUREAU OF STANDARDS

earlier Egyptian and Babylonian systems, particularly the former. These systems were similar in many respects but not identical. All units of linear measure were relatable to digit length or breadth. However, the manner of determining the finger size varied, not only between the various civilizations, but within each from time to time and place to place.

Another type of linear measure, which developed hand-in-hand with anatomical units, was botanical in origin. It developed from the requirement for units somewhat smaller or larger than the body-related units available. Since the smallest body unit was the finger, one way of subdividing the finger into smaller units was to relate it to one of several types of seeds. The barley grain was used in Europe and Asia for just such a purpose. Usually, four lengths of a grain of barley, or six widths, was equal to the width of a digit, about 18.5 millimeters or 1/54 meter.

In areas of the world such as Mesopotamia and the Nile delta, where there is considerable marshland, reeds were used. A small reed was made equivalent to four small elles (cubits) or twelve palms; a medium reed was defined as six medium elles (cubits) or twenty-four palms, and a large reed was equated to six large elles (cubits) or thirty palms. By the beginning of the Christian era, the digit, or finger, of approximately 1/54 meter (18.31 to 18.79 millimeters) was in use in Egypt, Assyria, Persia, Syria, Asia Minor, Greece, Italy, and the Roman colonies, including Great Britain. However, while apparently the dominant size, this was not the only digit in use. A somewhat later unit adopted by the Greeks that spread wherever Hellenic influence was strong was the finger (also referred to as the Parthenon or Olympic finger) defined as 1/16 Attic foot of 0.3083 to 0.309 meters or 19.27 to 19.31 millimeters. Even larger fingers than the Olympic came into use, some as large as 22.5 millimeters in breadth.

Itinerary Units of Measurement. All ancient linear systems had itinerary units related, at first, to human performance and later augmented to include the performance of animals such as the horse and camel. Some, for instance, defined the distance that troops could march in four hours without rest, or per day on a continuous basis, allowing for rest. Units such as the Roman mile, schoenus, parasang, and league came into being to express such distances. It was more convenient to say 12 miles than 12,000 paces or 60,000 feet, and it was still more convenient to express a longer distance as, say, six schoeni, or parasangs, than as the equivalent number of miles.

An important itinerary unit in the ancient world was the Greek stade, or stadion. This unit was originally defined as the distance a strong man could run without stopping for breath. Later, it became the standard length of the Olympic track and was equated to 100 fathoms, 500

Relationship between Greek Olympic and Roman Systems of Measure

GREEK OLYMPIC SYSTEM								ROMAN SYSTEM BASED ON ANCIENT GREEK SYSTEM					
Unit	Length in Meters	Finger	Palm	Foot	Cubit	Plethron	Stadion	Unit	Length in Meters	Digit	Foot	Pace	Stadium
Finger[a]	0.01929	1	1/4	1/16	1/24			Digit	0.0185185	1	1/16		
Knuckle	0.03858	2						Uncia	0.0247		1/12		
Palm	0.07716	4	1	1/4	1/6			Palm	0.074074	4	1/4		
Handbreadth	0.11574	6	1½		1/4								
Lick "Little span"	0.15432	8											
Handlength	0.1929	10	2½										
Span	0.23148	12											
Foot	0.30864	16	4	1	2/3			Foot (pes)	0.2963	16	1	1/5	
Pygme[b]	0.34722	18											
Pygon[c]	0.3858	20						Palmipes[e]	0.37037	20			
Cubit	0.463	24	6	1½	1			Cubit (ulna)	0.4444	24	1½		
Step[d]	0.7716	40	10	2½				Step	0.74074	40	2½		
Xylon	1.3888	72	18		3			Pace (passus)	1.48148	80	5	1	
Fathom	1.8518	96	24	6	4								
Pole	3.0864	160	40	10	6⅔			Pole	2.96296	160	10	2	
Cable	18.5184	960	240	60	40								
Plethron	30.864	1600	400	100	66⅔	1	1/6	Actus	35.556	1920	120	24	
Stadion	185.184	9600	2400	600	400	6	1	Stadium	185.185	10,000	625	125	1
Ride	740.736	38,400	9600	2400	1600	24	4						
Roman mile	1481.472	76,800	19,200	4800	3200	48	8	Roman mile	1481.48	80,000	5000	1000	8
								Miglio geografico[f]	1851.85	100,000	6250	1250	10

While the table shows only one value for each unit of measurement, a range of values actually existed to comply with the relationships shown. Other ancient cultures also had systems of measure incorporating the same units but assigning different values. The relationships shown between units apply for most systems based on larger feet such as the Babylonian (0.3142 to 0.31161 m) and the Drusian (0.3349 to 0.3415 m).

[a]Contrary to this widely accepted value, W. M. Flinders Petrie believed the Greek finger to be based on the Egyptian digit (0.018295 to 0.01879 m). He set 6 Olympic feet (4 cubits) equal to 100 Egyptian digits.
[b]One pygme = one lick + one handlength.
[c]One pygon = one foot + one palm.
[d]One step = one foot + one cubit.
[e]One palmipes = one palmus + one pes.
[f]Miglio geografico may date from a few centuries after the ancient Roman system proper.
SOURCE: After Fred F. Kravath, *Christopher Columbus, Cosmographer*, Rancho Cordova, Calif., 1987.

remens, or 600 Greek Olympic feet. Alexander the Great and his armies introduced the stade (stadion) into the Middle East and probably India. The Romans, in their zeal for standardization, made their own stadium equal to the Greek Olympic stadion. Strabo (62 B.C.–A.D. 19), the Greek historian and geographer, said eight stadia made the Roman mile, which yields a mile with a length of 1,481.5 meters.

Was the unit of measurement known as the Roman (Italian) mile—and defined as equivalent to 8 stadia, 1,000 paces, 5,000 feet, 80,000 digits, and 1,481.5 meters—the unit employed by Columbus at sea? Martinus Capella (fl.

third century), whose geography became somewhat of a standard in the medieval period, set the Roman mile at 1,000 paces, or 8 stadia; Macrobius (fl. c. 395–423), in describing Eratosthenes's and Ptolemy's differing metrologic conclusions, still set the Roman mile at 5,000 Roman feet or 1,000 paces; and Isidore of Seville (fl. c. 560–636) set the stadium at 625 Roman feet and the Roman mile at 8 stadia. There is, however, some evidence that in at least some areas the Roman mile grew to 1,488 meters (because of changes in the size of the basic foot, pace, and stadium); this measure was referred to as the "miglio Romano," in contrast to the "milliarium" or "mille pas-

Comparison of Various Stades (Stadions, Stadia) Found in the Literature

Historiographic Interpretation	Stade Length in Meters[a]	Stade Composition: Unit (Length in Meters) × Number	Stades per Roman Mile[b]
Herodotus-Gossellin stade[c]	99.75 m	Assyrian cubit (0.494 m) × 200	14.85
Pliny (interpreted by Macrobius) Pliny (interpreted by d'Anville)	148.2 m	Pelasgic foot (0.2963 m) × 500 Schoenus (5928 m) ÷ 40 Assyrian cubit (0.494 m) × 300	10
Pliny (interpreted by Hultsch) Pliny (interpreted by Dreyer/Stahl)	157.5 m	Schoenus (6300 m) ÷ 40 Royal cubit (0.525 m) × 300	9.41
Lehmann-Haupt	165 m	Plinian foot (0.275 m) × 600 Talmudic cubit (0.550 m) × 300	9
Polybius "Palesgic" stade	177.9 m	Pelasgic foot (0.2963 m) × 600	8.33
Strabo-Pliny Olympic stade and Roman stadium	185.2 m	Olympic foot (0.3086 m) × 600 Roman foot (0.2963 m) × 625 Egyptian remen (0.3704 m) × 500	8
Drabkin Philetaerian stade	197.6 m	Assyrian cubit (0.494 m) × 400	7.5
Ptolemaic or Royal Egyptian stade of Hultsch	210 m	Royal cubit (0.525 m) × 400	7
Lehmann-Haupt	296.4 m	Double Assyrian cubit (0.988 m) × 300	5
Babylonian and Assyrian ush (stadion)	355.68 m	Assyrian cubit (0.494 m) × 720	4.166
Klein's "superstadion"	1896 m	?	0.78

[a]One meter = 3.28084 U.S. customary feet.
[b]For this table, 1 Roman mile = 1482 meters.
[c]Based on an Egyptian itinerary measurement between Thebes and the mouth of the Nile River.
Source: After Fred F. Kravath, *Christopher Columbus, Cosmographer*, Rancho Cordova, Calif., 1987.

sus," the ancient Roman mile of 1,481.5 meters. There is also evidence that other Italian miles, such as the Tuscan (Florentine) mile and the "miglio geographico" (equal to 1,851 to 1,853 meters, essentially one minute of latitude, or of longitude at the equator), came into use for land measurements around Columbus's time or before. Closer to the Columbian era, Sacrobosco defined the Roman mile as equal to 10 stadia of 500 Roman feet each, which maintains the 5,000-foot equivalency.

Sometime during the period 1526–1528, some thirty-four to thirty-six years after Columbus's first voyage, Jean Fernel, the celebrated French physician known as "the modern Galen," undertook to measure the length of a degree of latitude on the Paris–Amiens road "where the road ran true north and south." In describing the reason for his undertaking, he indicated that authorities of his era considered Eratosthenes' degree of 700 stades to be equivalent to 87½ Italian (Roman) miles. Johann Müller (1436–1476, known as Regiomontanus), publisher of astronomical ephemerides used by Portuguese, Spanish, and Italian navigators, including Columbus, had reduced Eratosthenes' degree to 640 stadia or 80 Italian miles. Ptolemy's 500-stadia degree was in Fernel's time considered equivalent

to 62½ Italian miles; but Fernel himself accorded the degree only 60 Italian miles (the mariners' degree used by Columbus). Hence, the impetus to "straighten things out." After his measurement, which resulted in a degree length of 68,095¼ paces, Fernel equated this to 68 Italian miles and 95¼ paces (68.09525 Italian miles), or 544 Roman stadia and 95¼ paces (544.762 stadia).

Despite his insistence, for promotional purposes, that a degree measured 56⅔ Italian (Roman) miles, Columbus used the 60-Italian-mile degree that had adherents among not only mariners but also at least a modicum of sixteenth-century cosmographers. This mile was equivalent to 8 stadia, which unit was most likely used in estimating the speed of his ship, or one-quarter league (sometimes used for plotting a ship's course in dead reckoning). The league, however, unlike the Roman (Italian) mile, had an extremely variable value—over the years, from place to place, and even at a given place and time, depending on the context of its use. The literature reveals at least thirty-one values for this unit, from a low of 1.5 Roman miles to a high of over 4.58 Roman miles.

[See also *Circumference; Latitude; Longitude; Navigation,* article on *Instruments of Navigation.*]

BIBLIOGRAPHY

Berriman, A. E. *Historical Metrology.* London, 1953.

Delambre, J. B. J. *Histoire de l'astronomie du moyen âge.* Paris, 1821. Reprint, New York, 1965.

Gillings, Richard J. *Mathematics in the Time of the Pharaohs.* Cambridge, 1972. Reprint, New York, 1982.

Haws, Duncan. *Ships and the Sea.* Göteborg and New York, 1975.

Kravath, Fred F. *Christopher Columbus, Cosmographer.* Rancho Cordova, Calif., 1987.

Landstrom, Bjorn. *Columbus: The Story of Don Cristóbal Colón, Admiral of the Ocean Sea, and His Four Voyages Westward to the Indies.* New York, 1966.

Morison, Samuel Eliot. *Admiral of the Ocean Sea: A Life of Christopher Columbus.* 2 vols. Boston, 1942.

Phillips-Birt, Douglas. *A History of Seamanship.* New York, 1971.

Fʀᴇᴅ F. Kʀᴀᴠᴀᴛʜ

DOMESTICATED ANIMALS. Before Christopher Columbus crossed the Atlantic, the only domesticated animals in the New World were the dog, the turkey, the guinea pig, the alpaca, and the llama. Native Americans had no horses, cattle, sheep, goats, pigs, cats, or chickens. The North American cowboy and the gaucho of the Argentinian pampas developed only after cattle and horses reached the New World from Spain. Even the North American Plains Indians, commonly portrayed as horsemen in the modern popular media, did not have horses until the eighteenth century.

In 1493 Columbus brought twenty-four horses, ten mares, and three female mules to the New World, as well as cattle, sheep and goats, hogs, dogs, and probably cats and chickens. These were the first European domesticated animals to have a significant influence on the New World. The Vikings had brought horses, cattle, and other animals earlier to Greenland, but their animals did not survive the abandonment of that colony; and the English, Dutch, and French colonists did not bring their animals to northeastern North America until more than a hundred years after Columbus.

Every Spanish fleet after 1493 brought more animals. These animals multiplied and spread from the early ranches in the Caribbean to the mainland, reaching as far as New Mexico and Chile by the mid-1500s. As they spread, the animals brought about extensive and permanent ecological changes in the New World.

Routes to the New World. Spanish animals came to the New World by two main sailing routes. The first was via the Canary Islands to La Española. The voyage from Spain to the Canaries might be as short as eight to twelve days. At certain times of the year, the prevailing winds from the Canaries to the outer Antilles could be so steady and favorable that the voyage took as few as twenty days.

Another five days brought ships to La Española. Most of the animals brought to the Spanish colonies came by this route.

By Columbus's time, moving animals by watercraft was common, based on six thousand years of Mediterranean and north European maritime experience. The only difference between this early animal transport and that of the transatlantic passage was in the length of the voyages. As soon as mariners understood the patterns of winds and currents, they easily carried smaller animals to La Española from herds established on the Canaries, and they brought horses from Spain by this route until late in the sixteenth century.

Once in the New World, however, voyages between the islands of the Caribbean and along the mainland coasts could be very difficult. Although unfavorable winds and contrary currents on these routes took their toll of animals, livestock from La Española herds spread first to Puerto Rico and then to Jamaica, and from Jamaica to Honduras and to Nicaragua. La Española supplied stock for Cuba, and from Cuba animals were carried to New Spain. From there the animals moved north overland to what is now New Mexico. From La Española animals also moved to the north coast of South America and to Panama. Animals crossed the Isthmus of Panama, sailed down the west coast of South America to Peru, and then marched overland to Chile. This process took less than fifty years.

The second route from Spain and Portugal to the New World went via Cape Verde to the east coast of South America. This passage was very difficult because it crossed the doldrums and the so-called horse latitudes, those bands of windless sea at the intersection of major air patterns, where ships were becalmed for long periods and where dead animals were thrown overboard. On these voyages, the loss of animal life may have been as high as one-third, and perhaps one-half for horses.

Crossing the North Atlantic, the English, French, and Dutch ships met contrary winds and currents. These difficult and stormy voyages are much better known in North America than are the easier voyages of the Spanish ships. Confusion of the North Atlantic route and the route to South America with the favorable Middle Atlantic passage leads to an exaggeration of the difficulty of moving animals to the New World.

Growth of the Herds. The pattern of herd development in each of the Spanish colonies was similar. The conquistadores first brought their horses and dogs for war. They also brought some animals for provisions, but usually relied on foodstuffs provided by native Americans.

Once an area was under Spanish control, the land and its native American inhabitants were divided among the conquistadores. The ownership of a horse and arms was

GREENLAND

NORTH AMERICA

British
Isles

1750

1730

1770

1773

1719

1600

1690

Iberian
Peninsula

1540

1665

1665 from France

1629 from England

1660 from Flanders

1620 from England

ATLANTIC
OCEAN

1567

1520

1514

1519

La Española
(Hispaniola)

1493 from Spain

Canary
Islands

AFRICA

Jamaica

Puerto
Rico

Cape
Verde
Islands

Isthmus
of Panama

1509, from
La Española to
Puerto Rico and
to Jamaica

PACIFIC
OCEAN

Peru

SOUTH AMERICA

1530

1540

1560

1540 from Spain (failed)

1535

Chile

1580

INTRODUCTIONS AND DIFFUSION OF OLD WORLD
DOMESTICATED ANIMALS IN THE AMERICAS

sometimes prerequisite to receiving a land grant, and horsemen received a greater portion of treasure than did foot soldiers.

As the Spanish colonial economies developed around herding and ranching, the newly introduced domesticated animals increased dramatically in numbers. Although this increase can be attributed to the lush New World environment and its vacant ecological niches and to the lack of natural predators, the speed of the increase varied depending on the type of animal.

The increase in the herds was most immediate and obvious among pigs, sheep, and goats. Called *ganado menor*, these small animals have short breeding cycles, produce multiple births, and are relatively easy to transport. Mariners commonly left them to breed on uninhabited islands as future provisions for ships and expeditions. The small animals are rarely mentioned in the historical records, except in unusual circumstances.

Sheep spread to many areas of the New World, but they were never as important economically as they were in medieval Spain. Goats were usually found along with sheep and sometimes in great numbers where the land was poor. The pig's short reproductive cycle made it one of the most economically useful of all animals. Eating pork not only provided an important source of meat protein, but it also distinguished the Catholic Spaniard from Jewish and Muslim contemporaries. Hernando Cortés, Hernando de Soto, and Francisco Vázquez de Coronado all took swine on their expeditions, and Francisco Pizarro, known as a swineherd in Spain, had as many as three thousand to five thousand pigs in Peru.

Other small animals brought by the Spaniards included dogs, cats, and chickens. Dogs were greatly effective in war and interbred with indigenous breeds, multiplying so rapidly as to become a nuisance. We know of the presence and value of domestic housecats only from rare descriptions of their sale and their importance in the control of vermin.

Chickens may have spread throughout the New World the most rapidly of all the European animals because they were economically interchangeable with the indigenous turkey. Native Americans traded both fowl widely, and chickens arrived in northern New Spain well in advance of the Spanish explorers. Other small European animals present, but not mentioned directly in the historical sources, were rats, insects, parasites, and disease organisms.

Horses and cattle were called *ganado mayor*. It was very difficult to establish these larger animals in herds because they make a great physical investment in their offspring. Their reproductive cycle is longer than that of the smaller animals and they typically produce single births. The long period of dependency of the young on the mother makes the young more vulnerable to predators. Stock was also depleted when colonists consumed their animals during "starving times" and when native Americans added beef and horsemeat to their diets.

Horses are the best documented of all the animals brought to the New World because of their military and economic importance and because they occupied a special place in medieval and Renaissance European culture. To own and raise horses was a symbol of aristocracy; the words for *knight* in Romance languages—*caballero* in Spanish—are derived from the words for *horse*.

The conquistadores believed in the special effectiveness of their cavalry. Bernal Díaz del Castillo, Alvar Núñez Cabeza de Vaca, Pedro de Castañeda, Garcilaso de la Vega, and Bartolomé de las Casas all describe the formidable advantages of cavalry in war, although the usefulness of cavalry depended on compatible terrain and the ready availability of forage and water. In the early years of the Conquest, the Spanish explorers encouraged native Americans to believe horses to be divine. However, information regarding the limitations and mortality of horses quickly passed along indigenous trade and communication networks, and many native Americans were already familiar with large quadrupeds, such as the bison, the llama, and the alpaca. They quickly took advantage of the limitations of cavalry, practiced guerrilla warfare, avoided open combat, and cut off supplies.

Cattle followed the same paths in the New World as the other animals, although the herds of the pampas grew from cattle brought overland from Peru and Chile, not transported by the difficult transatlantic crossing from Cape Verde. As early as 1538, the cattle herders of New Spain established the *mesta*, modeled after the medieval Spanish sheepherders' association. The New World *mesta* organized cattlemen, held meetings, regulated brands, disposed of strays, and mediated disputes. Cattle from New Spain eventually reached Texas to become the foundation of the North American cowboy tradition.

The relationship between European animals and the environmental changes arising from their introduction is very clear in the example of cattle in New Spain. The discovery of silver on the northern frontier of New Spain increased the demand for leather, hides, and tallow. The resultant tremendous growth of cattle herds led to overgrazing that, along with the seasonal drought and the burning of scrub, created semidesert badlands. This ecological change in turn caused an inevitable decline in herding on the Mexican plateau and helped to create an accompanying economic depression.

Although herding and ranching were the foundation for colonial Spanish economies, the Spanish soldier-colonists considered most agricultural pursuits, except the raising of horses, to be of low social status. They relied instead on native Americans to supply labor for their ranches. As the herds and their attendant demand for labor increased and the native American populations drastically declined, black African slaves were brought to provide the necessary labor. Chroniclers also proclaimed the abundance and fertility of the New World in an effort to encourage farm laborers to emigrate from Spain to the New World.

Extensive ranches based on large land grants and their associated native American labor were absent in North America. The North American natural environment was comparatively hostile, and the native American populations were smaller, less dense, and not so highly organized as many Central and South American groups. The English, French, and Dutch economies were based on fur trading and farming, supported mainly by the colonists' own labor. Although it took longer to establish European animals in North America, they, too, ultimately displaced indigenous species and altered the precontact environment.

BIBLIOGRAPHY

Abbass, D. K. "Horses and Heroes: The Myth of the Importance of the Horse to the Conquest of the Indies." *Terrae Incognitae* 18 (1987): 21–41.

Abbass, D. K. "Herd Development in the New World Spanish Colonies: Conquistadors and Peasants." In *Themes in Rural History,* edited by Richard Herr. Ames, Iowa, 1991.

Crosby, Alfred W. *Ecological Imperialism: The Biological Expansion of Europe 900–1900.* Cambridge, 1986.

Denhardt, Robert Moorman. *The Horse of the Americas.* Norman, Okla., 1975.

Dusenberry, William H. *The Mexican Mesta.* Urbana, Ill., 1963.

Johnson, John J. "The Introduction of the Horse into the Western Hemisphere." *Hispanic American Historical Review* 23 (1943): 487–610.

Marcus, G. J. *The Conquest of the North Atlantic.* New York, 1981.

Patiño, Victor Manuel. *Animales domésticos introducidos.* Vol. 5 of *Plantas cultivadas y animales domésticos en América Equinoccial.* Cali, Colombia, 1970.

Roe, F. G. *The Indian and the Horse.* Norman, Okla., 1955.

Rouse, John E. *The Criollo.* Norman, Okla., 1977.

Varner, John, and Jeannette Varner. *Dogs of the Conquest.* Norman, Okla. 1983.

D. K. ABBASS

DOÑA MARINA. See *Malinche.*

E

ECONOMIC INSTITUTIONS. See *Social and Economic Institutions.*

ELCANO, JUAN SEBASTIÁN DE (1487?–1526), Basque navigator, member of Ferdinand Magellan's expedition, and first to sail around the world in one voyage. Elcano, the third son of Domingo Sebastián de Elcano and Catalina del Puerto, was born in the Cantabrian port town of Guetaria in the Basque province of Guipúzcoa. Little is known of his early life except that he followed a maritime calling and captained one of the ships that transported troops across the Mediterranean in Cardinal Jiménez de Cisneros's North African campaign in 1509–1510.

In late 1518, in Seville, Elcano joined Ferdinand Magellan's expedition. Magellan, though Portuguese, had received permission from Carlos I to seek an all-Spanish route to the Far East. Initially, Elcano held the post of *contramaestre* but was soon named master of *Concepción*, the third largest ship in the armada. The five-ship fleet sailed from the outport of Sanlúcar de Barrameda on September 20, 1519.

At Port St. Julian in southern Argentina where the fleet was wintering, Elcano, who believed that Magellan was not following a course in conformity with royal instructions, sided with Gaspar de Quesada, captain of *Concepción,* and more than forty other mutineers. Although initially condemned to death, Elcano and most of the others were pardoned and sentenced to hard labor for the remainder of the stay at Port St. Julian.

When the fleet continued its voyage, Elcano was restored to his post of master of *Concepción* and helped negotiate the strait later named after Magellan. On November 28, 1520, Magellan's flagship *Trinidad,* along with *Victoria* and *Concepción,* entered the Pacific Ocean.

After almost a hundred days at sea, they landed at Guam on March 6, 1521. From there, they proceeded to the Philippines where, on April 27, Magellan was killed. Elcano had missed the fateful sortie owing to illness.

Because of a lack of manpower and questions about her seaworthiness, *Concepción* was burned off the island of Bohol in the Philippines, leaving only *Trinidad* and *Victoria* to continue the voyage. Under the leadership of the Portuguese pilot, João Lopes de Carvalho, the expedition drifted from island to island, exploring, plundering, arranging treaties, and repairing the two ships. When Carvalho was deposed in the latter part of September, Elcano, who was now master of *Victoria,* was elected captain of the ship and treasurer of the expedition.

On November 8, 1521, the remnants of the Magellan expedition reached their destination of the Moluccas, landing in Tidore, where the local leader pledged allegiance to Castile. After loading both ships with cloves, the men decided that *Trinidad* should remain behind for repairs. On December 21, 1521, *Victoria,* under the leadership of Elcano and with fifty-nine others aboard, set sail for Spain via the Cape of Good Hope. Aided by Moluccan pilots, Elcano sailed through the maze of islands and, on February 11, 1522, began an epic voyage across the Indian Ocean, using a southwesterly route to avoid detection by Portuguese shipping, since that part of the world was off-limits to non-Portuguese. Fear of the Portuguese prevented Elcano from seeking aid in Mozambique, and the mariner had difficulty rounding the Cape of Good Hope. After five months of sailing in a leaking ship without fresh provisions, Elcano reached the harbor of Rio Grande on Santiago, a Portuguese Cape Verde island, pretending he had been blown off course coming from America. By then only thirty-five men remained aboard. The Portuguese gave them some supplies, but

COAT OF ARMS GRANTED ELCANO BY CARLOS I (CHARLES V). Embellished with cinnamon, cloves, nutmegs, and a globe with the words *Primus circumdedisti me* (You were the first to circumnavigate me).   AFTER F. H. H. GUILLEMARD, *THE LIFE OF FERDINAND MAGELLAN* (LONDON, 1890), P. 308.

seized thirteen men. Elcano and his crew quickly set sail for Spain via the Azores.

Fifty-four days later, on September 6, 1522, *Victoria* with Elcano, seventeen Europeans, and three East Indians arrived at Sanlúcar, a little less than three years after the voyage had begun. Elcano was well received by King Carlos I (Emperor Charles V), who, among other rewards, allowed him to use a coat of arms embellished with cinnamon, cloves, nutmegs, and a globe with the words *Primus circumdedisti me* (You were the first to circumnavigate me).

In the spring of 1524, Elcano served on the Castilian side of the mixed Commission of Inquiry that met to determine whether the Moluccas were on the Spanish or Portuguese side of the Line of Demarcation agreed upon in the 1494 Treaty of Tordesillas. (A fellow commissioner was Fernando Colón, son of Christopher Columbus.)

On May 24, 1525, a seven-ship expedition with 450 men under the command of García Jofre de Loaisa, with Elcano as pilot-major of the venture and captain of *Sancti Spiritus*, set sail from La Coruña for the Moluccas, following Magellan's route. Near the Strait of Magellan, Elcano's ship was wrecked and he transferred to Loaisa's flagship, *Santa María de la Victoria*. The lengthy voyage through the strait during winter and a stormy voyage in the Pacific took its toll: the overcrowded flagship separated from the rest of the fleet and sickness decimated the crew. On July 30,

1526, Loaisa died and Elcano succeeded him as captain-general. But Elcano, also ill, died just a few days later, on August 4, and was buried at sea about a month's sail from the Marianas.

Elcano's relative importance has been heatedly debated. Pro-Magellan writers have tended to denigrate the Basque navigator's achievements. One of the seventeen European survivors who reached Spain with Elcano in 1522 was the Italian chronicler Antonio Pigafetta, a great admirer of Magellan. His eyewitness account, the chief historical source for the voyage, fails to mention Elcano by name. On the other hand, some writers have tried to elevate the Spanish-born Elcano at the expense of the Portuguese-born Magellan, arguing that since he died in the Philippines, Magellan was not the first to sail around the world, that honor belonging instead to Elcano.

BIBLIOGRAPHY

Mitchell, Mairin. *Elcano: The First Circumnavigator.* London, 1958.

Morison, Samuel Eliot. *The European Discovery of America: The Southern Voyages A.D. 1492–1616.* New York, 1974.

Navarrete, Eustaquio Fernandez de. *Historia de Juan Sebastián del Cano.* Vitoria, 1872.

Nowell, Charles E., ed. *Magellan's Voyage around the World: Three Contemporary Accounts.* Evanston, Ill., 1962.

FRANCIS A. DUTRA

ENCOMIENDA. Creation of the formal, or legal, institution of the encomienda began during Nicolás de Ovando's rule as governor of La Española (1502–1509). During this period, Ovando systematically subjugated the native American chiefdoms of the island, placing their villages under the "care" of individual Spaniards who were to see that the Indians worked in the Spanish economy and lived "like Christians."

Ovando's model for this legal institution seems to have been the encomiendas that his military order, Alcántara, held in southern Spain. However, Columbus's demand that the Indians pay tribute, in gold, and earlier royal decrees requiring them to work and to receive Christian instruction had prepared the way for Ovando's actions. Another basis for the institution on La Española and in Paraguay was the service obligations of lower status kinsmen to the husbands of Indian women of high status. In both locations, Spaniards who took or were given the daughters of chiefs as their concubines discovered that her kinsmen began to offer food and labor services similar to those they owed the chief. In Paraguay, at least, this kin relationship tempered the exploitive nature of the institution.

The institution was legally formulated in a series of royal orders first drawn into a code in the Laws of Burgos of 1512 to 1514 and then in the New Laws of 1542. The orders and the law codes were responses to protests by Dominicans over the continuing abuse of Indian laborers and the rapid decline in the Indian population, a decline they attributed to the abuses.

Until 1542, Spanish law required the Indians to labor for their Spanish masters for fixed periods (as much as two-thirds of the year) in exchange for instruction in Christianity and Spanish ways of living and for legal and military protection. With the New Laws, the labor obligation was transformed into a tribute obligation, and personal service to the encomendero (master of a particular encomienda) was strictly forbidden. Supervision of the Indians' forced labor (to earn money to pay the tribute) was turned over to corregidores de indios, officials first appointed for New Spain in 1530. Native caciques, or village headmen, were made responsible for supplying the number and kind of laborers demanded by the corregidor. An attempt to abolish the encomienda system altogether provoked an insurrection by Spanish colonists in Peru. Elsewhere in the Spanish empire, the men charged with implementing the New Laws in fact suspended them to prevent insurrection. While continuing to award encomiendas to the descendants of the original conquerors, the Crown gradually brought more and more Indians into the "royal encomienda," or direct vassalage.

By 1600 the encomienda had largely ceased to be an important source of income for private persons. However, the derivative labor system, the mita, continued to be important in Peru as a method of supplying labor to the silver mines, especially at Potosí; elsewhere it was a source of seasonal labor for Spanish agriculture and public works projects. Although legally the encomienda was only a grant of the labor of a given group of Indians, it often provided a basis for the creation of haciendas as encomenderos obtained land and used the encomienda Indians as the labor on these properties.

BIBLIOGRAPHY

Chamberlain, Robert A. "Simpson's *The Encomienda in New Spain* and Other Recent Encomienda Studies." *Hispanic American Historical Review* 34 (1954): 238–250.

Keith, Robert G. "Encomienda, Hacienda, and Corregimiento in Spanish America: A Structural Analysis." *Hispanic American Historical Review* 51 (1971): 431–446.

Lockhart, James. "Encomienda and Hacienda: The Evolution of the Great Estate in the Spanish Indies." *Hispanic American Historical Review* 49 (1969): 411–429.

Simpson, Leslie B. *The Encomienda in New Spain: The Beginning of Spanish Mexico.* Rev. ed. Berkeley, 1966.

PAUL E. HOFFMAN

ENEA SILVIO. See *Pius II.*

ENGLAND. The earliest description of Tudor England was written by Polydore Virgil, an Italian historian who lived and worked at the royal court under the patronage of King Henry VII. Virgil divided the kingdom into four parts, "which all differ among themselves": the area south of the Thames, the Midlands south of the Trent, the six western counties "towards Wales," and the seven northern counties "towards Scotland." The key element in Virgil's description was his recognition of the extreme differences that set each area off from the others. Each sector had its own regional accents, traditions and ancient customs, unique agricultural patterns, communal organization, regional produce, and local industries.

Geographically, England rises slowly from the lowland southeastern shires to the northern highlands on the Scots border. In the southeast and southwest the land is best suited to fruit orchards, vegetables, and cereal crops with only a few cattle and almost no sheep. Until a climatic shift toward colder summers occurred in the fourteenth century, vineyards and a wine industry thrived in Kent. The Midlands and southern half of Yorkshire are composed of flat, well-drained, fertile land. Here, a variety of grain was grown, mostly wheat and oats. This area also contained a large number of cattle and huge flocks of sheep. In the far west and north—the regions that border on Wales and Scotland—the land is rocky and inhospitable. The large, crop-growing fields of the Midlands are replaced with broad expanses of meadow and grazing land that supported immense herds of sheep and the indigenous, long-haired highland cattle. Then as now, the land in the northern shires was distinctive for its emptiness, running on for mile upon endless mile of sheep runs separated by long, low-lying stone dikes and the occasional small stone shepherd's hut or larger stone cluster of monastic buildings.

England's organization of dwelling sites and patterns of landholding varied as much as did its geography. In the late fifteenth and early sixteenth centuries, the rural countryside was composed of innumerable villages, most of which traced their origins back through at least eight hundred to a thousand years of history. The villages in the southern shires of Kent, Sussex, and Hampshire were small, with house sites strung out in a linear pattern along innumerable High Streets. Peasant-farmers in this region owned individual, compact plots of land enclosed by high hedges. In contrast, the individual dwellings in Midland villages clustered haphazardly around a small stone church. Moreover, these villages sat in the center of a vast, unfenced, open-field system in which peasant-farmers owned strips of land. Life here was more communal for men and women in that all shared use of the village green, the central well, and the meadow and forest lands that surrounded the fields. Finally, the far west and north contained only hamlets and truncated, single farmsteads that supported a clan organization of clustered kinship groups, much like the Scots clan system. There was no recognizable village organization, and one parish church serviced a wide area of individual dwellings.

Population growth in this diverse land was slow. On the whole, the population of medieval England had suffered a dramatic decrease from the mid-fourteenth century through the early years of the fifteenth owing primarily to the devastating Black Death of 1348–1350 and the cyclical epidemics of bubonic plague that ravaged the kingdom thereafter. By the middle of the fifteenth century, however, population recovery was underway, and by 1485—when the first Tudor king succeeded to the throne—England as a whole already felt the quickening of the population growth. This increase continued unabated—despite the introduction of a new epidemic disease, the "sweating sickness," which first appeared in the late fifteenth century and was indigenous to the island.

The growing population was self-sufficient to a large extent. Practically all necessities of life—food, clothing, fuel, and housing materials—came from native resources of which the immense natural forests was the most important. Agricultural and industrial production was organized into innumerable small units, and peasant families lived on what they grew or made for themselves and on the sale of any surplus produce at local markets. Without doubt, population growth stimulated the proliferation of local town markets, which in turn contributed greatly to the development of the high level of economic prosperity that characterized life in late Tudor England, specifically during the reign of Elizabeth I.

On a broader economic level, sixteenth-century England was one of the primary producers of many of the raw materials that fueled various industries of continental Europe. Tin and lead mined in Cornwall and the Mendip Hills near Wales fed the smithies of southern Europe; and the cloth workshops of Flanders and northern Italy absorbed massive quantities of both raw wool and, later, finished woolen cloth.

But England had other "business" to accomplish on the continent in addition to the growth of commerce. As a nation-state, it played an increasingly important part in the continual power struggles that characterized diplomatic life at this time. When Henry VII ascended the throne in 1485 England was a virtual nonentity in European politics. But with an eye toward foreign alliances, Henry established his kingdom's presence as an important ally at the negotiating table or on the battlefield. In the early days of Tudor rule, captains of English ships, such as John and Sebastian Cabot, took part in the great voyages of discovery that had begun to chart the existence of whole "new worlds" far distant from the European continent. Later and throughout the Tudor century, English armed support was actively sought by France, Spain, and the Holy Roman Empire as well as the smaller Flemish and Dutch powers. In early Tudor years, England remained tied firmly to Spanish interests through an alliance sealed by the marriage of Catherine of Aragón to Henry VII's son Prince Arthur and after Arthur's death to his brother Henry VIII. This alliance of English and Spanish interests reached a high point in the mid-sixteenth century, when Queen Mary Tudor (1553–1558) married Philip II, king of Spain and Naples. But during the reign of the second Tudor queen, Elizabeth I, the relationship deteriorated quickly and finally ended when Spain sent its famed, albeit doomed, armada to try to destroy the smaller English navy and to land invasion troops on English shores in 1588.

In its social structure, early Tudor England was organized around the concept of a status hierarchy based on possession of land. A continuity that extended from the dawn of the Middle Ages, land was deemed valuable because it carried with it social status, economic wealth, and, most important, political power. Land ownership dictated the rank of each individual on the hierarchical ladder: the larger the amount of land owned by a single family, the higher the social status, the greater the wealth, and the more political power it could wield. Land possession was linked to territorial titles from a duke at the top of the pyramidal structure down through an earl or baron to a knight at the bottom of the land-owning strata. Because political enfranchisement was linked to possession of land—not the mere rental of land as a tenant—early Tudor England really consisted of only two classes: the politically enfranchised, land-based elite and everyone else in the lower reaches of the hierarchy.

Regardless of whether they were nobles or knights, merchants or farmers, all English men and women lived a life dominated by the liturgical rituals of the church. At the beginning of the Tudor century, this church was a single entity—Roman Catholic—led, technically, by the pope in Rome. But by the time the dynasty died out in 1603, the center of the Ecclesia Anglicana—the Church of England—had shifted from Rome to Canterbury in Kent, the supreme leadership over that church was now vested in the Crown, and instead of unity, religion in England varied in the extreme, from Anglican-Protestant to Puritan, including a small but committed group of secret Catholics. The constitutional break with Rome came in the reign of Henry VIII, and the doctrinal shift from a Catholic liturgy to a new Protestant liturgy centered primarily in the reign of Henry's son, Edward VI (1547–1553), and continued on into the reign of Elizabeth (1558–1603).

In political organization as in economic and industrial organization, England looked to locally powerful families to maintain social order and a modicum of peace and stability. Administration of the provinces was carried out through royal appointment of a single lord lieutenant, a single sheriff, and several justices of the peace who were chosen from among the male heads of landed, wealthy families. At the top of the hierarchy sat the Crown on the head of the current king or queen. Early Tudor monarchy was personal monarchy at its best: the monarch had the right to declare the law through arbitrary proclamation or through statute, made in tandem with Parliament. All men and women in *his* kingdom belonged to *him* and his will or whim was directly impressed upon all and sundry. Moreover, in line with continental monarchies, the individual who wore the Tudor Crown was believed to have been divinely chosen by God to reign over the realm. These Tudor monarchs—an extraordinary, glittering group of three men and two women—collectively built the strong base upon which their successors constructed an empire that one day would extend its rule to all corners of the globe.

[See also *Canada; Colonization,* article on *English Colonization.*]

BIBLIOGRAPHY

Bindoff, S. *Tudor England.* Harmondsworth, Eng., 1950.
Lockyer, R. *Henry VII.* New York, 1968.
Palmer, M. *Henry VIII.* London, 1971.

JOAN B. GOLDSMITH

ENRIQUE IV (1425–1474), king of Castile (1454–1474). Enrique's reign was a continuation of the chaos, factionalism, and monarchical weakness characteristic of that of his father, Juan II. Like his father, Enrique disliked the business of ruling and relied excessively on his close advisers Juan Pacheco and Beltrán de la Cueva. The questionable paternity of his daughter Juana provoked a crisis in the succession, which led to the accession of Isabel the Catholic as queen of Castile.

Enrique was born on January 5, 1425; little is known of his childhood. He married Blanca of Navarre in 1440 but the marriage was nullified in 1453 because Enrique was alleged to be impotent. The following year he married Juana of Portugal and a daughter, Juana, was born in 1462. Her paternity was not questioned until later, when it was alleged that Enrique was impotent and Juana was the daughter of Beltrán de la Cueva; hence she is known as "La Beltraneja." The issue of Juana's paternity never was resolved completely. Although Enrique maintained that Juana was indeed his daughter, his inconsistent support of her obscures the truth. Under pressure from his nobles,

ENRIQUE IV. Depicted on a Spanish coin.

AMERICAN NUMISMATIC SOCIETY

Enrique named his brother Alfonso heir in 1464. When Alfonso died in 1468, Isabel was declared heir, but Enrique repudiated her when, against his wishes, she married Fernando of Aragón in 1469.

Enrique's reign ended in failure and disgrace. He was unable to curb the power of a faction of rebellious nobles who dethroned him in a dramatic ceremony in Ávila in 1465, and the chaos of civil war dominated the last years of his reign. His death in 1474 followed a long illness.

BIBLIOGRAPHY

Amézaga, Elias. *Enrique Quarto.* Madrid, 1974.
Ferrara, Orestes. *Un pleito sucesorio: Enrique IV, Isabel de Castilla y la Beltraneja.* Madrid, 1945.
Miller, Townsend. *Henry IV of Castile, 1425–1474.* Philadelphia, 1972.
Phillips, William D., Jr. *Enrique IV and the Crisis of Fifteenth-Century Castile, 1425–1480.* Cambridge, Mass., 1978.
Sitges, J. B. *Enrique IV y la excelente señora, llamada vulgarmente Doña Juana la Beltraneja, 1425–1530.* Madrid, 1912.

THERESA EARENFIGHT

EQUIPMENT, CLOTHING, AND RATIONS. The equipment carried aboard Columbus's ships on his first voyage of discovery was limited to essentials. Life aboard ship in the Age of Discovery was not easy. Seamen had to put up with numerous privations and during foul weather perform hard physical labor for extended periods of time. To do this, they needed an ample supply of nourishing food and a reasonable level of assurance that, however indefinite the length of the voyage might be, they eventually would return safely to their homes. Thus, high on the list of priorities were those items needed to maintain the crew's physical ability to withstand the rigors of an ocean voyage and to temper their mental image of the dangers facing them in sailing off into the unknown.

Maintaining their physical well-being required adequate

means for preparing and serving food, and for providing necessary rest. On ships of this era, neither was easily accomplished. It should be understood that the serving of meals on these ships was for the basic purpose of providing nourishment rather than a pleasurable experience. The cooking stove called a *fogon* was an open square metal box with raised sides and back, lashed down somewhere on deck out of the weather. A layer of sand in the bottom of the box provided insulation for the wood fire. A cooking pot, hanging from an iron rod spanning the box, swung freely as the ship rolled. Food was ladled out of the pot into each crewman's wooden bowl, which he carefully held level against the rolling of the ship. He then ate with his fingers while sitting on a convenient coil of rope, one of the hatches, or on the deck wherever he could find room. He had no fork. If the food needed to be cut, the crewman used his personal knife, which he carried with him at all times for a variety of needs. If there was gravy or a heavy broth, he sopped it up with hardtack, a biscuit that needed some moistening to be edible. The only beverages available were water and wine, which became either unpalatable or unavailable after several weeks at sea.

The ship's watch schedule governed the time that food was served. Watches were of four hours' duration. In Columbus's time, the watch was changed at three, seven, and eleven o'clock day and night. In modern times, watches change at four, eight, and twelve around the clock, except the evening watch, which is commonly split into two watches, four to six and six to eight. This permits the evening meal to be served at the convenient time period of five to seven to one group of watch-standers just before they go on watch and to the other group just after they come off watch. These two-hour periods are called dog watches. They have the added advantage that their use staggers the watch schedule so that the same group of watch-standers does not always have the midwatch, the four-hour period from midnight to four in the morning. There is no indication that dog watches were used in the discovery era.

Although there is no historical comment as to when and how often the crewmen were fed, there are records of the food and drink carried by ships of the period. The basic staples were sea biscuits, or hardtack, salted flour, salt fish (cod, sardines, and anchovies), salt meat (beef and pork), olives, olive oil, vinegar, cheese, dry legumes (peas, chick-peas, black-eyed peas, and lentils), rice, garlic, almonds, raisins, honey, molasses, wine, and water. The olive oil, and perhaps olives, were carried in large earthenware jugs. All other provisions were stored in wooden casks, which occasionally, according to some reports, were of cheap and faulty construction, permitting the preserving brine to leak out of the meat casks and moisture to invade the casks of dry provisions. All were

stored in the hold, the driest section of which was normally reserved for those casks carrying dry provisions. The cooper was responsible for keeping the casks as tight as possible, with allowance made for their condition when loaded aboard.

Getting necessary rest was not easy. Cabins normally were available only to the admiral and the captain. The master and the pilot usually had open bunks in steerage under the raised quarterdeck clear of the massive tiller by which the helmsman steered the ship. Everyone else not on watch had to bed down somewhere out of the way on the main deck or in the hold. Some of the senior ratings had thin mattresses and others had straw mats, all of which were rolled up and stowed when not in use. The spare sails stowed in the hold would have been a favored spot for stretching out, particularly in foul weather.

Maintaining a healthy mental attitude among the crew was especially difficult on Columbus's first voyage largely because of the seamen's innate fear of the unknown. To assuage this fear, Columbus may have made use of a particular item of personal equipment. That was his copy of Toscanelli's chart from which, together with his study of Marco Polo, Ptolemy, and Marinus of Tyre, he had developed his firm belief that he would find Cipangu (Japan) only 750 leagues (2,115 nautical miles) west of Ferro in the Canary Islands. Since the three ships had on some occasions sailed as far as 50 leagues in a day, and could probably average 35 leagues per day, they should make a landfall within fifteen to twenty-two days, or so they probably were told.

Insistence by Columbus on careful use of the three principal navigational instruments available in the late fifteenth century would have been an important element in his efforts to develop his crew's confidence that the location of the ships was known at all times. These instruments were the compass, the half-hour sand glass, and the traverse board.

Compared to the modern compass, that of Columbus's time was very crude. The circular compass card, divided into thirty-two equally spaced compass points, had a magnetized needle fastened to it and a small, hollow, brass cone mounted over a small hole at the midpoint of the card. The complete assembly was suspended on a brass pivot mounted vertically in a wooden bowl by setting the hollow brass cone on the point of the pivot, about which the compass card was free to rotate. A black vertical line called the lubber line was drawn on the forward edge of the bowl. Since the magnetized compass needle always sought the earth's magnetic north pole, the point on the circumference of the compass card in line with the lubber line indicated the heading of the ship, subject to an important proviso: the orientation of the compass had to be fixed in a position such that a radial line from the center of the compass card passing through the lubber line was parallel to the keel of the ship. This was done by mounting the compass in a properly and securely aligned wooden box called the *bitacora,* or binnacle. In addition, to ensure that the compass card remained horizontal so that the compass card could rotate freely about its pivot despite the rolling and pitching of the ship, the compass was suspended within the binnacle by means of a brass gimble system. The binnacle was provided with a hood to protect the compass from the weather and with a small brass or copper oil lamp for illumination at night.

Two such binnacle assemblies were required, one on the main deck just forward of the tiller for the helmsman to steer by and the other on the quarterdeck for the captain or officer of the watch to monitor. There was an open hatch in the quarterdeck through which the officer of the watch called down to the helmsman the course to be steered. Other important items of equipment associated with the compass were the iron compass needles and the all-important lodestones needed to magnetize them. A number of each were carried on every ship.

In the Columbus era, and until the late sixteenth century, four items of shipboard equipment were used in conjunction with each other to indicate the approximate time of day. One was a simple diagram, sometimes referred to as the Polaris clock, for indicating time from the orientation of the axis of the Little Dipper as it appeared to rotate in a counterclockwise direction around the polestar. The second was an instrument called a nocturnal with which it was possible to measure with some precision the orientation of that axis. The third was an almanac that recorded that orientation at midnight for every night of the year, and the fourth was the half-hour sand glass, or *ampolleta.*

The Polaris clock diagram consisted of the figure of a man circumscribed by a circle with the time of day represented by twenty-four hourly points equally spaced around its circumference. The polestar, Polaris, at the end of the handle of the Little Dipper, was located at the man's navel, and a radial line from that point to Kochab, one of the two brighter stars at the Dipper's outer edge, defined the axis of the constellation. Thus, a ship's pilot, estimating the orientation of the axis of the Little Dipper and comparing it with the midnight orientation given in the almanac for that date could make a reasonable approximation of the local time. With the nocturnal, by sighting Polaris through a hole at the center of the instrument and rotating the movable radial arm until it was aligned with Kochab, it was possible to obtain a more accurate orientation of the axis of the Little Dipper and hence a more accurate estimate of the time. Obviously, use of these three items of equipment was limited to nights on which the Little Dipper was visible at least part of the time.

The only means available for keeping track of time on a continuing basis was the *ampolleta,* or half-hour sand glass. A gromet, or ship's boy, was assigned the tedious but essential task of watching the sand glass and turning it over promptly when all the sand had run out of the upper globe. These sand glasses were very fragile and each ship normally carried a dozen or more. Seamen of the period thought of time in terms not of hours but of *ampolletas* and guardias, sand glasses and watches, eight sand glasses to a watch. The crewmen of each ship were divided into two groups or watches, usually referred to as the port watch and the starboard watch. Every four hours, or eight *ampolletas,* the men on watch would be relieved of duty by the oncoming watch. At that time, the ship's pilot, sharing with the master the duty of being in charge of either the offgoing or the oncoming watch, would estimate the ship's position from the record of its estimated course and speed as recorded on the traverse board at half-hour intervals during the prior watch.

The traverse board consisted of a wooden compass rose with eight equally spaced holes drilled through the lines radiating from its center to each of the thirty-two compass points. Each hole represented one half hour of the watch. Each time the half-hour sand glass was turned over, the helmsman would call out his average course for the past half hour and a peg would be inserted in a hole for the specified compass course, starting from the center and working out toward the circumference as the watch progressed. Below the compass rose were eight horizontal lines with about ten equally spaced vertical lines superimposed on them. Each horizontal line represented one half hour of the watch and each vertical line one mile per hour of ship's speed and were so marked. The number of vertical lines was arbitrary and varied in accordance with the maximum speed a particular ship was capable of attaining. Holes were drilled at each intersection of the two sets of lines so that pegs could be inserted to record the estimated speed during each half-hour period.

These were the principal items of equipment used in the Columbus era for dead-reckoning navigation. During that period, the connotation of doom suggested by the term *dead reckoning* was not altogether false. Although the term is a contraction of *deduced reckoning* and is the presumed trace of the ship's course on a chart, the accuracy of this form of navigation diminishes markedly in direct proportion to the distance traveled from the known position of the point of departure and in inverse proportion to the skill of the master and pilot in estimating the true course and speed of their ship. The true course of a ship is dependent on several variables, which, in the uncharted waters of the discovery voyages, were of unknown size. For example, magnetic variation of the earth can cause the magnetic compass to be offset by several degrees either to the east or west from true north, and the direction and strength of the current can cause the true geographical course of the ship to differ significantly from its compass heading. The extent of these variables in the vast expanse of the Atlantic Ocean was completely unknown in the Columbus era. The diligence and skill of the helmsman in maintaining the assigned compass heading in variable wind and sea conditions was yet another factor. No instruments were available for determining a ship's speed, and its estimation totally depended on the experience and skill of the watch officer. Similarly dependent was the estimation of leeway, the amount that a ship is pushed sideways. These variables were cumulative, and as time and distance increased from a known location so too did the possibility of significant errors. The later increased use of celestial navigation made it possible to eliminate the cumulative effect of these errors.

The only two instruments available to Columbus for celestial navigation were the astrolabe and the quadrant. Although the cross-staff had been invented prior to 1500, there is no evidence that Columbus or any of his Spanish contemporaries ever used one. The astrolabe consisted of a disk of brass or bronze with degree markings from 0 to 90 etched into its upper semicircle. A small ring attached at the ninety-degree point permitted the astrolabe to be suspended so that a line connecting the zero-degree points would be horizontal. By sighting Polaris through the peepholes of the rotatable arm, the altitude of the polestar could be read from the etched degree markings, providing a reasonable approximation of the latitude of the viewer. The quadrant was a simple quarter-circle of hardwood or bronze with peephole sights attached along one edge, a light plumb line attached to the apex, and a scale of ninety degrees scribed into the arc. By sighting a star through the peepholes, its altitude could be read at the position of the plumb line. Accurate readings were difficult to obtain with these instruments when using them aboard a rolling and pitching ship. Even in calm weather a ship has enough motion so that the suspended instrument sways. Vasco da Gama, when attempting to establish the latitude of an important landmark during his voyage to India in 1497–1499, is said to have disembarked and hung his astrolabe from a tree in order to obtain an accurate reading. Columbus had very little success with either instrument, whereas his prowess as a dead-reckoning navigator has been acclaimed by many.

One item of equipment particularly important to historians was the ship's log book in which the ship's captain kept a record of each day's events. Entries in the log naturally depended on the writing skills of the captain and on his level of interest in events that occurred. In a well-kept log, the record would show the place and time of departure, courses and speeds for every watch, a daily estimate of the ship's position, weather conditions including wind direction and velocity, unusual conditions and sightings, occasional comments about the adequacy of

provisions and the health and morale of the crew, position and time of landfalls, place and time of arrival at destination, and any other happening that might be of historical interest.

Ships of the period normally carried seven anchors: four bower anchors, two of which were kept in readiness to let go on short notice with mooring cables attached, and two stowed either in the forecastle area or in the hold; one large sheet anchor for use in storm conditions, almost always stowed in the hold for reasons of ship stability; and two warping grapnels used for moving the ship around in a harbor. Occasionally a kedge anchor of moderate weight would be carried for use in hauling a grounded ship from a sandbar. The anchors had heavy wooden stocks and, in the case of Spanish anchors, relatively thin shanks and arms. As one would expect, the weights of the various sizes of anchors were related to the size of the ship on which they were carried. A bulky merchant nao such as Santa María carried bower anchors of about a thousand pounds each, whereas those of the smaller and less bulky caravels weighed only half as much.

In addition to the anchor cables fastened to the bower anchors in constant readiness, spare cables of various circumferences and lengths were stowed in the hold. Also stowed there were spare sails; various sizes of hemp rope for repair of rigging; tools and equipment for the carpenter, caulker, and cooper for effecting repairs to the ship; and the many casks of wine, water, salted fish and meat, hardtack, and other provisions. Two important items for the caulker, who was responsible for the watertightness of the ship, were tar and tallow with which the underbody of the hull was coated to protect it against shipworms. Other items required for the safe navigation of ships not only in the Age of Discovery but right up to the development of electronic instruments were the sounding lead and the deep-sea lead and their associated lead lines. The sounding lead, used for measuring depths of water of no more than twenty fathoms, weighed only a few pounds; the deep-sea lead, used for measuring depths of as much as two hundred fathoms, was heavier.

The one cabin on board, occupied by the captain or the admiral, was sparsely furnished. On the larger naos, with a cabin under the raised poop deck at the aft end of the half deck, there was enough room for a table, tableware, one or two chairs, a lamp, a seaman's chest, a built-in bunk with appropriate bed covers, a washstand, and perhaps a separate desk. Functional items of equipment included a shield, pieces of armor, a sword, an astrolabe, a quadrant, and perhaps a compass if the captain or admiral wished to monitor the course without having to go out to the quarterdeck to check the one there. The admiral had a royal standard and flags of Castile and León in readiness for carrying ashore when claiming possession of an island in the name of the Spanish sovereigns. He

FIFTEENTH-CENTURY CLOTHING OF SPANISH SAILORS. *Left:* A sailor caulking a hull. *Right:* Towing boats in Barcelona harbor.

may also have had a copy of Toscanelli's chart, or one of his own, hanging on the bulkhead, as well as an image of the Virgin Mary.

Clothing worn by seamen in the Columbus era could in no sense be described as uniform. Typically, clothing was of wool and loose fitting except for stockings, which, when worn, were of the leotard type. Some form of hat was always worn. Two general types were common: one, a red wool stocking cap from Catalonia and the other, also of red wool, a bonnet from Toledo. Blouses with full sleeves were favored and occasionally had hoods, which were useful in foul weather. Often, a lightweight sleeveless tunic was worn over the blouse.

Regardless of the weather, the Spanish always remained fully clothed, even in the tropics. This may have been the reason they were so astounded by the nakedness of the Indians, comments on which abound in every report. On board ship, when rousing the next watch to come on duty, there was no need to allow time for dressing. None would have undressed when coming off the previous watch.

In colder weather, an overcoat of coarse brown cloth was common. Columbus often wore such a coat, which some authors have referred to as a Franciscan habit, associating his choice of drab clothing with his fondness for that religious order. But whenever Columbus went ashore to claim new lands in the name of the Spanish sovereigns or to impress native caciques (chiefs), he invariably was royally adorned in red.

[See also *Arms, Armor, and Armament; Navigation; Timetelling.*]

BIBLIOGRAPHY

Landstrom, Bjorn. *Columbus.* New York, 1966.
Martinez-Hidalgo, José María. *Columbus' Ships.* Barre, Mass., 1966.

Morison, Samuel Eliot. *Admiral of the Ocean Sea: A Life of Christopher Columbus.* 2 vols. Boston, 1942.

WILLIAM LEMOS

ERICSSON, LEIF (fl. 1000), called the Lucky, Norse explorer and settler in Newfoundland. Leif Ericsson is widely accepted as the European discoverer of America in about A.D. 1000. During the Viking age, from shortly before A.D. 800, there was a special sea route, the western route across the North Atlantic, followed by the Norwegians and, after the discovery of Iceland, also by the Icelanders. The Norsemen sailed from island to island, farther and farther west, settling in the lands they reached. First they came to Shetland, Orkney, the Hebrides and the Faeroes; then Iceland and Greenland were found and settled; and as a final, logical consequence of the western route, none-too-distant America was reached.

Leif's father was Eric the Red, born about A.D. 950, who emigrated with his family from southwestern Norway to Iceland, where he settled and married. Leif Ericsson was born there. As the result of conflict with powerful families, Eric was outlawed and had to flee Iceland. He sailed westward, discovered Greenland, and explored its southwestern coast. He returned to Iceland three years later and in 986 led a large expedition of emigrants to the new land, which he called Greenland. Eric settled at Brattahlid, a favorable area at Ericsfjord and became the leader of the Greenland community, an independent state; this community existed for about five hundred years. When Leif came to Greenland with his family, he must have been a fairly young boy; he grew up in the new country, and became a Greenlander.

Two Icelandic sagas are our most important sources for Leif's discovery of Vinland and other regions in America. These sagas, which are found in thirteenth- and fourteenth-century manuscripts, are *Eiríks saga Rauða* (The saga of Eric the Red) and *Grœnlendingasaga* (The saga of the Greenlanders).

Eiríks saga relates that Leif Ericsson sailed from Greenland to Norway, where the Norwegian king Olafr Tryggvason commissioned him to Christianize Greenland. On his return voyage, Leif lost his way and came to an unknown country where he found vines and fields of wild wheat. That same summer he sailed to Greenland, where he preached Christianity. This version is probably largely unhistorical.

The *Grœnlendingasaga*, which is found in an Icelandic manuscript known as the Flatey Book (*Flateyarbók*, 1387), gives a radically different version. This saga states that Bjarni Herjulfsson lost his way when sailing to the colony in Greenland and sighted a strange coast that he followed to the north and east, finally reaching the eastern colony in Greenland. Leif Ericsson then set out on an expedition with a crew of thirty-five, in order to find the coasts Bjarni had seen, following the latter's route, but in the opposite direction. He came first to a barren, flat land with glaciers, which he called Helluland (Flatstone land, probably Baffin Island), then to a land that he gave the name Markland (Land of forests, presumably Labrador), and finally to a land with much grass, which he called Vinland (Land of meadows; the Old Norse syllable *vin* with a short *i*, meaning "meadow," was misinterpreted by Adam of Bremen to mean "wine" and accepted by the writer of the saga). Here he settled and built large houses.

The location of Leif's Vinland has been the subject of much discussion. The sagas state that Leif found vines and grapes, and therefore it has been fairly generally accepted that Vinland must lie comparatively far south, in parts where wild grapes grow. But after Helge Ingstad's discovery of a Norse settlement at L'Anse aux Meadows (51°35' N) in northern Newfoundland, a number of scholars agree that this site must be identical with Vinland. It is clear that Vinland was a good land with meadows that provided pasture, important to a people contemplating emigration with their livestock. There was a river here, and we know from the saga that it held salmon. Leif explored the land, but half his men always stayed near the houses; although they met no natives, they must have feared them.

Leif returned to Greenland after having spent a year in Vinland. During his return voyage he saved fifteen people wrecked on a reef and became known as Leif the Lucky. Now Leif, after succeeding his father as leader of the Greenland settlement, lived at Brattahlid. His advice must have been of decisive importance for the later expeditions to Vinland led by Thorfinn Karlsefni, by Freydis, Leif's sister, and by his brother Thorvald, who was killed by the natives.

We know little about Leif's person, although the *Grœnlendingasaga* describes him as "big and strong, of striking appearance, shrewd, and in every respect a temperate and fair-dealing man." It seems likely that he became a Christian, although his father, Eric the Red—and probably most of the other Greenlanders—remained pagans. Eric's wife, Thjodhild, however, was baptized, and built a church not far from Brattahlid. The remains of this church have been excavated by Danish archaeologists. It was built of turf and measured only 3.5 by 2 meters (11 by 6.5 feet). One of the 144 skeletons that have been excavated from its churchyard is probably that of Leif Ericsson, the European discoverer of America.

[See also *Icelandic Sagas; Vinland.*]

BIBLIOGRAPHY

Columbus, Ferdinand. *The Life of the Admiral Christopher Columbus.* Translated by Benjamin Keen. New Brunswick, N.J., 1959.

Ingstad, Helge. *Land under the Pole Star.* London and New York, 1966. English translation of *Landet under Leidarstjernen.* Oslo, 1959.

Storm, Gustav. *Studies on the Vineland Voyages.* Extraits des Mémoires de la Société royale des antiquaires du nord 1888. Copenhagen, 1889.

HELGE INGSTAD

ESPAÑOLA, LA. In December 1492 Columbus arrived at the western end of an island that he named "La Isla Española," known later by its Latin name, Hispaniola. Its native name was Ayti, meaning "mountainous land," and this is the name, spelled "Haiti," now applied to the western third of the island. The remaining portion comprises the Dominican Republic. The land is indeed mountainous, with five distinct ranges running from east to west. As on the other large West Indian islands, the central mountainous region is bordered by extensive plains, many of which are fertile.

By the late fifteenth century La Española was inhabited by about 600,000 Taínos, a subgroup of Arawaks, who had replaced earlier peoples. Those on La Española lived much like their neighbors in Cuba, except that they were more exposed to the hostile Caribs, who from their bases in the eastern Caribbean were at this time raiding Taíno settlements on the island. The Caribs, a warlike people, were skilled archers and were capable of ranging great distances in their swift canoes.

Columbus visited the island during his first voyage and was welcomed by the Taínos, whose gold ornaments particularly interested him. After *Santa María* had been wrecked, Columbus established a settlement at La Navidad and then sailed back to Spain, encountering some hostile Indians (perhaps Caribs) during his voyage along the island's northeastern coast. He returned in

© Carta

November 1493 to find the La Navidad settlement ruined; he then established a larger Spanish town at La Isabela and set about systematically subjugating the island's inhabitants.

Expeditions penetrated the different regions, and the Taínos were obliged to provide the Spaniards with food and to labor in the newly opened gold mines. As elsewhere, they were also inadvertently brought into contact with European diseases. The result was that by 1508 only about a tenth of the original 600,000 Indians were still alive. The survivors did their best to hold out in the mountains, and Africans were imported as laborers. Meanwhile, the conquest went on; it was consolidated during the governorship of Nicolás de Ovando (1502–1509) with the foundation of fifteen towns.

The site Columbus had chosen at La Isabela proved unsuitable, and so in 1496 the capital was moved to the south coast, where Nueva Isabela was founded on the left bank of the Ozama River. After this town was destroyed by a hurricane, the city of Santo Domingo was established in 1502 on the right bank of the river. Here the Spaniards constructed churches, monasteries, and public buildings, many of which survive to the present day, making Santo Domingo easily the oldest permanent city established by Europeans in the Western Hemisphere.

La Española continued throughout the sixteenth century to produce sugar and gold, and Santo Domingo became the center of an extensive administrative area known as an audiencia. Even after the Spanish conquest of the mainland in the 1520s and 1530s, Santo Domingo continued to enjoy a certain importance as the main Spanish base in the Caribbean; it was not until the late sixteenth century that it began to feel the effects of attacks by French, Dutch, and English pirates.

[See also *Indian America*, articles on *Taínos* and *Island Caribs*; *Settlements*, articles on *La Isabela, La Navidad,* and *Santo Domingo*.]

BIBLIOGRAPHY

Moya-Pons, Frank. *Historia colonial de Santo Domingo.* Barcelona, 1974.

DAVID BUISSERET

EUROPE AND THE WIDER WORLD IN 1492.
Educated Europeans in 1492 knew quite a bit about the universe they lived in, even before the voyages of Columbus. The great oceanic expeditions sponsored by Portugal and Spain would expand Europe's incomplete knowledge of Africa and Asia and introduce them to the vast American continents as well. Only a half century later a new view of the cosmos would prove to be equally fundamental. When Copernicus published his notion that the sun and not the earth was the center of the universe, he challenged ancient and medieval wisdom about the heavens quite as much as the voyages of Columbus and his successors challenged accepted knowledge about the earth.

Models of the Universe and the Earth

The astronomical knowledge of medieval Europe, and of the Islamic world as well, relied on the model proposed by the classical astronomer and geographer Ptolemy, a Greco-Egyptian trained in Hellenistic science who had lived in the second century A.D. His seminal work on astronomy had been translated into Latin in the twelfth century, although it generally continued to be known by the title of its Arabic translation, the *Almagest*. Ptolemy proposed a geocentric universe in which the moon, the planets, the stars, and the heavens all revolved around the spherical earth on perfectly formed, transparent crystalline spheres. Ptolemy's model included ten concentric layers around its earthly core: (1) the moon; (2) Mercury; (3) Venus; (4) the sun; (5) Mars; (6) Jupiter; (7) Saturn; (8) the firmament, or starry heaven; (9) the prime mover, or crystalline heaven; and finally (10) the empyrean, or habitation of God. Even if—as we know now—the basic theory was wrong, it held great importance throughout the Middle Ages in both the Christian and Islamic worlds.

Medieval astronomers were careful observers. Even if their basic geocentric model was incorrect, they knew that the moon had no light of its own and depended on reflected light from the sun. They also knew that eclipses of the moon occurred when the earth cast a shadow upon it and that eclipses of the sun occurred when the moon blocked the sun's light from reaching the earth. They had no telescope (the telescope was invented in the seventeenth century), but careful naked-eye observations persuaded them that the planets did not describe perfect circles in their seeming circuit about the earth. Medieval astronomers accounted for these discrepancies by accepting Ptolemy's suggestion that each planet described tiny circles (epicycles) on the surface of its crystalline sphere while the whole sphere revolved. By refining Ptolemy's model to account for observations that seemed to contradict it, medieval astronomers were able to retain a geocentric model of the universe for centuries.

The first frontal assault on that model came from the work of the Polish astronomer Nicolaus Copernicus (1473–1543), whose research and astronomical observations spanned the first decades of the sixteenth century—the very time that Iberian mariners were spanning the terrestrial globe. Copernicus's *De revolutionibus orbium coelestium*, published in 1543, placed the sun at the center of the solar system, but it took over a century and a half before the heliocentric idea would be widely accepted by scholars, and even longer before ordinary people would know about it. Because the English language was set while the geocentric model still held sway, we still speak of the sun rising and setting, although we know that our phrases describe only what our eyes observe, and not what is really happening.

The Spherical Earth. Educated Europeans, who had access to the cosmographical theorists such as Ptolemy, also knew perfectly well that the earth is a sphere. Popular works, too, made that knowledge more widely available among the literate. Around 1220, John Holywood, also known by the Latin version of his name, Sacrobosco, wrote a basic textbook called *De sphaera mundi*, based on his reading of a translation of the *Almagest* and various Muslim and Hellenistic geographers. Holywood's book was widely circulated in the later Middle Ages and went through many printings in the fifteenth and early sixteenth centuries.

Maps depicting the lands of the earth relied on the traditional medieval assumption that only a portion of the earth, well above the equator, was habitable. These maps also reflected the traditional Judeo-Christian idea that God had created the earth, and the Christian notion that spirituality continued to define it. Because Christian geographers believed that the most important event in human history was the death and resurrection of Jesus, they held that Jerusalem must be in the center of the inhabited world. In many medieval maps, the continents were arrayed around Jerusalem, with Asia at the top, Europe in the lower left and Africa in the lower right. Europe and Africa together were about the size of Asia by itself. Such depictions have come to be called T-O maps, because of their general layout, the Mediterranean forming the vertical base of a T with Jerusalem at its head, and the Nile River to the right and the Black Sea and the Don or Dnieper River to the left forming the arms of the T. Surrounding the land mass was an all-encompassing and uncharted ocean, the O of the map. To many scholars, these maps displayed Christian zeal but a profound ignorance of geographical reality. (In fact, similar maps were also produced by Muslim geographers in the Middle Ages.) More recently scholars are coming to suspect that the makers and users of medieval T-O maps knew quite well that they did not depict geographical reality. Instead they portrayed the spiritual reality of the world and its component parts, transcending the physical world.

That physical world was depicted fairly accurately in the late medieval period by another sort of map. The beautiful sailing charts called portolanos, common in Mediterranean countries, combined great aesthetic appeal with accurate depictions of the coasts and compass directions linking major ports. They are generally identified by their compass roses and rhumb lines emanating from the various compass points, so that mariners could use them

to sail from port to port. The so-called Catalan Atlas, attributed to the Majorcan Jew Abraham Cresques and presented to King Charles V of France around 1375, owed much to the portolano tradition. In addition, it contained information about the world beyond Europe and depicted it in a more accurate fashion than the T-O maps. Scholars, mapmakers, merchants, and mariners of late medieval Europe all profited from the advances made in academic geography and by the collection and dissemination of information about Asia and Africa by literate travelers. Full knowledge was still lacking, but sufficiently accurate, though incomplete, information circulated among scholars and informed laymen to inspire them to believe that ocean routes to India might be discovered.

Academic Geography. In 1268 Roger Bacon (c. 1214–1294) published his *Opus maius,* summarizing ancient geographical knowledge and integrating the contributions of Muslim geographers in the Middle Ages. He accepted the view of the world depicted in the T-O maps, specifically that the habitable portion of the world was composed of three parts (Asia, Africa, and Europe) and that the rest of the globe was covered by an encircling ocean. Earlier authorities had asserted that the "torrid zone"—lands located near the equator—would be too hot for habitation, but Bacon suggested that Africa and Asia were habitable south of the equator. Bacon's ideas influenced many other geographers between his time and the era of Iberian exploration.

In the early fifteenth century Pierre d'Ailly (1350–1420), a cardinal of the Roman Church, published a geography called *Imago mundi* that was to have a great influence upon Columbus. D'Ailly relied on geographical treatises by classical writers and Muslim scholars, but he disregarded the accounts of recent travelers such as Marco Polo. Perhaps because he seemed so careful with evidence, d'Ailly's conclusions carried great weight, although he made several fundamental errors. Two of these directly informed Columbus's mistaken conception of the world: that Asia covered much more of the globe from east to west than it actually does *and* that the oceans cover much less of the globe than they actually do.

As a geographical authority, d'Ailly's *Imago mundi* was greatly overshadowed by the translation of two works by Ptolemy. In addition to the *Almagest* on astronomy, Ptolemy also produced an influential geographical treatise, the *Geography,* translated into Latin in the early fifteenth century. As soon as it became available in that common language of European intellectual life, Ptolemy's *Geography* provided educated Europeans with a convenient framework for depicting the globe in a graphic form, particularly for those who already knew and trusted his work on the heavens. Ptolemy's division of the earth into 360 degrees became the basis for subsequent European maps. Ptolemy did, however, make two fundamental mistakes. First, he believed that Africa and Asia were joined by lands connecting their southern tips, making the Indian Ocean a landlocked sea, inaccessible to ships sailing from Europe around Africa. Fortunately for those who were trying to find just such a route, the humanist Enea Silvio Piccolomini, who became Pope Pius II, rejected the idea that the Indian Ocean was an enclosed sea when he published his own work summarizing much of Ptolemy's *Geography*. Columbus and others with dreams of global sea routes read Piccolomini's work and took inspiration from its conclusions. Ptolemy's other error, which did influence Columbus, postulated that the earth was about one-fifth smaller than it is.

The geographical ideas of the late fifteenth century found physical expression in a now-famous globe by Martin Behaim, made in 1492 (the earliest known globe to date), which presented a view of the world that was almost identical to the concept that Columbus had formed. The Americas are totally absent, of course. Cipangu (Japan) is located far distant from the mainland of Asia, and the ocean between Europe and the East is amply strewn with islands. Whether Columbus and Behaim had close contact with one another is unknown, but Behaim's depiction of the world and Columbus's concept of it both grew out of the academic geography available at the end of the fifteenth century. Both men had lived in Lisbon and had gained access to the Portuguese court, where courtiers and experts regularly discussed the latest geographical discoveries.

World Geography

The world depicted in the limited maps and geographies of the fifteenth century bore some relation to the world as it really was in 1492, but the vision was far from complete. Europe had quite limited information about the great civilizations that existed in Asia and Africa. Contacts with the Muslims had taught Europeans something about the interior of Africa, including that gold was obtained there. During the early fifteenth century, Portuguese voyages down the western shore of Africa added more direct practical knowledge as well. Europeans had no knowledge of the civilizations in the Americas, despite the Scandinavian voyages that had reached some part of North America around the year 1000. By the fifteenth century, however, Scandinavians were going no farther west than Greenland, and memory of their earlier voyages had not entered the mainstream of European thought. Implausible as it may seem, European scholars and merchants in the fifteenth century probably knew more about distant Asia than about any other part of the world outside Europe.

Asia. Despite the hostility felt by European Christians for the Islamic world, Muslim merchants served as crucial intermediaries between Europe and the vastness of Asia. Western Europeans had acquired first-hand knowledge of

the western fringe of Asia during the Crusades (1095–1291), when religiously motivated armies from western Europe established the Kingdom of Jerusalem and related principalities along the eastern shore of the Mediterranean, thus wresting control of Christian holy places from the Muslims. Even though the crusaders failed to maintain control of the Holy Land and lost their few strongholds eventually, their ventures spawned a long-lasting commercial development. During the Crusades, merchant communities from the Christian Mediterranean seized the economic initiative in the region from the Muslims and maintained it thereafter. The Crusades foreshadowed the worldwide expansion of Europe that began in the fifteenth century and gathered momentum with Columbus.

By the time of Columbus, the spice trade provided one of the most important motivations for European expansion. During the Crusades, Europeans had first developed a taste and demand for exotic spices, which improved the palatability of food in the thousands of years before the development of advanced preservation techniques. The European elite consumed increasing amounts of spices during the late medieval centuries. Most of the spices that entered European markets were grown in the Far East, especially in India and the South Asian islands, and were then brought by Muslim traders across the Indian Ocean to the Persian Gulf and the Red Sea. In eastern-Mediterranean ports, such as Alexandria, the most important emporium, Italian merchants bought spices from Muslims to resell in Europe, where they commanded high prices. The Venetian Republic, in particular, reaped enormous profits from this trade. Even if the buyers of Asian spices and other luxury goods formed only a tiny part of the total European population, their purchasing power helped to keep the entire structure of long-distance trade functioning. Because of the profits to be made from the spice trade, many other Europeans were eager to participate in it, but the Italians and their Muslim trading partners held an effective monopoly by their control of the eastern Mediterranean.

By the fourteenth century, many Europeans knew where spices came from. Indeed, many European missionaries and merchants had traveled to Asia—some as far as China—and had reported on what they had seen. They generally reached Asia by overland caravan routes through central Asia. Those routes were open to travelers during the thirteenth and fourteenth centuries because of what has been called the Pax Mongolica, the period when Mongol rulers held sway from North China to the Black Sea and guaranteed safety along the trade routes.

Mongol ascendancy began when Genghis Khan (1167–1227; born Temüjin, he assumed the title "ruler of the universe") secured the unity of the Mongols and related tribes in 1206. Fierce mounted warriors who relied for mobility on their powerful horses, the Mongols had a powerful bow and good steel arms and armor. From the Chinese, they learned the siege tactics necessary to capture fortified towns. All their military skills were put to good use in the rapid conquests of North China, Persia, and Russia. By the death of Genghis Khan in 1227, Mongol authority stretched from East Asia to eastern Europe.

Reports about the Mongols had filtered through to Europe, where, despite the horrifying and lurid nature of many of the tales, they inspired Western interest in contacting the Mongols, especially on the part of religious leaders. Although such interest may seem puzzling at first, it sprang from a logical source. The Mongols were a distant threat and not yet the enemies of Europe. The Muslims were close by and had been enemies for centuries. Consequently, popes and, later, kings thought that the Mongols might prove useful against the Muslims at a time when the crusader states faced increased Muslim pressure.

A joint Egyptian-Turkish army reconquered Jerusalem from the crusaders in 1244. In the next year, 1245, Pope Innocent IV sent an envoy, Giovanni da Pian del Carpini (c. 1182 or 1200–c. 1252) to the Mongol khan, charged with finding out more about these mysterious people. Carpini went by land from Kiev to the Mongol capital of Karakorum and was present at the coronation of Güyük (or Kuyuk) Khan. Carpini gave the khan the pope's letter calling on him to join an alliance against the Muslims and to recognize papal supremacy. Not surprisingly, the khan declined to recognize papal supremacy and nothing came of the military alliance, but Europe at least learned more about Asia. Carpini's written account of his journey found its way into the world history of Vincent of Beauvais (d. before 1264), court historian to Louis IX of France, who sought to strengthen contacts with the Mongols by sending other western ambassadors: Andrew of Longjumeau in 1248 and Willem van Ruysbroeck and Bartholomew of Cremona in 1253 to 1255. Their accounts, too, have survived. Taken together, the Christian missions to the Mongols prepared the way for the Christian merchants who soon followed.

In the later Middle Ages, many Italian merchants, especially Genoese and Venetians, were willing to try new ventures in the search for economic gain. One of the best known episodes began around the year 1260, when two Venetian merchants, Niccolò and Maffeo Polo, departed from the Crimean peninsula in the Black Sea, where other Italian merchants had been established for some time. Their trading expedition through Mongol lands eventually brought them to China. They returned to Venice in 1269 and left again for China a few years later, this time taking with them Niccolò's son Marco. Marco Polo (c. 1254–1324) remained for eighteen years in China, where he served as a bureaucrat in the court of the Mongol khan, Kublai. He traveled throughout China and returned to Europe after having visited India. At the same time other European merchants and missionaries also traveled to Asia. While Marco Polo resided at the Mongol court, Giovanni da Montecorvino arrived in Peking and later became its first Catholic archbishop, presiding over a large archdiocese but few Christians.

After Marco Polo returned to Venice, he was captured by the Genoese and spent several years as a prisoner of war. In prison he recounted the tale of his travels through Asia to Rustichello of Pisa. Although Rustichello embellished the story in places, and misunderstood some of it, his story of Marco Polo's travels provided one of the best and most accurate accounts of China and the east that Europeans had at their disposal, although many readers thought the tale more fanciful than real. Accounts by other travelers also appeared and spread through Europe, some of them genuine and others woven from legend rather than practical experience. John Mandeville (the name is a pseudonym) wrote a purported travel guide in the fourteenth century that included fabulous races of human beings with monstrous characteristics; some had no heads, others enormous tails, others extra limbs. Mandeville's book was extraordinarily popular, especially in the early days of printing in the late fifteenth century, and undoubtedly fed European enthusiasm for travel to real places, even as it confirmed ancient legends of monstrous humans and fanciful beasts. Based on the information from Marco Polo and others, Francesco Balducci Pegolotti was able to write a commercial guide in 1340 called *La pratica della mercatura* that included information about the spices and other products of Asia. He even provided a generally accurate indication of where those products originated. Both Polo and Pegolotti told their readers that it was possible to buy spices directly from their Asian sources, and Polo, at least, was an important inspiration for Columbus.

The Mongols suffered a series of reverses in the later thirteenth century and their empire broke up in the fourteenth. As long as it lasted, however, the Pax Mongolica opened Central and East Asia to a number of intrepid European missionaries and merchants, whose experiences taught them enough about Asia to spur great interest in long-distance trade and gave them a much greater knowledge of the world and a better idea of the extent of Muslim power. Unfortunately for Europeans who might wish to put the information about Asia and its markets to practical use, political conditions in the Middle East made it impossible.

After the collapse of the Mongol Empire, three new and aggressive Muslim empires gained importance in the Middle East. By the end of the fifteenth century they held sway from the Mediterranean to India. The Ottoman Turks in Anatolia and southeastern Europe had delivered the death blow to the Christian Byzantine Empire in 1453 by capturing Constantinople. Muslims now controlled the key ports and trade routes leading to the markets of Asia, and they severely restricted Christian trading opportunities: the Ottoman authorities permitted western merchants to frequent coastal markets such as Alexandria, but they would not allow them free passage along the routes they controlled. Consequently, some Europeans contemplated a bold alternative that had been discussed for centuries: to bypass the Muslims altogether by finding a sea route to India in order to purchase the spices directly at their sources.

Two adventuresome brothers from Genoa named Vivaldi had made a very early voyage out into the Atlantic to seek the sea route to Asia. In 1291 their small fleet sailed through the strait of Gibraltar with the aim of reaching India. They never returned, and left no traces of their fate except for some equivocal signs on the African coast opposite the Canary Islands. Although we can assume that the Vivaldis failed in their attempt, the hope of finding a sea passage to India remained alive to inspire the Portuguese and the Spaniards as they added new areas of Africa and the Atlantic to European knowledge in the fifteenth century.

With the benefit of hindsight, we know that Europeans would find a very favorable situation to develop their Asian trade once they had rounded Africa. Muslims from the Middle East—mostly Arabs and Persians—had established regular trade in the Indian Ocean. Making use of the annual cycle of monsoon winds, which blow from the northeast from October to March and from the southwest from April to September, they traveled from India in the east to the Red Sea, the Persian Gulf, and East Africa in the west. Although Muslim traders were able to maintain their monopoly in the northern reaches of the Indian Ocean, they did not dominate southeastern Africa or the ocean passage from there to India. Consequently they could not prevent the Portuguese and other Europeans from sailing to India. On Vasco da Gama's first voyage from Portugal to India, he picked up a skilled Muslim pilot in east Africa who guided the Portuguese fleet across the Indian Ocean.

Beyond India, China might have challenged European incursions into its sphere of influence, and could even have rivaled Europe on the unexplored oceans of the globe, but the Chinese chose not to. Chinese maritime technology and military capability easily equaled European achievements, and in the early fifteenth century, the Chinese had sent out seven large naval expeditions under the command of the admiral Cheng Ho. These spectacular Chinese fleets visited many Asian ports and islands, including places on the coast of India and Ceylon. They also reached the entrances to the Persian Gulf and the Red Sea and several places on the East African coast. After the last of these impressive voyages, however, the Ming emperors of China shifted the center of their operations away from the coast and made efforts to isolate China from the rest of the world. And Japan, the golden-roofed Cipangu of Marco Polo's tale, had not developed an important long-distance seafaring tradition. Once European voyagers learned how to sail around Africa, the markets of Asia lay open to them.

Africa. Although the 1291 voyage of the Vivaldi brothers aimed to reach India, their attempt to sail westward and southward from the Mediterranean exemplified the growing southern European interest in Africa and the Atlantic. In the late Middle Ages, Genoese, Catalans, and other Christian merchants of the Mediterranean had established a series of trading posts in the ports of North Africa from Egypt to Morocco. Through agreements with the local Muslim rulers, they were able to maintain residences, offices, and warehouses, usually in segregated districts. There they bought the products of North Africa and, in the eastern Mediterranean, Asian goods as well. In the western Mediterranean, they were especially taken with the goods of West Africa brought across the Sahara Desert by Muslim caravan traders.

Among the West African products available in North African ports was gold. Since the time of the later Roman Empire, western Europe had tried to increase its meager internal supplies of gold. Optimists kept hoping that alchemy would find a way to convert baser elements into the precious metal that served as the standard of wealth. Realists settled for trade to obtain it. The Muslim world was better provided with gold than Europe, largely by tapping into sources south of the Sahara. By the later Middle Ages, the most important gold supplies were in West Africa in three major mining areas: Bambuk, Boure, and Akan. Muslim caravan traders acquired gold in sub-Saharan Africa and took it across the desert to North Africa. In the exotic ports of the southern shore of the Mediterranean, European merchants, especially Italians and Spaniards, acquired it through trade, but often on unfavorable terms. Although the Muslims maintained a monopoly on the Saharan caravan routes, Europeans knew enough about Africa to realize that black Africans had rich kingdoms in the lands to the south of the Sahara, where the Muslims purchased slaves and gold, as well as other goods.

European knowledge of the black African kingdoms of West Africa can be gauged by the Catalan Atlas (c. 1375) mentioned earlier, attributed to Abraham Crescas and presented to King Charles V of France. On the map depicting Africa, the kingdoms of the Sudanic belt of grasslands south of the Sahara are represented by the figure of a black king, seated on a throne and holding a

DETAIL FROM THE CATALAN ATLAS, CIRCA 1375. This detail, an inset placed in northwestern Africa, depicts the king of Mali and an Arab trader on a camel.   BIBLIOTHÈQUE NATIONALE, PARIS

golden orb and scepter. The caption describes him as Musse Melly (Musa Mali), "lord of the Negroes of Guinea," and attributes his power to the abundance of gold found in his country.

By the fifteenth century, one of the primary Portuguese motivations for exploring the African coast was to intersect the gold trade. The city of Ceuta, on the Moroccan coast opposite Gibraltar, was closely linked with the trans-Saharan caravan trade, which was one factor in the Portuguese decision to conquer the city in 1415. Thereafter, the Moroccans diverted most of the trade away from Ceuta, although it remained an important outpost for the Portuguese. Later in the century they sought the gold-producing regions south of the Sahara, undercutting the Muslims' monopoly of the gold trade. Those early profits would help finance continuing Portuguese exploration.

Pseudo-knowledge of Africa coexisted with reality in European minds. Along with the real kings of Africa, a legendary king called Prester John—supposedly a powerful Christian monarch whose lands lay somewhere beyond the area under Muslim control—occupied a prominent position in the expansive dreams of the Portuguese. After completing the reconquest of their territory from the Muslims in the thirteenth century, the Portuguese thought to carry a Christian holy war to the heart of Islam. The curious legend of Prester John encouraged the Portuguese to think that, if only they could find him, he would become an ally in the struggle against Islam. The problem was that no one in Europe knew where to find him. Rumors in the twelfth and thirteenth centuries placed him in Asia; by the fifteenth he was believed to be in Africa. Portuguese captains on voyages down the Atlantic coast of Africa in the early fifteenth century had instructions to collect news or even rumors about Prester John's kingdom. In the late fifteenth century, contemporary with

Columbus, the Portuguese king João II sent an overland expedition into the Middle East to seek Prester John. The Portuguese did eventually find Ethiopia, a kingdom in East Africa whose people had been Christian since the fourth century, converted by the Copts of Egypt. But their ruler was a weak imitation of the legendary Prester John, totally lacking the resources to launch any sort of crusade against Islam. Given the scope of the Portuguese efforts, there is little doubt that the politico-religious goal of attacking the Muslims from the rear held an important place among European motives for expansion. That the results of their efforts did not measure up to expectations is beside the point.

The Portuguese had other reasons for their African and Atlantic ventures. For one, they sought to expand sugarcane production. European knowledge of sugarcane and the methods for growing and processing it had expanded greatly during the Crusades. After the Crusades were over, Europeans spread sugarcane cultivation throughout the Mediterranean areas they controlled. As the Spaniards and Portuguese discovered the islands of the eastern Atlantic, they found new opportunities for the expansion of sugarcane. Spaniards in the Canary Islands, and Portuguese in the Madeiras founded sugar plantations and mills, whose production could be sold very profitably in Europe. Sugarcane production was one of the ways that newly discovered lands might be used, and the profits derived from it helped to sponsor further explorations down the African coast.

A similar pattern applied to the slave labor acquired to work in cane fields and mills. Although cane could be grown in small plots or large, the need to process the cane immediately after harvest meant that large plantations with their own processing plants were the most profitable. Also, although the hard labor in the fields and the mills could be done by anyone, it was most profitably done by some form of coerced labor, whether slave or free. The opportunities for this kind of agricultural production were more plentiful outside Europe than within. For labor on their Atlantic island plantations, Europeans frequently used slaves, especially black slaves from Africa. At first, Portuguese voyages tended to raid native settlements for slaves, but soon they found that it was easier and more profitable to make agreements with local rulers to supply them with slaves in exchange for European trade goods. The slave trade soon produced profits that made continued exploration possible.

Much more ordinary motives for Portuguese expansion into Africa existed as well. Portuguese merchants bought wheat in North Africa, particularly Morocco, to supplement production at home and to trade for other goods in West Africa. In addition, both the Portuguese and the Castilians had well-established fishing fleets that provided for home consumption as well as for exports. They saw the Atlantic waters off Africa as suitable places to extend their fishing grounds. Like sugar plantations and the slave trade, the expanded fishing grounds and grain trade developed as part of a generalized search for profitable opportunities in Africa and elsewhere.

At some point, as the Portuguese explored and traded southward along the African coast, they began seriously to look for a sea route to Asia. As we have seen, the cosmography of the day held that the world's land masses were closely linked to one another, surrounded by vast oceans that covered the rest of the globe. To reach Asia by the most efficient sea route required a voyage around Africa, which was held to be much smaller than in fact it was. Luckily for the Portuguese, the African coastal trade and the products of the Atlantic island economies were profitable enough to finance continuing efforts to find a way around the vast continent.

The search went on decade after decade before Bartolomeu Dias finally reached the southern tip of Africa in 1488, which he appropriately dubbed the Cape of Good Hope. That hope came true when Vasco da Gama took a Portuguese fleet to India in 1497 and returned to tell the tale, revealing in the process extensive geographical knowledge about the southeast coast of Africa, the Indian Ocean, and India itself. The search for India also motivated Columbus and the monarchs of Spain who eventually backed his enterprise, and he began his first voyage in the years between Dias's discovery of the Cape and Da Gama's voyage to India. The difference was that Columbus proposed a westward approach to Asia, which was widely considered more dangerous and less promising among the experienced mariners of the day. A westward voyage would mean a confrontation with the still largely unknown Atlantic.

The Atlantic and the Americas. For centuries rumors and legends told of numerous islands out in the Atlantic. Many of these islands were only legendary: Hy Brasil, St. Brendan's Isle, and Antilia, for example, have never been found. But in the fourteenth and fifteenth centuries, Iberians found four island groups to conquer and settle, pushing back the southern and western frontiers of the known Atlantic. The Portuguese-held Azores, Madeiras, and Cape Verdes and the Castilian-held Canaries encouraged monarchs and mariners to hope that still more previously unknown islands could be found. The discoveries of islands in the eastern part of the south Atlantic had taught Iberian mariners the rudiments of the ocean's wind and water movements. Their later voyages would reveal the full range and extent of the oceanic patterns of winds and currents.

For the North Atlantic, the picture was murkier in 1492. The largest gap in European knowledge of the world was the nearly total ignorance of the American continents. Early in the Middle Ages Irish monks had journeyed out into the unknown North Atlantic, but their daring exploits, undertaken to find a quiet place to contemplate and serve God, had no known consequences. Around the year 1000 Scandinavian explorers traveled from island to island across the far north Atlantic, visiting the Shetlands and Orkneys, Iceland, and Greenland, and finally arriving in North America. But the exploits of Leif Ericsson and others did not usher in an era of general European expansion and global change. Instead, the voyages had no known effect on the wider European world and were very little known outside Scandinavia. Scandinavian settlements in North America were quickly abandoned, and the colony in Greenland existed in greatly reduced circumstances by the fifteenth century.

It is safe to assume that the only people with knowledge of the Americas in 1492 were the Americans themselves. The ancestors of human societies that Spanish explorers encountered in the fifteenth century had discovered America from Asia in prehistoric times. Their great trek across the land bridge between Siberia and Alaska, where the Bering Strait exists now, forms an important chapter in the ancient history of human migration, but it did not have the effect of linking America with the rest of the world. Instead, the descendants of the migrants lost contact with their Asian homeland, and America and its first human inhabitants developed in isolation from the Old World of Europe, Africa, and Asia.

Consequently, the Americas became strikingly different from the Old World in plants, animals, and human populations. By the fifteenth century, millions of people populated the continent from the Arctic Circle south to the tip of South America. They had settled in almost all the regions of the Americas suited for human habitation. Whether on plains, highlands, deserts, forests, jungles, or islands, native Americans had developed societies and economies that took good advantage of the topographies and the ecologies in which they lived. Their social organizations varied from groups of hunter-gatherers to highly developed urban civilizations. The latter had evolved in three areas: the Yucatán peninsula, the central valley of Mexico, and the highlands of the Andes in South America. The Mayas had built an advanced civilization, particularly learned in astronomy, in the Yucatán peninsula and the adjacent areas of Central America. They had reached their peak from about 400 B.C. to A.D. 1000 but had declined thereafter, perhaps because of soil exhaustion, perhaps from some other cause. In the central valley of Mexico, the Aztecs, or Mexica, created a large empire surrounded by tributary groups. Their empire was still flourishing in 1500, although many of the tributary groups chafed under the Aztec yoke. The empire of the Incas extended from what is today Peru north to modern Ecuador and south to Chile. Like the Aztecs, the Incas presided over a collection of tributary groups, and their empire was also flourishing in Columbus's time. As impressive as the great civilizations of the Americas were, their stone-age technology would prove to be no match for that of the Europeans, either on land or sea.

At the beginning of their global exploration in the fifteenth century, Europeans found the oceans of the world open to them, with no competing maritime powers anywhere on the face of the earth. The civilizations of the Americas lacked the technology for deep-ocean sailing. Similarly, the kingdoms of Africa south of the Sahara had no ocean-going vessels. Europe's strongest political enemy in the Old World—the Ottoman Empire—had only a Mediterranean navy. In the early sixteenth century the Ottomans would extend their sway to Egypt and North Africa as far west as Algeria. Their land attacks on Europe would reach as far as the gates of Vienna in 1529, and their Mediterranean navy would cause serious problems for the states of Italy and Spain in the sixteenth century. Nonetheless, the Ottoman Empire was in no position to challenge Portugal or Spain in the Atlantic or the Indian Ocean.

Beyond the Ottoman Empire to the east, the successor states to the Mongols were still gathering strength. In Persia, the Safavid Empire would be founded in 1502 and would continue in power for over two centuries. The Turkish Moguls, entering India from Afghanistan in the early sixteenth century, would carve out an empire that embraced much of northern and central India. Neither of these land-based empires could challenge European dominance of the world's sea lanes. The Portuguese and Castilians of the Iberian peninsula were ideally situated to lead European world exploration. Of all the peoples on earth in the late fifteenth century, they enjoyed the most effective combination of strong motives for overseas expansion and the maritime technology necessary to carry it out. They were encouraged to do so by what they knew and by what they suspected about the rest of the world. And no one else was in a position to challenge them.

The World after Columbus. Columbus was fortunate to have lived at a time when many Europeans were interested in exploring the oceans beyond Europe. Had he failed to obtain funding for his plan to reach Asia by sailing westward, other Europeans would have made the voyage and happened upon the Americas before too long. King João II of Portugal licensed at least one expedition to explore west from the Azores in the 1480s. English mariners probed the North Atlantic to the west in the same decade. Their efforts succeeded when John Cabot, a Genoese mariner, captained an English voyage to Newfoundland in 1497. In 1500 the Portuguese captain Pedro

Álvares Cabral reached Brazil, either by accident or design, as he sailed west and south to catch the winds for a voyage to southern Africa.

Columbus's voyages began the unification of the world, bringing the previously isolated Americas into the networks of trade and communication that already linked Asia, Africa, and Europe. The far-reaching consequences of his voyages, for good and for ill, have undoubtedly earned Columbus a place in world history. Nonetheless, he was not the first human being to discover America, or even the first European to do so. The ancestors of the Indians he encountered in the Caribbean had discovered and settled the land millennia before. Even among Europeans, Scandinavians had preceded Columbus by five hundred years.

Columbus was the first European to reach America since the Vikings, and his voyage occurred at a time when Europe as a whole was poised to exploit that discovery. Columbus had prepared his plans carefully, relying on his wide knowledge of contemporary European ideas—both correct and incorrect—about the world beyond Europe. His first voyage, and the later voyages he and others made during his lifetime, linked the Americas with the rest of the world, but they did not immediately allow Europeans to understand the true size of the earth or the relation of the continents to one another. The first circumnavigation of the globe between 1519 and 1522 did far more than Columbus's voyages to reveal the size and nature of the earth. That expedition, sponsored by Spain, begun under the command of Ferdinand Magellan and completed by his lieutenant Juan Sebastián de Elcano proved that vast oceans lay between the lands visited by Columbus and the kingdoms of Asia visited by Marco Polo.

Even after 1522, extensive exploration and observation would be necessary to map the earth fully and assign it its proper place in the universe. That work would not be complete until the twentieth century. By the mid-sixteenth century, however, some fifty years after Columbus's first voyage, all the global centers of high civilization and the major commercial networks had been connected directly or indirectly by sea. Geographers in Seville and Lisbon had a fairly accurate view of the earth and its parts. Although the details would change and although there were many unknown lands still to be explored, an educated European in 1550 could form a conception of world geography that would not differ in broad outlines from our own, although it would be startlingly different from the European conception of the world in 1492. In 1543 Copernicus allowed his heliocentric model of the universe to be published. Once his theory triumphed, Europeans could begin to explore the true nature of the heavens as well as the earth.

[See also *Cartography; Exploration and Discovery; Geography, Imaginary;* and biographies of figures mentioned herein. For more detailed discussions of particular places, see *Africa; Asia; China; Cipangu; England; Florence; France; Genoa; Naples; Ottoman Empire; Portugal; Rome; Spain; Venetian Republic; Vinland.* For discussion of the indigenous peoples and cultures encountered by Europeans in the Western Hemisphere, see *Indian America.*]

BIBLIOGRAPHY

Bovill, E. W. *The Golden Trade of the Moors.* 2d ed. Oxford, 1970.

Broc, N. *La géographie de la Renaissance, 1420–1620.* Paris, 1980.

Cassidy, Vincent H. *The Sea around Them: The Atlantic Ocean, A. D. 1250.* Baton Rouge, 1968.

Chaudhuri, K. N. *Trade and Civilisation in the Indian Ocean: An Economic History from the Rise of Islam to 1750.* Cambridge, 1985.

Chaunu, Pierre. *European Expansion in the Later Middle Ages.* Translated by Katharine Bertram. Amsterdam, 1979.

Dawson, Christopher, ed. *Mission to Asia: Narratives and Letters of the Franciscan Missionaries in Mongolia and China in the Thirteenth and Fourteenth Centuries.* New York, 1966. Reprint, Toronto, 1986.

Diffie, Bailey W., and George Winius. *Foundations of the Portuguese Empire, 1450–1580.* Minneapolis, 1977.

Fernández-Armesto, Felipe. *Before Columbus: Exploration and Colonization from the Mediterranean to the Atlantic, 1229–1492.* Philadelphia, 1987.

Jones, Gwyn. *The Norse Atlantic Saga.* 2d ed. London, 1983.

Mollat, Michel. *Les explorateurs de XIIIᵉ au XVIᵉ siècle: Premiers regards sur des mondes nouveaux.* Paris, 1984.

Olschki, L. *Marco Polo's Asia.* Berkeley and Los Angeles, 1960.

Parry, J. H. *The Age of Reconnaissance.* New York, 1963, and later editions.

Parry, J. H. *The Discovery of the Sea.* Berkeley and Los Angeles, 1974.

Penrose, B. *Travel and Discovery in the Renaissance, 1420–1620.* Cambridge, Mass., 1967.

Phillips, J. R. S. *The Medieval Expansion of Europe.* Oxford, 1988.

Rogers, Francis M. *The Quest for Eastern Christians: Travel and Rumor in the Age of Discovery.* Minneapolis, 1962.

Scammell, G. V. *The World Encompassed: The First European Maritime Empires c. 800–1650.* Berkeley and Los Angeles, 1981.

Southern, R. W. *Western Views of Islam in the Middle Ages.* Cambridge, Mass., 1962. Reprint, 1980.

Wolf, Eric R. *Europe and the People without History.* Berkeley and Los Angeles, 1982.

WILLIAM D. PHILLIPS, JR.

EXPLORATION AND DISCOVERY. [This entry includes three articles on overseas exploration:

Exploration and Discovery before 1492
European Exploration and Discovery after 1492
Basque Exploration and Discovery

For further discussion of European overseas interests, see *Atlantic Rivalry; Europe and the Wider World in 1492; Trade;* and entries on particular nations and city states. For discussion of overseas exploration and discovery by other civilizations, see *Africa; China.* See *Colonization* for discussion of the settlement efforts that followed European contact with the New World.]

Exploration and Discovery before 1492

Although the name Columbus is indelibly linked with European discovery of America, the Norsemen without question arrived in the New World five hundred years earlier, and other Europeans may have arrived a thousand years earlier. It does not minimize Columbus's achievement to put it in the context of Europe's knowledge of lands beyond the Atlantic from the time of the Greeks and Romans and perhaps earlier.

Some scholars postulate voyages to the Atlantic islands and even to the American continent by Stone Age or Bronze Age sailors from Europe. A thousand years later Phoenicians and Carthaginians ventured from the Mediterranean Sea to repeat the feats of these shadowy early navigators. Greeks and Romans followed. The Atlantic islands discovered were sometimes exuberantly reported as the site of the Hesperides (producer of golden apples), the Fortunate Islands, the Terrestrial Paradise, or other attractive locales. Although these early navigators are sometimes thought to have made transatlantic discoveries, most scholars limit their findings to islands in the Atlantic.

During the time of Alexander the Great, the Greek Pytheas of Massilia claimed to have visited an island called Thule, probably Iceland, which became known as the "ultimate," or farthest land from Europe; the sea around this land was often thought to be congealed. In medieval times (sixth to eighth centuries A.D.) Irish monks such as Saint Brendan (c. 520–578) set sail in seagoing, leather-skinned, willow-framed coracles, seeking variously the earthly paradise or solitude on deserted islands to which they were sometimes guided by a flight of birds. Because the earthly paradise was assumed to lie in the extreme East, the effort to sail west to reach it indicates a recognition of the sphericity of the earth and a belief that the width of the Atlantic separating Europe from Asia was not great. Reports of the voyages of Irish monks were to litter the maps of the period with mythical islands.

Norse Explorations and Settlements

Beginning in the eighth century A.D., Norsemen moved west from Scandinavia, often finding Irish already established on islands such as Iceland, which the Norse reached in the ninth century. The distance between Iceland and Greenland is much less than the distance between Iceland and the lands from which the settlers from Europe had come. Hence it is not surprising that, before the end of the tenth century, the Norsemen had reached Greenland and, shortly after, Vinland the Good (the North American continent). Some scholars assume the Irish were ahead of the Norse, even in America, but hard archaeological evidence is lacking to support the Irish claim, whereas it exists for the Norse.

That the Norse planted settlements—however briefly—on the mainland of North America has long been accepted, despite the fact that the Icelandic saga evidence upon which that assumption was based for many years was treated cautiously by scholars like Fridtjof Nansen because of its oral, folkloristic, and mythical elements. Indeed, the Massachusetts Historical Society, when asked to report on a nineteenth-century proposal to erect a statue in Boston to Leif Ericsson, responded, "There is the same sort of reason for believing in the existence of Leif Ericsson that there is for believing in the existence of Agamemnon; they are both traditions accepted by later writers, but there is no more reason for regarding as true the details related about his discoveries than there is for accepting as historic truth the narratives contained in the Homeric poems." But with the discovery in 1961 by Helge and Anne Stine Ingstad of some house ruins at L'Anse-aux-Meadows in northern Newfoundland containing European artifacts such as a Norse spindle-whorl dating from around A.D. 1000, the few remaining doubts about Norse pre-Columbian settlement in the New World were largely erased.

The Norse settlements on mainland America were an outgrowth of the activities of Eric the Red of Iceland who established a colony in Greenland in the late tenth century. Eric's son Leif may have been the first European to set foot on American soil, but the story of the accidental discovery and later occupation of a portion of "America" involves not only Eric and Leif but Bjarni Herjulfsson, Leif's brother Thorvald, and Thorfinn Karlsefni Thordarson.

The land west of Greenland that was discovered and temporarily settled (until conflict with the native inhabitants caused the Norsemen to withdraw) consisted of three distinct but apparently connected regions: Helluland, Markland, and Vinland. The first two areas are usually identified as Baffin Island and Labrador, but the last named is subject to great debate because of the assumption that vines grew there.

Questionable claims to pre-Columbian Norse sites have been made for New England, Minnesota, and other parts of Canada. Fourteenth-century voyages into the interior of Canada and the United States have periodically been reported—for example, as recorded on the Kensington Rune Stone found in 1898 near Kensington, Minnesota. This artifact occasioned a bitter debate among scholars and amateurs and was eventually judged to be a modern fraud, although theories of its authenticity periodically reemerge. The elastic character of ancient "inscriptions" on rocks can be judged from the fact that the puzzling inscriptions on the Dighton Rock near Taunton, Massachusetts, have been read to support both Norse and Portuguese pre-Columbian discoveries.

Another potential Norse site is on Kodlunarn Island (White Man's Island) in Frobisher Bay, where the English explorer Martin Frobisher led three expeditions in 1576, 1577, and 1578. The Arctic explorer Francis Hall in the mid-nineteenth century rediscovered the site and recovered an iron bloom from it, and a Smithsonian Institution expedition in 1981 excavated the site and discovered several additional iron blooms dating from the twelfth and thirteenth centuries. There are many explanations for the unusual dating of these objects that would preclude a Norse presence in the area during those centuries, but the possibility of a Norse presence cannot be ruled out. It is even conceivable that advocates of a pre-Columbian discovery by the legendary Welsh prince Madoc, around A.D. 1170, may, with the discovery of these artifacts, reemerge.

The fact that Vinland is clearly recognized by modern geographers as part of the North American mainland while Greenland and Iceland are identified as islands adjacent to the mainland but not necessarily within the Western Hemisphere, emphasizes the artificial nature of contemporary descriptions of what constitutes "discovery" of the "New World." Our present-day knowledge of the existence of a continent separated from both Europe and Asia by vast oceans impels us to consider any discovery within what we now know to be the mainland of that continent to be a discovery of the whole, while discovery of offshore islands is not given the same importance. Such thinking, indeed, is often used to rob Columbus of the distinction of discovering "America" because he discovered "only" outlying islands on his first two voyages and did not reach the mainland of South America until the third voyage, in 1498. But the explorations and settlements of the Norse on the mainland of North America, though known in Europe, had little impact on those who sought to reach the Asia described by Marco Polo, a land of immense, civilized, wealthy, and powerful populations. Rather, the reports that filtered back to Europe inspired at best curiosity about a cold and uninviting northern frontier similar to the northern reaches of the Scandinavian peninsula, with which the new discoveries were often confused in the telling and conjoined on some maps. [See also *Icelandic Sagas; Vinland; Vinland Map.*]

Classical Exploration

The Atlantic Ocean was the source of idyllic and paradisaical images for some classical writers but was described in forbidding terms by other classical and medieval writers as an impassable, shallow, muddy barrier to navigation. Such reports were derived principally from the story of Atlantis reported by Plato in the middle of the fourth century B.C. Atlantis, a powerful kingdom occupying a gigantic continent larger than Europe or Africa, had sought to conquer Europe but was destroyed in a cataclysmic series of earthquakes and floods, which caused it to disappear beneath the sea, leaving the Atlantic impenetrable because of the shoals of mud and dangerous reefs. In contrast to the tales of fortunate islands or isles of the blessed, other tales of giant sea monsters, huge eels, spouting whales, and the like were sometimes reported by fearful commentators, whose visions were later to adorn the maps of medieval Europe. The Roman poet Horace (first century B.C.) spoke of "godless ships bound madly in contempt o'er channels not allowed" and warned that the gods were appalled by this "violation" of strange seas and sacred waters.

It should be recalled that the Atlantic was thought by most classical and medieval scholars to be merely an arm of a great ocean surrounding the central landmass of Europe, Asia, and Africa. Prior to the efforts of those who sought to reach the East by sailing west, traders, diplomats, and explorers tried to reach the East by sailing east, starting from the eastern Mediterranean or the Red Sea (which were intermittently connected by a canal) and sailing across the Indian Ocean. Classical reports of attempts, some successful and some not, to sail around Africa, either from the east to the west or the west to the east, can also be found in the literature. The earliest known attempt to circumnavigate Africa from east to west was undertaken by Phoenician seamen at the beginning of the sixth century B.C. on the order of the Egyptian king Necho. Reported by Herodotus, the voyage, in the opinion of some modern scholars, did take place and did succeed in its mission.

In the second century B.C., Agatharchides of Cnidus in his *On the Erythraean Sea* (which included the Indian Ocean, Red Sea, and Persian Gulf) discusses the history of the area following Alexander the Great's conquests (336–323 B.C.), which opened up the area to Greek enterprise. Alexander's successors in Egypt, the four Ptolemies, promoted explorations down the African coast and into the surrounding ocean. By the first quarter of the second century B.C. the secret of the monsoon route to India from Africa had been discovered.

The Greek navigator Eudoxus of Cyzicus, in the last two decades of the second century B.C., twice sailed to India from Egypt's Red Sea ports, probably utilizing the hitherto closely held Arab knowledge of the monsoon seasons that facilitated such voyages. Subsequently, he tried to sail directly from the Mediterranean to India by circumnavigating Africa from west to east. He failed in his first attempt and made a second effort, during which he may

have been cut off by Carthaginians, who jealously guarded the Atlantic jumping-off places of the route around Africa, which they, as well as Phoenicians and Persians, had earlier—probably unsuccessfully—attempted to accomplish in a west-east direction.

Medieval Exploration

Voyages into the Atlantic, some with the goal of circumnavigating Africa, continued in the Christian Era. In 1291 the Vivaldi brothers, Ugolino and Vadino, of Genoa sailed into the Atlantic through the Straits of Gibraltar with the intention of reaching India and were never heard from again. The Venetians Niccolò and Antonio Zeno may have discovered land in the western ocean in the fourteenth century. Genoese navigators, in the service of Portugal in the fourteenth and fifteenth centuries, sailed to the Canaries and down the African coast. In the course of such voyages in the great ocean surrounding the land masses of Europe, Asia, and Africa, it is not inconceivable that sailors were blown off course, shipwrecked, or otherwise carried to "American" lands, in the same way that the Portuguese voyager Pedro Álvares Cabral "discovered" Brazil while sailing around Africa to India in 1500.

Periodic reports of Roman coins or other tantalizing evidence of a pre-Columbian presence in the New World, or in the islands lying between the New and Old Worlds, must always be treated with skepticism given the difficulty of establishing historical facts. The same must be said for the evidence of native American myths such as that of the white, bearded god Quetzalcoatl, expected to return from the East, whose assumed arrival in the form of the Spanish conquistador Hernando Cortés caused the Aztec ruler Motecuhzoma II (Moctezuma) effectively to disarm himself and lose his kingdom.

Pre-Columbian discoveries can also be attributed to explorers, navigators, fishermen, merchants, and others from Asia, who may variously have sailed, been blown off course, or been carried by the Japan Current northeast along the Aleutian Islands and down the West Coast of America. It is more difficult to conceive of a trans-Pacific route eastward across the southern Pacific to South America, though Polynesians have been given credit for the achievement by some; a more plausible route runs in the opposite direction, as has been demonstrated theoretically by Thor Heyerdahl. In any event, pre-Columbian contact between Asia and the western coast of North and South America has been hypothesized because of the similarity of pottery types in Japan during the early to middle Jomon period and the Valdivia pottery of Ecuador in the period 3500 to 2000 B.C. The similarity of pottery types on two sides of a vast ocean suggested trans-Pacific contact to Smithsonian anthropologists Betty Meggers, Clifford Evans, and their collaborator Emilio Estrada, though their thesis has been accepted by only a few scholars. But while images of Asian animals, similarities of items of clothing, pottery, and so forth can be used to demonstrate the possibility of transpacific exploration and discovery, the evidence is too insubstantial, and the effects too transient to threaten the importance of the first transatlantic discoveries that did have immediate and substantial consequences.

The Historians' Debate

Two scholarly vices, hypercriticism, on the one hand, and imaginative inferences, on the other, coexist in the historical profession, creating an ever-present tension between those who want to believe what cannot be proved and those who want to prove false what is in fact believable. The historian must steer a strict course between both extremes when dealing with the evidence for pre-Columbian contact between the Old World and the New.

Columbus's achievement has been denigrated by historians unwilling to concede that he had the ability or the luck to achieve his great enterprise. Skeptics have suggested that someone—possibly an anonymous pilot, possibly an Indian floating across the Atlantic, possibly a now-lost map—showed him the way. The presence of large islands such as Antillia in pre-Columbian maps of the Atlantic Ocean has encouraged some scholars to assume that these land masses represent pre-Columbian discoveries. Thus the island of Antillia—reputedly the refuge of seven bishops and their people who left Portugal in the eighth century to escape the Moors—on the 1424 map of Zuane Pizzigano (now in the James Ford Bell Library in Minneapolis) was judged in 1954 by the Portuguese scholar Armando Cortesão to represent the "forefront of America" and to reflect a pre-Columbian Portuguese voyage across the Atlantic.

Similar claims for pre-Columbian discoveries, particularly in the last quarter of the fifteenth century, have been made in behalf of the English (particularly those from Bristol), Danes, Flemings (in the service of Portugal), Basque fishermen from the Bay of Biscay, and Portuguese from the Azores. The documentation of each such claim is complex and clouded, as in the letter written in the winter of 1497–1498 by John Day, an English merchant in Andalusia, to the "Lord Grand Admiral" of Spain (Columbus) speaking of transatlantic discoveries by "men from Bristol in other times," which may or may not refer to pre-Columbian times.

Those who accept the various hypotheses of pre-Columbian discoveries of America frequently imply that Columbus does not deserve to be called the discoverer of America. Important scholars, particularly in an earlier era, frequently subscribed to such views, but they are increasingly rare among scholars of the late twentieth century.

Cortesão, for example, has received little support for his theory about the 1424 map from present-day Portuguese scholars.

More relevant, though not necessarily contradictory of the idea that Columbus discovered America, is the frequently voiced complaint that Columbus did not discover America because it had been discovered before, by its own inhabitants. Of course, it is true that ancestors of present-day Native Americans, who found, perhaps fifteen thousand years ago, a land bridge to the "New World," perhaps while hunting game, were the first men and women to discover the land geographers now categorize as the Western Hemisphere, or North and South America. But the term *discovery*, as used by Europeans, always meant "discovery by Europeans." It was not meant to suggest that the native inhabitants either did not know where they were or had not earlier discovered for themselves the lands now discovered by the Europeans. In each case the term is specific to the discoverers.

BIBLIOGRAPHY

Adam of Bremen. *History of the Archbishops of Hamburg-Bremen.* Translated with an introduction and notes by Francis J. Tschan. New York, 1959.

Agatharchides of Cnidus. *On the Erythraean Sea.* Translated and edited by Stanley M. Burstein. Hakluyt Society, 2d ser., vol. 172. London, 1989.

Cassidy, Vincent H. *The Sea around Them: The Atlantic Ocean, A.D. 1250.* Baton Rouge, La., 1968.

Fitzhugh, William W., and Jacqueline S. Olin. "Archeology of the Frobisher Voyages: Contributions to the Archeology of Kodlunarn Island, Frobisher Bay, N.W.T., Canada. Results of a 1981 Smithsonian Expedition." Report submitted to the Government of the Northwest Territories, Prince of Wales Northern Heritage Center, Yellowknife, N.W.T., Canada. Typescript. June 1990.

Ingstad, Helge. *Westward to Vinland: The Discovery of Pre-Columbian Norse House-sites in North America.* Translated by Erik J. Friis. New York, 1969.

Jones, Gwyn. *The Norse Atlantic Saga: Being the Norse Voyages of Discovery and Settlement to Iceland, Greenland, America.* London, 1964.

Keen, Benjamin. *The Aztec Image in Western Thought.* New Brunswick, N.J., 1971.

Magnusson, Magnus, and Hermann Palsson. *The Vinland Sagas: The Norse Discovery of America: Graenlendinga Saga and Eirik's Saga.* New York, 1966.

Oleson, Tryggvi J. *Early Voyages and Northern Approaches, 1000–1632.* Canadian Centenary Series. London, 1964.

Sauer, Carl O. *Northern Mists.* Berkeley, Calif., 1968.

Thiel, J. H. *Eudoxus of Cyzicus: A Chapter in the History of the Sea-Route to India and the Route round the Cape in Ancient Times.* Groningen, [1966].

Wahlgren, Erik. *The Kensington Stone: A Mystery Solved.* Madison, Wis., 1958.

Winsor, Justin. "Pre-Columbian Explorations." In vol. 1 of *Narrative and Critical History of America*. 8 vols. Boston, 1884–1889.

Wilcomb E. Washburn

European Exploration and Discovery after 1492

Following Columbus's first voyage to the Western Hemisphere and before the close of the fifteenth century, numerous non-Columbian expeditions sailed from Spain or England for the New World. Four of those departures are described in the recently discovered *Libro de Armadas* in the Archivo General de Indias, Seville. A fleet of four caravels commanded by Juan Aguado sortied in 1495 with supplies for Columbus's second settlement, La Isabela, on the northern coast of La Española (Hispaniola). A second supply fleet under Giannotto Berardi sailed in January 1496 but all its vessels foundered in a storm immediately upon leaving Cádiz; the *Libro* suggests that the business agent and chandler for that expedition, Amerigo Vespucci, sailed in one of Berardi's vessels. The same source records the departure for La Española of the ship *Catalina* and two caravels, *Santa María de Guía* and *Lázaro,* in June 1496, and the dispatch of the royal visitor Francisco de Bobadilla to the same island in 1499.

In the last years of the century three other expeditions departed Spain for the New World. Alonso de Ojeda, with three caravels and Vespucci and the mapmaker Juan de la Cosa among his passengers, left Cádiz in May 1499 with the intention of plundering and slaving in the pearl fisheries between Margarita Island and the Venezuelan mainland; he would return for the same purpose in 1502. La Cosa led two expeditions with similar goals to the region in 1504 and 1508. A second 1499 voyage was commanded by Peralonso Niño, who had commanded Columbus's *Santa María*. Niño left Palos in June in a single caravel and returned the following April with sizable treasure from the Pearl Coast. Other minor voyages to the same region followed in the next decade, such as that of Rodrigo de Bastidas in 1500; one of his passengers was Vasco Núñez de Balboa, who would cross the Isthmus of Panama in 1513 and sight the Pacific Ocean, on which the Portuguese were already sailing from the opposite direction.

The third and last significant non-Columbian Spanish effort of the century was commanded by Vicente Yáñez Pinzón, captain of *Niña* in 1492. From his native Palos in November 1499 Pinzón sailed down the African coast to the Cape Verde Islands and then in twenty days crossed the Atlantic to the shoulder of Brazil. After exploring the Amazon and loading a cargo of logwood (valued as a dyewood) and twenty native slaves, but having lost half his own men, he returned to Palos in September 1500.

Though his Brazilian landfall is not accepted by all historians, no one rejects his two subsequent voyages to the Caribbean, in 1502–1504 and 1508–1509; on the latter he was joint commander with Juan Díaz de Solís.

Another notable voyage in the 1490s was sponsored by Henry VII of England and commanded by the Venetian John Cabot. With one ship and a crew of eighteen, Cabot departed Bristol on May 20, 1497. Taking a high-latitude course in search of a northwest strait to the Indies, he raised the northern peninsula of Newfoundland in thirty-three days, explored the island's eastern capes, islands, and bays, and re-entered Bristol on August 6. In May of the following year he returned to "the newe founde lande" with five ships, four of which, with Cabot, disappeared without a trace. A son, Sebastian, who possibly sailed with his father in 1497, may have sailed to Newfoundland in 1508; it is certain that he reached the Río de la Plata on his own in 1525–1528.

In one of the most important voyages before the end of the decade, the Portuguese navigator Vasco da Gama sailed in a completely different direction, south and east around the Cape of Good Hope to the southwest coast of India, which he reached at Calicut in May 1498. A second Portuguese expedition in 1500 under Pedro Álvares Cabral was the first to exploit the newly opened Asian trade. Da Gama followed him in his second (1502) and third (1524) voyages to consolidate the Portuguese presence, particularly at Goa.

Credit is usually given to the Portuguese Cabral for the discovery of Brazil. Though he probably followed Pinzón by a few months, Cabral, having made an accidental landfall (he was bound around the Cape of Good Hope for India) on April 22, 1500, east of Monte Pascoal, formally opened Brazil to further exploration and commerce. He named the country, which he thought to be an island, Ilha da Vera Cruz. He thereupon proceeded around the Cape of Good Hope and returned to Lisbon, much depleted in ships and men, in summer 1501.

Several Portuguese and Anglo-Azorean expeditions made northern voyages in the period 1500 to 1536, among them the voyage in 1500 of João Fernandes, who conferred the name Lavrador (husbandman) to Greenland (a name later translated to eastern Canada), and others establishing a steady cod fishing industry on the Newfoundland banks.

The southern latitudes absorbed Iberian interest in the same period, and the peninsula's two most visible captains were the Florentine Amerigo Vespucci and the Portuguese Ferdinand Magellan. Having survived the wreck of Berardi's fleet off Cádiz in 1496, Vespucci sailed with Ojeda in 1499 and with the Portuguese Gonçalo Coelho in 1501. (There is no evidence for a western voyage that he claimed to have made in 1497.) The Coelho-

Vespucci fleet out of Lisbon made landfall on Brazil, where the Florentine made copious notation of native lifeways and the local flora and fauna. In 1503 he commanded a vessel in a second Coelho voyage that established a garrison on the Brazilian coast. In two widely circulated letters he described with some inflation his role and experiences in that *Mundus Novus,* leading the Lorraine cartographer Martin Waldseemüller to emblazon "America" across his 1507 depiction of South America. Spain continued to call the new lands Las Indias (the Indies).

In 1515, armed with a charter from King Fernando, the Spanish *piloto mayor* Juan Díaz de Solís sailed for Brazil and rounded Uruguay where he entered and gave a first European name to the Río de la Plata estuary: La Mar Dulce, later called Río de Solís, and still later Río de la Plata. Somewhere on the Uruguayan coast Solís and seven men went ashore where all but one were clubbed to death and eaten by natives. The remaining crewmen, less one ship of their three and one-third of their complements, returned to Seville in 1516.

Magellan, tantalized by tales of the Spice Islands (Moluccas) of Asia, and considering, it appears, that the Pacific was a narrow body of water, thought that those fabled sources of clove, cinnamon, and nutmeg might best be reached by a strait through Spanish America. Accordingly, on September 20, 1519, the five ships of his Armada de Molucca left Sanlúcar de Barrameda.

Sailing down the African coast to elude two fleets sent by a competitive Portuguese monarch to intercept him, Magellan crossed the Atlantic to the shoulder of Brazil, which he reached on November 29. His ships coasted south to Rio de Janeiro, Montevideo, and Patagonia, during which time he put down several mutinies. On November 1, 1520, he sighted the strait that he had sought, and made an unusually direct negotiation of its 334 nautical miles of tricky currents and dead ends. Although he named it Todos los Santos it soon acquired the name Strait of Magellan. On November 27 the fleet, now down to three ships, debouched into the trackless Pacific, which he also named.

Magellan hugged the Chilean coast north as far as Valdivia and then struck westward on a four-month crossing that took him past the Marshall Islands, through the Marianas, and finally to the Philippine archipelago at Leyte Gulf. At Mactan Island north of Mindanao, Magellan intervened militarily in a conflict on the side of the Mactanese against nearby Cebu. Tactical errors forced a Spanish withdrawal and Magellan, covering the retreat, was killed.

Down to two ships and a fraction of their force, the survivors succeeded in reaching the Moluccas on November 8, 1521. One ship, *Trinidad,* loaded with cloves from

Tidore, was captured by Portuguese ships sent around the Cape of Good Hope to deny the spiceries to Spain. The other, *Victoria,* captained by Juan Sebastian de Elcano, rounded the cape and, completing the first circumnavigation of the globe, put in at Seville on September 8, 1522, with enough spices to more than pay the monetary cost of the voyage, though hardly the cost in lives (227).

Meanwhile, Spain launched an ever-widening circle of voyages of discovery from her bases in the Caribbean Sea. Juan Ponce de León, who had sailed with Columbus in 1493, sailed northwest from Puerto Rico through the Bahama chain and on April 2, 1513, sighted the coastline of a large "island" to which he gave the name La Florida. Recent studies indicate that his landfall was probably south of Cape Canaveral. Sometime between 1514 and 1516 the slaver Pedrode Salazar reached the mainland at a higher but unknown latitude. In 1521 Ponce de León returned to what Alonzo Alvarez de Pineda had proved by that date to be a peninsula, but his landing party was repulsed, and he himself was mortally wounded by Calusa natives on the lower Gulf Coast.

Francisco Fernández de Córdoba sailed out of Havana in 1517 and discovered the Yucatán Peninsula of Mexico. His pilot, Antonio Alaminos, was the most experienced navigator of the region, having sailed with Columbus in 1493, Ponce in 1513, and numerous expeditions in between. Juan de Grijalba, with Alaminos aboard, followed to the Mexican coast in 1518. And in the same year Hernando Cortés, with Alaminos, left Baracoa, Cuba, for the lands that he would conquer and name Nueva España (New Spain).

Disaster met the expedition of Lucas Vázquez de Ayllón, which sailed from Santo Domingo in 1526 bound for La Florida with about six hundred settlers. After founding a town named San Miguel de Gualdape at Sapelo Sound, Georgia, on September 29, the colonists were quickly overcome by exhaustion, hunger, cold, and disease. What had been Europe's first settlement in territory that would later be part of the United States was abandoned after less than two months, and some 150 half-famished survivors (not including Ayllón) made their way by ship to various ports in the Antilles.

Pánfilo de Narváez landed at Tampa Bay in 1528 and explored the Florida interior as far as Apalache Bay, where, hungry and under incessant native attack, he and 245 of his men built barges and sailed west along the Gulf shore seeking refuge in Mexico. Most, including Narváez, were drowned in a storm. Four survivors among those who safely made the Texas coast eventually crossed by foot to the Pacific, then reached Mexico City in 1536. Their leader, Álvar Núñez Cabeza de Vaca, five years later walked nearly 950 kilometers (580 miles) across pathless Brazil from Santa Catarina Island to Asunción.

With a force of over six hundred people, some two hundred horses, and a herd of swine, the Extremaduran Hernando de Soto landed at Tampa Bay in 1539 and embarked on an overland reconnaissance that took his men through Florida and into areas comprising nine other present-day southeastern U.S. states, an exploration that covered 4,000 miles in four years. De Soto was the first European to reach the Mississippi River and died on its banks in 1542. About 310 survivors eventually reached Mexico City. A similar long march into the North American interior was led out of Mexico by Francisco Vázquez de Coronado, who penetrated as far as present-day Kansas in 1540–1542.

Sailing from Cádiz, Pedro Menéndez de Avilés founded St. Augustine, Florida, in September 1565. From there he explored the peninsular shoreline and the East Coast as far north as Santa Elena (Parris Island, South Carolina), where he established a second settlement (1566–1587). From Santa Elena in 1566 and again in 1567 Menéndez sent Captain Juan Pardo and 150 men to search the interior for an overland route to the mines of New Spain. Though he understandably failed in his primary mission, Pardo returned from both marches with the first significant information about the American interior since the expedition of De Soto a quarter century before. During the next half-century Spanish pilots out of St. Augustine conducted intensive reconnaissance of the coast northward. Typical were the expeditions of Fernández de Ecija in 1605 and 1609, which hunted details of the English settlement of Jamestown in Virginia.

Numerous navigators explored the coast of the Gulf of Mexico. On the basis of their information the Viceroy of Mexico authorized Tristán de Luna y Arellano to found a settlement at Pensacola Bay. After three difficult years (1559–1562), the colony failed. Spanish seaborne exploration continued, though it was left to a Frenchman sailing downriver in 1682, Robert Cavalier, sieur de La Salle, to discover the mouth and delta of the Mississippi. Despite additional Spanish attempts to pacify and settle the Gulf lands, particularly the expeditions of Luis de Carvajal y de la Cueva in 1580 to 1590, the expanse of shore between the Río Pánuco in Mexico and the Menéndez family claims in Florida remained unsubjugated wilderness at the close of the sixteenth century.

France had since 1504 exploited the cod banks of Newfoundland, but it was only after news of Magellan's strait that it began serious exploration of its own, and in a different region: the thirteen degrees of latitude north of Florida, where it was hoped her navigators could find a northern passage to Cathay. The first seeker to sail under French sponsorship was the Dieppe-based Florentine, Giovanni da Verrazano. With a single naval ship, *La Dauphine*, Verrazano made a landfall near Cape Fear, North Carolina, in early March 1524, then explored the Outer Banks, at one point fancying that across them he sighted the Pacific Ocean. Proceeding north he closed Barnegat, New Jersey, entered New York Harbor as far as the Narrows, then resumed coasting to Maine and the east coast of Newfoundland. Verrazano returned in July 1524 to Dieppe, where he mounted two more transatlantic expeditions, one in 1527 to cut logwood in Brazil and the second in 1528 to the Lesser Antilles, where Caribs killed him.

Obsessed by the search for a northern passage, France showed casual indifference to the great North American mainland that Verrazano was the first to explore, and subsequent French voyagers hunted instead in the far northern reaches of the present-day Maritime Provinces of Canada. Jacques Cartier made three such voyages. In the first, with two ships, he departed Saint-Malo in April 1534 and reached Newfoundland twenty days later. For three and a half months he explored the south coast of Labrador, the west of Newfoundland, Prince Edward Island, and the Gulf of St. Lawrence with its islands and bays. Cartier made the first contacts with the Hurons. He returned to these waters with three ships in the spring of 1535 and expanded his reconnaissance up the St. Lawrence River as far as the Rock of Québec and Montréal. Despite many hardships, including scurvy, the French survived the following winter in Canada and returned to France fourteen months after setting out.

Having opened up an east-west waterway that conceivably could be the long-sought strait, Cartier made a third and final voyage to establish a colony on its banks in 1541, though this time as subaltern to a nobleman, Jean-François de La Rocque de Roberval. Cartier reached the St. Lawrence ten months before Roberval, passed another severe winter above Québec, then on his way home met Roberval at Newfoundland and refused the latter's order to stay.

One winter proved enough for Roberval, too, and France abandoned interest in the far north for over half a century. In 1562 an expedition under Jean Ribault founded Charlesfort in Carolina, and two years later René de Laudonnière built Fort Caroline on the St. Johns River in Florida. The first was abandoned and the second was destroyed by Pedro Menéndez de Avilés in 1565. Not until 1604 to 1608, when Samuel de Champlain began the permanent settlement of Canada, did France take advantage of its Laurentian discoveries.

Spain, too, was active in the wake of Magellan. The Dominican García Jofre de Loaysa passed through the Strait of Magellan in 1525 but his seven vessels met disaster either at the strait or in the Pacific. Ending a long controversy with Portugal about the position of the Moluccas along the papal Line of Demarcation, Charles V in 1529 yielded the Spice Islands to Portugal in exchange for 350,000 gold ducats. In 1564 the Augustinian Andrés de Urdaneta oversaw a voyage from the west coast of Mexico to Cebu, which became Spain's first colony in the Philippines, not supplanted in importance until the foundation of Manila in 1571. By discovering the westerlies that brought him home to Acapulco by way of a California landfall, Urdaneta made possible the Manila galleon trade that opened in 1573.

Pedro de Mendoza followed Sebastian Cabot to the La Plata basin in 1534, founding Buenos Aires but losing his own life and about 1,850 others. An expedition commissioned by Bishop Gutiérrez de Varga Carvajal just barely negotiated the Strait of Magellan in 1540 to inaugurate trade with Chile and Peru. In 1557–1558 Juan Fernández Ladrillero from Chile proved that the strait could be traversed from west to east.

Cortés, conqueror of Mexico by 1521, began soon afterward to explore the Pacific coast northward. In May 1535 he discovered the lower tip of California. His lieutenant Francisco de Ulloa explored much of the Baja California littoral in 1539 and 1540. The first sighting of Alta California is credited to the expedition of Juan Rodriguez Cabrillo and Bartolomé Ferrelo, also out of Mexico, in 1542. The present state of California would not be seen by Europeans again until thirty-seven years later, by the crew of England's Francis Drake.

Drake's voyage in 1577 to 1580 began as a privateering expedition against Spain and resulted in the second circumnavigation of the earth. On his initial southwest course Drake by-passed the Strait of Magellan, rounded Henderson Island south of Tierra del Fuego, and made a wide sweep north into the Pacific. Only one ship, *Golden Hind,* of the original fleet of six survived. Perhaps seeking a western entrance to the northwest passage, which some called the Strait of Anian, Drake raised the coast of Oregon. He did not tarry long before turning south to northern California, where he found an agreeable bay and anchored from June 17 to July 23, 1579, naming the pleasant countryside Nova Albion (New England). Historians debate at which of three California bays *Golden Hind* anchored: Drake's Estero, San Quentin Cove, or Bolinas Lagoon. On his subsequent westerly passage Drake followed roughly the track of Elcano's *Victoria* fifty-eight years before, reaching Plymouth in September 1580.

The Englishman Thomas Cavendish circumnavigated the earth from 1586 to 1588, as did the Dutch Oliver de Noort from 1598 to 1601 and George Spilbergen from 1614 to 1617. The growing Dutch position among maritime powers was further demonstrated by the chartering of the Dutch East India Company in 1602, the establishment of the New Netherlands colony near Albany, New York, in 1614, and the discovery of Cape Horn by Wilhelm Cornelison Schouten and Jacob Le Maire in 1615–1617.

While Drake was exploring the Pacific, his countryman Martin Frobisher made three fruitless voyages (1576–1578) to the bay that bears his name, north of Labrador. Sir Humphrey Gilbert, financed mainly by his family and friends, and after one false start, explored the Canadian Maritime provinces in 1583, but lost his life off the Azores on the return. In three voyages between 1585 and 1587, the privateer and shipmaster John Davis explored the sounds and capes bordering Davis Strait between Greenland and Baffin Island in a fruitless search for a northwest passage, just missing the opening of one at Lancaster Sound.

In 1584 Humphrey Gilbert's half-brother Walter Raleigh, together with Philip Amadas and Arthur Barlowe, sailed from Plymouth to the temperate North American latitudes first sighted by Verrazano. On his return, having liked what he saw at the Carolina Outer Banks, Raleigh gave the region the name Virginia (the Spanish knew it as Jactán) and organized a fleet under Richard Grenville's command to establish a colony there, which its first governor, Ralph Lane, placed at Roanoke Island, in 1585. From that base Lane explored as far north as Chesapeake Bay. The colony faltered because of poor relations with the Indians, and after one year 103 survivors were withdrawn by Sir Francis Drake. Encouraged by nautical chronicler Richard Hakluyt and others, Raleigh sponsored a second Virginia colony in 1587, which settled at the same Roanoke site under governor John White. Unaccountably, it vanished almost without a trace.

The sixteenth century ended with only one European power, Spain, boasting a permanent toehold north of New Spain, at St. Augustine. In 1609, Santa Fe, New Mexico, was established. England founded Jamestown in Virginia in 1607. In the following year Champlain raised the fleur-de-lis above Québec. The Dutch opened New Netherlands in 1614. And in 1620 the Puritan Pilgrims established the second New England in Massachusetts. By then the stage was set for a three-nation struggle for hegemony over the continent that led to numerous new discoveries, both overland and downriver. In Mexico, the Central American isthmus, and South America the writs of Spain and Portugal ran unimpeded, and discovery there proceeded equally apace.

BIBLIOGRAPHY

Chaves, Alonso de. *Quatri partitu en cosmographia practica, y por otro nombre espejo de navegantes.* 1537. Reprint, Madrid, 1983.

Hakluyt, Richard. *The Principall Navigations, Voiages and Discoveries of the English Nation.* London, 1859.

Hanna, Warren L. *Lost Harbor: The Controversy over Drake's California Anchorage.* Berkeley, 1979.

Herrera y Tordesillas, Antonio de. *Historia general de los hechos de los Castellanos en las islas y tierra firme del mar Océano.* 4 vols. Madrid, 1601–1615.

Hoffman, Paul E. *A New Andalucía and a Way to the Orient.*
Baton Rouge, 1990.

La Roncière, Charles de. *Jacques Cartier.* Paris, 1931.

Libro de Armadas. Archivo General de Indias, *Contratación,*
legajo 3249.

Manzano Manzano, Juan. *Los Pinzones y el descubrimiento de
América.* 3 vols. Madrid, 1988.

Morison, Samuel Eliot. *The European Discovery of America: The
Northern Voyages A.D. 500–1600.* New York, 1971.

Morison, Samuel Eliot. *The European Discovery of America: The
Southern Voyages A.D. 1492–1616.* New York, 1974.

Paige, Paula Spurlin, trans. *The Voyage of Magellan: The Journal
of Antonio Pigafetta.* Englewood Cliffs, N.J., 1969.

Quinn, David B., ed. *North American Discovery, circa 1000–1612.*
Columbia, S.C., 1971.

MICHAEL GANNON

Basque Exploration and Discovery

Although Basques were renowned as competent seamen from early medieval times and though a Basque
navigator, Juan Sebastián de Elcano, was the first man to
return safely with his ship from a voyage around the world
(1519–1522), no fifteenth- or sixteenth-century Basque
ever claimed to have discovered America, as later legend
would claim. If there had been any genuine tradition of a
pre-Columbian Basque discovery of either North or South
America, the Basque historians Esteban de Garibay and
Lope de Isasti (both born in the sixteenth century), would
certainly have mentioned the fact. Instead, those writers,
as well as other contemporary documents, provide solid
evidence for the remarkable trading opportunities offered
by the New World and exploited by Basque merchant
mariners once "the navigation to Terranova had been
discovered" and once the Indies had been conquered. In
other words, Basques actively participated in but did not
initiate the exploration and exploitation of North America,
and Basques showed their genius more as merchants and
shipbuilders than as explorers and conquerors. The importation from the New World of vast quantities of dried
cod and whale oil and the exportation of iron and other
goods to the West Indies, for instance, were two highly
successful branches of commerce for Basques throughout
most of the sixteenth century, while from about 1505
onward their well-built ships formed the backbone of the
West Indies run.

Starting in the 1540s, several Basque navigators took
part in exploration along the Pacific Coast of North
America northward from Mexico. Probably the most
outstanding exploit of any Basque in the Pacific was that of
Andrés de Urdaneta who, at the king's bidding, left his
monastery in Mexico City to accompany another native of
the Basque province of Guipúzcoa, Miguel López de
Legazpi, on a voyage undertaken for the conquest of the
Philippines. The course from Mexico to the Philippines

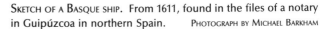

SKETCH OF A BASQUE SHIP. From 1611, found in the files of a notary
in Guipúzcoa in northern Spain.   PHOTOGRAPH BY MICHAEL BARKHAM

was relatively easy, but Urdaneta, in 1565, was the first
pilot to find an efficient return route via the coast of
California, so that the Manila galleons could thereafter
make a safe easterly passage from the archipelago to
Acapulco.

Unlike Urdaneta and Legazpi's expeditions, Basque
voyages to northeastern North America (from about 1517)
were entirely promoted by private enterprise. These
expeditions made a clear contribution to knowledge of
North American geography since many place names were
bequeathed by Basque fishermen and two small volumes
of sailing directions were written by Martin de Hoyarsabal
and Pierres Detcheverry "Dorre" (published respectively
in Bordeaux and Bayonne, in 1579 and 1677). The final
pages of the 1579 volume reflect the detailed knowledge
Basques possessed of the Atlantic coasts of Canada, from
Cape Breton Island and southeastern Newfoundland,
where many of their codfishing stations were located, to
the Labrador shore of the Strait of Belle Isle, where before
1550 they had established major whaling stations. Pilots of
other nationalities had left short descriptions of eastern
Newfoundland, but none at that date was as professional
as those of Hoyarsabal, while Detcheverry's description of
the island's west coast was only superseded a century later
by the surveys of Captain James Cook (1764–1767).

A larger number of Basque place names have survived
on the western side of Newfoundland than on any other
coast of North America because an almost exclusively
Basque seasonal presence was maintained there for nearly
two hundred years, while the rest of the Atlantic seaboard
was often shared by fishermen of various nationalities.
Although well over one thousand Basques went annually
to the Strait of Belle Isle whaling stations during the peak
years of the whaling industry (about 1565 to 1585), the
toponymy of the strait remained basically Breton as Breton

codfishermen had fished there before the Basques. During the 1580s, however, Basques were some of the first Europeans to use the Gaspé region and the north shore of the St. Lawrence River for fishing and fur-trading and were particularly successful as traders. References exist to the Montagnais Indians learning Basque during trading exchanges, while later Eskimo traders who often met Basques as far south as Portuchoa (now Port-au-Choix) incorporated Basque words into their trading language.

Since Basque whalers frequently stayed on the Labrador coast until January and occasionally wintered there, many deaths occurred in icebound harbors. The oldest known wills written north of Mexico resulted from these voyages, and as large sums of capital were invested in whaling vessels the voyages also spawned litigation. Early lawsuits, notarial records, and insurance documents testify to the importance of the Basque whaling industry, and archaeological evidence has supported the documentation. It is evident that the frequent impressment of Spanish Basque ships for royal armadas gradually undermined Basque shipbuilding and trading activities toward the end of the sixteenth century. However, a few Spanish and many French Basques continued to participate in transatlantic fishing and trading throughout the seventeenth and on into the eighteenth century.

BIBLIOGRAPHY

Detcheverry Dorre, Pierres. *Liburuhauda jxasoco nabigacionecoa: Martin de Hoyarzabalec egiña Francezes.* Bayonne, 1677. Facsimile edition, San Sebastian, 1985.

Garibay, Esteban de. *Compendio Historial.* 4 vols. Antwerp, 1571.

Huxley, Selma, ed. *Los vascos en el marco Atlantico Norte, Siglos XVI y XVII.* Vol. 3 of *Itsasoa.* San Sebastian, 1987.

Isasti, Lope de. *Compendio historial de la muy noble y muy leal provincia de Guipuzcoa.* Facsimile edition, Bilbao, 1972.

SELMA HUXLEY BARKHAM

EXPULSION FROM SPAIN. For discussion of the Expulsion of the Jews from Spain, see *Jews,* article on *Expulsion from Spain.*

F

FARGHANI, AL-. See *Alfraganus.*

FAUNA. The New World animals encountered by Columbus and those who followed him in the sixteenth century were diverse. The fauna commonly used by pre-Columbian peoples reflected a number of environmental factors. One major influence was whether they lived on an island or a continental mainland. Continental North and South America support a wide range of terrestrial animals, whereas the West Indian islands have very few. On the continents, climate and altitude are important factors. For example, animals living along the coast of Mexico or Peru are quite different from those found in the highlands of those countries. Although coastal peoples throughout North and South America used marine resources extensively, the ones they exploited depended upon whether there were salt marshes, reefs, banks, beaches, rivers, swamps, or other habitats nearby. Finally, the animals of South America are quite distinct from those of North America, with Central America serving as a bridge between them.

Since it is not possible to review the natural history of the entire New World, I will include here only those marine, aquatic, and terrestrial animals whose pre-Columbian use has been verified by archaeological evidence. And the discussion will be further restricted to those regions that were actively colonized by Spaniards during the sixteenth century: the West Indies, Spanish Florida, Mexico and Central America, and parts of South America.

One problem with archaeological evidence is that it is difficult to determine why a specific animal is found at a given site. The majority were probably eaten, but animals were used also for tools, drugs, rituals, jewelry, clothing, and shelter. Some, such as dogs and songbirds, were kept as pets or for protection, and animals used for these purposes might or might not also be eaten. Other animals were attracted to human residences and their refuse inadvertently became part of the archaeological deposit. Sometimes remains are found that appear to have been curios—for example, fossilized shark teeth. It is possible in some cases to determine the role animals played at a specific site, but it is unwise to assume that all animals were eaten, even though most probably were.

West Indies. The Gulf of Mexico and the Caribbean Sea define a subtropical and tropical basin. The islands of the West Indies separate this basin from the Atlantic Ocean while the coasts of North and South America form the continental rim. Although there are some differences between the animals of the Gulf of Mexico and those of the Caribbean, the Gulf Stream current unifies the marine animals of the West Indies and those of the adjacent continental coasts. The islands of the West Indies support terrestrial animals that are derived primarily from Central and South America rather than from North America. The Bahamas, Cuba, Jamaica, Hispaniola (La Española), Puerto Rico, and the Virgin Islands differ in faunal characteristics from the Lesser Antilles, which extend south from the Virgin Islands almost to continental South America. The islands of Grenada, Trinidad, Tobago, Margarita, and the Netherland Antilles are not considered part of the West Indies. The West Indies and the north coast of Venezuela are the only New World locations actually explored by Columbus.

The tropical waters of the Caribbean, as Columbus noted, support many fish, and these played an important role in pre-Columbian economies. Depending upon the site, over 90 percent of the animals were from the sea. Inshore or estuarine fish taken by West Indians included ladyfish, bonefish, porgies, mullets, puffers, and porcupinefish. Banks and reefs form the most common marine habitat in the West Indies and contributed sea basses, jacks, snappers, grunts, angelfish, wrasses, parrotfish, and surgeonfish. Sharks, tarpons, barracudas, mackerels, tunas, and triggerfish were also used. Columbus reported catching mullets and soles and also wrote that West Indians fished with remoras, which attached themselves to turtles and other fish. Remoras, however, are not common in pre-Columbian archaeological sites.

Caribbean waters support other marine animals used by pre-Columbian peoples. These include monk seals and manatees. Columbus thought that the three West Indian sirens (manatee) he saw were not as beautiful as they were usually pictured. He described sea turtles, which were commonly caught, as being like great wooden shields. Archaeological evidence of such invertebrates as mussels, arks, pearl-oysters, tree-oysters, lucines, jewelboxes, coquinas, venuses, limpets, topsnails, nerites, ceriths, conchs, slippersnails, murexes, whelks, and crabs are often found. Columbus wrote that conchs were tasteless.

Freshwater resources were occasionally used by West Indians. Although pond turtles were taken on some islands, freshwater fish have not been reported from West Indian sites. Marine fish that spend at least a portion of their lives in brackish waters or freshwater streams, such as eels, clingfish, needlefish, and sleepers, are sometimes found.

As Columbus noted, terrestrial mammals, although not numerous, were used by West Indians. These included insectivores, rice rats, an extinct family of rodents including *Quemisia,* hutias, and spiny rats. Some of these mammals had become extinct before 1492, but many survived into the sixteenth century only to become extremely rare or extinct during the post-Columbian period.

Other terrestrial and avian animals were used by West Indians. On some islands, iguanas and land crabs were consumed in large numbers. Columbus reported that some iguanas were six feet long and had white meat that tasted like chicken. Although he marveled at the large number of different kinds of birds, some of which sang very sweetly, birds do not appear to have been significant resources for West Indians. Those that have been found in West Indian sites include grebes, shearwaters, tropicbirds, boobies, herons, flamingos, ducks, rails, gulls, pigeons, doves, macaws, and owls. Columbus wrote in his log that some small birds were tamed and kept in houses

NEW WORLD FAUNA. Three drawings by John White of the Virginia colony, circa 1590: iguana, terrapin, flying fish.

and that there were so many parrots they darkened the sun. Among the foods and other presents given to him were parrots.

There is good evidence in the West Indies of animals introduced from South America and of West Indian animals transported to new islands within the Indies. Guinea pigs and a nonnative hutia have been reported on Hispaniola. Although the hutia might have been introduced to Hispaniola from Cuba, the guinea pig originated in South America. Other South American animals brought to the West Indies included opossums and agoutis. Perhaps the best known introduced animals are dogs, which probably came with peoples immigrating into the West Indies from South America. According to Columbus, some of these dogs could not bark and others were the size of mastiffs and pointers. Some hutias, a flightless rail, and a macaw might have been taken within the West Indies to islands where they were not native and hence were at least captive if not domesticated.

Spanish Florida. The coastal plain of what was once Spanish Florida is a low, flat region fringed by barrier islands and estuaries stretching from Texas into Virginia. The terrestrial and aquatic fauna are temperate North American animals, whereas marine animals are a combination of tropical and temperate species. Although occasional explorations were made into the upper coastal plain and beyond, the Spaniards generally stayed within the coastal mainland and islands for most of the three hundred years they occupied this area.

Marine resources might have contributed over 80 percent of the diet of natives living along the coastal fringe. The fish most frequently taken by these peoples were from the estuaries that border the coastal plain. In both the Atlantic Ocean and the Gulf of Mexico, tropical animals gradually decrease as temperate species increase. Tropical marine species may live in waters as far north as North Carolina, but only in the deeper waters of the continental shelf edge where water temperatures are more stable and warmer than closer to shore. Animals from the offshore area were not exploited by North Americans in Spanish Florida until several centuries after contact. Marine fish taken by coastal residents were primarily sharks, rays, sea catfish, sheepsheads, drums, and flounders. Although they were more common and abundant in warm Caribbean waters, sea basses, jacks, snappers, and porcupinefish were also taken. By far the most common fish used along the coast were members of the drum family, including silver perches, seatrouts, spots, croakers, black drums, red drums, and star drums.

Other marine resources were used in Spanish Florida. Porpoises and manatees are found occasionally in coastal sites. Sea turtles, common in the West Indies, also live in the area's warm waters and were taken on a seasonal basis. Diamondback terrapins were frequently used by coastal peoples. Invertebrates from coastal sites include mussels, arks, bittersweets, oysters, coquinas, stout tagelus, marshclams, quahog and venus clams, periwinkles, conchs, whelks, nassas, shrimps, and blue crabs.

Aquatic animals were used by coastal peoples as well as by those living farther inland. Beavers and otters were the primary mammals taken from this environment. Alligators, snapping turtles, pond turtles, musk and mud turtles, and softshell turtles are common freshwater residents, although some of these animals can live in estuarine waters. Freshwater fish found in archaeological sites include gars, bowfins, pikes, suckers, bullhead catfish, sunfish, and perches. Further inland, many species of the large freshwater mussel family Unionidae as well as campelomas, riversnails, rocksnails, and hornsnails are common.

Unlike the West Indies, continental Spanish Florida supported many terrestrial mammals. These include opossums, rabbits, squirrels, coyotes, foxes, bears, raccoons, weasels, minks, skunks, cougars, and bobcats. The white-tailed deer was an important part of the diet of North Americans living inland from the coast.

Other terrestrial and avian resources were also used. These include the terrestrial box turtles and gopher tortoises. The latter were frequently consumed by colonists in Spanish Florida, although apparently not often by native Americans. The gopher tortoise range extends north from peninsular Florida along the coastal plain to the Georgia–South Carolina border, but they are far more common in peninsular Florida than they are farther north. As in the West Indies, birds were not commonly used in Spanish Florida, although herons, ducks, quails, and common turkeys were found there. Inland sites sometimes contain a wider variety of birds, including the now-extinct passenger pigeon.

The only domestic animals in Spanish Florida were dogs, which may occasionally have been used for food as well as other purposes. Although the common turkey was domesticated elsewhere, this was not the case in Spanish Florida.

Mexico and Central America. Both North American and South American animals live in the Mexican–Central American region, with their ranges depending upon latitude, altitude, and rainfall patterns. This area is characterized by primarily temperate zone animals in Mexico and mostly tropical animals south of Mexico. There are significant altitudinal and climatic differences among the eastern coastal plain, the highlands, the deserts, the tropical rain forests, and the western coastal plain, and these are reflected in the animals living in each area. While the eastern coast of Mexico and Central America is inhabited by animals of the warm Gulf of Mexico and the Caribbean, the western coast is also bordered by warm tropical waters. These warm Pacific waters extend the length of Mexico and Central America to just south of the equator in South America.

A wide variety of fish were important in the economies of Mexican and Central American coastal communities, but the percentages are highly variable. The continental edge of the circum-Caribbean basin is frequented by many of the same fish found in the West Indies and Spanish Florida. Depending upon nearby habitats, people may have used sharks, sawfish, stingrays, eaglerays, tarpons, bonefish, sea catfish, toadfish, needlefish, snooks, sea basses, jacks, snappers, tripletails, mojarras, grunts, porgies, drums, wrasses, parrotfish, mullets, barracudas, sleepers, triggerfish, puffers, and porcupinefish. Different but closely related species were taken on the Pacific side of Mexico and Central America.

Other marine resources were available. On the Caribbean side of Mexico and Central America, manatees were used occasionally. Sea turtles are found off both the circum-Caribbean and Pacific beaches. Invertebrates from coastal sites include mussels, arks, oysters, jewelboxes, surfclams, marshclams, pointed-venus, nerites, hornsnails, periwinkles, queen conchs, moonsnails, crown conchs, melampus, blue crabs, and stone crabs.

Freshwater resources found throughout Mexico and Central America include reptiles, fish, and mollusks. Reptiles such as crocodiles, snapping turtles, pond turtles, and musk and mud turtles were often used. The region supports many species of freshwater characins, catfish, and cichlids that do not live farther north or in the West Indies. These are frequently found in sites adjacent to freshwater sources. Some freshwater mollusks, such as applesnails, were also used.

With few exceptions, the mammals of Mexico and Central America were rare or absent in Spanish Florida and none lived in the West Indies. Terrestrial mammals include opossums, armadillos, rabbits, Mexican porcupines, agoutis and pacas, foxes, raccoons, coatis, tapirs, collared and white-lipped peccaries, brocket deer, and white-tailed deer. These animals live on the coastal plain as well as in the highlands.

Other terrestrial animals included iguanas and birds. Iguanas live throughout Mexico and Central America. The use of birds by pre-Columbian residents of this area varied, depending upon cultural preferences for brightly colored feathers. In some locations, remains of boobies, frigatebirds, herons, wood storks, hawks, curassows, quails, wild common turkeys, ocellated turkeys, gallinules, coots, sandpipers, pigeons, parrots, owls, and songbirds are abundant. More often, birds found in archaeological sites are quails, turkeys, pigeons, doves, and parrots.

Two domestic animals were present in Mexico and Central America. One of these was the common turkey. Its range extends south into Mexico from the United States, in portions of which the birds were not domesticated. They were domesticated, however, in the southwestern United States, the highlands of Mexico, and the Yucatán. The common turkey should not be confused with the wild ocellated turkey which is confined to the Yucatán Peninsula and was not domesticated. Dogs were the other domestic animal. They have been found in contexts that indicate they were eaten by some groups and served as hunting companions, sacrifices, and protection for others.

South America. The South American fauna is largely a tropical one, although altitude and rainfall are important in the distribution of these animals. The animals of the Caribbean islands of Grenada, Trinidad, Tobago, and the Netherland Antilles are also South American. Many animals that are native to the continent but not found in the West Indies, such as monkeys, anteaters, and armadillos, are present on these islands and were used by islanders prior to 1492. Although the coastal plain of Venezuela, Colombia, and part of Ecuador is characterized by mangrove swamps, savannas, and tropical forests, the coastal plain from southern Ecuador to northern Chile is a desert virtually devoid of terrestrial animals. Beyond the coastal plain, the highland Andes have temperate and cold climates with distinct animals generally dissimilar to those living along the Pacific or Caribbean coasts. Unfortunately we know little from archaeological evidence of the resources used over much of this area.

Marine fish were very important in the Caribbean and Pacific coastal economies of South America. The coastal fish of Venezuela, the offshore islands, and Colombia east of Panama are Caribbean species similar to those found elsewhere in the circum-Caribbean basin. The fish in the warm waters off Colombia west of Panama are similar to those of Mexico and Central America. Just south of the equator there is a distinct change in Pacific fish. The waters off Peru and Chile are characterized by upwellings of nutrients, which support an abundant temperate and cold water marine life. Coastal sites in Ecuador contain the remains of more warm water animals than do sites farther south. Fish important to coastal populations in Ecuador include sharks, rays, herrings, sea basses, jacks, grunts, drums, mullets, barracudas, mackerels, tunas, and flounders. Fish important to coastal populations in Peru include different species of herrings, anchovies, sea basses, jacks, grunts, drums, mackerels, and tunas.

Other marine resources were also important. Sea turtles have been found in Ecuadorian collections, and whales, sea otters, fur seals, and sea lions were used by coastal peoples farther south. Invertebrates from coastal sites include mussels, scallops, thorny-oysters, surfclams, wedgeclams, venuses, limpets, tegulas, periwinkles, slip-persnails, rocksnails, chitons, lobsters, crabs, and sea urchins.

Aquatic resources are almost absent on the western side of the Andes below the equator, owing to limited rainfall and few freshwater sources. On the other hand, pond turtles and freshwater fish such as characins, catfish, and cichlids may be locally abundant in archaeological sites near lakes and streams.

The presence of coastal terrestrial mammals is also influenced by the presence of freshwater. The coast of Ecuador supports opossums, armadillos, rabbits, rice rats, agoutis, spiny rats, foxes, skunks, cougars, tapirs, white-lipped and collared peccaries, brocket deer, and white-tailed deer. In contrast, the Peruvian desert coast supports very few terrestrial mammals. These are primarily rabbits, mice, foxes, cougars, guanacos, and white-tailed deer.

Other terrestrial resources might be locally significant. Iguanas and *Dicrodon* lizards were more commonly used in Ecuador and on the north coast of Peru than farther south. Terrestrial tortoises have been found in two sites on the island of Trinidad. Although birds are not a common feature elsewhere in the New World, along the Pacific coast of South America many birds attracted by the marine upwellings are abundant in coastal sites. These include fulmars, shearwaters, penguins, boobies, pelicans, cormorants, and gulls. In Ecuador, more tropical birds such as tinamou, ducks, curassows, doves, and parrots were used.

A number of diverse habitats extend away from the coastal plain into the Andes. The upper valleys are separated from each other by altiplano grasslands and snow-capped peaks. Although the terrestrial fauna of the Andes is limited, some terrestrial mammals were extensively used. These included opossums, rabbits, guinea pigs, agoutis, viscachas, chinchillas, foxes, spectacled bears, kinkajous, skunks, otters, margays, cougars, guanacos, vicuñas, brocket deer, huemul deer, and white-tailed deer.

Other highland species are found in Andean sites. Iguanas have been identified occasionally. Birds from sites in the Andean highlands include tinamous, herons, ducks, vultures, hawks, pigeons, owls, and parrots, as well as birds more typical of the coast such as boobies, pelicans, cormorants, gulls, and terns. Aquatic fish and invertebrates are not common in the Andes, although some characins, catfish, and freshwater mussels have been identified.

In addition to dogs, several South American animals were domesticated. Chief among them were llamas and alpacas, members of the same family which includes the wild guanaco and vicuña. Although llamas and alpacas were originally domesticated in the Andean highlands,

they soon became common in coastal locations. Guinea pigs were also domesticated in the highlands and are found as domestic animals in sites on the Pacific coast and in the West Indies. Another South American domestic animal, the muscovy duck, has become widespread throughout the world.

[See also *Agriculture; Domesticated Animals; Flora.*]

BIBLIOGRAPHY

Chirichigno, Norma F. *Catálogo de especies marinas de interés económico actual o potencial para América Latina: Parte II, Pacífico Centro y Suroriental.* Rome, 1982.

Emmons, Louise. *Neotropical Rainforest Mammals: A Field Guide.* Chicago, 1990.

Fuson, Robert H., trans. *The Log of Christopher Columbus.* Camden, Maine, 1987.

Hoese, H. Dickson, and Richard H. Moore. *Fishes of the Gulf of Mexico.* College Station, Tex., 1977.

Landstrom, Bjorn. *Columbus.* New York, 1966.

Larson, Lewis H. *Aboriginal Subsistence Technology on the Southeastern Coastal Plain during the Late Prehistoric Period.* Gainesville, Fla., 1980.

Mares, Michael A., and Hugh H. Genoways, eds. *Mammalian Biology in South America.* Special Publication Series Pymatuning Laboratory of Ecology, vol. 6. Pittsburgh, 1982.

Meyer de Schauensee, Rodolphe. *A Guide to the Birds of South America.* Philadelphia, 1970.

Nowak, Ronald M., and John L. Paradiso. *Walker's Mammals of the World.* 4th ed. Baltimore, 1983.

Randall, John E. *Caribbean Reef Fishes.* Jersey City, N.J., 1968.

Wing, Elizabeth S., and Elizabeth J. Reitz. "Prehistoric Fishing Economies of the Caribbean." *Journal of New World Archaeology* 5 (1982): 13–33.

Woods, Charles A., ed. *Biogeography of the West Indies: Past, Present, and Future.* Gainesville, Fla., 1989.

ELIZABETH J. REITZ

FERDINAND. For discussion of Fernando of Aragón, see *Isabel and Fernando.*

FERNÁNDEZ DE CÓRDOBA, FRANCISCO (c. 1475–1526), Spanish explorer of Central America. The date of Fernández de Córdoba's arrival in the New World is not known, but around 1520 he participated in several campaigns as a lieutenant of Pedro Arias de Ávila (Pedrárias), first governor of Castilla del Oro. Since the discovery of the Pacific Ocean by Balboa, Pedrárias had sought to find a sea passage between the two oceans. In 1524, upon receiving news that Gil González de Ávila was exploring the coast of Honduras, Pedrárias formed an expedition to Nicaragua under the command of Fernández de Córdoba. The goal was to explore the Pacific coast to the north of the Isthmus of Panama and take possession of that

territory for Pedrárias, who had a claim to it based on an earlier expedition he had sent in 1516 under Hernando Ponce. Strictly following Pedrárias's instructions, Fernández marched inland and in 1524 he founded the town of Bruselas, near present-day Puntarenas, the first Spanish settlement in Costa Rica. He then discovered Lake Nicaragua, founded the city of Granada on its southwest shore, and began evangelizing the Indians. Continuing eastward, he founded the first city of León ("la Vieja"). Entering Honduras, he founded Segovia on the Yare River but then ran into the expedition of González de Ávila. In the ensuing clash, González skillfully overpowered Fernández.

A third party then intervened in the dispute: Cristóbal de Olid, sent from Mexico by Hernando Cortés (who was claiming the territory as part of New Spain). After landing in Honduras, Olid decided to break with Cortés, proclaiming himself governor. In a clash with González Olid managed to prevail. González was imprisoned together with Francisco de las Casas, who had been sent by sea to punish Olid, but who had been captured upon his arrival in Honduras. The two prisoners came to an agreement, broke free, executed Olid in January 1525, and then left for Mexico to inform Cortés. Fernández took advantage of their absence to proclaim himself governor of Nicaragua with the encouragement of Pedro Moreno, who had arrived from Santo Domingo to support González, but in González's absence decided to change sides. Fernández's own lieutenant, Juan Ponce de León, did not approve this independent move; he was arrested but managed to escape with the help of his fellow lieutenant Francisco de Campañón. Both returned to Panama to inform Pedrárias, who quickly arranged a naval expedition to punish Fernández. In a desperate move, Fernández then tried to get the support of Cortés, who had arrived in Honduras after the departure of González and Francisco de las Casas. Cortés seems to have been close to making an agreement with Fernández for a joint exploration of Nicaragua, but the deteriorating state of affairs in Mexico prompted Cortés's hasty departure from the area in April of 1526. Left alone, Fernández was not able to overcome Pedrárias, who had him executed in León, Nicaragua, in June of 1526.

BIBLIOGRAPHY

Alvarez Rubiano, Pedro. *Pedrárias Dávila*. Madrid, 1944.
Anderson, C. L. G. *Old Panama and Castilla del Oro*. Boston, 1946.
Gámez, José D. *Historia de Nicaragua*. Managua, 1889.

ANGEL DELGADO-GOMEZ

FERNÁNDEZ DE CÓRDOBA, GONZALO (1453–1515), Spanish army commander. Often known as the Great Captain—*el gran capitán*—Córdoba organized the

disciplined, professional army that built the Spanish empire during the sixteenth and seventeenth centuries. Córdoba was a tactician and military organizer who quickly identified combinations of troops, tactics, weapons, equipment, and organizational units that would be most effective in the various military situations he faced. He waged brilliant campaigns in both Spain and Italy. In Spain, he directed the last phase (1482–1492) of the Reconquista, the conquest of the Muslim kingdom of Granada, depending upon mobile light cavalry; he ended the conflict with an experienced army of battle-tested veterans. In 1495 he went to Italy to support the Aragonese monarchy of Naples against the invading army of King Charles VIII of France, who also claimed the Neapolitan throne. There he relied on mobile infantry and firearms in two campaigns (1495–1497 and 1501–1504) that effectively expelled French forces from Italy. By 1504 the weak dynasty of Naples had collapsed, and Córdoba incorporated the kingdom into the growing Spanish realm. From 1504 to 1506 he governed Naples as viceroy of the king of Spain. Though he had no direct connections with Christopher Columbus or Spanish expansion overseas, his work contributed to the success of Spanish forces in America, for many of the early conquistadores acquired their military discipline and gained battlefield experience in Córdoba's armies in Spain or Italy.

BIBLIOGRAPHY

Elliott, J. H. *Imperial Spain, 1469–1716*. New York, 1963.
Parker, Geoffrey. *The Military Revolution: Military Innovation and the Rise of the West, 1500–1800*. Cambridge, 1988.

JERRY H. BENTLEY

FERNÁNDEZ DE OVIEDO, GONZALO. See *Oviedo, Gonzalo Fernández de*.

FERNANDO. For discussion of Fernando of Aragón, see *Isabel and Fernando*.

FIESCHI, BARTOLOMEO (c. 1470–c. 1530), captain on Columbus's fourth voyage. Bartolomeo Fieschi was a member of a noble Genoese family that belonged to the Fregoso party, the political party of which Columbus's father, Domenico Colombo, was also a member. The fortunes of Columbus's father were tied to this party; his moving from Genoa to Savona was occasioned by its final eclipse. His successes, especially the lucrative post as warden of the Olivella gate, came about because of the influence of the Fieschi family. It is therefore not surprising to find Bartolomeo Fieschi a companion of Columbus and a participant on the fourth voyage.

In 1503, while Columbus and his crew were marooned on Jamaica, Bartolomeo Fieschi and Diego Méndez made a daring canoe voyage from Jamaica to La Española to secure help. Their trip was later recorded in detail in Fernando Colón's biography of his father. After returning to Spain, Fieschi remained with Columbus, helping him draw up his will on May 19, 1506, at Valladolid, signing it as a witness, and helping on the occasion of his death the next day.

The historian Cesare de Lollis believes that Fieschi went home immediately after the Admiral's death, identifying him with the Bartolomeo Flisco who, according to Agostino Giustiniani, was an instigator of a popular uprising in Genoa in July 1506. The uprising resulted in Fieschi and his family going into exile and Louis XII of France sending troops to intervene. In 1525, having returned to Genoa, Bartolomeo Fieschi was elected captain of a fleet of fifteen Genoese ships that sailed to fight France. In 1527, he was declared *padre del comune* (city father).

BIBLIOGRAPHY

Morison, Samuel Eliot. *Admiral of the Ocean Sea: A Life of Christopher Columbus.* 2 vols. Boston, 1942.

Taviani, Paolo Emilio. *I viaggi di Colombo.* Vol. 2. 2d ed. Novara, 1990. Spanish ed., Barcelona, 1989.

PAOLO EMILIO TAVIANI

FILM. For discussion of Columbus as a figure in film and motion pictures, see *Iconography,* article on *Film.*

FIRST VOYAGE. See *Voyages of Columbus.*

FLORA. [This entry includes three articles on native American flora and on crop exchange between the Old World and the New:

An Overview
Psychotropic Flora
Tobacco

For related discussions, see also *Agriculture; Domesticated Animals; Fauna.*]

An Overview

When Christopher Columbus made landfall in 1492, he set in motion an exchange of plants between the Old and New Worlds, landmasses that had been separated since the breakup of Pangaea (the ancient supercontinent) nearly 200 million years before. Although in the years to follow useful plants would move both ways across the Atlantic and Pacific oceans, changes in the flora of the New World were the most profound. Alfred W. Crosby has pointed out that the long geographic isolation of the New World rendered its inhabitants, human, plant, and animal alike, vulnerable to Old World diseases and ill-adapted for competition. Humans fell victim to smallpox and other contagions; native vegetation succumbed to the pressures of grazing by cattle, pigs, and horses. Soon the New World began to resemble the Old, with European crops, herds, and weeds spreading into all hospitable environments.

What plants did Europeans bring to the New World? Which species did they carry back to Europe and across the Pacific? In both instances, economically useful plants, especially foods, formed the core of the exchange. These transplanted crops had significant impacts on the diet, health, and economic well-being of the inhabitants of both hemispheres. To understand this phenomenon, it is necessary to begin with the plants themselves.

Crops of the New World. The pre-Columbian flora of the New World was tremendously varied; so too were the manipulations of it by humans. The history of crop domestication in the New World is centered largely in the tropical latitudes. Jack Harlan has described two independent areas of domestication in the tropics, one in Mesoamerica (central Mexico and Guatemala) and another, larger area in South America. The major crops native to these regions include:

Grain: maize (corn)
Root crops: manioc (cassava), sweet potato, white potato
Pulses: common bean, lima bean, peanut, jack bean
Vegetables: squash, tomato, quinoa, amaranth
Fruits: avocado, pineapple, papaya, guava, passion fruit
Spices/stimulants: chile pepper, cacao, tobacco, coca
Utility: cotton

Plant domestication in South America probably occurred in many locations, with crops evolving both in the lowland zones (manioc, sweet potato, peanut) and the highland zones (white potato) of the continent. The earliest stages of plant domestication are difficult to document, but by 5000 B.C. fully evolved crops were present in both Mesoamerica and South America. Maize was domesticated in Mesoamerica, but spread early into South America. Species of beans, chile peppers, squashes, and cotton were domesticated independently in both areas. Recent research has also documented a temperate zone area of New World plant domestication, in eastern North America. By the time of contact, however, most of the indigenous crops of this region—small-seeded annuals like chenopod and sumpweed—had been replaced by maize.

Crops of the Old World. Four independent areas of crop domestication existed in the Old World: in the Near East (NE: eastern Mediterranean), Africa (A: tropical Africa), north China (C), and Southeast Asia and the South Pacific (SEA: eastern India, southern China, Southeast Asia, south Pacific). In addition, central Europe (E) was a secondary area where several local crops evolved from weeds growing in fields of introduced grains. The major crops of Old World origin include:

Grains: wheat, barley (NE); sorghum, finger millet, pearl millet (A); rice, broomcorn millet, foxtail millet (C); sugarcane, rice (SEA); oats, rye (E)

Root crops: beet, turnip, carrot, radish, onion (NE); yams (A); taro, yams (SEA)

Pulses: lentil, pea, chick-pea, broad bean (NE); cowpea (A); soybean (C); rice bean, mung bean (SEA)

Vegetables: lettuce, cabbage (NE); cucumber (C); eggplant (SEA)

Fruits: fig, olive, apple, grape, melon (NE); watermelon (A); peach (C); banana, plantain, mango, breadfruit, citrus fruits, plum (SEA)

Spices/stimulants: coffee (A); tea (C); clove, black pepper, nutmeg, turmeric (SEA)

Utility: flax (NE); cotton, gourd (A)

By the fifteenth century, many of these Old World crops had spread far from their areas of origin. Citrus fruits—lemons, limes, and oranges—were domesticated in Southeast Asia but were known in Europe by the thirteenth century; bananas and plantains were introduced into Africa early in the Christian era. Many crops domesticated in the Near East spread millennia earlier into Europe. Einkorn wheat, for example, spread to central and western Europe during the fifth millennium B.C., attaining a wide distribution during the Bronze and early Iron Ages. Olives were known to the Romans; figs to the ancient Greeks. The foods carried by the first Europeans traveling to the New World were thus a mixture of plants from many regions of the Old.

European Crops in the Americas. The history of European crops in the Americas begins with the second voyage of Columbus. As Crosby relates, Columbus, on his return to La Española, brought seeds and cuttings for wheat, chick-peas, melons, onions, radishes, salad greens, grape vines, sugarcane, and fruit trees, including the olive. Here, with the vegetable mainstays of Mediterranean cuisine, the newcomers set about re-creating the gardens and orchards of home.

The Caribbean is not the Mediterranean, however, and not all the new crops prospered. Wheat, barley, olives, and grapes would not grow, for example. Other orchard crops, such as figs, oranges, and lemons, did well, as did melons and some vegetables. Sugarcane, and a slightly later introduction, the banana, did very well in the hot climate of the Caribbean.

The success of the early introductions of European crops to the Caribbean depended on the temperature,

rainfall, and day-length requirements of the individual species. Because he made his first landfall in the tropical latitudes of the New World, Columbus missed the region preferred by many of the European staples, especially grains—the temperate zone. But sugarcane, banana, and citrus, among other crops of the Old World tropics, prospered in the new setting.

Six examples will serve to illustrate how and where European crops adapted to the New World and the impact of the vagaries of plant geography on indigenous peoples and colonists alike. Wheat, grapes, and two legumes (peas, broad beans) illustrate the pattern for the temperate zone crops; sugarcane, bananas, and yams, for the tropical crops.

Wheat (*Triticum* spp.) is the most important cereal in the world today, followed closely by rice. It is essentially a temperate zone crop, but can be grown successfully at higher elevations in the tropics. In the mountains, one finds the cooler temperatures needed for wheat's successful growth and development. There are five species of cultivated wheats—common or bread wheat, spelt, durum, emmer, and einkorn. Their domestication and evolution under cultivation occurred initially in the Near East and continued as the species spread throughout the temperate regions of the Old World.

Attempts were made in the sixteenth century to grow wheat in the Caribbean and Spanish Florida, but these largely failed, owing to the combination of high summer temperatures and high humidity in this region. To grow wheat under such conditions requires cultivation during the drier, cooler season, with irrigation to provide the necessary moisture. This was not the cultivation practice in Europe.

As the Spanish exploration of the tropical New World progressed, however, higher elevation lands suitable for growing wheat were soon discovered. One of the first successful introductions of wheat was to the highlands of Mexico in 1529. Wheat was carried soon after into the Andes of South America, where it found a productive niche: the higher elevation zone favored by the potato. Peru became the wheat breadbasket for the Spanish New World, supplying wheat flour to the lower, wetter regions. The English settlers of North America had less trouble establishing this mainstay of diet; it was introduced successfully early in the seventeenth century and spread westward with the settlers.

The case of the domesticated grape (*Vitis vinifera*) is less the story of a crop finding its natural range in a strange land and more a story of adaptation. Grapes prefer regions with Mediterranean climates: hot, dry summers and cool, rainy winters. Grapes were carried on all the early voyages of discovery and were introduced into the eastern United States, Spanish Florida, Mexico, and South America. Mediterranean climates were eventually found in California and the southern Andes, but grapes were successful in other regions as well. This was in large part due to the hybridization of the cultivated grape with native, wild grapes. Such crosses resulted in vigorous offspring, better adapted to the local growing conditions. In eastern North America the concord grape developed; in the Caribbean, crosses with a local species produced grapes that were resistant to disease and tolerant of heat and moisture.

The pea *(Pisum sativum)* and the broad bean *(Vicia faba)* are two temperate latitude pulses introduced into the New World by Europeans. Peas were domesticated in the Near East and introduced early into the northern Mediterranean and Europe. They spread east to India and China and south into central Africa before the age of European exploration. Because peas require a cool, humid climate, they do poorly in the tropics except at higher elevations. Like wheat, however, they can be grown as a winter crop at lower elevations if sufficient moisture is present. Peas are one of the four most important seed legumes today and are an excellent source of vegetable protein.

The broad bean, or field bean, like the pea, is a very old Near Eastern domesticated plant. It was the only edible bean known in Europe before the discovery of the New World and the introduction of the American *Phaseolus* beans. It is a crop that does poorly in hot weather, even in the temperate zone, when it may flower but not produce fruit. It can be grown in the summer at higher elevations in the tropics or as a winter crop at the edges of the tropical zone.

In contrast to temperate zone crops like wheat, grapes, peas, and broad beans, for which only high-elevation terrain proved productive in Spanish and Portuguese America, Old World crops of tropical origin were preadapted to the extensive lowlands of the New World. With the exception of some fruits and spices, however, these African and Asian crops were not at the core of European cuisine. Why, then, did the Spanish and Portuguese introduce crops like sugarcane, bananas, and yams to the New World? The answer is twofold: for profit and to feed the African slaves introduced to replace the dying indigenous populations.

Sugarcane *(Saccharum officinarum)* was domesticated in the islands of Southeast Asia, where its stems, or canes, were chewed for their sweetness. The practice of extracting the juice and boiling it down to make sugar probably originated in India. Sugarcane had spread as far as Persia by the sixth century, where it was adopted by Arab peoples, who carried it to northern Africa and eventually to the northern Mediterranean and Spain. By the time of Columbus's voyages, sugar was a lucrative industry in the Iberian Peninsula and the recently conquered Canary Islands. Demand in Europe was high, but land suitable for cultivation limited.

Sugarcane requires hot weather, plenty of rain and sunshine, a long frost-free period, and well-drained soil. It is a perennial crop that can be planted on the same land for many years. These characteristics combined to make sugarcane cultivation one of the most powerful forces for vegetation change in the tropical New World. Forests were clear-cut for cane fields that never went out of production; deforestation led to erosion, reduced rainfall, and more vegetation change. Soon after their discovery, the islands of the Caribbean were transformed into vast sugar mills. Sugarcane cultivation was introduced in the early sixteenth century into Mexico, Peru, and Brazil, with similar results.

As native peoples died from disease and hardship, African slaves were brought in to work the cane fields. Feeding these workers required staple crops that would produce abundantly in the lowland tropics. In their explorations of West Africa in the fifteenth century, the Portuguese encountered a variety of such crops, some of which they introduced into the Canary Islands. Among these was the banana, which was taken from the Canary Islands to La Española in 1516.

Bananas *(Musa* spp.) originated in Southeast Asia. They were introduced into Africa perhaps as early as the fifth century A.D. Ripe bananas are sweet and easily digested raw. Unripe fruits are starchy and must be cooked. In this

BANANAS. Sketch of an Old World plant made in the New World, circa 1590, by which time species of bananas had already become well-established in the Caribbean region. From *Histoire naturelle des Indes,* often called the Drake Manuscript; perhaps a sketch from Sir Francis Drake's own hand.

THE PIERPONT MORGAN LIBRARY, NEW YORK; M.3900, F.11v

form they are often called plantains, but there are also true plantains, strains that are starchy even when ripe. Plantains are high in carbohydrates (about 35 percent) and a good source of vitamins and minerals. They have been important staples in many parts of Africa for centuries, supplementing the native and Asian yams and the introduced New World tuber, manioc.

Yams (*Dioscorea* spp.) evolved independently as cultivated plants in the New World, African, and Southeast Asian tropics. Like the banana, the Asian, or greater yam, was introduced into Africa from the East during the first millennium A.D. and spread across the continent. Readily accepted by agriculturalists accustomed to the native yellow or Guinea yam, the greater yam became an important West African food. Yams were used for victualing of slave ships sailing from West Africa and were carried to both the Caribbean and Brazil soon after contact.

The African slaves who worked the sugarcane fields subsisted on a diet high in starches—a combination of New World crops, including the highly productive manioc, and introduced crops familiar to them, such as bananas and yams. As the temperate latitudes and higher elevation tropics began to mirror Europe, the lowland tropics were transformed by the plantation system and the blending of African, Asian, and indigenous crops.

American Crops in the Old World. In the years following the discovery of the New World, food plants from the Americas were carried back to Europe with the other fruits of conquest. First viewed as curiosities, some of these crops came to play major roles as food staples. Crosby suggests that the introduction of new food crops into sixteenth-century Europe resulted in an increase in the quantity and quality of food, which in turn contributed to population growth. Many New World crops found productive niches in the Old World, where they complemented native crops. Maize, for example, is a genetically plastic grain, able to adapt to many different growing conditions. From its hearth in Mesoamerica, it had spread prehistorically throughout the New World, from the Amazon basin to the Great Lakes region of North America. In the Old World, it was suitable for land too wet for wheat and too dry for rice, thriving in both the temperate and tropical latitudes.

Many New World plants had an impact on European, Near Eastern, African, and Asian cuisines and customs. Chili peppers spice up food around the world; chocolate (from cacao) transformed candy; the tomato is indispensable in Italian cooking; smoking tobacco is a common practice around the world. Food staples have had the greatest impact on health and nutrition, however. Maize, bean, manioc, and potato will serve as illustrations.

Maize, or corn (*Zea mays*), is the most important cereal in the world after wheat and rice. In tropical regions, it is

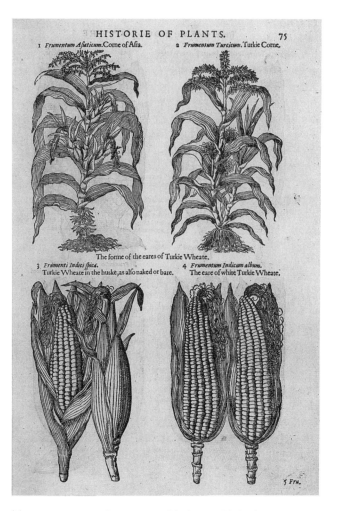

MAIZE. Engraving of a New World plant published in Europe in 1597, by which time maize had been established in temperate regions of the Old World. From J. Gerarde's *The Herball*.

LIBRARY OF CONGRESS

used primarily as a starchy staple for human consumption; in the temperate regions, its primary role is as livestock feed. European settlers throughout the New World survived on maize when their own crops failed.

The first European reference to maize was made by Columbus, who recorded its cultivation on Long Island in the Bahamas. He took seeds back to Spain, where the plant was described and grown as a garden curiosity. Sixteenth-century herbals illustrate two varieties, one similar to the flint corn of eastern North America, the other to Caribbean maize. The potential of maize was quickly recognized, however, and cultivation spread from Spain around the Mediterranean and into North Africa. Both Spanish and Portuguese explorers carried maize with them on their explorations of the tropics; it was introduced into West Africa in the early sixteenth century and was carried by Ferdinand Magellan around the world, becoming established first in the East Indies and the Philippines and then spreading to the Asian mainland. Maize was introduced into India either by sea by the Portuguese or overland from the Near East by Arab peoples.

Maize quickly became a dietary staple in the warm temperate regions of the Old World, where its cultivation rivaled that of the traditional Near Eastern grains. In the tropics—for example, in Africa—maize also replaced traditional grains, which here were sorghum and the millets, and during the height of the slave trade (seventeenth and eighteenth centuries), it became a major cash crop. Maize assumed these roles because it is high yielding and nutritious for the labor required and is compact and easily stored or transported. In Asia, rice remained the preferred grain, but maize found a role, replacing lower-yielding native millets on terrain too dry for rice.

The major New World bean species, the common bean *(Phaseolus vulgaris)* and the lima bean *(Phaseolus lunatus)*, are among the most important sources of vegetable protein in the world today. Domesticated independently in Mesoamerica and South America, beans were grown throughout the temperate and tropical regions of the New World. The common bean was introduced into Europe in the sixteenth century and carried around the world by Spanish and Portuguese explorers. A genetically plastic crop, the common bean thrived throughout the temperate zones of the Old World and in areas of medium rainfall in the tropics. It was cultivated widely in Europe by the seventeenth century and became an important source of vegetable protein there.

Lima beans were introduced into the Philippines and Asian mainland by Spanish explorers. They were also introduced into Africa, along with the common bean, where they became the major pulse crop in wetter regions. Lima beans tolerate higher rainfall than the common bean. They fulfilled an important dietary function in wet tropical Africa, providing protein to complement the high-starch diet of grains, root crops, and plantains. The native African pulse, the cowpea, is primarily a crop of the drier, savanna habitat. Neither of the New World beans became very important in tropical Asia, where two native *Phaseolus* species, mung bean and rice bean, were already established.

Two root crops, manioc and potato, round out the picture of the role American crops played in Old World agriculture. The story of manioc is primarily African, the potato European.

Manioc, or cassava *(Manioc esculenta)*, originated in the low-elevation tropics of South America. It was the primary carbohydrate source of the tropical-forest agricultural

system. Manioc is a highly productive crop that can tolerate prolonged drought and soils of marginal fertility. It is often grown as the last rotation under shifting cultivation, after soil is too depleted to grow maize. Some strains, referred to as bitter manioc, have high levels of hydrocyanic acid (HCN), which must be destroyed by cooking or fermentation. The toxin serves to protect the plant from animal and insect predation.

These characteristics—high yield, ability to tolerate drought and low soil fertility, and natural pest protection—make manioc an attractive choice in tropical regions with uncertain rainfall and depleted soils. Manioc was introduced into Africa and elsewhere in the tropics by the Portuguese late in the sixteenth century. It had a relatively limited distribution and use from then through the eighteenth century, however, becoming widespread only in the mid-nineteenth century and after. African agriculturalists preferred the yam. Manioc production increased dramatically only after its cultivation was encouraged as protection against famine and locust attacks. It performed well, but with manioc now dominating agriculture in some regions of Africa, protein deficiency and HCN toxicity have become serious problems.

The white potato *(Solanum tuberosum)* has also been a mixed blessing to Old World agriculture. Overdependence on the potato led to the death of a million people in nineteenth-century Ireland when blight destroyed the crop; nevertheless, today potatoes rank fourth in world food production, behind wheat, rice, and maize.

Originating in the central Andes of South America, in the Lake Titicaca region, the potato spread south into Chile and north into Ecuador and Colombia before European contact. The Andean potato was a crop of short days and cool growing conditions. Its spread to the north was checked by the heat of the Central American lowlands. It was only after contact that potato cultivation spread to Mesoamerica and North America. In the latter case, the potato arrived in the seventeenth century by way of Europe, after strains adapted to long daylight conditions had been developed.

The potato was introduced into Europe twice, first from Colombia to Spain in about 1570 and then to England sometime around 1590 with goods seized from Spanish treasure ships. The potato was illustrated in herbals of the period and by late in the sixteenth century was grown in Spain, Italy, and southern France, where it was suitable as a winter (short-day) crop. By the seventeenth century the potato had been introduced into Ireland, but it was not until the late eighteenth or early nineteenth century that potato cultivation spread throughout Europe, where it became a mainstay of peasant agriculture.

With maize and the potato among the top four food crops of the world, it is clear that the New World has contributed crops vital to the life and health of people around the globe. Plants domesticated by native Americans are grown today both under mechanized production and on small peasant farms, expanding the land that can be cultivated and providing essential components of the human diet. The crops of the New World were among its greatest gifts to the Old.

BIBLIOGRAPHY

Burton, W. G. *The Potato: A Survey of Its History and of Factors Influencing Its Yield, Nutritive Value, Quality, and Storage.* Wageningen, Holland, 1966.

Chadha, Y. R., ed. *Maize in India.* New Delhi, India, 1977.

Crosby, Alfred W. *The Columbian Exchange.* Westport, Conn., 1972.

Crosby, Alfred W. *Ecological Imperialism.* Cambridge, 1986.

Finan, John J. *Maize in the Great Herbals.* Waltham, Mass., 1950.

Harlan, Jack. *Crops and Man.* Madison, Wisc., 1975.

Hawkes, J. G. *The Potato: Evolution, Biodiversity, and Genetic Resources.* Washington, D.C., 1990.

McAlister, Lyle N. *Spain and Portugal in the New World, 1492–1700.* Minneapolis, Minn., 1984.

Purseglove, J. W. *Tropical Crops: Dicotyledons.* New York, 1974.

Purseglove, J. W. *Tropical Crops: Monocotyledons.* 2 vols. London, 1972.

Root and Tuber Crops, Plantains and Bananas in Developing Countries: Challenges and Opportunities. Food and Agriculture Organization of the United Nations (FAO). Plant Production and Protection Paper, no. 87. Rome, 1988.

Simmonds, N. W., ed. *Evolution of Crop Plants.* London, 1976.

DEBORAH M. PEARSALL

Psychotropic Flora

Soon after Columbus and his men set foot on land in what came to be called the West Indies, they were confronted by a phenomenon that, like everything else the native inhabitants believed and practiced, was unfamiliar and shocking to them: to contact their gods the Taínos intoxicated themselves with a potent snuff. Commissioned by Columbus on his second voyage in 1496 to record Taíno ceremonies and "antiquities," Ramón Pané described rites in which the natives inhaled cohoba, an intoxicating herb that was "so strong that those who take it lose consciousness," believing themselves to be in communication with the supernatural, while "sorcerers" customarily inhaled the drug together with their patients so as to learn the cause and proper treatment of the affliction.

Since then, ethnobotanists have identified more than a hundred ritual plant hallucinogens, not counting tobacco, which the Spaniards identified with cohoba. Because the custom soon died out in the West Indies, along with

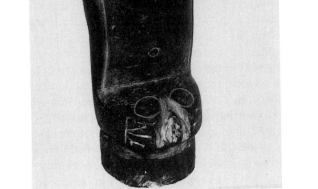

CEREMONIAL SNUFF HOLDER. From the West Indies.

virtually the entire native population, the identification of cohoba as tobacco was accepted until 1916, when an influential American botanist, William A. Safford, insisted that cohoba could not have been tobacco but was the same as *yopo,* the hallucinogenic snuff Indians in Colombia and elsewhere in northern South America derive from the seeds of a leguminous tree, *Anadenanthera peregrina.* Recent research, however, suggests that the Spaniards may well have been right, and that the West Indian cohoba may indeed have been pulverized tobacco of the potent species *Nicotiana rustica.*

The genus *Anadenanthera* also has a highland species, *A. colubrina,* from whose seeds Andean Indians prepared a snuff called *willka. Willka* was used not only in Peru: from bone-dry burials in the Atacama Desert of northern Chile, archaeologists and looters have recovered *willka* powder as well as hundreds of beautifully carved hardwood snuff tablets dating to around A.D. 800.

Snuffs were derived from the *Virola* tree in addition to the two species of *Anadenanthera*. On the Upper Orinoco, some Yamomami Indians and their neighbors prepare a vision-inducing powder from the dried shavings of the inner bark. This is mixed with the powdered leaves of an acanthaceous weed, *Justicia pectoralis,* and the ash of the bark of a leguminous tree, *Elizabetha princeps.* The former, a powerful hallucinogen, is also cultivated and used by itself.

In western Amazonia, Indians brew a powerful hallucinogenic beverage from *Banisteriopsis caapi* and related species, often with the addition of other plants that also contain psychoactive compounds. The drink has many names—Quechua-speakers call it *ayahuasca,* "vine of souls," a name adopted by some non-Quechua peoples east of the Andes. Others call it *caapi, mihi, dapa, pinde,* or *natéma.* The most common admixture is an extract of *Brugmansia,* a tree *Daturas* with showy trumpet-shaped flowers. *Brugmansia* is also used by itself. Shrub *Daturas,* including *D. stramonium,* the so-called jimsonweed of the eastern United States, and *D. inoxia,* the *toloáche* of Mexico and California (from the Aztec *toloátzin*), were employed in divination and curing by Mexican Indians, and in initiations and vision seeking by Indians in California, just as Virginia Indians used *D. stramonium. D. inoxia* is sacred and retains a divinatory use even today among the Pueblo Indians. *Datura* use is not without a certain danger, however. Of all the ritual plant hallucinogens now employed by American Indians, only the solanaceous *Daturas* are so toxic as to pose physiological risk. On the other hand, none is addictive.

Another ritual hallucinogen, of importance in the southern plains at the time of Spanish exploration and, on the archaeological evidence, for more than ten thousand years before, was *Sophora secundiflora.* The red and black seeds were widely employed in the initiation rites of ecstatic-shamanistic medicine societies. Caches of the beans have been found in Texas rock shelters in association with the remains of a long extinct giant bison and projectile points dating between 8400 and 8120 B.C., making *Sophora* the oldest continuously used hallucinogen in the New World. The mescal bean cults died out only in the late nineteenth century A.D.

First mentioned by sixteenth-century Spanish chroniclers among the divine intoxicants of the Aztecs, the little peyote cactus, *Lophophora williamsii,* remains at the core of the indigenous religion of the Huichols of the Sierra Madre Occidental. But it has also achieved a unique role north of Mexico, as a sacrament of a pan-Indian religion, the Native American Church, which has some 250,000 adherents from the Río Grande to the Canadian plains.

Peyote is a veritable factory of alkaloids. More than thirty have been identified, but the one chiefly responsible for the color-saturated visions it induces is mescaline. This is also the principal hallucinogenic alkaloid in San Pedro, *Trichocereus pachanoi,* a tall columnar cactus with a very long history in Andean ritual. First depicted on Peruvian pottery and textiles dating to 1000 B.C., San Pedro continues to play an important role in the curing rituals of Andean folk medicine.

The Spanish colonial authorities tried in vain to stop Mexican Indians from using peyote. But they had no more success with the little cactus than with *ololiuhqui,* as the Aztecs called the revered seeds of the white-flowered morning glory *Turbina corymbosa.* What brought on the extraordinary effects described by the Indians was a matter of controversy until the 1960s, when the Swiss chemist Albert Hofmann identified the hallucinogenic compounds as lysergic acid derivatives, closely related to the synthetic LSD-25 he and an associate had discovered in 1938. *Ololiuhqui* is still used by some Mexican Indians today, as are the seeds of the purple morning glory *Ipomoea violacea.*

Nor were the Spaniards able to stamp out the sacred mushrooms the Aztecs called *teonanácatl,* "divine flesh." At the time of the Conquest, at least half a dozen species seem to have been in ritual use in Mexico, but many more, previously unknown, species have been identified in recent years in Mexico and elsewhere, all of the genus *Psilocybe* and related genera. Several indigenous peoples continue to employ them for divination and curing. In any event, stone sculptures of mushrooms dating to the first millennium B.C. in highland Guatemala and pre-Columbian mushroom effigies of cast gold found in Colombia confirm that veneration of mushrooms was already ancient in the New World when the Spaniards first encountered it nearly five centuries ago and that it was far more widespread than formerly assumed.

BIBLIOGRAPHY

Furst, Peter T. *Hallucinogens and Culture.* San Francisco, 1986.
Schultes, Richard Evans, and Albert Hofmann. *Plants of the Gods.* New York, 1979.

PETER T. FURST

Tobacco

Although the genus *Nicotiana* occurs naturally not only in the Americas but also in parts of Africa, Oceania, and Australia, nowhere but in the New World were any of its more than sixty species cultivated or used for tobacco. Moreover, the largest concentration—almost 60 percent—is in South America. And it is from the South American continent that the genus is believed to have dispersed naturally millions of years before two of Columbus's men, Luis de Torres and Rodrigo de Jerez, became, according to the Admiral's journal entry of November 6, 1492, the first Europeans to see Indians smoke cigars made of the herb called *tabaco* in the Arawakan language.

It was not long before Europeans took up this curious custom and promptly became addicted. "I have known Spaniards in this isle of Hispaniola who were wont to take them," wrote Bartolomé de las Casas of the Indian cigars in his *Apologética historia de las Indias* (c. 1527), "and being reproved for it and told that it was a vicious habit, they replied that it was not in their power to stop taking them." Because Las Casas's work and Columbus's journal were not published until considerably later, the first printed description of tobacco smoking appeared in Gonzalo Fernández de Oviedo's *Historia general y natural de las Indias, islas y tierra-firme del mar océano*, dated 1535. The first books, however, to depict native American tobacco ritual were not European but the Mixtec *Codex Vindobonensis*, or *Codex Vienna*, and a handful of other pre-Hispanic pictorial manuscripts that survived the conquest of Mexico.

Johannes Wilbert, in *Tobacco and Shamanism in South America*, a book on tobacco as a ritual intoxicant of South American shamans and the biochemistry of nicotine intoxication, comments that "man's historic interest in *Nicotiana* has been exclusively because of the nicotine alkaloid it contains." Not all *Nicotianas* synthesize nicotine; some contain it in large amounts, others in small, and some none at all. Hence, writes Wilbert, Indian peoples selected only a dozen or so for tobacco cultivation, of which two, *Nicotiana rustica* and *Nicotiana tabacum*, became widely disseminated throughout the Americas. The former, with a nicotine content as high as 18.76 percent, many times that of Virginia blends, achieved almost the same wide distribution as maize—from the southern limits of agriculture in Chile to Canada. *N. tabacum*, which contains up to half as much nicotine as *N. rustica*, never made it beyond the tropics in pre-Columbian times. Botanically, the *Nicotianas* belong—along with such food plants as the pepper, eggplant, tomato, and potato, and such psychoactive and medicinal species as *Datura*, mandrake, deadly nightshade, and *Atropa belladonna*, and such garden flowers as the petunia—in the family of the Solanaceae (ironically, petunia derives from *petún*, the name the Tupían-speaking Indians of Brazil apply to tobacco).

The designation *Nicotiana rustica* notwithstanding (*rustica* is Latin for "wild"), both it and *N. tabacum* are cultigens, and both are hybrids whose parent species may have been the earliest plants to be cultivated by South American Indians, earlier even than the beginnings of agriculture some eight thousand years ago. *N. rustica* is

almost certainly the older as well as the hardier and more potent; its center of origin is thought to be north-central Peru. *N. tabacum* may have begun on the eastern slopes of the Bolivian Andes, from where it diffused into Amazonia, the Guianas, and ultimately the West Indies, possibly, but not certainly, as late as the early sixteenth century. *N. tabacum* also became the basis of the commercial blends, *N. rustica* having been found to be too potent for general consumption. In any event, if, as Columbus's men thought, the potent snuff with which they saw the native people of the West Indies intoxicate themselves in visionary rituals was tobacco, it would have had to be the nicotine-richer *N. rustica*, the species of choice in South American tobacco shamanism as well as the *piciétl* of the Aztecs and the "Indian tobacco" of eastern North America.

South American Indians ingest tobacco in many more ways than inhaling its smoke or taking it in powder form. Wilbert lists the following: snuffing, smoking, drinking, chewing, licking, sucking, sniffing, and eating. Tobacco is made into poultices, pastes, jellies, juice, and enemas. It is absorbed through the mucous membranes, skin, intestines, eyes, nose, and ears. It is given to the gods and spirits as their sacramental, indeed, their only proper food, blown in the shaman's spit or as therapeutic smoke on his patients, pressed on wounds and stings and foodstuffs as a magical as well as practical disinfectant, burned for divination, and used externally against insects and internally against worms and intestinal parasites. It is taken to enhance vitality, reduce pain, induce vomiting for physical and ritual purification, relieve hunger and thirst, conjure the spirits, exorcise demons, and cure disease. Above all, it is smoked or otherwise ingested by shamans in enormous quantities to trigger the ecstatic-visionary trance state that is everywhere the hallmark of shamanism and that other practitioners of the shamanic arts attain with the hallucinogenic flora or by nonchemical means.

As Wilbert notes, the action of nicotine absorbed into the system in such prodigious quantities is deeply implicated in almost every characteristic of South American shamanism, from the experience of initiatory sickness, death, and resurrection, and other ordeals of the shaman's novitiate to various bodily transformations, such as the shaman's special guttural and dark-timbered speaking and singing voice, the experience of "magical heat," distinctive sight and improved night vision, and combative behavior.

Generally speaking, tobacco did not become a recreational drug until it was adopted by Europeans and rapidly diffused throughout the Old World. Ironically, only after it had circled almost the entire globe and arrived among tribal Siberians did it once again attain some of the magico-religious status and the connection with shamanism it had enjoyed and, at least in the case of *N. rustica*, still enjoys, among Native Americans.

BIBLIOGRAPHY

Furst, Jill L. *Codex Vindobonensis Mexicanus I: A Commentary.* Albany, N.Y., 1977.

Las Casas, Bartolomé de. "Apologética historia de las Indias." In *Nueva Bibliotéca de Autores Españoles,* edited by M. Serrano y Sanz. Madrid, 1909.

Oviedo y Valdés, Gonzalo Fernández de. *Historia general y natural de las Indias, islas y terra-firme del mar océano.* Asuncíon del Paraguay, 1944.

Wilbert, Johannes. "Tobacco and Shamanistic Ecstasy among the Warao Indians of Venezuela." In *Flesh of the Gods: The Ritual Use of Hallucinogens.* Edited by Peter T. Furst. New York, 1972. Revised edition, Prospect Heights, Ill., 1990.

Wilbert, Johannes. *Tobacco and Shamanism in South America.* New Haven, Conn., 1987.

PETER T. FURST

FLORENCE. When Columbus was born in 1451, Florence was one of the premier cities in Italy and, indeed, in Europe. Its urban population of some fifty thousand placed it among the five largest cities in Italy; it governed a territory of forty-five hundred square miles. Florence had a republican government, though its polity was gradually drifting under the control of the Medici family in the later fifteenth century. As one of the five most powerful states on the Italian peninsula, it had been involved in a long series of debilitating wars, which finally ended in 1454 with the Peace of Lodi. Thereafter, the city enjoyed a forty-year period of peace, broken only sporadically by minor conflicts.

Florence's power and reputation were based upon its productive and diverse economy, which for centuries had played an important role in European and Levantine commerce. The city had developed a thriving cloth industry, specializing in the production of fine woolens and silks. Its merchants were active in every major port in the Mediterranean and in European markets from London to Budapest. In the fifteenth century, Florentine galley fleets regularly sailed to England, the Low Countries, and the Levant. The most prosperous segment of the city's economy was banking, which involved particularly the papal finances. The wealth of the Medici and that of other leading families (Strozzi, Pazzi, Bardi, Salviati, Altoviti) came largely from the profits gained from the papal fisc.

In 1300, Pope Boniface VIII had called the Florentines the "fifth element" in the universe, referring to their economic power and their ubiquitous mercantile presence throughout Christendom. Two centuries later, the city was still known for its entrepreneurial activities, but even more for its cultural achievements. In the early 1400s,

Florence was the laboratory for the creation of a new Renaissance culture based upon the revival of classical antiquity. Later in the century, when Lorenzo de' Medici was Florence's leading citizen, the city became (in Eugenio Garin's words) "the cultural capital of the world." It counted among its artists such luminaries as Andrea del Verrocchio, Filippo Lippi, Leonardo da Vinci, and Michelangelo, and among its scholars Marsilio Ficino, Angelo Poliziano, Christoforo Landino, and Paolo del Pozzo Toscanelli. On June 25, 1474, Toscanelli, a distinguished scientist, wrote a letter to a Portuguese cleric, Fernam Martins, in which he suggested the possibility of reaching the Orient by sailing westward. A copy of this document survives in Columbus's handwriting; it was a key piece of evidence used by the Genoese explorer to justify his Atlantic voyage.

After Lorenzo de' Medici's death in 1492, Florence's fortunes declined. The city was occupied in 1494 by the French army of King Charles VIII, and for the next four decades it experienced almost continuous warfare, political upheavals, and economic disruption, culminating in its siege and occupation by imperial forces in 1530. Florence's republican government was replaced by a Medici principate under Duke Cosimo I (r. 1537–1574). In these troubled years, many Florentines chose to pursue their fortunes abroad. Two of the city's most illustrious exiles were Amerigo Vespucci (1454–1512) and Giovanni da Verrazano (1480?–1527?), who participated in early voyages to the Americas.

BIBLIOGRAPHY

Brucker, Gene. *Renaissance Florence.* Berkeley and Los Angeles, 1983.

Butters, Humfrey. *Governors and Government in Early Sixteenth-Century Florence.* Oxford, 1985.

Garin, Eugenio. *Portraits from the Quattrocento.* New York, 1972.

Hale, John R. *Florence and the Medici: The Pattern of Control.* London, 1977.

Weinstein, Donald. *Savonarola and Florence.* Princeton, N.J., 1970.

GENE A. BRUCKER

FLORIDA, LA. For discussion of the Indians of La Florida, see *Indian America,* article on *Indians of La Florida.*

FONSECA, ALFONSO DE (1418–1473), archbishop of Santiago and Toledo. A descendant of a noble and influential Galician family, Alfonso (or Alonso) de Fonseca began his ecclesiastical career as archdeacon of the cathedral of Santiago de Compostela, a see that, by the late fifteenth century, had almost become the private fief of the Fonseca family. Fonseca rose to prominence as chaplain to the Infante Enrique, heir to the Castilian throne, being named bishop of Ávila in 1445 and archbishop of the wealthy see of Seville in 1453. In 1460 his nephew, also named Alfonso de Fonseca, the archbishop of Santiago de Compostela, faced popular unrest and opposition in his diocese. Uncle and nephew exchanged ecclesiastical dignities, supposedly because the elder Fonseca had the energy and connections to deal more successfully with the problems. Once the disturbances were quelled, however, the younger Alfonso refused to vacate the see of Seville, and his uncle had to seek legal recourse from the pope to recover his position in Seville. This he finally did in 1463.

Active in Castilian politics during the reigns of Juan II and of Enrique IV, Fonseca often found himself opposing the royal favorite, the enigmatic Álvaro de Luna, during the turbulent years of the early and mid-fifteenth century. After Enrique IV's ascent to the throne in 1454, Fonseca served him well during the first years of his reign, but the archbishop joined the rebellious magnates in their anti-royal league (the League of Burgos) in 1464. That same year, Fonseca played an important role in the "farce of Ávila," the ritual and theatrical dethroning and humbling of Enrique IV's effigy. Nevertheless, although opposed to the king, Fonseca worked for the reconciliation of the king and his half-brother, the Infante Alfonso, the magnates' candidate. At the death of the latter, the archbishop of Seville returned to Enrique's allegiance. It was in this later role as the king's adviser that Fonseca was instrumental in the drawing up of the Pact of the Toros de Guisando, the agreement that served as the legal basis for Isabel's claim to the Castilian throne upon Enrique IV's death in 1474.

BIBLIOGRAPHY

Fernández, Luis Suárez. *Nobleza y monarquía: Puntos de vista sobre la historia castellana del siglo XV.* Valladolid, 1975.
Mariéjol, J. H. *The Spain of Ferdinand and Isabella.* Translated and edited by Benjamin Keen. New Brunswick, N.J., 1961.
MacKay, Angus. "Ritual and Propaganda in Fifteenth-Century Castile." *Past and Present* 107 (1985): 3–43.

TEOFILO F. RUIZ

FONSECA, ANTONIO DE (d. 1533), financial adviser to the Spanish Crown. The brothers Antonio de Fonseca and Juan Rodríguez de Fonseca dominated the administrative and accounting affairs of the Indies between the years 1493, when Juan was in charge of provisioning and outfitting Columbus's second voyage, and 1533, when Antonio died. Antonio, the older, was lord of the towns of Coca and Alaejos in the north of Castile. A close ally of

King Fernando, he negotiated the marriage contract between Princess Juana and Philip of Burgundy in 1495 and became chief auditor (contador mayor) of Castile in 1503. As auditor of the Castilian royal revenues from the royal patrimony and the Indies, Antonio influenced the policies of the new king, Juana's son Charles. Together, the Fonseca brothers enjoyed a considerable income from the Americas in the form of monopolies and encomienda revenues. When Charles needed cash to secure election as Holy Roman Emperor, Antonio advanced him large sums (some speculate as much as 16,000 ducats), drawn against future revenues from the Americas. The Fonseca brothers opposed efforts to reform Spanish administration of American Indians, which would have reduced their own income. In May 1520 Charles left the government of Castile under the administration of a royal council that included both Antonio, as captain general of the Kingdom of Castile, and Juan. Antonio's military and political blunders during the Comunero Revolt, the tax rebellion that swept over Castile in 1520–1521, weakened the influence of the Fonseca brothers over American affairs, although Antonio became grand commander (comendador mayor) of the Order of Santiago in 1526.

BIBLIOGRAPHY

Giménez Fernández, Manuel. *Bartolomé de las Casas.* Vol. 2, *Capellán de s.m. Carlos I, poblador de Cumaná (1517–1523).* Seville, 1960.
Haliczer, Stephen. *The Comuneros of Castile: The Forging of a Revolution, 1475–1521.* Madison, Wis., 1981.
Lovett, A. W. *Early Habsburg Spain, 1517–1598.* Oxford, 1986.

HELEN NADER

FONSECA, JUAN RODRÍGUEZ DE (1451–1523), prelate and adviser to the Spanish court. Fonseca was born in the city of Toro, son of the lord of the towns of Coca and Alaejos and his second wife. His family intended him for a career in the church and was sufficiently close to the monarchy to place him at the seat of power from the beginning of his education as a priest and apprenticeship for a prelacy. They sent him to the royal court, where he became a member of the household of Queen Isabel's confessor, Hernando de Talavera. He received several benefices that gave him a comfortable income and in 1492 formed part of the team that negotiated Aragón's annexation of Rosellón and La Cerdagne from France. Juan accompanied Fernando and Isabel to Barcelona, where he was ordained as a subdeacon on March 2, 1493, and as a priest on April 6.

Fonseca was present when Columbus arrived at the royal court to report on his first voyage to America, and on May 20 the monarchs appointed Fonseca to create a fleet in Seville for Columbus's second voyage. Certainly he succeeded—the fleet counted seventeen ships and twelve hundred men—but Columbus had preferred a smaller fleet that could leave right away. The two men were locked in conflict from then on, because the monarchs entrusted Fonseca with responsibility for supervising the European side of Spain's transatlantic trade.

In April 1495, Fonseca established regulations and procedures for trade with the Americas. These included government contracts with joint stock companies to systematically explore the South American coast (these expeditions are called the Andalusian voyages), restriction of the Americas trade to ports where royal customs officials could inspect the cargoes, posting of royal customs officials to the Americas to inspect the loading and unloading of cargoes there, and issuance of government clearances for individuals to travel to the Americas.

The Americas trade grew so much that on January 1, 1503, the monarchs established a branch of the royal treasury, the House of Trade (Casa de la Contratación), in Seville to house the customs, mint, navigation, licensing, and judicial offices. Fonseca probably recommended the regulations that went into effect on that date, as well as the expanded and revised regulations for the House of Trade that were issued on June 13, 1510, and March 18, 1511. Fonseca shaped policy for all the Americas trade until his death in 1523. The next year, Charles V created a royal council, the Consejo de Indias, to replace the position Fonseca had held.

Although the Americas had been Fonseca's principal responsibility, he had also carried out many diplomatic assignments for the monarchs and advanced his career in the church. He escorted members of the royal family to and from the Netherlands and England in 1499, 1500, and 1501; acted as witness of Queen Isabel's will in 1504 and carried the news of her death to the Netherlands; attended King Fernando on his deathbed in 1516; and welcomed the new king Charles in Aguilar in 1517. In 1518, he organized the fleet for Ferdinand Magellan's expedition to circumnavigate the world, and the next year he organized the fleet that transported the royal court to Germany for Charles's coronation.

BIBLIOGRAPHY

Alcocer y Martínez, Mariano. *Juan Rodríguez de Fonseca.* Valladolid, 1926.

Giménez Fernández, Manuel. *Bartolomé de las Casas.* 2 vols. Seville, 1953–1960.

"Ordinances for the Casa de la Contratación, 1503." In *The Conquerors and the Conquered.* Vol. 1 of *New Iberian World: A Documentary History of the Discovery and Settlement of Latin America to the Early 17th Century.* Edited by John H. Parry and Robert G. Keith. 5 vols. New York, 1984.

Helen Nader

FONTANAROSSA, SUSANNA (c. 1425–c. 1480), mother of Christopher Columbus. Daughter of Jacobi de Fontanarubea (Giacomo Fontanarossa), Susanna Fontanarossa was born to an affluent Catholic family. The name Susanna was very common in the Catholic families of Liguria, owing, in part, to the fact that in the middle of the fifteenth century a Genoese pope had restored the church of Santa Susanna in the center of Rome.

Her family owned substantial real estate in Quezzi, a little village in the low-lying valley of Bisagno (part of the present-day city of Genoa). In the fifteenth century, it was necessary to go through the Olivella gate, where Christopher Columbus's father was custodian for two terms, in order to travel from the valley of Bisagno to Genoa.

Susanna Fontanarossa brought to her marriage to Domenico Colombo a dowry of a house with land. This property was soon sold; a record of the sale, dated May 25, 1471, is in the State Archives in Genoa. (Columbus's mother is also mentioned in two other documents, dated August 7, 1473, and January 23, 1477, which are found in the State Archives in Savona.)

The marriage between Susanna Fontanarossa and Domenico Colombo was apparently harmonious. The names of five children are known: Christopher (Cristoforo), Giovanni Pelegrino, Bartolomé (Bartolomeo), Diego (Giacomo), and Bianchinetta. It is likely that she bore other children, for, at this time, child mortality exceeded 50 percent. The exact date of her death is unknown, but it is probable that she died around 1480.

BIBLIOGRAPHY

"Albero genealogico della famiglia Colombo." In part 2, vol. 1 of *Raccolta di documenti e studi pubblicati dalla R. Commissione Colombiana pel quarto centenario dalla scoperta dell'America.* Rome, 1896.

Genoa, City of. *Christopher Columbus: Documents and Proofs of His Genoese Origin.* English-German ed. Bergamo, 1932.

Taviani, Paolo Emilio. *Cristoforo Colombo: Genius of the Sea.* Rome, 1990.

Paolo Emilio Taviani

FOOD. See *Equipment, Clothing, and Rations.*

FOURTH VOYAGE. See *Voyages of Columbus.*

FRANCE. In the Age of Exploration, France was a monarchy ruled by the Valois dynasty. Except for Charles VIII (r. 1483–1498), whose strong-willed sister Anne of Beaujeu governed during his first years, the kings of this era—Charles VII (r. 1422–1461), Louis XI (r. 1461–1483), Louis XII (r. 1498–1515), Francis I (r. 1515–1547), and

Henry II (r. 1547–1559)—came to the throne as adults and provided France with generally strong rule. The kingdom they governed was the most populous and largest in western Europe. It had a population of perhaps as many as 14 million people in 1500, and the number was rapidly increasing. Containing much of the best agricultural land in Europe, France exported considerable grain and, of course, wine. French was the language of most of the people; but in Brittany, Gascony, and the Midi, local dialects were in use, and the rural folk probably understood only a few phrases of French.

France had begun to expand beyond its long-term medieval borders but still was about 20 percent smaller than the modern republic. Provence and Dauphiné had recently been incorporated into the realm, but many regions of modern France—Calais, Flanders, Artois, Lorraine, Alsace, the Franche-Comté, Savoy, Roussillon, and northern Navarre—remained outside of it. All were the objects of much diplomatic and military activity.

Before France could expand its borders farther, the monarchy had to gain greater control over the feudal magnates. Louis XI did much in that respect by crushing the League of the Common Weal in 1465. His skillful intrigue and diplomacy led to the death of Charles the Bold of Burgundy at the hands of the Swiss at the Battle of Nancy in 1477. Louis seized control of the duchy of Burgundy, but he was not able to pressure Charles's heiress, Mary of Burgundy, into marrying his son. Instead she married Maximilian of Habsburg and passed most of Charles's lands, including Flanders and the Franche-Comté, to the House of Austria. When Charles VIII married Anne of Brittany in 1491, the last autonomous principality of medieval France passed under royal control.

The Hundred Years' War had come to an end in 1453, but continued English control of Calais and its claim to the French throne resulted in numerous episodes of war until 1559. Nonetheless, by 1494 Charles VIII was secure enough to lead an army of thirty thousand men and the best artillery train yet seen in the first French invasion of Italy. His goal was to make good a two-hundred-year-old French claim to the Kingdom of Naples. Brushing aside ineffective Italian resistance, Charles marched to Naples and proclaimed himself king. It was a member of the House of Aragón whom Charles ousted, however, and Fernando of Aragón organized an anti-French league against Charles. Although Charles quickly returned to France, the army he left behind to occupy Naples remained there until 1503, when a Spanish force crushed it in the Battle of Cerignola.

The second French invasion, led by Louis XII in 1499, and the third invasion, led by Francis I in 1515, centered on Milan. When Francis claimed the title of duke of Milan

FRANCIS I. Portrait by Jean Clouet.

after his victory at Marignano (1515), he gave Holy Roman Emperor Charles V a pretext for war, since the duchy was nominally an imperial fief. The Valois-Habsburg feud was fought in Flanders, the Franche-Comté, Roussillon, and Navarre, but Milan was still the main prize. The Battle of Pavia in which Francis was captured was fought near there in 1525. His ransom, agreed upon in 1530, required paying 3 million crowns and giving sovereignty over Flanders and Milan to Charles V. Nonetheless, hostilities continued, and the French sought to balance the vast array of Habsburg forces with a tacit alliance with the Ottoman Empire, extending to the use of Toulon as a base for the Turkish fleet in 1542. The war continued into the reigns of Henry II and Philip II, but it ended with the Peace of Cateau-Cambrésis in 1559. France conceded Spanish control of Italy but gained Calais and the three bishoprics of Lorraine.

The French army that fought those wars had undergone vast change in a century's time. In 1439 Charles VII had created fifteen lance companies, each to consist of one hundred armored lancers and five mounted support troops for each lancer, paid for by the king. Recruited from the nobility, the lance companies remained the heart of the French army until 1559, but by then the use of mounted pistoleers was threatening their primacy. Efforts to create a native infantry foundered on the long-ingrained fear among French nobles of putting weapons in the hands of their peasants. France had to depend on foreign mercenaries, mostly Swiss and German. The special strength of the French army was its artillery. A vast number of high-quality bronze guns, which fired iron balls instead of stone, gave the French an extraordinary ability to reduce fortifications until the design of forts began to change after 1500. The French also developed the first mobile gun carriages, permitting the artillery to keep up with the army.

The major French contribution to war at sea was the gunport. French seamen began to raid Iberian transoceanic shipping shortly after 1492. Their success led Charles V to create the flota system with its galleons for transporting treasure and goods from the Americas. The acquisition of Provence in 1480 provided the French with several ports to base a galley fleet for use in the Mediterranean. In the 1500s this fleet made its mark largely in joint operations with the Turkish fleet.

The revenues for the enhanced French military came largely from a property tax, the taille. In 1444 Charles VII gained the power to levy it without permission of the Estates General, and it quickly became permanent, but by 1465 the nobles and the clergy had obtained a permanent exemption. In 1550 the taille provided 80 percent of royal taxation. The clergy irregularly provided a "gift" of 10 percent of its income; this *décime* became annual under Francis I. Although taxes and the traditional revenues from tolls and the royal domain reached 8.3 million livres by 1547, royal expenses always exceeded revenues, and the kings resorted to borrowing. In 1559 royal indebtedness totaled some 43 million livres.

The Estates General was supposed to control taxation, but the inability of its three constituent bodies, the clergy, the nobility, and the commoners, to work together undercut its effectiveness. It met only sporadically until 1506 and then not again until 1561. The existence of provincial estates in most of the realm, which were far more likely to agree to royal demands for revenues, also undermined the Estates General. Far more powerful a factor in French government was the Parlement, the law court. The Parlement had authority to register royal edicts, which could not take effect until it did so, but the king retained the right to go in person to require that edicts be registered. The chief administrative officer of the state, the chancellor, usually was chosen from among the presidents of the Parlement. His appointment was for life, and his purview extended to virtually all the routine matters of government. Issues of special importance were decided by the royal council, over which the king usually presided and which varied in size from one reign to the next.

The theoretically absolute power of the monarchy was also limited by the presence of numerous corporate bodies in the realm such as the nobility, the cities, and the guilds. The most powerful was the church. The French church was imbued with Gallicanism and claimed autonomy for itself from the papacy in such matters as finances and episcopal appointments. The key Gallican document was the Pragmatic Sanction of Bourges of 1439, which ended the payment of funds to Rome and papal appointment of bishops for French sees. The papacy regarded the situation as schismatic and was quick to accept Francis I's offer to negotiate a new arrangement in 1515. The resulting Concordat of Bologna, which remained in effect until 1790, gave the right to nominate bishops to the king with papal approval and permitted the transfer of funds to Rome.

The concordat provided the French monarchs with a powerful incentive to remain Catholic, since there was now little benefit in their becoming Protestant. The kings did little to correct the abuses in the church, where corruption and ignorance among the clergy were commonplace. Early French Protestantism, however, was disorganized and had little success until John Calvin, himself French, began to provide strong leadership and an attractive theology. After 1550 the number of Huguenots, as French Protestants became known, began to increase rapidly, and by 1559 they may have reached 15 percent of the population.

The monarchy's efforts to repress religious dissent, the attraction of many nobles to the new religion, and the weakness of the monarchy after Henry II's accidental death in 1559 all contributed to the Wars of Religion that wracked France until 1598. Until they were concluded, they distracted the French from overseas exploration. French interest in the lands revealed by Iberian expeditions was limited in the years after 1492. Charles VIII had ignored a request from Bartolomé Colón for aid for a voyage across the Atlantic. Having no claim to any newly discovered lands, France was left out of the papal Line of Demarcation of 1493. Francis I would later ask to see "where in Adam's will the world was thus divided." French fishermen worked the waters off Newfoundland before 1500, but little is known of their voyages. Frenchmen also had reached Brazil before 1504. Royal support for exploration began only in 1523 with Giovanni da Verrazano's voyage along the east coast of North America. It was followed by Jacques Cartier's voyages to eastern Canada from 1534 to 1542. Under Henry II, Nicolas de Villegaignon attempted to found a colony in Brazil, but Portuguese attacks and the death of the king doomed it.

Thus in the century after Columbus discovered the New World, France was little involved in the discovery and conquest of the new lands. Only after 1600 did the French follow up on the claim to Canada that Cartier's voyages had created.

[See also *Colonization,* article on *French Colonization.*]

BIBLIOGRAPHY

Baumgartner, Frederic J. *Henry II, King of France.* Durham, N.C., 1988.

Bridge, John. *A History of France from the Death of Louis XI.* 5 vols. New York, 1929.

Febvre, Lucien. *Life in Renaissance France.* Translated by Marian Rothstein. Cambridge, Mass., 1977.

Kendall, Paul. *Louis XI: The Universal Spider.* New York, 1971.

Knecht, R. J. *Francis I.* Cambridge, 1982.

Labande-Mailfert, Yvonne. *Charles VIII et son milieu.* Paris, 1975.

Lavisse, Ernest. *Histoire de France.* Vols. 4–5. Paris, 1900–1911.

Quilliet, Bernard. *Louis XII: Père du peuple.* Paris, 1986.

Vale, Charles. *Charles VII.* Berkeley, Calif., 1977.

FREDERIC J. BAUMGARTNER

FUNCHAL. The capital city of the Madeira Islands, Funchal is a seaport situated on the south coast of Madeira Island, 978 kilometers from Lisbon. It was officially recognized as a town *(vila)* in 1452 by Afonso V, king of Portugal. On November 1, 1450, the duchy of Funchal had been granted by royal charter to João Gonçalves Zarco, whose family ruled as lord proprietors until 1497. The city's population in 1480 is estimated at eight thousand. It was designated a city in 1508 by Manuel I. Funchal is named for *funcho,* or fennel.

Italians dominated the sugar trade in Funchal from 1470 through the 1480s. Among these merchants were Baptista Lomelino, Francisco Galvo, Micer Leão, João Antonio, Bartolomeu Marchioni, Jeronimo Sernigi, Luis Doria, and Christopher Columbus. Columbus visited Funchal at least three times and spent from one to two years (1479–1481) using it for his base of operations while representing Genoese firms in Lisbon.

On his first visit in 1478, Columbus represented Paolo Di Negro, a powerful Jewish financier, for whom Columbus purchased a cargo of sugar to deliver to Genoa. When he arrived in Genoa, the firm hailed him before a notary to explain under oath why the order was not complete. On August 25, 1479, Columbus gave his age as twenty-seven, related that he was sailing to Lisbon the next morning, and testified that he had not been given credit to cover the whole order.

Before his second visit to Funchal, Columbus married Felipa Perestrelo Moniz in 1479 in Lisbon. Their son Diego was born the next year while he was living with his brother-in-law, the governor of Porto Santo, an island to the northeast of Madeira.

During this time, Columbus made friends with Jean de Esmenaut (João Esmeraldo), a Flemish merchant exporter from Picardy who owned extensive lands southwest of Funchal. It is traditionally claimed that Columbus lived at the residence of Esmeraldo when he was in Funchal. Columbus visited Funchal late in 1481 when he joined Diogo d'Azambuja on a voyage to the Gulf of Guinea, and then many times from 1483 to 1484 as master or officer of trading expeditions to São Jorge da Mina. His last visit to Funchal, in 1498, was at the beginning of his third voyage across the Atlantic. The landfall was for the purpose of taking on water and wood, and Columbus remarked, "In the town I was given a fine reception and much entertainment, for I am well known here, having been a resident for some time."

[See also *Madeira.*]

BIBLIOGRAPHY

Carita, Rui. *História da Madeira, 1420–1566.* Funchal, 1989.

César, César Figueira. *Ilha da Madeira.* Funchal, 1982.

Cossart, Noël. *Madeira: The Island Vineyard.* London, 1984.

Farrow, John, and Susan Farrow. *Madeira: Pearl of the Atlantic.* London, 1987.

Silva, J. Donald. *Bibliography on the Madeira Islands.* Durham, N.H., 1987.

J. DONALD SILVA

G

GALLO, ANTONIO (d. around 1510), Genoese chronicler. Gallo recorded the most reliable information we have about the early years of Columbus's life. A notary public, he lived and worked in the second half of the fifteenth century and the beginning of the sixteenth. From 1491 to 1510, he was chancellor in the office of the San Giorgio Bank. Gallo wrote three Latin commentaries on Genoese history, to which he added a fourth on Columbus's voyages. They were published by the historian Lodovico Antonio Muratori in his *Rerum Italicarum scriptores* (1723–1738). The importance of these commentaries as a source of information on Columbus has been demonstrated by Gianbattista Spotorno in his *Literary History of Liguria* and was confirmed by a little codex found in the State Archives of Genoa. This codex attests to the relationship, based on interests and friendship, between Gallo and the relatives of Columbus. Gallo declares that he saw a letter signed by Columbus, from which he took some of the information he records. His commentary was compiled between 1496 and 1498—that is, after Columbus's second voyage and before his third.

Gallo's testimony is of exceptional value, for it confirms the many notarial documents that have been found in the Archives of Genoa and Savona. He notes, for example, Christopher and Bartolomé were brothers of Ligurian nationality who were born of plebeian parents in Genoa and that their father was a wool weaver who lived in the quarter of Sant' Andrea's Gate.

BIBLIOGRAPHY

Belgrano, L. T. *Relazione sulla casa abitata da Colombo.* Genoa, 1887.
Gallo, Antonio. *De navigatione Columbi per inaccessum ante Oceanum comentariolum.* Manuscript of 1506, published by A. Muratori, in book 23, part 1 of *Rerum Italicarum scriptores,* edited by E. Pandiani. Città di Castello, 1910.
Colombo, Fernando. *Le historie della vita e dei fatti dell' Ammiraglio Don Cristoforo Colombo.* Vol. 8 of *Nuova Raccolta Colombiana,* edited by Paolo Emilio Tavaini and Ilaria Caraci. Rome, 1991.
Staglieno, M. *Il borgo di S. Stefano ai tempi di Colombo e le case di Domenico Colombo.* Genoa, 1881.
Taviani, Paolo Emilio. *Christoforo Colombo: Genius of the Sea.* Rome, 1990.

Paolo Emilio Taviani
Translated from Italian by Rodica Diaconescu-Blumenfeld

GAMA, VASCO DA (1460?–1524), discoverer of the maritime route to India. Da Gama was admiral of the Indian Ocean, the first count of Vidigueira, sixth governor of Portuguese India, and its second viceroy. The date and place of his birth are uncertain, but he may have been born at Sines, a seaport in the south of Portugal, where his father, Estêvão da Gama, became civil governor after 1478. His mother, Isabel Sodré, was a granddaughter on her mother's side of a Sudley, who settled in Portugal.

Nearly ten years after Bartolomeu Dias rounded the Cape of Good Hope (1488), King Manuel I made plans to continue that historic voyage. To that end, he appointed Vasco da Gama commander of a fleet of four ships, which departed from Lisbon on July 8, 1497. Books, maps, and charts were supplied by Diogo Ortiz de Vilhegas, titular bishop of Tangiers and one of the three royal commissioners who had discredited Columbus's plans for a voyage to Cipangu (Japan).

On July 15 the fleet sailed past the Canary Islands. The following night the ships became separated in a fog but came together July 26 at the Cape Verde island of Santiago, where they remained for a week. Leaving the Cape Verdes on August 3, they steered southwestward into an unknown ocean. To escape from the doldrums and currents of the Gulf of Guinea, where Dias's experience had shown that unfavorable weather might be expected, Da Gama conceived the bold idea of shaping a circular course through the Atlantic in order to reach the Cape of Good Hope. In September, the fleet reached its westernmost limit, coming within six hundred miles of South America, and then headed back to the cape. On November 7 the ships dropped anchor at St. Helena, a bay on the west coast of Cape Province. Since leaving the Cape Verdes the fleet had spent ninety-six days in the South Atlantic and had sailed fully forty-five hundred miles. No navigator of whom there is any authentic record had ever completed so long a voyage without sight of land. Columbus himself had covered only twenty-six hundred miles between his departure from the Canary Islands and his first landfall at San Salvador.

Da Gama's fleet remained at St. Helena for eight days to careen the ships, and on Thursday, November 16, the voyage was resumed. Owing to contrary winds, however, they were unable to double the cape until the twenty-second. Three days later they anchored in Mossel Bay, where they remained for thirteen days, breaking up the

VASCO DA GAMA. From *O sucesso dos visoreis*, by Lizuarte de Abreu, mid-sixteenth century. Colored ink drawing.

store ship and transferring its contents to the other vessels. On December 8 the fleet set sail but soon encountered a dangerous storm that forced them to run under bare poles. Eight days later they passed the Great Fish River, the farthest point reached by Dias. During the next five days they encountered considerable difficulty because of the Mozambique current, which at times made them run backward. They got past this obstacle and on December 25 reached Natal, whence they followed the coast. On January 11 they stopped at the mouth of the Limpopo River, and on the twenty-fourth they anchored in the estuary of the Kilimane where they saw the first signs of Eastern civilization. For thirty-two days, from January 24 to February 24, they remained there, careening and repairing the ships and nursing the crew through an epidemic of scurvy. They stopped successively at Mozambique on March 22, at Mombasa on April 7, and at Malindi on April 13. Contrary to what had happened to them in Mozambique and Mombasa, where they had to defend themselves against Muslim machinations, they were well treated in Malindi. The sultan there gave them a Gujerati pilot with whom they departed on April 24.

On May 20, less than a month later, they anchored in front of Calicut, India, where Da Gama spent several months in negotiations over trade with the local rajah, or *samuri*, as he was called. At first, the Portuguese were made welcome, but later the *samuri*'s attitude changed, probably owing to the intrigues of the local Muslim merchants who feared the loss of their trade monopoly. Finally, Da Gama decided to return home, convinced that only a stronger expedition than his would have the power to bring negotiations to a successful conclusion.

At the end of August 1498, the fleet turned homeward. This time, the crossing of the Indian Ocean took three months and was beset with almost insuperable difficulties—calms, contrary winds, and violent attacks of scurvy, which decimated the crews. On January 7, 1499, the fleet anchored at Malindi where, for lack of hands, *São Rafael* was burned and the crew distributed between the other two ships. On March 20 the ships, *São Gabriel* and *Berrio*, rounded the cape together, but a month later they were parted by a storm. *Berrio* held on its way and entered Lisbon harbor on July 10, 1499, two years and two days after it had left, while Vasco da Gama proceeded to Cape Verde. From there he dispatched *São Gabriel* to Lisbon, while he took his dying brother Paulo da Gama (in a hired ship) to the Azores, where he expired the following day. Vasco da Gama reached Lisbon on September 8, 1499, and made a triumphal entry into the city nine days later, receiving many honors and rewards from King Manuel I.

There is no doubt that Da Gama's outward voyage was the finest feat of seamanship recorded up to that time, far greater than Columbus's. It took 209 days and covered a distance of over twelve thousand miles, five times that

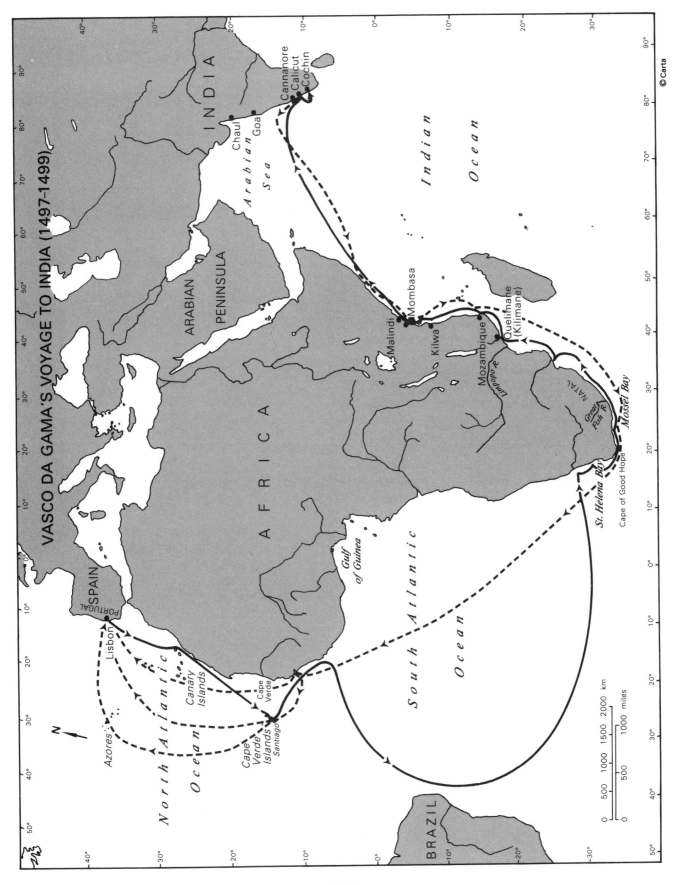

VASCO DA GAMA'S VOYAGE TO INDIA (1497-1499)

INDIA

Cannanore
Calicut
Cochin

Chaul
Goa

Arabian
Sea

Indian
Ocean

Mombasa

Malindi
Kilwa

Mozambique
Quelimane
(Kilimane)

Limpopo R.

NATAL

Great Fish R.

Mossel Bay

St. Helena Bay

Cape of Good Hope

South Atlantic
Ocean

AFRICA

Gulf
of Guinea

ARABIAN
PENINSULA

SPAIN

PORTUGAL

Lisbon

North Atlantic
Ocean

Canary
Islands

Cape
Verde

Cape Verde
Islands
Santiago

Azores

N

BRAZIL

500 1000 1500 2000 km
0   500   1000 miles

© Carta

289

traversed by Columbus. Not only did Columbus have a much shorter distance to travel, but, favored by the wind, he could proceed almost straight from the Canaries to the Caribbean. In scientific knowledge, Da Gama also proved himself the superior, for the accuracy of his charts was in marked contrast to the errors made by Columbus. In the late fifteenth and early sixteenth centuries, the general goal was to reach the spice countries. Thus the results of Columbus's voyages were disappointing, but the news of the arrival of the Portuguese at Calicut stirred the minds of people in every country and filled them with wonder, envy, or alarm. Though his diplomatic mission was a failure, owing to the enmity of the Muslims, he had found India and brought back samples of its products.

Vasco da Gama made two more voyages to India, in 1502 as commander of a fleet of twenty ships, and in 1524 as viceroy of Portuguese India. The highlights of his second voyage included a stop at Kilwa on July 12, 1502, where he forced the East African sultan to become tributary to Portugal, though according to historian Fernão Lopes de Castanheda, the tribute was paid by the hostage himself, who knew he would not be ransomed. On his approach to the coast of India, Da Gama captured a ship underway to Mecca, confiscated the cargo, and set it afire, killing most of the occupants, with the exception of twenty children who were later baptized. He committed many other cruel and barbarous acts against the Muslims and bombarded the unfortunate city of Calicut, all in the name of avenging the ill treatment accorded Pedro Álvares Cabral two years before. In Cochin he signed a treaty of friendship with the rajah and set up a factory, and he did the same in Cannanore. His ships fully laden, on December 28, 1502, Da Gama left for home with a squadron of thirteen ships. After passing Mozambique, he was struck by a storm during which one of the ships became separated from the fleet, but apart from that, the rest of the voyage home was uneventful. He reached Lisbon on September 1, 1503, where he paraded his accomplishments before an admiring crowd, preceded by his page who was carrying a basin full of the gold tribute he had exacted from the sultan of Kilwa as well as the two treaties he had signed with Cochin and Cannanore. In addition to many other honors and emoluments, King Manuel I rewarded him with the titles of admiral of the Indian Seas and count of Vidigueira.

Twenty-one years later, when the affairs of Portuguese India had begun to decline, Vasco da Gama was again called on, this time by King João III (r. 1521–1557), in the hope that he could improve matters. On April 9, 1524, he departed from Lisbon, with an appointment as viceroy of Portuguese India, at the head of a fleet of fourteen ships. After losing two vessels on the way, he anchored at the Indian port of Chaul on September 5, 1524, and reached Goa, then the capital of Portuguese India, at the end of the month, where he arrived with great pomp befitting his station. He tried to do away with corruption, but his harsh policies spread fear and dread among the inhabitants, many of whom fled inland. Three months later, on the night of Christmas, 1524, the viceroy died, more feared than loved. His body was transferred to Portugal in 1538, where he received more honors than had ever been given to anyone of nonroyal blood.

BIBLIOGRAPHY

Castanheda, Fernão Lopes de. *História do descobrimento e conquista da Índia pelos portugueses.* Edited by M. Lopes de Almeida. 2 vols. Porto, 1979.

Cortesão, Armando. *The Mystery of Vasco da Gama.* Coimbra, 1973.

Góis, Damião de. *Chronica do felicíssimo rei Dom Manuel.* 4 vols. Coimbra, 1949–1955.

Jayne, K. G. *Vasco da Gama and His Successors, 1460–1580.* Lisbon, 1910.

Ravenstein, E. G. *A Journal of the First Voyage of Vasco da Gama, 1497–1499.* Hakluyt Society Publications, 1st ser., vol. 99. London, 1898.

Sanceau, Elaine. *Good Hope: The Voyage of Vasco da Gama.* Lisbon, 1967.

REBECCA CATZ

GEMMA FRISIUS (1508–1555), Dutch mathematician, cosmographer, cartographer, and instrument maker. Gemma Frisius was born in Dokkum, Friesland. The name Gemma (Latin for "gem") was evidently an allusion to his intellectual abilities and his small stature. His father's name was Reynier, and the son was sometimes referred to as Gemma Reyneri or Reinerus Gemma. He was slight, frail, and born crippled, a condition of which he was miraculously cured at the age of six. He got his early education in Groningen and enrolled as one of the "poor students" in Lily College of Louvain University in 1526. He took his master's degree in 1528 and at the age of twenty-one was well enough grounded in geography and astronomy to publish an edition of the popular book of cosmography authored by Peter Apian (Peter Bennewitz). Gemma's version enjoyed a long and useful life, going through thirty-three editions in five languages over the course of the next eighty years. In 1530 Gemma published a pair of globes (terrestrial and celestial), although neither has survived.

The booklet that accompanied these globes is extant, however, and includes a prescient paragraph on a method for determining the longitude of places, a serious problem in all oceanic voyaging. Gemma's solution was to carry a timepiece set to local sun time at the point of origin. Comparing the difference between the time shown on the clock and the local sun time at the remote location would yield the longitude. As Gemma explained (in Richard Eden's translation of 1555):

> We see that in these owre dayes certeyne lyttle clockes are verye artificially made the whiche for theyr smaule quantitie are not comberous to be caryed abowt in all vyages. These often tymes moue continually for the space of xxiiii houres: and may with helpe continewe theyr mouynge in maner perpetually. By the helpe therefore of these the longitude may bee founde after this maner. Before wee enter into any vyage, wee muste fyrste foresee that the sayde clocke exactly obserue the houres of the place from whense we departe: And ageyne that in the way it neuer cease. Accomplysshynge therefore xv. or xx. myles of the vyage, if wee desyre to knowe howe much in longitude we are dystant frome the place of owre departure, we must tary untyll the poynt or style of the clocke do exactly come to the poynt of sum houre: and at the same moment by our Astrolabie or globe, owght wee to seeke the houre of the place where we bee.... And so shall the longitude bee founde. And by this arte can I fynde the longitude of regions althowgh I were a thousand myles owt of my attempted course & in an unknowen distance. (*The Decades of the Newe Worlde*, London, 1555, p. 361)

Gemma's technique was correct in principle, but the "lyttle clockes" and watches of the day, although they might run twenty-four hours on a winding, were not sufficiently accurate to yield usable results. The practical solution of the longitude problem had to await the chronometers of John Harrison in the eighteenth century.

In 1533 Gemma published the second of his vital contributions to cosmography, a description of the use of triangulation in surveying. The geometrical bases of triangulation were, of course, well known, but he was the first to print a full description of the technique for mapping purposes, including the measurement of base lines, the means for setting the scale of a map, and the use of resectioning for orienting the instrument (which was very like a modern surveyor's compass). Within a few years after the appearance of Gemma's description, all the provinces of the Netherlands had been mapped using the new technique, and its wide dissemination ushered in a new era in the making of large-scale regional maps.

In 1534 Gemma married and, presumably to better provide for his family, embarked on the study of medicine. He continued to be involved in the production of globes and, together with the young Gerardus Mercator and another engraver, Gemma produced a new pair of globes in 1536–1537. The terrestrial globe shows a wide bay in North America that connects with the South Sea. Labeled "Arctic Straight or Straight of the Three Brothers by which the Portuguese attempted to sail to the Orient & Indies & Moluccas," this may have been a reference to a voyage of Sebastian Cabot and his brothers.

Gemma published an influential world map in 1540. No copy has survived, but we know from contemporary descriptions that it was a nautical chart, with radiating rhumb lines, a wind rose, and scales. The map continued to be sold for at least twenty years. Gemma's most popular work was a handbook of practical arithmetic, which was first published in 1540. With seventy-five editions printed over the next one hundred years, it was the most widely read arithmetic book of its day.

Gemma was awarded the degree of doctor of medicine in 1541, and although he became a highly respected physician, he continued to write and publish in the field of cosmography and navigation. He also established a considerable reputation as a maker, or at least designer, of instruments. No surviving instrument bears his name, but he certainly designed an improved cross-staff, made of brass, which he hoped would make it possible to read angles with sufficient exactness to determine lunar distances for calculating longitude. This method was also theoretically correct but, as with the clocks, required a level of accuracy and precision unobtainable in the sixteenth century. Gemma's version of the cross-staff came into rather general use in England. His last book, published posthumously, dealt with the astrolabe, the standard instrument of navigators until the seventeenth century.

Gemma Frisius died in 1555 in Louvain, aged only forty-six years. His theoretical solution of the longitude problem, his perfection of triangulation as a surveying technique, his work as a cartographer and instrument maker, and his contribution to the spread of mathematical knowledge make him a figure of major importance in the annals of navigation and cosmography in the sixteenth century.

BIBLIOGRAPHY

Bagrow, Leo, and Robert W. Karrow, Jr. *Mapmakers of the Sixteenth Century and Their Maps: The Catalog of Cartographers of Abraham Ortelius, 1570.* Chicago, forthcoming.

Ortroy, Fernand G. van. *Bio-bibliographie de Gemma Frisius.* Académie Royale de Belgique, Classe des lettres et des sciences morales et politiques. Mémoires, 2d ser., vol. 11, fasc. 2. Brussels, 1920. Reprint, Amsterdam, 1966.

Pogo, A. "Gemma Frisius: His Method of Determining Differences of Longitude by Transporting Timepieces (1530) and His Treatise on Triangulation (1533)." *Isis* 22 (1935): 469–505.

Smet, Antoine de. "Gemma Frisius." *National biografisches woordenboek* 6 (1974): 315–331.

Vocht, Henry de. "Gemma Cosmographer." In Part 2 of *History of the Foundation and Rise of the Collegium Trilingue Lovaniense, 1517–1550.* Volumes 10–13 of Humanistica Lovaniensia. Louvain, 1953. Vol. 11, pp. 542–565.

ROBERT W. KARROW, JR.

GENOA. In the mid-fifteenth century, when Christopher Columbus was born, Genoa was about to become, as Fernand Braudel has put it, a "metropolis of European capitalism." For centuries Genoa, endowed with a perfect harbor and overlooking a deep bay almost in the center of the Mediterranean, had been a maritime capital. It had successfully fought for control of the Tyrrhenian Sea against the Saracens and against Pisa, Provence, and Catalonia. Freedom of movement and control over the sea routes to the Ligurian Sea were indispensable for its men and ships. The Genoese moved about the Mediterranean in search of strongholds from which they could travel farther inland in the quest for goods and markets. Since the early eleventh century, the Genoese had been in Sardinia and Corsica, and then along the coastlines of Tunis and Spain. They were thus established in the West before they made contact with the East, where they arrived only with the First Crusade, whose fleets embarked from their harbor.

In this way a Genoese colonial empire was formed, although it was an economic, not a political empire. Its private citizens sent capital, ships, men, and commercial ventures to various parts of the Mediterranean, going so far as to act against the directives and political alliances of their mother country. Genoese settled in Spain, in North Africa, and in the Aegean and Black seas. Their intricate network of interests extended both west, toward Portugal, England, and Flanders, and east, toward Persia, India, and China.

From this Mediterranean perspective, the West and the East appeared not so much antithetical worlds as potential markets in the vast Genoese commercial circuit, and subject to the Republic's vigilant attention. It was not at all strange, then, that even before he landed in Spain, Columbus had made a voyage to Chios, the island in the archipelago of the Southern Sporades that was one of the pillars of the Genoese colonial empire.

By the fifteenth century, Genoa had an economic regime that could be defined as capitalistic, or, if one prefers, mercantilistic. It had already emerged from the feudal Middle Ages, which knew nothing of free enterprise except what was carried on occasionally or surreptitiously. The young Christopher Columbus grew up in this mercantile world, hearing around him the language of money-making—purchases, sales, interest, percentages, commissions, profits. He left Genoa with this kind of economic background and then, having traveled the British seas, engaged in commerce with the Portuguese and Spanish islands in the Atlantic and off the coast of Africa and lived in Portugal, where he entered into negotiations with the king before leaving for Seville and Córdoba.

In Spain Columbus found a substantial Genoese settlement of Adornos, Dorias, Centuriones, Grimaldis, Pinellis, Spinolas, De Maris, and Di Negros—the best names of the rich class of merchants from that richest of cities, Genoa. The political and economic power the Genoese had accumulated in Seville and Córdoba was nothing short of incredible: they lent money to the court and to the municipal administrators, and they allocated local taxes. There were so many Genoese nationals that in 1473 Genoa dared to solicit the pope to appoint a Genoese bishop in Seville in order to better safeguard the Republic's interests. Some Genoese took advantage of a law granting citizenship after ten years of residence in the kingdom and became citizens of Seville or Córdoba. Others, in exchange for services rendered to the Crown, hoisted their ships' flags with the royal coat of arms. A Genoese company obtained a monopoly over the mercury trade from the sovereigns. Francesco Pinelli was especially successful; he was an adviser and confidant to the Catholic monarchs, the financier for the sovereigns' Granada venture, the director of the Treasury of Santa Hermandad, and a friend of Christopher Columbus and of the Catalonian minister Luis de Santángel, whom he supplied with part of the capital necessary to finance the first voyage of discovery.

But a paradox emerges here. Christopher Columbus, the progressive who looked forward to the Renaissance, could also be a reactionary who looked back to the Middle Ages in economic matters. In Genoa, Portugal, Seville, and Córdoba, Columbus was the typical man of mercantilism, or incipient capitalism. He dealt in percentages,

GENOA. Woodcut, from *Liber chronicarum*, 1493.

commissions, interest, and profits with the king of Spain and his ministers, with his Genoese compatriots, with the Florentines, and with converted Jews. But when in 1499–1500 in Santo Domingo he had to choose a political and social system that could be implemented in the newly discovered lands—and found himself trapped in the struggles between the Indians and the colonists as well as the Castilian conquistadores—he had to resort to establishing the encomienda. The encomienda was an institution inherited from the Castilian Middle Ages. The encomendero—the colonist or landowner—had and would have for centuries in the Spanish Empire of the Americas the same rights over Indian workers that the medieval feudal vassals had had over their serfs. These workers were not marketable slaves—unlike those in the colonies of Portugal, England, and Holland, countries that were already capitalistic and mercantile—but servants bound to the land. Hence, even Columbus's economic practices can be traced to Genoa, just as his ideas in another field—geography—can.

In the fifteenth century Genoa was among the capitals of nautical cartography, along with Venice, Mallorca, and the Arabian schools. When the young Columbus attended the school of the wool weavers' guild, he learned the basics of geography and the nautical arts in a city with great sensitivity toward and knowledge of these subjects. Genoa, then, can be seen as the cultural homeland of the discoverer of the Americas.

BIBLIOGRAPHY

Bradford, Ernle. *Christopher Columbus.* New York, 1971.

Howard, Edmund. *Genoa: History and Art in an Old Seaport.* Genoa, 1971.

Taviani, Paolo Emilio. *Christopher Columbus: The Grand Design.* London, 1985.

Taviani, Paolo Emilio, Piero Sanavio, Adriana Martinelli, and Caterina Porcu Sanna. *Cristoforo Colombo nella Genova del suo tempo.* Turin, 1985.

PAOLO EMILIO TAVIANI

GENOCIDE. See *Pacification, Conquest, and Genocide.* See also *Disease and Demography.*

GEOGRAPHY, IMAGINARY. When Columbus made his first voyage to America in 1492, he met the inhabitants of the West Indies and was surprised to find that contrary to what he had expected, they were physically similar to Europeans. Since he was entering a region of exotic geography, it had seemed likely that he would find there fabulous beings as well. Agreeably surprised, he insisted over and over again on the physical attractiveness of the

inhabitants by the standards of his own world. Later, in a letter to Fernando and Isabel, Columbus reassured them that whatever earlier geographers might have said, there were no "monstrous" men in America, only "savage" men.

Monstrous men and animals were such an important feature of the legendary geography of Columbus's age that they were a commonplace of any exotic travel narrative. Columbus's assumptions about the appearance of the people of the New World were much like those of "Europeans" from antiquity to the late Middle Ages who made real or imaginary voyages to places such as India or Africa. Beyond the boundaries of the European known world were believed to live monstrous races of beings whose oddity, according to some thinkers, was caused by climatic extremes of heat or cold in their habitat. These monstrous beings invariably differed in physical appearance, such as possessing extra body parts, and in social practices from the person describing them, who often gave them names derived from these qualities. Their diet was particularly important in characterizing their otherness. Chroniclers told of races who lived solely on the smell of apples; of troglodytes who dwelt in caves and ate their prey raw; of beings who were physically or socially unusual but not anomalous, such as pygmies, giants, and Amazons; and of others who were truly fabulous, such as the Four-Eyed Maritime Ethiopians or the Blemmyae, men with their faces on their chests.

The exotic geographical inheritance of Columbus contained about fifty distinct races, living always far from Europeans, for distance was a precondition of their existence. They inhabited places like India, Ethiopia, Albania, or Cathay, whose outlines were vague to the medieval mind but whose names evoked mystery. As

BLEMMYAE. Illustration from a manuscript edition of John Mandeville's *Travels,* fifteenth century.

BIBLIOTHÈQUE NATIONALE, PARIS

geographical knowledge grew through the voyages of Columbus and others, the existence of these people was disproved by actual experience and the monstrous races were consigned to less well known regions, such as Lapland.

These fabulous peoples posed a number of theological and cosmographical questions for Europeans. Even their humanity became an issue. Did they have souls? Were they rational? Were they descended from the line of Adam as were all other members of the human family, or did they have a separate lineage? How had they survived the Flood? Could they be converted to Christianity? Was their existence a portent of God's intentions toward humankind? If so, what was their significance in the Christian world scheme?

The monstrous beings whom Columbus expected to find in the New World were races—that is, they would possess inherited physical and cultural characteristics. He

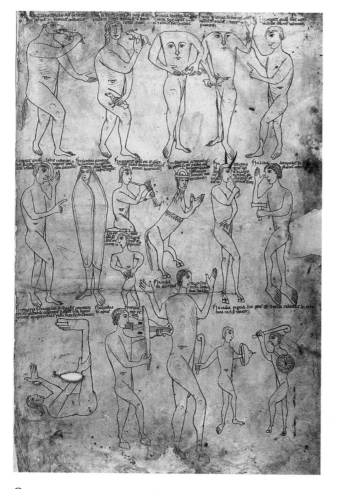

CATALOG OF MONSTROUS TYPES. From a manuscript from the Middle Rhine, late twelfth century.

did not anticipate supernatural or infernal beings, or the polymorphic creatures found in Romanesque and Gothic art, who were chiefly animal in composition, each differing from the next. Nor were they to be simply ordinary humans monstrous because of birth defects, though classical and medieval discussion of them often involved matters more properly associated with embryology.

The term *monster* (Latin, *monstrum*) to Columbus and his age had three different senses. Chiefly, it meant something outside the existing order of nature. Aristotle considered anomalous births as monsters (*terata*) who were defects of nature, which had deviated from the mean; he examined their physiological causes and classified them by type. The Romans discussed these births as portending the will of the gods because they showed (*monstrare*) something to humankind. Both of these senses signified individual unusual beings rather than races. It remained for the Roman encyclopedist Pliny the Elder to see both individual prodigies of the womb and the legendary races of the East as indicating God's power and desire to revitalize humanity's sense of the marvelous. Monsters, individual or as a species, fascinated and terrified the antique and medieval worlds because they challenged human understanding and pointed up the fragility and uncertainty of traditional conceptions of human beings.

The first Western accounts of these beings came from two Greek geographers, Ctesias who lived in the early fifth century B.C. and Megasthenes who lived in the fourth. They described their voyages in India in works of dramatic anthropology, focusing on the way such races were unusual or dissimilar to Greeks. Pliny described thirty distinct races in his *Natural History,* and Latin versions of the legends of Alexander the Great, who was believed to have encountered many hostile monstrous men in his Eastern exploits, were another important source for descriptions of perhaps twenty more. The conqueror was believed to have written a *Letter of Alexander to Aristotle on the Wonders of the East.* A new feature of Pliny's collection was the idea that many of the races lived in Ethiopia, which was confused with India. Indeed, the names of these two regions in medieval travel works and world maps should really be understood as vague literary terms rather than as denoting specific places.

Although there is no early medieval tradition of illustrated editions of Pliny's *Natural History* or of the Alexander cycle, portrayals of the monstrous races were quickly adopted by the compilers of medieval world maps. The two main kinds were the Noachid, or tripartite maps, sometimes called T-O maps, and the Macrobian zone maps. The former showed the world as a flat pie-like shape, with the world disk surrounded by a ring of ocean forming the shape of a letter O. Within the O and dividing it into three parts was a shape resembling the letter T, whose stem was formed by the Mediterranean imagined as a narrow vertical mass (north being generally to the left and east to the top in these maps) and whose cross bar was formed by the rivers Don and Nile. The area within the O was thus divided into three continents believed to have been created by Noah when he gave Europe, Asia, and Africa to his sons Japheth, Shem, and Ham, respectively, after the Flood. The continent of Africa on these maps usually contained at its outermost edge a band of monstrous races.

Macrobian zone maps were more theoretical; they divided the globe into regions of excessive cold or heat with two temperate zones suitable for human habitation between them. Some zone maps added an austral continent, which was the home of such monstrous beings as the sciopod, or shadow-footed man, who reclined with his foot over his head serving as an umbrella. The Antipodes also gave rise to a race of men believed to have their feet turned backward, or to be literally "opposite-footed."

Thus theories about the monstrous races were highly ethnocentric from the beginning. As the Aristotelian ideal of a mean between extremes gave rise to the notion of a mean climate found at the middle of the earth, extreme climates whether hot or cold had of necessity to be "un-ideal," deforming the inhabitants in mind and body. Each European nation thought of itself as a "middle people" superior in appearance, manners, and climate to all other peoples. Indeed, a Frenchman, Guy de Bazoches, observed that because of its climate and geographical situation, "France alone has no monsters, but abounds in wise, strong, and eloquent men." Another Frenchman, Benoît de Sainte-Maure, suggested that where the days are hot and burning there are various races "who have no law, religion or reason, justice or discretion; not knowing the difference between right and wrong, they are more felonious than dogs." Men in these torrid regions, he went on, are large, black, chinless, horned, and hairy right down to the ground with hanging ears, long noses, and huge feet. These features were the result of the extremes of temperature at the world's edges.

Much the same Aristotelian ideal was applied to the Plinean peoples' habitats. Visual depictions of them—for example, the illustrations in the very popular *Travels* of Sir John Mandeville—place them on mountains or crags that deviate from the norm in height. Mountains inspired great fear and distaste in the medieval populace. Antique fondness for landscapes that show the influence of art over nature made mountains unattractive for aesthetic reasons. The Bible associates topographical height with pride and with Satan, and in the Midrash, mountains are the earth's punishment for the sin of Adam. In the ninth-century Latin text *Liber monstrorum*, however, mon-

strous races live not only in the mountains and forests but in swamps, at the bottoms of deep pools, and in the vast wilderness of deserts and other hiding places at the edges of the world. They have deservedly been banished from the centers of civilization, their deviation from the physical appearance and social customs of Europeans responsible for their exile and their danger to humans. For example, races called the unclean peoples of Gog and Magog were believed to live in the Caucasus Mountains, safely walled up by Alexander the Great behind a great gate of brass. They ate their own afterbirths and periodically broke free of their gate to do terrible harm to Europeans. Although a contrary tradition made certain of the races, such as the Indian Bragmanni, or naked wise men who engaged in philosophical dialogue with Alexander, into noble savages and saw them in the light of romantic primitivism, even these lived not in cities and houses but in caves or waste places and had no political organization beyond simple kingship.

In the medieval *mappaemundi*, or world maps, available to Columbus, the monstrous men were always marginalized at the farthest point—usually eastward—from the center of the disk. Thus they were symbolically farthest in creation from Christ and hence from Jerusalem, the center of Christianity, which was usually represented in the exact center of the disk on the T-O maps. This metaphoric positioning eventually came into conflict with geography.

On the eve of the great discoveries, the chief problem of the Christian thinkers who took the geographic lore of Pliny seriously and expected to find monstrous races in the New World was how to fit them into the narrative of events recorded in scripture. If they descended from Adam, how had they survived the Flood and how had they gotten to the New World? Many theologians of Columbus's day wondered if it would be possible to convert them to Christianity. Were they redeemable like others? If they had descended from Adam, Augustine said, they must have souls, and if they had souls, they could be saved by grace. But were they so descended? This seemed questionable. As only hairy men and pygmies are mentioned in the Bible, the Plinean peoples seemed to have no scriptural genealogy and thus were not included in the single-family creation theory of *Genesis*.

Some said the monstrous races were distorted in form and manners and lived in remote places because they descended from children of Adam who disregarded his warning not to eat certain herbs. Others took them to be descendants of either Cain or Noah's rebellious son Ham, whose crimes had earned them exile in the waste places of the earth. A more extreme idea, found in the Midrash, was that the Plinean races' supposed ancestral father, Cain, was not Adam's child at all but the offspring of Eve's copulation with Satan. The curse that Noah laid upon his son Ham was also a genealogical explanation, for many theorized that this curse was blackness and physical deformity, so that black peoples, especially the supposed Ethiopians, and later the Moors and Saracens, were assigned a descent from Ham.

Another line of thought, which stemmed from Roman legal interpretations of monstrous births, also questioned the humanity of the Plinean races and of their actual counterparts in the New World. The legal and religious status of those of anomalous birth was of considerable interest to medieval jurists commenting on Roman law and to their contemporaries the canon lawyers. The former, as might be expected, considered *monstra* with respect to human form, laws of inheritance, and place in society, whereas the latter were concerned with their salvation as rational creatures having souls. The Cynocephali, or dog-headed men, and the pygmies particularly interested medieval thinkers in this way because their physical shape or size and social customs raised questions concerning their human status.

In Roman law, monstrous births, such as hermaphroditic babies, were instantly killed because they suggested a breakdown in cosmic order and portended an imminent danger to the state. Thus the Laws of the Twelve Tables, dating from as early as 450 B.C., stated that a father should immediately put to death a son who was a monster or who had a form different from members of the human race. For the Romans, human form was a prerequisite for human social or legal status. Not only did the *monstrum* reveal the gods' anger and serve as a focal point of danger to all; it lacked a place in society because it was unable to perform within it. The great legal commentators of the Middle Ages like Baldo Ubaldi slightly broadened this narrow definition of humanity: since form gives essence to a thing, that which does not have the form of a man is not a man, but if the creature has something of human form—like the dog-heads—he has civil status. The parish priests' manuals, popular embodiments of canon law, counseled how to baptize a creature with two heads: ought it to be baptized as one being or two? The answer: two heads meant two separate souls and so baptism as two persons.

The Scholastic philosophers of Columbus's immediate intellectual background speculated on the humanity of creatures like the Cynocephali who supposedly lived naked or wore animal skins and on pygmies who departed from the mean in human size. Albertus Magnus, for example, advanced the argument that the pygmy is the most perfect of animals, as he makes use of memory and understands by audible signs. In this he seems to imitate reason without truly possessing it, for he cannot through syllogistic reasoning elicit universals from past experience and apply them to similar cases in matters of art and learning. Pygmies, then, are subhuman because they lack the true reason inseparable from the forms of Aristotelian thought.

All these philosophical speculations as well as the literary conquests of Alexander the Great provided the underpinnings of the pattern of Western conquest and subjugation in the New World. Immodest dress, sexual license, and a lack of written history and laws—traits that had long offended the West in its dealings with the peoples of fabulous geography—were assumed to characterize the New World natives as well.

These qualities in New World monsters were dealt with by the sixteenth-century Aristotelian thinker Juan Ginés de Sepúlveda, who in 1550 engaged in a celebrated argument with Bartolomé de las Casas on the correct methods of propagating Christianity and Spanish capitalism in the New World. Las Casas argued for benign treatment and peaceful conversion to Christianity of the wild men, who were New World forms of the Anthropophagi, Donestre, and Hairy Wild Men of the Alexander legends; Sepúlveda countered that these men—if they were not more beasts than men—were the natural slaves of whom Aristotle spoke in the *Politics* and that their servitude to the conquerors and their conversion should be induced by force, stressing as part of his argument their sinful sexuality and their lack of written history and laws. Sepúlveda had in effect exported the ethnocentrism of the earliest Greek accounts of the fabulous geography of India and Africa to the New World and transformed the Indians of the Americas into Cynocephali, pygmies, and Hairy Wild Men. The myths of the monstrous races, though geographically obsolete by Columbus's day, were too vital to discard, for they provided a ready and familiar way of looking at the inhabitants of the New World.

[See also Cartography; Travel Literature.]

BIBLIOGRAPHY

Campbell, Mary. *The Witness and the Other World: Exotic European Travel Writing, 400–1600.* Ithaca, N.Y., 1988.

Friedman, John Block. *The Monstrous Races in Medieval Art and Thought.* Cambridge, Mass., 1981.

Kappler, Claude. *Monstres, démons et merveilles à la fin du moyen âge.* Paris, 1980.

Wittkower, Rudolf. "Marvels of the East." *Journal of the Warburg and Courtauld Institutes* 5 (1942): 159–197.

JOHN BLOCK FRIEDMAN

GERALDINI, ALESSANDRO

GERALDINI, ALESSANDRO (1455–1525), bishop of Santo Domingo. Columbus, thinking that a region of the coast of Venezuela was an island, named it "Isla de Gracia." This name, which did not survive, was an expression of appreciation to the Umbrian bishop,

Alessandro Geraldini, who had supported Columbus's cause at the court of the Spanish monarchs. The name of Geraldini's mother was Gracia.

She had married Andrea del Segale and then, having become widowed, Pace Busitani. She had two sons: from the first husband, Antonio; from the second, Alessandro. The stepbrothers were adopted by their maternal uncle, Angelo Alessandrini.

Antonio Geraldini, papal nuncio at the court of the Catholic monarchs, long supported Columbus's projects. When he died in 1488, his stepbrother, Alessandro Geraldini, was nominated by Pope Innocent VIII to be his delegate at the Spanish court. After the discovery of the lands across the sea, he was named bishop of Santo Domingo, thereby becoming the first bishop to reside in the New World. When he died in Santo Domingo in 1525, he left behind a work of Columbian bibliography that is considered among the best from the point of view of chronology: *Itinerarium ad regiones sub aequinoctiali plaga constitutas* (1631).

Alessandro Geraldini was especially helpful during the Council of Santa Fe, which was convened in the winter of 1492 to decide on the feasibility of the enterprise proposed by Columbus. The council was composed primarily of prelates rather than geographers and cosmographers. On that occasion, Columbus had many supporters, but Geraldini's arguments were particularly important in surmounting the doubts regarding the cosmography that was at the heart of Columbus's proposal to sail westward to reach the East.

Geraldini recorded his intervention in his *Itinerarium*:

Christopher Columbus, of Italian nationality, had his origins in the city of Genoa, in Liguria; he is an expert in Cosmography, Mathematical Sciences, and in the knowledge of the dimension of the sky and of the earth; above all he is renowned for his great courage. . . . In the process of measuring the sky's circuit, he realized, during his long navigations on the Ocean, that he could reach the lands of the Equinox, that is, the Antipodes. But such an expedition was rejected by King John of Portugal. Columbus decided to go to Spain where King Fernando and Queen Isabel were in those days waging war against the Arabs.

Thereupon, Antonio Geraldini, my brother, papal nuncio and most esteemed person, who had recently come back from the legation to the Sovereign Pontiff Innocent the VIII, offered his very powerful help to Columbus. But once my brother's death had taken place, Columbus had remained without any human succor whatever, and came to such dire circumstances that he went, dejected and entreating, to a monastery of Saint Francis where he might be given the food necessary for life.

Thereupon Fra Giovanni de Marchena, a man esteemed everywhere for his life, religion and sanctity, seeing Columbus, a man remarkable in every aspect, and having had compassion for him, left for Granada in order to see

King Fernando and Queen Isabel. These, moved by the authority of such an honorable person, called for Columbus. Nonetheless, many Spanish bishops were judging him guilty of heresy, because Nicholas of Lyra had maintained that there was no land in the Southern Hemisphere, and because Saint Augustine had asserted that there existed no Antipodes. Then I approached Cardinal Mendoza, and had him reflect on the fact that Saint Nicholas of Lyra and Saint Augustine were great for their sanctity and doctrine, yet lacking in cosmographical science; for so much was true, that the Portuguese had already reached the regions below the Southern Hemisphere.

This argument by Alessandro Geraldini, meant to resolve the conflict between science and faith, helped dispel Queen Isabel's concern regarding the heretical implications of Columbus's enterprise.

BIBLIOGRAPHY

Baggio, Sebastiano. *Alessandro Geraldini di Amelia, primo vescovo residente nelle diocesi riunite d'America.* Grotte di Castro, Italy, 1985.

Geraldini, Alessandro. *Cristoforo Colombo ed il primo vescovo di Santo Domingo mons. Allassandro Geraldini d'Amelia.* Amelia, Italy, 1986.

Geraldini, Alessandro. *Itinerarium ad regiones sub aequinotiali plaga constitutas.* Vols. 12 and 14. Rome, 1631.

Masetti, P. "L'amicizia fra Cristoforo Colombo e Alessandro Geraldini." *Columbus '92* (Genoa) 2, no. 7–8 (1986).

Tisnés, R. M. *Alejandro Geraldini, primer obispo residente de Santo Domingo en la Española. Amigo y defensor de Colón.* Santo Domingo, 1987.

PAOLO EMILIO TAVIANI
Translated from Italian by Rodica Diaconescu-Blumenfeld

GERMANUS. See *Martellus, Henricus.*

GLOBES. Arab astronomers and geographers were making celestial globes in the Middle Ages. Though no European medieval globes survive, scholars such as Gebert of Aurillac (c. 945–1003; later Pope Sylvester II) used celestial globes and armillary spheres in teaching the astronomical sciences. The earliest extant European celestial globe is that made by Nicholas of Cusa at Nürnberg in 1444. The revival of Ptolemy's *Geography* (written around A.D. 150), first published with maps in 1477, reinforced the concept of a spherical earth. The cosmographer Nicolaus Germanus (c. 1420–1490), famous for the Ulm edition of Ptolemy's *Cosmographia* (1482), made a pair of terrestrial and celestial globes for the Vatican in 1477. They were presumably lost in the sack of Rome in 1527.

The earliest surviving terrestrial globe is the "Erdapfel" (Earth apple), which Martin Behaim (1459–1507) made at

Nürnberg in 1492 (and which is now preserved in the city's National Museum). The geographical features were drawn on vellum by the miniaturist Georg Holzschuler, and the map was pasted on a sphere about fifty centimeters (twenty inches) in diameter. The globe is famous as the only one now known that dates from before Columbus's discovery of America.

Scholars have puzzled over the fact that the globe appears to reflect the ideas of Columbus, yet there is no evidence that Columbus and Behaim had met. The explanation is found in records indicating that Behaim received payment for "a printed *mappamundi* embracing the whole world," which he used for the globe. This has been identified as the large world map of Henricus Martellus of about 1490 (now in the Beinecke Rare Book Library of Yale University). Columbus apparently consulted this map or a prototype for planning his voyage. Behaim's globe is also notable for its depictions of Portuguese discoveries along the coast of Africa, derived partly from information Behaim obtained in Portugal.

Globes were essential geographical instruments in the age of discovery, for they depict direction, distance, and area more accurately than does the plane chart. Columbus's papers include references to globes as well as to charts, and his brother Bartolomé Colón was skilled in making or painting spheres.

John Cabot's discovery of North America for Henry VII in 1497 was recorded on both a globe (probably the first English one) and a map, as the ambassador of the duke of Milan reported in a letter of December 18, 1497: "This Messer Zoane has the description of the world in a map, and also in a solid sphere, which he had made, and shows where he has been. In going towards the east he passed far beyond the country of the Tanais [i.e., the Don]." On this globe Cabot's discoveries in the region of Newfoundland must have been shown as located on a cape of Asia.

The earliest printed globe gores, or triangular sections, are those made by Martin Waldseemüller, professor of cosmography in Lorraine, dated 1507 and probably published at Strasbourg. The globe is a simplified version of Waldseemüller's large world map of 1507 and is described in an accompanying text, *Cosmographiae introductio* (St. Dié, 1507). On both the map and the globe Waldseemüller names the southern part of the New World "America" in honor of Amerigo Vespucci, who navigated the coasts of South America from 1499 to 1501. By the time Waldseemüller recognized Columbus's priority of discovery, the name of America was firmly established (such is the power of the printed word). The globe, like the map, shows the New World as a separate landmass, divided by a strait.

The Lenox globe in the collections of the American Geographical Society has been described as the oldest extant post-Columbian globe. An engraved copper ball, unsigned and undated, it was probably made about 1510. The New World, shown as South America, is named "Mundus Novus, Terra Sancta Crucis." To the north are islands and open ocean between Europe and Asia; there is no North American continent. The gilded copper globe, 7.3 centimeters in diameter, in the Jagellonian University Library, Cracow, is similar in its geographical features.

The "Globe Vert," or Green Globe, in the Bibliothèque Nationale, Paris, named for the bright green color of its seas, is a painted wooden sphere twenty-four centimeters in diameter, unsigned and undated, probably from about 1515. It bears similarities to Waldseemüller's globe gores and is the earliest cartographic document to give the name of America (which appears four times) on both the northern and southern continents of the New World. A legend names Columbus as the discoverer of the Antilles. To the south of South America an unnamed southern land is similar to that named "Brasilie regio" on Schöner's globe of 1515.

Johann Schöner (1477–1547), mathematician and geographer, was the most influential globe maker of his day. He was the first to undertake globe production on a considerable scale and in association with many astronomical and cosmographical publications. His woodcut globe made in 1515 ranks as the earliest printed and mounted terrestrial globe. Two of these survive, in

ANONYMOUS GLOBE GORES, INGOLSTADT, CIRCA 1518. Facsimile, mounted as a globe.

Weimar and in Frankfurt. An accompanying pamphlet dated 1515 reveals Schöner's authorship. The strait that appears between "America" and the southern landmass "Brasilie regio" has prompted the speculation that Ferdinand Magellan was familiar with this globe and that it guided him in 1520 to the discovery of the strait named after him. Globe gores, published about 1518, probably in Ingolstadt, show America in a form similar to that on Schöner's globe—without a southern continent.

Schöner's manuscript globe of 1520 provides another interpretation of the discoveries of the time. The New World comprises five landmasses, from Terra Corterealis in the northeast to Brasilia Inferior as a substantial southern continent in the south. In 1523 Schöner issued another globe, now apparently lost, which he refers to in his treatise *De nuper . . . repertis insulis ac regionibus . . . epistola* (An epistle concerning islands and regions recently discovered). The text seems to suggest that Schöner now gave North America ("Parias," as he called it) an Asiatic connection.

F. C. Wieder identified the lost globe of 1523 with the Stuttgart globe gores, but this is no longer accepted. The gores, which would make a globe thirty-five centimeters in diameter, appear to date from about 1535 and to have been made in Nuremberg. They display the track of Magellan's ship *Victoria* around the world. The artist may have been from the school of Schöner. The Gilt, or De

Bure, globe in the Bibliothèque Nationale is similar to the Stuttgart globe gores and also shows the track of *Victoria*. In both these works America is joined to Asia, whereas most globes of the period are notable in showing the New World as a land or lands independent of Asia. The globe gores by Georg Hartmann, published at Nuremberg in 1535, illustrate a typical conception of America.

Another globe depicting Magellan's voyage and identified for some years mistakenly as Schöner's lost globe of 1523 is that known in the form of globe gores in the New York Public Library. In its mounted form, it is called the Ambassadors' Globe, from its inclusion in Hans Holbein's portrait of ambassadors at England's Hampton Court in 1533. It is notable in displaying the Line of Demarcation between the Spanish and Portuguese spheres as determined by the Treaty of Tordesillas, 1494. The instruments in the picture, including a celestial globe (probably that by Peter Apian first published in 1530), express in graphic form the theme of Henricus Cornelis Agrippa's book on the vanity of the arts and sciences, *De incertitudine et vanitate omnium scientiarum & artium liber,* first published at Antwerp in 1530.

The invention of printing and engraving techniques gave mapmakers and artists as well as instrument makers the opportunity to take up globe making. The artist Albrecht Dürer (1471–1528) proposed in 1525 the globe-biangle (gore) as a means of transferring the sphere to a

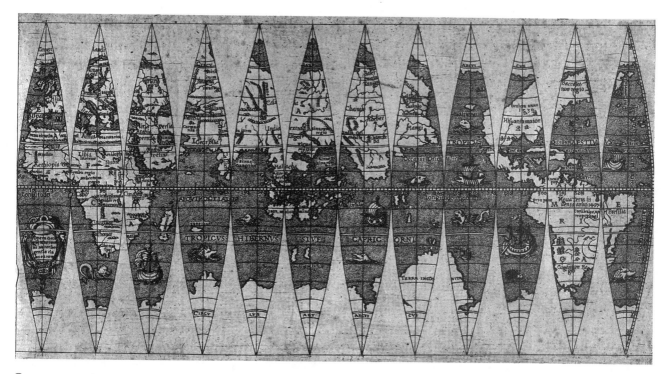

GLOBE GORES BY GEORG HARTMANN. Nürnberg, 1535.

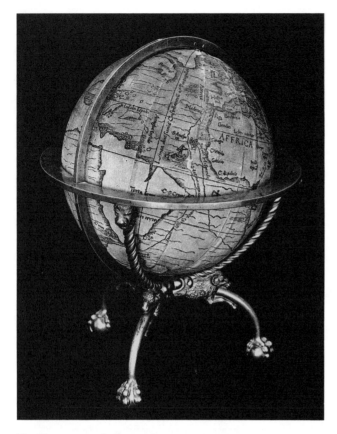

THE AMBASSADORS' GLOBE. Mounted facsimile of globe gores published possibly in Nürnberg, circa 1530.

NORDENSKJÖLD COLLECTION, UNIVERSITY OF HELSINKI

GEMMA FRISIUS. Constructing a celestial globe at his workshop in Louvain.

BIBLIOTHÈQUE ROYALE DE BELGIQUE, BRUSSELS

flat surface. The Swiss professor Henricus Loritus Glareanus in 1527 was the first to explain how to construct globe gores. His *Poetae laureati geographia liber unus* (Basel, 1527, with later editions to 1542) includes a chapter, illustrated by a diagram, that describes the method. The construction is simple but not completely correct mathematically.

As geographical studies advanced in the sixteenth century, globe makers became interested in exploring the relationship between the terrestrial and celestial spheres. They found that the most effective way of conveying the relationship was to make a matching pair of terrestrial and celestial globes, often accompanied by a book on their use. Gemma Frisius, professor of mathematics at the University of Louvain, made the earliest pair now extant, 36.5 centimeters in diameter, the terrestrial dated 1536, the celestial, 1537. They were engraved by Gemma Frisius's celebrated pupil Gerardus Mercator. The globes became well known throughout Europe and were of particular interest in England because the terrestrial showed the northwest passage Sebastian Cabot claimed to

have discovered while in English service many years before.

Mercator's pair of globes, forty-one centimeters in diameter, the terrestrial published in 1541, the celestial in 1551, superseded the globes of Gemma Frisius and were in standard use in the later part of the sixteenth century. The terrestrial globe displays innovative features. Loxodromes, or rhumb lines, are marked from the numerous compass roses as a guide for seamen, and these became a standard feature on globes. The second device was the depiction of stars as seen at various places on land and sea to help the traveler orient himself at night. This did not inspire others to follow suit, however.

In England the first pair of globes was published to great acclaim in 1592. They were made by Emery Molyneux, a Lambeth mathematician and instrument maker, with the help of Cambridge mathematician Edward Wright, engraved by the Dutchman Jodocus Hondius, and produced at the expense of the London merchant-adventurer William Sanderson. Measuring two feet two inches in diameter, they were the largest printed globes yet made.

Terrestrial (left) and celestial (right) globes by Émery Molyneux. First published in London, 1592. Second edition in 1603.

The terrestrial globe provided a full record of England's explorations and discoveries abroad, and the arms of Elizabeth on the continent of North America were designed to encourage her plan for an English empire there.

Globes featured in pictures and portraits of the sixteenth century as emblems of statecraft. They symbolized the territorial ambitions and spiritual power of the monarch. Henry VIII, for example, had a great hall built at Calais for a banquet to entertain Emperor Charles V on July 12, 1520, after their meeting at the Field of the Cloth of Gold. Eight hundred feet around, the hall contained "the whole sphere" on its roof.

In more mundane affairs geography was taught using globes, and ships on voyages of discovery were equipped with them. At international conferences, such as the Council of Badajoz to settle the territorial disputes between Spain and Portugal, the diplomats had globes as well as maps to consult.

[See also *Cartography.*]

BIBLIOGRAPHY

Babicz, Józéf. "The Celestial and Terrestrial Globes of the Vatican Library Dating from 1477, and Their Maker Donnus Nicolaus Germanus." *Der Globusfreund* 35–37 (1987): 155–168.

Krogt, Peter van der. *Old Globes in the Netherlands: A Catalogue of Terrestrial and Celestial Globes.* Utrecht, 1984.

Muris, Oswald, and Gert Saarmann. *Der Globus im Wandel der Zeiten.* Berlin, 1961.

Nordenskiöld, A. E. *Facsimile-Atlas to the Early History of Cartography.* Stockholm, 1889. Reprint, New York, 1961.

Ravenstein, E. G. *Martin Behaim: His Life and His Globe.* London, 1908.

Shirley, Rodney W. *The Mapping of the World: Early Printed World Maps, 1472–1700.* London, 1983.

Stevenson, Edward Luther. *Terrestrial and Celestial Globes.* 2 vols. New Haven, 1921.

Wallis, Helen. "Some New Light on Early Maps of North America, 1490–1560." In *Land- und Seekarten im Mittelalter und in der frühen Neuzeit,* edited by Cornelis Koeman. Munich, 1977.

Wieder, F. C. *Monumenta cartographica.* Vol. 1. The Hague, 1925.

Helen Wallis

GRANADA. Granada in the time of Christopher Columbus was transformed from the capital city of the last Muslim kingdom in the Iberian Peninsula into a defeated and deeply divided outpost on the periphery of Castile. From 1482 to 1485, Castilian frontal attacks against the city itself failed; the surrounding terrain was too rugged for a rapid Christian advance, and the Christian supply line ran through hostile territory. Finally, Fernando and Isabel isolated the city of Granada from its seaports and surrounding farmland. They besieged and captured the coastal city of Málaga in 1487, enslaving eleven thousand to fifteen thousand of its citizens because the city had resisted so fiercely. The lesson was not lost on the Granadines. As one port after another fell to the Christian armies, citizens of the capital escaped to Africa. After Granada was surrounded, it surrendered without a fight, receiving very favorable terms of capitulation. The defeated Muslim ruler, Boabdil, formally transferred sovereignty to Fernando and Isabel, who entered the city on January 2, 1492.

Under the terms of the capitulation agreement, the Muslims were allowed to retain their religion, laws, and customs. But the taxes they once paid to Muslim rulers they now paid to the Christian monarchs. In religion, too, the old dues *(habices)* that had previously supported Muslim religious and charitable institutions now went to support the Christian cathedral and churches. Only after accomplishing this conquest and transfer did the Catholic monarchs turn their attention to Christopher Columbus's proposal for his voyage of discovery, which they agreed to in a contract signed in the royal encampment of Santa Fe, outside the walls of Granada.

From this point on, Granada began a long decline punctuated by episodes of crisis. The most serious effects were loss of population and a decline in silk manufacturing. In 1499–1500, Fernando and Isabel crushed a Muslim uprising by military force and ordered all Muslims to convert to Christianity or leave the Kingdom of Castile. The archbishop of Toledo, Cardinal Francisco Jiménez de Cisneros, launched a successful military attack on North Africa, which inspired counterattacks on Spanish ports and shipping all along the Granadine coast. A serious food shortage in 1506 and an epidemic (probably typhus) in 1507 devastated the local population and discouraged immigration to the city from other parts of Castile. Silk production dropped, and the traditional trade patterns with North Africa were broken. The population of about 100,000 at the time of the conquest had dropped by half by the end of the sixteenth century, with a corresponding decline in production levels and rate of economic transactions. But silk thread and cloth continued to be the largest exports, and the silk tax was the monarchy's principal income from Granada.

The old Muslim consumer economy, epitomized in the luxuriously decorated Alhambra Palace overlooking the city, was replaced by an administrative service economy. The palace was the captain-general's headquarters for the Kingdom of Granada and housed a large portion of the military personnel and their families. The archbishop of Granada and the cathedral's staff supervised the ecclesiastical administration of eastern Andalusia, and the royal appellate court for southern Castile, the *chancillería*, moved permanently to Granada in 1505. The minutes of the Granada city council, which survive almost intact from 1497 to the present, show that, though the city was amply provisioned with food from the surrounding countryside, the variety and volume of manufactures shrank during the sixteenth century.

BIBLIOGRAPHY

Domínguez Ortiz, Antonio, and Bernard Vincent. *Historia de los moriscos: Vida y tragedia de una minoría.* Madrid, 1984.

Grabar, Oleg. *The Alhambra.* London, 1978.

Ladero Quesada, Miguel Angel. *Granada: Historia de un país islámico (1232–1571).* Madrid, 1969.

Rosenthal, Earl E. *The Palace of Charles V in Granada.* Princeton, 1985.

HELEN NADER

VIEW OF GRANADA. Woodcut from Pedro Medina's *Libro de grandezas de España*, 1548.

LIBRARY OF CONGRESS, RARE BOOK DIVISION

GRAND KHAN. "Khan" was the title given by Turkish and Mongol tribes to the man whom their warriors proclaimed the leader. Although khans were frequently descendants of previous khans, the title was not hereditary or continuous but apparently activated by the exigencies of combat. When on occasion a number of tribes banded together, usually for military purposes, they chose a common leader who bore the title "gurkhan." Throughout the early medieval period, western Europe was buffered from the periodic westward thrusts of these nomadic peoples by the intermediary civilizations of Byzantium and Islam. Accurate knowledge of inner Asia and the Far East was negligible. What information Europeans had was derived from ancient sources and the legends and romances based upon them.

Early in the thirteenth century, however, a Mongol of noble descent named Temüjin (1167–1227) consolidated control of the Mongols, Kairites, and Uighur Turks of outer, eastern, and western Mongolia. In 1206, he took the name Genghis (Chingis) and the title "kah khan," or "the emperor of mankind." In his quest to conquer the world he amassed an army of nomadic horsemen capable of traversing the great steppes of inner Asia with extraordinary speed and efficiency. A series of campaigns in the second and third decades of the thirteenth century gave him control of northern China, Manchuria, and the central Asian Muslim empire of Khwarazm.

Direct contact between the forces of Genghis Khan and central Europeans occurred in the second decade of the thirteenth century when Hungary, Poland, and Silesia were overrun in a Mongol offensive that reached the shores of the Adriatic Sea. These fierce hordes receded rather abruptly before the mobilizing armies of western Europe could engage them, probably in the aftermath of the death of Genghis in 1227. A subsequent Mongol offensive in 1240 resulted in the conquest of Christian Romania.

The sudden, devastating appearances of these horsemen terrified Europeans, who called them "the scourge of God" and "the devil's horsemen." Such apocalyptic apprehensions did not, however, prevent Pope Innocent III from seeking to establish diplomatic relations with Genghis's successor, the Grand Khan Güyük (or Kuyuk). The legate chosen by the pope to journey eastward to meet the Grand Khan was the Franciscan friar Giovanni da Pian del Carpini (1180–1252). After a rapid passage across inner Asia on relay teams of horses, Carpini and a companion were received at the court of Güyük. Upon his return, he wrote an account of his journey of 1245 to 1247 titled *History of the Mongols*. This work marks the beginning of a new phase in European knowledge of the peoples of central Asia and the Mongol empire.

Carpini was followed by another Franciscan, Willem van Ruysbroeck, who in 1253 was sent by the French king Louis IX to locate and proselytize the communities of Nestorian Christians presumed to exist in parts of Asia. The two-year expedition culminated with eight months spent in the court of Güyük's successor, Mangu Khan. Willem provided a detailed account of his experiences in a work known as *The Journey* and also informed other

writers such as Roger Bacon, who made use of the information in parts of his *Opus maius*.

In 1260, two Venetian merchants, Niccolò and Maffeo Polo, seeking to establish new trade networks in Russia and Persia, were stranded by local conflicts in the important Muslim trade center of Bukhara. They were invited by Barak, the Muslim khan of Turkestan who controlled Bukhara, to accompany him on a diplomatic visit to his overlord, the Grand Khan Kublai, whose court was located near present-day Beijing (Peking). The Polo brothers returned to Italy in 1269 as envoys from Kublai Khan to the pope. Upon finding the pope recently deceased and the papacy vacant, the brothers in 1271 elected to return to the court of Kublai Khan, taking with them Niccolò's son Marco, then probably around fifteen years old.

Marco Polo spent almost two decades in China and southeastern Asia. His activities and movements during this period are not altogether clear, though he does appear to have been associated with the court of Kublai Khan. In 1292 he returned to Venice not by the ancient overland routes established by silk and spice traders but by sea from Southeast Asia to the Persian Gulf port of Ormuz and thence by land to the shores of the Mediterranean. Some six years later he was captured and imprisoned by the Genoese in a sea battle with the Venetians. While in prison he dictated his story of his years in the Far East to a fellow inmate, one Rustichello of Pisa. The *Travels* (also known as *Il milione*), originally written in French, enjoyed great popularity from the time it began to circulate and was soon translated into other vernaculars. Many manuscripts and early printed editions survive; the work generated an important pictorial tradition as well.

The title grand khan disappeared in the late fourteenth century with the demise of Mongol power, but western Europeans, unaware of such dynastic shifts, continued to believe that this at once alluring and terrifying leader ruled the Far East. Marco Polo's exotic and opulent description of the court of Kublai Khan, contained in the famous third chapter of the *Travels*, was an important stimulus to the Spanish and Portuguese voyagers of the fifteenth and sixteenth centuries. Prompted by a desire to find a sea route to India and the Far East that would bypass the routes controlled by Muslim traders, Prince Henry the Navigator (1394–1460) masterminded a series of Portuguese expeditions down the west coast of Africa beginning in 1510. These culminated in Vasco da Gama's circumnavigation of the Cape of Good Hope in 1497–1498 and the subsequent establishment of Portuguese maritime trade networks in the seas once traveled by Marco Polo on his return journey from China to Italy some two hundred years earlier.

The Portuguese successes in discovering new sea routes to what Marco Polo called the "marvels of the East" undoubtedly played an important part in Fernando and Isabel's decision to underwrite Columbus's voyages. And Columbus, who read and heavily annotated a copy of Marco Polo's *Travels,* clearly expected to find the riches described therein by sailing west. His own letters and various other sources indicate that he was particularly interested in reaching Cipangu (Japan), described by Marco Polo as being even richer than the territories held by Kublai Khan, who coveted it.

On his first voyage Columbus took a converso named Luis de Torres whom he thought would serve as an interpreter in the interviews he expected to have with the Grand Khan. According to Bartolomé de las Casas, Columbus thought that the Tainos whom he encountered on the island of Cuba spoke of "El Gran Can." He dispatched a diplomatic party headed by Luis de Torres to meet this nonexistent leader in a land he did not yet know existed, poignant proof of the enduring power of the legend of the Grand Khan in the age of European expansion.

[See also the biographies of Carpini and Polo.]

BIBLIOGRAPHY

Chambers, James. *The Devil's Horsemen: The Mongol Invasion of Europe.* New York, 1985.
Dawson, Christopher. *Mission to Asia.* Toronto, 1980.
Polo, Marco. *The Travels.* New York, 1958.
Rossabi, Morris. *Khubilai Khan: His Life and Times.* Berkeley, 1988.
Wittkower, Rudolf. "Marco Polo and the Pictorial Tradition of the Marvels of the East." In *Allegory and the Migration of Symbols.* London, 1977.
Yule, Henry. *Cathay and the Way Thither: Being a Collection of Medieval Notices of China.* Taipei, 1966.

PAULINE MOFFITT WATTS

GRAVE OF COLUMBUS. See *Burial Places.*

GRIJALBA, JUAN DE (1489–1527), Spanish explorer. Juan de Grijalba and his uncle Diego Velázquez, Cuba's first governor, were both from Cuellar in Spain. In Cuba, Velázquez heard about the riches of a land known as Culhua, recently discovered in 1513 and 1516 by Juan Ponce de León, who had been appointed adelantado of Bimini and Florida. Under this title, he had exclusive rights to explore and settle territory extending from the Río de Palmas, forty leagues north of Panuco, up to Newfoundland's Grand Banks.

Lacking such a title to Culhua, Velázquez was allowed to outfit expeditions only for the purpose of barter with the Indians. Ponce de León complained to King Fernando that Velázquez had illegally taken off some three hundred

Indians from the territory he had been granted, so on July 22, 1517, a 1502 decree declaring that all Indians were free men was reconfirmed.

Velázquez then tried to obtain a grant to explore Culhua from the Hieronymite friars who governed La Española, while sending Friar Benito Martín to Spain to seek his appointment as adelantado (a title granted so far only to Bartolomé Colón, Columbus's eldest brother, and Ponce de León).

Although lacking such a grant, Velázquez dispatched in 1517 three ships under Francisco Fernández de Córdoba with pilot Antón de Alaminos, who had served as pilot when Ponce de León explored these coasts. While bartering with the Indians, however, the expedition was attacked, and the captain wounded. It was forced to return to Cuba by way of Florida, landing where Alaminos said he had been with Ponce de León.

Next, in May 1518, Velázquez sent four ships with 160 men to Culhua in an expedition captained by his nephew, the "young and beardless" Juan de Grijalba. He was ordered to barter with the Indians, seek gold, and deliver a full report of the land (called Mayab, but named Yucatán, meaning "don't understand"). He landed at Cozumel Island and then at Asunción and San Juan de Ulúa bays, so named by Ponce de León. They bartered for gold and Indian objects, which Grijalba sent to Velázquez. He then sailed toward Campeche. There the party was attacked by Indians and was forced to return to Cuba; the trip was considered a failure.

Velázquez organized yet another expedition under Grijalba and his secretary, Hernando Cortés, in a three-man private partnership. Because he still lacked a grant, the expedition was supervised by a government overseer and a treasurer. In October 1519 Cortés led ten ships to explore and settle "the islands of San Juan de Ulúa, Ponce, and Yucatán." They were also to barter with the Indians and rescue shipwrecked and captive sailors. Grijalba falsely claimed that Spaniards had not sailed along those shores before, hoping to be recognized as the pioneer explorer. He was demoted by Velázquez and died in Nicaragua.

BIBLIOGRAPHY

Wagner, H. R., trans. *Discovery of New Spain in Fifteen Eighteen by Juan de Grijalva.* 1942. Millwood, N.Y., 1969.

AURELIO TIÓ

GUZMÁN, ENRIQUE DE (d. 1492), second duke of Medina-Sidonia. Enrique de Guzmán inherited the richest of the Castilian duchies in 1478, having been recently legitimized by his father. The estate, which included vast territories around the mouth of the Guadalquivir River, was contested unsuccessfully by the counts of Alba de Liste, who were descended from a legitimate daughter of the first duke.

The second duke spent most of his career in a bitter feud with the marqués of Cádiz, who regarded him as "my enemy incarnate." This struggle, which occasionally degenerated into open warfare, was a major concern of the Catholic monarchs who were able to secure only a temporary truce. Medina-Sidonia nevertheless came to the aid of his enemy in 1482 when the marqués was besieged by the Moors after capturing Al-Hamma. The duke's refusal to accept a share of the booty earned him the respect of other grandees, but the feud was revived in later years. For the remainder of the Granadan war, Medina-Sidonia participated chiefly in local defense, though his son commanded the family's troops in several major campaigns.

Shortly after Columbus arrived at Seville in 1485, he approached the duke in the hope of securing his support. He was encouraged to do so by Antonio de Marchena, who was no doubt aware of Medina-Sidonia's investment in the Canaries campaign. Negotiations were abandoned when the duke returned to his estates after yet another outbreak of his feud with the marqués of Cádiz. Medina-Sidonia died on August 25, 1492, only three days before the passing of his mortal enemy, Cádiz.

BIBLIOGRAPHY

Ladero Quesada, Miguel Angel. *Spain in 1492.* Bloomington, Ind., forthcoming.

Vassberg, David. *Land and Society in Golden Age Castile.* Cambridge, 1984.

WILLIAM S. MALTBY

H

HENRY. For discussion of the Castilian king Henry IV, see *Enrique IV*.

HENRY THE NAVIGATOR (1394–1460), prince of Portugal. Born in Oporto, Henry was the third surviving son of João I, founder of the Aviz dynasty, and Philippa, daughter of John of Gaunt of England. Prince Henry played a seminal role in the early stages of European overseas expansion. He was a patron of pioneering voyages to Madeira, the Azores, and the west coast of Africa, and his private court at Sagres was responsible for notable advances in cartography, navigational instruments, and ship design. His elusive goal—not realized until Vasco da Gama's epic voyage some four decades after the prince's death—was the maritime passage to Asia, the coveted prize for a spice-starved and Christian Europe eager to outflank the middlemen of the Levant trade while extending the crusade against Islam.

Henry's biographer, Gomes Eanes de Zurara, states that the prince and his brothers, Duarte and Pedro, convinced their father to continue the crusade against Islam in North Africa so they might win their knightly spurs in true combat. The Portuguese Crown was also no doubt eager to win a share of the trade in slaves and gold that had hitherto proved so lucrative for the Moors. An expedition sailed for Ceuta in July 1415. Prince Henry played a prominent role in the capture of this place and was promptly named governor. This position gave him access to ships, and he soon began to sponsor voyages of discovery. Between 1418 and 1420 his squires, João Gonçalves Zarco and Tristão Vaz Teixeira, rediscovered the islands of Porto Santo (destined to play a notable role in the life of Columbus) and Madeira.

After the prince returned to Portugal, he was given the titles of duke of Viseu and lord of Covilhã and was appointed governor of the Algarve. He left Lisbon in 1419 to take up this post in Portugal's southernmost province, selecting the windswept and rocky promontory of Sagres, near Cape St. Vincent, as the site for his court. There he gathered sailors, cartographers, astronomers, and shipbuilders to help in his quest for exploration and discovery.

In 1420 Prince Henry's projects received welcome support when he was named grand master of the Order of Christ, the successor in Portugal to the crusading order of the Templars. Henry used revenues from this order to finance his expeditions. Thereafter, his ships bore the red cross of the order on their sails and had as an ancillary objective the conversion of pagans to Christianity.

In the decades that followed, Prince Henry dispatched scores of ships from the nearby port of Lagos. According to Zurara, Henry had six motives for his grand enterprise: to learn what lay beyond the Canaries and Cape Bojador, to open profitable new trades with Christian peoples, to investigate the extent of Islamic power, to win converts, to make alliances with any Christian rulers who might be found (e.g., Prester John), and to fulfill the predictions of his horoscope, which compelled him to engage in "great and noble conquests" and to seek "the discovery of things which were hidden from other men." During the 1420s the prince's expeditions explored the Azores and Canaries and colonized the Madeira Islands. These activities suggest that Henry may have been considering a western passage to Asia of the type that Columbus would later attempt.

Before King João died in 1433, he exhorted his son not to abandon his quest. The following year Gil Eannes succeeded in doubling Cape Bojador, and by 1436 Henry's

HENRY THE NAVIGATOR. From *Crónica do descobrimento e conquista da Guiné*, by Gomes Eanes de Zurara, 1543.

BIBLIOTHÈQUE NATIONALE, PARIS

caravels had nearly reached Cape Blanco. But renewed warfare in Morocco (including a disastrous 1437 attack on Tangier), King Duarte's death in 1438, and Afonso V's stormy minority with Pedro as regent hindered Henry's work.

Exploration began anew in 1441 when Antão Gonçalves returned with the first slaves and gold from the Guinea coast and Nuno Tristão reached Cape Blanco. A burst of maritime activity characterized the remainder of the 1440s: Nuno Tristão reached the Bay of Bight in 1442, Tristão and Dinis Dias reached the mouth of the Senegal and Cape Verde in 1445, Alvaro Fernandes pushed on to Sierra Leone in 1446, and Prince Henry in 1448 had a fort and warehouse built on Arguin Island to exploit the Guinea trade, perhaps the first European trading post established overseas.

The year 1449 witnessed the culmination of the struggle between Afonso V and Pedro. After trying without success to act as peacemaker in this feud, Henry sided with his young nephew without taking part in the bloody skirmish at Alfarrobeira (May 1449) that ended with Pedro's demise.

The final decade of Henry's life was dominated by the colonization of the Azores and Madeira, the further exploitation of the Guinea trade, a last campaign in Morocco, and the sponsorship of more voyages along the African coast. In 1458 Henry accompanied Afonso V (flush with crusading zeal but little enamored with the work of maritime discovery) in the campaign against Alcacer Ceguer. Earlier, he had dispatched the Venetian Alvise Cadamosto, who between 1455 and 1456 explored Senegal and Gambia, discovered the Cape Verde Islands, and mapped a significant section of the African coast beyond Cape Vert.

When Prince Henry died in 1460 in his town near Cape St. Vincent, he was in the midst of preparations for additional voyages. Although late medieval conventions of propriety had prevented him from personally embarking on exploratory voyages, his patronage of such trips justly ensured his place as the initiator of the great Age of Discovery. Prince Henry's activities made Portugal the leading European power in the quest for overseas conquest and the center of navigational and geographic knowledge of the age. This legacy attracted the young Columbus to Lisbon and exerted a profound influence on his life and theories. The prince's voyages also ensured Portuguese dominance of the African route to the Indies, thus compelling Columbus to search for a western passage.

BIBLIOGRAPHY

Dinis, A. J. Dias, ed. *Monumenta Henricina.* 8 vols. Coimbra, 1960–.

Godinho, V. M. *A economia dos descobrimentos Henriquinos.* Lisbon, 1962.

Major, R. H. *The Life of Prince Henry of Portugal, Surnamed the Navigator.* London, 1868. Reprint, London, 1967.

Prestage, Edgar. *The Portuguese Pioneers.* London, 1933. Reprint, New York, 1966.

Zurara, Gomes Eanes de. *Chronicle of the Discovery and Conquest of Guinea.* Translated and edited by C. R. Beazley and Edgar Prestage. 2 vols. London, 1896–1899.

GLENN J. AMES

HENRY VII (1457–1509), king of England. Henry Tudor succeeded to the English throne in 1485 at a time when the kingdom was racked by the Wars of the Roses—a series of dynastic battles fought between the feuding families of York and Lancaster since mid-century. When the head of the Lancastrian faction, Henry VII, married the Yorkist Princess Elizabeth, he cemented the two factions together, ending more than thirty years of civil war. He then rebuilt the strength and power of the monarchy and amassed a fortune, replenishing the royal treasury.

Henry increased and protected English commercial interests through a series of skillfully negotiated trade

HENRY VII. Bust by Torrigiano.

HENRY VIII (1491–1547), king of England. Henry VIII, probably the best known of English monarchs, has been portrayed as a glittering Goliath who hovered menacingly over those around him—particularly the women. Popular views aside, Henry VIII is best understood as a study in contrasts.

In his early years Henry was noted for his beauty, height and athletic prowess. He exercised daily in the tiltyard or on the tennis court (a game he made popular in England). He enjoyed the hunt and regularly outrode his companions. But by the end of his life, ill health had made it impossible for him to sit a horse and, as his suits of armor illustrate, he had grown obese. When he died there was little trace of the energetic young man who had captured the hearts of his subjects.

Henry VIII was a deeply pious and orthodox Catholic. In 1520 he wrote a treatise defending the Roman Catholic church against Martin Luther's accusations, which prompted the pope to award him the title "Defender of the Faith." Yet he also engineered a constitutional revolution within the English church and, with Parliament, enacted laws that broke with Rome and created an English catholic church with himself as supreme head in place of the pope. Although he allowed little doctrinal change in

treaties and political alliances with continental countries. Because of his awareness of the importance of trade, Henry in 1496 issued a license to John Cabot and later to his son Sebastian to search for "unknown lands beyond the . . . seas." By the end of his reign he had helped write laws that dealt with standardization of weights, measures, and coinage—all of which encouraged the growth of internal and external commerce.

In foreign policy, Henry VII was motivated by his desire to place England on a par with the great continental powers of France, Spain, and the Holy Roman Empire. To this end he allied himself with Spanish interests through the marriage of his eldest son, Arthur, to Catherine of Aragón, princess of Castile and daughter of Fernando and Isabel. After Arthur's early death, Henry refused to return Catherine's dowry and kept the young widow in England, close to the throne through unofficial promises and plans to marry her to his second son and heir, the future Henry VIII. By the time of his death in 1507, Henry's pragmatic political negotiations in combination with England's growing prosperity and slowly centralizing royal power had made the kingdom an important player in the complex game of maintaining the balance of European power.

BIBLIOGRAPHY

Alexander, M. *The First of the Tudors*. Totowa, N.J., 1980.
Lockyer, R. *Henry VII*. New York, 1968.
Storey, R. L. *The Reign of Henry VII*. London, 1968.

JOAN B. GOLDSMITH

HENRY VIII. Portrait by Hans Holbein.

the catholic liturgy, the nationalization of church wealth, dissolution of monastic houses, and publication of an English Bible loosened ties to the old church and opened the way for the Protestant Reformation during the reigns of his children Edward VI and Elizabeth I.

Henry VIII perceived himself as a patriarch, loyal to the institution of marriage. During his marriage to his first wife, Catherine of Aragón, he wrote a work defending the sacrament of marriage in reaction to its exclusion in the new Lutheran faith. Yet by the end of his life, Henry had been married six times, divorced twice, and widowed three times—twice at the hands of the royal executioner. In the words of a contemporary, he was "the greatest Prince in Christendom" and "the uncommonest man who ever lived!"

BIBLIOGRAPHY

Scarisbrick, J. J. *Henry VIII.* Los Angeles, 1968.
Smith, L. B. *The Mask of Royalty.* London, 1971.

JOAN B. GOLDSMITH

HERALDRY. See *Coat of Arms.*

HERNÁNDEZ. See *Fernández.*

HERRERA Y TORDESILLAS, ANTONIO DE (1549–1624),

Spanish historian of the Indies. Herrera, who was appointed Chief Chronicler of the Indies and Chronicler of Castile and León by Philip II of Spain, is best known for his *Historia general de los hechos de los castellanos en las Islas y Tierra Firme de el Mar Océano* (General history of the deeds of the Castilians in the Islands and Mainland of the Ocean Sea), first published in 1601. Preceded by his study of the West Indies, *Descripción de las Islas y Tierra Firme de el Mar Océano que llaman Indias occidentales,* the *History* is divided into eight sections or decades, chronicling the discovery, exploration, and colonization of the New World from the era of Columbus until 1554.

Influenced by the Roman historian Tacitus, whose *Annales* he translated, Herrera supplied his history with a multitude of details, always striving to magnify the Spanish enterprise and to minimize anything untoward, harsh, cruel, or unjust. He has been accused of plagiarizing from many authors, including Bartolomé de las Casas, Gonzalo Fernández de Oviedo, and Fernando Colón. In reply to the complaint that he had never visited the Indies, he pointed out that neither Livy nor Tacitus had seen all the lands they wrote about. Despite these criticisms, his description and history of the Indies still provide a useful overview of the establishment of the Spanish overseas empire.

BIBLIOGRAPHY

Herrera y Tordesillas, Antonio de. *Historia general de los hechos de los castellanos en las Islas y Tierra Firme de el Mar Océano.* Edited by Antonio González Barcía. Madrid, 1726–1730. Reprint, 2 vols., Asunción, 1944–1947.
Prescott, William H. *History of the Reign of Ferdinand and Isabella.* 3 vols. Philadelphia, 1872.

JOSEPH F. O'CALLAGHAN

HISPANIOLA. See *Española, La.*

HORSES. See *Domesticated Animals.*

HOURGLASS. See *Timeglass.*

HOUSE OF TRADE. See *Casa de la Contratación.*

HUASCAR (d. 1532),

Inca emperor, successor to Huayna Capac and rival of Atahualpa. Huascar was the son of Huayna Capac and Rahua Ocllo, Huayna Capac's sister but not his *coya* (queen). Huayna Capac had left Huascar in charge of the Inca state in Cuzco while he was campaigning in Ecuador, but Huascar was never designated coruler. After the deaths of Huayna Capac and his son and designated successor, Ninan Cuyuchi, there was much dissension among the *orejones* (Inca ruling class). The rivalries between the surviving sons led to the formation of factions. Because of Rahua Ocllo's influence, Huascar obtained court and administrative support in Cuzco and was elected successor to Huayna Capac as emperor of Tahuantinsuyu (the Inca state). However, Huascar did not maintain good relations with his supporters and antagonized the powerful lineages of Cuzco by threatening to confiscate their lands and property and to end their autonomy. He had a reputation for being tactless, violent, cruel, and cowardly. He finally rejected the nobles of Cuzco and surrounded himself with foreigners, especially the Cañaris and the Chachapoyas (northern ethnic groups), who formed his personal bodyguard.

Huascar feared that his brother Atahualpa was organizing a rebellion in the north and sent a militia army to invade Quito. The Inca army supported Atahualpa and repulsed Huascar's troops. Subsequently, Atahualpa took the title of Inca emperor. Huascar's army was definitively defeated at the battle of Huanacopampa, west of Cuzco, and Huascar was captured. Atahualpa's army triumphantly entered Cuzco. Huascar was killed shortly after Atahualpa was captured by Francisco Pizarro at Cajamarca.

BIBLIOGRAPHY

Hemming, John. *The Conquest of the Incas.* San Diego, 1970.
Rostworowski de Díez Canseco, María. "Succession, Coöption to Kingship, and Royal Incest among the Inca." *Southwestern Journal of Anthropology* 16 (1960): 417–427.

JEANETTE SHERBONDY

HUAYNA CAPAC (d. 1525?), Inca emperor. Huayna Capac was born Tito Cusi Hualpa in Tumipampa (Quito) while his father, the Inca Tupac Yupanqui, was conducting the campaign for the northern expansion of Tahuantinsuyu (the Inca state) into what is today southern Colombia. He was quite young when he succeeded to the throne. His mother, the *coya* (queen) Mama Ocllo, begged him to stay close to Cuzco, where for several years he inspected the many ethnic groups near the capital that had already submitted to Inca rule.

He essentially maintained the vast territory his father had conquered, which extended from central Chile to southern Colombia. While he was leading his armies through the southern quarter of Tahuantinsuyu, he heard of rebellions in the north and marched to Quito. The northern ethnic groups formed a strong alliance against the Inca troops, among whom there was much dissension. At one point Huayna Capac's troops even dropped his litter, which angered him for many years. Huayna Capac personally led his army and spent many years in Tumipampa fighting against and finally incorporating the northern ethnic groups into the Inca state.

He heard reports of the arrival of Francisco Pizarro's expedition along the coast of Ecuador in 1526. Shortly thereafter he died in Quito during an epidemic of smallpox and measles that also killed most of his court, the generals of his major military command, and the son he had named as his successor, Ninan Cuyuchi. He was succeeded by his son, Huascar.

BIBLIOGRAPHY

Hemming, John. *The Conquest of the Incas.* San Diego, 1970.
Rostworowski de Díez Canseco, María. *Historia del Tahuantinsuyu.* Lima, 1988.

JEANETTE SHERBONDY

HUMBOLDT, ALEXANDER VON (1769–1859), German naturalist, traveler, and statesman. Friedrich Wilhelm Heinrich Alexander von Humboldt was born in Berlin, the son of a major in the Prussian army who later became a royal chamberlain. Originally destined for a financial career, while at the universities of Frankfurt an der Oder, Berlin, and Göttingen, Humboldt's passion for travel and his early interest in geology and botany redirected him into a lifelong study of the natural sciences. In 1790 he traveled to Holland, England, and France with George Forster. In 1792 he entered the Prussian mining service, and was appointed a mining superintendent in Upper Franconia. Moving to Paris in 1798, he contributed to the first relatively conclusive determination of magnetic inclination. Later that year he journeyed to Spain and thereafter undertook a scientific expedition in company with the French botanist Aimé Bonpland, traveling during the next six years through the Spanish colonies in Venezuela, Cuba, Colombia, Peru, Ecuador, and Mexico, gathering plant specimens, mapping the regions, recording observations of natural phenomena, and studying volcanoes, the origin of tropical storms, and the igneous origin of certain rocks. On his return journey in 1804, he visited the United States, meeting several times with President Thomas Jefferson and cabinet members, to whom he reported on his travels. In 1829 he made a long-postponed scientific expedition to Russian Asia. In his later years he was often employed on diplomatic missions for the Prussian government. He died in Berlin after a prolonged illness at the age of ninety.

Humboldt's travel journals, never completed, were published in thirty-four volumes over a period of twenty-five years. Among his most important works was *Kosmos* (1845–1862), in which he provided a description of the physical universe. In a five-volume work that appeared in 1814–1834 entitled *Examen critique de l'histoire de la géographie du nouveau continent aux XV* et *XVI* siècles (A critical examination of the history of the geography of the new continent in the fifteenth and sixteenth centuries), Humboldt directed attention to a generally overlooked passage in Washington Irving's biography of Columbus in which Irving noted that the name America had been invented in 1507 by Martin Waldseemüller and his associates and first published in *Cosmographiae introductio*, as well as in a set of globes and a world map.

BIBLIOGRAPHY

Dictionary of Scientific Biography. Vol. 6, pp. 549–555. New York, 1972.
Encyclopaedia Britannica. 11th ed. Vol. 13, pp. 873–875.
Humboldt, Alexander von. *Examen critique de l'histoire de le géographie du nouveau continent aux XV* et *XVI* siècles. 5 vols. Paris, 1814–1834.
Irving, Washington. *The Life and Voyages of Christopher Columbus.* New York, 1828.
Nouvelle biographie générale depuis les temps les plus reculés jusqu'à nos jours. Vol. 25, cols. 510–525. Paris, 1861.
Terra, Helmut de. *Humboldt: The Life and Times of Alexander von Humboldt.* 6th ed. New York, 1968.

SILVIO A. BEDINI

I

ICELANDIC SAGAS. The sagas of Iceland are relevant to the story of Columbus in two ways: they recount the explorations by Europeans who preceded him to the New World and there is a hint in the records that Columbus may have visited Iceland. The Icelandic sagas indisputably document the presence of Icelanders and other Norsemen on American shores several centuries prior to Columbus. The term *saga* is an Old Norse word meaning "tale," originally an oral narrative, which began to be committed to writing in the twelfth century by Icelandic scribes. The sagas are of various kinds; they range from sober historical accounts of past events, primarily relating to happenings in which Icelanders were involved, to more fanciful stories that must be identified as romances. The chroniclers of Iceland were keenly aware of their special history as an island colony of Scandinavian (primarily Norwegian) enterprise. After their gradual Christianizing in the tenth and eleventh centuries, they began busily recording past and contemporary events in their history. Preservation of these sagas was at first casual but became systematic in the sixteenth century with the collecting of documents in the royal libraries of Scandinavia, especially in Denmark, which at this time held dominion over Iceland. An Icelandic repository did not come into being until well into the twentieth century.

Information about the Icelandic discovery was actually available before the sagas, in the *History of the Archbishopric of Hamburg* (c. 1070) by the German cleric Adam of Bremen. Adam wrote that the king of Denmark had told him of an island in the North called "Winland," which had the peculiar quality that "vines grow wild there which yield the best of wine" as well as "grain unsown." Around 1130 a Christian historian of Iceland, Ari Thorgilsson, known as "the Learned," wrote his *Íslendingabók* (Book of the Icelanders) in which he mentioned "Vinland" and

its native inhabitants, whom he called "skraelingar," apparently a derogatory term referring either to American Indians or Eskimos.

For our purposes the most valuable sources are the Icelandic sagas that were written between 1100 and 1300, some of which deal specifically with the discovery of America. They offer two differing versions, which we distinguish by the manuscript compilations that contain them, called the "Hauk's Book" and the "Flatey Book." These are both from the fourteenth century. A third version, "AM. 537 qto." from the fifteenth century, is largely identical with the Hauk's Book. Scholars have long debated the relative merits of the two versions without coming to any definite conclusion.

The Flatey Book version concentrates on the family of Eric the Red and his son Leif Ericsson, who was the first to explore Vinland. Eric was born in Norway and became the first Norse settler of Greenland, having emigrated as an outlaw from Iceland in 986, but he held back from exploring Vinland. The first person to view Vinland was Bjarni Herjulfsson, who skirted its coast after losing his way from Norway to Greenland. His sighting of the unknown coast encouraged Leif to undertake an expedition that is recounted in some detail in the Flatey Book. Because of his exploration and his success Leif came to be known as "the Lucky." He was also commissioned by the king of Norway, Olafr Tryggvason, to convert the natives to Christianity (including his recalcitrant father). Leif was the first to apply Norse names to the American coast: from north to south, Helluland, "land of rocks"; Markland, "land of forests"; and Vinland, "land of vines" (possibly "of wine"). Just which part of the American coast was designated by these names is still a matter of discussion.

According to the Flatey account, Leif was not the only son of Eric to explore America. His brother Thorvald became a victim of the natives' arrows and lost his life. A third brother, Thorstein, also made the attempt but was driven back by storms. A sister named Freydis followed because "people fell to talking of the journey to Vinland, for this seemed an open road to wealth and honor." Freydis apparently had nothing but wealth in mind, for her expedition resulted in the massacre of many participants.

The Hauk's Book version (also known as Eric the Red's Saga) is more interested in the family of the later explorer Thorfinn Karlsefni, who was the first to make a serious attempt to settle the new land. One suspects that the saga writer's interest was determined by the fact that Thorfinn and his wife, Gudrid, were direct ancestors of Hauk Erlendson, the compiler of Hauk's Book. Thorfinn was an Icelandic trader who came to Greenland and equipped a fleet of three ships with 160 men, many accompanied by their wives. He brought "all sorts of livestock" with him and did not head directly to Vinland, but crossed the Davis Strait and sailed down the coast of Labrador at least as far as Newfoundland. Like Leif he found lands that he named Helluland, Markland, and Vinland.

But he also found and named other areas: a headland named Kjalarnes (Keelness), long, sandy beaches named Furdustrandir (Wonderstrands), Straumfjord (Stream-fjord), a mysterious area named Hvitramannaland (White Men's Land), and finally an area named Hop, where he encountered natives with whom he first traded and later fought. This encounter can be seen as the first clash between Indians and Europeans, and it was disastrous for the outnumbered Icelanders; after their third winter they retreated back to Greenland. In the words of historian Gwyn Jones, "They were unwilling to woo and unable to conquer." The Norse settlements in Greenland have left abundant remains in the form of dwellings and churches, which were abandoned only with the extinction of the Norse colonies in the fourteenth century or possibly the early fifteenth.

There can be no doubt that the expeditions to Vinland actually took place in the tenth and eleventh centuries, but the exact location of their "Vinland" is still in doubt, in spite of the assurance of the sagas. Vinland has been sought in modern times from Labrador in the north to Florida in the south. In 1965 a new angle was offered by scholars at Yale University in the form of a purported "Vinland Map." The map got its name by including on a rectangular mappamundi a figure to the west and south of Greenland representing a "Vinlanda Insula" (Island of Vinland). Its appearance in a sumptuous Yale publication was a scholarly sensation.

In the meanwhile an experienced Norwegian explorer, Helge Ingstad, who had been pondering the problem of the Norse colonies in the New World, undertook explorations in northern waters from 1961 to 1968. He first announced his findings in *National Geographic* (November 1964) and published his first book on the subject, *Westward to Vinland*, in 1969. Ingstad was the first to locate Norse remains on an American coast, at a place in northern Newfoundland known as L'Anse aux Meadows. This was an even more startling discovery than the Vinland Map, for it concentrated attention on a more northerly area than had been customary. It had the merit of reflecting more accurately the directions of the sagas in terms of days' sailings. After exploring the American and Canadian east coasts thoroughly, Ingstad came upon sites that had never been excavated and that proved to contain indubitable evidence of Norse settlement around A.D. 1000. He and his archaeologist wife, Anne Stine Ingstad, spent seven summers, assisted by other experts, digging up the remains.

In Ingstad's words: "The results may be briefly summarized as follows: Eight larger or smaller house-sites . . . one of them a smithy, four boat-sheds, three large outdoor pits of which two may have been cooking pits. Various finds have been made at the sites and in the many test trenches." Among the rather sparse finds Ingstad mentions stone tools, nails, fragments of iron, a stone lamp, a whetstone for needles, and a soapstone spindle-whorl. A larger publication edited by Anne Stine Ingstad appeared in 1977, detailing the finds with an abundance of maps and illustrations, plus carbon datings. The Ingstads are convinced that this was the Vinland of the sagas, but questions remain about the fact that the sagas also include expeditions to more southerly climes. Ingstad admits the possibility. Otherwise we have to dismiss the sagas' stories of grapes and self-sown wheat and the active contact with the Skraelings.

The possibility of Columbus's having visited Iceland is based on a passage in his son Fernando Colón's biography of his father. He cites a letter from Columbus stating that in February 1477 he sailed "a hundred leagues beyond the island of Tile" (i.e., Thule, Iceland). But there is no reference to his having stopped in Iceland or spoken with anyone, and in any case it is unlikely that anyone he spoke to would have known about the Icelandic discovery of Vinland. More significant may be the fact that he refers to Bristol, England, as the starting point of this voyage; Bristol had connections with Iceland. On the whole, however, it is hardly important. If Columbus had learned anything, he would have mentioned it in his plans for exploration.

[See also *Vinland*; *Vinland Map*; and the biography of Ericsson.]

BIBLIOGRAPHY

Haugen, Einar. *Voyages to Vinland: The First American Saga.* New York, 1942.

Ingstad, Anne Stine. *The Discovery of a Norse Settlement in America.* Oslo, 1977.

Ingstad, Helge. *Westward to Vinland.* New York, 1969.

Jones, Gwyn. *The Norse Atlantic Saga.* London, 1964.

Magnusson, Magnus. *Viking Expansion Westwards.* London, 1973.

Skelton, R. A., Thomas E. Marston, and George D. Painter. *The Vinland Map.* New Haven and London, 1965.

EINAR HAUGEN

ICONOGRAPHY.

[This entry includes five articles that explore the Columbian legacy in painting, coins, stamps, and motion pictures:

Early European Portraits
American Painting
Numismatics
Philately
Film

For further discussion of visual representations of Columbus, see *Monuments and Memorials.* See *Literature* for explorations of the Columbian theme in literature.]

Early European Portraits

As far as we know, Columbus was never painted in his lifetime. Yet virtually every book about him contains a portrait, and many general textbooks do as well. The 1893 World's Columbian Exposition in Chicago displayed seventy-one portraits of Columbus, which William Eleroy Curtis discussed in *Christopher Columbus: His Portraits and Monuments.* None could be considered authentic, and few even remotely resembled extant descriptions of his physical characteristics.

The only firm evidence about Columbus's appearance comes from a few brief descriptions written by persons who knew him or at least were his contemporaries. The descriptions have a good deal in common and may have borrowed from one another. They describe a strongly built man of more than average height for the time. All agree that he had a ruddy complexion; he may have had freckles as well. His hair is variously described as bright red or blond when he was a young man and as having turned gray when he was about thirty. His face was oblong, neither full nor thin and distinguished by an aquiline nose and lively eyes. The commentaries in Italian describe their color as *bianchi* (pale or light). One Spanish commentator uses the word *garzos,* which nowadays is usually translated as "light blue," but which seems to have connoted "light gray-green" or "hazel" to Columbus's contemporaries. These distinctive physical characteristics provide a standard by which to evaluate the portraiture of Columbus.

PORTRAIT BY SEBASTIANO DEL PIOMBO (1485–1547). Oil on canvas.
THE METROPOLITAN MUSEUM OF ART, GIFT OF J. PIERPONT MORGAN, 1900.(00.18.2)

Only a few representative portraits will be discussed here, but they served as models for scores of others. Sculpture and other art forms will not be discussed, nor will the large historical scenes and murals that feature events in Columbus's life.

The most representative portraits of Columbus fall within several families or types. The first, and probably the best known, is the Piombo type, based on Sebastiano del Piombo's portrait in the Metropolitan Museum of Art in New York. The man in Piombo's portrait has a fleshy face and nose, large round eyes, dark hair, full lips, and a double chin. He is wearing a black angled hat, a full dark cape, and a vertically pleated shirt. An inscription across the top of the painting gives the date as 1519 and reads, "Haec est effigies liguris miranda Columbi antipodum primus rate qui penetravit in orbem" ("This is the likeness of the Ligurian mariner Columbus, the first in the world who penetrated the antipodes").

There is no doubt that the portrait is by Piombo, who was a younger contemporary of Columbus, and the inscription on the painting would seem to identify it conclusively. Nonetheless, the face does not reflect the written evidence we have about Columbus, and art historians have recently questioned its identification on

ENGRAVING FROM THÉODOR DE BRY'S *GRANDS VOYAGES.* Piombo type.

LIBRARY OF CONGRESS

depictions associated with the Italian Paolo Giovio (1483–1552), archbishop of Nocera in the early sixteenth century. The archbishop's palace on Lake Como displayed a large and important art collection, and his portrait of Columbus, probably commissioned between 1530 and 1540, was copied by many other artists. Unfortunately, the location and identity of the painting owned by Archbishop Giovio are no longer certain, and several paintings have been claimed as the original over the centuries.

Further confusion relates to a book Giovio wrote called *Elogia virorum bellica virtute illustrium* (1549). An edition published in Basel by Petrus Perna in 1575 contained an engraving commonly attributed to Tobias Stimmer that is often claimed to be the oldest firmly dated portrait of Columbus. There is no evidence, however, that Stimmer ever saw the portrait owned by Giovio or indeed that the engraving bears any resemblance to that portrait. The engraving shows a man with a firm expression, short curly hair, and large round eyes, dressed in what appears to be

other grounds. Michael Hirst, in his book about Piombo, says the inscription "is a later addition and there is, therefore, no reason to suppose that it is the likeness of the navigator or that the painting was done in about 1519–20." He concludes that a stylistic analysis of Piombo's development hints that "the picture may one day prove to be of one of the clerics present in the winter of 1529–30 at Bologna."

During the sixteenth century, however, the Piombo type of likeness became accepted as authentic. Théodore de Bry's *Grands voyages,* published in Frankfurt in 1595, included an engraving of the Piombo type, which Bry claimed was based on a copy of a portrait commissioned by King Fernando of Aragón before Columbus's voyage. Portraits of the Piombo type continued to be popular in the succeeding centuries. Constantino Brumidi's two paintings of Columbus in the U.S. Capitol Building, painted in the mid-nineteenth century, clearly used Piombo as a model, and twentieth-century artists have found inspiration in Piombo and his followers as well. Nonetheless, Piombo's painting cannot be taken as an authentic or even plausible representation of Columbus.

Another family of Columbus portraiture stems from two

PORTRAIT BY CONSTANTINO BRUMIDI. Piombo type. Adorns a ceiling in the Senate wing of the U.S. Capitol.

ARCHITECT OF THE CAPITOL

a monk's robe. It does not actively contradict the evidence from contemporary descriptions of Columbus, although no one ever wrote that he had curly hair.

Thus, there are two types of Columbus portraiture associated with Paolo Giovio, although many authors seem unaware of the distinction. One type descended from the painting owned by Giovio or its numerous copies; the other, from the engraving in his *Elogia virorum.*

The painting is best exemplified by the so-called di Orchi portrait, named for Dr. Alessandro di Orchi of Como, who owned the portrait in the late nineteenth century. Many claim this is the original portrait of Giovio's collection, because the Giovio male family line died out in 1849, and this portrait passed to Antonia Giovio, wife of di Orchi. The unknown artist shows the worn face of a man in later middle age, with dull eyes and a firm expression. His garb is semiclerical. The di Orchi portrait has inspired many imitators over the years. Whether or not it depicts Columbus in old age, it seems to represent a real person rather than an idealized hero.

THE SO-CALLED DI ORCHI PORTRAIT. An anonymous work named for Alessandro di Orchi, who owned the portrait in the nineteenth century. Giovio type. The work presently hangs in the Museo Civico, Como.   SCALA/ART RESOURCE

ENGRAVING ATTRIBUTED TO TOBIAS STIMMER. Capriolo subtype. From the 1575 Basel edition of Giovio's *Elogia virorum bellica virtute illustrium.*   PAR/NYC, INC.

In 1552 Cristofano dell'Altissimo was sent to Como by Cosimo de' Medici to copy the Giovio portrait. His copy has hung in the Uffizi palace in Florence ever since, belying the sometime claim that it is the original Giovio portrait. The Florentine/Uffizi portrait is very similar to the di Orchi portrait, but the subject has a thinner face and harsher expression. It seems to have been painted by a less skilled hand than the di Orchi portrait, which reinforces the notion that it is a copy rather than the original owned by Giovio.

The type of Columbus portrait descended from the engraving in Giovio's *Elogia virorum* is best represented by Aliprando Capriolo's engraving in *Ritratti di cento capitani illustri,* first published in Rome in 1596. Capriolo's rendering of the facial features, expression, and garb of Columbus is similar to Stimmer's, although Capriolo depicts Columbus's hair as long and straight rather than short and curly.

Many later portraits clearly descend from the Capriolo engraving, including a painting in the Museo Naval in Madrid. The Spanish government commissioned the portrait in 1838 from Charles Le Grand, who added age lines

FLORENTINE/UFFIZI PORTRAIT. Presumed to be a copy of the original
Giovio portrait.   LIBRARY OF CONGRESS

and a more anxious expression to the face but followed the general aspect and garb set out by Capriolo. The artist shows Columbus with a noble head, round light eyes, a very high forehead, a receding hairline, straight blond hair, and a long straight nose with flaring nostrils. Many other artists since have used Capriolo and Le Grand as models.

Another commonly used depiction of Columbus is the Cevasco portrait, named for the donor who gave it to the city of Genoa. The Cevasco portrait fits in no obvious category, although it bears more resemblance to the Capriolo family of portraiture than any other. The artist depicted Columbus with a round, soft face, round, rather dull eyes, a soft cap, and a simple tunic. The portrait has been attributed to Ridolfo Ghirlandaio (1483–1561), although most sources simply say the artist and date are unknown.

The last family of Columbus portraiture to be considered here descended from a portrait by Lorenzo Lotto, signed and dated 1512. The portrait was discovered in Europe in the late nineteenth century and, despite the doubts of some scholars, soon gained a reputation as the most authentic likeness of Columbus. The portrait shows a young man with a very high forehead, a long face, straight fair hair, and fair skin. The reputation of the Lotto portrait relates not only to its close adherence to contemporary descriptions of Columbus but also to its provenience. Lotto painted it for Domenico Malipiero, a Venetian senator and historian, on the recommendation of Angelo Trevisan, secretary to the Venetian ambassador in Granada in 1501. Both Trevisan and his ambassador knew Columbus well, which puts the Lotto portrait closer to its subject than any other painting known. An engraving of the Lotto portrait by T. Johnson in 1892, contained in an article by John C. Van Dyke for Century magazine, gave Columbus a suspicious, piercing glance and an aspect rather different from the original.

The Lotto family of Columbus portraiture includes two distinguished paintings. One is The Virgin of the Navigators by Alejo Fernández, a Spanish artist active in Seville from 1508 and in Córdoba before that. Fernández could have met or at least seen Columbus before the latter died in 1506, though there is no proof that the two had any contact. The Virgin of the Navigators, painted in 1531–1536, hangs in the Reales Alcazares in Seville and depicts several famous explorers at the Virgin's feet. They have been variously identified, but the figure in lavish robes in the left foreground has often been identified as Columbus. Whether or not Fernández ever saw Columbus, it is likely that he used a local model for the painting, because his Columbus greatly resembles King Melchior in the Epiphany that Fernández's workshop painted for the cathedral of Seville. In other words, however closely Fernández's portrait may resemble descriptions of Columbus, one cannot argue that it is an authentic likeness.

The other distinguished portrait of the Lotto type was painted by the Spanish artist Joaquin Sorolla y Bastida (1863–1923). Sorolla's Departure of Columbus from the Port of Palos was commissioned by the American collector Thomas Fortune Ryan and currently hangs in the Mariner's Museum in Newport News, Virginia. Besides doing research, the artist used a descendant of Columbus, the duke of Veragua, as his model. In Sorolla's masterful full-length portrait, Columbus has sharp features and a penetrating gaze, which reflect his character far better than the mild and noble visages depicted by Lotto and Capriolo.

Dozens of other portrayals of Columbus follow these four families of portraiture—Piombo, di Orchi, Capriolo, and Lotto—either singly or in combination. Others span the range of European physical types and bear little or no relation to contemporary descriptions of Columbus. Depending on the source, Columbus can be depicted as a bearded buccaneer, a corpulent burgher, a brooding intellectual, a dashing cavalier, or a pensive ascetic. He can be clean-shaven or bearded; thin or fat; blond,

ENGRAVING BY ALIPRANDO CAPRIOLO. From his *Ritratti de cento capitani illustri*. Rome, 1596. Capriolo subtype.

ENGRAVING AFTER THE LE GRAND PORTRAIT. This engraving by Henri Lefort (France, 1891) closely follows the 1838 portrait by Charles Le Grand in the Museo Naval, Madrid. Capriolo subtype.

OIL PORTRAIT BY LORENZO LOTTO. Signed and dated 1512.

ENGRAVING BY T. JOHNSON. From *Century Magazine*, 1892. Lotto type.

OIL PORTRAIT BY JOAQUIN SOROLLA Y BASTIDA. Lotto type.   COURTESY OF THE MARINERS' MUSEUM, NEWPORT NEWS, VIRGINIA

ALEJO FERNÁNDEZ, *THE VIRGIN OF THE NAVIGATORS*. Oil, 1531–1536. The figure in lavish robes in the left foreground is often identified as Columbus.   MAS, BARCELONA

brunet, red-headed, totally gray, or nearly bald. Because we have no portraits painted from life, and none even dated in his lifetime, there is no authentic portrait of Columbus. Nonetheless, a comparison of written descriptions with the available portraiture suggests that the best approximations of his appearance are the Lotto or Capriolo type of portrait for the prime years of his life and the di Orchi type for his old age.

BIBLIOGRAPHY

Berenson, Bernard. *Lorenzo Lotto*. London, 1956.
Bianconi, Piero. *All the Paintings of Lorenzo Lotto*. Translated by Paul Colacicchi. New York, 1963.

Curtis, William Eleroy. *Christopher Columbus: His Portraits and Monuments*. Chicago, 1893.
Hirst, Michael. *Sebastiano del Piombo*. Oxford, 1981.
Honour, Hugh. "L'image de Christophe Colomb." *Revue du Louvre* 26 (1976): 255–267.
Peel, Edmund, et al. *The Painter Joaquin Sorolla y Bastida*. London, 1989.
Van Dyke, John C. "The Lotto Portrait of Columbus." *Century* 44 (October 1892): 818–822.
Volpe, Carlo, ed. *L'opera completa di Sebastiano del Piombo*. Milan, 1980.

CARLA RAHN PHILLIPS

American Painting

Depictions of Christopher Columbus in American art are diverse because artists have imagined his likeness so differently. But they are also monotonously similar because painters portray identical incidents. Such events as his meeting with clerical scholars in Salamanca, his departure from Palos, his landing at San Salvador, his triumphal appearance before the Spanish court, and his return in chains after being arrested by Spanish authorities frequently found their way into paintings and prints. During the nineteenth century the landing at San Salvador was by far the most popular Columbus subject, perhaps because it best seemed to embody the metaphor of "discovery" by picturing the first permanent European presence on American shores.

One of the earliest depictions of Columbus by an American artist was Benjamin West's *An Indian Cacique of the Island of Cuba* (Chicago Historical Society), created as an illustration for Bryan Edward's *History of the British West Indies*, published in 1794 shortly after the tercentenary of Columbus's first voyage. Six years later Edward Savage and David Edwin issued a large engraving entitled *The Landing of Columbus* (American Antiquarian Society, Worcester, Mass.), which features a large burly figure of the Admiral in Renaissance attire accompanied by a priest and several soldiers. Three immigrant artists—Michael Corne (private collection), Frederick Kemmelmeyer (National Gallery of Art, Washington, D.C.), and John James Barralet (Library of Congress)—created Landing of Columbus scenes in the early years of the nineteenth century. All three of these artists placed an unprecedented emphasis on the Catholic orientation of the landing party and stressed the importance of American commerce. Around 1825, an anonymous folk artist rendered a most unusual version of the *Landing of Columbus* (New York State Historical Association, Cooperstown), featuring two natives, one playing a flute, the other aiming a bow and arrow at a landing party in the background. Were it not for the inscription attached beneath ("Christopher Columbus

FREDERICK KEMMELMEYER, *FIRST LANDING OF CHRISTOPHER COLUMBUS.* Oil on canvas, 1800–1805.

NATIONAL GALLERY OF ART, WASHINGTON, D.C.

Landing upon the Island of St. Salvador; October 12, 1492"), one would have no way of identifying the subject, especially since the setting looks a great deal like the rocky coast of New England.

After Washington Irving's popular *History of the Life and Voyages of Christopher Columbus* was published in 1828, artists interpreting events from the Admiral's life patterned their compositions after the many descriptive passages in the biography. John Vanderlyn acknowledged that he consulted Irving's text when painting *The Landing of Columbus on San Salvador,* which was installed in the Capitol rotunda in 1847 and has become the most famous Columbus painting in the United States. After he received the commission from Congress in 1836, Vanderlyn (then in his sixties) traveled to the Caribbean to make sketches of the foliage and the terrain before renting a studio in Paris to complete the painting. While the work was in progress, Americans visiting the French capital sent home glowing reports, no doubt realizing that the composition—with the heroic Columbus planting the standard of Fernando and Isabel on the tropical shore—epitomized the discovery as did no other painting that preceded or followed it.

Vanderlyn's work became such a familiar icon of popular culture that copies appeared on U.S. stamps, souvenirs, advertisements, and even the side panel of a turn-of-the-century circus wagon (Circus Museum, Baraboo, Wis.).

Among other unusual American works from the mid-nineteenth century are William James Hubard's *The Dream of Columbus* (Valentine Museum, Richmond), which pictures the Admiral as a youthful dreamer envisioning his future empire, and four versions of *Columbus at Salamanca* by Robert Walter Weir (West Point Museum), William Henry Powell (Kennedy Gallery, New York City), Frank Duveneck (Cincinnati Art Museum), and William Merritt Chase (private collection). Between 1842 and 1855, the German-American artist Emanuel Leutze executed a series of paintings devoted to episodes from Columbus's life, including *The Return of Columbus in Chains to Cadiz* (1842, Masco Corporation, Detroit, on loan to U.S. State Department), *Columbus before the Queen* (1843, Brooklyn Museum), and *The Departure of Columbus from Palos* (1855, Fumi International Collection, Tokyo). All of Leutze's compositions are theatrical spectacles that exaggerate the Admiral's lonely heroism and dramatize his mistreatment by the Spanish court. *The Departure from Palos,* which depicts the dramatic moment on the deck of *Santa María* just as the large sail was being hoisted, is perhaps the most riveting because Columbus in the center of the composition points westward toward the lands he will "discover." In the early 1880s, William Morris Hunt created an allegorical mural entitled *The Discoverer* for the New York State capitol in Albany, featuring a brooding figure of Columbus accompanied by several goddesses. Shortly after its completion, Hunt's painting began to deteriorate and subsequently had to be covered.

The 1892 quadricentenary inspired many American painters and printmakers to delineate episodes from Columbus's life. Thomas Moran and Albert Bierstadt painted tropical landscapes with tiny representations of Columbus and his crew, Thomas Eakins made a sketch of *Columbus in Prison* (Kennedy Gallery), and James A. McN. Whistler designed a *Discoverer* mural for the Boston Public Library, although the project was never completed. In the early twentieth century, the illustrators Edward

ANONYMOUS, *LANDING OF COLUMBUS.* Watercolor, circa 1825.

NEW YORK STATE HISTORICAL ASSOCIATION, COOPERSTOWN

JOHN VANDERLYN, *THE LANDING OF COLUMBUS ON SAN SALVADOR.* Installed in the Rotunda of the U.S. Capitol in 1847.

ARCHITECT OF THE CAPITOL

ROBERT WALTER WEIR, *COLUMBUS AT SALAMANCA*.   WEST POINT MUSEUM, NEW YORK

EMANUEL LEUTZE, *COLUMBUS BEFORE THE QUEEN*. Oil on canvas, 1843.   THE BROOKLYN MUSEUM, NEW YORK

ROBERT COLESCOTT, *KNOWLEDGE OF THE PAST IS THE KEY TO THE FUTURE: SOME AFTER THOUGHTS ON DISCOVERY*. Acrylic on canvas, 1986. COURTESY OF THE PHYLISS KIND GALLERY, NEW YORK AND CHICAGO; PHOTOGRAPH BY ADAM REICH

Austin Abbey (Yale University) and N. C. Wyeth (Annapolis Museum) created dramatic landing scenes that featured a fair and youthful Columbus claiming the "New World" for Spain. By the 1930s, films began to replace paintings as the major source for Columbus imagery, while at the same time adherence to modern trends seemed to end the long history of narrative paintings devoted to episodes from Columbus's life. But the subject has not vanished entirely, even though such recent works as Robert Colescott's *Knowledge of the Past Is the Key to the Future: Some After Thoughts on Discovery* (1986, Metropolitan Museum of Art, New York City) and Alexander M. Frankfurter's *Columbus Triptych* (1980s, property of the artist) have responded to ethnic and racial sensitivites and thus attempted to counteract the very myths that once motivated artists in the United States.

BIBLIOGRAPHY

Abrams, Ann Uhry, and Barbara Groseclose, eds. *Christopher Columbus/U.S.A.* Forthcoming.
Brown, Milton W. et al. *American Art: Painting, Sculpture, Architecture, Decorative Arts, Photography.* New York, 1979.

ANN UHRY ABRAMS

Numismatics

Christopher Columbus was not widely depicted in coins or medals until the twentieth century. The 1592, 1692, and 1792 anniversaries of his first voyage passed without numismatic notice, although a medal struck by the Columbian Order (Tammany Society) of New York City in 1789 may have honored Columbus. The first medal to salute him specifically was a French bronze piece issued by Amedée Durand in 1819 as part of a series of medals honoring the world's famous men. The first coin to depict Columbus was an eight-real (dollar) piece issued by Guatemala in 1854.

The four-hundredth anniversary of the first voyage was commemorated by four nations. The United States, Colombia, and El Salvador issued half-dollar coins (approximately 31 millimeters in diameter) in 1892; the American coin was reissued in 1893 and the Salvadoran coin in 1893 and 1894. The United States also issued a silver quarter-dollar in 1893 portraying Queen Isabel. El Salvador placed Columbus's effigy on its 37-millimeter silver pesos issued between 1892 and 1914. The fourth nation, Costa Rica, named its new monetary unit the colón in 1897 and placed

COLUMBIAN SILVER DOLLAR. Minted by the United States in 1892 and 1893, the world's first coin of general circulation to honor Christopher Columbus. Over 2,500,000 pieces were struck at the Philadelphia mint. Size: 31 mm.

ALL COINS ILLUSTRATED IN THIS ARTICLE ARE FROM THE COLLECTION OF RUSSELL RULAU.

SILVER QUARTER DOLLAR. Honoring Queen Isabel, minted by the United States in 1893. Only 24,000 pieces were struck at the Philadelphia mint. Size: 25 mm.

FIFTY-CENTAVO COIN, COLOMBIA. Colombia struck only 4,800 pieces of this 1892 denomination honoring Columbus. Size: 31 mm.

ONE-PESO COIN, EL SALVADOR. This coin honoring Columbus was struck from 1892 through 1914 at the Central American Bank. Size: 37.5 mm.

Columbus's portrait on its gold two-, five-, and ten-colón coins issued from 1897 to 1928.

There were no other Columbus coins until Italy pictured Columbus's three ships (without naming them) on its silver five-hundred-lire coins between 1958 and 1987. Other nations began to honor Columbus on coins intended for collectors in the 1960s. The Bahamas, where Columbus first landed in the New World, very likely on Watlings Island (Guanahani or San Salvador), issued a gold one-hundred-dollar piece in 1967; other Bahamian issues

appeared between 1971 and 1988. Haiti issued Columbus coins between 1967 and 1974, Jamaica between 1972 and 1989, the Turks and Caicos Islands between 1975 and 1986, the Cayman Islands in 1988, the Dominican Republic between 1984 and 1988, the Cook Islands in 1989, Cuba in 1981, Belize in 1989, Nicaragua in 1989, Italy in 1990, and El Salvador between 1984 and 1988.

In 1989, Spain issued a set of four gold and eight silver coins to honor Columbus, his discoveries, and the times in which he lived. Each coin was struck to the standards of

Two-thousand peseta coin, Spain. This large (40-mm) silver coin was struck in an issue of 235,000 at the Madrid Mint in 1989. Its value approximates the eight-real "Spanish dollar" of the sixteenth century.

Two-hundred peseta coin, Spain. An astrolabe such as that used by Columbus is featured on this small (20-mm) 1989 issue, approximately equal to one real in sixteenth-century coinage. This and the two-thousand peseta coin are part of a twelve-coin issue initiating a massive memorial minting saluting the 1992 Quincentennial.

Ten-thousand cordoba coin, Nicaragua. This 1989 silver coin recalls the discovery of the country by Columbus during his final voyage in 1502. Ten thousand pieces were struck. Size: 38 mm.

the fifteenth century. The U.S. Congress authorized gold five-dollar, silver one-dollar, and nickel-clad fifty-cent coins for the five-hundredth anniversary in 1992.

BIBLIOGRAPHY

Eglit, Nathan N. *Columbiana: The Medallic History of Christopher Columbus and the Columbian Exposition of 1893.* Chicago, 1965.

Forrer, Leonard. *Biographical Dictionary of Medalists.* 9 vols. Reprint, London, 1987.

Hibler, Hal E., and Charles V. Kappen. *So-Called Dollars.* New York, 1963.

Hobson, Burton. *Historic Gold Coins of the World.* London, 1971.

Krause, Chester L., and Clifford Mishler. *Standard Catalog of World Coins.* Iola, Wis., 1990.

Rulau, Russell. *Discovering America: The Coin Collecting Connection.* Iola, Wis., 1989.

RUSSELL RULAU

Philately

From the first issuance of postage stamps in Great Britain in 1840 to the present day, many countries of the world have honored Christopher Columbus with designs on their stamps; over fifteen hundred such stamps have been issued. The first country to so honor Columbus was Chile, which used his portrait on its first postal issue in 1853—a five-centavo denomination in brown-red. In fact, all of Chile's postal issues until 1900 utilized his portrait in the design.

The initial stamp issued by the United States to commemorate Columbus was the fifteen-cent bicolor stamp of the 1869 regular postage series, which showed a classic landing scene of Columbus's discovery of the Americas. This particular denomination has also been found with the center inverted, which is a very scarce and valuable stamp. Its value ranges from $17,500 to $145,000, depending on condition and color, and whether used or unused.

The nineteenth century was a period of considerable movement of people from Europe to the United States and then westward across the continent. In the course of this expansion, more than forty towns named Columbus were established, of which only nineteen have survived with an operating post office into the latter half of the twentieth century.

A major event commemorating Columbus's discovery of the New World was the World's Columbian Exposition held in Chicago, Illinois, from May 1 to October 30, 1893. In that year the U.S. Post Office issued an unusual series of sixteen commemorative stamps in horizontal format, in denominations of 1¢ to $5.00, for a total face value of $16.34. These stamps depicted various scenes pertaining to Columbus and his voyages to the New World. Quantities issued included 1.4 billion of the two-cent denomina-

UNITED STATES, ISSUES INCORPORATING THE "LANDING SCENE." *Above:* Pictorial issue of 1869, fifteen-cent denomination engraved and printed in brown and blue by the National Bank Note Company. *Below:* Columbian commemorative issue of 1893, two-cent violet engraved and printed by the American Bank Note Company. Both issues use an engraving after *Landing of Columbus* (1842–1844), a painting by John Vanderlyn commissioned for the Rotunda of the U.S. Capitol.

ALL STAMPS ILLUSTRATED IN THIS ARTICLE ARE FROM THE COLLECTIONS OF JIM DOOLIN AND GORDON BLEULER. PHOTOGRAPHY BY THE STEVE IVY STAMP & COIN CO.

tion and 26,000 to 55,000 of the five different dollar values in the series. The designs in this set were engraved and printed by the American Bank Note Company. A complete set of these stamps is considered one of the key series of U.S. philatelic collectibles.

One of the many firsts associated with the Columbian Exposition was the release of a series of beautifully lithographed souvenir postal cards. It consisted of twelve designs printed in full multicolor. These cards, printed on the back of the one-cent, black U. S. Grant postal card, were released as the official world's fair souvenir cards through a concession contract held by Charles W. Goldsmith. Approximately two million of Goldsmith's cards

UNITED STATES, POSTAL ITEMS FROM THE 1893 WORLD'S COLUMBIAN EXPOSITION. *Above:* Columbian Exposition postal stationery; one-cent blue entire postmarked with machine cancellation of the Exposition's postal station. *Middle:* One-cent Ulysses S. Grant postal card with machine cancellation of the Exposition's postal station, dated September 1, 1893. This is the postal card stock on which the multicolor Goldsmith designs (below) were printed. *Below:* Lithographed, multicolor souvenir postal card, showing a portrait of Columbus and a view of the Exposition's Fisheries Building. These souvenir cards were printed by the American Lithographic Company and distributed by Charles Goldsmith.

UNITED STATES, COLUMBIAN COMMEMORATIVE ISSUE OF 1893. Complete set of sixteen denominations, from one cent to five dollars, with various Columbus-related scenes. These are impressions from the original plates. *Top to bottom, left to right:* one cent, a clean-shaven Columbus, as pictured by artist William Powell, is shown in sight of land from the deck of *Santa María*; two cents, only a day later, Columbus lands, in an engraving after John Vanderlyn, but he now has a full beard; three cents, *Santa María*; four cents, *Niña, Pinta*, and *Santa María*; five cents, Columbus asks Isabel to finance his trip; six cents, Columbus is welcomed in Barcelona after his return from the first voyage; eight cents, Columbus restored to favor after meeting with Isabel; ten cents, Columbus presents a group of American Indians to Isabel; fifteen cents, Columbus relates his discoveries (the platform from which he spoke can still be seen at the Cathedral of Barcelona); thirty cents, Columbus at La Rábida (the first time a dog was ever pictured on a stamp); fifty cents, Columbus is recalled to Barcelona by Isabel prior to the first voyage; one dollar, depiction of legendary scene in which Isabel pawns her jewels to finance the first voyage; two dollars, Columbus is returned to Spain in chains; three dollars, Columbus tells the Spanish court of his discoveries after his third voyage; four dollars, portraits of Isabel and Columbus (this is the first time a U.S. stamp featured portraits of royalty or someone who was not a U.S. citizen); five dollars, Columbus and allegorical figures in a design taken from a commemorative half-dollar issued for the 1893 World's Columbian Exposition.

were sold during the fair, and many were mailed to foreign destinations, thus publicizing the Columbian Exposition. Although printed on U.S. government postal stationery, they are considered to be the first illustrated postal cards in the United States.

The Columbian Exposition also maintained and operated a World's Fair Station post office. Mail collected from various points on the fairgrounds was taken to the station for canceling and handling. Special World's Fair Station machine and hand-stamp markings were applied on this mail. Thus, there are a range of U.S. postal markings under this category for the collector of Columbian material.

Other privately printed Columbian four-hundredth anniversary postal cards and stationery as well as illustrated envelopes and letterheads were issued during this period. A special "Puck" postal card (*Puck* magazine) was given away to visitors at the Puck Building on the fairgrounds.

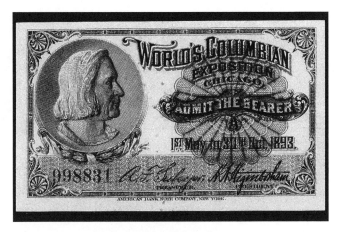

SOUVENIR TICKET, WORLD'S COLUMBIAN EXPOSITION OF 1893. Showing a medallion portrait of Christopher Columbus. From a group of six designs that were engraved and printed by the American Bank Note Company.

OTHER ITEMS OF FOUR-HUNDREDTH ANNIVERSARY VINTAGE. *Top left*: Wells Fargo domestic frank commemorating the anniversary. *Top right*: Unusual use of three Columbian entires that have been overlapped as one cover to make the five-cent foreign mail rate. Mailed from New York to Christiania, Norway. *Bottom*: Trade card published by Ayer's Sarsaparilla.

COLUMBIAN COMMEMORATIVE ISSUE STAMPS ON SELF-PROMOTIONAL BUSINESS ENVELOPES. *Top*: Stewart Fruit Company, Baltimore; postmarked 1894. *Bottom left*: W. F. Snyder of Mifflintown, Pennsylvania, evidently in the furniture-moving business. *Bottom right*: J. F. Collins, dry goods retailer, Smith, North Carolina; postmarked 1894.

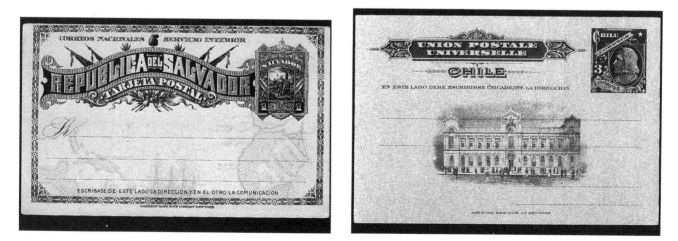

TURN-OF-THE-CENTURY ISSUES FROM CENTRAL AND SOUTH AMERICA. The four-hundredth anniversary inspired many postal designs in the Spanish-speaking countries. *Left:* El Salvador, one-centavo postal card with printed frank showing the landing of Columbus; issued 1892. Background design shows ships with a map of the route of one of Columbus's voyages. *Right:* Chile, government postal card. Three-cent denomination with portrait of Columbus; issued 1905.

Another interesting Columbian Exposition collectible is a series of six beautifully engraved and printed souvenir admission tickets, each with a different portrait. These tickets were engraved and printed by the American Bank Note Company. One has a portrait of Christopher Columbus.

In 1893 the U.S. Post Office also issued four envelopes (entires) in denominations of one cent, two cents, five cents, and ten cents. This commemorative postal stationery group has embossed portraits of Columbus and Liberty against a background of the Eastern and Western Hemispheres.

Other countries, including Argentina, Chile, Honduras, El Salvador, Nicaragua, and Venezuela, also issued stamps and postal stationery in observance of the four-hundredth anniversary. Interestingly, Spain was not among them. The first stamp issued by Spain in recognition of Columbus's achievement was included in a series issued for the Seville and Barcelona Exposition in 1929. The one-centavo greenish blue stamp shows the flagship of Columbus, *Santa María*, offshore from the city of Seville.

In 1930, Spain allowed a privately produced postage set

and two airmail sets commemorating Christopher Columbus to be used. Limited quantities of these sets were given to the Spanish postal authorities, who placed them on sale for a short time. They are attractive, large-size stamps with designs relating to Columbus. Several of the series were printed in multicolor.

During recent years a number of countries, primarily in South and Central America but also elsewhere, have issued Columbus stamps that may be considered as early commemoratious of the five-hundredth anniversary. And in 1990, the United States tentatively scheduled several souvenir-type sheetlets bearing "stamp on stamp" designs taken from those included in the 1892 series of U.S. World's Columbian Exposition commemoratives.

It is interesting to compare how the European countries Columbus knew most intimately have commemorated him on their stamps in the nineteenth and twentieth centuries. For example, Portugal has never recognized Columbus on its postage or commemorative issues and has expressed no intent to do so for the quincentenary. Spain recognized Columbus with issues in 1929 and 1930, and it has already started issues for the quincentenary.

POSTMARKS OF U.S. CITIES NAMED COLUMBUS. *Top left*: North Carolina, 1932; design of envelope shows Columbus at court of Isabel. *Top right*: Kansas, 1894. *Bottom*: Louisiana, 1932.

SPAIN, 1930. Various denominations and designs from the three Columbus sets issued in September 1930.

Though Italy has released many special issues over the past seventy-five years, Columbus has received little recognition. Emphasis has, rather, been placed on the achievements of Marco Polo. There are, however, indications that Italy will recognize Columbus with an issue in 1992.

BIBLIOGRAPHY

Bleuler, Gordon, and Jim Doolin. "Columbian Exposition Revisited." *American Philatelist* 94, no. 8 (1980): 713–726.

Bomar, William J. *Postal Markings of U.S. Expositions.* North Miami, Fla., 1986.

Doolin, Jim. *1893 Columbian Exposition Admission & Concession Tickets.* Dallas, 1981.

Maineri, Ronald J. *Checklist of Christopher Columbus Related Postage Stamps.* 2d ed. San Bernardino, Calif., 1987.

GORDON BLEULER AND JIM DOOLIN

Film

Christopher Columbus has been the subject of a wide variety of motion-picture productions throughout the twentieth century, ranging from one-reel films in the early silent era to scientific expeditionary footage, animated educational short subjects, a television miniseries, and a major feature film in the age of sound.

The importance of motion pictures is often ignored in assessments of the cultural landscape of the twentieth century. Films, in all their variety, have played an important role in perpetuating the iconography of Columbus that was established in Europe and America, through the end of the nineteenth century. Indeed, it is the entire body of those pre-cinema stereotypes and iconographic depictions, which began accumulating during Columbus's lifetime and were nurtured and polished in popular expressions between the sixteenth and nineteenth centuries, that became the grist for motion pictures of all kinds in the twentieth.

Christopher Columbus was of interest to early filmmakers because of his obvious link to the origins of America. But there was another more direct reason why Columbus was regarded by the first film producers as a historical figure of particular interest to contemporary audiences. The age of commercial development of motion pictures began the year after America celebrated the quadricentennial of Columbus's discovery in 1892. During this period of precinematic popular entertainment, an enormous output of amateur and professional plays, novels, songs, poems, and other works was produced on the life of Columbus. (The outpouring of these works actually began prior to 1880 and continued to appear with unusual frequency through the early part of the twentieth century.) In the decade of the 1890s alone, the United States Copyright Office registered over forty dramatic compositions based on the life of Columbus, plus numerous biographies, historical novels and other written and graphic works as well.

By the end of the nineteenth century, filmmakers began turning to fictional and historical subjects for plot and character ideas that could be made into short entertainment films. These early productions, though primitive by modern standards, were nevertheless usually based on scripts or scenarios that were derived from existing source materials that had already demonstrated, to some degree in a nonfilm venue, their popularity with a mass audience. Early film producers looked toward all the precinema, large audience entertainments for successful works that could be adapted to film. No good narrative idea or plot was ignored regardless of its original venue or format: grand opera, the Broadway theater, novels, popular songs and poems, magazines and pulp fiction, and vaudeville or burlesque sketches.

The commercial development of motion pictures, particularly in America, grew therefore directly out of the ideas and subjects that formed the content of popular entertainments as they existed at the end of the nineteenth century. When the makers of film entertainments discovered that all that had gone before them was adaptable to the screen, Columbus was among the prime group of historical figures whose life stories were virtually already prepared for endless adaptations to the motion picture medium.

The first feature-length American motion picture about Columbus was the three-reel production *The Coming of Columbus*, released by the Selig Polyscope Company of Chicago in May 1912. The scenario was written by C. E. Nixon and the starring roles were played by Charles Clary, Thomas Santschi, Bessie Eyton, and Herbert Rawlinson. The film is of special interest because the producer, William N. Selig, filmed many scenes on board replicas of *Niña, Pinta,* and *Santa María* that had been presented to the United States by the queen regent, María Cristina of Spain, for display at the World's Columbian Exposition of 1893. In an effort to achieve authenticity and publicity, Selig also secured the use of the log of the first voyage as a prop in the film.

The earliest extant theatrical motion picture about Columbus known to be in an American film archive is a 1910 French production by the Gaumont Company entitled *Christopher Columbus,* in the collection of the Library of Congress. It was imported and released by George Kleine, a Chicago-based film distributor. The most widely distributed and best-known English-language, sound-era feature film on the life of Columbus is the 1948 J. Arthur Rank production, *Christopher Columbus,* starring Fredric March and Florence Eldridge. Though the Gaumont, Selig,

FROM *THE COMING OF COLUMBUS*, UNITED STATES, 1912. The three-reel Selig Polyscope production. *Top*: Columbus is made an admiral by Isabel and Fernando before taking command of his ships. *Bottom left*: Reproductions of *Niña, Pinta,* and *Santa María,* which were given as gifts by the Spanish government to the World's Columbian Exposition of 1893 and refitted by the Selig company for the film. *Bottom right*: Columbus is received at the court of Isabel and Fernando after the first voyage.

FROM *CHRISTOPHER COLUMBUS*, FRANCE, 1910. The Gaumont Company production. *Above*: Columbus persuades Isabel and Fernando to sponsor his voyage. *Below:* Columbus quiets his rebellious crew. LIBRARY OF CONGRESS

and Rank productions span almost forty years, they depict the identical dramatic events of Columbus's life in the same reverent and conventional manner that characterized mainstream commercial biographical films until the 1960s.

Short-subject productions from the same period created humor by incorporating Columbus's name in their titles. Examples include the 1911 Thanhouser one-reeler *A Columbus Day Conspiracy,* the 1933 Vitaphone short *Double Crossing of Columbus* (starring the vaudeville act Vanessi and the Maxellos), the 1934 Walter Lantz cartoon *Chris Columbus, Jr.* (with animation by Tex Avery), and the 1938 Terrytoon *Chris Columbo.*

As with the majority of important historical figures whose lives have been dramatized in motion pictures, Columbus has also been the target of occasional satires, as in Chico Marx's fine cameo burlesque in the otherwise forgettable *The Story of Mankind* (Warner Bros., 1957).

In addition, motion pictures have been directed to purposes other than theatrical entertainment since the making of narrative films began in the early 1900s. In 1923, for example, the Yale University Press Film Service produced a biographical film entitled *Columbus,* based on

FROM *CHRISTOPHER COLUMBUS*, UNITED STATES, 1948. The J. Arthur Rank production. Two scenes of Columbus at court. *Above:* Columbus (Frederic March) entreats Isabel (Florence Eldridge) and Fernando. *Below:* Columbus's triumphal return after his first voyage. THE MUSEUM OF MODERN ART, FILM STILLS ARCHIVE

FROM *CHRISTOPHER COLUMBUS*, UNITED STATES, 1948.   The J. Arthur Rank production. Columbus (standing), before his arrest, is interrogated by Bobadilla.

THE MUSEUM OF MODERN ART, FILM STILLS ARCHIVE

Irving Berdine Richman's book *The Spanish Conquerors*. This film, along with others in the series Chronicles of America Photoplays, was produced partly as a rebuttal by the academic community to the costume melodramas of commercial producers in New York and Hollywood, who were criticized at the time for their lack of regard for historical facts. The series was also intended to promote the use of film as an educational medium.

One of the more interesting noncommercial applications of motion pictures was made in 1939 by the historian Samuel Eliot Morison, who used the medium to record his expedition retracing the first voyage of Columbus.

Numerous short films and filmstrips about Columbus and other explorers have also been produced for educational markets, especially in the period following World War II. Productions of this type that continue to be circulated by distributors of educational films include *Christopher Columbus* (BBC/Time-Life, 1976), *Christopher Columbus* (Churchill Films, 1982), and *Christopher Columbus—The Voyage of Discovery* (American Films, 1989).

Two notable productions on the life of Columbus have appeared on American television networks. The first is the 1971 CBS Television News broadcast *You Are There: Columbus and Isabella,* which was hosted by Walter Cronkite. The second is the six-hour miniseries *Christopher Columbus* (1985), also broadcast by CBS. Produced by Radiotelevisione Italiana with international financing, the series was widely seen throughout Europe and the Americas.

BIBLIOGRAPHY

Dramatic Compositions Copyrighted in the United States, 1870–1916. 2 vols. Washington, D.C., 1918.

Educational Film and Video Locator. 4th ed. 2 vols. New York, 1990.

Filmography

Christopher Columbus. Gaumont Film Company, France, 1910.

The Coming of Columbus. Selig Polyscope Company, 1912.

Columbus. Yale University Press Film Service, 1923.

Harvard Columbus Expedition, 1939. Samuel Eliot Morison/ Richard S. Colley.

Christopher Columbus. J. Arthur Rank Productions, 1948.

PATRICK LOUGHNEY

IMAGINARY GEOGRAPHY. See *Geography, Imaginary.*

INCAS. See *Indian America,* article on *Incas and Their Neighbors.*

INDIAN AMERICA. [This entry provides an overview of the peoples and cultures of the Western Hemisphere that figure prominently in the earliest phases of European presence in the Americas. The lead article, *First Visual Impressions in Europe,* surveys the earliest representations of what to Europeans was a new world. It is followed by twelve articles on particular peoples from the Caribbean region, South America, and North America:

Taínos
Island Caribs
Arawaks and Caribs
Tupinambás
Indians of the Spanish Main and Central America
Chibchas
Incas and Their Neighbors
Mayas
Aztecs and Their Neighbors
Indians of Northern Mexico, Baja California, and Southwestern North America
Indians of La Florida
Indians of New England, Roanoke, Virginia, and the St. Lawrence Valley

For further discussion of the Western Hemisphere before Columbus's voyages across the Atlantic and the consequences of encounter, see *Agriculture; Colonization; Disease and Demography; Encomienda; Fauna; Flora; Mineral Resources; Pacification, Conquest, and Genocide; Settlements; Slavery; Syphilis; Trade,* article on *Caribbean Trade; Women in the Americas.*]

First Visual Impressions in Europe

There is no evidence that Columbus or anyone on his voyages made pictures of what they saw in America, nor are any pictures known of the people or the natural and artificial curiosities they took back to Europe. However, the earliest illustrations that claim to show American subjects do appear in editions printed before 1500 of Columbus's letter announcing his discovery. One of

these, issued in two versions in Basel in 1493 and 1494, shows a Mediterranean forty-oared galley approaching "Insula hyspana" (La Española), where there is a waiting crowd of about twelve natives, entirely unclothed as Columbus reported the men to be, but with short hair and at least one man bearded, as were no Indians seen or described by Columbus. No artifacts are shown, and no distinctive flora or fauna. The other woodcut, which was first issued in 1493 with G. Dati's Italian verse translation of Columbus's letter, also shows a crowd of Indians, the men bearded and unclothed, the women wearing leafy girdles, and both with long wavy hair. The women's girdles reflect Columbus's brief verbal description, as do a badly depicted palm tree beside the Indians and two large branched trees behind them. There are also two roofed sheds, which are pure inventions of the (unknown) artist. This scene was repeated without useful variations in three other Italian editions of this poem, published in 1493 and 1495.

Illustrations of Vespucci's Account. The next known published European illustrations of America are woodcuts accompanying various versions and translations of accounts by Amerigo Vespucci. One is a variant of the Dati scene. In the others most of the elements are based on

FRONTISPIECE OF GIULIANO DATI'S *LETTERA.* Published in Florence, 1493. King Fernando of Spain points across the Atlantic to the landing of Columbus. None of the details is based on American reality.

LIBRARY OF CONGRESS, RARE BOOK DIVISION

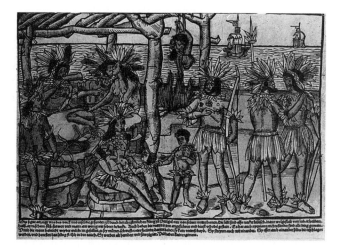

FROSCHAUER WOODCUT, AUGSBURG, 1505. Tupinambá Indians of Brazil in a hand-colored woodcut. This is the first picture of New World natives to contain some relatively accurate details.

NEW YORK PUBLIC LIBRARY

Vespucci's verbal descriptions of South American Indians, especially their nakedness, or on the artists' conventional preconceptions, and do not directly reflect or depict American reality. Several of them include clearly non-American elements, such as curly hair, full beards, and the wrong kinds of clubs, buildings, and canoes. However, there are one or two exceptions that provide the first true, or approximately true, European images of America.

The best known is a woodcut on a broadside probably printed by Johann Froschauer in Augsburg in 1505; it is accompanied by four lines in German that paraphrase Vespucci's description of the Tupinambá Indians of coastal Brazil. Much of the scene is invented by the anonymous artist, either following his European preconceptions (for example, the full beards on three of the men, the composition of a mother with three children, the stalk probably meant to represent maize but with milletlike seeds), or following Vespucci's overly brief verbal descriptions (the cannibalistic cooking and eating, probably the stone ornaments inset in the men's chests and faces). But several of the feather ornaments worn by the Indians resemble known examples from the Tupinambás or from much later Brazilian Indians in details that cannot be based solely on verbal descriptions. Examples are a rosette-shaped bustle, crowns of upright feathers, short feather capes or collars, perhaps ankle and arm bands, and perhaps the skirts of long feathers. Almost certainly these details are based on actual examples brought from Brazil that were available to the artist in Augsburg (or perhaps Nürnberg). Only two examples of this woodcut survive, in Munich and New York; they are impressions

from the identical block, although the text beneath has slightly varying type settings.

The broadside was evidently once common, for it served as the model for a crude, simplified version used by Jan van Doesborch in Antwerp on two broadsheets printed about 1510 to 1515. It may have influenced another woodcut illustrating Vespucci's Mundus Novus printed in Leipzig or Nürnberg in 1505 or 1506; this also survives in only two examples, different impressions from the same woodblock, one of them appearing above a long text in German after Vespucci. The latter print may well be based also on Brazilian objects brought to Germany as souvenirs or trophies that provided ideas about the appearance of feather crowns, skirts and leg bands, and long clubs. Another related woodcut, by Jörg Breu the Elder, was printed in Augsburg in 1515 to depict the inhabitants of Sumatra described in a German translation of the Itinerario of Ludovico Varthema. Some of Breu's feather ornaments and the postures are related to those on the 1505 woodcut. But one headdress with a vertical feather resembles a form known from nineteenth-century Brazil

DRAWING BY ALBRECHT DÜRER, 1515. From the Gebetbuch Maximilians. The figure wears a Tupinambá feather skirt, a feather collar, a downy feather cap, and holds a feather scepter.

BAYERISCHE STAATSBIBLIOTHEK, MUNICH

TUPINAMBÁ MEN AND WOMEN. Tupinambá feather ornaments, clubs, and bows and arrows in a woodcut by Hans Burgkmair from the *Triumph of Maximilian*, circa 1516-1519. American monkeys, a macaw, and the first clear illustration of maize are included. LIBRARY OF CONGRESS

but not otherwise documented for the sixteenth century. Other indications of the presence of Tupinambá Indian objects in Augsburg to serve as models are three feather skirts and a long feathered scepter in Breu's woodcut, which resemble examples depicted in a beautiful 1515 drawing by Albrecht Dürer of an unidentified man. The skirts reappear on many figures in a woodcut scene of a triumphal procession done in 1516 to 1519 by Hans Burgkmair.

More Tupinambá Models. Soon after 1519 Burgkmair or another in his circle painted two watercolors of Indians wearing very similar skirts, and also feather capes, crowns, and downy caps, which seem accurately drawn Tupinambá objects, although one crown is worn backward and

the skirts may in fact have been capes, for one is too short to go fully around the model's waist. This misunderstanding may be the origin of the skirt of long feathers that became part of the European visual symbol representing Indians and America in general. Although there is no evidence for eastern Brazilian Indians wearing such skirts in recent times, and they seem impractical for everyday wear, there are a few examples of Tupinambá Indians shown wearing them—in particular in a ritual dance—in illustrations on sixteenth-century maps where other details seem quite accurate reflections of ethnographic reality.

Another very early accurate European illustration of Tupinambá objects is a panel painted in oils for the high altar in the cathedral at Viseu, Portugal. This is attributed to Vasco Fernandes and dated about 1505 (or even 1501); it is an Adoration of the Magi in which the usual African king is replaced by a figure with brown skin (but not otherwise especially Indian in appearance) who wears rich European clothing (Tupinambá nudity being inappropriate in the context), carries a long heavily fletched arrow that is Brazilian in form, and wears a feather crown, feather necklace, belt of short feathers, and a downy feather cap, which are all probably accurate depictions of objects brought from Brazil.

Indians on Early Maps. The first depictions of American topics made from life reflect visits to the coast of Brazil after it was discovered by Cabral in 1500, and not the voyages of Columbus in the Caribbean region. The emphasis on the Tupinambás in European depictions continued throughout the first century after 1492. Some fifteen manuscript French and Portuguese maps drawn between 1525 and 1579 bear colored figures of Indians and Indian activities in America, many of them very skillfully done. Although Indians in northern South America, Mexico, and around the mouth of the St. Lawrence are also shown, only scenes of Tupinambás seem to be based directly on observations. The best, in the amount of detail and the apparent accuracy, are on a map of Brazil by Jean Rotz, 1542 (in his *Boke of idrography* preserved in the British Library). Other excellent depictions are on maps by Nicolas Vallard (1547), Pierre Desceliers (1553), Guillaume Le Testu (1555), and Jacques Vaudeclaye (1579). Less accurate, but not wholly invented, are Tupinambás depicted by Pedro and Jorge Reinel in the Miller Atlas (c. 1525), on maps by Juan Vespucci (1526) and Diogo Ribeiro (1529), on the Harleian world map in the British Library (c. 1544), and on maps by Pierre Desceliers (1546, 1550), Sancho Gutiérrez (1551), Diogo Homem (1558, 1568), and Sebastião Lopes (1565). Less reliable are figures on a woodcut map published by Giovanni Ramusio in 1556 and on a large map by Sebastian Cabot printed probably in 1544. Non-Brazilian Indians are shown in the Miller atlas

ADORATION OF THE MAGI, CIRCA 1501-1505. Oil pànel depicting the Epiphany attributed to Vasco Fernandes. The central figure, taking the place of the traditional African king, evidently wears Tupinambá feather ornaments and carries a Tupinambá arrow.

MUSEU GRAO VASCO, VISEU, PORTUGAL

(northern South America, fictional), in the Rotz atlas (fictional in most of eastern North America and South America, but with accurate wigwams and possible tailored clothing in Labrador), by Desceliers (1546, imaginary St. Lawrence scene; 1550, fictional North American Indian houses and clothing), Vallard (fictional figures in northern South America and in North America), Gutiérrez (invented figures in North America), Cabot (several figures may be based ultimately on Mexican Indian clothing, although they are misplaced), Le Testu (invented figures in southern South America, Peru, Mexico, and eastern North

America, along with surprisingly accurate snowshoes and an impossibly accurate painted tepee), Ramusio (imaginary structures and clothing along the St. Lawrence, plus some canoes that may remotely reflect observations of Indian birchbark canoes), and Fernão Vaz Dourado (1568, dubious Patagonian archers).

Tupinambá Reality. There are two very early depictions of a Tupinambá village filled with figures engaged in various typical activities that were done from life not in America but in France. An elaborate imitation Brazilian village set up in Rouen for the entry of King Henry II in 1550 included among the occupants fifty Brazilian Indians and 250 Frenchmen said to have learned how to act like Indians while living with the Tupinambás in Brazil (as many Normans had, but probably not 250). There are two contemporary illustrations of this scene, a watercolor that shows few details although it does indicate the customary red body paint worn by the otherwise naked Indians (and Frenchmen); and a woodcut that is crowded with details that are quite small and rather poorly executed, but obviously only one or two removes from observed reality.

Much more accurate details of Tupinambá artifacts and activities (although the compositions and scale are distorted) appear in forty-two small crude woodcuts illustrating a book published in 1557 in which Hans Staden tells how he escaped being sacrificed and eaten by Tupinambás during his captivity among them in 1553 and 1554, and ends with a brief but systematic account of Tupinambá customs. The illustrations obviously reflect Staden's own observations; while they cannot be versions of drawings done directly from life, they may reflect his own sketches done later or at least must have been prepared under his critical supervision.

More skillfully done, but hardly more accurate, are seventeen woodcuts published by André Thevet in 1557–1558, 1575, and 1584. These are based on Thevet's own observations during some three months in Brazil in 1555 and 1556, and perhaps on some Tupinambá objects he is known to have brought back to France. Some of Thevet's illustrations are derivatives of works in other sources, and a few obviously have no basis in reality (for example, war between Amazons; a view of Trinidad; some Patagonian giants), while others are quite dubious ("portraits" of Motecuhzoma and Atahualpa; three views of Indians of New France and Newfoundland that are largely imaginary but include snowshoes and houses only several removes from Canadian reality).

Better depictions of Tupinambá Indians than Thevet's were published by Jean de Léry in 1578, in a work based on his own experiences in Brazil in 1557. Léry criticized Thevet's work, largely justifiably, but used one of Thevet's engravings as the basis for an improved version, and in a second edition in 1580 added three new woodcuts copied from Thevet without improvements. French knowledge of Tupinambás is also reflected in two woodcuts showing a man and woman with quite accurate feather ornaments in a costume book by François Deserps (or Desprez) published in Paris in 1562 and reissued and copied later. A woodcut of a Tupinambá man with accurately depicted feather cape and leg bands was published in 1599 by Ulisse Aldrovandi in a book on ornithology. The watercolor that lies behind this illustration survives in Bologna. It was certainly based on Brazilian objects in Aldrovandi's natural history collection, as was another watercolor and engraving of a woman of Florida (probably a Timucua Indian), which is more difficult to evaluate because no examples of the clothing and ornaments she wears survive. Other engravings published by Aldrovandi show, quite accurately, Mexican Indian artifacts in his collection.

An anonymous Portuguese painting in oils of about 1550 shows the Devil presiding in hell over the vividly depicted torturing of the damned. Curiously, among the strange accoutrements of the Devil are a feather crown, a feather skirt, and perhaps a short feather cape that seem to be influenced by Tupinambá examples, although he also wears an entirely invented tailored feather shirt and perhaps also feathered trousers.

The Allegorical Figure of America. From these and perhaps other, now lost, depictions of Tupinambá Indians

was derived the long-standard allegorical figure of America, which then underwent diffusion and stylistic development entirely divorced from American reality. America's career begins with the invention of allegorical personifications of the four continents, which appeared almost simultaneously in Flanders, Italy, and France in the 1570s. America is usually an undraped female figure wearing a feather crown and often a feather skirt, sometimes a feather collar or cape, based on Tupinambá originals (usually at several removes). She often carries a bow and arrows, not especially Brazilian in form, and frequently has a long club shaped like the Tupinambá club used to sacrifice victims in cannibalistic rituals, and she is often shown with a severed human head or another body part alluding to cannibalism. Each of the continents is usually accompanied by a typical animal; for America there is an alligator, a large South American armadillo, or sometimes a parrot. This kind of figure came to represent America for Europeans in many contexts well into the nineteenth century, while in America itself in the seventeenth and eighteenth centuries it usually was understood to be an Indian. What has been termed the Tupinambization of eastern North American Indians resulted when they adopted the crown of upright feathers from the non-Indian stereotype. Finally, in the late nineteenth century the older feather crown influenced the adoption of the

VESPUCCI DISCOVERING AMERICA.   An allegorical ink drawing by Jan van der Sreet, called Stradanus, 1589. A remote descendant of a Tupinambá club leans against the tree at left.

THE METROPOLITAN MUSEUM OF ART, GIFT OF THE ESTATE OF JAMES HAZEN HYDE, 1959. (1974.205)

AMERICA. Allegorical drawing by Marten de Vos, 1594. The armadillo is American (although far too large), as is the anchor axe. The rest is imaginary.

ings by Gonzalo Fernández de Oviedo, some of which were converted into woodcuts illustrating his books on the natural and civil history of America that were published between 1526 and 1547. Most depict artifacts, including a fire drill, tobacco-snuffing tube, and two houses. A few show activities, including canoe paddling and gold mining. Oviedo was not a skilled artist, but he succeeded in producing informative illustrations of the Indian cultures of La Española, Central America, Peru, and Patagonia, as well as many pictures of the flora and fauna of these regions. Other good illustrations of the Indians of the West Indies, the Spanish Main, Central America, and Peru are the sixteen published in 1565 in Girolamo Benzoni's Italian history of the New World, based on his own observations between 1541 and 1556. A few other illustrations of South American topics—Indians and their

DRAWING OF A PINEAPPLE BY FERNANDEZ DE OVIEDO. From the original manuscript of his natural history, created before 1547.

Plains Indian war bonnet of sloping eagle feathers to stand for Indians in many contexts.

Accurate Representations. In the earliest period after Columbus, American Indians were occasionally pictured as fantastic figures transferred from other regions imagined by Europeans. These included humanoid figures without heads but with faces on their chests, figures with dog heads, giants, Amazons living without men, and wild men with heavy body hair wearing leaves and carrying large crude clubs.

The first relatively accurate illustrations of the aborigines of the Greater Antilles are among twenty-odd draw-

excellent standing colored figures of Indians in an entirely European style. There are many illustrations of Mexican Indians influenced to varying degrees by the native manuscript-painting tradition. Probably the best known are the hundreds drawn by Mexican Indian artists for the use of the Franciscan missionary and proto-ethnographer Bernardino de Sahagún between 1558 and his death in 1590.

There are very few sixteenth-century depictions of North America. All those done by Jacques Le Moyne de Morgues in Florida in 1562 and 1564–1565 survive only in the many engravings based on them published by Théodor de Bry in 1591, and in excellent manuscript copies done by John White about 1580 of two Le Moyne drawings of a standing Timucua Indian man and woman. White's

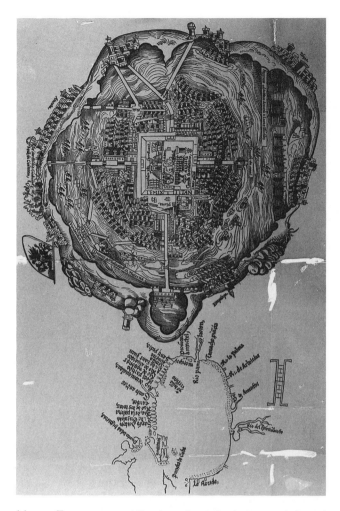

MAP OF TENOCHTITLAN. Woodcut, from the Latin translation of Hernando Cortes's letter to Charles V published in Nürnberg, 1524. The temple precincts are shown clearly, with Motecuhzoma's zoo adjoining one corner.

NEW YORK PUBLIC LIBRARY, RARE BOOK DIVISION

artifacts, plants, animals—are in a manuscript by Galeotto Cey describing his travels between 1539 and 1552, and in a curious manuscript work in French by an unknown shipmate of Francis Drake that must have been compiled soon after 1586.

There are more good sixteenth-century illustrations of Mexico than of any other part of America. They begin with a 1524 woodcut map of Tenochtitlan with some recognizable details. There follow eleven fine, detailed colored drawings of Aztec Indians brought by Cortés to the court of Charles V in 1529, where they were depicted by Christoph Weiditz, a visiting German artist. Another manuscript source is the Codex Tudela (1553), which includes both copies of native Mexican paintings and six

NATIVE MEXICAN PAINTING OF TLALOC. From the Codex Ixtilxóchitl. The Aztec deity was rendered in a very Europeanized style by a native artist working in Texcoco in 1580.

BIBLIOTHÈQUE NATIONALE, PARIS

KING AND QUEEN OF FLORIDA.   Engraving by Théodor de Bry, 1591, after a lost original watercolor by Jacques Le Moyne de Morgues, showing a Timucua couple, circa 1564-1565.

THE SMITHSONIAN INSTITUTION

own depictions, based on his observations near Roanoke, North Carolina, in 1584 to 1587, are among the very best and most important sixteenth-century illustrations of American subjects. Of these, eighteen original watercolors survive, and there are many more quite accurate engraved derivatives of White's drawings published by De Bry in 1590. The subjects include plants and animals as well as Indian figures and scenes. White also painted some Baffinland Eskimos captured by Martin Frobisher in 1576 and 1577, either as a member of Frobisher's expedition or as an observer of the captives in England, where they were drawn by two or three other artists. There is an earlier portrait of Eskimos, a woodcut in several versions done in Antwerp showing a Labrador woman and child exhibited there in 1566.

Depictions of Flora and Fauna. Another genre of illustrations of America are botanical drawings. Three herbals, in addition to those already mentioned, are by Mexican Indian artists. The Badianus manuscript was written in Nahuatl in 1552 by Martín de la Cruz and translated into Latin by Juan Badiano. La Cruz probably is responsible for the 184 small paintings, in a mixed Aztec and European style, of plants and trees of medicinal importance. Other Mexican botanical drawings are among those in the works

of Sahagún. The massive work on plants, animals, and minerals compiled in Mexico between 1571 and 1577 by the Spanish physician Francisco Hernández, which contained hundreds of illustrations, many by named Indian artists, was burned in 1671. Many woodcuts based on the drawings were printed in 1651. A medical work by Nicolas Monardes depicted American plants that he grew in Spain, including the first printed illustration of tobacco. The English translation, *Joyfull Newes Out of the Newe Founde World* (London, 1577) is perhaps better known than the more conservatively titled Spanish original (Seville, 1569).

American plants appeared with Old World Plants in several sixteenth-century herbals. Their origins were sometimes unknown, since the drawings, paintings, and woodcuts were usually based on plants grown in Europe rather than dried specimens or drawings imported from America. Among the works including American plants are those by Otto Brunfels (1530; woodcuts by Hans Weiditz, a pupil of Dürer), Leonhart Fuchs (1542; illustrations by Albrecht Meyer), Pierandreo Mattioli (1544, 1554), Plantin (about 1565–1573; the main artist was Pierre van der Borcht), and John Gerard (1597; with perhaps the first printed illustration of the potato). Early illustrations of several American plants, including maize, pineapple, and prickly pear, appeared in G. B. Ramusio's collection of voyages published in Venice in 1556. Konrad Gesner (Conrad Gessner; 1516–1565) did many drawings of American plants and animals. One of his students, Ulisse Aldrovandi (1522–1605), employed painters, draftsmen, and engravers in Bologna to illustrate his huge collection of natural history specimens. Thirteen large folio volumes were eventually published between 1599 and 1688, illustrated with woodcuts of many American plants, mammals, birds, fishes, reptiles, and minerals, along with Aldrovandi's text descriptions. For early illustrations of American mammals and birds (especially the macaw) maps are among the most important sixteenth-century sources, including most of those mentioned above.

[See also *Geography, Imaginary*.]

BIBLIOGRAPHY

Alegría, Ricardo E. *Las primeras representaciones gráficas del Indio Americano, 1493–1523*. San Juan, Puerto Rico, 1978.

Honour, Hugh. *The New Golden Land: European Images of America from the Discoveries to the Present Time*. New York, 1975.

Honour, Hugh. *L'Amérique vue par l'Europe*. Paris, 1976. Corrected version of *The European Vision of America*, 1976.

Hulton, Paul. *America 1585. The Complete Drawings of John White*. Chapel Hill, N. Car., 1984.

Kohl, Karl-Heinz, ed. *Mythen der Neuen Welt: Zur Entdeckungsgeschichte Lateinamerikas*. Berlin, 1982.

Robertson, Donald. *Mexican Manuscript Painting of the Early Colonial Period: The Metropolitan Schools*. New Haven, Conn., 1959.

Sturtevant, William C. "First Visual Images of Native America." In *First Images of America: The Impact of the New World on the Old*, edited by Fredi Chiappelli. Berkeley, 1976.

WILLIAM C. STURTEVANT

TURKEYS. A woodcut after a painting by Pierre Gourdelle, from Pierre Belon's *L'Histoire de la nature des oyseaux*, Paris, 1555. Belon thought the bird originated in Asia.

HOUGHTON LIBRARY, HARVARD UNIVERSITY

BISON. The first published picture of the North American bison; a woodcut perhaps based on a sketch from life. From López de Gómara's history of the Indies, 1552.   THE SMITHSONIAN INSTITUTION

Taínos

The Taíno Indians, who lived in the Bahama Islands and the Greater Antilles (Cuba, Jamaica, La Española [Hispaniola], and Puerto Rico), were the first people of the New World to have contact with the Spanish explorers and conquerors. Their culture was the first to be described by European explorers and chroniclers such as Cristopher Columbus, Bartolomé de las Casas, Gonzalo Fernández de Oviedo, and Pietro Martire d'Anghiera.

The Taínos descended from Arawakan Indians, who approximately 2,500 years ago began to migrate from the coasts of South America (Venezuela and Guyana) to the archipelagoes of the Antilles. Evidence of this migratory movement has been discovered in the region of the Orinoco River, on the coasts of Venezuela, on the island of Trinidad, and in the Lesser Antilles. Archaeology reveals that by the sixth century A.D. the culture of these Indians in Puerto Rico had already attained characteristics that differentiated them from their South American predecessors; there is evidence of a cultural expansion by the tenth century in Puerto Rico and La Española, from which they began to emigrate to Jamaica, Cuba, and the Bahamas.

Archaeologists such as Irving Rouse have distinguished the Taínos of Puerto Rico, La Española, and eastern Cuba, who attained a more complex level of cultural and political development, from the Indians of central Cuba, the Bahamas, and Jamaica, who are considered Sub-Taíno. The Sub-Taínos of the Bahamas were called Lucayos.

The term *Taíno* was used by the Indians of La Española to indicate to the Spanish conquerors that they were "good, noble" Indians, as opposed to the Caribs, the warlike Indians of the Lesser Antilles. The word *Taíno* has been used by archaeologists and ethnohistorians since the nineteenth century as the name of the Indians of Arawakan origin who lived in the Greater Antilles at the time of the Discovery.

It is difficult to determine the population of the Greater Antilles at the time of the European discovery. Some chroniclers, such as Las Casas, say that in La Española there were over a million inhabitants and that in Puerto Rico and Jamaica there were more than 600,000 Indians. Modern knowledge of the indigenous economy and historical data on the number of Indians distributed among the colonists suggest that these figures are exaggerated. As early as 1509 the conquerors recount that because in La Española and Puerto Rico there were few Indians, they had to import Indian slaves from the Bahamas, the South American coast, and the Lesser Antilles. New demographic studies are needed to reach a realistic conclusion, which will undoubtedly show a much smaller figure than Las Casas's. In the case of Puerto Rico the population was probably not larger than sixty thousand.

The Taínos were agriculturists who had brought with them from South America to the Antilles the cultivation of the yucca, with which they made their cassava bread, together with corn, sweet potatoes, yautia (malanga), peanuts, and numerous other food plants. They also grew fruit trees such as guava, soursop, sweetsop, yellow mombin, mammee, papaya, and other plants such as pineapple, annatto, red pepper, tobacco, and cotton. High yields of manioc and sweet potatoes were obtained by planting them in rows of low mounds of dirt heaped up in the fields, or *conuco*s.

Besides agricultural products, the Taínos complemented their diet with birds and a small rodent similar to a rabbit that they called *jutía*. They also hunted manatees, snakes, large iguanas, and sea turtles. Taínos fished with bone and shell fishhooks, with nets, and with bows and arrows. They also used a plant extract that numbed fish and brought them to the surface. They also ate oysters, clams, and conchs from the coastal reefs, as well as mute dogs that they bred.

Taínos lived in settlements near the coasts of the islands and in the interior valleys near rivers. According to Las Casas some of these villages, which the Taínos called *yucayeque*s, contained hundreds of *bohío*s (communal houses), each of which housed an extended family. The *bohío*s were made of tree trunks, reeds, and straw roofing. Taínos used hanging nets called *hamaca*s as beds.

The Taínos, like other inhabitants of the tropical regions, wore almost no clothes. Men and unmarried women walked about completely naked. Married women used some small aprons woven of cotton called *nagua*s. The caciques and the shamans sometimes used cotton mantles and clothing made of feathers of various colors. Taínos frequently painted their bodies totally or partially with drawings of red, white, and black pigments derived from annatto (*Bixa orellana*), genipap, and earth and ochre coloring. Body ornaments of stone, bone, shell, clay, seed, feather, cotton, and straw included counting necklaces made of tubular granite or marble beads, pendants or amulets that often had anthropomorphic and zoomorphic representations, radial crowns with feathers of different colors, and woven-cotton belts and head ornaments. They also worked gold nuggets into thin sheets that they shaped and embossed. The cacique wore a golden disk as a sign of his status in the social hierarchy.

Taíno society was governed by a cacique, or hereditary chief, who was the political and religious authority. The office was matrilineally transmitted; as a result, the cacique's mother and sisters enjoyed high prestige. The caciques in the Greater Antilles acquired great political power and their authority extended over several villages. According to some chroniclers, the cacique Agueybaná was the most important cacique of the island of Boriquén (Puerto Rico) and other caciques were subordinate to him. Las Casas says that in La Española there were five powerful caciques and numerous minor caciques under them. There was also a social class called *nitaíno*s that the Spanish colonists called the nobles; they functioned as subcaciques in the villages, directing the *naboria*s (workers) who attended to agricultural activities, fishing, and hunting.

The caciques were permitted many wives; some marriages were the results of alliances with neighboring caciques. The cacique was privileged in dress, ornaments, and food. He was the owner of the most powerful idols. In some cases, when the cacique died, he could be turned into a demigod and his remains could become part of an idol. The chroniclers tell us that, in some cases, when the cacique died, some of his favorite wives were buried with him.

The Taínos were the heirs of an ancient and complex magicoreligious tradition that had its sources in the Amazon regions of South America. It included a rich mythology about the origins of islands, of plants, of animals, and of human beings. Some aspects of Taíno mythology were collected by Ramón Pané at the beginnings of the conquest of La Española. They believed in a supreme being or creator called Yocahu Maorocón and in a goddess who was associated with fecundity and known by several names, including Apito and Atabei.

The Taínos' principal cult concerned the tutelary spirits

INDIAN AMERICA

North Atlantic Ocean

Jamestown (founded 1607)
Roanoke Island

Gulf of Mexico

Cuba

Jamaica

La Española
(Hispaniola)

Puerto Rico

Caribbean Sea

SPANISH MAIN

Trinidad

Tenochtitlán

Pacific Ocean

Orinoco R.

Amazon R.

South Atlantic Ocean

Cuzco

Paraná R.

Río de la Plata

ETHNIC AND LANGUAGE GROUPS

Ais & Tequestas (1)
Algonquians. *See* Beothuks;
  Micmacs; Passamaquoddies;
  Roanoke Island Algonquians;
  Virginia Algonquians.
Apaches (2)
Arawaks (3)
Aztecs (4)
Beothuks (5)
Calcusas (6)
Caribs (7)
Cenus, Dabeibas, & Quimbayas (8)
Chibchas (9)
Chinchas (10)
Conchos (11)
Dabeibas, Cenus & Quimbayas (8)
Guaranis (12)
Hochelegans. *See* Iroquois.
Hokan Language Family. *See*
  Seris; Yumans.
Hopis (13)
Huastecs (14)
Incas (15)
Iroquois (St. Lawrence River
  Region: Hochelegans &
  Stadaconans) (16)
Island Caribs (17)
Karankawans (18)
Lencas (19)
Lucayos (20)
Mayas (21)
Mayos (22)
Micmacs (23)
Mississippian Chiefdoms
  Apalachees, Casquis, Chicazas,
  Cofitachequis, Coosas,
  Guales, Ichisis, Naguatezes,
  Ocutes, Pacahas, Quigualtams,
  Tascaluzas (24)
Mixtecs (25)

Mocozos & Ozitas (26)
Navajos (27)
Ocales & Urriparacoxis (28)
Opatas (29)
Otomís (30)
Ozitas & Mocozos (26)
Passamaquoddies (31)
Payas (32)
Pimas (33)
Piplis (34)
Pueblos (35)
Quimbayas, Cenus, & Dabeibas(8)
Roanoke Island Algonquians (36)
Seris (37)
St. Lawrence Iroquois. *See*
  Iroquois.
Stadaconans. *See* Iroquois.
Taínos (38)
Tarahumaras (39)
Tarascans (40)
Tepehuans (41)
Tequestas & Ais (1)
Timucuans. *See* Ocales;
  Urriparacoxis; Utinas; Yustegas.
Totonacs (42)
Tulas (43)
Tupinambás (44)
Urriparacoxis & Ocales (28)
Utinas (45)
Uto-Aztecan Language Family.
  See Conchos; Hopis; Mayos;
  Opatas; Pimas; Tarahumaras;
  Tepehuans; Yaquis.
Virginia Algonquians (46)
Waraos (47)
Xincas (48)
Yaquis (49)
Yumans (50)
Yustegas (51)
Zapotecs (52)

© Carta

347

TAÍNO CERAMIC EFFIGY JAR OF A MAN. Eleventh to fifteenth century, La Española. Surviving Taíno pottery is mostly unpainted bowls and jars decorated in low relief. Effigy vessels are rare, and this is perhaps the finest known example.

(cemíes) of their ancestors. Statuettes were carved from wood, stone, bone, and shell or made of clay and woven cotton. These objects, which were associated with the magicoreligious cult, manifest the high level of Taíno art. The idols and paraphernalia used in the cohoba ceremony represent some of the best examples of Taíno art. Other objects of high artistic value were the cacique's dujos (ceremonial chairs), low benches, generally with four legs, carved from wood or stone. They were also enriched by incrustations of sheets made of gold and shell. Trigonolites (three-pointed stones) found in Puerto Rico and the Dominican Republic often represent a humanoid head or the head of an animal at one end and "frog legs" at the other.

The Taínos were relatively peaceful and, according to the chroniclers of the conquest, they fought among themselves only on rare occasions. They resorted to war in order to defend their villages from the frequent attacks carried out by the Island Caribs from the Lesser Antilles.

Their weapons included spear throwers, bows and arrows, and the macana, a kind of wide sword made of the hard wood of the corozo palm that was used as a club for hand-to-hand combat. They also used noxious gases produced by throwing pepper into clay pots full of burning coals.

They were good sailors, using boats called canoas that they carved from the trunks of big trees and propelled with paddles. They traveled from island to island to exchange products.

It was among the Taínos that the conquerors saw for the first time a ball made of rubber. It was used in batey, a game that had both a ceremonial and a recreational character, occasionally being played to discern the gods' desires. One of the representative objects of the Taínos of Puerto Rico, the stone belt, is associated with the batey game. These monolithic arcs, which in the past were called "stone yokes," attest to the high level of Taíno stoneworking technology. Among the best examples of Taíno art were these monolithic belts and codos (elbow stones), which were part of a belt, completed with a wooden arc.

The Spanish conquest and the colonization of the Greater Antilles began in La Española in 1494. The Spaniards soon established the encomienda system in which between fifty and three hundred Indians, under a cacique,

TAÍNO CEREMONIAL STOOL. Thirteenth to fifteenth century, La Española. This example, reportedly preserved in a dry cave, is one of the finest known, and the only one to show gold leaf (in the eyes and mouth and on the shoulders of the figure). Such stools, called dujos, were the property of chiefs, who occupied them on important occasions.

were assigned to work for a colonist, who was obliged to contribute to their conversion to Christianity and to their adjustment to Spanish customs. Such policies were harshly criticized by the Dominican friars, especially Las Casas, because they facilitated abuses against the Indians who, although they were vassals of the Crown by Spanish law, suffered from an exploitation that was equivalent to slavery. The Lucayo Indians (Sub-Taínos) of the Bahamas were forcibly uprooted from their islands to work in La Española, Puerto Rico, and Cuba, since the Spaniards considered their islands *inútiles* (useless) and never colonized them. The conquest and the colonization of Puerto Rico began in 1508, that of Jamaica in 1509, and that of Cuba in 1510. The encomienda system that began in La Española and was responsible for the deaths of thousands of Indians was also introduced into Cuba. The Taínos of La Española, Puerto Rico, Cuba, and Jamaica tried to free themselves from the oppressive yoke of the Spanish conquerors, but their weapons and their knowledge of war could not compete with the conquerors' powerful weapons, horses, and dogs.

In 1512 to 1513, even before the Dominican friars protested to King Fernando, the Laws of the Indies were meant to correct some of the abuses, but they did not abolish the encomiendas, thus permitting the extinction of the indigenous society of the Antilles. Until 1518 there were attempts to establish free Indian villages in the Greater Antilles, but they did not succeed and the indigenous population continued to diminish rapidly. In 1542, Spain granted total freedom to the Indians. For the Taínos of La Española, Cuba, Jamaica, and Puerto Rico, however, it was already too late, since there was only a small number of them left. In Puerto Rico, the bishop in charge of granting freedom to the Taínos reported that he could only find sixty native Indians.

The wars against the conquerors, who robbed them of their land, their freedom, and their magicoreligious beliefs; the European and African diseases against which they had no natural defense; the mistreatment they suffered when they were obliged to work in the mines; the change in diet that was imposed on them by the conquest; and the collective suicide they sometimes committed to free themselves from their sufferings: all these factors contributed to the disappearance of Taíno society in little more than a century after the initial contact. However, because the Spaniards were used to racial miscegenation, they cohabited with the Indians from the beginning of contact, and so there soon arose a mestizo society that retained many cultural characteristics of the Taínos. Its language influenced the Spanish spoken in Cuba, the Dominican Republic, and Puerto Rico, and some Taíno words have entered English and other modern European languages: *hamaca* (hammock), *savana* (savan-

nah), *tabac* (tobacco), *maíz* (maize), *huracán* (hurricane), *cayo* (cay), and cacique. Their physical type, their diet, some of their handicrafts (such as the weaving of baskets and hammocks), the use of the maraca, and other characteristics of their culture still survive among the populations of the Greater Antilles.

BIBLIOGRAPHY

Alegría, Ricardo E. *Ball Courts and Ceremonial Plazas in the West Indies.* New Haven, 1983.

Fewkes, J. Walter. *The Aborigines of Porto Rico and Neighboring Islands.* Washington, D.C., 1907.

Las Casas, Bartolomé de. *History of the Indies.* Translated by Andree M. Collard. New York, 1971.

Loven, Sven. *The Tainan Culture of the West Indies.* Göteborg, 1935.

Morison, Samuel Eliot, ed. *Journals and Other Documents on the Life and Voyages of Christopher Columbus.* New York, 1963.

Pané, Ramón. *Relación acerca de las antiguedades de los Indios.* Edited by José J. Arrom. Mexico City, 1974.

Rouse, Irving. "Prehistory of the West Indies." *Science* 144 (1964): 499–513.

Rouse, Irving. "The Arawak." In vol. 4 of *Handbook of South American Indians.* Washington, D.C., 1948.

Willey, Gordon R. *An Introduction to American Archaeology.* Vol. 2. Englewood Cliffs, N.J., 1966.

RICARDO E. ALEGRÍA

Island Caribs

The word *carib* is unknown in the language of the inhabitants of the Lesser Antilles, who have been called Caribs since the discovery of America. The term, a corrupt form of *cariba, caniba, caribata,* is borrowed from Taíno, a language of western Hispaniola (La Española), where Christopher Columbus landed in November 1492. According to Douglas R. Taylor, the word meant "harmful, hurtful nation" or "quarrelsome people," which the inhabitants of the northwest coast used to designate the peoples of the east. These aggressive and redoubtable neighbors were said to be dogfaced, one-eyed monsters who ate humans. These details were related by Spaniards who evidently did not understand the native language well, and who were guessing, fantasizing, and embellishing, influenced by European literary descriptions of fantastic peoples, especially in the writings of Pliny.

During his first stay on La Española, Columbus had encountered inhabitants of the northeastern peninsula, who with their very long hair, black facial paint, and bows and arrows differed in appearance from the natives he saw around him; he quickly concluded that these were the "Caribs." In November 1493, on the second voyage, Columbus and his companions went ashore on Guadeloupe, where they found human bones in villages deserted by their inhabitants, who had fled into the forest. They were therefore convinced that they had found those "cannibals" of whom they had been told the previous year. From that time the word *carib* was applied to the islanders of all the Lesser Antilles, and subsequently also to the cannibals of the mainland, with whom they were for a long time confused. The mainland peoples are known in anthropological literature as the Karinyas or the "true Caribs." They speak a language of the Cariban family, which bears no relation to the native language of the Island Caribs of the Lesser Antilles.

Contrary to the Spanish interpretations of Taíno tales, it is doubtful that the Caribs of the Lesser Antilles carried out raids on La Española since extremely strong currents flowing from west to east in the Caribbean Sea would have made it impossible for them to return home in their canoes. It is more likely that, besides their traditional annual expeditions to the Orinoco and farther to the east on the South American continent, they made forays onto the island of Borinquén (now Puerto Rico), to the northeast of their territory. Such raids were documented during the sixteenth century, Puerto Rico being by then a Spanish colony. Borinquén and La Española shared the same language and culture; it is possible that the inhabitants of La Española knew of the raids carried out on Borinquén and mentioned them to the Spaniards. However, there is no proof that these raids took place in pre-Columbian times and that they were not attributable, in the sixteenth century, to the presence of Europeans. One must in any case disregard the myth of the Carib raids on La Española and acknowledge that the sociopolitical system of the Lesser Antilles was aligned with the South American continent, and the inhabitants were more closely linked by war and trade with local populations than with the Taíno group of the Greater Antilles, which was close geographically but quite distant socially and culturally.

From St. Christopher in the north to Grenada in the south, all the small islands were inhabited by peoples who spoke a language that belonged to the same Arawakan family as did Taíno, shared the same institutions and rituals, and who visited one another frequently from island to island. They comprised more than just one ethnic population; rather they formed a social and political unit occupying the archipelago that was bounded on the north by the Virgin Islands (uninhabited during the fifteenth century, except St. Croix) and Borinquén, and on the south by the island of Chaleibe (present-day Trinidad). This society was composed of networks of alliances, both matrimonial and political, which united the local groups. These groups were for the most part exogamous and composed of one single extended uxorilocal family, the headman of which was the father of married daughters and lived with his sons-in-law. Thus a man of common

status after marrying would go to live in the village of and under the authority of his wife's father. He would establish his own village when his father-in-law died, and he himself became a father-in-law when his own daughters married. This fluctuating structure, by which the village populations were spatially redistributed with each generation, was based on the ties between the wife's father and the daughter's husbands, not between kin of the same sex. Sisters were quite likely to live separately when their husbands became village chiefs. Hence, it would be inappropriate to speak of matrilocality or, especially, matrilinearity in this cognatic society that did not recognize lineal descent.

Some villages were more important and more populous than others. In these more important villages the headman was recognized as a war chief because of his feats, the number of prisoners he had taken on his expeditions, and, consequently, by the magnitude of the anthropophagic rituals he held in which the prisoners were sacrificed. To acquire this status the prospective war chief had to undergo a lengthy initiation, which included fasting, flagellation, being bitten by ants, and seclusion. Once attained, this status remained tenuous and had to be maintained by frequent expeditions. The war chief, whose status was tenuous, had to be able to forge for himself a clientele with his kindred as its nucleus. The more expeditions he made the more prestige and partisans he gained and the more privileges accrued to him. He was exempt, for example, from the "bride service" obligatory in uxorilocal villages. Warring expeditions were directed not toward the Antilles but toward the South American continent around the mouth and the valley of the Orinoco and the Guyanas where the islanders had both long-term and occasional allies and enemies. The wars were accompanied by trading, as the result of a system of partnership by which the warriors had "friends" in the enemy villages with whom they traded and whom they never took prisoner. Most of their enemies were cannibalistic and went out on expeditions and abducted women. Thus, on the continent, the island peoples participated in a polity structured by war and the exchange of goods, women, and values, in which social and ideological communication was characterized by reciprocal positions and relationships.

The long-time confusion between the islanders and their Karinya or Kalinya allies (the "true" Caribs) of the continent springs from a remarkable social practice that has been misinterpreted. It was said that the men and the women of the islands spoke two different languages—the women's language belonging to the Arawakan family and the men's language belonging to the Cariban family. It was suggested that the abduction of Arawak women by Carib invaders explained this oddity. In reality the maternal language of all of the islanders was Arawakan. In this language their name for themselves was *Kaliponam*. The men, who by their overseas expeditions and trading had close links with continental groups, notably with the Karinyas, made numerous lexical borrowings from their language. Among themselves, at their gatherings at the men's house (in the central plaza of the village), they used this mixed speech, with its Arawakan structure and partially Karinya vocabulary, which one can consider to be a social marker of the hierarchical difference between the sexes. Moreover, on the continent a pidgin was spoken in interethnic relations to permit communication between groups who often spoke unrelated languages. It appears that Karinya was the dominant element, which explains how it influenced the speech of male islanders to the extent that they called themselves Kalinago, from the name of a mythical ancestor who invoked a link with the Karinyas.

Though they were doubtlessly weakened by epidemics and deadly battles with the Europeans, the Kaliponams/Kalinagos (the so-called Island Caribs) were able to continue their traditional social life and their continental expeditions throughout the sixteenth century. The Spaniards were occupied with conquering Mexico beginning in 1519 and with conquering Peru beginning in 1532. Aside from some attempts at establishing a settlement in Dominica, which was a stopover point for their fleets, they did not seek to colonize the Lesser Antilles, which lacked the richness in minerals they sought and which were staunchly defended by warlike and terrifying natives. The situation changed radically in 1624 when the English and the French simultaneously decided to establish colonies in the Lesser Antilles as strategic bases supporting their colonial undertakings to the north (in Virginia) and to the south (in the Guyanas). The first island to be conquered was St. Christopher, which the English and the French shared, and where, in 1629, they carried out the partial massacre of the island Indians. Those who survived took refuge on the other islands, especially on Guadeloupe. The French settled there in 1635, at the same time that they settled on Martinique. Until 1678, there were incessant attacks throughout the archipelago followed by bloody retaliation between the colonists and the Indians, who defended themselves with the energy born of despair, but who succumbed in great numbers to the bullets, swords, and diseases of the Europeans. In 1678 a treaty was signed by, on one side, the French and English, and on the other side the "Caraibes," which stipulated that the Indians had to abandon all the islands except Dominica and St. Vincent, which were recognized as their property. This treaty was not honored by the colonists, who continued to settle on St. Vincent and to bring African slaves there. Many fugitive slaves from plantations found refuge with the Indians, but the latter disappeared little by little from St. Vincent during the eighteenth century, absorbed by intermarriage with blacks whose population was rapidly increasing. The black Caribs carried out a guerrilla war of harrassment against the colonists until they were defeated and deported en masse in 1797 to the British colony of Honduras (now Belize) where they settled. The Indian population of Dominica dwindled, and the social structure collapsed, deprived of its political framework, which had been dependent on wars, rituals, and long-distance trading.

BIBLIOGRAPHY

Breton, Raymond. *Dictionnaire françois-caraïbe.* Auxerre, 1666.

Dreyfus, Simone. "Historical and Political Anthropological Interconnections: The Multilinguistic Indigenous Polity of the 'Carib' Islands and Mainland Coast from the 16th to the 18th Century." *Antropológica* 59–62 (1983–1984): 39–55.

Dreyfus, Simone. "Territoire et résidence chez les Caraïbes insulaires au XVIIe siècle." In vol. 2 of *Actes du XLIIe Congrès international des Américanistes.* Paris, 1977.

Taylor, Douglas R. "Carib, Caliban, Cannibal." *International Journal of American Linguistics* 14 (1958): 156–157.

Taylor, Douglas R. "Kinship and Social Structure of the Island Carib." *Southwestern Journal of Anthropology* 2 (1946): 180–212.

Taylor, Douglas R. "The Place of the Island Carib within the Arawakan Family." *International Journal of American Linguistics* 24 (1958): 153–156.

SIMONE DREYFUS
Translated from French by Elizabeth Keller

Arawaks and Caribs

At the time of the European discovery, the islands of Trinidad and Tobago, the coastal zone of Guiana and the lower and middle reaches of the Orinoco River in Venezuela were inhabited by Amerindian groupings of varying ethnicity, linguistic affiliations, subsistence strategies, and levels of sociopolitical integration. Most of these peoples spoke languages belonging to three major linguistic families, Arawakan, Cariban, and Waraoan; the two former language stocks are still widely dispersed on the South American mainland, especially in the Amazon Basin. Waraoan forms an isolated speech community, without known linguistic relations, found today exclusively in the Orinoco Delta and the adjoining portion of Guyana. It may be the survivor of an originally widespread substratum language, which was displaced by Arawakan and Cariban.

Although sixteenth- and seventeenth-century written sources reveal a multitude of Amerindian names, each claiming to refer to a particular ethnic unit, it is likely that the actual situation was much less complicated. Apart from Waraos, two major Amerindian ethnic groups can be distinguished in the Southeast Caribbean: Arawaks and Caribs, along with a variety of smaller groups such as Guaianas, Nepoios, Yaios, Shebaios, Chaimas, and Paragotos.

The Amerindian people referred to in the early documentary sources as the Aruacas or Aroacas represent a grouping that in the period of initial contact inhabited South Trinidad, the lower Orinoco Valley and parts of the Guiana coastal zone. Sixteenth-century maps suggest that the Arawaks originally occupied the lower reaches of the major rivers, especially in the western portion of the latter area. They are mentioned for the first time in 1520 when a Spanish report speaks of a region, situated beyond the Gulf of Paria, "que dize de Aruaca" (that is called Aruaca). Under Spanish pressure the Arawaks disappeared from Trinidad and the Orinoco Valley in the seventeenth and eighteenth centuries and their numbers became greatly reduced. The present Arawaks, who still live in scattered settlements in Guyana, French Guiana, and Suriname, call themselves Lokono (the [own] people); the alternative name, Arawak, is probably derived from the name of a major Lokono settlement on the lower Orinoco, called Aruacay. The Spaniards of the pearl-producing islands of Cubagua and Margarita maintained close trading contacts with Aruacay throughout the sixteenth century. The Lokono language is documented since the 1590s, when Dutch and English sailors collected Arawak word lists in South Trinidad. The ethnographic literature often refers to the Lokono as the "True" or "Mainland" Arawaks, in order to distinguish them from the Taíno or "Island" Arawaks who occupied the Greater Antilles in the period of contact. The two Amerindian groupings are unrelated except for a linguistic bond which can be compared to that between English and German or Dutch.

The supposed "traditional enemies" of the Arawaks were the Cariban-speaking Kalinas. Sixteenth-century documentary and cartographic evidence suggests that the ancestors of the Kalinas, Indians whom the Spaniards called Caribes, occupied the northern third of Trinidad, the reaches of the Guiana rivers upstream from the Arawak, and the middle Orinoco Valley. The name Caribes is derived from Caniba or Canaiba, both Spanish corruptions of *kalinago*, the word (a combination of *kalina*, "the [own] people," and the honorific suffix *-go*) that the male Caribs of the Lesser Antilles used to refer to themselves.

The fierce resistance that the Caribs of the West Indies made against European colonization and slave raiding earned them a negative reputation in the documentary sources, whereas the Arawaks tended to be shown in a favorable light by Spaniards. This obviously resulted from their sixteenth-century trade relationships.

Most Amerindian peoples of the southeast Caribbean were organized sociopolitically as tribes, that is, as egalitarian societies consisting of a series of semi-independent villages, each normally having some three hundred to five hundred inhabitants. The livelihood of most people depended on a form of subsistence that combined swidden (slash-and-burn) cultivation with hunting for small game, fishing, and the unspecialized collecting of edible wild plants, seeds, and shellfish. Only a few peoples, including the Waraos, specialized in nonagricultural subsistence strategies. Political organization was typically tied to kinship and did not extend beyond the village. The village headman was chosen for his abilities as a leader of war and trade expeditions. A few communities of the southeast Caribbean had a more complex type of political organization, with a principal chief and subordi-

NATIVE OF TRINIDAD. Working an elaborate parrot trap, which uses the cries of a captive parrot to lure other birds. From *Histoire naturelle des Indes*, known as the Drake manuscript, which contains sketches and drawings of the Caribbean region made at the behest of Sir Francis Drake.

THE PIERPONT MORGAN LIBRARY, NEW YORK; M.3900, F.83.

nate chiefs. The Lokono town of Aruacay on the lower Orinoco is an example. Sixteenth-century Spanish sources note that Aruacay consisted of some four hundred large round houses, each forming the dwelling of a *parentela*, obviously a kinship group, perhaps a localized clan. Furthermore, Aruacay is described as being ruled by nine chiefs, subordinate to one principal chief, who also functioned as the main shaman. The town probably owed its preeminent position to its strategic geographical position at the apex of the Orinoco Delta, which was conducive especially to maintaining extensive ties of ceremonial exchange and trade with other peoples.

The boundary between exchange and war was ambiguous, however. Although constant warfare characterized the Amerindian societies of the southeast Caribbean in pre-Columbian times, the hostilities between traditionally antagonistic peoples such as the Caribs and Arawaks never interrupted their mutual trade. Major items of Caribbean ceremonial exchange, the famous *kalukulis* (zoomorphic or crescent-shaped breast and nose ornaments made of a gold-copper alloy) found their way from the mainland of South America into the Antilles through peaceful exchange between the Arawaks of the lower Orinoco Valley and Trinidad and the Caribs of the Lesser Antilles. These ties of Arawak-Carib trade show that, among the Amerindian societies of the southeast Caribbean, exchange and war could be considered merely two different expressions of the same reciprocal pattern of social interaction.

BIBLIOGRAPHY

Boomert, Arie. "The Arawak Indians of Trinidad and Coastal Guiana, ca. 1500–1650." *Journal of Caribbean History* 19 (2) (1984): 123–188.

Sued Badillo, Jalil. *Los Caribes: Realidad o fábula*. Río Piedras, P.R., 1978.

Whitehead, Neil L. *Lords of the Tiger Spirit: A History of the Caribs in Colonial Venezuela and Guyana 1498–1820*. Dordrecht and Providence, R.I., 1988.

ARIE BOOMERT

Tupinambás

The name Tupinambá refers to the Indians inhabiting the coast of Brazil from the region of São Paulo to the mouth of the Amazon River. Closely related to the Guaranis of southern Brazil and Uruguay, Tupinambás were divided into a number of tribal groupings that, although culturally similar and speaking mutually intelligible dialects, were often in a state of bitter and perpetual warfare with one another. In fact, the Tupinambás were recent migrants to the coastal regions, having displaced earlier occupants.

The first recorded contact between Tupinambás and Europeans occurred in 1500 when Pedro Álvares Cabral, a Portuguese captain on his way to India, anchored briefly off the Brazilian coast. Subsequent European contacts were generally friendly, often involving the exchange of European manufactures for raw materials from the Brazilian coast. Serious efforts at colonization by the Portuguese began in the 1530s. After 1550 colonization intensified along much of the Brazilian coast, both on the part of the Portuguese and the French. At first the Tupinambás welcomed contact with the Europeans, finding the economic exchanges beneficial. Various Tupinambá groups formed trading and military alliances with the French and Portuguese, incorporating the Europeans in their internecine warfare. Over time, however, Portuguese expansion put greater and greater pressure on the Tupinambás and their way of life.

Tupinambá subsistence was based on a mixed economy of swidden horticulture, hunting, fishing, and gathering. Horticultural work was done primarily by women, while men dedicated themselves to hunting, fishing, and warfare. Villages were moved often, due primarily to the deterioration of local agricultural lands caused by swidden agriculture.

Tribal groupings resided in dispersed, fortified settlements throughout well-demarcated tribal areas. Tribes lacked any sort of overarching, centralized political structure. Each individual community was theoretically independent of the others, although there were long-standing alliances forged by kinship, friendship, common interests, feasting, and mutual aid in warfare. The local community or village consisted of four to seven *malocas*, long houses composed of various extended families and housing between forty and several hundred people. Each *maloca* was presided over by a *morubixaba* (principal), to whom the resident members were related through kinship or close friendship. Each nuclear family occupied its own area within the *maloca*. Village leadership was provided by a chief, usually the *morubixaba* of one of the *malocas*, but some villages had more than one such chief. Leadership was exercised through persuasion and prestige. Village chiefs had no power to compel compliance in day-to-day activities, although their counsel and supernatural power were greatly esteemed. The *morubixabas*, almost invariably older men who had demonstrated great valor and success in warfare, formed a village council that deliberated important matters related to village activities, particularly with respect to warfare and village movement. Also essential in village leadership were the *pajés* (shamans), whose divinations were necessary before any important undertaking.

Law among the Tupinambás was based primarily on the principles of *lex talionis* (law of retaliation) and private justice. Since no police or formal judicial system existed for redress of grievances, the Tupinambás emphasized strongly the principle of retribution and revenge for offenses. If one Tupinambá injured another, the guilty party or a close relative should suffer the same injury, and it was up to the aggrieved person and his or her relatives to press for settlement of disputes. In the case of capital offenses, the kinsmen of the perpetrator were required to themselves kill the guilty party in recompense or face feud and warfare. Thus, feud was always a threat and occasionally broke out among groups that had once been allies and kinsmen. The retributive principle was one of the major causes of warfare among the Tupinambás.

Tupinambá warfare, driven by ideology, demographic pressure, and economic and social factors, was chronic. By means of success in warfare, men gained prestige and political influence in society. One of the primary motivations for warfare was to take vengeance for relatives killed or eaten in religious rituals by their enemies. Consequently, much Tupinambá warfare took on the aspect of continual feud in which the losers always sought to revenge themselves on the winners.

Great importance was placed on the capture of enemies. A captive was taken to the village of the captor, incorporated into his household and, if a male, married to his daughter or other close female relative. Female captives generally became the wives of the captor. Captives were treated in many respects as if they were a member of the household, playing roles similar to those of other members of the local community. However, their fates were quite distinct, since at some time in the future, they would be ceremonially executed in the public square and then roasted and eaten.

The process of revenge warfare was closely integrated into other aspects of Tupinambá culture. Warfare could be static, the contending parties engaging in an endless series of raids and counter raids. Warfare also had a dynamic aspect. At times, tribal groups were able to drive their enemies from their lands, occupying the areas thus vacated. Given the lack of political centralization, this occupation did not lead to larger and larger territorial control by successful tribes. Rather it took the form of groups migrating from less desirable or ecologically overused lands to more productive ones. These migrations, often under the leadership of *pajés*, took on the guise of messianic movements in search of a legendary earthly paradise; there were also powerful demographic and ecological motivations behind these movements. Tupinambá subsistence practices led to a deteriorating ecological balance, which necessitated shifting cultivation. With population growth, migration and warfare became mechanisms for alleviating such pressures on local tribes.

Much warfare took the form of raids, which involved relatively small forces making incursions into enemy territory, with the intent of seizing prisoners and then fleeing back to friendly territory. Weaponry was simple but effective, consisting of bows and arrows and the *tacape* (hardwood club). But very large expeditions, involving several thousand warriors, also took place, often involving siege tactics against enemy villages, which, because of the constant threat of attack, were characteristically palisaded and contained other defensive features. This form of larger-scale battles was intensified as a result of European contact and incursion in the form of colonization, slaving, and attempts to subdue the native groups and seize their lands.

Kinship was a central principle of social organization among the Tupinambás. The *maloca*s were composed principally of kinsmen, and the preferential forms of marriage—mother's brother with sister's daughter and cross-cousin—reinforced kin relations based on affinal ties. Kin ties, together with success in warfare, were the primary means by which a man built a following and gained prestige and influence in the community and tribe. Men were not generally allowed to marry until they had captured and ritually killed an enemy in warfare. Even then it might be difficult for young men to marry, as it was customary to marry young, nubile daughters and sisters to older, accomplished males, thus extending or enhancing the father's or brother's ties to important people. As it was common for older males to practice polygyny, a young man often was not able to find an acceptable wife until he had gained some renown. Thus, there was a strong gerontocratic aspect to both kinship and political power. When finally able to marry, a young man was usually required to live in the *maloca* of his in-laws, and to labor on behalf of his father- or brother(s)-in-law, and to serve under their direction, until such time as he could recompense them by providing a daughter in marriage. Thus daughters were greatly esteemed, as their marriages enabled a man not only to free himself from heavy obligations to his in-laws, but to make important alliances within the community and tribe.

There was considerable inequality in status between males and females. Although status differences existed within each gender, women were generally subordinate either to their fathers or brothers, or to their husbands. The husband's considerable authority and power over his wives was checked to some degree by the wife's male relatives, who might react adversely if she were mistreated. A woman's status was derived primarily by ascription—a daughter or sister of a renowned warrior or principal had high status and tended to marry a male of high status. However, some women, particularly female shamans, could gain prestige and status in their own right. Females cultivated the fields and carried out practically all the domestic chores. Such was the division of labor that a male was virtually unable to function without a spouse or female relative to care for him.

PORTRAITS OF TUPINAMBÁ MAN AND WOMAN, CIRCA 1640, BY ALBERT ECKHOUT. Portuguese colonization rapidly changed Tupinambá life and culture to conform to the needs and values of colonial society. Such changes are reflected in the dress and personal adornment of the two subjects. The man holds a a typical Tupian bow and arrows, with which the native Brazilians were exceptionally proficient. Acculturated or mixed-blood Tupinambás were often employed by Europeans as hunters or auxiliaries in war.

NATIONAL MUSEUM OF DENMARK, DEPARTMENT OF ETHNOGRAPHY

Shamanism was an important religious function. Through auguring, divination, and healing, individuals and groups could discern the outcome of events and restore health. Tupinambás believed in and feared a great number of spirits, including the spirits of the dead, who, if not properly buried and reverenced, could cause injury and death to the living. The souls of the dead who had exemplified the ideals of society, especially bravery in warfare, were believed to journey to a land of happiness, abundance, and joy where a man was reunited with his ancestors, especially his male ancestors. Wicked or cowardly persons could never attain this land.

The effects of European contact on Tupinambá culture were dramatic. At first, rival tribes aided the Europeans in raids against their traditional enemies, but the colonists soon made little distinction among the groups they would raid for slaves. Moreover, epidemic diseases, to which the natives had little resistance, devastated Indian peoples, as did the practice of slavery. As a result of this process, Indians were able to avoid assimilation or death only by fleeing farther and farther into the interior. Thus, as European colonization ensued over several centuries, Tupinambá culture disappeared except in the most remote areas of Brazil.

BIBLIOGRAPHY

Brandão, Ambrósio Fernandes. *Dialogues of the Great Things of Brazil*. Translated and annotated by Frederick H. Hall, William F. Harrison, and Dorothy W. Welker. Albuquerque, N.Mex., 1987

Hemming, John. *Red Gold: The Conquest of the Brazilian Indians*. Cambridge, Mass., 1978.

Metraux, Alfred. "The Tupinamba." In *Handbook of South American Indians*. Vol. 3. Washington, D.C., 1963.

Staden, Hans. *Hans Staden: The True History of His Captivity 1557*. Translated and edited by M. Letts. London, 1928.

DONALD W. FORSYTH

Indians of the Spanish Main and Central America

The term *Spanish Main* was the English phrase applied in part to the mainland territory opposite the islands of the West Indies. It included the south coast of the Caribbean Sea from the Paria Peninsula, opposite Trinidad, and west along the coast of northern South America to and including lower Central America. At the time of first European contact this environmentally diverse coastal region (including northern Venezuela, northern Colombia, Panama, eastern Costa Rica, eastern Nicaragua, and eastern Honduras) was populated by several dozen native societies, most of which were organized into chiefdoms of varying sizes and degrees of political complexity.

The majority of the population in each of these chiefdoms consisted of commoners, who were governed in political and religious matters by a small group of aristocratic elites. In addition, war captives worked as laborers and servants and sometimes were absorbed by marriage or adoption into the general population. Elites and commoners were differentiated in part by the relative honor accorded their respective ancestors and in part by overall lifestyles. Elites displayed rare and valuable ornaments made of gold alloys and precious and semiprecious stones and wore robes and mantles of exceptionally fine woven textiles. They were carried in litters by retainers, lived in large, elaborately decorated houses located in ceremonial centers, and were buried in tombs richly stocked with items reflecting wealth. Commoners, in contrast, lived in the countryside surrounding the elite center in plainer and smaller homes, had fewer and less elaborate ornaments and clothing, and were more simply buried.

Commoners focused their lives on daily subsistence activities and kin group affairs. To raise manioc and other root crops such as maize, peanuts, chili peppers, and various tree crops, including pejibaye palm, they cleared and burned agricultural land and planted it with the aid of pointed sticks; mountain slopes and hillsides were sometimes terraced and irrigated by canals. Commoners

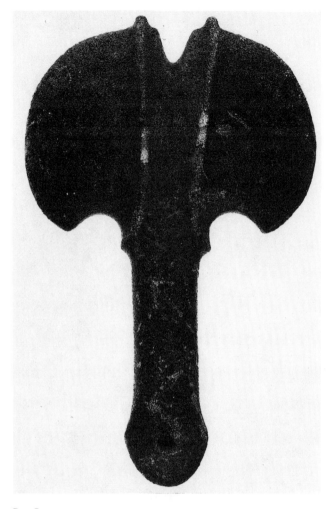

PRE-COLUMBIAN DOUBLE-HEADED STONE AXE. From present-day Costa Rica.   REPRODUCED BY COURTESY OF THE TRUSTEES OF THE BRITISH MUSEUM

hunted abundant land and aquatic animals including deer, peccary, iguanas, ground birds, turtles, water fowl, and manatee and fished in rivers and ocean, providing food for themselves, for the elite, and for ceremonial occasions. They also worked agricultural lands for their lords and built the chiefs' compounds and ceremonial centers, but they paid no taxes or other formal tributes.

Elites focused their attention primarily on foreign affairs, creating complex regional networks of high-level contacts through diplomatic marriages (chiefs were polygynous), warfare, and trade with lords of other polities. Trade involved a wide range of crafted and natural goods, including salt, raw cotton, woven textiles, raw gold, finished gold jewelry, dried fish, emeralds, seashells, and pearls. By such means, ties were established between Panamanian elites and lords of the mountains and lowlands of northern Colombia (e.g., Dabeiba, Quimbaya, Cenu), between chiefs of coastal Colombia and chiefs of interior highland peoples (e.g., Chibchas), between elites of northwest Venezuela (including the Lake Maracaibo area) and those of northeast Colombia and the Venezuelan Andes, and between lords of northeast coastal Venezuela and the grassland (llanos) peoples of the interior.

Spanish contact had a devastating effect on many of the indigenous cultures of the Spanish Main. Expeditionary raids and forays in search of portable wealth (gold, gems) and exportable slaves quickly depleted many of the sizable native populations as people became victims of the raids and of new diseases. Survivors sought refuge in the more inhospitable depths of mountains and forests. The Spaniards then utilized select ports along the Caribbean, most notably Cartagena and Portobelo, as jumping-off points for expeditions farther into the interior and as transshipment points for the crucial trade that eventually linked the South American colonies with Europe.

BIBLIOGRAPHY

Gordon, B. LeRoy. *Human Geography and Ecology in the Sinu Country of Colombia.* Berkeley, 1957.

Helms, Mary W. *Ancient Panama: Chiefs in Search of Power.* Austin, Texas, 1979.

Helms, Mary W. "The Indians of the Caribbean and Circum-Caribbean at the End of the Fifteenth Century." In *Colonial Latin America.* Vol. 1 of *The Cambridge History of Latin America.* Edited by Leslie Bethel. Cambridge, 1984.

Sauer, Carl O. *The Early Spanish Main.* Berkeley, 1969.

MARY W. HELMS

Chibchas

The Chibchas lived in the high valleys of the eastern cordillera of the Andes in what is now central Colombia, an area of year-round cool climate, moderate rainfall, and fertile soils. Estimates of the preconquest population have run as high as one million. The Spanish conquest of the Chibchas began in 1537, when about 170 men led by Gonzalo Jiménez de Quesada arrived via the Magdalena Valley. Two years later, two more expeditions arrived: one, from Venezuela, under Nicolás Féderman, and the other, from Ecuador, led by Sebastián de Belalcázar, each apparently unaware of the other. The three leaders returned to Spain to claim the rewards of conquest, leaving Hernán Pérez de Quesada in charge. So-called "rebellions" that followed probably constituted the main Chibcha resistance; they were put down with considerable bloodshed, especially for the Chibcha nobility. Smallpox epidemics, starting about 1560, also claimed many lives. However, a considerable Chibcha population remained through the colonial period.

Colonial-period sources describe the Chibchas as organized into two kingdoms, which were probably fairly loose confederations of towns headed by caciques (local chieftains), who may have had some hierarchical relationships among themselves, but any hegemony of the Zipa of Bogotá and the Zaque of Tunja (the "kings") was probably recent and weak. The division may reflect some kind of dual organization not understood by the Spaniards. The local communities (towns) were internally divided into a variable number of entities called (in English) parts, each having a hereditary leader (captain); the cacique was captain of his own part. Inheritance of part membership and of leadership positions was strictly matrilineal and remained so for three hundred years after the Spanish conquest. The parts were neither exogamous nor endogamous, but may have been localized.

The food supply was based on agriculture; corn, potatoes, and a variety of other crops were grown in an extensive system of raised-bed fields, traces of which have been discovered in recent years. Deer, guinea pigs, and other animals were hunted, and fishing was important, perhaps to the extent of fish-farming in the ditches between the raised-bed fields. Cotton was grown in the lower-altitude parts, and was spun and woven into fine textiles decorated with painted as well as woven designs. Besides serving as clothing, textiles were important items of trade; their use for such purposes as ceremonial gifts, prizes, and religious offerings suggests that weaving and textiles may have had symbolic values similar to those reported ethnographically for the linguistically related Kogi. Other crafts included pottery, woodworking, and metallurgy, mainly in gold and copper and for ornamental and religious purposes rather than for tools. Gold was obtained by trade, which was an important activity; established marketplaces and specialized traders are reported. Besides textiles, the main trade item was salt, produced abundantly at several localities, especially Zipaquirá, still an important source of this mineral.

Houses and temples were built of wood with thatch roofs, circular in plan; early colonial-period maps sometimes have little drawings of them. Little architectural use of stone has been found, and the perishable building materials have left no monumental ruins. However, the numerous palisaded settlements were impressive enough to remind the first Spaniards of Moorish fortresses in southern Spain; they called the Bogotá region Valle de los Alcázares.

Chibcha religion involved a considerable pantheon of divinities, the chief of whom seem to have been a creator god, Chimingagua; the Sun, Xue; his wife the moon, Chía; and a culture hero, Bochica or Nemquethaba, who traveled through the country teaching the people to spin and weave and live good lives, and then disappeared. Relations with these and other spiritual beings were the responsibility of specialized priests, whose lengthy training started in boyhood, and who led celibate and very ascetic lives. They made offerings of gold objects, emeralds, miniature textiles, and other objects in temples and other places. Temples, large and small, public and private, were numerous; the most important was located at Sogamoso, north of Tunja. Future caciques were secluded in temples for training. An elaborate ceremony at Lake Guatavita for the cacique of that town seems to be the origin of the legend of El Dorado.

BIBLIOGRAPHY

Broadbent, Sylvia M. "The Formation of Peasant Society in Central Colombia." *Ethnohistory* 28 (1981): 259–277.

Broadbent, Sylvia M. "A Prehistoric Field System in Chibcha Territory, Colombia." *Nawpa Pacha* 6 (1968): 135–147.

Broadbent, Sylvia M. "The Site of Chibcha Bogotá." *Nawpa Pacha* 4 (1966): 1–13.

Simón, Pedro. *Noticias historiales de las conquistas de Tierra Firme en las Indias Occidentales.* 1625. 9 vols. Bogotá, 1953.

SYLVIA M. BROADBENT

Incas and Their Neighbors

Tahuantinsuyu (Tawantinsuyu), the Inca state, was no more than a century old in 1532 when, after a short campaign, 155 Europeans overthrew it. Such a swift collapse convinces some observers that it had been a state without coherence, a makeshift ethnic conglomerate. Protracted military campaigns far from familiar geographic conditions had certainly enfeebled it, particularly in the equatorial north. Dynastic squabbles between royal lineages also contributed to the European victory. But considering what had been achieved in the century before the European invasion, the Inca state was a remarkable socioeconomic and technological structure.

In 1532 the Incas ruled over twelve million people, including dozens of ethnic groups speaking at least twenty different languages. Tahuantinsuyu stretched from present-day northern Ecuador to Mendoza in west-central Argentina and the Maule River in central Chile. What impressed the Europeans most and very early were the roads—more than 25,000 kilometers (15,500 miles) linking territories that today are part of five modern republics—and the thousands of warehouses, strung along the roads and in the administrative centers, full of food and textiles. One of the best early sources on the Americas, Gaspar de Espinosa, member of a prosperous slave-trading and banking family, who had financed the invasion of the Andes by Francisco Pizarro and Diego de Almagro, wrote to Charles V in 1533 that these Indians were good candidates to be made to serve the Spaniards in light of their experience as members of the Inca state, and that "these Indians of the provinces of Peru are very skilled at making and opening roads and causeways and fortresses

and other buildings of stone and earth and at opening water canals and at this building it is said that they are far in advance of us."

The Inca state also transferred populations for productive or strategic purposes. In the last few decades before the arrival of the Europeans, when the Inca armies found themselves fighting farther and farther from home, special measures had to be taken to ensure the supply of commodities that the troops expected as their reward. While high-altitude tubers and their conversion to storable, freeze-dried *chuñu* formed the bulk of the food supply, maize and its by-product, beer, were held in much higher esteem and were expected by the troops. Eventually state maize plantations were set up in present-day Bolivia, worked by highlanders sent down on rotation. Because soldiers also expected regular issues of high-status cloth, state manufactures were established using as many as a thousand carders, weavers, and feather ornamentors. The European chroniclers who reported these exotic features of Inca military organization noted that the troops were likely to rebel if they did not receive regular issues of commodities rare in the villages.

Since Inca rule outside the Cuzco region was so recent, many ethnic groups, large and small, were still distinguishable and retained their sense of identity within Tahuantinsuyu. Some of them still recalled a time, less than a century before 1532, when their own lords competed with Cuzco for political hegemony. And since the Incas were not the first overarching polity to emerge in the Andes, the dynastic oral traditions of each ethnic group recalled periods in the past when their own lords had achieved power beyond their immediate valleys and pastures. Some of them also recalled decades of "war of all against all," as described by Guamán Poma de Ayala (Waman Puma), an Andean writer. In 1615, Poma finished a twelve-hundred-page "letter" to the Spanish king Philip III, describing not only Inca glories but also his own ancestors' rule in pre-Cuzco times. This memory of past independence also encouraged many local lords to favor the Europeans against the Incas; they lived to regret it.

Although the Incas were a high-altitude, mountain dynasty, the political structure they eventually cobbled together included many coastal polities. While some of these had resisted Inca rule, others were folded into the Inca state without resistance. Some of these coastal polities were small, others made up of several valleys; all depended on irrigation, since the Peruvian coast is a desert. As these polities expanded in pre-Inca times, so did their irrigation network; in some cases waters from the rainy highlands were diverted at will from one valley to another. Several languages and ethnic groups prevailed on the Andean coast. Their achievements are better understood—even though their descendants no longer speak the mother tongue and frequently have no histori-

EFFIGY VESSEL, STANDING MUSICIAN. From Chimu, fourteenth to fifteenth century. Silver and turquoise.

THE METROPOLITAN MUSEUM OF ART, THE MICHAEL C. ROCKEFELLER MEMORIAL COLLECTION, GIFT OF NELSON A. ROCKEFELLER, 1969. (1978.412.219)

lord's identity, the interpreter explained that he was the "lord of Chincha, master of 100,000 rafts on the sea." While the exact number of these craft need not detain us, the sea-borne traffic is startling both for the number quoted and distances traveled.

The balsa wood used to build the rafts came not from the arid Peruvian coast but from the distant warm waters of the Gulf of Guayaquil, in present-day Ecuador. The sailors maneuvered their craft with the help of sails and a keel. Cabins to protect the goods and the crew were built on the raft; some had crews of as many as twenty sailors. The rafts carried vast amounts of spondylus shells; like the balsa wood, these mollusks did not grow in the cold waters of the Peruvian coast. It is unclear what the southerners, like the Chincha (who used spondylus shells to encourage rainfall and to feed the gods) sent north in exchange. María Rostworowski, a leading Peruvian scholar of Andean history, suggests that in exchange for spondylus, metals—arsenic alloys for bronzes at an earlier stage and the more familiar tin bronzes in Inca times—were shipped north.

The Inca dynasty was aware of the strength of ethnic diversity throughout the realm and the separatist dangers implicit in such differences. The royal road and the army were only some of the methods used to foster coherence. The cult of the sun, identified originally with the Incas in their Cuzco homeland, was extended to the rest of the realm, sometimes incorporating local deities, at other times repressing them. Another tactic was to ignore local ethnic and linguistic differences and loyalties and to impose a decimal system for reorganizing and governing conquered groups. This decimal system reflected the organization of the official Inca historical and accounting records, quipu, made by knotting strings. The conquered peoples were divided into units of ten to ten thousand "households." Surviving records for part of the Huánuco region imply that a "hundred households" unit was composed of five hamlets in close geographic proximity. This method of classifying subjects was ignored by the Europeans, but occasionally the decimal vocabulary does appear in North Andean records, where this method of accounting apparently originated. Finally, there was an attempt to impose Runa Simi, the language of Cuzco, as the common language for the whole realm. Today some ten million people in four republics speak variants of this language (called Quechua), but much of its spread occurred after the colonial period, when the Spaniards continued the Inca campaign against local dialects and languages.

Sun worship was the state religion of the Incas, but the religious beliefs and practices of other pre-Incan peoples continued in some form up to the time of the Spanish conquest. In addition to Inti, the sun god, the Inca pantheon contained his wife Mama-Kilya, the moon

cal awareness of their past—because archaeologists have long preferred to concentrate on the desert coast, and the presence of gold, emeralds, and other treasure in the graves has favored the study of coastal civilizations over Inca civilization.

One coastal society that has received attention from historians, even though its metallic treasure was rare, is the Chincha. Eyewitnesses of the Inca defeat in 1532, at Caxamarca, reported that only one lord other than King Atahualpa was carried in a litter. When asked about the

goddess; Viracocha, the creator god; and Apu Illapu, the rain giver. Priests presided over the Inca religion and resided at all important shrines and temples. The Incas held monthly religious festivals, performed divination, and practiced sacrifice ranging from daily offerings of burnt corn for the rising sun to human sacrifice at times of defeat, famine, or pestilence.

The Inca version of their history cannot be readily studied because they apparently did not write. The quipu decimal records are said to be limited to matters that could be expressed in quantitative terms. Eyewitnesses of the invasion refer to "maps" kept by the state's record keepers. At an early moment in the invasion these "maps" had permitted the Europeans to learn of ethnic groups, their size, their geographic distribution, and their leaders before they had ever seen them. As late as 1575, the viceroy Francisco de Toledo sent to Philip II in Madrid a collection of four "maps" kept by descendants of Andean authorities, but these have not yet surfaced. Both quipu and the use of ethnic "maps" were abandoned by the Spaniards soon after the invasion, possibly because the office of custodian was a religious office.

Knowledge of Inca history is thus severely limited when compared, for example, with contemporary knowledge of the Maya past. Inca history may be illuminated in two ways, by examining the archaeological record (many Inca cities are still standing along the Qhapaq Ñan, the royal highway), and by searching for additional sixteenth-century administrative and ecclesiastic records, which were compiled by eyewitnesses but remain inaccessible, locked up in convent and private libraries.

[See also *Cuzco*.]

BIBLIOGRAPHY

Hemming, John. *The Conquest of the Incas*. San Diego, 1973.
Hyslop, John. *The Inka Road System*. San Diego, 1984.
Hyslop, John. *Inka Settlement Planning*. Austin, Tex., 1990.
Morris, Craig, and Donald Thompson. *Huánuco Pampa: An Inca City and Its Hinterland*. London, 1985.
Murra, John V. *The Economic Organization of the Inka State*. Greenwich, Conn., 1980.
Murra, John, Nathan Wachtel, and Jacques Revel. *Anthropological History of Andean Polities*. New York, 1986.
Steward, Julia H., ed. *Handbook of South American Indians*. Vol. 2: *The Andean Civilizations*. Washington, D.C., 1946.

JOHN V. MURRA

Mayas

The Maya region stretches from Tabasco and Chiapas in Mexico to the western parts of El Salvador and Honduras. It includes all of Yucatán, Guatemala, and Belize. In the late twentieth century there were about 2.5 million Maya Indians, but there were between six and seven million in 1519. After the Spaniards arrived, the native population declined, dropping 80 to 90 percent in some areas and becoming extinct in others. The Maya region is composed of three main geographical zones: the highlands, the lowlands, and the Pacific coastal plain and piedmont.

The Classic Mayas

During the Classic period (A.D. 250 to 900), the Mayas developed one of the most complex and sophisticated civilizations in the Petén lowlands of Mexico and Guatemala. The elite class of rulers and higher administrators formed the upper level of a diverse society that consisted of lesser bureaucrats, merchants, craftsmen, farmers, and unskilled laborers.

Carved monuments called altars and stelae document the histories of the rulers of many of the important sites such as Tikal, Copan, Yaxchilan, Calakmul, and Quirigua. At one time Maya scholars thought the depictions on these monuments were priests and that the accompanying hieroglyphs mainly dealt with religion and the passage of time. Classic Maya society was perceived to be basically theocratic and peaceful. More recent work and increasing ability to read Maya texts have demonstrated that Maya society was quite militaristic and that the monuments record dynastic histories and conquests as well as astronomical information. Emblem glyphs, or those that identify individual sites, show that some of the larger sites, such as Tikal, dominated smaller nearby centers.

Architecturally, lowland Maya structures are some of the finest produced in ancient Mesoamerica. Vast trade networks spanned the Petén leading to the Gulf of Mexico, the Pacific coast, highland Guatemala and southeast to Copan and Quirigua. Classic Maya civilization was already declining by the late ninth century. By the early tenth century, most of the sites had been abandoned, and the jungle had begun to encroach upon the ruins. The Mayas of the Petén region were not to be rediscovered until the nineteenth century.

Maya Culture at Contact

In 1519 the Mayas were fragmented into many small, autonomous polities that engaged in constant warfare. There were around sixteen of these in northern Yucatán and several in highland Guatemala and Chiapas. Boundaries between adjacent groups were not clear and were often disputed. Other causes of war were desire for tribute, trade routes, land, and slaves. Walled, palisaded, and moated centers were common. In the Guatemala highlands major sites (*tinamit*) were located on mountain slopes and hilltops for defense. The larger Maya sites were residences of the elite and centers of political, ritual, and economic activities. Commoners inhabited smaller villages scattered throughout the countryside.

The Petén (central lowlands) was not densely populated. The most important sites were located on islands in

Lake Petén-Itzá and Yaxhá. The elite lived in these island centers, and the commoners inhabited scattered mainland villages. The Itzás of Tayasal had a political system similar to that of Yucatán and warred against their neighbors. Other Petén groups, such as the Lacandóns, seem to have had a village-level political organization.

Maya sites in highland Chiapas were small. Some were politically aligned with the Chontal Mayas, but others were independent and ruled by local nobles. Centers in the Chiapas Plateau, such as Zinacantán, faced Aztec intervention and encroachment from the nearby Chiapanecs.

Sociopolitical System. Throughout the Maya area the most important groups had a corporate form of lineage organization. The lineages were ranked, and the highest political offices were held by male leaders of the highest-ranking lineages. The lineages were grouped into a larger entity known generally as the *chinamit*. Members were not always related, but the *chinamit* was called by the surname of the highest-ranking male. A territorial and political unit, the *chinamit* was responsible for its members' actions. It was a resource and land-holding group, and the members lived together within a walled area. Highly ranked members married outside the *chinamit* and sometimes out of their center. Commoners married within the *chinamit*. In highland Guatemala principal lineages were associated with multifamily dwellings called big houses. Such dwellings were also constructed in Yucatán, Acalán, and Tayasal and probably characterized most Maya groups.

Socially, the Mayas were divided into two main groups, the nobles who received tribute and the commoners who paid it. The nobles dominated the higher offices, wore fine clothing, and lived in large houses in major centers. Commoners, who were lesser officials, farmers, fishermen, unskilled laborers, foot soldiers, craftsmen, and burden bearers, lived in outlying villages. Warriors, merchants, and skilled artisans formed a middle status group but still paid tribute. There were also serfs who originally seem to have been conquered people who were attached to and inherited with the land. Some became trusted servants, warriors, and guardians of valuable lands and rose in society. Slaves were war captives, criminals, debtors, and those sold into slavery.

Economic System. The Maya economic system consisted of local agricultural and crafts production, commercial agriculture, local and long distance trade—the latter primarily involving luxury products—and tribute. Local agricultural products consisted of such crops as maize, beans, chili, honey, cotton, and salt and fish. These were the staples of daily life along with such craft products as pottery, obsidian and flint tools, and weaving and rush mats. Other crops, such as cacao and cotton, were raised on large plantations.

There were many local and regional markets, the most important ones being held in major centers. People selling the same items were grouped together, and luxury as well as everyday items were sold. Markets in important centers were located near temples, and there were judges to settle disputes. Cacao was the most common medium of exchange, but salt and gold were also used.

There were several long-distance trade networks. Much of the sea trade route that stretched from the Chontal area, around Yucatán, and down to the Sula plain of Honduras was controlled by Chontal traders who had large canoes. One such canoe was sighted by Columbus in 1502, and it was filled with trade goods. The Chontals received such goods as cloth, gold ornaments, copper and obsidian items, cochineal, rabbit furs, and slaves from the Aztecs. Aztec merchants had enclaves in Chontal territory, especially at the port of Xicalango. They took cacao, jaguar skins, carved tortoise shells, feathers, and precious stones back to Mexico. Salt, fish, cotton, slaves, honey, and beeswax came to Acalán from Yucatán. The Chontals had extensive cacao plantations in Potonchan, Chetumal, and Honduras. They had enclaves and ports in Cozumel, Chetumal, Nito, and Naco. Another trade route probably passed overland through the Petén, to Tayasal and on to the Caribbean, and one went from Yucatán south to northern Belize.

In Guatemala the most important trade network involved the highland and Pacific coastal exchange. Maize, lime, timber, salt, obsidian, copper, and fish were highland products which were exchanged for lowland cacao, feathers, shrimp, turtles, iguanas, cotton, and fruit. Quetzal feathers were exported from Verapaz and jade from the Motagua area. Gold was imported from Soconusco and Honduras.

Tribute payers ordinarily paid items grown or made in their local area. They paid prescribed amounts over fixed periods of time, and the tribute does not seem to have been a severe hardship. Labor service to the lords was given and involved such activities as working in the lords' fields or building their houses.

Arts and Architecture. The period immediately preceding the Conquest was one of decay in Maya arts and architecture. Much construction was shoddy, and art forms often imitated past styles. In architecture Maya style was combined with such Mexican elements as twin temples placed on a single substructure, round temples, dance platforms, skull racks, colonnaded multiroomed structures, and ball courts in the shape of a capital *I*. Buildings at major centers were usually made of stone and were arranged around plazas.

Mixteca-Puebla influence appears in murals found at several Maya sites. The walls of the palace of the Quiché Cawek lineage at Utatlán were covered with such frescoes portraying important events in the lives of the lords. The best preserved are at Tulum in a two-story building where Xux Ek, the Venus deity, is portrayed. The style is Mixteca-Puebla, but the content is Maya.

During this period, most pottery was local or regional although some Mixteca-Puebla pieces turn up in Maya sites. Chinautla polychrome, a red-and-black-on-white ware from the Guatemala highlands, was traded as far south as El Salvador. Incense burners are found throughout the Maya area. Most pottery and monumental stone sculpture were undistinguished and poor in quality. At Naco, pottery used by the elite living in the central precinct differed from that used by the common people and suggests the higher class had ties with the lowland regions to the north. Other important arts were woven cotton textiles, feather garments, gold, silver and jade items, and painted hieroglyphic books.

Religion. The Mayas had some deities who had been worshiped for a long time, such as Itzamná (a reptilian diety), the Chacs (or rain gods), Ix Chel (the rainbow deity), and Ek Chuah (the merchant god). Mexican-derived gods, such as Kukulcan, and the gods of impor-

THE QUICHÉ IDOL IK.

FROM LEONHARD SCHULTZE, *LEBEN, GLAUBE UND SPRACHE DER QUICHÉ VON GUATEMALA, JENA, 1933.*

tant lineages were also prominent in the period immediately before the conquest. The Maya religious system was polytheistic, and many local deities and spirits were also worshiped. Shrines and pilgrimage centers, such as that dedicated to Ix Chel on Cozumel, also existed.

The gods were portrayed in sculpture and painted hieroglyphic books (codices). They were also worshiped in the form of effigies made out of wood, clay, or stone. The effigies were believed to speak to their people through chosen interpreters or prophets. Dressed in fine clothing and adorned with precious stones and gold, the effigies were kept in temples or were hidden in caves and were the focus of rituals involving fasting, dancing, drinking, and burning incense. The gods were fed food, drink, and human blood. The hearts of living victims were removed by priests, and the victims' blood was smeared on the idols. Birds and animals were also sacrificed by individuals who hoped to attain health, fortune, or some other desire.

The religious organization was headed by a high priest who was assisted by many subordinate priests. They resided in a multiroomed structure near the temple. Priests were in charge of the hieroglyphic books that contained the 260-day divinatory and the 365-day calendars and other religious texts. The *Popol Vuh*, the sacred book of the Quiché Mayas, contains mythology and legends as well as historical accounts of the Quiché forefathers and their Mexicanized gods that are remnants of a much larger body of sacred material that existed before the Conquest. In Yucatán the cult of the *katuns* (twenty-year periods) involved prophecies based on the idea that whatever happened in the past would happen again in another *katun* of the same name. In highland Guatemala sacred bundle cults, such as that of the Pizom Qáqál mentioned in the *Popol Vuh*, were important.

Post-Contact Maya Culture

The period of fighting in the Maya area lasted around twenty years. Some areas were quickly subdued, and others, such as Yucatán (northern lowlands) and the Petén (central lowlands), took longer to conquer.

The Conquest Period: 1517–1542. It was not until 1542 that Francisco de Montejo, father and son, were able to found a capital in Yucatán at Mérida. The conquest of Yucatán was difficult because there was no supreme native ruler to defeat and the provinces defended themselves with guerrilla warfare. Revolts continued throughout the sixteenth century in Yucatán. The conquest of the eastern Maya area around the Gulf of Honduras was achieved quickly, and the Indians were almost entirely obliterated at Nito and Naco. Chetumal held out until 1544; most of its inhabitants fled after the conquest.

Diego de Mazariegos began the conquest of Chiapas in 1528 and rapidly subdued the population. Pedro de

Alvarado entered Guatemala in 1524 and soon conquered the highland groups. He established a permanent capital at the foot of Agua volcano in 1527. This capital was destroyed in an eruption of 1541, and a new capital was founded at present-day Antigua. In 1524 Alvarado also conquered Cuzcatlán (El Salvador), and Honduras was taken by Cristóbal de Olid. The Itzás of the Petén were the last Maya group to remain independent and were not conquered until 1697.

The conquest of the Mayas was facilitated by the superior arms and military strategies of the Spaniards, by the failure of the Indians to put aside local conflicts and join together to fight the common enemy, and by the willingness of both Mexican and Maya Indians to give aid to the Spaniards.

The first Spanish institution imposed on the Indians by the Crown was the encomienda, a grant of a certain number of Indians to reward a conqueror for his service to Spain. The encomendero had the right to receive tribute and labor service from his encomienda Indians. The conquerors tended to exploit their encomiendas as they wished, and there were few limits on their demands. The turbulent times and the small number of Crown officials in the Maya area made it impossible to curb the excesses of the conquerors, whose goals were to become wealthy as quickly as possible and return home to positions in Spain. Sources of gold, silver, and precious stones were quickly exhausted, and the encomienda was used to deplete the Indians rapidly of their wealth.

The upper level of the native sociopolitical structure was greatly affected by the Conquest. Rulers lost their independence and could no longer conduct war and were reduced to the level of local authorities as regional units were dissolved. Agriculture remained in Indian hands as the Spaniards were not initially interested in farming. The conquerors did, however, take over long-distance trade networks. Some of these, such as the sea route from Yucatán to the Gulf of Honduras, were disrupted, but not all the trade was destroyed.

By the 1540s it was becoming clear that the situation could not continue as before. Severe population decline had occurred as a result of fighting and diseases introduced by the Spaniards, reducing the value of encomiendas. Initial sources of wealth were exhausted, and colonists resented the removal of Indians because their labor was needed in local areas.

Establishment of Spanish Authority: 1542–1600. Beginning in 1542, with the passage of the New Laws, which abolished Indian slavery and prohibited the colonists from interfering in most aspects of native life, the Crown took steps to ensure its control and protect the remaining Indians. A new administrative structure was imposed, and more priests were sent to Christianize and protect the natives. The New Laws were resisted, but by 1550, control passed to the audiencias, administrative bodies staffed by officials from Spain. The Audiencia de los Confines, established in 1543, included the area from Chiapas to Costa Rica, except Yucatán, which was initially a part of the Audiencia of Mexico.

Two policies in particular established the basic format of Indian life throughout the sixteenth century: congregation (the gathering of scattered native settlements into focal towns) and the implementation of the Indian town-government system. Many hilltop and remote villages were abandoned for more accessible sites. Towns were laid out according to the Spanish town plan with the church, cabildo (town council), and other main buildings being placed around the plaza. Indian houses surrounded the central area.

The Guatemala and Chiapas highlands received more Spanish colonists than tropical areas and Yucatán. Both Yucatán and Chiapas remained areas of Indian agriculture. By 1550 many Spaniards had left Chiapas or had begun to raise cattle and sugar in the Grijalva River valley. As they took more land, Indians were forced to leave home in search of work. This migration, also found in the Guatemala highlands, destroyed the lineage structure in towns, such as Zinacantán and possibly Atitlán, which were severely affected by loss of men. Many died in tropical areas working on cacao plantations. More remote towns, such as Chamula and Sacapulas, retained the pre-Hispanic social organization.

The Spaniards transferred the people of Itzamkanac to coastal Tixchel in 1557 as the interior had few Indians left. This severely weakened the trade system linking the southern and northern lowlands, and few wealthy Acalán merchants survived by the end of the sixteenth century. The Pacific coastal piedmont area became a focus of Spanish exploitation. Indians owned and cultivated cacao, but most of the harvest was drawn off as tribute or in trade. Because of steep population decline, external competition, and the lack of proper attention, the piedmont cacao plantations gradually declined, and the area was eventually impoverished.

By the mid-sixteenth century, most of the Indians resided in remote highland areas of Chiapas and Guatemala and northern Yucatán. The majority of Spanish colonists resided in a few large towns in temperate areas and lived off encomiendas, through trading, or on government salaries.

Another important local institution introduced by priests after 1550 was the *cofradía* (religious sodality). *Cofradías* were dedicated to a patron saint, and became the focus of Indian religious life. By this time priests had destroyed most of the Maya effigies and hieroglyphic books and had ended human sacrifice. Some of the aspects of aboriginal religion objectionable to the Spaniards went underground, however, and did not completely disappear in the sixteenth century. The Mayas were allowed to retain much of their religious life, as long as they were outwardly Catholic. They mixed pagan beliefs with Catholicism through *cofradía* rituals. Drinking, dancing, fasting, incense, sacred bundles, and diety worship in the form of a cult of the saints continued.

By the end of the sixteenth century, the Spanish had implemented the colonial system that was to exist for the next two hundred years in the Maya region. Indian culture was not destroyed in all areas, and many aspects of pre-Hispanic life endured. Indians living close to Spanish towns or in the lowlands experienced more disruption and exploitation than those inhabiting remote highland areas. Loss of traditional lands and migration also affected the continuity of Maya social organization. Many of the methods used by the Spaniards to control the Indians were variations of aboriginal practices, but they were often much harsher. Along with the introduction of epidemic diseases, these methods led to the gradual lowering of Indian society to a peasant level and to the destruction of ancient sources of wealth.

BIBLIOGRAPHY

Carmack, Robert M. *The Quiché Mayas of Utatlán: The Evolution of a Highland Guatemala Kingdom.* Norman, Okla., 1981.

Edmonson, Munro. *The Book of Counsel: The Popol Vuh of the Quiché Maya of Guatemala.* Middle American Research Institute, no. 35. New Orleans, 1971.

Hill, Robert M., and John Monaghan. *Continuities in Highland Maya Social Organization: Ethnohistory in Sacapulas, Guatemala.* Philadelphia, 1987.

Lovell, George W. *Conquest and Survival in Colonial Guatemala: A Historical Geography of the Cuchumatán Highlands, 1500–1821.* Kingston, Ont., and Montréal, 1985.

MacLeod, Murdo J. *Spanish Central America: A Socioeconomic History, 1520–1720.* Berkeley and Los Angeles, 1973.

Morley, Sylvanus G., and George W. Brainerd. *The Ancient Maya.* 4th ed. Revised by Robert J. Sharer. Stanford, Calif., 1983.

Orellana, Sandra L. *The Tzutujil Mayas: Continuity and Change, 1250–1630.* Norman, Okla., 1984.

Roys, Ralph L. *The Indian Background of Colonial Yucatán.* Norman, Okla., 1972.

Scholes, France V., and Ralph L. Roys. *The Maya Chontal Indians of Acalán-Tixchel. A Contribution to the History and Ethnography of the Yucatán Peninsula.* Norman, Okla., 1968.

Wasserstrom, Robert. *Class and Society in Central Chiapas.* Berkeley and Los Angeles, 1983.

SANDRA L. ORELLANA

Aztecs and Their Neighbors

Although, strictly speaking, *Aztec* (Nahuatl, *Azteca*, Person of Aztlan, the legendary homeland) designated only the ancestors of the Mexica of the twin cities of Mexico Tenochtitlan and Tlatelolco, it has proved useful as a generic term for the late pre-Hispanic peoples of Central Mexico. Most spoke dialects of a common language, Nahuatl, shared an essentially similar culture, and were organized into a number of city states that were dominated by a coalition of the three most powerful: Mexico Tenochtitlan, Tetzcoco, and Tlacopan (in Spanish these Nahuatl names became, respectively, Tenochtitlán, Texcoco, and Tlacopán)—constituting what is usually referred to as the Triple Alliance or Aztec empire.

Traditional History. Mexico Tenochtitlan achieved the supreme position in the coalition. According to one version of Mexica official history, their ancestors were commanded to leave Aztlan, described as an island in a lake, by their patron deity, Huitzilopochtli, in 1116. After a long migration, which included a period of servitude in Colhuacan, they encountered the sign that signaled the end of their wandering, an eagle perched on a nopal cactus growing from a rock. This occurred on a swampy island in the western portion of the saline lake that covered much of the floor of the Basin of Mexico. There they founded their city, Mexico Tenochtitlan (Place of the Mexica–Next to the Stone Nopal Cactus Fruit) around 1325. A divisive group of Mexica leaders established a short distance to the north another city, Tlatelolco (Place of the Globular Islet), that eventually became a serious rival of its southern sister city.

This lake zone was controlled by the Tepaneca of Azcapotzalco, on the western shore, capital of the city-state that had superseded Colhuacan as the paramount power in Central Mexico. Although still tributary to the Tepaneca, the Mexica of Mexico Tenochtitlan, now also called the Tenochca, were able in 1376 to crown their first official ruler, Acamapichtli, a part-Mexica scion of the Toltec-descended royal dynasty of Colhuacan.

At the outset of the reign of the fourth Tenochca ruler, Itzcoatl (r. 1428–1440), a general revolt of most of the Central Mexican city-states tributary to Azcapotzalco was successful. In the early 1430s a new imperial order, the Triple Alliance, was formally established. Mexico Tenochtitlan was joined by Tetzcoco, which under its part-Mexica ruler, the famed "poet king," Nezahualcoyotl (r. 1431–1472), controlled the eastern Basin of Mexico, and Tlacopan, the junior partner, which had inherited the remnant of Tepanec power. This coalition generated great military strength and under a succession of able and aggressive rulers, particularly the nephew and successor of Itzcoatl, Motecuhzoma I (r. 1440–1469), steadily expanded the territory subject to its control. At the time of the Conquest, the Triple Alliance imperium included most of Central and Southern Mexico, and into its capitals regularly flowed a huge amount of rich tribute from hundreds of communities within this extensive territory. Mexico Tenochtitlan, ruled by Motecuhzoma II (r. 1502–1520), the great-grandson of Motecuhzoma I, had, with its twin city, Tlatelolco (which it had conquered in 1473), grown to a great, canal-laced island metropolis, connected by four main causeways to the mainland, with perhaps as many as a quarter-million inhabitants.

Although Motecuhzoma II continued to extend the boundaries of the empire, focusing particularly on the Mixtec-speaking polities of southwestern Oaxaca, the era of spectacular Triple Alliance military expansion was nearly over. Soon after his accession, the first vague reports of the operations of the Spanish in the Caribbean drifted into his realm (Columbus himself, on his fourth and final voyage, in the summer of 1502, reached the Bay Islands off the north coast of Honduras). According to post-Conquest tales, various signs and portents of impending catastrophe plagued Motecuhzoma's last years. The ruler of Mexico Tenochtitlan's chief imperial partner, Nezahualpilli of Tetzcoco, who had succeeded Nezahualcoyotl in 1472, died in 1516, reputedly prophesying dire events to come. A favorite of Motecuhzoma, Cacama (r. 1516–1520), one of Nezahualpilli's sons by a Mexica wife, was chosen the new lord of Tetzcoco—and Mexico Tenochtitlan's preponderance in power within the Triple Alliance became steadily more manifest.

In 1517, two caravels from Cuba were blown off their course and found themselves off a low, unknown shore, the northeastern corner of Yucatan (Spanish, Yucatán). The next year a small fleet of four ships cruised up the coast of Motecuhzoma's Gulf Coast dominions. His representatives there, after engaging in trade with the strangely attired newcomers, reported this unexpected visitation to their emperor. When they returned to the coast, bearing Motecuhzoma's gifts and official message of greeting, the "houses that floated on the water" had sailed away.

In 1519 a much larger fleet of thirteen ships appeared off the same coast. On Good Friday, April 22, Hernando Cortés stepped onto the sandy shore at the edge of Cemanahuac Tenochca Tlalpan (The Whole Earth, the Land of the Tenochca). A little over a year later the most powerful native ruler in North America, a bewildered prisoner in his father's palace, fell under a hail of stones hurled by his own people. Huitzilopochtli's children rallied for a desperate defense of their empire, but, in spite of their stoic heroism, most of their leaders perished in the flaming ruins of the great city that had grown up on the spot where their ancestors had encountered the eagle on the cactus on the rock. Nezahualpilli's prophecy had been fulfilled.

The Triple Alliance Empire. The imperial territory was divided into a number of tributary provinces, comprising various towns and their dependencies. One of the main towns served as the headquarters for the *calpixqui,* the imperial official and his staff, who supervised the collection of the tribute and forwarded it to the capital(s). Provinces of particular strategic importance were governed by high ranking military officers, who commanded garrisons of imperial troops.

A wide range of products constituted the regular tribute levies, which were most commonly collected every eighty days. Various pictorial and textual sources, particularly the *Matrícula de tributos* and its cognate, Part II of the Codex Mendoza, provide itemized lists of them, province by province. Large quantities of foodstuffs and condiments were exacted, mainly from the more centrally located provinces. The prized cacao, the source of chocolate, was collected from certain lowland provinces. Both male and female clothing of cotton and maguey fiber was a standard item, as were elaborate warrior costumes and shields and jade, rock crystal, amber, and gold ornaments. A greater amount of tribute was demanded of provinces that had militarily resisted the Triple Alliance armies. As long as the provinces paid their tribute on time and did not otherwise create problems for their masters, they were allowed a high degree of internal autonomy.

The empire of the Triple Alliance was an intricate mosaic of numerous peoples speaking many different languages, among which Nahuatl—which also served as a lingua franca throughout most of Mesoamerica—was clearly dominant. Another important language of Central Mexico was the unrelated Otomi and its linguistic congeners (Matlatzinca, Mazahua, Ocuilteca), whose center of gravity was to the west and north. To the southeast, centered particularly in Oaxaca and neighboring territory, other languages were spoken, most of them at least remotely related to the Otomian family, the most important of which were Mixtec and Zapotec. To the east, in the Gulf Coast region, were Huaxtec (only their southernmost communities had been added to the empire), Tepehua, and Totonac. Directly to the west was a large block of Tarascan (Purepecha)-speaking communities, which had been organized into an extensive empire, ruled from Tzintzuntzan. This powerful polity had successfully resisted the westward thrust of the Triple Alliance, inflicting on Axayacatl (r. 1469–1481) the greatest military defeat ever suffered by the imperial army. The southeastern border of the empire touched on the territory of the speakers of the Mayance languages. However, although some Triple Alliance dynastic marital alliances had apparently been entered into with the Quiche- and Cakchiquel-speaking polities of Highland Guatemala, any more serious moves to extend the empire in this direction were forestalled by the Spanish Conquest.

The imperialistic thrusts from the Basin of Mexico had radiated out in a somewhat irregular fashion, often leapfrogging or bypassing still-resisting areas, and, at the time of the Conquest, there were various enclaves of unconquered territory within the extensive area dominated by the Triple Alliance. The most important of these were three populous city-states and their lesser allies just to the east of the Basin of Mexico: Tlaxcallan, Huexotzinco, and Cholollan. Just before the Conquest, Tlaxcallan and Huezotzinco had had a serious falling out, resulting in the former dominating the latter, and Cholollan had entered into an uneasy truce with Mexico Tenochtitlan. Tlaxcallan, however, was still a formidable military power, as became evident when in 1519 it formed a pact of friendship with Cortés, and the Tlaxcaltecas long served as the most potent and faithful native allies of the Spaniards. Other significant enclaves were Yopitzinco, along the Costa Grande of Guerrero, east of Acapulco, and a cluster of Mixtec-speaking polities, headed by Tototepec, in southwestern and coastal Oaxaca.

Subsistence. Aztec subsistence was based primarily on intensive agriculture, with some subsidiary hunting, gathering, and fishing. A variety of crops was cultivated, with maize, beans, and squash preeminent. Cotton and maguey provided most of the fiber for the weaving of clothing. The fermented saccharine exudate of maguey constituted the standard intoxicating beverage, pulque (Nahuatl, *octli*). Cacao, which provided the elite, luxury drink, chocolate, was cultivated in certain favored tropical locations.

The simple digging stick was the basic agricultural tool. Intensive rainfall cultivation was widespread in the semi-arid highlands, while the slash-and-burn (swidden) system prevailed in the tropical lowlands. Where feasible, irrigation, flood-water farming, and terracing were employed on a limited scale. Food-storage facilities were well developed, with large, sturdily constructed granaries of both quadrangular pole and adobe vasiform (*cuezcomatl*) types.

Economy. Large agricultural surpluses could be produced both for satisfying tribute obligations and for commercial purposes. Aside from routine domestic household production, particularly the weaving of clothing by the women to satisfy family needs, small-scale "industrial" production featuring numerous specialized crafts played a significant role in the economic system.

In general, commerce, both local and long range, was of great importance. Although most transactions were conducted by barter, cacao beans and standard-sized cotton mantles served as a kind of supplemental currency. The major metropolitan centers held organized markets daily, the lesser communities normally every five days. The two most important Central Mexican markets were in Tlatelolco, where, according to Cortés, sixty thousand persons gathered daily, and Cholollan (Cholula), in the Basin of Puebla, a special holy city and pilgrimage center that also served as a great mercantile emporium. The highly

organized professional merchants (*pochteca/oztomeca*) joined with the merchants of other communities in undertaking great trading caravans that penetrated as far east as Guatemala and even beyond. They were much favored by the Triple Alliance rulers, who employed them as commercial agents and gatherers of useful military intelligence.

Sociopolitical Structure. The fundamental sociopolitical unit was the city-state, a dominant major town (*altepetl*) or group of allied towns that politically controlled a number of smaller dependent satellites. Even if the city-states paid tribute to more powerful polities—as most of them did within the Triple Alliance empire—they typically were permitted to manage most of their internal affairs. The larger communities were subdivided into smaller units (*calpolli, tlaxilacalli*), largely endogamous residential wards that exercised various corporate functions, particularly those involving land tenure.

All family members cooperated closely in subsistence and economic activities. By the age of ten most boys left their families to attend either the ward's military school (*telpochcalli*) or, particularly if they were members of the nobility, temple schools (*calmecac*). Some girls also attended the temple schools, but most were instructed in domestic skills by their mothers in their homes. Girls normally married quite early, boys somewhat later, after a period of military service. Polygyny was standard among the aristocracy, while most commoner marriages, mainly for economic reasons, were monogamous.

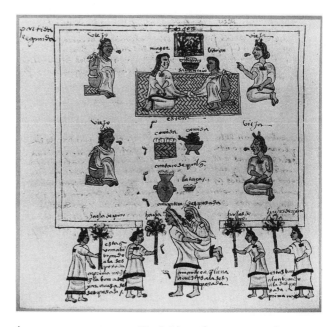

AZTEC MARRIAGE CEREMONY. The bride and groom, seated on a mat, literally "tie the knot," as his shift is tied to her blouse. From the Codex Mendoza, folio 61r.   LIBRARY OF CONGRESS

The society was highly stratified, with two major classes, the nobility *(pipiltin)* and the commoners *(macehualtin)*, with various distinctions of rank within each stratum. Most of the former possessed their own patrimonial lands, which were worked for them by commoners as well as tenants attached to them. All other commoners were required to pay taxes and fulfill additional obligations, including corvée labor on public works and military service. Nobles were usually free from local tax levies but were expected to serve in various leadership roles, particularly in the military sphere. Slaves *(tlacotin)* were owned mainly by the upper class and performed many of the more menial tasks. However, they possessed definite legal rights and were not considered mere chattel property.

Most of the major city-states at the core of the empire were governed by a ruler *(tlatoani,* speaker) who possessed great power as the earthly representative of his community's patron deity but was expected to consult with an advisory council composed of the highest ranking nobles before making important decisions. An extensive bureaucracy administered both local and imperial affairs, particularly the collection of taxes and tribute. Many of the higher officials also performed judicial duties, functioning within a complex, hierarchically organized system of local and imperial courts. They applied a rich body of traditional law based on both formal codes as well as recognized precedents.

Religion. The pervasive role of religion has long been recognized as one of the leading features of pre-Hispanic Mesoamerica. Typically, the Aztec religious and ritual system was extraordinarily rich and complex. From birth to death, the individual was immersed in incessant religious activities. Aside from a considerable amount of household ritual, most religious activities focused on the temple *(teocalli)*. In the larger communities, a highly organized professional priesthood *(teopixque)* served in these temples. The priests lived together, practicing sexual abstinence, in monastic-type establishments *(calmecac)* that also served as schools for the sons of the nobility. In addition to the priest who served his community as a whole, there was also the practitioner of both white and black magic *(nahualli)* who mainly served individuals, especially in divination and curative medicine.

The rich theatrical ritualism was largely regulated by the two principal calendric cycles, the (13×20) 260-day cycle *(tonalpohualli)* and the (18×20+5) 365-day cycle *(xihuitl)*, geared to the vague tropical year. The former was primarily employed for divination, each day and its numerical coefficient possessing a fortunate, unfortunate, or neutral connotation. The latter regulated the principal public ceremonies that honored the major deities. The typical ceremony involved a preparatory fasting period, offerings (especially food), processions, deity imperson-

ation, dancing, singing, and often human sacrifice with attendant ritual cannibalism.

The most striking feature of Aztec cosmogony was the concept of four great cosmic eras, or "suns," that had preceded the present age and had terminated with different types of cataclysmic destructions. The current era, the fifth and last, was to be terminated with mankind's final destruction by great earthquakes.

Aztec cosmology conceived the earth as a quadrangular land mass surrounded by ocean. From its center four quadrants extended to the cardinal directions. The celestial sphere consisted of thirteen tiers, the highest of which constituted the abode of the supreme creative divinities. Beneath the earth's surface were nine levels, the lowest, Mictlan, being the final resting place of most of deceased humanity.

An extensive pantheon of individualized deities was believed to control the various spheres of the universe. The majority expressed different aspects of certain fundamental themes, three of the most important being celestial creativity, agricultural fertility, and war/sacrifice/sanguinary nourishment of the sun and earth. The major supernaturals included Tezcatlipoca, the omnipotent "supreme god," Huitzilopochtli, the patron "war god" of the Mexica, Tlaloc, the ancient rain/fertility god, Ehecatl Quetzalcoatl, the wind deity, Chicomecoatl, the principal maize goddess, and Teteoinnan, the earth mother.

Writing. An embryonic writing system was employed, both for religious and secular purposes. It was essentially pictographic but contained some phonetic elements, utilizing the principle of the rebus, or "phonetic transfer," in place and name signs. Besides divinatory and ritual manuals, Aztec writings covered a wide range of subjects, including histories, genealogies, maps and plans, and

COLOSSAL STONE JAGUAR. A *cuauhxicalli*, or ritual vessel for human hearts, in the form of a jaguar. Discovered one block north of the Cathedral of Mexico City in 1901.

MUSEO NACIONAL DE ANTROPOLOGÍA, MEXICO CITY

administrative records such as taxation and tribute lists, censuses, and cadastres.

Aztec culture constituted the final synthesis of the ancient civilization of Mesoamerica. Cut off in full flower by the sudden, wholly unexpected Spanish invasion, much still survives of the lifeways of the indigenous peoples of Central Mexico, albeit in considerably modified form. Certainly no satisfactory understanding of modern Mexico can be achieved without full appreciation of the importance within its cultural fabric of the heritage of Mexico Tenochtitlan, today's Mexico City, and the many peoples over which this great New World Venice once ruled.

BIBLIOGRAPHY

Anderson, Arthur J. O., and Charles E. Dibble, eds. and trans. *Florentine Codex: General History of the Things of New Spain, Fray Bernardino de Sahagún.* Monographs of the School of American Research, Santa Fe, N.Mex., No. 14, Parts 1–13. Salt Lake City, 1950–1982.

Barlow, Robert H. "The Extent of the Empire of the Culhua Mexica." In vol. 28 of *Ibero-Americana.* Berkeley, Calif., 1949.

Berdan, Frances E. *The Aztecs of Central Mexico: An Imperial Society.* New York, 1982.

Carrasco, Pedro. "The Social Organization of Ancient Mexico." In vol. 10 of *Handbook of Middle American Indians,* edited by Robert Wauchope. Austin, Tex., 1971.

Clark, James Cooper, ed. and trans. *Codex Mendoza: The Mexican Manuscript Known as the Collection of Mendoza and Preserved in the Bodleian Library, Oxford.* 3 vols. London, 1938.

Davies, Nigel. *The Aztecs: A History.* Reprint, Norman, Okla., 1980.

Davies, Nigel. *The Aztec Empire: The Toltec Resurgence.* Norman, Okla., 1987.

Gillespie, Susan. *The Aztec Kings: The Construction of Rulership in Mexíca History.* Tucson, Ariz., 1989.

Gillmor, Frances. *Flute of the Smoking Mirror: A Portrait of Nezahualcoyotl, Poet-King of the Aztecs.* Reprint, Albuquerque, N.Mex., 1968.

León-Portilla, Miguel. *Aztec Thought and Culture.* Norman, Okla., 1963.

Matos Moctezuma, Eduardo. *The Aztecs.* New York, 1989.

Nicholson, H. B. "Religion in Pre-Hispanic Central Mexico." In vol. 10 of *Handbook of Middle American Indians,* edited by Robert Wauchope. Austin, Tex., 1971.

Nicholson, H. B., with Eloise Quiñones Keber. *Art of Aztec Mexico: Treasures of Tenochtitlan.* Washington, D.C., 1983.

Pasztory, Esther. *Aztec Art.* New York, 1983.

H. B. NICHOLSON

Indians of Northern Mexico, Baja California, and Southwestern North America

The human landscape encountered by Spanish explorers in northwestern New Spain in the sixteenth century was even more varied than the arid physiographic area that sheltered it. Ranging across mountains, plateaus, canyons, river valleys, and deserts were Uto-Aztecan speakers (among them, Tepehuan, Tarahumara, Concho, Yaqui, Mayo, Opata, Pima, and Hopi Indians); Pueblo Indians of the Tanoan, Keresan, and Zunian linguistic groups; Apache and Navajo speakers of Athapaskan languages; and Seri and Yuman subgroups of Hokan speakers.

Nor did these peoples exhibit cultural unity. Although the native groups within this vast region had trade and exchange ties in the late prehistoric period (perhaps extending into Mesoamerica) and some of them had hierarchical sociopolitical structures, at least by 1600, the indigenous peoples of northern New Spain were characterized by relatively small, predominantly egalitarian communities that were independent of one another economically and politically. Their economies rested on varying combinations of agriculture (carried out by both men and women), gathering (mainly by women), and hunting (by men). Pueblos lived in compact adobe villages and practiced intensive irrigated and dry-farm agriculture. Roving-band peoples could be hunters and gatherers exclusively (as in Baja California) or, like the Navajos and some Apaches, also engage in limited agriculture. The largest number of northern Indians lived in scattered settlements of noncontiguous dwellings called rancherías where they practiced dry farming and floodplain agriculture, depending upon their location. Some changed ranchería locations within the course of the year and supplemented farming with hunting and the gathering of wild foods. In spite of differences in subsistence, kinship organization, and habitat, many inhabitants of this region (particularly the Uto-Aztecan groups) shared some common features, cultivating maize, beans, and squash; twilling baskets and mats; making pottery; and weaving cotton. Elders of individual communities constituted a type of moral authority in peacetime; tribal war leaders emerged in times of conflict. Shamans, whose power derived from dreams, predicted future events and possessed supernatural powers related to weather and curing. Ceremonial life included ritual dancing and the use of intoxicants. A common cosmological framework included belief in stages of creation, a universal flood, dominant male and female supernatural beings related to heavenly bodies, and opposition between supernatural beings who controlled wet and dry seasons.

Estimates of population at the time of contact range from one to two million. Within a hundred years after contact (a process that itself occupied a century), these numbers diminished by more than 90 percent due primarily to epidemic diseases such as smallpox, measles, and typhus. The demographic decline was the greatest ally of the Spaniards in bringing Indian peoples under their control. Hopis, Navajos, Apaches, and Yumans, living at the margins of Spanish empire, successfully resisted incorporation, but even they underwent profound changes in material culture. The introduction of Spanish livestock nearly everywhere diversified small-scale subsistence. Most groups experienced attempts by Franciscans and Jesuits to reorganize them in mission communities where native subsistence strategies and cosmologies clashed with Spanish coercive practices designed to extract surplus production and inculcate Christianity. Indigenous responses, often initially receptive, eventually took varying forms of accommodation and resistance, resulting in a wide range of acculturation.

BIBLIOGRAPHY

Hall, Thomas. *Social Change in the Southwest, 1350–1880.* Lawrence, Kan., 1989.

Ortiz, Alfonso, ed. *The Southwest.* Vols. 9 and 10 of *Handbook of North American Indians,* edited by William C. Sturtevant. Washington, D.C., 1983.

Spicer, Edward H. *Cycles of Conquest: The Impact of Spain, Mexico and the United States on the Indians of the Southwest, 1533–1960.* Tucson, 1962.

SUSAN M. DEEDS

Indians of La Florida

The Spaniards who explored sixteenth-century La Florida—roughly the southeastern United States—encountered a large number of native societies that differed in language, culture, and social structure. Many, but not all, had been powerfully shaped by an economic and social transformation that began about five hundred years before the Spaniards arrived. Beginning around A.D. 1000, this Mississippian transformation entailed a shift from hunting and gathering wild food to a significant dependence on corn grown in cleared fields. The native people of the Southeast had been cultivating several plants on a small scale for 3,000 years or more, but the food from these cultivated plants was little more than an accessory to the wild food they procured from hunting and collecting. Even in the Mississippian period (A.D. 1000–c. 1550), the cultivation of corn, beans, and squash never completely supplanted hunting and gathering. But the demands of corn dependency shaped the Mississippian way of life in a way that previous cultivation had not.

Only a small percentage of the soils in the Southeast are rich enough to have been cultivated without a heavy investment of labor. These favored soils—especially the alluvial soils along the margins of rivers and ox-bow lakes—became crucially important to the Indians of the Mississippian era and were worth fighting for.

Along with this economic change, there were far-reaching social changes during the Mississippian period. Most notably, many people in the Southeast organized themselves into chiefdoms that were hierarchical in structure. The people of a chiefdom were ranked in terms of their birth-order distance from the chief.

Chiefs and their closest relatives and retainers were supported by "gifts," which were voluntarily given, though they could be informally sanctioned, but the chiefs of larger chiefdoms were supported by tribute extracted by coercion or the threat of coercion. The chiefs of the larger Mississippian societies were set apart in life by special clothing, special ritual treatment, and possession of finery; in death they were set apart by burial in sanctified places accompanied by elaborate grave goods.

Just as the members of chiefdoms were ranked with respect to each other, so too were their communities ranked. The typical Mississippian chiefdom was not more than about twenty miles in diameter, and its population numbered in the thousands or low tens of thousands. The central town of a Mississippian chiefdom, which was not always the largest town in size or population, was normally a site with one or more flat-topped mounds on which there were buildings in which the chief lived, where councils and rituals were held, and where venerable things were kept. But chiefdoms might also include secondary towns with mounds, as well as smaller villages and homesteads with no mounds.

In addition, in a number of places in the interior of the Southeast, chiefs gained ascendancy or influence over other chiefdoms, becoming paramount chiefs. Notably unstable because of internal and external conflict, paramount chiefdoms could be short-lived.

One of the principal concerns of Mississippian chiefdoms was the waging of warfare. Southeastern warriors were most adept at one-on-one combat using bows and arrows and warclubs, but they also organized units of combatants against distant enemies. They were devotees of the swift attack from ambush, and they symbolically identified themselves with the cougar and the peregrine falcon. Warfare between some chiefdoms was so endemic and so long-lasting, the combatants were separated by very large uninhabited wildernesses. The Indians warily entered these wildernesses to hunt, fish, and collect wild foods.

The Indians of the Mississippian Southeast created a variety of technically proficient and aesthetically pleasing art forms. This included wooden and stone temple statuary, repoussé copper, engraved shell, and, most particularly, pottery. In the early Mississippian era a complex of symbols known as the Southeastern ceremonial complex became widespread in Mississippian chiefdoms.

The expeditions of Hernando de Soto (1539–1543), Tristán de Luna (1559–1561), and Juan Pardo (1566–1568) all penetrated the interior of the Southeast and came into contact with the paramount chiefdoms. The most notable of these paramount chiefdoms were Coosa, dominating the ridge and valley area of Tennessee, northwestern Georgia, and northeastern Alabama; Ocute, on the middle Oconee River in Georgia, and with probable influence over people living on the western headwaters of the Savannah River, the Guale on the coast, and perhaps Ichisi below the falls at the Ocmulgee River; Cofitachequi, controlling the Wateree River in South Carolina, and with influence over societies between the mountains and the coast; Tascaluza, whose domain lay along the Alabama River; Apalachee, commanding the area between the Aucilla and Ochlockonee Rivers; Chicaza, dominating the middle course of the Tombigbee River and its western tributaries; Pacaha, commanding both sides of the Mississippi River from perhaps thirty miles above and below present Memphis; Casqui, commanding the upper St. Francis River in Arkansas; Naguatex, commanding the great bend of the Red River in southwestern Arkansas; and Quigualtam, commanding the Mississippi River below the mouth of the Arkansas River down to about the mouth of the Yazoo River.

In addition, the European explorers encountered a number of smaller chiefdoms that may not have been incorporated into paramount chiefdoms. The most important of these were Capachequi and Toa on the Flint River in Georgia; Guatari, on the Yadkin River in North Carolina; Apafalaya, on the Black Warrior in Alabama; Quiguate, on the middle St. Francis River in Arkansas; Coligua, on the upper White River in Arkansas; Cayas, on the upper Arkansas River; Quipana, on the upper Ouachita River; Autiamque, on the middle Arkansas River; Anilco, on the lower Arkansas; Guachoya, on the Mississippi River below the mouth of the Arkansas River; and Aminoya, on the Mississippi River above the mouth of the Arkansas River.

Finally, on the margins of the Southeast there were a number of small chiefdoms and tribal societies that were based on hunter-gatherer economies, or societies that were agricultural but not fully Mississippian. The most notable of these were the buffalo-hunting Tula of northwestern Arkansas; the hunter-gatherer Karankawans of the coast of east Texas, among whom Álvar Núñez Cabeza de Vaca and his companions suffered; the Tequesta and Ais of southern Florida, both small societies of hunter-gatherers; the Calusa of southwestern Florida, a chiefdom with a hunter-gatherer economy; and the Ozita and Mocozo of Tampa Bay, who appear to have relied mainly on hunting and gathering. In addition, there were several who in later times were loosely called Timucuans, the most important of whom were the Urriparacoxi and Ocale, agriculturalists in the Withlacoochee River wetlands; the agricultural Yustega of northern Florida; and the Utina of eastern Florida.

Spain had a continuous presence in the Southeast after 1564. But Spain's sphere of influence never extended much beyond the missions of northern Florida and the Georgia coast. The missionaries were effective within this sphere, converting the Indians to Catholicism and instructing them in the Spanish language and in useful skills. But the diseases that the Spaniards brought from the Old World to the New had a catastrophic impact on the native people. One disease after another struck in the late sixteenth century and throughout the seventeenth century. The native population declined precipitously, the paramount chiefdoms fell apart, and the survivors reorganized themselves into new societies to face the challenge of the eighteenth century.

BIBLIOGRAPHY

Dye, David H., and Cheryl Anne Cox, eds. *Towns and Temples along the Mississippi*. Tuscaloosa, Ala., 1990.

Galloway, Patricia, ed. *The Southeastern Ceremonial Complex: Artifacts and Analysis*. Lincoln, Neb., 1989.

Hudson, Charles. *The Southeastern Indians*. Knoxville, Tenn., 1976.

Milanich, Jerald T., and Susan Milbrath, eds. *First Encounters: Spanish Exploration in the Caribbean and the United States, 1492–1570*. Gainesville, Fla., 1989.

Smith, Bruce D., ed. *The Mississippian Emergence*. Washington, D.C., 1990.

Thomas, David Hurst, ed. *Columbian Consequences: Archaeological and Historical Perspectives on the Spanish Borderland East*. Vol. 2. Washington, D.C., 1990.

CHARLES HUDSON

Indians of New England, Roanoke, Virginia, and the St. Lawrence Valley

At the time of Columbus's explorations, the natives of the northern and mid-Atlantic coast and the St. Lawrence Valley of North America were a large and varied array of communities and cultures. Natives of the St. Lawrence River basin and northern New England were members of two distinct cultural traditions, one the northern Algonquian maritime-hunting cultures such as the Beothuks, Micmacs, and Malecite-Passamaquoddies. The other tradition was Iroquoian and included groups known collectively as the St. Lawrence Iroquoians.

The St. Lawrence Iroquoians practiced a mixed economy, including farming, hunting, and fishing. First encountered by French explorers in 1534, these natives occupied two distinct territories, one centering around the Île d'Orléans, and the other on Montréal Island, and they may have been divided into correspondingly separate political and cultural entities. They are today sometimes known as Stadaconans and Hochelagans, after their principal fortified towns. By 1535, the Stadaconans had established themselves as trading intermediaries between the French and native groups farther inland. Rivalry between them and the equally powerful Iroquoian and Algonquian groups to the west probably led to their defeat and dispersal in the late sixteenth century.

The Algonquian-speaking people of the St. Lawrence basin and northern coastal regions were also hunters, subsisting mainly on game, fish, wild vegetable foods, nuts, and seeds. Their material culture was well-suited to the harsh climatic conditions of their territory; they exhibited superior workmanship in hide clothing, snow shoes, and hunting and fishing gear. Coastal groups, such as the Micmacs of the Gulf of St. Lawrence and Maritime provinces, and the Passamaquoddies of the lower St. John River valley, were sea-mammal hunters, while inland groups hunted moose, caribou, and other game. Religious ritual was shamanistic, with emphasis on divination, healing, and the accumulation of personal spiritual power. The northern Algonquians were organized into bands with leaders chosen for their skill at hunting and diplomacy and sometimes for their shamanistic abilities as well. In the late sixteenth century, some of these leaders were exploiting long-distance coastal trade routes for the benefit of their lineages and bands, and it was these men who first negotiated with Europeans in the early decades of the seventeenth century.

Natives of southern New England and the Atlantic seaboard were also Algonquian speakers, but, unlike their northern relatives, they were more sedentary, with women's agricultural products providing a large portion of their diet. Many were organized into communities led by hereditary leaders, known in some areas as sachems, who were entitled to tribute and empowered to allocate land, conduct diplomacy, and wage war. Their cosmology included a belief in an afterlife and in the efficacy of *manitou* (spirit helpers) in gaining success as providers, warriors, and leaders.

Some of the earliest known illustrations of eastern woodlands people are of the Indians of Roanoke Island, completed by the artist John White in 1585. The Roanoke Indians were Algonquian-speakers, and, like the natives of coastal Virginia, were farming people, ruled by elected or hereditary chiefs. The religious ceremonies of the Virginia and Roanoke Algonquians included an elaborate burial cult and belief in frightening and powerful spirits to whom ritual sacrifices were made.

At the time of the establishment of Jamestown in 1607, the natives of eastern Virginia were united into a confederacy under a paramount chief known as Powhatan, a confederacy perhaps influenced by previous encounters with Europeans, particularly the Spanish, who had established an ill-fated Jesuit mission on the York River in 1576.

The size of the aboriginal population in the Northeast varied with ecological conditions. Northern and inland

DEPICTION OF AN INDIAN VILLAGE BY JOHN WHITE. The type of village commonly found along the Atlantic seaboard south of New England at the time of first contact with Europeans. This engraving, after a drawing by White, appeared in Thomas Hariot's *A Brief and True Report of the New Found Land of Virginia*. Frankfurt, 1590.

NEW YORK PUBLIC LIBRARY, RARE BOOKS DIVISION

regions may have supported as few as three to ten people per one hundred square kilometers, while the same area supported as many as one hundred people in more temperate and coastal regions. Contact with Europeans after 1492 led to a series of disastrous epidemics throughout the native populations of the Northeast, with losses up to 95 percent in certain regions. These debilitating losses, accompanied by political instability and exacerbated by early trade rivalries, severely affected but did not destroy the majority of native cultures in the region.

BIBLIOGRAPHY

Fitzhugh, William W., ed. *Cultures in Contact: The European Impact on Native Cultural Institutions in Eastern North America A.D. 1000–1800.* Washington, D.C., 1985.

Quinn, David. *North America from Earliest Discovery to First Settlements: The Norse Voyages to 1612.* New York, 1977.

Trigger, Bruce C. *The Northeast*. Volume 15 of *Handbook of North American Indians*, edited by William C. Sturtevant. Washington, D.C., 1978.

KATHLEEN BRAGDON

INDIES, THE. For Europeans of the fourteenth and fifteenth centuries, India was a vast, poorly defined territory of the Orient, subdivided into India Major and Minor (India below and above the Ganges). India was important because it was the source of spices that made the European diet palatable. Pepper and clove, cinnamon, mace, and ginger were shipped from parts of Hindustan to Europe, mainly from Calicut. Most of them were shipped through India from other parts of South Asia. Pepper and cinnamon did come from India, but clove originated in the Moluccas and mace in the Banda Islands. There were other products besides spices: dyes (such as anil), medicinal plants (such as cardamom), precious stones (such as rubies, pearls, and emeralds), silks, musk, lacquer, and many other goods that found a ready market in Europe. Europeans paid premium prices for these products because kings and territorial lords along the trade routes between the centers of production and consumption added surcharges in the form of imposts or duties on transit rights.

In the last centuries of the Middle Ages and until the end of the fifteenth century, the distribution of such merchandise was mainly in the hands of the Muslim traders who transferred it from parts of India, especially from western Hindustan, to Genoese or Venetian ships in ports of the Near East or the Black Sea. European merchants, especially those who came from the small states or cities of the Italian peninsula tried at times to establish direct ties with the producers of spices, though with little success.

The most famous of these merchants was Marco Polo (1254–1324), who went to Asia personally at the end of the thirteenth century in order to take direct charge of his business affairs. He was relatively well acquainted with India, although he was based in China. The importance of Marco Polo for fifteenth-century Europe can be attributed to his sometimes confused description of the areas from which much-sought-after luxury products were imported into Europe. *The Description of the World* (also called *The Book of Marco Polo*) enjoyed a wide readership in the Western world during the fourteenth and fifteenth centuries and was eventually translated into the vernacular languages. It attracted the attention of travelers who, like Christopher Columbus, elaborated plans to make contact with the Orient that the Venetian adventurer described in his work, at times with some exaggeration.

The plan to reach the East Indies directly, thereby eliminating the Muslim intermediaries, took shape only during the second half of the fifteenth century as the result of the Portuguese expansion along the west coast of Africa. In effect, the so-called India plan (meaning direct access to the Indies by sea) was laid only after Prince João (1455–1495; after 1481 King João II) assumed responsibility for the administration of overseas affairs in 1473. The plan became reality only after he encouraged southward voyages along the African coast in the hope of finding, despite the ideas of Ptolemy, a maritime link between the Atlantic and Indian oceans. Between 1481 and 1488 two or three voyages under the command of Diogo Cão (fl. 1480–1486) explored the African coast. In 1488 Bartolomeu Dias (c. 1450–1500) sailed into the waters of the Indian Ocean, off southeast Africa.

King João based his expectation of the success of the India plan on many sources of information on the Indies and the Orient that were known in Europe even in the early fifteenth century, before European expansion began. Marco Polo was the first source of much of the information about the Orient disseminated throughout the Western world. But there were other sources of knowledge available to scholars and merchants as well as to the simple curious reader.

Among written sources were *Liber Tartarorum* of the Franciscan Giovanni da Pian del Carpini (c. 1180–1252), a curious account of the lives and customs of the Tatars mixed with some fabulous reports, and the description of the itinerary of the Franciscan Odoric of Pordenone (c. 1265–1331), whose report contained objective observations but was also permeated with symbols, myths, and marvels.

Oral traditions were as important—if not more important—than written documents and pseudogeographical novels. Oral relations were rooted in antiquity and were widely disseminated. Kings and great lords had occasional recourse to storytellers, though not all of them deserved the confidence placed in them. Because their accounts often gave free rein to the imagination, whenever projects related to India were planned, it was considered indispensable to obtain precise information directly from trustworthy persons.

João II was absolutely sure of being able to reach India by way of the Cape, perhaps as a result of the information obtained from Diogo Cão, who believed that he had almost reached the Indian Ocean on his first voyage. For that reason, in 1487, King João sent two men, Afonso de Paiva and Pero de Covilhã, to the Orient to gather accurate information on Ethiopia and the spice markets (the king suspected that Ethiopia and India were different places). Covilhã accomplished his mission, visiting the Malabar Coast (Calicut), Kanara (Goa), and Hormuz and perhaps following the Muslim maritime commerce along the East

African coast as far as Sofala (on the central coast of Mozambique). Paiva died before he reached Ethiopia, and Covilhã took his place after transmitting to the king his impressions of the world of active commercial exchange with which he had come into contact in the Indian Ocean. That the news sent by Covilhã was a determining factor in the king's plan is proven by the fact that in 1498 Vasco da Gama sailed directly to the port of Calicut and stayed there from the middle of May to the end of August.

Muslim merchants had reached India many years before Da Gama. They carried the message of their religion but did not forcibly convert followers of other religions. Because of their tolerance, they were able to gain markets without arousing opposition. Perhaps for that reason they gained faithful followers and eventually dominated the economy of the Indian hinterland. The Muslims followed all the routes of local commerce from the Red Sea to Malabar, Bengal, Malacca, Kanara, the Banda Islands, and Java. They navigated the Strait of Hormuz to follow routes along the east coast of Africa as far as Sofala. Eventually they came to enjoy enormous influence in all the major commercial entrepôts. Such accomplishments were achieved without difficulty or friction, and without claiming for themselves exclusivity or privileged treatment.

In the first half of the fifteenth century, when, for reasons even today only partly understood, Chinese overseas expansion ended (though their ships still continued for several years to visit Malacca, where the Portuguese encountered them), the Muslims dominated commerce in this active world of trade that included Gujaratis, Malays, Bengalis, and Javanese, among others. Muslim merchants were aware of their ability to dominate trade in India, but, recognizing the greater complexity of Indian culture, they had little difficulty in adapting to it and deriving economic benefits from supplying its products to Western markets.

The Portuguese operated much differently. Although the offensive capability of Da Gama's fleet was obviously insufficient in 1498, the first Portuguese in India employed the artillery mounted on their ships to force open markets and engage in a commerce that would have been impossible for them to win otherwise. In a short time, Portuguese activity brought about a reaction: the Turks appeared in Cambay, descending the coast in the direction of Calicut. They attacked and besieged the bar of Chaul (1508); in the ensuing battle, Lourenço de Almeida, son of the viceroy of India, was killed. The Portuguese realized that their foothold in India was vulnerable, and their sense of vulnerability was confirmed in the sixteenth century. They never succeeded in occupying Aden (on the southwest coast of Arabia) and Turkish galleys ran freely along the coast of Arabia and penetrated the Strait of Hormuz. Afonso de Albuquerque had captured Hormuz and con-

structed a fortress there; other fortresses were built in strategic Arabian ports. But the Portuguese presence in Arabia (which guarded the routes to India) was placed in jeopardy when Ottoman armies descended the Euphrates and captured Basra in 1547. The Turks besieged the Portuguese fortress of Diu (in northwestern India) in 1538 and supported a second attack, by the king of Cambay, in 1546.

In view of this situation, the Portuguese government of India felt compelled to develop a new commercial policy. Instead of allowing freedom of trade, it adopted a permanent control of merchants and merchandise. Navigation was permitted only to holders of a *cartaz* (license to sail, or safe conduct). On the other hand, various products (such as pepper from Malabar, horses from Iran, and cinnamon from Ceylon) were traded on a monopoly basis by the Portuguese.

Portuguese mercantile policy encountered innumerable difficulties. The Portuguese offended a great number of merchants, Muslim and non-Muslim alike, who usually become their declared enemies. In addition, they lacked the military power and population to impose their policy.

Christopher Columbus was in Lisbon in 1485 and he must have followed with great interest the steps taken to implement the India plan. In view of the uncertainty of rounding southern Africa, he conceived an alternative plan based on his readings of Nicole d'Oresme (c. 1325–1382), Pierre d'Ailly, and other writers: to sail westward across the Atlantic to Asia. But Columbus's calculation of the circumference of the earth was incorrect; he assumed that the earth is smaller than it is and therefore that the distance west from Europe to Asia is smaller than it is. And he did not suspect the existence of a vast continental landmass between western Europe and eastern Asia.

King João II had at his disposition better estimates of the dimensions of the earth. He also knew, or thought he knew, that the route via the Cape of Good Hope would be the most convenient. He therefore rejected Columbus's project. Considering his immediate objectives, King João was right; it was impossible to know the importance of Columbus's voyages in the fifteenth or early sixteenth century. The Portuguese wanted to reach the Indies, and, at the time, João II was the great victor in the race to get there. Columbus failed after enduring great hardship and being imprisoned, yet he was convinced that he had visited parts of Asia. Vasco da Gama had actually reached Asia and won for Lisbon the means of trading with the East. At that time no one had as yet the least idea of the importance that America would assume later.

If Columbus never reached India, he did reveal to the world the existence of new continents. So insistent was he that he had reached Asia that the whole group of islands in the Caribbean were designated as the "West Indies" or the "Indies of Castile." His error also prevented the two continental masses from being named after him. They are called the Americas after Amerigo Vespucci, because he, and not his fellow Italian, Columbus, succeeded in demonstrating that the lands they explored were continents and not islands off the coast of Asia.

[See also *Trade.* For discussion of uses of the name Columbus, see *Columbianism.* On the name America, see *America, Naming of.*]

BIBLIOGRAPHY

Albuquerque, Afonso de. *Albuquerque, Caesar of the East.* Translated and edited by T. F. Earle and John Villiers. Warminster, England, 1990.

Cortesão, Armando. *The "Suma Oriental" of Tomé Pires and the "Book of Francisco Rodrigues."* Hakluyt Society Publications, 2d ser., vols. 89 and 90. London, 1944.

Danvers, Frederick Charles. *The Portuguese in India,* 2d ed. 2 vols. New York, 1966.

Lach, Donald F. *Asia in the Making of Europe,* vol. 1, bks. 1 and 2. Chicago, 1965.

Prestage, Edgar. *The Portuguese Pioneers.* London, 1933.

Whiteway, R. S. *The Rise of Portuguese Power in India, 1495–1550,* 2d ed. London, 1967.

LUÍS DE ALBUQUERQUE
Translated from Portuguese by Rebecca Catz

INNOCENT VIII (1432–1492), pope. Born in Genoa, Giovanni Battista Cibò was educated at Padua and Bologna and during his early career in Naples fathered an illegitimate son and daughter. Entering the clerical state, he was employed by Cardinal Filippo Calandrini and was named bishop of Savona (1466–1472), of Molfetta (1472–1484), and datary (1471–1473), before becoming a cardinal (1473–1484). He owed his rapid promotions to Cardinal Giuliano della Rovere, who at the conclave of 1484 also secured his election as pope.

Amiable and kind, Innocent VIII was also frequently ill, lacking in financial resources, and subject to the influence of Cardinal della Rovere. As a result, he accomplished little as pope. Civil rulers took advantage of his weakness to gain greater control over local churches. Much of his time and energy was consumed in a protracted (1484–1492) military and diplomatic conflict with Ferrante I (1458–1494) of Naples over disputed territories, unpaid tribute, and independent church appointments. Threats of French intervention and of relocating the papacy outside Italy, coupled with the mediating services of Fernando and Isabel of Spain, led finally to the settlements of 1486 and 1492.

Although dissension and death among Christian princes undid his earnest efforts to launch a crusade against the Turks in 1490, his obtaining custody in 1489 of Cem, brother of Sultan Bayezid II (Bajazet), who lived as a

INNOCENT VIII. Papal medal, 1484.   AMERICAN NUMISMATIC SOCIETY

hostage in the Vatican palace and could be used to stir up civil war in the Ottoman Empire, led Bayezid to sue for a truce. He paid tribute to keep his brother as prisoner and presented the relic of the Holy Lance to the pope as a gift.

To encourage the Reconquista efforts of Fernando and Isabel in Spain, Innocent issued in 1486 the bull *Orthodoxae fidei* extending their traditional ecclesiastical patronage rights to bishoprics and major benefices in the conquered lands of Granada, the Canary Islands, and the town of Puerto Real recently founded by the Spanish monarchs near Cádiz. When Granada fell in 1492, the pope is said to have confirmed their traditional title of *los Reyes Católicos* (the Catholic monarchs).

According to a story told in the circles of Martín Alonso Pinzón of Palos, captain of *Pinta,* Pinzón visited Rome during the reign of Innocent VIII and found in the Vatican library an ancient account of a transatlantic voyage to Japan that so impressed him that he tried on his own to organize such a voyage. He is said to have shared this information with Columbus, encouraged him to seek royal authorization and financing, and put together the fleet Columbus eventually used for his first voyage of discovery. There is no evidence that Columbus himself had contact with his fellow Genoese countryman Innocent VIII.

BIBLIOGRAPHY

Brezzi, Paolo. "Innocenzo VIII, papa." In *Enciclopedia Cattolica.* Vol. 7. Vatican City, 1951.

Burchard, Johannes. *The Diary of John Burchard, Bishop of Orta.* Vol. 1. Translated by Arnold H. Mathew. London, 1910.

Morison, Samuel Eliot. *Admiral of the Ocean Sea: A Life of Christopher Columbus.* 2 vols. Boston, 1942.

Paschini, Pio. *Roma nel Rinascimento.* Vol. 12 of *Storia di Roma.* Bologna, 1940.

Pastor, Ludwig von. *The History of the Popes from the Close of the Middle Ages.* Vol. 5. Translated by Frederick Ignatius Antrobus. St. Louis, 1923.

Rodocanachi, Emmanuel P. *Histoire de Rome: Une cour princière au Vatican pendant la Renaissance (1471–1503).* Paris, 1925.

NELSON H. MINNICH

INQUISITION. The Spanish Inquisition was an ecclesiastical tribunal established in 1478 by Isabel and Fernando to determine whether the conversos were practicing Christianity and not their former Jewish rites. This definition, however, requires an explanation of what is meant by the Inquisition's being Spanish, as well as of its origin, structure, procedures, and goals.

The first inquisition was established in 1231 as a juridical tribunal. When Pope Gregory IX (r. 1227–1241) saw the inactivity of the bishops of southern France in pursuing the Cathars, or Albigensian heretics, he appointed members of the newly founded Dominican order as his direct representatives to deal with them. This inquisition was thus a papal, and not a royal, institution, although its activities did contribute to the definitive French domination of the region, which had been hesitating between France and Aragón.

Whereas the French tribunal was never an organ subordinate to the French Crown, the Spanish Inquisition was a department of government. In other nonpolitical aspects, however, it was essentially a continuation of the French, or papal, inquisition, and adopted its provisions and by-laws regarding arrest of defendants, trial procedures, confiscation, secrecy, witnesses, and other procedures. The medieval inquisition was dominant in France especially in Languedoc. In Spain the Inquisition extended only to the Crown of Aragón comprising the three kingdoms of Aragón proper, Catalonia, and Valencia, but never to Castile. It was dormant in the fifteenth century. The *Directorium inquisitorum* written by the Catalan inquisitor Nicolau Eymerich (1376) was the primary procedural guide of the Spanish Inquisition, so much so that some scholars contend that there was only one Inquisition.

In order to deal with the alarming number of conversos who some people believed to be Marranos (Jews who submitted to forced conversion but maintain Jewish practices in secret) several proposals were advanced in the fifteenth century by the constable, Alvaro de Luna, and King Enrique IV, either to extend the Aragonese Inquisition to Castile or to establish a new one with a special orientation. The new Inquisition, however, seems to have been a personal initiative of King Fernando based on reports by anticonverso friars like Alonso de Espina in his *Fortalitium fidei* (1460) and on the alarm raised by Pedro González de Mendoza, archbishop of Seville, who discovered important groups of secret Judaizers in that city and in Andalusia. It took the shrewdness of the king and the greed of Pope Sixtus IV to agree on the terms of the bull *Exigit sincerae devotionis* (November 1, 1478), which authorized the monarchs to appoint inquisitors. Nothing was done for several months until the accidental discovery of a plot of Jews and conversos in Seville set in motion the machinery that resulted in the first *auto de fe* ("act of faith," a term used for the formal announcement of the Inquisition's judgment and the execution of its sentence) held in that city on February 6, 1481.

Many of the suspect conversos fled the city and even Spain; some protested in writing (most interesting is a famous letter, now lost, by the humanist Juan de Lucena) to the sovereigns or to the pope, and others in person. But the king was adamant and obtained royal control of the Inquisition from the pope with a strong letter of May 13, 1482, and with more money. Out of the group of the first inquisitors active in various cities, Tomás de Torquemada was appointed the first inquisitor general in 1483. His authority as a Castilian and his introduction of the new Castilian Inquisition in Aragón was strongly protested by the Aragonese conversos and by the Cortes; the ancient *fueros* (special laws) of that kingdom prohibited torture and secret witnesses and forbade foreigners from taking posts in its administration. This led to the assassination of Pedro Arbués, one of the first two Aragonese inquisitors, in the cathedral of Saragossa on September 15, 1485, a crime used by the king and by the local Inquisition to eliminate entire families of conversos, some prominent, and to obtain the popular support they needed. While the Castilian Cortes usually voiced opposition to the legal and moral abuses of the Inquisition, the Aragonese Cortes had legal grounds to attack its very existence publicly, not only politically but also theologically, because the Cortes felt that heretics could be sufficiently controlled by a revived medieval, papal, or episcopal tribunal.

The Inquisition was governed by a centralized Supreme Council (Suprema), headed by the inquisitor general, who enjoyed a status equal to—though in fact superior to—a government minister. The inquisitor general supervised the activity of a network of fifteen district tribunals that covered the whole of Spain. At the peak of inquisitorial activities, tribunals were created in 1569 in Mexico and Lima and in 1610 in Cartagena. Each of the tribunals was served by a group of "familiars," laymen or clergymen, and also of "commissaries," always members of the clergy. All were scrupulously prepared to receive and transmit information and accusations, to assist in the arrest and transportation of defendants, and to participate in the official ceremonies and *autos de fe*. Each tribunal consisted of at least three local inquisitors, specialists in canon law, some attorneys for the prosecution and the defense, several notaries who produced hundreds of thousands of documents (today preserved mostly in the Archivo Nacional in Madrid), and guards. There were also several consultors, clergymen well versed in theology, who evaluated the propositions attributed to the defendants' speech or writings, many times out of context.

Such a complex structure was meant to be financially self-supporting. According to the *Instrucciones* of Torquemada and the subsequent body of inquisitorial jurisprudence, when a person was jailed by the Inquisition, his or her possessions were confiscated, to be returned at the time of release. This was one of the reasons that many trials were lengthy and that the inquisitors sometimes felt compelled to be stringent in their verdicts, especially at the Inquisition's beginnings. As the numbers of conversos diminished, from about 1520, Pope Paul IV decreed in 1559, during the tenure of the famous inquisitor Fernando de Valdés, that the revenues from at least one of each of the cathedral canonries and collegiate churches be appropriated to the Inquisition. Even when added to revenues from confiscations and other resources, these monies were never sufficient. The Inquisition was always a bankrupt operation, and the study of the political and diplomatic intricacies of the inquisitorial finances has become its own field of study.

The exact numbers of conversos prosecuted and of those executed in the first forty years, roughly 1481 to 1520, will never be known. Most of the extant documents are too vague, and the figures supplied by historians such as Juan Antonio Llorente are suppositions. Nothing more accurate can be said than that "several thousand" conversos, but no more than between five and six thousand, were put to death, usually by burning at the stake. The figures for later periods are better documented. Although many original documents from the district tribunals are lost or were destroyed in the course of the many Spanish revolutions, the *relaciones de causas,* annual summaries of the current and completed cases that the local tribunals sent to the Supreme Council, can supplement the missing documents. The computerization of these data may some day yield more exact figures. A provisional conclusion is that in the period from 1540 to 1700 the tribunals in Spain and its dependencies prosecuted 5,007 conversos; 11,311 moriscos (Muslim converts to Christianity); and 3,499 Protestants; and that 49,092 cases for all kinds of offenses were examined. The total number of persons executed in this period for all kinds of crimes was 776 in person and 707 in effigy. These figures show that the activity of the Inquisition declined after the violent first period, which was directed specifically against the conversos.

The inquisitorial tribunals worked in absolute secrecy, and most of their decisions were communicated to the interested parties in private *autos de fe.* Public *autos de fe* were much less frequent. Since they were expensive, they were undertaken only when it was believed that such a spectacle would serve as a warning, but the populace soon lost interest in them. They took place either in a large church or in an open plaza, and consisted of a solemn procession followed by a mass during which the accusations and penalties were read to those convicted after a sermon of indoctrination: this was the essential "act of faith." If any execution had been decreed, lay guardsmen took the condemned to the *quemadero* (place of execution) to be burnt.

The Inquisition had jurisdiction only over baptized persons, including Marranos and conversos. The few Jews that appeared before the Inquisition prior to the Expulsion acted either as witnesses against conversos or as defendants in cases of intentionally anti-Christian blasphemy or impeding the activity of the Inquisition. Modern studies have shown, ironically, that the majority of the people prosecuted were old Christians (people who were not of Jewish descent). Between 1540 and 1700, 14,319 persons were accused of advancing "scandalous propositions"; other crimes sufficient for prosecution included blasphemy, bigamy, superstitions of various kinds, and solicitation of women by priests in the confessional.

In general, the Inquisition was the main instrument of social control by the establishment in Spain and to a more limited extent in Hispanic America for four centuries. It changed the scope of its attention according to the needs of each period, from conversos to Erasmians and Lutherans, biblical scholars with progressive ideas, spiritual reformers with suspicious attitudes, satirical writers, liberal thinkers, and whatever threatened the status quo. The Inquisition has become famous because it was established to inquire into the sincerity of the *judeoconversos.* But it is important above all because its repression halted the progress of Spain. Especially after the discovery of the New World, it was prepared as no other country was to lead the whole world in the enterprises of the Renaissance; it soon became paralyzed by the "pedagogy of fear"—as Bartolomé Bennassar called it—that the Inquisition exercised. Temporarily suppressed by the liberal Cortes of Cádiz in 1813, the Inquisition was finally abolished by royal decree in 1834. It was a miracle of inner spiritual resources that, the Inquisition notwithstanding, Spain was able to produce its remarkable Golden Age and to create in Spanish America a world after its own image.

BIBLIOGRAPHY

Alcalá, Angel. *Los orígenes de la Inquisición en Aragón.* Zaragoza, 1984.

Alcalá, Angel, et al. *The Spanish Inquisition and the Inquisitorial Mind.* Highland Lakes, N.J., 1987.

Bennassar, Bartolomé. *L'inquisition espagnole XVᵉ–XIXᵉ siècle.* Paris, 1979.

Kamen, Henry. *Inquisition and Society in Spain.* Bloomington, Ind., 1985.

Lea, Henry Charles. *A History of the Inquisition in Spain.* 4 vols. New York, 1906. Spanish edition, 3 vols., Madrid, 1984.

Llorente, Juan Antonio. *A Critical History of the Inquisition of Spain.* 1823. Reprint, Williamstown, Mass., 1967. An abridgment of the following title.

Llorente, Juan Antonio. *Historia crítica de la Inquisición española* (1822). 4 vols. Reprint, Madrid, 1980.

Pérez Villaneuva, Joaquín, and Bartolomé Escandel, eds. *Historia de la Inquisición en España y América.* Vol. 1. Madrid, 1984.

ANGEL ALCALÁ

ISABEL (1470–1498), princess of Castile; queen of Portugal. The eldest child of Fernando and Isabel of Castile, Isabel traveled throughout Spain with her mother and was witness to the important events of her parents' reign—the war against Granada, the Inquisition, the expulsion of Jews from Spain, and the return of Columbus from his first voyage to the New World.

Born at Dueñas near Valladolid, Isabel had an abiding affection for her mother, and they remained close throughout her life. She possessed a serious disposition and was deeply religious. The Italian humanists Antonio and Alessandro Geraldino and Lucio Marineo Siculo served as her tutors, educating her well in both religion and classical literature and language.

Isabel married Afonso, son of King João II of Portugal, in Lisbon on November 22, 1490. She was widowed in July 1491 when Afonso died following a fall from his horse. She returned to Castile and spent the next six years in mourning, rejecting all offers to remarry. Finally she consented to marry King Manuel I of Portugal, but stipulated that the Jews be expelled from Portugal. Manuel complied with her wishes, and the wedding took place on September 30 in Valancia de Alcántara. That same month her brother, Prince Juan, died, making Isabel and Manuel heirs to the Castilian throne.

Isabel was in the early months of pregnancy when she and Manuel traveled to Castile for the formal declaration of their Castilian inheritance. But Isabel would never rule Castile: she died in childbirth on August 23, 1498.

BIBLIOGRAPHY

Azcona, Tarsicio de. *Isabel la Católica: Estudio crítico de su vida y su reinado.* Madrid, 1964.
Miller, Townsend. *The Castles and the Crown: Spain 1451–1555.* New York, 1963.
Prescott, William H. *History of the Reign of Ferdinand and Isabella the Catholic.* Boston, 1838.
Sanceau, Elaine. *The Reign of the Fortunate King, 1495–1521.* Hamden, Conn., 1969.

THERESA EARENFIGHT

ISABELA, LA. See *Settlements*, article on *La Isabela*.

ISABEL AND FERNANDO. Isabel of Castile (1451–1504), queen of Castile from 1474 to 1504 (as Isabel I), and Fernando of Aragón (1452–1516), king of Aragón (as Fernando II) from 1479 to 1516 and king of Castile (as Fernando V) from 1474 to 1504, ruled Spain as joint monarchs at a time of momentous change. Owing as much to the personal qualities of these monarchs as to the press of events, their rule is exemplified by four significant developments in 1492. Known later as the Catholic monarchs, Isabel and Fernando conquered the Muslim Kingdom of Granada, expelled the Jews from Spain, and sent Christopher Columbus on his mission of exploration. The year 1492 also marks the completion by Antonio de Nebrija of the first Spanish grammar, which is dedicated to Isabel. This standardization of the language facilitated the introduction of Spanish into the regions of the New World that came under Spain's influence. The king and queen are discussed together here because of the interplay of their personalities and policies, their shared genius for seizing opportunities, and the great abilities demonstrated by both in their joint rule. Many of their actions and motives are not considered praiseworthy today—in part because of changed perceptions of political morality, in part because of the hindsight of five hundred years.

Isabel was born at Madrigal de las Altas Torres, in Castile, on April 22, 1451. Fernando was born in Sos, in Aragón, on March 10, 1452. In 1453, the Christian city of Constantinople, considered Europe's bulwark at the eastern end of the Mediterranean, fell to the Muslim Turks. Throughout the lifetimes of the queen and king and for a century or more after, Christian Europe perceived Muslim Asia and Africa as a threat. The Spanish kingdoms, neighboring Muslim Granada and separated from Africa only by the Strait of Gibraltar, were viewed as a frontier outpost of Christianity. The rulers and chroniclers of the largest of the Iberian kingdoms, Castile, had, since the Muslim conquest eight centuries earlier, identified the monarchy with the effort to regain lost territory in what is known as the reconquest.

Hereditary kings (and an occasional queen) in Spain exercised authority as did others in medieval Europe—as mediators within society and dispensers of titles, wealth, and honors, the extent of their power depending on a combination of the force they could command and the loyalty they could instill, one often dependent on the other. Castile's kings, in particular, presented themselves as military leaders with a God-given mission. They claimed in the cause of reconquest nearly unlimited personal power and, in practice, owed much of their effectiveness among clergy, nobles, and commoners to their role as head of a community united against the other world power, Islam. From the royal point of view, the ruler, as head of the community, had to carry out God's wishes (and thwart Satan's stratagems). And although Muslims and Jews had long resided within Castile and the other Iberian kingdoms, theoretically they did so as royal wards, outside the dominant community and at the sufferance and service of the Crown. The Castilian monarchy was paid for principally by booty and by sales taxes on internal and foreign trade. War and commerce were thus integral to royal power.

When Isabel and Fernando married on October 19, 1469, at ages eighteen and seventeen, respectively, Isabel was heir apparent to Castile, its *princesa,* and Fernando was prince of Aragón and king of Sicily. They were cousins, both of them children of kings of the Trastamara dynasty. Isabel's grandfather, Enrique III, had been king of Castile, and his younger brother, the grandfather for whom Fernando was named, had ruled Aragón. Isabel was the daughter of Enrique's only son, Juan II of Castile, and Juan's second wife, Isabel of Portugal. A brother, Alfonso, had been born in 1453. On July 21, 1454, Isabel's father died. Her older half brother, Enrique IV, succeeded him. (Alfonso was, since male, by custom next in line for the Crown, followed by the infanta Isabel.) The modest household of the dowager queen moved to nearby Arévalo, where Isabel spent her childhood. Arévalo was a provincial center, the market town for a region devoted to farming, yet in contact with Castile's larger towns and cities and linked to a commercial network encompassing all of the Mediterranean basin as well as northern Europe.

The infanta's formal education is undocumented, though it is recorded that at Arévalo Isabel had contact with Franciscan friars known for their austerity and learning. Her informal education would have included exposure to the culturally distinct communities of Muslims and Jews in Arévalo, separate from but tolerated by the Christian majority. From Arévalo the royal chancery, which wintered there in 1454, prepared Enrique IV's expedition against the Muslim kingdom of Granada. The enterprise was meant to strengthen his authority among Castilian nobles, clergy, and commoners by taking charge of the reconquest and to pressure the Granadans into remembering their agreement to pay tribute to the king of Castile.

Isabel and Alfonso were brought to Enrique's court when she was ten or eleven, by late 1461. A first child, daughter Juana, was born to the king and queen the following February. Her birth induced a party of dissident nobles led by Alfonso Carrillo, archbishop of Toledo and head of a powerful noble family, to step up previous demands for reforms, to spread rumors that the child was not the king's, and to insist that the infante Alfonso be recognized as the royal heir. Protracted negotiations between the parties failed. At Ávila, on June 5, 1465, the

The Castilian Succession from Juan I to Carlos I

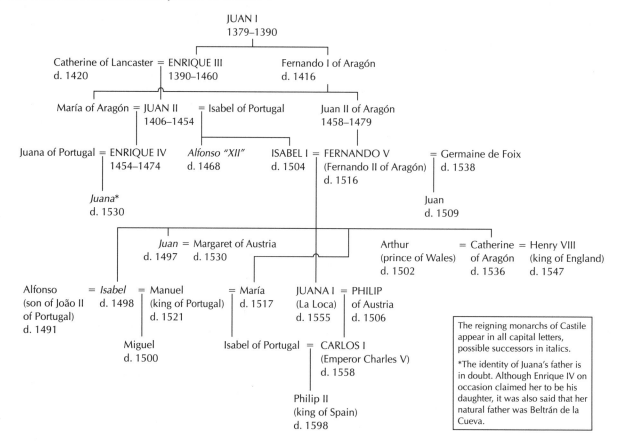

The reigning monarchs of Castile appear in all capital letters, possible successors in italics.

*The identity of Juana's father is in doubt. Although Enrique IV on occasion claimed her to be his daughter, it was also said that her natural father was Beltrán de la Cueva.

dissidents deposed Enrique in effigy and proclaimed the twelve-year-old Alfonso king. Civil war ensued, lasting three years, until, on July 5, 1468, Alfonso died suddenly, purportedly of plague. His supporters turned to seventeen-year-old Isabel, who rather than take up Alfonso's title won Enrique's agreement to end the war and to recognize her as his heir. Thereafter, the critical issue was her marriage. When the king revealed himself to be seeking a husband for her who would remove her from Castile or be unacceptable to its people, Isabel, backed by Carrillo, made her own choice. She chose Fernando of Aragón, who had expressed willingness to come to Castile. Castilians had indicated an acceptance of Fernando, in terms of his birth and reputation, as a suitable husband for an aspirant to the Crown. The engagement was arranged without consulting Enrique.

At age seventeen, Fernando already enjoyed renown as a hero of several sieges. As his father's lieutenant, he had had a taste of governing, and he had fathered two, perhaps three, children by two mothers. His father, Juan II of Aragón, had been born and raised in Castile, became through marriage king of Navarre, then succeeded to Aragón's Crown in 1459. His mother, Juan's second wife, Juana Enríquez, was also Castilian, the daughter of Castile's admiral, Fadrique Enríquez. Reputedly head-strong and ambitious, she had, though not yet its queen, made certain Fernando was born in Aragón, coming to the village of Sos just before his birth, and then put off his baptism for nearly a year, until his father had become regent of Aragón and the ceremony could be held with royal pomp in the cathedral in Zaragoza. An older half brother, the king's son Carlos of Viana, fortuitously died when Fernando was nine. That year, his father named Fernando royal lieutenant in Catalonia; his mother was to exercise authority for him. She did so with a high-handedness that led to mother and son being expelled from Barcelona and retreating to Gerona, where she directed the repulse of a Catalan siege. Four years later, at age twelve, Fernando himself led forces in defeat of the Catalans. With his valorous feat, a well-phrased appeal, and Valencia's delight in his victory over its chief rival, Barcelona, he gained from Valencia's council large annual loans for his father's hard-pressed government. When his mother died of cancer in 1468, Fernando gave her funeral eulogy. He had just finished presiding over the *corts*, Aragón's parliament, when Isabel's emissaries arrived to escort him to Castile and their wedding.

Isabel and Fernando first met in Valladolid on October 14, 1469, and they married there five days later. Both were well aware that Castile was the prize, and that they were jointly gambling for it—Enrique was only forty-four years old, and Isabel's claim and requisite aristocratic backing were shaky. Isabel's supporters had beforehand required

of Fernando and his father an agreement that, while in tone suggesting that Fernando would wield a good deal of power, acknowledged that Isabel alone had the right to become proprietary ruler of Castile. Juan and Fernando thus forbore asserting a claim to the Crown of Castile based on the fact that Juan was the male next in line of succession to Enrique IV. Isabel and her advisers never lost sight of that relationship. The birth of a daughter, Isabel, on October 2, 1470, made the principle of female succession vital to both parents. Isabel and Fernando had discovered an immediate affinity in working together, indeed a mutual love and respect, and both showed themselves mindful of the advice of Juan of Aragón, that neither was powerful without the other.

From late 1469 to 1474, the fortunes of the young couple seesawed. Enrique, furious at their marriage, reinstated his purported daughter, Juana de Castilla (known as La Beltraneja), as heir apparent. Isabel and Fernando relied upon the power and purse of the archbishop, Carrillo; upon Fernando's grandfather, the admiral; and upon their position as king and queen of Sicily, which permitted them to form international alliances and to receive crucial funding from taxes on the sale of the island's abundant grain. To their advantage in Castile was the worsening economy and Enrique's wavering response to it. Showing themselves to be astute and capable, while seeking popular support, they slowly gained the backing of some key Castilian towns and nobles. Slowly Enrique was prevailed upon by his counselors, notably the Mendoza clan, to come to terms with his sister and his cousin, her husband. They reconciled at the end of 1468; Isabel was once more to be designated royal heir. When, on December 12, 1474, Enrique died, Fernando was in Aragón, fighting the French. Isabel, in Segovia, upon hearing the king had died, observed the proper rites of mourning, then, on December 13, had herself acclaimed queen of Castile. Fernando hurried back and was acclaimed king, but the arrangement that would remain in force had been proclaimed throughout the land: Isabel was the proprietary ruler of Castile.

The land, however, had first to be won. Raising the banner of Juana, who may or may not have been Enrique's daughter and who was then thirteen years old, Afonso, king of Portugal, resolved to marry her and gain back her inheritance. He invaded Castile, joined by some of its chief nobles. Again there was civil war, its end signaled by Afonso's return to Portugal after being bested by Fernando's forces outside Toro on March 1, 1476. Although Isabel and Fernando spent several more years gaining effective control, after Toro the realm was substantially theirs.

In the course of this crisis they had established the characteristics of their reign. They had taken on proven

ISABEL OF CASTILE AND FERNANDO OF ARAGÓN. Anonymous portraits, Flemish school.

REPRODUCED BY GRACIOUS PERMISSION OF HER MAJESTY QUEEN ELIZABETH II

advisers, most notably Pedro González de Mendoza, then archbishop of Seville and cardinal of Spain, who served them until his death in 1495 as chief minister, and Hernando de Talavera, the Hieronymite friar who became Isabel's chaplain and who was a principal architect of the monarchs' treasury arrangements and their administrative bureaucracy. They had found, too, a source of revenue and manpower in establishing under royal supervision a national hermandad, or brotherhood, a permanent league of the towns. The business of winning support during the war had reinforced their belief in the importance of public opinion and had developed their skill at molding it. They also had successfully forged what would become a lifelong practice of working in tandem.

The royal motto they shared, *tanto monta*, "as much one as the other," came to signify their cooperation. Fernando took as his emblem the double yoke, the *yugo* (its initial letter, *y* , standing for Isabel), worn by a team of oxen. Her emblem was a sheaf of arrows, *flechas* (the *f* standing for Fernando); the barbs of those arrows were held at ready, a warning to Castilians not acknowledging the reach of royal authority or that greatest of royal functions, the right to mete out justice.

In mid-April of 1476, they first convened the Cortes, or parliament, at Isabel's birthplace, Madrigal. Representatives of seventeen towns were called and nobles and high clergy were assembled to confirm the Princess Isabel in succession, to vote revenues, and to set up the Santa Hermandad, which would come to supplant the Cortes as a source of royal funding. These measures pointed to the future, as did more stringent restrictions on Muslims and Jews, who were ordered to wear distinguishing insignia and were forbidden their own communal justices. Afterward, Isabel went to reinstate royal authority in Extremadura, a seat of rebellion (and the region from which came a number of the future conquistadores of America), and

Andalusia, a center of noble autonomy crucial to Castile's relations with the Mediterranean and the Atlantic. In the great port city of Seville, so long under the sway of two dominant noble families, the Guzmán and the Ponce de León, the queen undercut their power: she had the hermandad established, royal administrators imposed, and castles and forts put under royal authority. She entered the city in state. She meted out justice severely, quickly, and publicly and reestablished respect for the monarchy. Under royal license, maritime expeditions then went out from Seville and the adjoining Andalusian coast with the purpose of challenging the Portuguese in the Atlantic Ocean, along the African coast, and in the Canary Islands.

Fernando joined Isabel in Seville in the fall of 1477. On June 30, 1478, Isabel gave birth to a son and heir, Prince Juan. That fall, at royal solicitation, a papal bull conceded to the Crown the right to appoint two or three priests as inquisitors. Isabel immediately appointed an investigatory commission in Seville, which reported widespread and adamant heresy among converts from Judaism. First in Seville, in early 1480, inquisitors appointed by the Crown began to try accused heretics, sentencing some to penance and loss of property, others to execution. Fernando, king of Aragón after his father's death in 1479, instituted a similar system there. A new Inquisition, encompassing all of Spain, was instituted with goals analogous to the royal policies made patent in the Cortes held at Toledo in 1480: to unify administration, to centralize power, to produce revenues, to instill fear and respect for the monarchy, and to create a climate of opinion supportive of a strongly national church identified with a state intent on crusade against the Muslims of Granada and even beyond. The overarching purpose was for Spain under its monarchs to regain the balance lost by the fall of Constantinople and, ultimately, to retake Jerusalem, the center of the faith and the goal of all previous crusades.

When, on December 27, 1480, Granadans took the Christian town of Zahara by surprise, Isabel and Fernando called their realms to war. The story of the next ten years is carved into the choir stalls of Toledo's cathedral. They depict over fifty of the Muslim towns taken in annual campaigns, beginning with Alhama in the heart of Granada. Its three great mosques were converted into churches. Isabel herself is said to have created ornaments for Santa María de la Encarnación, the first church consecrated in the first conquest. The monarchs counted on both a reinvigorated chivalry and a new army, on nobles and on royal appointees; as time went on, however, they relied more and more on recruits from the towns and less on the private armies of the nobility. Scaling operations gave way to heavy artillery, which battered walls, set fire to towns, and terrorized inhabitants into surrender. That Granada was rent internally by civil war was used to advantage (as similar situations among the Aztec and Inca would be used by the conquistadores in America).

To help fund the massive ongoing war, the Spanish monarchs received from the pope the right to the tithe and to the revenues from sale of bulls of crusade. The Inquisition turned over confiscated wealth—how much it took in and how much of it passed on no one knows, just as no one knows the amount of booty the Crown received from captured towns. The monarchs levied forced loans on nobles and clergy and on Jewish and Muslim communities. They sent out agents to set quotas and to collect men, money, and provisions from the towns and their hermandades. Andalusian towns, above all Seville, bore the brunt of this war effort.

Fernando commanded the armies. He and Isabel made policy decisions jointly and in council. She directed provisioning and recruiting, and at crucial junctures joined Fernando in camp before a besieged stronghold, by her presence enheartening the armies. Hers was the steady, relentless determination in fielding the annual campaigns. When in early 1484 Fernando decided that making war against the French threatening Aragón was more important than a campaign against Granada, Isabel chose to go south herself to direct that year's effort on land and to set a naval blockade of aid to Granada from Africa. Fernando, unable to fund a campaign against the French, arrived in time to attack and take Alora and Setenil. From then on the first matter of business for both monarchs was the war against Granada. In 1485 Ronda fell, and with it the western third of the kingdom. That winter they gave a brief audience to a Genoese sailor, Christopher Columbus, who made an unusual proposal, but they were occupied by the war. As for Aragón, the monarchs paid it sporadic attention, governing largely through viceroys. In 1486 Fernando, through the *sentencia de Guadalupe*, freed peasants in Aragón who were still tied to the land.

The populations of defeated towns were dealt with in various ways. The most cooperative simply came under Castilian domination; others were exiled, to be replaced by Castilian settlers. In 1487, the monarchs made an example of Granada's main port of Málaga. When it capitulated only after a grueling siege of four months, they carried through on an earlier ultimatum by enslaving and selling off most of its inhabitants. In November of 1491 the surrender of the city of Granada was formally arranged. Granadans might remain in the city and retain their property and religion. They would become subjects of the Crown of Castile. The Spanish entered the Alhambra on January 1 or 2, 1492, a momentous beginning for a momentous year. Thereafter, Talavera, as Granada's first archbishop, energetically sought to convert the populace to Christianity.

Double excelente coin. Bearing likenesses of Isabel and Fernando, this coin was introduced in 1497 and minted until 1536. It was part of a new system of national coinage introduced after the absorption of Islamic Granada in 1492 and the arrival of quantities of gold and silver from the New World. The Latin inscription reads: (obverse) "Fernando and Isabel, by the grace of God, king and queen," (reverse) "Protect us under the shadow of Thy wings."   American Numismatic Society

Royal initiatives after Granada's fall were all of a piece: preparations for the pursuit of conquest into Africa, the expulsion of the Jews, the expedition of Christopher Columbus and another to the Canary Islands, an alliance with Egypt against the Turks, and the marriages of their five children. The overriding vision was an imperial one—to achieve hegemony over Christendom and to bring as much of the world as they could to the Roman Catholic faith.

An advance into Africa was the next step against Islam, and African gold was a powerful lure. Accordingly, Isabel and Fernando secured royal control of key ports facing Africa: Cádiz, Málaga, and, in 1500, Gibraltar. The 1479 peace treaty with Portugal had recognized Spanish economic interests in Africa east of Gibraltar (principally in the kingdom of Fès). In 1494 the Treaty of Tordesillas, which drew a line of demarcation between Spanish and Portuguese spheres of expansion, further acknowledged Spain's control. The royal couple planned to take Melilla (in present-day Morocco), a hub of the gold trade. By 1496 expeditions had occupied all the Canary Islands and from there were probing the nearby African coast. A visitor to Spain wrote in 1494, upon seeing preparations for an expedition to Africa, that no doubt Africa would soon belong to the Crown of Castile, and that then, with Africa conquered, it would be easy for the monarchs to take Jerusalem.

A decree dated March 31, 1492, signed by Isabel and Fernando in Granada, ordered all Jews to convert or leave the country by the end of July. It gave as principal reason the pernicious influence of some of them on the New Christians, recent converts from Judaism. It did not mention that Jews in Spain had decreased in number, wealth, and value to the Crown, nor that they had become ever more unpopular in the years of religious war.

Delegates at Madrigal in 1476 had stated the prevailing belief that Jews refused to acknowledge the divine will: "Well you know your highnesses, that following divine law, by the coming of the Holy of the Holies [the Messiah] the authority and jurisdictions of the Jews cease."

The decree presented the expulsion as the last step in a slow and steady progression, directed by royal policy, toward an extreme religious homogeneity. A document of 1477 signed by Isabel, forbidding certain acts against the Jews, had reflected a traditional royal stance: "The Jews are mine and they are under my protection and power." The Crown had over the centuries both stoked latent hostility to Jews and kept it tamped down: royal disdain had reinforced popular prejudice; royal power had held it in check. From 1480 the war, popular opinion, the growing strength and acceptance of the Inquisition, and ebbing royal intercession on behalf of Jews had foreshadowed the decree. Jews who proselytized were subject to the Inquisition, and Jews were in fact sentenced to burn at the stake in cases at Huesca in 1489 and at La Guardia in 1491. Against this background, it was but a step to argue that Spanish Jewry must be expelled.

Isabel and Fernando were accustomed to thinking about communities as corporate entities and to moving people en masse. Within this context, their decision can be understood as the fruit of a war-nurtured ruthlessness and a hardening of their shared conviction, their moral certainty, that the promptings of the royal hearts emanated from God. In 1492, as Spain's monarchs were accorded a place among Europe's foremost for defeating the Muslims, the presence of Jews showed Spain to Europe as old-fashionedly heterodox. To the Crown, the edict was more than anything else a mopping-up operation, subsidiary to the work of the Inquisition. That it happened so late was an embarrassment to Spain at the time; that it happened at all would subsequently become one.

In the quest for unity and orthodoxy, the rulers promoted within Spain a moral cleansing, beginning with the clergy, who expected in turn to raise the general level of morality and devotion to faith and crown. The year 1492 also marked the beginning of the rapid ascent to first minister of the brilliant and forceful Franciscan friar Francisco Jiménez de Cisneros. Cisneros succeeded in influence both Hernando de Talavera, who devoted himself to Granada as its first archbishop, and Cardinal Pedro González de Mendoza, who died in January of 1495. The king and especially the queen relied upon Cisneros for his skill in administration and his strength of belief and commitment to reform.

With Spain ascendant in 1492, the extravagant scheme of Christopher Columbus appeared worth risking. We have only hints as to what he proposed to the monarchs. They had been intrigued by Cristóbal Colón from the first

THE MADONNA OF THE CATHOLIC KINGS. Unknown artist. On the right is Isabel. On the left is Fernando and their son Juan.

MUSEO DEL PRADO

audience, in late 1485 or early 1486, when—according to the chronicler Andrés Bernáldez—he showed them a world map and "awakened in them a desire to know those lands." They most likely heard then of his plan to seek the rich and strategic eastern part of India and to find the Grand Khan by sailing around the globe. This account of Columbus's scheme accords with informed court opinion of 1493, when Peter Martyr (Pietro Martire d'Anghiera) wrote of Columbus having discovered an archipelago, new to Europeans, off the Malay peninsula of Asia.

Between the initial meeting and 1492, Fernando ordered a copy of Ptolemy's *Geography*. Isabel recalled Columbus to court, talked to him over time and at length, and held out hope of sponsorship once the war was won. With Granada conquered, the royal reputation was so high that even a failed expedition would not dim it. Within three weeks of the decree against the Jews, a concession to Columbus was signed by the king and queen, stating, "We send Cristóbal Colón with three caravels through the Ocean Sea to the Indies on some business that concerns the service of God and the expansion of the Catholic faith and our benefit and utility."

The enterprise cost the Crown little, and the funds were drawn from the two agencies that had managed wartime funding: the *cruzada*, that is, the sale of indulgences, and the hermandad. Isabel probably did offer to pawn her jewels, yet doing so was, in today's terms, only a question of cashflow, as she was offering not prized possessions but customary collateral. Columbus sailed for Castile, which had long laid claim to Atlantic places. The monarchs interpreted his initial discovery as "lands toward India" and the immediate royal interest was in clearing title with Portugal, which was accomplished at Tordesillas in 1494. The second voyage, sponsored primarily to strengthen the Spanish presence in the newfound lands, had profit as a motive as well. Thus, while Columbus wielded delegated political authority, the Crown retained an economic monopoly, and royal treasury officials sailed with the expedition. The monarchs' view on conquest overseas prevailed. They asserted lordship over native rulers and the royal right to seek material and spiritual recompense, through native labor and tribute and through missionary activity. The right to sponsor exploration was itself a royal monopoly, forbidden to nobles and all others unless by royal license.

Isabel, hoping that Columbus had found East Asian lands (a discovery that would promise both riches and a route that would allow competing with the Portuguese and outflanking the Muslims) as well as out of a natural curiosity, wrote Columbus in 1494 for more information on geography, flora, and fauna. Lacking a satisfactory answer, and with rumors circulating of mismanagement, little gold, and a wealth mostly in souls, Fernando and Isabel in 1495 sent a royal agent to investigate. The following year, they were furious to hear that Columbus had brought back three shiploads of wealth, which turned out to be Amerindians he was selling as slaves. They ordered the Indians seized until it was ascertained whether they had been justly enslaved (that is, for cannibalism or for attacking Spaniards), and, if so, they would claim the profits for themselves. They dispatched missionaries in 1497, and from then on their interest in the Indies was royal oversight of self-sustaining settlements, including plantations and sugar mills. Native peoples were to become Christian and to provide settlers and Crown with labor and tribute. Still, despite their disillusionment with him, the king and queen showed a continuing fondness for Columbus. His sons came to court as pages. Even so, step by step the Crown imposed royal governors to supersede him and his family in what would be called America.

The expansive spirit of 1492 was caught by Elio Antonio Nebrija, who dedicated the first Spanish grammar to Isabel with the explanation that "language is the companion of empire." The postwar atmosphere was one of power and grandeur. The court now traveled—there was as yet no fixed royal residence—in a retinue over one thousand strong, including grandees, young nobles at court school, musicians and chaplains, household retainers, and a burgeoning administrative staff made up chiefly of *letrados*, who were lawyers and clergy, an increasing number of them educated at the University of Salamanca. The *letrados* staffed the royal councils: those of state (from 1494), justice, finance, hermandad (until disbanded in 1498), and Inquisition (established by 1488). The chancery sat permanently at Valladolid, and a second court of justice (audiencia) was instituted in Granada. The nobility retained seats on the council of state and enjoyed a resurgence of power, especially those who had served in the war. The economy flourished, especially in the south and in Barcelona, with an upsurge in trade with the Mediterranean and northern Europe. In Barcelona, on October 25, 1492, Prince Juan received, as he had elsewhere in his parents' realms, the formal oath as crown prince of Aragón. This promised a Spain unified in his person, and, indeed, at bottom all the measures taken that year had at their root dynastic hope and dynastic aspiration.

The five royal children had their own households. The oldest, the infanta Isabel, however, was much with her parents. When her husband, Afonso, heir to João of Portugal, died within eight months of their marriage in 1490, she returned to Castile, until in 1497 she wed Manuel, Afonso's cousin and Portugal's new king. The marriages arranged for all the children reflected a policy of alignment with some of Europe's chief states, directed toward hemming in the most powerful of all, France. In 1497 Prince Juan married Margaret of Austria, whose mother had inherited the duchy of Burgundy and whose father, Maximilian of Habsburg, controlled an extensive domain in Germany and Austria. Juan's sister, the infanta Juana, married Margaret's brother, Archduke Philip. Catalina wed first Arthur, heir to Henry VII of England, in 1501, and, after he died, his brother, Henry, in 1509. Isabel and Fernando did not live to see Henry VIII divorce this last child of theirs, known to the English-speaking world as Catherine of Aragón, yet misfortune had arrived even earlier. Prince Juan, never strong, died in 1497, within six months of his wedding, his doctors concluding it was from overfondness for Margaret and their connubial bed. Margaret shortly after was delivered of a stillborn child. Within a year, young Isabel died in childbirth and her infant son, Miguel, survived less than two years. Her widower, Manuel, then married her sister, María, and the couple succeeded to Portugal's throne. From 1500, Juana and her husband, Philip, were heirs apparent to their parents' realms.

Family tragedy, appearing to doom the vision of dynastic continuity and Spanish unity, was paralleled by delay in the plans for an African expedition, because of embroilments with France in Italy. In 1494, when Charles VIII of France invaded Italy to take Naples, Fernando and Isabel leagued with Venice, Milan, Maximilian of Habsburg, and Pope Alexander VI. Spain sent an expeditionary force to Italy. Its leader, Gonzalo Fernández de Córdoba, con-

firmed the monarchs' reputation for genius in appointments. Known to history as the Great Captain, he retook Naples and showed himself a master of strategy, timing, and military discipline. The pope and the curia, in appreciation of Spanish intervention at Naples and in acknowledgment of Isabel's and Fernando's services to Christendom, bestowed upon them the honorary title of *los Reyes Católicos* (the Catholic monarchs). In 1498 a new French invasion of Italy caused a Spanish expedition poised for Africa to sail for Naples once again.

It is probably not unrelated that as the century ended four royal heirs had died, Isabel had been critically ill, and more stringent measures against social deviation had been imposed. A royal edict of 1499 declared death to any Jew entering Spain unless for the express purpose of being baptized. In 1500 and 1501 Jewish slaves were ordered deported or converted to Christianity. Legislation attacked gypsies. Homosexuality was punishable by death. Laws were enacted against luxurious dress. In 1502 all books were ordered reviewed and licensed, blasphemy was harshly punished, a campaign against priests living with concubines was launched. Further, no reconciled converso, until the fourth generation, was permitted to sit on the royal council, signaling the onset of an official policy of *limpieza de sangre*, purity of blood. In 1499, Cisneros, echoing the expulsion of the Jews, instituted a similar royal policy for Castile's Muslims: they were to be baptized or to emigrate. From 1499 through 1501, Fernando put down outbreaks of armed resistance to the policy in Granada. By 1502, through mass baptisms, most Muslims had become moriscos, and many others had left, chiefly for Africa.

Isabel died on November 26, 1504. Reportedly she had not been well since the death of her oldest daughter and had worsened with each subsequent tragedy, up to the last, which was Juana's patent lack of inclination to rule,

TOMB OF ISABEL AND FERNANDO. Royal Chapel, Granada.

her mounting mental instability, and her beloved husband's obvious dislike of Castile and affection for France. The queen was buried, as she had instructed, in Franciscan garb, in Granada.

After Isabel's death Fernando was no longer king in Castile, but, with Philip's death in 1506 and with Juana's mental instability, he ruled Castile as regent from 1508. In 1510 his armies conquered Tripoli. He proposed conquest of the eastern Mediterranean and planned to lead a crusade against the Turks, but once again troops were deflected to Italy in a campaign against the French. In 1505 he married Germaine de Foix, the niece of Louis XII of France. They had one son, in 1509, who lived less than a day. Fernando died on January 23, 1516. By the terms of his will, he was buried beside Isabel, in Granada.

Isabel and Fernando's reign was a model to their grandson and successor, Charles V, who made of Spain an empire, and to his son, Philip II, who tried mightily to carry on what they had begun. Fernando and Isabel have in the intervening five centuries been interpreted and reinterpreted in accord with the times and the writer's predilections. Today, Isabel has come to stand for religious devotion; Fernando, for Machiavellian statecraft. Both monarchs were in fact deeply devout and both excelled as rulers, though they never separated (as did Machiavelli's prince) the exigencies of statecraft from the promptings of morality. At issue, rather, is their concept of morality. Operating within it, they established one of Europe's most powerful nation-states and set Spain on the road to world empire. Most remarkable of all was their sharing of royal power, their success in lifelong cooperation.

[See also; *Columbus, Christopher,* article on *Columbus in Spain; Jews; Inquisition; Muslims in Spain; Reconquista; Spain; Treaty of Tordesillas,* and biographies of numerous figures mentioned herein.]

BIBLIOGRAPHY

Contemporary Chronicles

Anonymous. *Crónica incomplete de los Reyes Católicos (1469–1476).* Edited by Julio Puyol. Madrid, 1934.

Bernáldez, Andrés. *Memorias del reinado de los Reyes Católicos.* Edited by Manuel Gomez Moreno and Juan de la Mata Carriazo. Madrid, 1962.

Enriquez del Castillo, Diego. *Crónica del rey Don Enrique el cuarto.* Edited by Cayetano Rosell. Vol. 70 of *Biblioteca de Autores Españoles.* Madrid, 1953.

Palencia, Alfonso de. *Crónica de Enrique IV.* Edited by Alfonse Paz y Melia. 4 vols. Madrid, 1973–1975.

Pulgar, Hernando de. *Crónica de los reyes católicos.* Edited by Juan de la Mata Carriazo. 2 vols. Madrid, 1943.

Santa Cruz, Alonso de. *Crónica de los Reyes Católicos.* Edited by Juan de la Mata Carriazo. 2 vols. Seville, 1951.

Valera, Diego de. *Crónica de los reyes católicos.* Edited by Juan de la Mata Carriazo. Madrid, 1927.

Historical Studies

Azcona, Tarsicio de. *Isabel la Católica.* Madrid, 1964.

Clemencin, Diego. *Elógio de la Reina Católica Doña Isabel.* Madrid, 1821.

Fernández-Armesto, Felipe. *Ferdinand and Isabella.* New York, 1975.

Ladero Quesada, Miguel Angel. *España en 1492.* Madrid, 1978.

Liss, Peggy K. *Isabel the Queen.* Forthcoming.

Mariejol, Jean Hippolyte. *The Spain of Ferdinand and Isabella.* Translated and edited by Benjamin Keen. New Brunswick, N.J., 1961.

Suárez Fernández, Luis. *Los Reyes Católicos.* 5 vols. Madrid, 1989–1990.

Vicens Vives, Jaime. *Historia crítica de la vida y reinado de Fernando II de Aragón.* Zaragoza, 1962.

PEGGY K. LISS

ISIDORE OF SEVILLE (c. 560–636), Roman Catholic saint; Hispano-Roman theologian and encyclopedist; bishop of Seville (584–600). Isidore was a man of great learning with broad intellectual interests, especially the secular learning of the Greek and Roman civilizations. He is noted for his theological, ecclesiastical, and historical writings and his biographical essays of ecclesiastical and secular figures of his age.

Two secular works, *Etymologiae* and *De natura rerum,* were of great importance for the organization of the field of science and influenced later medieval conceptions of astronomy and geography. *Etymologiae,* an encyclopedic compilation of the remnants of secular learning up to his age, provided a wide range of information in a concise and accessible form for a time desperately in need of it. *De natura rerum* is a longer and more detailed examination of Books III, XIII, and XIV of *Etymologiae.* It is an important exposition of the physical sciences of the early Middle Ages, specifically astronomy, cosmography, and physical geography. Early medieval science relied not on systematic observation or reasoned proof but rather on the learning of the past or on divine authority. Therefore, *Etymologiae* and *De natura rerum* often contain serious contradictions, particularly concerning the sphericity of the earth and the existence of certain undiscovered, perhaps mythical, islands in the Atlantic Ocean near the coast of Africa. Isidore's works were used as the foundations for later research and as such were important sources for late medieval cartographers such as Paolo del Pozzo Toscanelli and Martin Behaim.

BIBLIOGRAPHY

Díaz y Díaz, Manuel C., ed. *Isidoriana: Colección de estudios sobre Isidoro de Sevilla, publicado con ocasión del XIV centenario de su nacimiento.* León, 1961.

Fontaine, Jacques. *Isidore de Séville et la culture classique dans l'Espagne wisigothique.* 2d ed. Paris, 1983.

Fontaine, Jacques, ed. *De natura rerum, Isidore de Séville: Traité de la nature, suivi de l'Epître en vers du roi Sisebut à Isidore.* Paris, 1960.

Perez de Urbel, Justo. *San Isidoro de Sevilla: Su vida, su obra y su tiempo.* Barcelona, 1940.

Theresa Earenfight

ISLAND CARIBS. See *Indian America*, article on *Island Caribs.*

ITALY. For discussion of Italian republics and city states, see *Florence; Genoa; Naples; Rome; Venetian Republic.*

ITALY IN THE FIFTEENTH CENTURY

J, K

JAMAICA. Jamaica is the third largest of the Greater Antilles, after Cuba and Hispaniola (La Española), and like them has a mountainous central area and shallow plains rimming the coast. The island is about 240 kilometers (150 miles) long and nearly 80 kilometers (50 miles) across at its broadest point; the highest mountain reaches an impressive 2,245 meters (7,400 feet). During the fifteenth century the island seems to have supported a population of about 60,000 Taínos, a subgroup of the Arawaks.

The Taínos lived in villages under chiefs, or caciques, and liked to choose sites close to the sea, for they were great fishers. For starch they had the omnipresent cassava bread; they also hunted a variety of small animals. Their canoes were sometimes very large, and they shared with the other Arawak groups the use of hammocks and tobacco. A little gold was to be found on Jamaica, and they made ornaments from it.

Christopher Columbus visited Jamaica on his second voyage, anchoring in what is now Saint Ann's Bay, which he called Santa Gloria. He was astonished by the island's beauty, calling it "the fairest that eyes have beheld." However, the Taínos in Saint Ann's Bay, and in the next port westward, Río Bueno, did not appear friendly, and Columbus chose to discourage an attack by shooting some, using his crossbowmen, and threatening others with a savage dog. These were tactics the Spaniards had already used on the native inhabitants of the Canaries.

Columbus then sailed off from Montego Bay, but after reconnoitering the south coast of Cuba returned to Jamaica. He made landfall at Montego Bay and then sailed round the island's west and south coasts; here he encountered nothing but friendliness from the inhabitants. He did not return to Jamaica until June 1503, at the end of his fourth voyage, when he was forced to beach his two water-logged caravels at Saint Ann's Bay. Here he was marooned for just over a year, until a vessel from Santo Domingo fetched him and his men away.

During this enforced stay, Columbus succeeded in remaining on friendly terms with the Taínos from a neighboring village, who supplied him with food. He had great difficulties, however, in controlling his crews, who mutinied, set up roving bands, and caused all manner of trouble. In reading about the problems within this quite small group, we can better understand the way in which the Spaniards ran riot throughout the Americas. Columbus had used his beached ships as his base, and their remains may one day be found at Saint Ann's Bay.

The Spaniards returned to Jamaica in 1510, when the first governor, Juan de Esquivel, founded the city of Sevilla la Nueva close by the place where Columbus had been marooned. Here a small town with a substantial stone fort and a church grew up, though the capital was moved in

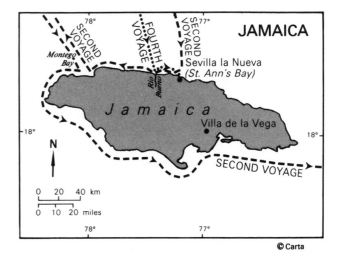

387

1534 to the south side of the island, where Villa de la Vega was built on the banks of the Río Cobre. Jamaica proved to have little gold and to be of value chiefly for its agricultural products: cassava bread, sugar, hides, and lard. The relations between the Spanish settlers and the Taínos do not seem to have been too bad, but the normal pattern of population decline through disease prevailed, until the native inhabitants were virtually extinct. Jamaica survived as a backwater of the Spanish empire until the British seized the island in 1655.

[See also *Indian America*, article on *Taínos; Settlements*, article on *Sevilla la Nueva*.]

BIBLIOGRAPHY

Black, Clinton V. *The History of Jamaica*. Kingston, Jamaica, 1983.
Osborne, Francis J. *History of the Catholic Church in Jamaica*. Chicago, 1988.
Padrón, Francisco Morales. *Jamaica española*. Seville, 1952.

DAVID BUISSERET

JAPAN. See *Cipangu*.

JEWS. [This entry includes four articles that focus on Jewish life and culture relative to events in the period of overseas European expansion:

Jews in Spain
Conversos
Expulsion from Spain
Jews in the New World

See also *Inquisition; Muslims in Spain; Religion*, article on *European Traditions*.]

Jews in Spain

The first Jewish settlements in Spain probably date back to the destruction of the Second Temple in A.D. 70. No historical document mentions them before the Council of Elvira (Illiberis, near present Granada) around the year 305. The laws the council adopted set the tone for later ones, outlawing marriage outside the ethnic group, providing for excommunication for sexual intercourse between Jew and Christian, as well as for clerics eating with Jews, and prohibiting the blessing of Christian agricultural products by Jews. Under the Visigothic monarchy (419–711) several kings decreed open persecution of the Jews, and even accused them of treason and conspiracy against the throne. The Muslim conquest was greeted by Iberian Jews who expected the new Semitic rulers to extend to them the limited tolerance of other religions prescribed in the Qur'an.

Not much is known about the life of the Jewish communities in the first centuries of Islamic rule. With the disintegration of the Córdoba caliphate in 1031 into twenty-three small *taifa*, or independent kingdoms, some Jews acted as prime ministers. The most famous were Samuel ha-Nagid (993–1055 or 1056) in Granada and Yekutiel ibn Hassan in Saragossa. As the Jewish physician Hasdai ibn Shaprut (c. 915–975) had done while serving as one of the ministers of Caliph 'Abd ar-Rahman III in the tenth century, these leaders encouraged the intellectual development of their coreligionists, competed for artists and writers, and attracted those Jews skillful in the techniques of agriculture and tannery to their states. Some historians rightly speak of this period, until the end of the thirteenth century, as the Jewish golden age in Spain.

It was in this milieu that writers like Solomon ibn Gabirol (c. 1022–c. 1070), Bahya ben Joseph ibn Pakuda (eleventh century), and Judah ha-Levy (c. 1075–1141) in Saragossa; Moses ibn Ezra (c. 1060–1139) and Abraham ibn Ezra (c. 1090–1164) in Toledo; and the great Moses ben Maimon (Maimonides; 1135–1204) in Córdoba produced works that influenced Western philosophy and Christian biblical scholarship and theology. These and other Spanish Jewish writers—except Judah ha-Levy—wrote in Arabic and had to be translated into Latin and Hebrew. Some of them led a wandering life because of the successive waves of Muslim invaders, the Almoravids in 1086 and the Almohads after 1174. Maimonides left Spain at age seventeen never to return; he died in Egypt. The Christians maintained a peaceful, although restricted, coexistence with Jews through the next century.

In Toledo, Murcia, and other cities, the so-called schools of translators were founded, in which teams of Christians and Jews, fluent in several languages, translated several Greek classic works from Arabic into Latin and Spanish. After the early medieval period, when most Spanish Jews lived in small towns and made their living in agriculture, the Jews slowly moved to cities under the personal protection of the kings, and though some continued rural activities, most engaged in small-scale commerce (cloth, cattle, grain, dried fish), craftsmanship (builders, silversmiths, shoemakers, tailors, tanners), and money lending. Spanish Jews were not on the whole bourgeois, and only a few reached high social echelons as financial advisers, tax contractors, doctors and *bayles*, administrators of the royal patrimony with jurisdiction over Christian subjects. *Juderías* (Jewish settlements) were organized in *aljamas*, Jewish communities juridically structured under the authority of a *nasi*, a chief justice; the *aljamas* were relatively independent microsocieties within the surrounding Christian society. In the thirteenth and fourteenth centuries, there were many instances of cooperation between Christians, Moors, and Jews under kings

READING THE TORAH IN A SPANISH SYNAGOGUE. From a fourteenth-century Hebrew Haggadah.

who enjoyed and sometimes used the title "emperor of the three religions."

The *Siete partidas* of Alfonso X, "the Wise" (1252–1284), a juridical doctrine in seven parts that was promulgated as law in 1342, manifests the ancient ambivalence of Christians about Jews: relative protection of the Jews as special subjects is juxtaposed with the hope that "those who come from the lineage of Christ's crucifiers" will soon be convinced to accept baptism. This increasingly restrictive attitude resulted from both external and internal motives. Spain felt the influence of two church councils, Lateran IV (1215) and Vienne (1311–1312), which legislated a set of statutes that weakened the peaceful coexistence of Christians and Jews. Successive regional councils, like one in Zamora (1312) and another in Salamanca (1335), aligned the church of Castile with the church at large. This official attitude was greatly enhanced by the new mendicant orders, especially the Dominican Order, which had been founded by a Spaniard. Christian enmity toward Jews in general as well as Jewish and Christian enmity toward those Jews who either individually or in groups were converting to Christianity, especially in times of persecution, became more apparent.

Among the devices used by Christians against the Jews were formal disputations that offered Christians the opportunity to convince Jewish scholars of the truth of Christian doctrine. The most famous occurred in Barcelona (1263) between Moses ben Nachman (Nachmanides) and Pau Christiá, a converso, and a century and a half later in Tortosa (1413–1414) between the converso Jerónimo de Santa Fe and almost twenty rabbis from all over Aragón. The results were disastrous for the Jews: all the rabbis who participated in the dispute of Tortosa converted except Joseph Albo (c. 1380–c. 1444), who retired to Soria and wrote his pietist *Book of the Principles*.

Popular persecutions of Jews usually occurred during the tenure of weak monarchs or at the death of those who had most protected and used them. Such was the case after the death of Jaime I of Aragón (1276) and after the deaths of Alfonso X (1284), Pedro I (1369), and Juan I (1390) of Castile. The persecutions and mob killings of Jews that took place in 1391 throughout Spain started in Seville, encouraged by an overly zealous cleric in temporary charge of that important see, and it quickly spread to other cities and towns. The great Rabbi Hasdai ben Abraham Crescas (1340–1410), author of *Or Adonai* (The light of the Lord), escaped death because he was in Zaragoza with the Aragonese court, but his son was killed in Barcelona together with many Jews, who were buried in the cemetery in Montjuïc (the mount of the Jews). Thousands were killed in hundreds of cities and towns, and many more thousands converted. That year marks the beginning of the end of Spanish Jewry. Many of the medieval *aljamas* never recovered; they either dispersed or disappeared.

By the beginning of the fifteenth century, the fate of Spanish Judaism was sealed. A new series of *taqqanot* (ordinances) agreed to in Valladolid in 1432 tried to reconstruct it, again allowing the *aljamas* to have their own schools, special jurisdiction, and penal authorities. Jews were allowed to practice usury within the legal limits, since the marginal social positions into which they had been compelled to retire forced them into the service industries. But there were many other political interests at stake: the status of the conversos was becoming more and more ambiguous and the Jewish minority was becoming negligible in numbers and in power and, therefore, politically disposable. According to lists of the *aljamas* and of the royal taxes allocated proportionally to them, in the second half of the fifteenth century there were in Castile only 224 *aljamas*, most of them in very small towns. Toledo did not have more than forty Jewish families. The kingdom of Aragón had only twenty-five *aljamas*: three in Catalonia (Lleida, Girona, Cervera), three in modest towns in Valencia (Murviedro, Castellón, Burriana), and the rest in Zaragoza and other towns in Aragón proper.

Despite the historical importance of the Jewish presence in Spain for centuries, and of the role it played in Jewish history, the Jews did not leave a permanent mark on Spanish literary culture, both for religious and linguistic reasons. The great Jewish scholars were unknown even to the best Spanish Christian scholars. The Spanish language retains no more than twenty words of Hebrew origin, almost all of biblical import. There were no Jews of note who wrote in Spanish, with the exception of Rabbi Sem Tob of Carrión, who wrote *Proverbios morales* in the mid-fourteenth century. Even connections between the Jews and Christopher Columbus—for instance, that he used maps produced by the so-called Jewish school of cartographers from Majorca; or that he was helped by Abraham Zacuto, the Jewish professor at the University of Salamanca, and by his *Almanach*—need careful scrutiny. The general Jewish influence on Spain was social and financial rather than cultural. In the second half of the fifteenth century, that influence was very much diminished although three Jewish leaders of the time—Abraham Seneor, Mair Melamed, and Isaac Abravanel—were the financial advisers to the Crown. Even so, the Jewish people as a group paid a high price in terms of a general antipathy that ultimately determined their expulsion.

BIBLIOGRAPHY

Ashtor, Eliyahu. *The Jews of Moslem Spain*. 3 vols. Philadelphia, 1973–1984.
Baer, Yitzaak. *A History of the Jews in Christian Spain*. 2 vols. Philadelphia, 1961.
Borchsenius, Paul. *The Three Rings: The History of the Spanish Jews*. London, 1963.
Neuman, Abraham Aaron. *The Jews in Spain: Their Social, Political, and Cultural Life during the Middle Ages*. 2 vols. Philadelphia, 1944.
Suárez Fernández, Luis. *Judíos españoles en la edad media*. Madrid, 1980.

ANGEL ALCALÁ

Conversos

A Spanish expression for convert or converted, *conversos* or *cristianos nuevos* (new Christians as distinguished from old Christians) or *confesos* (those who confessed the Christian faith) was the name given to those individuals who were known to have converted to Christianity from Judaism or Islam. Since the Muslim converts were also called *moriscos*, the word *conversos* was applied almost exclusively to *judeoconversos*. One would be considered a converso if one converted personally or if a conversion could be documented within the last four generations of a family. Hence there arose the popular Spanish expression "por los cuatro costados" (from four sides). Cervantes

uses this image in Sancho Panza's famous line about "men that have four inches of old Christian fat in their souls" (*Don Quixote* 2.4).

There were always notable Jewish converts in Spain. The most famous are Moses Sephardi, converted in Huesca as Petrus Alphonsi in 1106, who was the author of important scientific works and of *Disciplina clericalis,* an influential collection of Oriental tales; Rabbi Abner of Burgos, baptized in 1321 as Alfonso de Valladolid; and Rabbi Solomon ha-Levi, who converted with his brothers and children as Pablo de Santa María in 1390, and later became bishop of Burgos, chancellor of Castile, and the author of biblical commentaries and anti-Jewish polemics. But Jews started to convert in great numbers during and after the persecutions of 1391. By the mid-fifteenth century some conversos had reached high positions in Christian society through marriage into the nobility, through careers in the church, or through achievement in the professions open to them. Old Christians, infuriated at being dominated by former Jews now exacting high taxes from them for the king, revolted in Toledo in 1449, when for the first time a popular uprising tried to prevent conversos from occupying any post in the municipal administration, a precedent of what was known later as statutes of *limpieza de sangre* (purity of blood, i.e., of ancestry), strongly opposed by some converso scholars like Alfonso de Cartagena (son of Pablo), Juan de Torquemada, and others. The accusation that conversos were judaizing (observing Jewish practices) in secret was common, though it was without evidence; nonetheless, the Inquisition was founded to investigate such claims. How many conversos actually were *judaizantes* is still much discussed. Some Jewish historians (Yitzaak Baer, Isaac S. Révah, Haim Beinart) hold that the vast majority of conversos were Marranos (Jews who submitted to forced conversion but maintained Jewish practices in secret). In this case, the accusations of the Inquisition would have been accurate. Other historians (Benzion Netanyahu and others) believe that the vast majority of conversos were almost assimilated into the Christian majority by 1492 in social and religious habits, and that because of the influence and social prestige of the conversos, the *juderías* (Jewish settlements) had been dwindling long before. In fact, the Inquisition prosecuted hardly more than 5 percent of the estimated converso population of 600,000 in a country of less than six million. Of course, there were always pockets of heroic Jewish resistance, instances of which occurred well into the eighteenth century. Most of the conversos, however, assimilated so quickly and profoundly into the mainstream of the country that dozens of them wrote classics of Spanish literature of the Golden Age, while practically all the spiritual writers, reformers, and mystics of sixteenth- and seventeenth-century Spain—such as John of Ávila,

Teresa of Ávila, John of the Cross, Fray Luis de León—were descended from conversos.

Whatever the probability that Columbus might have been of distant converso descent (it would be wrong to say Jewish descent), it is true that from the very beginning of his activities in Spain he was helped by some Jews (Isaac Abravanel, Abraham Seneor) and by a group of conversos, either clerics (Diego de Deza, later archbishop of Seville and the second Grand Inquisitor, and Hernando de Talavera, later first bishop of Granada) or courtiers. When Columbus was dismissed by Isabel in Granada on January 10, 1492, after his third and last attempt to win her support, he was recalled by an emissary of Fernando, who had been convinced by four of his Aragonese courtiers—Luis de Santángel, Gabriel Sánchez, Juan Cabrero, and Juan de Coloma, all of them prominent conversos—that Columbus's venture was worthy of support. Conversos were active on every level of Spanish society, and as courtiers they participated in the enterprise of discovery.

BIBLIOGRAPHY

Benito Ruano, Eloy. *Los orígenes del problema converso.* Barcelona, 1976.

Domínguez Ortiz, Antonio. *Los judeoconversos en España y América.* Madrid, 1971.

Manzano, Juan Manzano. *Cristóbal Colón: Siete años decisivos de su vida, 1485–1492.* Madrid, 1973.

Netanyahu, Benzion. *The Marranos of Spain from the Late Fourteenth to the Early Sixteenth Century according to Contemporary Hebrew Sources.* 2d revised and enlarged ed. New York, 1973.

Serrano y Sanz, Manuel. *Orígenes de la dominación española en América: Los amigos y protectores aragoneses de Cristóbal Colón.* Madrid, 1918.

ANGEL ALCALÁ

Expulsion from Spain

On March 31, 1492, Fernando and Isabel signed a decree ordering the Jews of Spain either to be baptized or to leave the country by July 31. The decree was in fact the culmination of a series of experiments by the Crown to deal with the social and political problems concerning Jews. While it put an end to the long coexistence of Christians and Jews in Spain, the Expulsion also tried to prevent backsliding by the conversos. Ironically, this problem was to prove even more intractable. The decision was unexpected and it even astonished the prominent Jewish leaders in close contact with the court such as Isaac Abravanel, administrator of the royal tax system, and Abraham Seneor, chief rabbi of Castile, but several steps had been taken at court that should have forewarned them.

The Cortes of Castile that met in Madrigal in 1476 had reiterated laws issued in 1461 and earlier prohibiting Jews, especially women, from dressing richly in silk or displaying gold or silver and ordering them to wear "a distinctive round red cloth in the chest near the shoulders"; this was afterward changed into "a red star with six legs". The Cortes also curtailed the independent jurisdiction of the *aljamas* (Jewish communities) with regard to several issues. In 1480 the Cortes that met in Toledo confined the Spanish Jews in separate walled neighborhoods for the first time; their gates had to be shut at night. In the same year several Jews and conversos were discovered in Seville plotting to help African Moors to reinforce Granada against the Christian campaign; this discovery led to the first *auto de fe* in February 1481, and also to a first, partial expulsion of Jews from Andalusia decreed on January 1, 1483. Three years later Fernando ordered all Jews expelled from the Aragonese dioceses of Zaragoza and Albarracin, though these decrees were not fully carried out.

The text of Fernando's decree makes an explicit statement of the goal of expelling the Jews and says that the sovereigns had hoped "that by such separation the situation would be remedied." The situation they allude to is the status of the conversos.

The recovery of the *juderías* (Jewish settlements) after 1432 had raised apprehension on the part of some clerics that hundreds of thousands of converts might either return to Judaism or become an uncommitted mass of passive, agnostic, and syncretistic unbelievers, unable to be sincere Christians if the Jewish minority was allowed to stay. According to the decree of expulsion, in its first ten years of operation (1481–1491), the Inquisition had been ineffective "because of the contact, intercourse, and communication that they [conversos] have with the Jews." The text makes clear that the Expulsion, if painful, was a decision imposed on the Crown by the failure of the Inquisition to control the conversos socially, economically, or religiously, a control much more important politically for the internal peace of the country than keeping the few thousands of reluctant Jews on its soil.

The Crown decided to solve the internal social unrest caused by the divisions among old Christians, Jews, sincere new Christians, and Marranos by sacrificing a minority that had already become politically disposable. A careful study of the decree shows that the Expulsion had been decided long before and was to take place when the circumstances would allow. The end of the Granada war on January 1, 1492, and the consequent release of formerly needed funds made it possible to yield both to the long-standing demands of Columbus for his venture as well as to the pressures of the Inquisition to suppress the Jews.

The lists of tax contributions by the *aljamas* that have

been preserved for the years immediately before the Expulsion show that the majority of Jews were poor and lived mostly in rural areas. Estimates of the number of Jews in Spain in 1492 are much lower than the 800,000 proposed by the Jesuit Juan de Mariana (1536–1624) and taken for granted by Juan Antonio de Llorente (1756–1823) in his *History of the Inquisition;* they are lower than the 160,000 proposed by Yitzak Baer (1966). There were probably about 100,000 (fewer according to some scholars) Jews out of a total population of nearly six million. Given the small numbers and the poverty of the Jews, it is unlikely that greed on the part of Fernando and Isabel was a motive for the Expulsion; the rulers sometimes confessed that it would have been more advantageous to keep the Jews as taxpayers and workers.

The Decree of Expulsion was directed against Jews as adherents of a religion; there is in the text of the decree no trace of the so-called Spanish anti-Semitism that found expression in statutes of *limpieza de sangre* (purity of blood, i.e., of ancestry). At that time, few objected to accepting as full Spaniards those Jews who abandoned Jewish practices. Everything suggests that, in view of the massive and constant conversions since 1391, the monarchs and their advisers expected the majority of Jews to convert. Their expectations were partly vindicated when entire *juderías*, such as the one in Murcia, converted. In addition, many exiles returned to be baptized, and of the three leading Jews at that time, two converted— Abraham Seneor and Mair Melamed —leaving Isaac Abravanel as the sole important leader of the Sephardim (Jews of Spain). Abravanel sailed from Valencia at the head of those who chose to go to Italy.

As the July 31 deadline approached, all Jews felt pressed to dispose of their property. Since the decree of Expulsion forbade them to take gold and silver out of the country, land and houses were sold for movable property, such as mules or donkeys. About two-thirds of the Sephardim left; they underwent much suffering as they migrated to the countries where they settled: Portugal, North Africa, France, the Low Countries, the Papal States, Naples, Venice, and the Ottoman Empire.

The social importance of the Jews in 1492 and the numbers of Jews expelled have been exaggerated by some historians. The Expulsion did not cause the so-called decadence of Spain. The few important positions held by Jews and the professions in which Jews were active were filled either by new converts or by descendants of earlier converts. In any case, the Inquisition, because of its support of the statutes of purity of blood, made it impossible for the conversos and for Spain to succeed in the long run.

It was a coincidence that Columbus embarked on his first voyage across the Atlantic at dawn on August 3, just two days after the official deadline for expulsion. August 2, a Thursday, was the Ninth of Ab, a Jewish holiday, when, as a Jewish saying says, "those who work will never see a blessing therefrom." Hypothetical arguments have been constructed from this fact, suggesting the possible converso lineage of Columbus, who might have wished to keep the holiday as an ancestral family habit. But other scholars have suggested that the town of Palos, which he could not offend, celebrates on that day the festivity of its patron, the Virgin. To infer that he had a "Jewish agenda" or that he wanted to explore new lands of freedom for his fellow "Jews" sounds from a historical point of view absolutely preposterous.

BIBLIOGRAPHY

Baer, Yitzak. *A History of the Jews in Christian Spain.* 2 vols. Philadelphia, 1966.
Kriegel, Maurice. "La prise d'une décision: L'expulsion des juifs d'Espagne en 1492." *Revue Historique* 240 (1978).
Netanyahu, Benzion. *Don Isaac Abravanel.* Philadelphia, 1982.
Suárez Fernández, Luis. *Documentos acerca de la expulsión de los judíos.* Valladolid, 1964.

ANGEL ALCALÁ

Jews in the New World

Jews, Moors, and recent converts to Christianity were barred from immigrating to the Spanish Indies. This prohibition was included in the first instruction sent by Queen Isabel to Nicolás de Ovando, first royal governor of La Española (Hispaniola), Spain's first colony in the New World, in 1501. Reiterated over the years, the prohibition was expanded to include the children and grandchildren of converts. Enforced both by royal officials and by the transplanted Holy Office of the Inquisition, the policy remained in force throughout Spain's rule in the Americas. In this way, the Spanish Crown continued the dual policy it had developed with respect to Jews and persons of Jewish descent over the course of the fifteenth century: Spanish Jewry was to be converted or expelled from Spain; converts from Judaism and their descendants were not to be accorded equal status with other Spanish Christians either at home or in the New World.

The policy was put into effect through laws of *limpieza de sangre* ("clean blood") that barred conversos from engaging in any honorable public activity: to enter a university, practice a profession, hold public office, ride a horse, or sail to the Indies. Under these laws, descent from a Jewish ancestor became an indelible stain in one's blood which nothing, not even baptism, could eradicate. The old religious distinction between Jew and Catholic now became a racial distinction between New Christians of Jewish descent and Old Christians who had been converted from paganism in earlier centuries.

These legislative and social barriers led to the emergence of a new social class, the *conversos* (converts), who stood midway between Catholics and Jews and were wholly accepted by neither. The conversos were distrusted and resented by Old Christians who fought to retain their own superior status in society. Conversos were condemned by contemporary Jews as apostates. But Jewish history later enshrined the conversos as crypto-Jews or Marranos, on the supposition that, although forced to conform outwardly to Catholicism, they really remained loyal to their Jewish faith.

The Jews were expelled from Spain at the same time that Columbus set sail on his first voyage in the summer of 1492. Despite the obstacles placed in their way, unknown numbers of Jews and conversos followed in the explorer's wake. The new lands now coming into view beyond the sea gave hope to some conversos that they could disappear into a life free of harrassment by the Inquisition, which continually suspected them of backsliding into Judaism. Other conversos were motivated by the same desire for wealth and glory that drove their Old Christian countrymen to join the profitable enterprise of the Indies. Such a man, for example, was Simon Vaez Sevilla, a merchant of New Spain who was denounced to the Inquisition as a Jew but who survived several trials by torture to emerge a free man. Professing Jews found their way to America because of the pressing need for a refuge imposed upon them by the order of expulsion. At that time, Jews were prohibited from entering most countries of Europe and pirates stood off the coast of Spain to capture shiploads of refugees heading for Africa. In these desperate circumstances, some Jews came to America in the hope of finding some distant place where they could practice Judaism without being molested. Luis de Carvajal the Younger, his mother, and five sisters died at the stake for this miscalculation. Crypto-Jews like the Carvajals, or Tomás Treviño de Sobremonte and Francisco Maldonado de Silva are honored in Jewish history as martyrs to their faith.

A variety of stratagems were employed by Jews, conversos, and their descendants to enter areas prohibited to them. Certificates of clean blood could be bought from complaisant priests; soldiers, sailors, and servants did not need to show these at all. And from time to time, the Spanish Crown, sunk in debt and increasingly corrupt, sold the privilege of immigration to classes of persons whom it legally excluded. There were conversos in Columbus's successive crews and among the conquistadores. In 1528 one Hernando Alonso, who had fought with Hernando Cortés, had the dubious honor of being the first person in the New World to be burned at the stake for

Judaizing (practicing Jewish customs though a baptized Catholic). Alonso was accused of having baptized a child in wine, not a Jewish custom. From the record, it is unclear whether he was a secret Jew, a converso and thus vulnerable to his personal enemies, or the victim of a political plot—the first, but certainly not the last, instance in which an accusation of Judaizing was to be used to destroy a political opponent.

Most Jews and conversos followed less dramatic occupations. The records of the Inquisition show that those brought before it on charges of Judaizing followed the whole gamut of trades of that day—from shoemaker to clergyman, from merchant to weaver to the vicar-general of the Mexican province of Michoacán. Necessary as their skills may have been, persons of Jewish descent were not permitted to take their place in society. The revelation that someone had Jewish ancestry was enough to arouse a paranoid perception that society was being infiltrated by "Jews," whom the church inveighed against unceasingly. Weekly sermons and periodic autos de fe where presumed heretics were incinerated either in person or in effigy primed the populace constantly to be on the lookout for signs of the presence of Jews. Judaic concepts such as monotheism, and the prohibition against graven images found no place in these warnings. Rather, congregations were exhorted to report persons who changed their underwear on Friday or stripped a tendon from a leg of lamb before cooking it. Such admonitions placed every household at the mercy of gossip, particularly as informers were rewarded by receiving a portion of the goods confiscated from the accused. As in the conquest of the indigenous peoples, faith mingled companionably with greed. The most spectacular case occurred in Lima in 1635, when sixty-four suspected Judaizers, most of them prosperous merchants, were arrested in one coordinated operation. The arrests led to the immediate flight of capital from the viceroyalty, the deaths and imprisonment of the accused in an auto de fe four years later, and the emergence of the Lima branch of the Inquisition as the wealthiest in the world.

Portugal, a nation of some one million people on the eve of the encounter with the New World, faced the imperial necessity of holding down Brazil as well as its global galaxy of commercial entrepôts in India, Africa, and China. Under these circumstances, the Crown could not afford to sacrifice too many of its subjects. Having forcibly converted all Portuguese and Spanish Jews within its borders in 1497 in order to evade a contractual obligation to expel them, the Crown proceeded, within limits, to permit its *novo cristãos* (New Christians) to colonize Brazil. The Inquisition was never established in Brazil itself; nevertheless, suspected Judaizers could be, and were, sent to Lisbon or even Goa to be tried by tribunals there. Inquisition records show that in Brazil also, New Christians were engaged at all levels of the economic and social structure, including the church. Economically, they were especially important as owners and managers of sugar mills. Interestingly, although *novo cristãos* were free to travel, and frequently did, to places such as Amsterdam and Hamburg where they would have been free to revert to Judaism, most chose to return to their homes under Portuguese rule, with all the risks that entailed, and even helped defend coastal cities against raids by the Dutch.

Only in the Dutch dependencies and, from time to time, in the French- and English-ruled islands, was it possible to live openly as a Jew in the New World. Those individuals who left Brazil for the safety of Curaçao, Bonaire, or Aruba took their skills with them, spreading the technology for manufacture of sugar out of cane to the various islands where it is still a staple industry. The Jewish community of Curaçao also included shipowners, sailors, slavers, and merchants who were at the core of the island's thriving oceanic trade in the seventeenth and eighteenth centuries.

Spanish America benefited from the talents of personalities of "tainted" ancestry such as Sister Juana Inés de la Cruz, dubbed the "Tenth Muse" by admirers of her poetry; Bernardino de Sahagún, the Franciscan monk who transcribed what we know today of Nahua (Aztec) culture; Antonio de León Pinelo, the polymath who laid the foundations for scholarship in Latin America. Brazilian culture was enriched by Bento Teixeira Pinto, author of the *Prosopopeia*, who died after four years in an Inquisition prison and public humiliation as a Judaizer; and the eighteenth-century Portuguese poet Antonio José da Silva, burned in Lisbon in 1739 as a pertinacious Jew.

These persons and unknown others, against great odds, lived creative lives while undergoing traumatic transformation from Jew to Catholic. Neither Jews nor Jewish culture survived the sustained attack of the Inquisition. There is thus no continuity between conversos and crypto-Jews who lived under Spanish or Portuguese colonial rule and contemporary Latin American Jewish communities.

BIBLIOGRAPHY

Böhm, Günter. *Nuevos antecedentes para una historia de los judíos en Chile colonial.* Santiago, 1963.
Cohen, Martin. *The Martyr. Luis de Carvajal: The Story of a Secret Jew and the Mexican Inquisition in the Sixteenth Century.* Philadelphia, 1973.
Emmanuel, Isaac S., and Suzanne A. Emmanuel. *History of the Jews of the Netherlands Antilles.* 2 vols. Assen, 1970.
Lewin, Boleslão. *El judío en la época colonial: Un aspecto de la historia río-platense.* Buenos Aires, 1939.
Liebman, Seymour B. *The Inquisition and the Jews in the New World: Summaries of Procesos, 1500–1810, and Bibliographic Guide.* Coral Gables, Fla., 1974.
Novinsky, Anita. *Cristãos novos na Bahia.* São Paulo, 1972.

JUDITH LAIKIN ELKIN

JIMÉNEZ DE CISNEROS, FRANCISCO

JIMÉNEZ DE CISNEROS, FRANCISCO (1436–1517), Spanish prelate and statesman. During his long life, Cisneros occupied the most important political and spiritual offices of the Crown of Castile: cardinal-archbishop of Toledo, inquisitor-general, and governor of the realm. No Castilian prelate has since possessed such power. Judgments about his achievements are contradictory. To some, he was an intransigent, overzealous friar; to others, a model prelate and statesman.

For the first fifty-six years of his life, Cisneros gave little indication of future greatness. A graduate of Salamanca with a bachelor's degree in law, he went to Rome to pursue an administrative career in the church. His nomination by Paul II in 1471 to a benefice in the archdiocese of Toledo angered the archbishop of Toledo, Alfonso Carrillo, who placed him in jail. But Cardinal Pedro González de Mendoza intervened on behalf of Cisneros and appointed him chaplain of the bishopric of Sigüenza in 1480. Four years later, Cisneros decided to retire from the world and took orders as an Observant Franciscan, living in the convents of La Salceda and El Castañar. But in 1492 he was persuaded by Queen Isabel to replace Hernando de Talavera, now archbishop of Granada, as her personal confessor. With this appointment, Cisneros began his rise to prominence; three years later he was appointed archbishop of Toledo.

Cisneros, like the Catholic monarchs Isabel and Fernando, wished to improve the education, discipline, and morale of the clergy, both regular and secular. His most energetic church reform was that of his own order, where he forced the lax *conventuales* to join the more rigorous and edifying Observant Franciscans in honoring their vows of poverty, chastity, and obedience. Female orders were also visited to ensure that their convents were adequately endowed and had edifying spiritual direction. Cisneros held two synods in the archdiocese of Toledo (Alcalá de Henares, 1497; Talavera de la Reina, 1498), and much of the legislation of these synods, which urged parish priests to catechize their parishioners, to teach children the Christian doctrine, and to keep records of baptisms, anticipated the Tridentine reforms. Evidence in present-day Toledo suggests that this legislation was implemented by many parish priests.

The foundation of a new university at Alcalá de Henares in 1498 formed part of the prelate's reform program. This university was to be a center for the teaching of theology, and the curriculum included not just Thomas Aquinas but also Duns Scotus and nominalism. Cisneros was enthusiastic about what was called the New Learning, and he employed at Alcalá a bevy of humanists, translators, and philologists to study the various translations of the Bible. The culmination of their efforts was the magnificent but ill-fated Complutensian Polyglot Bible that included texts in Hebrew, Latin, and Greek printed in parallel columns. Quick to recognize the utility of the printing press for his reform efforts, Cisneros encouraged the translation and printing of many religious and mystical works, thus making them accessible to a new public.

With the death of Queen Isabel in 1504, the political situation in Castile deteriorated. In 1505 Fernando retired to Italy after ceding the government of Castile to his son-in-law, Philip I of Flanders, who died a year later. Cisneros acted as regent until Fernando returned in 1507, when he presented to Cisneros a cardinal's hat, a worthy accompaniment to the title of inquisitor-general he had received earlier that year. In 1516, after Fernando's death, Cisneros again served as regent until the new heir, the future emperor Charles V, arrived in Castile. That Cisneros was able to survive and rule during these turbulent periods, when powerful nobles split into opposing factions and sought to advance their own interests, suggests that he possessed political skills of a high order.

Cardinal Cisneros has been described as the last of the crusading prelates, and this phase of his personality is best seen in the North African campaigns. In 1507 he financed the conquest of Mazalquivir (in present-day Algeria) and in 1509 personally supervised the conquest of Oran, accompanying the fleet and praying while the soldiers fought—"behaving like a new Moses," according to one observer. The New World did not escape the prelate's purview. After 1500 he was active in organizing expeditions of Franciscan missionaries and in the creation of the first episcopal sees. In response to the problems associated with the Indian labor communes (encomiendas), Cisneros sent to the Antilles three Hieronymites with instructions about the reorganization of the Indian population and the administration of the new territories.

Cisneros's attitude toward the minorities of Castile—the Jews and Muslims—seems to have been mixed. His lack of patience with the moderate, humane methods of Cardinal Talavera in the treatment and conversion of Muslims in the newly conquered Kingdom of Granada is well known. Cisneros implemented a policy of coercion and mass baptism, which eventually led to an uprising of the Granada moriscos that was barely contained. In other cases, however, the record differs. Although a strong supporter of the Holy Office and its prerogatives, Cisneros as inquisitor-general ushered in a more temperate period after the fanaticism of the inquisitor Diego Rodríguez Lucero. The prelate had Arabic books burned in Granada, but he claimed a large collection of Arabic books plundered in Oran for his new university in Alcalá. His treatment of conversos, or Jewish converts, in the city of Toledo was far from intolerant. After he became inquisitor-general, several Toledo conversos who had been arrested earlier by the Holy Office were absolved and freed, most notably the maestrescuela of the Toledo cathedral, Francisco Álvarez de Toledo-Zapata, who became a friend of the prelate. Cisneros encouraged a new confraternity, La Virgen y Madre de Dios, composed largely of conversos who met in the archbishop's palace. And on the roster of those employed to work on the famous Polyglot Bible were many Jewish converts whose knowledge of Hebrew was indispensable to the undertaking.

BIBLIOGRAPHY

Azcona, Tarsicio de. La elección y reforma del episcopado español en tiempo de los reyes católicos. Madrid, 1960.

Elliott, John H. Imperial Spain 1469–1716. New York, 1966.

García de Oro, José. Cisneros y la reforma del clero español en tiempo de los reyes católicos. Madrid, 1970.

García de Oro, José. "Francisco Jiménez de Cisneros." In vol. 2 of Diccionario de historia eclesiástica de España. Edited by Quentín Aldea et al. 5 vols. Madrid, 1972–1987.

Gómez de Castro, Alvar. De las haçanas de Francisco Jiménez de Cisneros. Edited and translated by José Oroz Reta. Madrid, 1984. Originally published as De rebus gestis a Francisco Ximenio Cisnerio. Alcalá, 1569.

LINDA MARTZ

JIMÉNEZ DE QUESADA, GONZALO (1492/1506–1579), conqueror of New Granada (Colombia). Born in either Córdoba or Granada, Jiménez de Quesada was educated in law and served for a time in the Chancery of Granada. In 1535 he was named superior justice (alcalde mayor) in Pedro Fernández de Lugo's expedition to occupy Santa Marta.

Once established at Santa Marta, Fernández de Lugo commissioned Jiménez de Quesada to ascend the Magdalena River until he found its source. A force of six hundred men, one hundred horses, and six ships set out on April 5, 1536. The expedition found little of note until it reached the Magdalena's confluence with the Opón, where the native peoples had salt cones that the Spaniards guessed had come from a developed culture in the interior.

Jiménez de Quesada abandoned exploration of the Magdalena River and took the remaining men, numbering under two hundred, up the Opón and into the mountain valleys. Venerated by the Indians as children of the sun and moon, the Spanish were allowed to pass until they reached the Bogotá valley. There they began to loot the gold jewelry of the inhabitants, even robbing tombs. The Indian province of Tunja (roughly the modern department of Boyacá) was also raided. Santa Fé de Bogotá was founded on August 6, 1538, as part of Jiménez de Quesada's preparations to leave the province and go to Spain to seek a royal grant of its government. The Spanish city provided a juridical basis for his pretensions and rewards for his followers in the form of land and encomiendas.

Before Jiménez de Quesada could depart for Spain, Nicolás Federmann arrived from Venezuela, to be followed not many months later by Sebastián de Belalcázar, who had crossed the mountains from Quito. Federmann joined Jiménez de Quesada but Belalcázar attempted to overthrow his power on behalf of Francisco Pizarro, whose royal grant included part of southern Colombia, but not the Bogotá area. When that failed, he withdrew to Quito.

Jiménez de Quesada sailed from Cartagena on July 8, 1539. He was unable to secure appointment as governor of New Granada and spent a number of years in other parts of Europe before returning to Spain. Eventually granted the title of Marshal of New Granada and certain incomes, he returned to the province in 1555. A popular leader of the Spanish residents, he did not leave Bogotá until 1569, when he lead an ill-fated expedition in search of El Dorado. Jiménez de Quesada worked his way east as far as the Venezuelan Llanos before turning back. He spent the final years of his life writing an account of his conquests and a book of sermons, both now lost. In 1575 he participated in a campaign against rebellious Indians. He died of Hansen's disease in 1579 at Mariquita, New Granada.

BIBLIOGRAPHY

Arciniegas, German. *The Knight of El Dorado*. Translated by Mildred Adams. 1942. Reprint, Westport, Conn., 1968.
Cunninghame-Graham, R. B. *The Conquest of New Granada, Being the Life of Gonzalo Jiménez de Quesada*. London, 1922.
Markham, Clements R. *The Conquest of New Granada*. London, 1912.
Parry, J. H. *The Discovery of South America*. New York, 1979.

PAUL E. HOFFMAN

JOÃO II (1455–1495), king of Portugal (1481–1495). A man of exceptional intelligence and strength, João II, "the Perfect Prince," ruled Portugal after the death of his father, Afonso V, in 1481. João brought prosperity to Portugal, which enabled him to concentrate on exploration and to build a Portuguese overseas empire founded on the economic and political benefits from the voyages of discovery.

JOÃO II OF PORTUGAL.   KUNSTHISTORISCHES MUSEUM, VIENNA

During the last years of Afonso's reign, João was virtually co-ruler with his father. He managed the Crown's monopoly of the trade with Africa and was put in charge of the Junta dos Mathemáticos. The Junta, a maritime advisory committee responsible for overseas expansion, created a comprehensive plan for the discoveries, incorporating both land and sea exploration. He focused his attentions eastward, primarily on Asia and Africa. During João's reign Diogo Cão explored central Africa (1482) and Bartolomeu Dias rounded the Cape of Good Hope (1487).

Columbus brought his petitions for support of his westward voyages to João in 1484 and 1488. João rejected Columbus's theories as incorrect and mathematically improbable, so Columbus took his petitions to the court of Castile where he eventually received financing from Fernando and Isabel. When Columbus returned from his first voyage in 1493, weather conditions forced him to land in Portugal, not Castile as he had planned. Upon hearing the details of Columbus's voyage, João asserted that because the lands discovered were south of the Canary Islands, they were not within the jurisdiction of Castile but rather belonged to Portugal, according to the Treaty of

Alcáçovas (1479). Pope Alexander VI, in his bull *Inter caetera* (1493), attempted to resolve the dispute by pushing westward the Line of Demarcation. (Although there is no evidence of prior visits to Brazil by European navigators, it is likely that João suspected its existence since he knew of Paolo del Pozzo Toscanelli's map indicating possible islands in the Atlantic and suggesting a westward route to the Indies.) João disputed the papal bull, and in 1494 the disagreement was resolved by the Treaty of Tordesillas, which granted Columbus's discoveries to Castile but moved the Line of Demarcation farther west, allowing Portugal later to claim Brazil.

João married Leonor of Viseu, a member of one of the most powerful noble families in Portugal. In 1491 their only son, Afonso, married Isabel, daughter of Fernando and Isabel of Castile, but the marriage was tragically brief. After only a few months, Afonso died in a riding accident. João turned to his young cousin Manuel, the duke of Beja, and began grooming him for succession.

João strengthened royal authority by limiting the power of the nobility. Even his wife's family connections did not stop his ruthless treatment of his brothers-in-law, the powerful dukes of Bragança and Viseu; he ordered the execution of Bragança and murdered Viseu with his own hands. He harbored Spanish Jews exiled by Fernando and Isabel in 1492, including Abraham Zacuto, the famous astronomer from Salamanca. His motives were not entirely altruistic: the Jews were allowed to stay for eight months only and were taxed for the privilege of entrance to the kingdom. Just before his death in 1495 João completed plans for Vasco de Gama's voyage to India, work that was brought to fruition during the reign of Manuel I.

BIBLIOGRAPHY

Domingues, Mário. *Di João II, o homen e o monarca: Evocação histórica.* Lisbon, 1960.
Gaspar de Naia, Alexandre. *D. João II e Cristóbal Colón: Factores complementos na consecução de um mesmo objectivo.* Lisbon, 1951.
Oliveira Marqués, A. H. de. *History of Portugal.* 2 vols. New York, 1972.
Oliveira Martins, Joaquim Pedro. *O principe perfeito.* 3d ed. Lisbon, 1923.
Sanceau, Elaine. *The Perfect Prince: A Biography of the King Dom João II.* Porto, 1959.

THERESA EARENFIGHT

JOHN. For discussion of Spanish kings, see under *Juan.* For discussion of Portuguese kings, see under *João.*

JUAN (1478–1497), crown prince of Spain; the only son of Isabel and Fernando. Juan's birth in Seville was greeted with extraordinary enthusiasm, for he would inherit the united kingdoms of Castile and Aragón, to which later would be added the kingdoms of Navarre and Granada. He and his children thus would be the first monarchs in nearly eight hundred years to rule a united Spain. Juan's education was wide ranging and firmly grounded in Renaissance humanism; his tutors included Lucio Marineo Siculo and Pietro Martire d'Anghiera (Peter Martyr). Juan, who learned the art of governance as he accompanied the peripatetic court of Fernando and Isabel, later established his own court in Almazán. He was present at the fall of Granada in 1492 and the royal reception in Barcelona on April 20, 1493, which celebrated the return of Columbus from his first voyage to the New World.

Juan's marriage on April 3, 1497, in Burgos to Margaret of Austria, daughter of Emperor Maximilian I, was part of a double matrimonial alliance that joined the royal family of Castile and Aragón with the Austrian House of Habsburg. The alliance, which was designed to offset the power of France, also united Juan's sister Juana with Maximilian's son and heir, Philip the Handsome. The carefully crafted alliance lasted only a matter of months, however. Juan's health had been fragile since childhood, and he died suddenly on October 6, 1497, in Salamanca. The only child of the marriage was a stillborn daughter. Juan was buried in Ávila at the monastery of Santo Tomás.

BIBLIOGRAPHY

Camón Aznar, J. *Sobre la muerte del príncipe Don Juan.* Madrid, 1963.
Maura, Duque de. *El príncipe que murió de amor, Don Juan, primogénito de los reyes católicos.* Madrid, 1944.
Miller, Townsend. *The Castles and the Crown: Spain 1451–1555.* New York, 1963.
Suárez Fernández, Luis, and M. Fernández Álvarez. *La España de los Reyes Católicos (1474–1516).* Vol. 17 of *Historia de España.* Edited by Ramón Menéndez Pidal. 2 vols. Madrid, 1966.

THERESA EARENFIGHT

JUAN II (1397–1479), king of Aragón (1458–1479). Juan, son of Fernando I of Antequera and Leonor of Albuquerque, was already an experienced monarch when he inherited the Crown of Aragón in 1458 following the death of his brother King Alfonso V (Alfonso the Magnanimous). He had ruled Navarre since 1420 by right of his first wife, Blanca, and had served as lieutenant in Aragón during Alfonso's extended absence in Naples.

Juan's rule of the realms of the Crown of Aragón was turbulent and marked by a decade of bitter civil war (1462–1472), which devastated the economy of Barcelona. He clashed with France over possession of the counties of Roussillon and Cerdagne, an issue that would not be resolved until the reign of his son Fernando the Catholic.

His dealings with Castile were equally stormy, dating to 1420 when he and his brother, Enrique, the infantes of Aragón, interfered in Castilian affairs. As king of Navarre he attempted to manipulate the Castilian succession, hoping to unite the various Spanish kingdoms within his own family. His quarrel with his son Carlos of Viana brought Navarre close to war with Castile. When Carlos died in 1461, murder was suspected, but there was no evidence to accuse Juan of the crime.

Carlos's death cleared the way for Fernando, Juan's son by his second wife, Juana Enríquez, to inherit the Crown of Aragón. At Juan's death in 1479 the Crown of Aragón was a far-flung domain, which included the peninsular realms of Aragón, Catalonia, and Valencia as well as the Mediterranean kingdoms of Mallorca, Sardinia, Sicily, and Naples.

BIBLIOGRAPHY

Bisson, Thomas N. The Medieval Crown of Aragon: A Short History. Oxford, 1986.

Vicens Vives, Jaime. Juan II de Aragón (1398–1479): Monarquía y revolución en la España del siglo XV. Barcelona, 1953.

Vicens Vives, Jaime. La politique méditerranéenne et italienne de Jean II d'Aragon entre 1458 et 1462. Bern, 1950.

Vicens Vives, Jaime. Els Trastàmares (segle XV). Barcelona, 1956.

THERESA EARENFIGHT

JUANA DE CASTILLA (1462–1530), princess of Castile and alleged daughter of King Enrique IV of Castile, known as Juana la Beltraneja. Juana was the central figure in a prolonged crisis concerning the succession to the throne; it fractured the kingdom and led to nearly a decade of civil war in Castile. The problem of the succession centered on the uncertainty of Juana's parentage, an issue that has never been definitively resolved, although no convincing evidence exists to prove the claims of her illegitimacy. King Enrique was alleged to be impotent, and his first marriage to Blanca of Navarre was nullified on those grounds. He was wed again, to Juana of Portugal, but it was six years before a child was born on February 28, 1462. Soon after her birth, rumors began to circulate concerning the king's impotence and the queen's indiscretions. It was said that Juana was the illegitimate daughter of the king's closest adviser, Beltrán de la Cueva—hence her derogatory nickname "la Beltraneja."

Although on May 9, 1462, the Cortes of Castile judged Juana to be heir to the throne, the controversy did not subside. When a faction of nobles and clergy in the court pressured Enrique to repudiate Juana, he began to waver on the question of her legitimacy and she became a pawn in the ensuing struggle. The Sentence of Medina del Campo (1465), which repudiated Juana in favor of

Enrique's brother Alfonso, was a tacit admission by Enrique of Juana's illegitimacy, but he later revoked his repudiation. In the civil war that followed, rival factions rallied behind either Juana, supported by Beltrán de la Cueva and the Mendoza family, or Prince Alfonso, who had the formidable support of Alfonso Carrillo, the archbishop of Toledo. When Prince Alfonso died in 1468, Juan Pacheco and Carrillo pledged their support to Enrique's sister, Princess Isabel. Enrique conceded to the strength of Pacheco and Carrillo and signed the Treaty of Toros de Guisando (September 18, 1468), which designated Isabel as heir. This action temporarily pacified the situation and shifted the balance of power in favor of the Isabelline faction. But the calm was broken in 1469 when Isabel married Fernando of Aragón and a serious rift developed in relations between her and Enrique. In 1470 Isabel was repudiated once again in favor of Juana, who was declared true heir and was betrothed to the duke of Guienne, the younger brother of Louis XI of France; the duke, however, died before the marriage. Isabel and her supporters, in an alliance with the majority of the nobles and townspeople, were gaining strength.

At the time of Enrique's death in 1474 he had neither firmly settled the issue of Juana's legitimacy nor declared anyone as heir. Isabel was proclaimed queen, but Juana's partisans, especially King Afonso V of Portugal, did not give up the cause. Juana was betrothed to Afonso; they called themselves the king and queen of Castile, and the civil war continued. Fernando's defeat of Afonso's Portuguese troops at Toro in 1476 and the birth of a male heir, Juan, in 1478 to Fernando and Isabel signaled the end of Juana's attempts to gain the throne of Castile. She retired to the convent of Santa Clara in Coimbra, calling herself queen of Castile until her death in 1530.

BIBLIOGRAPHY

Ferrara, Orestes. Un pleito sucesorio: Enrique IV, Isabel de Castilla y la Beltraneja. Madrid, 1945.

Miller, Townsend. The Castles and the Crown: Spain 1451–1555. New York, 1963.

Phillips, William D., Jr. Enrique IV and the Crisis of Fifteenth-Century Castile, 1425–1480. Cambridge, Mass., 1978.

Sarasola, Modesto. Isabel la Católica y el destino de doña Juana, la Beltraneja. Valladolid, 1955.

THERESA EARENFIGHT

JUANA I (1479–1555), queen of Castile (1504–1555), known as La Loca. Juana, called the "mad queen of Castile," was the third child of Isabel I and Fernando V. She succeeded to the throne of Castile after the death of Isabel in October 1504 because of the vacancy created by the untimely deaths of her brother, Juan (1497), older sister, Isabel (1498), and Isabel's son, Infante Manuel (1500). Her incapacity to rule provoked a series of succession crises that ensued after the deaths of her husband, Philip (1506), and her father (1516).

Juana's marriage to Philip the Handsome, archduke of Austria and duke of Burgundy, in 1496 was part of a double matrimonial alliance between Castile and Emperor Maximilian I, in which her brother Crown Prince Juan was betrothed to Philip's sister Margaret. Among the six children of Philip and Juana were Charles and Ferdinand, each of whom successively bore the title of Holy Roman Emperor.

Juana had been moody and temperamental since childhood, and her marriage to Philip exacerbated her emotional instability. She was devoted to him and was particularly jealous of his numerous infidelities. The first clear signs of serious mental illness were evident as early as 1502, when because of her pregnancy she was forced to remain in Castile when Philip returned to Flanders. Her condition steadily worsened, so that when Isabel died in 1504 she named Juana as successor to Castile but stipulated that if Juana was incapable of ruling, Fernando should serve as regent for Charles, then six years old.

When Philip returned to Castile in 1506, he asserted that Juana was sane and declared that as her husband he was within his rights to rule as king. But because Philip was not especially interested in the Spanish kingdom, Fernando feared that he would be an absentee king. Juana retreated into seclusion, and the animosity between Philip and Fernando intensified. Many prominent nobles, seeking to use the easily manipulated archduke for their own political advantage, allied with Philip against Fernando, and he

bowed to their strength. On June 23, 1506, he signed the Agreement of Villafafila, which granted Philip full rights to rule Castile and denied Juana any role in government. Philip's reign was brief, however. He died in September of the same year, and Castile was faced with a succession crisis.

Fernando, who had left Castile for his kingdom in Naples, ordered the Castilians to obey Juana. But in the absence of strong royal authority, civil unrest grew as nobles asserted their independence and towns rebelled. Juana's mental state deteriorated markedly after Philip's death. She refused to let his casket be entombed and ordered that it accompany her throughout her nocturnal travels in Castile. When she abandoned all responsibilities as queen, Cardinal Francisco Jiménez de Cisneros assumed control as regent until Fernando's return in 1507. Fernando ruled Castile, with Juana as nominal queen, until his death in 1516. Castile once more was threatened with civil unrest, and a faction of the nobility tried to rule in Juana's name. The cardinal again served as regent until Charles was recognized as king in 1518. Juana, queen in name only, withdrew completely from the world and lived under guard as a recluse in the royal castle at Tordesillas until her death in 1555.

BIBLIOGRAPHY

Dennis, Amarie. *Seek the Darkness: The Story of Juana la Loca*. Madrid, 1953.
Imann, Georges. *Jeanne le Folle*. Paris, 1947.
Pfandl, Ludwig. *Juana la Loca*. 7th ed. Madrid, 1955.

THERESA EARENFIGHT

KAMAL. The first European to mention the *kamal* was probably Niccolò de' Conti, around 1440. The Portuguese historian João de Barros, describing Vasco da Gama's first encounter with the Muslim navigator *(mu'allim)* from Gujarat who was to show him the way to India, reported that the navigator was not impressed by Da Gama's large wooden astrolabe and others of metal used for finding solar and stellar altitudes. The navigator told Da Gama that the mariners of "Cambaya" (Cambay, a formerly important port in Gujarat) and India used an instrument of "three tablets," one of which he had in his possession. In Book 4 of *Décadas de Asia* (1552–1615), Barros compares the use of this exotic instrument to the *balestilla* (cross-staff). The Portuguese called the *kamal: tavoletas* (or *tábuas*) *da Índia* and *balestilha do mouro*. *Tavoletas* were brought back to Portugal, and the sixteenth-century works of João de Lisboa and André Pires mention them; it has been suggested that the revival in the sixteenth century of the cross-staff as a nautical instrument was influenced by knowledge of the *kamal*.

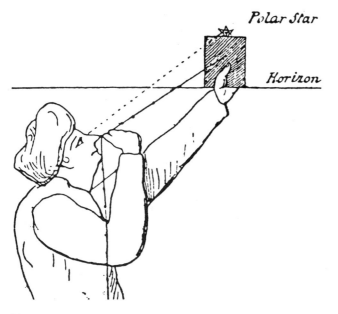

Polar Star

Horizon

USE OF THE *KAMAL*.   AFTER CONGREVE, 1850

The tablets of a *kamal* were of horn or of wood and of different sizes, and each had a central hole where a string was attached. The string was divided by appropriately placed knots, giving readings in numbers of *isba'* (finger [breadth]). In use, the bottom edge of the tablet (chosen for being of appropriate size) was aligned on the horizon, and the top edge was aligned on the celestial body, the altitude of which was to be measured (compare the use of the cross-staff). The knot that, when held between the teeth or to the nose of the observer, kept the string taut indicated the altitude. The *kamal* was used primarily to measure stellar altitudes (*qiyas*) in order to ascertain directly or by analogy the altitude of the polestar, and thus the latitude. In a variant form of *kamal*, the knots on the string indicated not *isba'*, but the altitude of the polestar at various places on the western coast of India. The few *kamal*s that have been described and illustrated in the literature can no longer be located.

It seems clear that the *kamal* was paralleled in China by the *qian xing ban* (guiding star stretch-boards), twelve ebony plates and an ivory piece, measuring *zhi*, mentioned by a sixteenth-century Chinese author, Li Zu, and in use, presumably, earlier. Some transmission from China to India seems probable. The name *kamal*, which James Prinsep learned from a navigator on a ship from the Maldives, has not been found in any other source and may not be the original term or form. Apart from the Portuguese names, the only alternative name that has been found is *khashaba* (a piece of wood), used by the Arab *mu'allim*s Ahmad ibn Majid (fl. 1460–1550) and Sulayman al-Mahri (first half of the sixteenth century); the former also uses in poetry the variant *khadaba*. The Arabic word *kamal* means "perfection, completion," but in this case might represent the assimilation of the New Persian, Arabic, Turkish, and Urdu word *kaman* (bow, arch, arc) or a derivative of the Greek word *kámilos* (rope), possibly through another Indo-European language such as Hindi or Maldivian, or even of a loan word from a South Indian Dravidian language; the Chinese might also be connected. The individual tablets were called *lawh* in Arabic.
[See also *Cross-Staff*.]

BIBLIOGRAPHY

Congreve, H. "A Brief Notice of Some Contrivances Practised by the Native Mariners of the Coromandel Coast, in Navigating, Sailing and Repairing Their Vessels." 1850. Reprinted in vol. 3 of *Instructions nautiques et routiers arabes et portugais des XVe et XVIe siècles*, edited by Gabriel Ferrand, pp. 24–30. Paris, 1928.

Maddison, Francis. *Medieval Scientific Instruments and the Development of Navigational Instruments in the XVth and XVIth Centuries*. Agrupamento de estudos de cartografia antiga, vol. 30. Coimbra, 1969.

Needham, Joseph, Wang Ling, and Lu Gwei-Djen. "Civil Engineering and Nautics." Part 3 of vol. 4 of *Science and Civilisation in China*. Cambridge, 1971.

Prinsep, James. "Note on the Nautical Instruments of the Arabs." 1836. Reprinted in vol. 3 of *Instructions nautiques et routiers arabes et portugais des XVe et XVIe siècles*, edited by Gabriel Ferrand, pp. 1–24. Paris, 1928.

Tibbetts, G. R. *The Navigational Theory of the Arabs in the Fifteenth and Sixteenth Centuries*. Agrupamento de estudos de cartografia antiga, vol 36. Coimbra, 1969.

Tibbetts, G. R. *Arab Navigation in the Indian Ocean before the Coming of the Portuguese, Being a Translation of* Kitab al-Fawa'id fi usul al-bahr wa'l-qawa'id *of Ahmad b. Majid al-Najdi*. Oriental Translation Fund, new series, vol. 42. London, 1971.

FRANCIS MADDISON

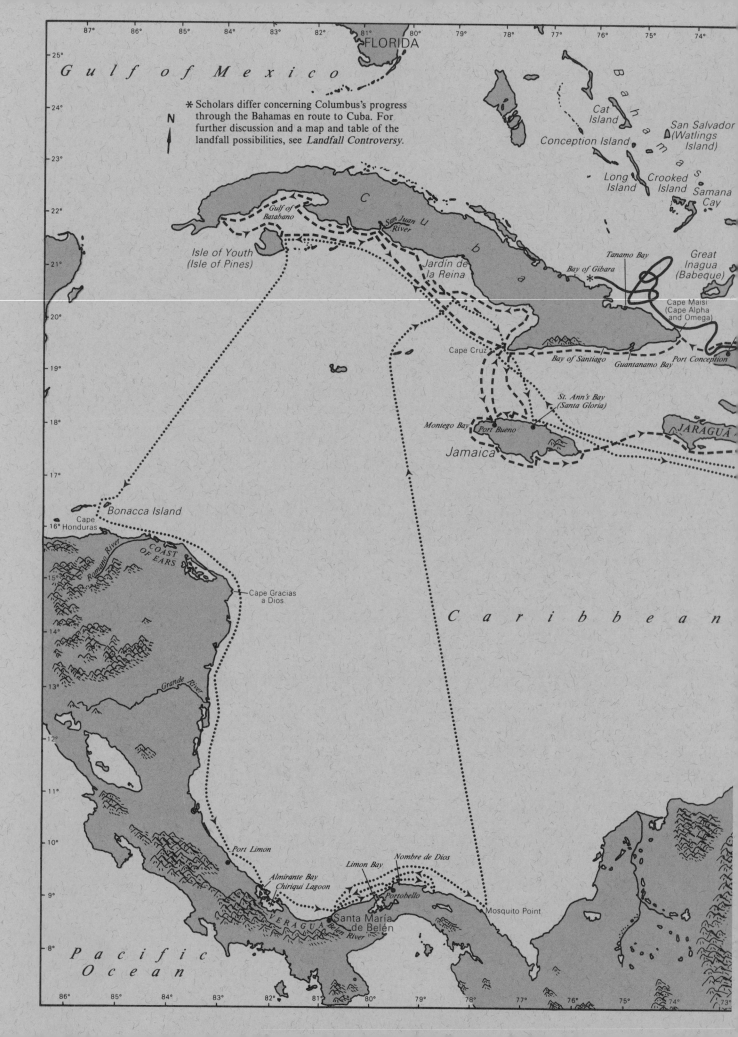

Gulf of Mexico

FLORIDA

27° 86° 85° 84° 83° 82° 81° 80° 79° 78° 77° 76° 75° 74°

25°

24°

✱ Scholars differ concerning Columbus's progress
through the Bahamas en route to Cuba. For
further discussion and a map and table of the
landfall possibilities, see *Landfall Controversy*.

N

23°

22°

Cat
Island

San Salvador
(Watlings
Island)

Conception Island

C

Gulf of
Batabano

Isle of Youth
(Isle of Pines)

San Juan
River

U

Long
Island

Crooked
Island

Samana
Cay

Jardín de
la Reina

b

Tanamo Bay

Great
Inagua
(Babeque)

Bay of Gibara
✱

a

Cape Maisí
(Cape Alpha
and Omega)

Cape Cruz

Bay of Santiago

Guantanamo Bay

Port Conception

St. Ann's Bay
(Santa Gloria)

Montego Bay
Port Bueno

JARAGUÁ

Jamaica

Bonacca Island

Cape
Honduras

Romano River

COAST
OF EARS

Cape Gracias
a Dios

C a r i b b e a n

Grande River

Port Limon

Nombre de Dios

Limon Bay

Almirante Bay
Chiriqui Lagoon

Portobello

VERAGUA
Belen River

Santa María
de Belén

Mosquito Point

Pacific
Ocean